At the End of Military Intervention

The Changing Character of War Programme is an interdisciplinary research group at the University of Oxford, and was funded by the Leverhulme Trust between 2003 and 2009.

At the End of Military Intervention

Historical, Theoretical, and Applied Approaches to Transition, Handover, and Withdrawal

Edited by
Robert Johnson and Timothy Clack

OXFORD
UNIVERSITY PRESS

Great Clarendon Street, Oxford, OX2 6DP,
United Kingdom

Oxford University Press is a department of the University of Oxford.
It furthers the University's objective of excellence in research, scholarship,
and education by publishing worldwide. Oxford is a registered trade mark of
Oxford University Press in the UK and in certain other countries

First Edition published in 2015
Impression: 1

Published in the United States of America by Oxford University Press
198 Madison Avenue, New York, NY 10016, United States of America

British Library Cataloguing in Publication Data
Data available

Library of Congress Control Number: 2014941216

ISBN 978–0–19–872501–5

Printed and bound by
CPI Group (UK) Ltd, Croydon, CR0 4YY

Foreword

Lieutenant General JD Page CB OBE
Commander Force Development & Training, Headquarters Army

> In a world of drastic change it is the learners who survive; the 'learned' find themselves fully equipped to live in a world that no longer exists.
>
> Eric Hoffer, *Reflections on the Human Conditions*

Militaries of the twenty-first century must be adaptive and learning organizations. In addition to conventional war-fighting, the skills to contest low-intensity conflict and insurgencies, counter threats from terrorism and proliferation, and deliver enterprises in upstream security and capacity must be refined. To be effective, militaries require components, not least in the intelligence sphere, which demonstrate continual enterprise and robust expertise. Successful military operations are, after all, most often defined by who anticipates, learns, and adapts the fastest. This remains contingent upon understandings of the context, including but not limited to adversarial forces, human and geospatial terrain, and conflict enablers and drivers. Therefore it is commonsense to suggest that operational outcomes are enhanced through the possession of the kinds of disciplinary, temporal and geographic understandings which the research community can endow. Of course, whilst it is ideal for militaries to possess expertise internally, it is pragmatic to 'reach out' to credible sources in order to explore and address identified gaps in knowledge. Knowledge may be an object but learning is practice, requiring the capacity and attitude to recognize and incorporate insight.

Principally, this volume results from the ongoing collaboration between the Land Forces Intelligence Fusion Centre (LIFC) and the Changing Character of War Programme (CCW) at the University of Oxford. So fruitful has this relationship proven itself to be, that it is worth providing some institutional background. The LIFC is a relatively nascent, albeit now established, component of the British Army. In the main it is dedicated to the provision of tactical and operational intelligence support to the Field Army. It was established in 2010, in response to operational requirements linked to the campaign in Afghanistan. The unit provides, through an immersive environment, what military doctrine casts as 'Understand'. Acting as something akin to a 'clearing house' of intelligence, one of the important ways in which understanding is amassed and then disseminated to those being deployed on operations, is through academic outreach. This outreach activity has taken a number of guises, in particular fellowships for senior and junior staff, educational packages delivered in the UK and Germany, and conference events. One key and ongoing academic relationship—didactic and research—has been forged with the CCW Programme. Housed at Pembroke College with core staff and a vibrant cadre of visiting fellows, this is an interdisciplinary and policy-relevant academic programme, which focuses on the research of war and armed conflict.

This was the context and rationale behind the 'Understanding Transition and Transitioning at the Land Tactical Level' Workshop held at Merton College, Oxford, 17–19 December 2012. The Workshop was a collaborative event, co-delivered by the LIFC and Oxford's CCW Programme. The occasion, attended by over one hundred academic, crown, and military delegates, aimed to enhance understanding of the operational environment, inform concepts, doctrine and policy, and prepare transition planners and implementers for current and future roles. The frank and honest discussions to be heard throughout the three days, equally in the sessions and in the sidelines, demonstrated perhaps how useful the Workshop was as a model for critical outreach. Certainly, the feedback from the event rated highly the open, transparent nature of the engagement as well as the willingness of participants to explore innovative, counter-narrative trains of thought.

Inevitably and rightly, the role of the UK military as a component of ISAF (International Security Assistance Force) in the transition of security in Helmand, Afghanistan, was a prime focus. Indeed, this gave the Workshop immediate value: lessons, risks, and concepts identified at the event were pushed into the Operational Theatre and promulgated amongst personnel of Task Force Helmand (TFH) and the Helmand Provincial Reconstruction Team (HPRT). There was also, however, an obvious relevance beyond current operations. As no intervention is intended to endure indefinitely and no operation takes place in a vacuum, future interventions will face analogous parameters of tactical exit and power transfer.

During the course of the Workshop a number of testing themes recurred: importance of the correct models of intervention/entry and governance; problems of insufficient or dwindling equipment and manpower; deteriorating loyalty and the fate of loyalists; local agencies opposing the agenda of the withdrawing forces; breakdown of civil government and authority; loss of intelligence for security forces and deteriorating morale amongst transitional forces. Thus history records clearly how transitions embody risks and compromises. Operational management must account for these dimensions but must also recognize that they do not encompass the full picture. It is more difficult to recognize achievement than limitation. In the real world, amidst an absence of 'control' conditions and for that matter the veracities of media and political agendas, focus tends to be diverted from 'strengths' to 'weaknesses'. This can ensure, in a productive sense, that planners and implementers learn lessons and recover delivery. Yet it is crucial to recognize that considerable accomplishments also characterize transitions and these must be considered and learnt from too. Thus development of indigenous capacity, calibre of the security forces, context of handover, advancements in infrastructure, governance, education, and rule of law, and progress in the economic sector, might all be proposed as relevant measures of satisfaction.

How the concert of these factors, positive and negative, relates to local circumstance together with their tactical and operational impacts must be priority considerations for all commanders tasked to deliver transition, now and in the future. It is for these reasons that this volume, offering greater clarity on many of the relevant themes and written by leading scholars and practitioners, is especially welcome. I commend it to all those engaged in Transition.

Finally, I am heartened by the ongoing associations between LIFC and CCW and it is more than appropriate that this edited monograph is being published in the 'Changing Character of War' Series with Oxford University Press. I am grateful for CCW's support to the Army.

Acknowledgements

The origins of the present collection are found in the organization of the 'Understanding Transition and Transitioning at the Land Tactical Level' workshop held at Merton College, Oxford in winter 2012. The Land Forces Intelligence Fusion Centre (LIFC) deserves acknowledgement for initiating and funding this event. Whilst the LIFC and the Changing Character of War Programme (CCW) co-delivered the workshop, a number of other institutions also provided crucial support of one kind or another. These included: the Department for International Development (DFID); the Development Concepts and Doctrine Centre (DCDC); Foreign and Commonwealth Office (FCO); Helmand Provincial Reconstruction Team (HPRT); Ministry of Defence (MOD); and the Stabilisation Unit (SU). The numerous delegates at that event should be mentioned as their input has continued to offer insight and mould interests. Particular thanks go to those speakers who gave generously of their time and insight but, for a number of reasons, were unable to develop their papers for publication: Dr Tim Bird, Professor Richard Caplan, Dr Toby Dodge, Sir Jeremy Greenstock, Brigadier Rupert Jones, Mr Patrick Moody, Major General Andrew Sharpe and Professor Sir Hew Strachan. The event itself ran with exceptional efficiency due to the unfailing efforts of Lieutenant Alex Crisp, Ms Elisa Torrequebrada and a cohort of stoic volunteers from the Oxford University Officer Training Corps.

Media Operations at Army HQ gave approval for use of the cover image and Figures I.1, I.2, and I.3 used in the editors' introduction. We are also grateful to the Ministry of Defence for reproductive permissions linked to Mark Beautement's contribution and Figures 15.3 and 15.4.

Putting together a volume of this size is no small undertaking. Indeed, this collection would not have been possible without several very important supporters of the project. From the outset Lieutenant General 'Jacko' Page, Colonel Nicolas Baker, Lieutenant Colonel Andrew Perrey, Mrs Nicola Budd, Major Rosalind Diamond, Mrs Catriona Laing, Dr Peter Rundell, and Mrs Jo Baldwin played significant respective parts in shepherding and facilitating. The publishers and copy-editors provided exemplary advice and assistance. Nicole Hartwell helped enormously with the production effort. We must also thank the volume's many contributors for all their hard work and commitment. They have been incredibly intelligent and stimulating companions not only throughout this project, but also in a myriad of other ventures.

Sadly, during the final stages of editing this collection, we received the news that our friend and colleague, James Dunsby, had died on a training exercise with the Army Reserves. Recently married, James was a gregarious character of untiring energy and enthusiasm. He served as an Intelligence Analyst at the LIFC, a Reservist with the Yeomanry, and was a former Visiting Fellow of the CCW Programme, where he refined his research into transition logistics. In all these roles and despite his age, he left a huge and positive impact. He will be sorely missed.

This book is dedicated to James, his wife, Bryher, and the people of post-transition Afghanistan.

TC and RJ
Oxford, November 2014

Contents

List of figures

List of tables

List of tables

List of contributors

David Anderson is Professor of African History at the University of Warwick. He took his BA in History at the University of Sussex (1978), and a doctorate at Trinity College, University of Cambridge (1982). His interests span the wider eastern African region, with a particular focus on Kenya, Uganda, Ethiopia, and Somalia. His most recent books include *Histories of the Hanged* (2005), *The Khat Controversy* (2007), *The Handbook of African Politics* (edited with Nic Cheeseman). He is now researching on the history of the Cold War in Africa; comparative histories of collaboration across the British Empire; conflict and insurrection in eastern Africa from 1950 until 1990; and current political violence in the region.

Mark Battjes is a Major in the US Army. He served four tours in support of Operation Iraqi Freedom, including as a company commander and Military Transition Team chief in Baghdad, Iraq during 2007 and 2008. As an Art of War Scholar at the Command and General Staff College, Fort Leavenworth, Kansas, he authored *Protecting, Isolating and Controlling Behavior* in the 'art of war series' published by the Combat Studies Institute Press. He has recently been selected for the US Army Advanced Strategic Planning and Policy Program and will begin work on his PhD in the fall of 2014.

Mark Beautement was the District Political Officer (POLO) in Sangin, Helmand Province, Afghanistan, between September 2009 and July 2010, deploying with the UK Government's Stabilisation Unit. He served alongside the UK's 3 RIFLES and 40 Commando battlegroups, and the incoming US Marines, in the run up to the Sangin Accord.

Sir Rodric Braithwaite is a writer and former diplomat. He served in military intelligence in Vienna in 1951–52, studied French and Russian at Cambridge and joined the Diplomatic Service in 1955. He had postings in Jakarta, Warsaw, Moscow, Rome, Brussels, and Washington. He was British Ambassador to Moscow 1988–92. In 1992–93 he was Foreign Policy adviser to Prime Minister Major and Chairman of the Joint Intelligence Committee. He is an Honorary Fellow of Christ's College, Cambridge and Honorary Doctor and Professor of Birmingham University. His latest book *Afgantsy: The Russians in Afghanistan, 1979–89* was published by Profile in 2011.

Lieutenant Colonel Andrew Britton is a serving Army Officer with operational COIN experience in Northern Ireland and Iraq. He has also completed two tours in Afghanistan (2008 and 2012) in operational planning roles in multinational NATO headquarters (HQ Regional Command South and HQ Task Force Helmand). He currently commands his Regiment of 'Tankies' (1RTR) and lives in Suffolk.

Contributors

Timothy Clack is a Senior Research Fellow of the Changing Character of War Programme at the University of Oxford. He took a doctorate from the University of Manchester in 2006, held research and teaching positions at the University of Oxford between 2006 and 2013, and has current research interests into various conflict drivers, including the ownership of the past, cultural hybridization, and trans-border migration and exchange, primarily related to areas in the Horn of Africa. During 2011–12 he worked in a liaison capacity with the UK Stabilisation Unit.

Lindsay Clutterbuck is a Research Leader at RAND Europe in Cambridge. Prior to joining RAND he served for over 20 years at New Scotland Yard in the Specialist Operations Department of the Metropolitan Police, specializing in terrorism and counter-terrorism. Since 2008, he has carried out field research into the role of police and policing during counter-insurgencies, travelling to both Anbar Province in Iraq and across a number of provinces in Afghanistan. He received a PhD in 2002 from the University of Portsmouth for his research into the early origins and evolution of terrorism and counter-terrorism in the UK.

John Darwin is Beit University Lecturer in the History of the British Commonwealth, Nuffield College, University of Oxford. He is a recognized authority on the British Empire, decolonization and the End of Empires. His numerous books include: *The Empire Project* (Cambridge University Press, 2009); *The End of the British Empire* (Blackwell, 1991); and *Britain and Decolonization* (Macmillan, 1988).

James Dunsby was an Intelligence Officer with the Land Intelligence Fusion Centre between 2010 and 2013. He took a BA from the University of Tasmania (2005), a PGCE from Buckingham (2007), and a Masters in International Relations from Sussex (2009). During the early part of 2013, he undertook a CCW Visiting Fellowship at Pembroke College, Oxford to research the changing role of contractors through military transitions.

Aaron Edwards is a Senior Lecturer in Defence and International Affairs at the Royal Military Academy Sandhurst. Awarded his PhD in politics from Queen's University Belfast in 2006, he has written widely on the challenges to British security posed by terrorism and insurgency. Responsible for overseeing counter terrorism studies at Sandhurst, he has lectured to military and civilian audiences across the world on various aspects of international security. A Fellow of the Higher Education Academy and a member of the Insurgency Research Group at King's College London, his most recent book is *Defending the Realm? The Politics of Britain's Small Wars since 1945* (Manchester University Press, 2012).

Martin Evans is Professor of Modern European History at the University of Sussex. He has written numerous books on Algeria, including *Algeria: Anger of the Dispossessed* (Yale, 2007), *The Memory of Resistance: French Opposition to the Algerian War 1954–62* (Berg, 1997), and most recently *Algeria: France's Undeclared War* (Oxford University Press, 2012). The latter work is the result of a Senior Research Fellowship at the British Academy (2007–08).

Antonio Giustozzi is an independent researcher. He took his PhD at the London School of Economics and Political Science (LSE) and is currently associated with the

IDEAS (International Affairs, Diplomacy, Strategy), LSE. He is the author of three books on Afghanistan, *War, Politics and Society in Afghanistan, 1978–1992* (Georgetown University Press, 1999), *Koran, Kalashnikov and Laptop: The Neo-Taliban Insurgency, 2002–2007* (Columbia University Press, 2008), and *Empires of Mud: War and Warlords in Afghanistan* (Columbia University Press, 2009), as well as editor of, *Decoding the New Taliban* (Columbia University Press, 2009). He is currently researching the insurgency and issues of governance in Afghanistan from a wide-ranging perspective, which includes understanding the role of the army, police, sub-national governance, and intelligence system.

Karl Hack is Director of the Ferguson Centre for African and Asian Studies at the Open University, having previously taught at Singapore's Nanyang Technological University for more than a decade. His areas of expertise are the British Empire, Southeast Asia (especially Malaysia and Singapore), and insurgency and counter-insurgency. Related books include (edited with C.C. Chin), *Dialogues with Chin Peng: New Light on the Malayan Communist Party* (Singapore University Press, 2004), and (authored with Kevin Blackburn), *War Memory and the Making of Modern Malaysia and Singapore* (NUS Press, 2012).

Robert Johnson is the Director of the Oxford Changing Character of War Programme and Senior Research Fellow of Pembroke College. A former army officer, he is the author of *The Afghan Way of War* (Hurst, 2011) and a specialist on historical and current conflicts in the Middle East and Asia.

Saul Kelly is a Reader in International History at the Defence Studies Department, King's College, London, at the Joint Services and Command College, Shrivenham. He received his PhD from the London School of Economics and Political Science in 1995. His recent publications include: *Fighting the Retreat from Arabia and the Gulf: The Collected Essays and Reviews of J.B. Kelly, Vol. 1* (New English Review Press, 2013); *Imperial Crossroads: The Great Powers and the Persian Gulf* (co-edited with Jeffrey R. Macris, Naval Institute Press, 2012); and 'Britain, the United Arab Emirates and the Defence of the Gulf Revisited' (co-authored with Gareth Stansfield).

Anthony King is Professor of Sociology at the University of Exeter and was a Visiting Fellow at All Soul's College, Oxford 2012–13. His most recent books are *The Transformation of Europe's Armed Forces* (Cambridge University Press, 2011) and *The Combat Soldier: Infantry Tactics and Cohesion in the Twentieth and Twenty-First Centuries* (Oxford University Press, 2013). He has acted as a mentor and adviser to the armed forces including ISAF's Regional Command South 2009–10, where he was a member of the Prism Cell.

Oliver Lewis is a civil servant in the Ministry of Defence. In 2012 he deployed as the Prism Advisor to the Commander of Task Force Helmand for Operation Herrick 16 and 17. Prior to joining the Ministry he lectured on critical security studies in London and was educated at Oxford, Aberystwyth, Leicester, Brown, and Cambridge.

Roger Mac Ginty is Professor of Peace and Conflict Studies at the Humanitarian and Conflict Response Institute, and the Department of Politics, University of Manchester. His latest book is *International Peacebuilding and Local Resistance: Hybrid Forms of Peace* (Palgrave, 2011). He edits the journal *Peacebuilding* and a book series entitled 'Rethinking Political Violence'. He is currently developing Everyday Peace Indicators.

Piers Robinson (Senior Lecturer in International Politics, University of Manchester) has an international reputation for his research on the relationship between communications and world politics. His most recent book, *Pockets of Resistance: The British Media and the 2003 Invasion of Iraq* (Manchester University Press, 2010), analyses UK media coverage of the 2003 invasion of Iraq. His book *The CNN Effect: The Myth of News, Foreign Policy and Intervention* (Routledge, 2002) analyses the relationship between news media, US foreign policy, and humanitarian crises. Other work on media and international politics has been published in leading journals including *Journal of Communication, Journal of Peace Research, European Journal of Communication, Review of International Studies* and *Media, Culture and Society*, amongst others. He is also an editor of the journal *Critical Studies on Terrorism* (Routledge).

Peter Rundell has since 1979 worked in international development, up to 2005 mainly in Africa. He has worked in the Western Balkans, Iraq, Afghanistan, and Libya—where he led the first British stabilization and humanitarian teams in Benghazi after UNSCR 1973. As Director (Policy & Programmes) in the Helmand Provincial Reconstruction Team, and later as Strategy Advisor, he led both delivery of international assistance in the most violently contested Province in Afghanistan and review of lessons there. He is currently Deputy Head of the EU border assistance Mission in Tripoli.

Georgina Sinclair is a Research Fellow at the International Centre for Crime, Policing and Justice at the Open University. She has substantive interests in the policing of the British Empire and Commonwealth and international policing (1945–present). Since 2010 she has assisted ACPO International Affairs with policy development in relation to international policing and is a member of IPAB.

James Worrall is Lecturer in International Relations at the University of Leeds. He specializes in Levantine and Gulf politics, counter-insurgency, and international organizations. His book, *State Building and Counter Insurgency in Oman: Political, Military and Diplomatic Relations at the End of Empire*, is published by IB Tauris (2014). Dr Worrall is currently exploring Hizbollah's media strategy during the Arab Spring while also writing a book on the international organizations of the Middle East. He is joint reviews editor for the academic journal *Civil Wars* and a founding member of the Terrorism and Political Violence Association (TAPVA).

Introduction

Principles, Themes, and Problems in Transitions

Timothy Clack and Robert Johnson

The focus of much of the scholarship and comment on Western military operations in recent years has been on the decisions, manner, and relative success of interventions, and there has been considerable interest in, and criticism of, the subsequent insurgencies and counter-insurgency measures these created in Iraq and Afghanistan between 2001 and 2014. Rather less attention has been paid to the practical problems at the end of military intervention, namely, transition, handover, or withdrawal. This is perhaps ironic since there is, amongst civilian organizations, a great deal of experience of working with regional governments and passing responsibility back to local authorities after a crisis, although coordination of their efforts has often been problematic. Moreover, the defining European experience of the post-1945 period in international affairs, other than the Cold War confrontation, was decolonization of Africa and Asia involving the transfer of powers and responsibilities, training of local elites, the building of institutions, and, at times, conducting fighting withdrawals. The majority of conflicts that Europeans fought from 1945 to 1990 were wars of counter-insurgency and extraction. In fact, the Europeans sought, where possible, to avoid fighting in order to leave behind sovereign states with which they could do business in the future. They were not always successful in that regard. Nevertheless, some former colonial powers, like Britain and France, were able to establish better relationships and long-term cooperation with many other countries in Africa and the Near East. For Britain, the Commonwealth emerged as an assemblage of freely associated states linked by history and shared interests.

The United States and its Coalition allies sought to establish a similar benign, democratic dispensation in Afghanistan and Iraq in the early 2000s. The initial hope was to set up new representative institutions amongst local political elites, subject to democratic principles, but without the enormous commitment of nation-building. The circumstances of these interventions are well documented but the development of insurgencies in both countries jeopardized the chances of peaceful processes of stabilization. Nevertheless, it was the incomplete and unsatisfactory nature of the stabilization efforts, and protracted violence, that, ironically, accelerated transition. Handovers had, of course, been envisioned from the outset, but withdrawal proved more problematic when stability was precarious, democratization still embryonic, and, despite new local security forces, the drivers of the fighting had merely been suppressed.

Transition is a term that conceals a multitude of activities and objectives. It implies rather more than 'withdrawal' in that it points towards the establishment or reconstitution of local authority, responsibility, and ownership. It is a transfer of power rather than the abandonment of it. For military personnel, transition is the progressive transfer of security functions and responsibilities so as to ensure a sustainable level of stability for a nation, and one which no longer depends on a substantial international operational contribution.[1] In the United Kingdom, security transitions at the operational and tactical level are governed by four principles: a political focus, legitimacy, capacity building, and sustainability.[2] Taken together they suggest that there are two objectives, that is, to create a political settlement and to build capability. British doctrine emphasizes the need for military personnel to ensure that plans and operations serve a political settlement and that legitimacy must be built amongst the local population. In building capacity and capability, practitioners are reminded that their efforts must enable local security forces to recruit, train, equip, manage, and sustain themselves. Sustainability requires much more than providing a training team or a liaison officer, as it implies that there must be development of processes and resources, and integration with local political objectives and the constitutional apparatus. To gauge the appropriate level of support, the doctrinal advice is to retain flexibility, to identify and understand the motivations of the key actors, and make balanced judgements over the degree to which local or international advice is prioritized. The conclusion highlights the practical difficulty of working with embryonic local institutions: while trying to avoid 'impositions' by outsiders, all too often the experience is one of partisan local agendas being asserted over one group or another.

[1] Joint Doctrine Publication (JDP) 6/10 *Security Transitions* (2010).
[2] JDP 6/10, pp. ix, 1–6 and 1–7.

There are considerable risks inherent in transition. Local actors may feel that transition occurs before processes are fully embedded or their staffs are confident or even competent in their role. Nevertheless, local leaders are often impatient for change. One of the most critical risks is where these contradictory aspirations produce situations where local security provision fails. Such an occurrence at the point where efforts are underway to integrate former combatants can threaten to unravel the entire process. Moreover, there appears to be a pattern where states which have endured a conflict in the recent past are more likely to experience a return to violence: in general terms, the longer the post-conflict period, the greater are the chances of an enduring peace. Nevertheless, there are risks of perpetual human rights abuses and violent conflicts of interests during and after transition.

Whilst acknowledging the historical and contextual specificity of each case in time and space, there are four unifying subordinate themes that span different periods and places and which support the definition offered here. First, transition is a dynamic process requiring flexibility and agility from its participants. It is not necessarily a linear activity where neat timelines can predict its outcomes. Second, it is a process that entails a gradual loss of the control by the intervening power. It is therefore, as noted above, a period of considerable risk. Third, its significance and its complexity have been overlooked compared with entry or the operations that occur in support of erecting some new authority. The inherent difficulties of transition mean that it requires considerable effort to get the formula right, unless the policy is one of scuttle. The fourth observation is that, if transition is contested, the implication is that the intervening power has not entirely succeeded. Yet, this assumption, which is often made, needs to be tested against the ability of the intervening power to create legitimation amongst its co-opted allies and former enemies. It is possible that, in spite of some residual violence, warlords can become courtiers. Indeed, it may be reasonable to assume that, after the withdrawal of the intervening power, the new local authority will attempt to assert itself, and whatever residual levels of violence occur, its failure is by no means automatic.

In states or regions affected by civil war, peace-building efforts can be considerably more effective with the presence of international negotiators, trainers, aid agencies, and military forces. Many experienced field operatives, drawn from these organizations, speak candidly about the fundamental importance of physical security as the first step in building stability. A functioning government, judiciary, police, and, where necessary, gendarmerie or military forces, are essential. Critical services providing water, food, energy, and transport are vital, as are the infrastructural components required for economic activity and recovery. Reconstruction is considerably easier if the fighting has ceased. Observations of Sri Lanka and Angola, where government forces achieved decisive victories over rebel groups, meant recovery was more rapid even if government systems were 'illiberal'.[3] States where Western forces intervened and achieved equally decisive results, such as Sierra Leone and Mali, also accelerated transition and reconstruction. Where an outright military success was not achieved, there were significant challenges for stabilization.

One of the most striking characteristics of military personnel is their willingness to endure all manner of hardships, physical, mental, and emotional, and to risk their lives in the pursuit of a mission. It is this mission-focus, euphemistically called a 'can do' mentality, which enables collective bodies to go forward into danger, to take casualties and yet still achieve a specific objective. It is, in short, an essential element for combat operations. Nevertheless, in those missions where the destruction of an enemy force in combat is not the priority, such as the stabilization of fragile states, an entirely new set of skills and characteristics are required. While tactical imperatives do not diminish, their relative importance to strategic outcomes can be reduced. As one counter-insurgency specialist put it, 'sometimes it is better to do nothing'.[4] In fact the more certain advice would be to pause and reflect, to assess the situation from the point of view of local people, and to weigh up a vast array of non-military considerations about the local economy, parochial politics, and the cultural parameters of a given society. There is a tendency for armies to pursue the 'achievement of the mission' as if it were merely a tactical objective, such as the control of a region, or the possession of an urban space, thus ignoring the indisputable fact that all armies are extensions of the political will of their governments, reflect the societies from which they themselves are drawn, and that their actions are judged by a variety of social groups including, today, the global media. The character of the Western approach to wars in Iraq and Afghanistan between 2001 and 2014 was a tendency, at least initially, to 'tacticize' the mission of stabilization and to concentrate on combat against an ill-defined enemy. The establishment of security, while managing a tactical transition, became one of the most difficult phases in these campaigns, but it was essential if military forces were to fulfil the political task they had been set. The ability to gather and fuse information, to develop insight and understanding of the local people and their socio-economic environment, was a significant feature of these wars.

Civilian critics of the military efforts in Iraq and Afghanistan concentrated primarily on the legitimacy of the intervention and particularly the objectives,

[3] Ricardo Soares de Oliveira, 'Illiberal peacebuilding in Angola', *Journal of Modern African Studies* 49, no. 2 (2011): pp. 287–314.

[4] John Nagl, *Counterinsurgency Field Manual* FM3-24 (Chicago: University of Chicago Press, 2007), 1–152, p. 49. See also David Kilcullen, 'The Twenty-Eight Articles', in *Counterinsurgency* (London: Hurst, 2010), pp. 22–49.

and methods, of American foreign policy.[5] At the tactical level, a rather different set of complaints developed. Those NGOs engaged in development and aid projects were alarmed when military personnel seemed to trespass on their territory. There was dismay that methods regarded as obsolete and culturally insensitive were readily practised by well-intentioned but inexperienced military officers. Aid organizations with considerable experience of long-term humanitarian intervention and responsible exits were highly critical of the 'quick fix' culture of Western militaries and appalled by their instrumentalist attitude to bringing succour to local populations, specifically making aid and relief dependent on supporting a Western-approved indigenous government, merely as part of a policy of 'winning hearts and minds'.

More broadly, critics were concerned that a military-led approach generated violence and civilians were being caught in the cross fire. They pointed out that military formations either ignored or were not designed to implement legal and governance systems on which stabilization depended. When advisors and specialists deployed, the security situation often dictated when and where, and at what tempo, change could be affected, leading to exasperation on both sides. Military personnel argued that their civilian counterparts were too hide-bound by risk-averse peacetime regulations rendering them ineffective, while civilians were frustrated by what they regarded as military high-handedness and error. Despite warm assurances about the integrated character of a 'comprehensive approach' where the military and civilian agencies all worked towards a common goal, the reality was that cooperation depended on individuals, their tolerance, team-working skills, and their personality.

When a military interventionist force has to hand over control to a host nation government, what happens at the 'grass roots' of these strategic recalibrations? The tactical and operational dimensions of making a transition are informed by the framework of an exit *strategy*, and Richard Caplan's excellent edited volume on this subject has been the starting point of our own work.[6] With regard to the Western interventions in Afghanistan and in Iraq in 2001 and 2003, it is fascinating to recall how much optimism prevailed and how widespread the assumption was that military operations would be concluded swiftly with transition made almost immediately to an indigenous government. Caplan notes that references to state-building were more frequent from the 1990s but, in 2001 and 2003, the United States had specifically set

[5] See, for example: Thomas E. Ricks, *Fiasco: The American Military Adventure in Iraq* (New York: Penguin Books, 2007); Ali A. Allawi, *The Occupation of Iraq: Winning the War, Losing the Peace* (New Haven, CT: Yale University Press, 2007); Larry Diamond, *Squandered Victory: The American Occupation and the Bungled Effort to Bring Democracy to Iraq* (New York: Times Books, 2005); Larry Diamond, *The Spirit of Democracy: The Struggle to Build Free Societies Throughout the World* (New York: Henry Holt and Company, 2008).

[6] Richard Caplan, ed., *Exit Strategies and State Building* (Oxford: Oxford University Press, 2012).

out to avoid becoming embroiled in any long-term commitments of 'nation-building' and certainly not in any counter-insurgency operations. Before the invasion of Iraq, the US government, which was deprived of crucial local intelligence, had consulted expatriate Iraqis to ascertain whether the Western invasion would be greeted as liberation or not. There was considerable faith in the idea that the Iraqi armed forces would defect to the protection of the West and that army officers might even stage a coup against President Saddam Hussein. These 'allies' and partners would be the personnel who would assume power and ensure a smooth transition, allowing the United States to withdraw. In Afghanistan, the initial plan was simply to pursue the forces of Al Qaeda, enlist local militias in that mission and to eschew any prospect of occupation, which was seen as the folly of the Soviet Union. Niall Ferguson noted that the United States was engaged in a form of 'Empire Lite', reminiscent of British gunboat diplomacy of the nineteenth century but without the willingness or 'strategic patience' to commit to the construction of states or to build any lasting legacy.[7] To the critics of the United States, it seems the Americans were using their military power in an aggressive and rather absent-minded manner.

The West's preference for international intervention has a long historical precedent, and, rather uncomfortably, draws its antecedents from the colonial era. In turn, the Western experience of transition has derived from the period of decolonization after 1945. New impetus was given to intervention and transition by the Cold War as the Superpowers and their allies attempted to maximize their security. As failing or unstable states in the developing world had the potential to escalate conflict between the Superpowers, considerable effort was made to stabilize and consolidate them. The major powers set out either to localize and suppress civil conflicts, support proxies, or make direct interventions (including, for example, Hungary and Suez 1956; Vietnam 1961; Czechoslovakia 1968; Afghanistan 1979; Angola 1974; and Grenada 1983). The end of the Cold War produced a brief unipolar hegemony for the United States but also a period of considerable uncertainty about the future.[8]

The shocking terrorist attack on the United States in September 2001, launched from the failed state of Afghanistan, illustrated how difficult it was to monitor new, more clandestine threats. The attack compelled the CIA to establish an 'ungoverned areas project' and to examine capacity-building efforts that might prevent the establishment of safe havens for international

[7] Niall Ferguson, *The Rise and Fall of the American Empire* (New York: Penguin, 2004).

[8] Christopher Layne, 'The Unipolar Illusion: Why New Great Powers Will Rise', in *The Cold War and After: Prospects for Peace*, edited by Sean M. Lynn-Jones and Steven E. Miller (Cambridge MA: MIT Press, 1993), pp. 242–90; Christopher Layne, 'The Unipolar Illusion Revisited: The Coming End of the United States' Unipolar Moment', *International Security* 31, no. 2 (2006): pp. 7–41.

terrorist groups like Al Qaeda.[9] The final report of that project, published in 2008, called for an assessment of the interaction of geography, politics, civil society, resources, and other factors that caused states to be ungoverned, misgoverned, under-governed, contested, and exploited.[10] It concluded that there must be a unified, coordinated, and cooperative effort by all agencies and the use of defence, diplomacy, development, and law enforcement to build capacity in vulnerable states. It is interesting that neither the report, nor the discourse about enhancing American security, acknowledged the turbulence caused by Western economic penetration, its progressive liberal ideology, or by its overwhelming military power.[11] The problem, to use a post-modernist expression, was always 'the Other'. Nevertheless, there was considerable and renewed interest in stabilization and how it could be achieved. This at least had the potential to acknowledge the pressing need for research prior to intervention, the matching of the most appropriate form of intervention to local requirements and the chance to consult local authorities. The concern though was that the West was interested in stability at the expense of transformation, at a time when the pace of change in the Global South, demographically, economically, educationally, and culturally, was at its greatest tempo.

The Western military interventions in Afghanistan and Iraq encountered the problem of highly diverse and divided societies suddenly thrown into turmoil by the removal of the existing tyrannical national authority. The immediate release of previously suppressed forces encouraged factions to assert themselves, often violently. In Iraq, Western analysts struggled to understand the 'insurgent ecosystem' amidst the score-settling of sectarian death squads, the terrorism of former regime loyalists, the opportunism of patriotic volunteers, a murderous campaign against traditionalist elders by the internationalist brigades of Al Qaeda, and sponsored violence from neighbouring states. Transition to a new, democratic Iraqi government based on an agreed constitution took far longer than originally imagined. In Afghanistan, there was even more work to do. After decades of civil war, government institutions had to be built from scratch while the levels of illiteracy, lack of experience, and clan or warlord parochialism meant training a new cadre of national authorities would be a very long-term project indeed. Again, initially the hope in the West was to hand over to locals who would determine these matters for themselves, but lawlessness by interim security forces, excessive corruption (itself fuelled by a huge injection of Western funds) and

[9] Robert D. Lamb, *Ungoverned Areas and Threats from Safe Havens: Final report of the Ungoverned Areas Project* (Office of the Under Secretary of Defense for Policy, Department of Defense, 2008).

[10] Lamb, *Ungoverned Arenas and Threats*, p. 50.

[11] For more detail on this problem, see James Putzel and Jonathan Di John, *Meeting the Challenge of Crisis States* (Crisis States Research Centre, London School of Economics, 2012).

the regeneration of insurgency meant an early Western withdraw was an impossibility. Critics of the Western campaign in Afghanistan failed to acknowledge that it was not through preference that the militaries remained in place, but the fact that an immediate withdrawal would have returned the country to anarchy and civil war. Having embarked on a project of giving Afghanistan workable governance, a viable economy, and security for its people, there was a moral imperative to remain committed at least until the processes and institutions in place were 'good enough'.

Transition is a problematic term in theory and even more difficult to implement in practice. If, in essence, it is about the transfer of power, then it is important to acknowledge that powerful states cannot alone determine the outcome of transition. At the 'tactical' level, power is transitory and contested, and always subject to the dynamics of interaction and friction. Local people, while apparently weak, have agency and can accelerate the withdrawal of more powerful forces by their actions. Perceptions of where power is located will influence strongly the allegiances of all actors in the process. The military desire to control, to plan, and to intervene has often been upset by the failure to grasp the dynamic effect of the collision of wills and perceptions, and by a failure to listen or adapt to local needs or political imperatives. All international intervention in a sovereign territorial space, particularly a military intervention, creates a dynamic effect in local populations, and withdrawal or transition, will also, in turn, create a new dynamic. Some local groups choose to collaborate with the new dispensation, and others will invariably resist. The decision will be based on a myriad of factors and perceptions, from pure opportunism to principled belief. It is easy to assume that national resistance to foreign occupation was the overwhelming characteristic of the wars in Iraq and Afghanistan, but it is striking that, in both cases, more sided with the international forces to create security, functioning governance, and to generate a working economy than to fight for some nebulous patriotic or ideological cause.

Richard Caplan pointed out in his work on *Exit Strategies* that, despite more than 70 United Nations (UN) peacekeeping operations since 1948, it has often been unclear when international interventionist forces should exit: what are the benchmarks? How does one know whether their achievements are 'sustainable'? Western practitioners and policy-makers referred to the contrasts of conditions-based withdrawal and handover, as opposed to the setting of timelines 'where', as one soldier put it, 'the *only* "condition" is time'.[12] The tendency to prioritize international agendas over local needs has been much criticized, on the grounds that it subverts sustainability. In fact, historical

[12] Interview with the authors [name withheld], Kabul, March 2010.

examples suggest that international agendas have invariably been prioritized, and that timetables for withdrawal have galvanized local elites to end petty disputes and concentrate on the pragmatic business of allocating or sharing power. In 2009 President Obama set out the plan for the withdrawal of the United States from Afghanistan in part to placate an angry and impatient American electorate, but it was also designed to drive all parties in the war, including his own armed forces, towards a specific resolution of the conflict that had developed there. Caplan notes that, for the UN, operations are always planned with the exit in mind, but progress towards peace does not always follow a set of defined 'conditions': there are instead many constraints and the struggle is to obtain consensus in order to define 'success'. Exit strategy is often a *process* of transition, from peacekeeping to peace building operations, handovers to national institutions, or the withdrawal of various components of international involvement. Even after transition, there may be considerable international engagement and continuity in processes.

If peace, democratization, a viable economy, and stability are the ultimate objectives of a Western intervention, this might be characterized as a 'positive peace'. On-going instability and injustice are, by contrast, regarded as the characteristics of a 'negative peace'. But, as Paul Collier notes, Western institution-building may not address the root causes of instability that led to the intervention in the first place.[13] Despite the aspirations of Western and UN actors, some dictatorships are better at preserving peace while democratization can create a great deal of instability. In assessing the record of UN interventions that did not sustain peace, it is striking that the objectives of the UN, while laudable, were frequently too broad. Poverty, for example, is assumed to be a universal cause of instability and conflict which, some insist, must be tackled by intervention, but it is not the cause of civil war in every region of the world. Even relative disparity in wealth and power, long assumed to be a driver of bitter social unrest, can be sustained without civil war. Instead, the focus needs to be on the specific fault lines of each conflict. Acknowledging the budgetary and political limits of intervention by the UN, Caplan also criticizes the lack of agreed benchmarks or of a common approach. At times, it appears that the UN's insistence on the observation of human rights and its own legal standards hinders its efforts at stabilization as they contradict local needs for peace and stability. The priority is to stop the fighting first rather than conflate this with the requirements of a subsequent sustainable peace, which might take many years, even decades to fulfil. Moreover, in a somewhat counter-intuitive sense, transitions and exits require a period of increased

[13] Paul Collier, *Breaking the Conflict Trap: Civil War and Development Policy* (Washington, DC: Oxford University Press, 2003).

effort, specifically as *appropriate* training and resources, rather than merely a steady reduction.

There are few shortcuts in transition. In building capacity, it is easy to assume that, since providing security is the priority of military forces and law enforcement units, security is the basis of capacity building. Yet any state will require a functioning criminal justice system through which police forces can pass suspects, including a trained judiciary, prosecution and defence personnel, penal code, incarceration facilities, courts, and rehabilitation programmes. Furthermore, transition cannot be limited solely to the staging of democratic elections, for there needs to be systematic follow on measures, the maturing of checks and balances, an acceptance of the idea of 'opposition' within a broader notion of 'consensus', the full development of civil society, and preferably the involvement or tolerance, where possible, of regional powers. While crucial for democratization, elections are the achievement of democracy, implying an acceptance of representation and power-sharing, rather than being the sole driver of the process. Moreover, scholars now suggest that, since democracy is culturally variable, it must necessarily differ in form amongst the people. They posit that tolerance of 'alternative democracies' are the solution.[14]

Transition is in part the process of 'exit', specifically the disengagement and ultimate withdrawal of external actors from a state or territory, but it is also a transformation involving the transfer of power, authority, and legitimacy, and perhaps significant changes in the power relationships of those left behind. Transition is a transformative change in politics and security but one which also implies socio-economic alterations too. Historical case studies suggest the manner of intervention, particularly the nature of the entry and initial efforts in consolidation, will have a significant impact on the success of the transition. Evidently, if the political objectives of a military intervention have been accomplished, a successful transition will make a successful consolidation more likely. If, however, the objectives and missions have not been attained, successful exits will entail measures to preserve the partial gains or minimize losses, including reputational costs to the interventionists and their surrogate actors. From the outset it is worth noting that the failure to achieve a durable political settlement can only produce stability so fragile that it will be unable to sustain itself without the continued support of external actors. This might also be the case in economic terms, a feature historians refer to as 'informal empire' or the creation of 'rentier' states. The result of such state fragility or dependence is often a greater likelihood of economic unrest and civil conflict. Even where the interventionist power is eager to exit, limited

[14] Julia Paley, *Democracy: Anthropological Approaches* (Santa Fe: School for Advanced Research Press, 2008).

local support for transition or its successor dispensation will similarly imperil stability. Exits can similarly be jeopardized by 'loyalists' attempting to gain advantage as interventionists depart. A particular problem is posed by those who had collaborated or were employed directly by intervention organizations as they seek to protect their gains and interests.

To be sustainable, transition will require a political settlement that, at the very least, offers the best chance of a stable future. It will also require organizational sustainability, where institutions have the ability to deliver, be logistically enduring, and have appropriate accountability mechanisms. Processes need to be sustainable, in that they serve the interests of locals, can be resourced and are fully 'owned' by them. Resources might reasonably include financial and economic sustainability, although in practice this is rarely achieved at all in the short-term. Dependency but with the expectation of local financial responsibility might be anticipated.

The international context is often the most critical variable affecting the timing and outcome of an exit and thus the processes of transition. Favourable geo-politics will have significant impact on the legitimacy and endurance of a transition. In contrast, interference from regional 'spoilers' can jeopardize stability even where transition is successful in the short-term. No stabilization or state-building operation can remain unchanged as the process develops, of course, for that is the nature of 'transition'. It follows that while an exit is envisioned from the outset, the precise character of that exit evolves according to changing circumstances. To some extent transition is 'path dependent', in that it is inextricably linked to entry and the evolving process of the transfer of authority, but it is also subject to the *dynamic interactions* of conflict and shifting power. The way an intervention begins, the objectives set, and agreements forged, will set expectations and conditions for the subsequent transition, and strongly affect the form of its termination, but it will not determine it entirely. Adaptability and flexibility for those involved are critical, with all agencies working towards a common 'end state' rather than merely an 'end date'. If end dates for intervention are deemed unavoidable then the strategy will usually have to shift towards stability over the longer term. In these cases, the military components of transition will be subordinated to economic and diplomatic elements, although the security situation may not allow it. Indeed, it is an irony that an insurgency, designed to 'liberate' a territorial space, may actually prolong an occupation because of the difficulties of making a viable transition possible. Consequently, even 'end date' scenarios cannot be defined in terms of a single event. Through a variety of obstacles, processes, and events, end states are, in fact, often unavoidably left 'unfinished'.

Transitions are complex operations because it is difficult to deal with every aspect of the process concurrently and symmetrically. 'Exit' is likely to occur in stages, with different actors, including diplomatic and political staff, aid agencies, security forces, mentors, intelligence teams, and logisticians reduced in number and withdrawn at different times. The coordination and management of the transitions between these different operations and actors can be crucial. Ironically, extraction from a difficult transition may entail a temporary increase of effort or at least need to produce a greater effect locally in order to 'break clean' at the tactical level. Nevertheless, there may be military operations in support of a new political dispensation long after the moment of withdrawal, even if there is a lower profile for the personnel involved. The Soviet Union continued to support the successor regime in Kabul after its withdrawal of 1989 with munitions, advisor personnel, and significant funding. Pakistan's interest in the future of Afghanistan also lasted well beyond the date of the Soviet departure as it sponsored a number of Mujahedeen groups. Both the Soviets and Pakistan avoided direct confrontation, but waged a war by proxy. There was concern to calibrate very precisely the means and the ways of the continued involvement in Afghanistan, to reinforce their achievements and prevent adverse developments. While the Soviet economy remained robust, it could continue to supply arms, including aircraft and Scud missiles, and financial support; the Pakistani intelligence services tried to sustain the momentum of a Jihadist war of liberation against the secular, communist authorities in Kabul although it found no solution to the deep factionalism amongst Afghan resistance groups. It was the sudden termination of Soviet support that tilted Afghanistan decisively in Pakistan's favour. This example alone typifies the fact that 'exit' rarely marks the cessation of international involvement, support, and influence.

Planning the transition process, including the character of the exit, is essential. Military personnel pose five key questions in their planning: why is transition taking place? What functions are critical enablers of the security transition? Who are the potential partners and key stakeholders in transition? When should the security transition take place? And how will transition options be developed, negotiated, and implemented?[15] That planning entails the continual re-evaluation of objectives against the ends and some honest assessments of progress. Security and stability are often represented as the priorities in this regard. However, there are no 'hard' metrics or indicators of consolidated stability. The ultimate test of sustainable security and stabilization comes necessarily after the fact; that is, after the exit has been enacted. The best measures available to assess progress before the exit are context dependent but tend to link three foundational requirements: establishment and maintenance of basic security; effective and legitimate governance and rule of law; and management of the conditions affording economic and social

[15] JDP 6/10, p. xi.

productivity. Put another way, the ability to make governance and society 'functional', with its commensurate obedience of the law, participation in local and national government, and vibrant economic activity, is the ideal set of conditions for a successful transition. It is crucial to recognize that the acquisition of 'threshold institutional capability' takes place over the long-term. Forms of governance in societies compromised by violence, often underpinned by attitudinal and cultural change, can take generations to transform. It is important to recognize that no particular level of development or normative system is implied here: it will be beyond the capacity of an intervening authority like the UN to 'lift society out of poverty' or to create a highly developed political system such as a fully functioning and mature democracy. Rather, the purpose is to create a working stability and to restore the sovereignty of the people to determine their own future without the tyranny of conflict or an economy so crippled that it does not function at all.

In a post-colonial world, where the sovereignty of self-determined peoples is the norm, it follows that transition plans have to incorporate local needs, beliefs, and sensibilities. Western nations and humanitarian agencies that become involved in international state-building have a tendency to be ideologically liberal in outlook.[16] This liberal agenda may not always be compatible with the position and aspirations of local elites, who have their own agencies, interests, and plans. Lobby groups in the West are eager to ensure that the principles of liberal ideology with regard to the protection of children, the rights of women, and the prevention of discrimination on the basis of race or sexual orientation are upheld, and there is no reason why interventions by liberal powers should not advocate these as their own principles. However, the international standards of the UN and Geneva are far better aspirations because of their universality. Moreover, it is merely pragmatic to desist from imposing Western liberal constitutional arrangements where this jeopardizes the objectives of stability, peace-building, and transition. It is an uncomfortable fact that progressive liberal structures are not always suitable in the aftermath of civil war: at the grass roots, the overwhelming desire is for security for oneself, one's family, and one's home.

Sovereignty and legitimacy must be restored at the earliest opportunity during transition. Invoking a Gramscian idea, the Organisation for Economic Cooperation and Development (OECD) notes that: 'state legitimacy matters because it provides the basis for rule by consent rather than by coercion'. Their report continues: 'Lack of legitimacy is a major contributor to state fragility

[16] Astri Suhrke, 'Reconstruction as Modernisation: The "Post-Conflict" Project in Afghanistan', *Third World Quarterly* 28, no. 7 (2007): p. 1301; see also Astri Suhrke, 'The Dangers of a Tight Embrace: Externally Assisted Statebuilding in Afghanistan', in *The Dilemmas of Statebuilding*, edited by Roland Paris and Timothy Sisk (New York: Routledge, 2009), p. 233.

because it undermines the processes of state-society bargaining that are central to building state capacity.'[17] Legitimacy is eroded by foreigners adversely affecting sovereign control, corruption in state systems, abuses by government, and economic or systemic state failure. Legitimacy implies a faith, or a degree of consent, in a particular form of governance. To build legitimacy, for transition, it must be developed by local government; there must be the provision of fundamental services; there must be representation and protection; there needs to be a morally correct government; and it must either be patriotic or at least refer to the local history and culture. Crucially all these elements must take place at the grass roots as well as at the national level. In Afghanistan, where provincial governors held their local police forces to account, engaged the public through weekly *shura* (consultative meetings), made available a 'hotline' for complaints, established a monitoring team and then acted on any misdemeanours, there was greater acceptance of state governance. In Helmand, the Ministry of Justice, Ministry of Women's Affairs, the Huquq (civil rights group), prisoner review *shuras*, and district justice committees reduced episodes of arbitrary arrest, and restored a degree of faith in the state criminal justice system. Justice was perhaps more important to local people than security in many regions of Afghanistan, but its development at the national level had been rather slow after the intervention of 2001. Nonetheless, many Afghan citizens expressed a desire for justice to remain at a local level, where traditions of restorative justice underpinned by Sharia law were accepted, a not uncommon feature in other parts of the world.[18]

A historical survey indicates that the post-civil war environment is inhospitable to either the transition toward democracy or its survival. Once again, history is contingent and specific to each example, but in general terms former belligerents fear a loss of security, be that physical, political, or economic, and thus marginalization in a democratic system where they do not possess a majority or where certain elites retain power. It has often been the case that the side that wins an election in a post-war state uses its power to dismantle the institutions of democracy in order to preserve control. In revolutionary states, a similar pattern emerges, but majorities of a population may also opt for the restoration of order over the fruits of democracy if they perceive that instability and violence would otherwise be the result. Revolutions may therefore create civil war, but they may also create dictatorships, either by individual elites or by sections of society that prefer stability to civil rights.

[17] OECD-DAC, *The State's Legitimacy in Fragile Situations*, January 2010, <www.oecd.org/dataoecd/45/6/44794487.pdf>.

[18] In the 1920s, the British accepted local justice in the frontier districts of the North-West Frontier of India. Under the terms of the Frontier Crimes Regulation Act, only the most serious offences were dealt with by the colonial authorities while all minor ones were handled by the communities themselves.

Purpose and scope of this volume

This book was the result of a three-day academic conference between 17–19 December 2012 at Merton College, Oxford, delivered by the Changing Character of War (CCW) research programme at Oxford University and funded by the British Army, specifically the Land Intelligence Fusion Centre (LIFC). The aim of the conference was to explore the tactical aspects of transition processes, exit, and power transfer by bringing together faculty from history, sociology, international relations, and politics, along with ambassadors, members of the Foreign and Commonwealth Office (FCO), the Department of International Development (DfID), and British Army personnel, including infantry officers from the sharp end to Lieutenant Generals responsible for future development and training. Uppermost in our minds was the fact that transition planning and operations in Afghanistan were going on at the time of the conference (Figure I.1), and several delegates had flown in specifically to attend the event. It was therefore vital that the conference delivered tangible benefits, not only to enhance our general and theoretical understanding of the issues, but also, as our military colleagues pointed out, ideas and techniques that could be applied immediately. Despite the focus on ISAF (the International Security Assistance Force) and the specific role for Britain,

Figure I.1. Mann Recovery/Demolition Vehicles en route to PB 2 (Green Zone), February 2014 (Crown copyright)

namely the transition of power in Helmand Province, effort was taken to ensure wider relevance. The result was a global perspective, which, in fact, enhanced considerably our insights into the best and worst practice that might appear in Afghanistan. Thus, this edited volume is the result of a very specific conference, but it is one that, we hope, is intrinsically of interest to the academic and policy world. Readers will be able to reflect on the past, but also develop new understanding, inform concepts, doctrine, and policy, and apprise transition planners and implementers in the near future.

Given the context, in this introduction we seek to give no more than an overview of the themes and draw out a selection of insights. The chapters that follow will each give a more comprehensive examination of case studies, specific issues, and theoretical approaches. They are arranged in accordance with a number of core themes: of strategy and entry; definition of objective; primacy of the political agenda; flexible planning; and risk management. The volume works outwards from the global and thematic but permits a number of case studies to show specificities. There are also a select number of chapters that make reference to the transition of Afghanistan. As editors we became increasingly aware of gaps and omissions in the volume. It is apparent, for example, that the American withdrawal from Vietnam gets scant treatment in this work; there are numerous other examples, no less significant perhaps, which also do not appear here. Critics will have cause to point to the paucity of theoretical models, or the absence of certain regions of the world as case studies, or thematic lacunae. Our only defence is that in one short, multi-disciplinary volume and one brief conference we were able to do no more than sketch the outline for more detailed, scholarly work.

History and theory: insight and understanding

Historical studies can add experience that inform our judgements and creates what Clausewitz called *coup d'oeil* ('insight'). Equally, theoretical models can clarify understanding, and enable us to assess and measure progress, to compare various cases and draw judgements. They cannot be applied as templates. Historical examples provide useful guidance but they are specific to their time and place and consequently cannot substitute for the decisions that pertain to specific operations. As Hegel once noted, 'The owl of Minerva only spreads her wings at the gathering of the dusk'; meaning, we are always wise after the event. Theory always follows practice. Suggestions of what is relevant from history or the theories of social science have to be treated with caution. If we take one example, where a 'light footprint' might have been appropriate in one context, the same would leave a force too vulnerable and ill-protected in another. Gerald Templer, the British plenipotentiary for Malaya in the

Emergency of the 1950s, argued that the answer to the insurgency there was not 'pouring more and more men into the jungle'.[19] He advocated the promise of *merdeka* (independence) with the restoration of peace and the cultivation of the relationship with ethnic Malays as the successor government elite. This also appealed to a government at home that lacked the resources for a major military campaign but which wanted favourable continuities in their post-colonial relationship, an area that Karl Hack deals with in his chapter in this volume on the long-term transition of Malaya. By contrast, the American counter-insurgency strategy in Iraq could not have achieved a suppression of violence with insufficient manpower: it was the ability of the United States to augment its effort with vast resources in manpower and money, the effect of 'mass', that ensured other elements of its strategy could prevail. Nonetheless, despite the need for specificities to be acknowledged, there are some general trends from history and theory that can aid understanding.

There are six main mechanisms of transition apparent in the period after 1945. The first is the 'cut and run'. This is the obvious response to an intervention which is costly and failing. The process is a simple one of withdrawal, with little or no consideration of the consequences locally. It is often seen as a negative calculation and cast pejoratively, but it is one which characterized the British withdrawal from Palestine in 1948. The failure to get local actors to accept a UN plan, pressures at home, and the desire to wind up a troublesome mandate authority meant that Britain left rapidly in May that year.

The second type is the 'phased withdrawal'. This is an exit in stages, with the pace of withdrawal often being commensurate with the achievement of targets that ensure strategic objectives are fulfilled. For obvious reasons, most interventions would be planned to end this way. Both Soviet and Western transitions from Afghanistan characterize this approach.

The third type is the 'deadlines' approach. The timetable of an exit may be determined in advance. These fixed timetables are often problematic. They encourage 'spoilers' and can make responses to unanticipated obstacles more difficult. Yet timetables sometimes galvanize local elites to join the process of transition, ensuring local security forces and institutions can be tested and 'inoculated' to their role. The importance of time and particular deadlines featured strongly in the British colonial withdrawal from Malaya.

A related type, and fourth, is the 'benchmarking' approach. The framework of pre-established standards of achievement is applied as a mechanism to manage the configuration of the interventionist forces and the character of political relations. The focus is often on outputs, such as the number of trained personnel, rather than outcomes, such as the establishment of an independent

[19] Brian Lapping, *End of Empire* (New York: St. Martin's Press, 1990), p. 224.

security force. There is significant risk that benchmarks become distorted through political manipulation and subject to the dynamics of the withdrawal process. Various UN missions have attempted to utilize this approach.

A fifth type is dependence on elections. Elections are considered important instruments of peace consolidation as they restore sovereignty to the people, mark a symbolic conclusion to violence as the means to resolve contested power-sharing, and help identify and legitimate political elites that external actors regard as sovereign representatives in international relations. It must be noted that elections cannot in themselves deliver stability and should be considered as just one element, if an important one, of a transitional strategy. Indeed, elections offer no guarantee of peace, particularly if sections of a society feel disenfranchised, subordinate to a majority, or there are obvious and odious irregularities in the electoral system. To go further, the ability to ensure local representation, by whatever system, is preferable to holding elections that do no more than confer legitimacy on an incompetent or unrepresentative regime.

The sixth type of transition involves continued military operations. Such operations may or may not be conducted by the original intervention forces, or there may be a form of more clandestine or distant support through the supply of arms, intelligence assets, or training, but all are used to consolidate gains made, assist the new state authorities to build on their powers, or to complete the suppression of unrest, resistance, or insurgency. British operations in Borneo in support of their allies in Brunei in the 1960s or in Dhofar in support of the Omanis in the 1970s exemplify this type.

While examining the intellectual problem of transition through a typology such as this can be useful, it tells us very little of the detail. Theoretical models cannot reveal what human doubts, hesitations, calculations, and passions governed the decision-making of transition while it actually took place. Retrospective assessments are convenient, sanitized, and manipulated to prove an agenda was correct or incorrect. The headline in *The Chronicle Herald* in Canada in February 2013 was 'Let's face it we didn't win in Afghanistan'.[20] Nevertheless, while making dramatic headlines, such contemporary assessments are selective. It is rare to find analyses that posit a balanced verdict, showing, for example, that the West had achieved its objectives of apprehending Osama bin Laden as the architect of the '9/11' 2001 terrorist attack on the United States, established a national, constitutional government and a nascent local government apparatus, the embryo of a criminal justice system, a new

[20] 'Let's face it: We didn't win in Afghanistan', *The Chronicle Herald*, 10 February 2013, <http://thechronicleherald.ca/novascotia/677174-let-s-face-it-we-didn-t-win-in-afghanistan>; see also Stephen Walt, 'Lessons of two wars: we will lose in Iraq and Afghanistan', *Foreign Policy*, 16 August 2011, <http://walt.foreignpolicy.com/posts/2011/08/16/lessons_of_two_wars_we_will_lose_in_iraq_and_afghanistan>.

transport infrastructure, improved health services (such that life expectancy for Afghan citizens increased and child mortality rates fell steeply), and made inroads into education at primary, secondary, and tertiary level.[21] Negative assessments, which were far more frequent, were valid in identifying continued conflict and instability, layers of corruption, inadequate protection of individuals or minority communities, a weak and dependent economy, and foreign interference. Too few articles in Western media outlets identified the same issues about which Afghan journalists and citizens complained, which begs the question of *who* 'won' or lost, and by what criteria such a simple assessment can be drawn. If the United States had indeed 'lost' the conflict in Afghanistan by 2013 then it is striking that America was far less affected by its 'defeat' than Afghanistan. In almost all respects, America has been unscathed by its protracted struggle with insurgents. To give our assessments greater depth than those of the contemporary media, comparative work can be very helpful, particularly where historical patterns are concerned. To illustrate this, two cases, set in contrasting historical and thematic contexts, specifically transitions at the end of empire and the operations in Iraq, now follows.

Transitions at the end of empire

In trying to describe patterns at the end of European colonial rule in Africa and Asia it is important to recognize that decolonization varied widely: some were peaceful handovers, others were conducted amidst considerable violence. Moreover, some transitions stood the test of new, independent nationhood or confederation, while others descended into anarchy, civil war, sectarianism, or dictatorship. Nonetheless, from this maelstrom of changes, various themes are still discernible. The first is that the end of European imperialism was closely linked to changes in the geo-political circumstances of the time. European empires existed because of a belief that they were beneficial, strategically and morally justifiable, and the associated costs of security and administration were bearable. After 1945, the geo-strategic landscape was transformed as Europe's relative power was eclipsed by the ascendency of the United States and the Soviet Union. In European politics, democratization and a more intense focus on social improvement meant there was far less appetite for colonial rule, and in the colonies themselves democratic and nationalist movements were becoming more assertive. Moreover, European

[21] From 2001 and 2013 maternal mortality came down from 16 to 14 (per 1,000) and child mortality from 131 to 101 per annum (per 1,000). See 'Afghanistan: Mortality rate', accessed 8 March 2014, <http://www.indexmundi.com/facts/afghanistan/mortality-rate>. Moreover, in the same period life expectancy rose from 46.2 years (2001) to 60.5 years (2013). See 'Afghanistan Statistics', *Unicef Website,* accessed 8 March 2014, <http://www.unicef.org/infobycountry/afghanistan_statistics.html>.

economic change, with a relative loss of the share of world trade it had once dominated, made burdensome administration of the colonies unattractive compared with investment in the developed world. In short, transformation in Europe was driving the process of decolonization. Nevertheless, the United States backed the late imperial agendas of France and Britain as better alternatives to Soviet expansion: the strategic imperative was global stability with democratization where viable. There were limits and caveats. It was not prepared to allow Britain and France unilateralism over the Suez crisis in 1956 when these nations attempted to impose a military solution on Egypt. Nevertheless, the Americans prioritized anti-communist policies and regarded their European allies as crucial elements in that ideological struggle.

Despite the clarity of the West's strategic agenda, the hallmark of most European colonial transitions was haste, a paucity of resources, and improvisation. In some cases, there was considerable resistance to European authority, including protracted insurgencies. The history of decolonization therefore provides some interesting observations which John Darwin draws out in his chapter. The first observation is that the idea that a timetable of transition could be controlled proved illusory. Local actors, especially the elites, demanded full independence and power in relatively short periods of time whereas, in general terms, the Europeans had hoped for gradual transitions which would allow them the chance to retain economic and security privileges, develop permanent and perhaps client relationship links with the successor authorities, and protect minorities. Rob Johnson illustrates this outcome, driven also in part by British domestic politics, with his chapter on India and Pakistan in 1947.

The second observation is the prospect of gaining power after the departure of Europeans led to a scramble for positions of authority between a variety of individuals, parties, factions, and groups. This tended to increase divisions in society and politics, and could sharpen and deepen ideological, ethnic, or sectarian consciousness. In this volume, Aaron Edwards examines the attempts to conduct robust operations amidst the shifting sands of British foreign policy at the chaotic end of colonial rule in Aden in 1967. We might deduce that to obtain the compliance from local elites required incentives and consistent good faith. This sometimes posed a moral dilemma about whether liberal principles could be forced on to leaders whose priorities were very different. Colonial officials were often uneasy about involvement in negotiations with those linked to 'direct action' or, far worse, those associated with violence. Home governments were less likely to allow local colonial concerns to change the agenda of decolonization and often drove the initiative, sometimes regardless of opposition by settler populations.

The third observation is that in order to preserve influence after transition, significant resources, particularly financial support and direct aid had to be invested well beyond the period of colonial control. The United Kingdom's aid programme to India, for example, commencing before independence in 1947, was only terminated in 2013. It is also striking that the Europeans were eager to transfer power to a government of a 'viable' state with appropriate state-level functions, and a friendly elite that could exercise control within its own borders. Where it had doubts about this viability or where minorities were threatened by a more powerful group, Britain attempted to create confederations. Not all of these survived for long, but there were successes including the confederation of Canada (1837) and the union of South Africa (1910). Unity and tradition were particularly valued by the British in transition planning. In this volume, James Worrall shows the relative success of ending counter-insurgency operations and the building of legitimacy in Oman in the 1970s through strong relationships and commitment, effectively reuniting quite distinct communities in the country.

The fourth observation is that the colonial powers were quite prepared to 'cut and run' when their respective national interests were at stake. France faced a serious constitutional crisis over the protracted and unpopular war in Algeria and despite the colony's status as part of metropolitan France, it was jettisoned to preserve the integrity of the metropole. Britain discarded its control of the Gulf States, Palestine, and several African colonies to cut costs and avoid international criticism, even when arrangements for the internal security of these nascent states was far from certain. Saul Kelly's chapter on southern Arabia and the Gulf exposes the contradictions and bad faith of British governments in their withdrawal calculations in the period 1964–71.

The key criticism of imperialism was not only the denial of freedom to colonial peoples, but also the violence inflicted on them. Nevertheless, colonial states were not governed solely by the lash. It was the logic of all states that a single authority required local collaboration and ultimately a monopoly of violence. Consequently, European colonial powers invested significantly in their security apparatus and made much use of local manpower to augment their own military forces. This had two effects: one, these security forces required continued support as part of the transition in order to guard against violent unrest, and, two, it could in some circumstances empower particular elites, especially those in the armed forces who subsequently saw it as their duty to protect the state not only against external enemies but subversive elements, corruption, and unreasonable oligarchies. Such aspirations were not always pre-planned or fulfilled as David Anderson explains in his chapter on the heavy handed ending of British rule in Kenya between 1952 and 1963.

In theory, Britain was particularly concerned to make the transfer of power conditional on the willingness of local leaders to accept the Westminster democratic model and a version of the British legal system, but it was also keen to ensure a lasting, cordial relationship with its newly independent partners. Nevertheless, preferential treatment of the new elites precluded any continuing responsibility for colonial minorities, including those loyalists on whom the colonial state had relied. It also made it difficult to make any form of representation against repression by post-colonial regimes. The new elites, who needed to create myths of liberation to reinforce their independent national identity, refused to acknowledge any imperial magnanimity and often distanced themselves from the colonial past. In Europe, a lack of interest in the fate of the colonies made it easier to make the psychological shift that followed the loss of 'Great Power' status. While colonial agendas influenced the way the transfer of power was debated and then realized, it proved far more important to satisfy opinion 'at home'. This was just as true of the French experience in Algeria and the British departure from India.

Furthermore, anti-colonial sentiment has proved a powerful political instrument in the post-colonial world. Post-colonial political failings are often reconfigured as historical or contemporary external interferences. Some narratives, of course, are more powerful and enduring than others, especially when based on accepted narratives of past 'oppression'. Even episodes of 'colonial abuse' which occurred more than one hundred years ago are invoked to explain current setbacks or failures, and conspiracy theories are popular tools of explanation for seemingly any event. Such discourse makes even the most benign intervention or transition process less than straightforward.

The ending of the campaign in Iraq, 2004–11

The conventional invasion of Iraq by a multistate 'coalition of the willing' in 2003 was soon overshadowed by the complexity of a widespread insurgency, complicated by criminal elements, foreign subversion, and opportunists. Over the seven years of the campaign, the United States struggled to impose order, establish a new Iraqi government, rebuild its security apparatus, restart its economy, and repair the country's infrastructure. The invasion was controversial and the conflict proved unpopular with Western governments, and the American electorate, which combined to push the administration of President George W. Bush to consider a series of exit strategies. The campaign was still unresolved when President Barack Obama was elected, but his new administration assured the American public that the United States would seek an early withdrawal by handing power over to the Iraqi government.

The United States struggled to find a solution to the insurgency that had developed, but the greatest number of security incidents, which had peaked by 2006, involved sectarian or communal violence rather than actions against the Coalition. Whilst some clearly fought what they regarded as a foreign occupation, volunteers from outside Iraq poured in to sacrifice themselves as suicide bombers or make opportunistic attacks on the Coalition forces, Iraqi government units, or sectarian rivals. Death squads, vigilante groups, and criminal elements using police uniforms to kidnap middle class Iraqis for ransom all added to the complex 'insurgent eco-system'. Journalists spoke of a civil war engulfing the centre of the country, and the rise of Sunni resistance in the Tikrit-Baghdad 'triangle'. Meanwhile, British operations in southern Iraq provoked the formation of Shia militias, and these enjoyed the backing of Iran. In response to the deteriorating situation, the American approach was to surge in with fresh troops to dominate the capital and central Iraq, while in peripheral regions, such as Al Anbar province and the Kurdish north, arrangements were made with local community leaders to form self-defence militias against outsiders.

Stung by criticism at home, the British government, by contrast, attempted to accelerate the departure of its forces through accommodations with the largest militia, the Jaish al-Mahdi. The British deal failed disastrously. Basra, the second largest city of the country, fell into the hands of the insurgents and it took a combined American and Iraqi Army operation (ironically, one planned by the British Army) to drive the insurgents out.[22] Britain had been humiliated by the government's decision to withdraw its units at the critical moment of the campaign, and a belated return to the city did little to restore confidence in the British approach. Noticeably, British expertise in counter-insurgency techniques, which they had claimed stemmed from long years of experience from Malaya to Northern Ireland, was largely dismissed by American personnel as false or exaggerated.

The manner of entry, where the absence of a specific UN Security Council resolution authorizing the invasion, which was condemned as a breach of international law, had precipitated unfavourable conditions for exit. UN cooperation was limited which meant that finding a diplomatic or political solution through international agreements was unlikely. For the sake of their reputation, the American government regarded it as imperative to leave the country in a stable condition with a functioning democratic government. Yet the military situation was also highly problematic. The toppling of Saddam Hussein and the dismantling of his regime was achieved skilfully and with overwhelming force in a matter of weeks. The decision to dismiss the entire civil service, police, and armed forces as 'regime elements' nevertheless deprived thousands of their livelihood and gave them no option but to resist the occupation. Moreover, whilst the Coalition troops trained in conventional warfare could provide a modicum of security, they were neither trained nor equipped for a protracted insurgency. Worse still, the invasion plan had not envisaged a prolonged occupation or reconstruction. Consequently, there were almost no arrangements made to provide basic services. The realization

[22] Hew Strachan, Jonathan Bailey, and Richard Iron, eds, *Blair's Wars and Britain's Generals* (Oxford: Oxford University Press, 2013).

of the mounting cost, both financial and in terms of casualties, deepened the unpopularity of the war with the American public and put further pressure on Washington to find a rapid solution.

The Iraq case makes clear that the planning for interventions and their termination has a tendency to grossly overestimate the transformatory capacity of armed forces, and revealed the absence of any suitable agency to carry out reconstruction. In the British government, the Foreign and Commonwealth Office and the Department for International Development had quite limited roles which ordinarily depended on working through an existing national government. They had no experience or capacity to deliver the sort of services that were urgently required, including the repair of electricity power stations, food distribution, and local administration.[23] Coalition military forces attempted to fill the gap, but had to learn on the job while trying to contain a deteriorating security environment.

The exit, driven by the domestic political agendas of interventionist nations, proved very costly to the fulfilment of the mission and to the population under occupation. Even the electoral process, on which great hopes for an early resolution to the conflict had been pinned, contributed to corruption and anger amongst Iraqis. Fears of being disenfranchised, a refusal by Sunnis to participate in a system imposed by the Coalition, and the desire for revenge against sectarian rivals damaged the process of democratization. Iraqi parties and certain leading politicians stripped the assets of the ministries under their control and appointed their friends and allies. Unsurprisingly, their victims and their rivals retaliated.

A number of plans for exit from Iraq evolved cumulatively and in response to worsening security conditions.[24] These exit plans were in sequence. The first, envisaged in 2003–04, was the policy of 'plug and play'. The concept was that the Iraqi Army would be defeated but the other institutions of state would survive. In essence security would continue to be delivered by the Coalition while Iraqi ministries underwent significant reform. This was to ensure a speedy exit of interventionist forces from Iraq. The plan soon disintegrated and was replaced by 'seven steps to sovereignty'. This policy aimed to develop new state capacities with criteria and timelines, yet it was found to be quite unrealistic. At the core of the plan was de-Ba'athification, particularly the eradication of the old ruling elite from the upper echelons of the technocratic civil service. These men were to be replaced by Washington's favoured Iraqi exiles. In addition, de-Ba'athification involved the disbandment of the Iraqi Army, which meant the compulsory redundancy of 400,000 trained personnel who, inexplicably, were allowed to keep their weapons. There was to be the

23 Hilary Synot, *Bad Days in Basra* (London: I.B. Tauris, 2008).

24 Toby Dodge, 'Iraq', in Caplan, ed., *Exit Strategies and State Building*, pp. 242–58.

gradual re-building of the political system following the American model which would enable Coalition forces to drawdown in stages. The plan was abandoned when it became clear the ambitious pre-departure benchmarks were never going to be met.

The subsequent plan was the 'November 15 Agreement'. The concept was to limit the commitment of the United States to Iraq, without totally abandoning state reform, by transferring power to a handpicked cohort of Iraqi expatriates and their partners. Essentially, this meant subcontracting the complex task of state building to unproven and deeply unpopular exiles and outsiders. Linked to the agreement were long-term financial commitments which would be subject to rigorous American scrutiny. In the south, the British had proceeded with their own separate plan. Here the emphasis was on 'Provincial Iraqi Control'. The British approach in Basra, in contrast to the national state-building effort in Baghdad, even at the height of their capacity, could at best be described as 'conflict mediation'. Extended negotiations with Jaish al-Mahdi, the primary militia force in the city, ensured a secure withdrawal on the basis of payments and commitments not to return. Subsequent abuses by Jaish al-Mahdi were ignored for reasons of political expediency. Even if the negotiations had produced an interim authority, the failure to make this dependent and conditional on the approval of the administration in Baghdad condemned the project to failure. Coordination across the Coalition was therefore woefully inadequate at the political and strategic level.

The final phase involved 'strategic negotiations and mass'. The concept was to prioritize security by surging forces (171,000 troops in 2007) and deploy them across much larger areas of central Iraq. This new military posture, being much more interventionist in the pursuit of insurgents into their base areas, but also dominating the ground and protecting the civilian populations within designated areas, helped to turn the tide of the conflict. Crucially, cooperating with Sunni groups that wanted to drive out Jihadist extremists and Shia gunmen also changed the situation. Nevertheless, strategic negotiations with the Iraqi government did not succeed. It had become clear, for example, that American expectations about the long-term use of military bases, prisoner detention, immunity from prosecution for American troops and contractors, and unfettered operational freedom, were unacceptable in Baghdad. The United States struggled to secure a satisfactory 'state of forces agreement'. It was these strategic negotiations which resulted in fixed timelines for extraction of American forces, for, without the full cooperation of the new Iraqi government, the American occupation had become unviable. In this volume, Mark Battjes examines the tactical aspects of the Iraq case through the fortunes of the 25th Infantry Division, the last US Army division to leave in 2011, and how American personnel managed new legal constraints, domestic political pressures, restrictive rules of engagement, and slender logistics.

Implications for Afghanistan's long-term stability

This volume was written at a time when the future of Afghanistan, after Western military intervention, was unknown. As authors, our concern was to assert historical, theoretical, and applied approaches in other contexts to gain some better insight and understanding that could be brought to bear on the issues in Afghanistan. Nevertheless, we recognized from the outset that the situation in Afghanistan was obviously unique. All we could really hope to do was offer reflections, scope analogous tactical and operational circumstances and pose further questions. The first and most logical step was to engage Sir Rodric Braithwaite, Britain's former ambassador to the USSR who has used his background to write a history of the Soviet War in Afghanistan, and he has contributed a chapter on the Soviet withdrawal showing how the gap between official rhetoric and reality created a strategic setback, despite a competent military withdrawal.

It was Basil Liddell Hart who once wrote: 'The objective in war is a better state of peace—even if only from your own point of view. Hence it is essential to conduct war with constant regard to the peace you desire'.[25] Defining the end state for Afghanistan has been far more difficult than originally thought. Expectations that Afghanistan could be rebuilt and turned into a democracy with a fully functioning economy proved hopelessly over-optimistic. 'Nation-building' became, with a degree of weariness in the expression, 'Afghan good-enough'. The desire to create a modern army that could take over from the ISAF forces by 2014 at times looked to be foundering because of illiteracy, corruption, and the lack of a professional officer corps. 'Green on blue' (later 'insider threat') incidents, where Afghan security forces turned their weapons against members of ISAF, were the result not only of infiltration by insurgents, but also frustration and irritation with foreign methods, or drug abuse. Afghan civilians in the Pashtun south frequently expressed their anger with corrupt government officials, including police officers who sexually assaulted children. ISAF was often regarded as a force that simply enabled the corrupt to get away with their crimes and operations that resulted in civilian casualties were criticized in every quarter. Moreover, Coalition nations that had agreed to take a lead on a particular aspect of nation-building in some cases seemed to make the situation worse. Germany's early efforts to create a new police force were deemed too slow and complex, necessitating the creation of auxiliary police units. These proved so predatory they had to be abandoned and police reform lagged far behind the development of the Afghan National Army until new impetus was given by the American takeover of all security sector reform.

[25] Basil H. Liddell Hart, *Strategy* (New York: Praeger Publishers, Inc., 1967), p. 338.

The United Kingdom had offered to take the lead on counter-narcotics, and although there was some success with eradication in the north, the policy generated significant resistance in Helmand when it was introduced there in 2006.[26]

The term 'transition' refers to a long process of change, involving the transfer of authority, space, capability, and responsibility. Whilst an Afghan national government apparatus was created and some progress had been made with local governance, the Afghans had reason to doubt that the West would sustain its commitment when President Obama announced, in 2009, that there would be a timetable for withdrawal and that all combat operations would cease by 2014. For the Americans and for the other Coalition partners, national interests invariably override all other considerations, and exit would threaten the ability to provide security and thus sustain development unless the Afghan government could establish control across the country by its own means. Where perhaps the West's mission was 'to secure, in order to develop', transition required a new and clear definition. ISAF's multinational character complicated the lines of command and control, not least because national agendas took precedence. Simplicity was the solution to restore clarity in ISAF's collective purpose. Each nation had to strive for a dignified, timely, and well organized withdrawal, wherever possible without casualties. Above all, the success of the entire campaign depended ultimately on the resilience of the structures left behind, which included the Afghan security forces, the viability of the Afghan economy, and the preservation of democracy.

It was clear that there were major weaknesses in the Afghan government and its security apparatus, but the Western Coalition had to be pragmatic about who it transferred power to. Efforts had to be made to cultivate local leaders, including insurgents, to encourage their participation in government rather than leaving them 'outside' the dividends of peace. Nevertheless, the explicit facilitation of insurgency or acquiescence in the return of warlordism was unlikely to be tolerated by the international community nor welcomed by Afghans. Historically, and perhaps in a manner distinct from the United States or other European nations, Britain had often co-opted its former enemies and critics into government, including the successor regimes to the colonial administrations. Britain bargained transfers of power or degrees of power sharing through negotiations with, for example, Abdur Rahman Khan in Afghanistan, Mohandas Gandhi and Jawarhawal Nehru in India, Aung San in Burma, Jomo Kenyatta in Kenya, Kwame Nkrumah in Ghana, the National Liberation Front in Aden and South Arabia, and Gerry Adams in Northern Ireland. Nevertheless, the United States made clear in 2013 that the

[26] Frank Ledwidge, *Losing Small Wars* (New Haven, CT: Yale University Press, 2012).

conditions on which it would determine Taliban participation in Afghan governance would be their acceptance of the Afghan constitution, with its protection of minority rights, a recognition of the sovereign position of the president, Hamid Karzai, and a cessation of violence. The Taliban reiterated its refusal to accept the government of Kabul and pledged to continue its struggle, and yet it did not rule out the possibility of negotiations once all foreign forces had been withdrawn.

The insurgency in Afghanistan that developed in 2003 was not a monolith but rather a loose association of different commanders and 'front' networks that possess overlapping interests and agendas but also display varying degrees of adherence to their senior leaders. Interviews in 2012 and 2013 revealed the Taliban did not believe it had the capacity to overrun the country or ensure compliance to its will in the way it had done in the mid-1990s. It was for this reason that it entered into tentative phases of negotiations with the Americans from 2011, although there were repeated statements of the desire not to negotiate with the regime of Hamid Karzai in Kabul. On the other side, ISAF, the International Security and Assistance Force, although sanctioned by the UN, was always regarded by Afghans as an American organization and, at worst, an occupation force carrying out exactly the same sort of mission as the Soviets while backing the corrupt and apparently secular regime in the capital.

In order to develop the idea of how Afghanistan's transition and subsequent transformation may unfold beyond 2014, and to offer a comparative framework in order to assess other cases, the remainder of this introduction utilizes the theory and principles of transition and matches them against options and scenarios that have occurred in the past in various regions of the world. While this examination cannot capture the dynamic processes that would undoubtedly occur, nor give any firm predictions, it can offer some observations for assessing areas for contingencies and subjects that would require similar planning.

Approaches to transition in Afghanistan

It is in the nature of institutions to focus on predictable processes in transition at the expense of the rather more unpredictable elements, namely local people and their agendas. Nevertheless, the situation in Afghanistan has been typical in that local sensibilities, sculpted by a patronage system, respond to particularly influential personalities rather than any post or appointment. Local government officials can find themselves isolated and ignored in rural areas if they do not cultivate good relationships with men of influence and power. Authority can often depend on the ability to deliver tangible improvements to people's lives, to provide security and to create incomes. Moreover, historically in Afghanistan there has been a long-standing association between notions of 'small government' and 'good government': national agendas were considered too remote to be relevant or beneficial in rural communities and the predatory character of Kabuli regimes meant that *hokumaat* (the government) was a pejorative term in the southern and eastern Pashto language. In times of crisis, when central direction is needed, it seems counter-intuitive to suggest that minimizing the influence of a national government, or international agencies, could be a solution, but this is precisely the case with Afghanistan. There is a strong cultural expectation that local actors would not only be consulted, but actively involved in the decision-making and processes of reconstruction. Naturally this produces tensions and contradictions with all external bodies, including international aid agencies and foreign military forces. The art of transition at the tactical level is nevertheless dependent on the careful coordination of local aspirations and the multitude of bodies, often with competing priorities, who wish to intervene. It is an obvious but important point that all international organizations need to foreground their insight and understanding of areas that require transition, including knowledge of the local languages, history, and culture in order to make informed decisions.

In 2013, a senior figure of the British Foreign and Commonwealth Office identified four tenets for transition in Afghanistan that could frame an organization's decision-making, summed up in the words: Fight, Build, Talk, and Commit. The 'fight' referred to the provision of security and security-sector reform. Training and mentoring of local police and military units reduces the unwelcome footprint of foreigners and offers new employment opportunities. A gradual reduction of foreign trainers and advisors can occur, if circumstances permit, where numbers are 'lower for longer' rather than being surged in the short-term. The testing and inoculation of new local units is crucial, with remedial support offered to those that fail under pressure. The provision of foreign or external reinforcements that act as 'quick reaction forces' is of paramount importance to prevent the collapse of efforts that may have taken years to establish. The transition of intelligence and support systems should take place as early as possible to establish and develop capabilities without which local forces will be unable to function. Oliver Lewis and Andrew Britton, in their chapter, show there are often gaps between the rhetoric and practice, and in clarity and understanding, which underscore the importance of listening and responding to local requirements.

This introduces the second tenet of 'build'; a reference to capacity in physical terms but also the training of local personnel. Investments and development projects must be coordinated, and should be part of a long-term plan. Short-term goals can then be plotted and prioritized according to the operational needs of security, the aspirations of local communities, available resources, and local government direction. Care must be taken to think through the secondary effects of all interventions, since uncoordinated if well-meaning efforts can have detrimental consequences. One village in southern Afghanistan was provided with sixteen wells its population did not need because aid agencies were unable to unite their efforts.[27] Attempts to provide impoverished farmers on the periphery of a drugs eradication zone in southern Afghanistan with tools and free fertilizer caused deep resentment amongst farmers who lived within the proscribed zone. They were furious that the newcomers cultivated opium and were the beneficiaries of free hand outs. In simple terms, during transition the consolidation of security and justice, and viable economic activity, should be given primacy over health and education, important though the latter are in the long-term. It is also true that, education and justice have been concerns that give rise to unrest that may lie at the heart of an insurgency. For many Afghans, the provision of education and justice has influenced strongly their allegiance between the government and the insurgents. However, as Peter Rundell shows in his chapter on the Helmand Plan, despite the 'seven deadly sins' of economic and political development by outsiders, Provincial Reconstruction Teams provide examples of good practice for transition too.

The third tenet, 'to talk', while simple in theory, is often the most difficult to initiate and sustain in practice.[28] National governments and their international supporters need to engage with regional neighbours both to reassure them that the new transitional dispensation does not contest their own regional interests, and to gain recognition, or establish bilateral agreements on trade, justice, and security. When possible, reconciliation and reintegration should be put in local hands, albeit with the provision of eternal assistance when required. The most controversial component is the engagement of armed actors, such as insurgent or rebel groups, or the management of negotiations with a national government set on the repression of a portion of its own population. Negotiations during a civil war or insurgency, in common with military strategies, have a variety of purposes, and fulfil the Clausewitzian dictum of being 'an extension of politics by other means'. Negotiations can be designed to end conflict, but can also make it possible to gain an advantage in a future peace even if the military campaign is going badly. Negotiations enable belligerents to buy time, or to sow discord and divide their enemies. Initiating discussions, even if they are no more than window-dressing, can mollify internal critics of a conflict or powerful external third

[27] Sippi Azarbaijani-Moghaddam, Mirwais Wardak, Idrees Zaman, and Annabel Taylor, *Afghan Hearts, Afghan Minds: Exploring Afghan perceptions of civil–military relations* (British and Irish Afghan Assistance Group, 2008).

[28] The chapter by Mark Beautement regarding Sangin in Helmand Province, in this volume, exemplifies this problem.

parties. In short, negotiations, whilst often welcome as the roadmap to peace, are not always sincere.[29] In this volume, Mark Beautement gives a case example of Sangin in Helmand where specific circumstances, and detailed knowledge of local aspirations, opened the opportunities for negotiations.

The final tenet is to commit beyond the 'end date' of transition. Failure to do so leads to a scramble by local actors to maximize the benefits in the remaining period of external control, which may lead to looting, seizures of property or institutions, an increase in corrupt financial practices, and even *coup d'etat*. Civil and economic efforts by interventionist agencies ought therefore to continue through the transition process and beyond. There is a clear peace dividend that comes with investment. In common with many other developing countries after civil war, in southern Afghanistan, the most important issues are the protection of the immediate family, water supply, land ownership, maintaining networks for political power through influence, and, ultimately self-respect through personal prestige. Through transition local people will always seek to protect their interests and they require guarantees. They will calculate how to maximize their personal survival, and their security should be linked to local security forces and cooperation with law enforcement agencies. Citizens will also seek the biggest share of available resources which requires space and opportunities for peaceful negotiation. Unsurprisingly, the disbursement of funds by intervention organizations, both civilian and military, can cause the greatest ambition, anxiety, and resentment. Transparency is essential. In extreme cases, interventionist organizations may need to strike local accords for safe passage but due to the fragility of such agreements and activities by spoilers and rivals, such arrangements can never substitute for proper security.

Tactical transition

In addition to the four tenets listed above, there are some features of transition at the grass roots which, while perhaps self-evident, must be acknowledged as vitally important. It is essential that a clear strategy, based on sound policy, must drive operations and tactics; the 'tacticization' of strategy, where the minutiae of events, concerns about reputational costs, or the desire to act, regardless of the consequences, cannot be allowed to determine the process of transition. David Galula, the French counter-insurgency theorist, noted in 1964 that: 'Essential though it is, the military action is secondary to the

[29] Rob Johnson, '*Mizh der beitabora khalqi-i*': A Comparative Study of Afghan-Pashtun Perspectives on Negotiating with the British and the Soviets, 1839–1989', *Journal of Imperial and Commonwealth History*, Special Edition, 39, no. 4 (November 2011): pp. 551–70.

political one, its primary purpose being to afford the political power enough freedom to work safely with the population.' He continued: '"A revolutionary war is 20 per cent military action and 80 per cent political". [This] is a formula that reflects the truth.'[30] Critics of Western military intervention have repeated their concerns over many years that governments have tended to act, often to assist countries in crisis, without a considered political plan. Coalition states that have participated in Afghanistan's reconstruction now recognize that they must abandon the idea that their military forces alone could provide a solution to the conflict there. Even security sector reforms have proved far more difficult to implement in practice than originally thought. International agencies are even less willing to attempt reconstruction or nation-building, and they are more wary of trying to introduce new innovations. It is well known that there were inconsistencies and gaps in the Afghan governance system prior to transition but this was to be expected. Controversies raged about the Afghan electoral system and there were significant concerns that members of the Afghan government were involved in the Kabul bank scandal or other episodes where donor money was siphoned off to private off-shore accounts. Nonetheless, the Western plan for Afghanistan's development was less idealistic by 2009 and adopted the more pragmatic notion that the country only had to be left in a resilient condition to manage its own security, develop its economy, and thus decide its own fate.

For the international assistance forces in Afghanistan, it was clear that they had to accept political primacy throughout the final phase of transition. In counter-insurgency operations, as the British politician and European envoy Paddy Ashdown once noted, it is often the case that military forces can do no more than, 'hold the ring' until a political settlement can be thrashed out.[31] This has a very practical purpose when international forces find themselves deep inside the territory where a conflict has not been resolved: a political settlement which concludes conflict can ensure the safe passage of those forces and holds out the prospect of a more enduring and workable peace. Military withdrawal can, of itself, be a useful bargaining tool in peace negotiations. Deception and psychological operations, while important tactical military devices, must also the serve the political agenda of transition. Consultation with locals must be genuine and sincere. Clearly stated objectives, the smooth passage of information, and incorporation of local aspirations, are imperative. Transition makes it important that withdrawing intervention forces do not make promises they cannot keep, and it is far easier to offer

[30] David Galula, *Counterinsurgency Warfare: Theory and Practice* (London: Praeger Security International, 2006), p. 63.

[31] Paddy Ashdown, *Swords into Ploughshares: Bringing Peace to the Twenty-First Century* (London: Orion, 2007).

withdrawal to elicit local cooperation. Yet, any cooperation will be short-lived and conditional so it is imperative that 'handovers' are efficient, and keep to established timetables. Divisions in conflict-ridden societies and amongst rival insurgent groups make small-scale bargains feasible and attractive for departing troops, but the local government would need to be involved in order to retain its legitimacy and authority after transition.

As transition approached for ISAF in Afghanistan, there was a pervasive belief amongst Afghans that power was invested in 'foreigners' and the government of Karzai was 'weak'. There was a strong feeling that those in power in Kabul would do everything they could to retain power, even at the expense of national reconciliation. Insurgent groups labelled the administration of Karzai as the 'government of slaves', suggesting that all its actions were really driven by the Americans. On the other hand, Afghans' statements about transition could not be taken entirely at face value. From the announcement of the end date for combat operations by international forces, Afghans were described as 'hedging', specifically diverting assets out of the country, making connections as insurance against becoming isolated, and, whilst not something that could be easily proved, they opened communications with insurgent groups even in areas where there were sectarian or ethnic antagonisms.[32] There was, by 2013, a widespread recognition that Western troops were leaving, the evidence was in plain sight (Figures I.2 and I.3), but most Afghans believed reasons would be found for ISAF to remain.[33]

Transition requires the development of local, well-trained security forces. In Afghanistan, these had to be built from scratch, not least because the auxiliary units that existed were often predatory and unreliable. The British have a particularly strong track record in this sort of training activity, which is modelled on their own military culture and phased into a logical sequence for transition. In the first phase in southern Afghanistan, the British in Helmand assumed responsibility for security themselves, using some local 'legacy' forces as auxiliaries while new units were formed up out of contact in American training centres. Western personnel were then embedded in nascent Afghan units as either Operational Mentoring and Liaison Teams (OMLTs), the British title, or Embedded Training Teams (ETTs), the American title. This work proved challenging for both Western and Afghan personnel, generating a fair degree of frustration, anger, humour, and absurdity, but also some remarkable bonds of friendship and mutual respect. The British clung to their model of small unit mentoring for some time, but the logic was to gradually permit tactical formations to function on their own, eventually

[32] See Antonio Giustozzi's chapter in this volume.

[33] Mike Martin, 'War on its Head: An Oral History of the Helmandi Conflict, 1978–2012' (PhD Dissertation, King's College London, 2013).

Figure I.2. Manual demolition of section perimeter at FOB PRICE, October 2013 (Crown copyright)

Figure I.3. Demolition of Hesco Bastion Perimeter at FOB PRICE, October 2013 (Crown copyright)

concentrating on advisory work at brigade and corps level. General Allen, as Commander ISAF, encouraged the Afghan security forces to be inoculated into their role, and expected that some might fail initially. His reasoning was that the Afghan Army and police needed to be tested progressively and faults rectified while ISAF was still in a position to support them. While there were significant concerns about the mobility, logistics, and professionalism of the officer corps, individual Afghan units often performed better than expected in the last two years of ISAF combat operations, namely 2012–14.

Western democracies tend to work to short-term cycles, imposed by adherence to elected governance and the need to produce tangible results within the lifespan of one or two parliaments or Congressional assemblies. By contrast, insurgents following a Maoist model of protracted war generally prefer a slower timescale for planning and operations. Nevertheless, in the time they have they must avoid defeat, marshal their resources, maintain the security of their personnel, and drain the strategic patience of their adversaries. Consequently, time is a crucial variable for transition, allowing governments to regain the initiative and force their enemies to reach a decision about future compromise or long-term resistance. Time can be denied to the insurgents by a series of political and diplomatic initiatives. Insurgents can be left behind and rendered irrelevant by reforms that resolve the grievances of the population or which remove interventionist troops. Transition can also impose a pressure on local governments, making them realize that they cannot rely indefinitely on the support of international donors or foreign military forces. The tempo and gradient of change induced by transition will rarely be linear and will invariably be dynamic. This implies that no political or military plans can be conclusive, particularly as to timetables, but they must provide sufficient directive detail.

There is a possibility that, in transition, there will be some unexpected and uncomfortable outcomes, including the risk that a local military force, perhaps built up by an intervention, may seize power.[34] Research suggests that, despite Western ideological reluctance to accept such an outcome as a success, autocratic forms of government usually outlast elected ones in the period after a civil war. Moreover, if one is to leave aside the obvious objection to military dictators' recourse to coercion, historical examples point to the great value of pro-consular figures with unfettered executive control when it comes to reconstruction and recovery. If this was to occur in Afghanistan post-transition, it could damage the reputation of the countries that invested heavily in the democratization and liberalization of the Afghan constitution. The solution was to ensure that Afghan National Security Forces commanders understood the importance of the primacy of civil authority, and the establishment of common goals. In terms of internal security, the security forces could be authorized to act against insurgents but would need to seek a return to civil control as soon as possible.

It is a feature of transition that the closer the deadline of handover, and the nearer one gets to the transfer of power, the more limited are the options to

[34] Edward Luttwak, *Coup D'Etat* (London: Penguin Press, 1968).

the international organizations and forces involved. It was clear to many of those with experience in development that Afghanistan would take decades to achieve even the modest goals of post-war reconstruction, even without an insurgency. It was also established many years ago that aid agencies could not hope to avoid a culture of dependence in the country they supported if they insisted on carrying out development work themselves. Projects that enhanced the prestige of the donor, with the donor's identity emblazoned across new schools and institutions, did not guarantee long-term sustainability, meeting the needs of the recipients or local acceptance of the work carried out. These lessons were learned the hard way from the 1960s in Africa, but it was depressing to see them repeated in Afghanistan and often by military forces trying to compensate for the absence of civilian or official bodies who could lead on development. The lesson of dozens of failed projects that went over budget was that Afghans had to reach their own solutions and they needed appropriate technologies and systems to meet their needs. In terms of transition, like development projects, much will appear unfinished at the date of departure, but this will not be a problem where Afghans have assumed full responsibility for the project in good time. It is a simple fact that 'end states' are often unfinished at the time the foreign civil or military effort is withdrawn. The end of the military phase of transition is but the opening of a new period in a process: warfare and peace-building are both hybrid processes and not absolute phenomena. Roger Mac Ginty demonstrates in his chapter that we need to avoid linearity in thinking and expectations to incorporate local agency, avoid value-laden categorization and focus, not only on elites, but on entire populations.

It is perhaps paradoxical that relationships between international and local actors can shift decisively. The way adversaries define their enemies and partners changes over time as transition, fighting, negotiating and peace-building unfolds. The key is to make the idea of cooperation normative. Disarmament and security sector reform measures which are in place before the final moment of transition can enhance the idea of future cooperation and reconciliation. Training Afghan Army soldiers the skills that can be transferred to civilian peacetime jobs would go a long way to foreground the inevitable demobilization of soldiers beyond 2020, absorbing the unemployed and equipping them with skill sets ideal for the development of Afghan light industry such as food processing. Moreover, there must be a reasonable prospect of a secure and better life after transition to prevent local actors flocking to the 'spoilers' as insurgents, looters, or bandits. Nevertheless, any attempt to prevent changes in the structure and dynamics of a society that has emerged from civil war and transition just for the sake of stability is doomed to failure. Chis Cramer notes in his work that civil conflict has produced as many beneficial outcomes as negative ones.[35] Western liberal ideology, with its preference for peace, bureaucratic governance, and stability, is often a cause of confusion to conservative Afghans, who are de-sensitized to conflict and its losses, more familiar with the value of patronage and networks for local advantage, and accept a greater degree of instability and uncertainty in their political economy.

There are several tactical and operational, military considerations in transition. Having established the strategic context, military personnel have to identify the functions required for a sustainable level of security, the key stakeholders, options for transition, and the parameters for negotiation. These require close liaison with civilian authorities. Moreover, there needs to be a clear understanding of the political drivers and the legal mandate of the military contribution to transition. There is often a great deal of confusion with overlapping 'reporting lines' in multinational and multiagency operations, but much can be achieved with good working relationships, regular contact, and a willingness to withhold coercive force in the interests of building 'normalcy', and taking the 'heat' out of a local conflict. In this, the importance of trained local police cannot be gainsaid. Georgina Sinclair shows that United Kingdom Ministry of Defence police are particularly valuable in training their counterparts in conflict zones and Lindsay Clutterbuck shows what challenges exist now and in the future for the policing of regions experiencing civil war.

Military forces are nevertheless useful in providing protection for citizens and basic levels of human security throughout transition. Their technical expertise can reduce threats, support government officials in their work, and bring relief to suffering populations, covering gaps where local state functions are not yet in place. They can provide border security against external aggressors. They can train local officials to design policy and allocate resources, manage those resources, and assist local authorities to deliver improvements at the tactical level. Military officials need to review at frequent intervals the agencies they should be working with and which reporting lines are the most appropriate for each task. Establishing a sense of what the key milestones are in the process of transition, rather than focusing on an illusory 'end state', and being clear on the sequence of activities are crucial.

The military aspect of transition is the most short-lived: economic and political transitions will take place over a longer period. Transition offers the opportunity for peaceful dialogue and a vision of the future that all sides can invest in. Reaching a negotiated settlement is only one step in that process since the goal must be finding agreement on how to end the dependence on

[35] Christopher Cramer, *Civil War is not a Stupid Thing* (London: Hurst and Co., 2006).

armed factions and restore security through civil policing, how all sides can share in the generation of wealth, and, ultimately how to govern the country. In Afghanistan, there are alternative routes to conflict resolution. Certain insurgent demands could, potentially, be aligned with those of the Afghan government and local communities. These might include agreement on land reform, systems of justice, and wealth distribution. There are also economic solutions which avoid enriching only the elites. Areas of cooperation include: the offer of development aid, alternative livelihoods, and work creation schemes that absorb unemployment; the creation of physical security at village level, the control of routes, access and economic conditions; and the evolution of improved communications through mobile telephone technology. All of these areas indicate how the appeal of the insurgents might wither away and how a government might be made more accountable to its people. Material gain, moral security, and evident Afghan military power will, ultimately, determine the loyalty of the majority of Afghans toward the transitional government.

Despite the preference of Western governments for 'narratives' of success in intervention and transition, the international media assert that they prefer an empirical basis to any claim that a transition has achieved its objectives. Narratives are not substitutes for tangible improvements, although it is noticeable that the quiet drawdown of an intervention, with prosaic if important improvements to the lives of local people, is unlikely to draw much international media interest. The media is driven by the need to acquire the latest, most newsworthy and up to date information, packaged as a story, and, with the advent of 24-hour rolling news, preferably short in duration and detail. The derailment of a peaceful transition in Afghanistan by a handful of adverse incidents provides the media with not only an immediate story, but also continuity in a more critical editorial, namely, that of cumulative and overall failure. In this volume, Piers Robinson shows how important perception management and narratives can be.

With a casualty-averse domestic population in the West, and a large number unsympathetic to the idea of humanitarian or preventative intervention, criticism increases with any significant casualties amongst foreign troops. This implies that the protection of personnel becomes a higher priority for foreign intervention forces. Nevertheless, at the local level, physical improvements in material and moral terms are far more effective and lasting than international stories. Despite the seduction and promise of 'influence operations', credibility remains essential. The overall verdict is that a quiet handover of control is far more preferable than even a minor incident which could be presented as evidence of a much greater failure. It is striking that the 'black hawk down' incident in Mogadishu in 1992 precipitated an American withdrawal from

Somalia and overshadowed a less sensational process of transition and peacekeeping, a process which was to enjoy a new impetus after 2002.

Insurgency is rendered politically irrelevant by the ability of governments and their counter-insurgents to defuse the insurgent strategy, rather than the defeat of insurgent forces. Measures that de-militarize a situation, gradually handing over control to civilian agencies responsible for policing, education, medical care, and the economy, are the criteria of success. If the insurgent tactics are provocation, intimidation, protraction, and exhaustion, then these require responses that can defuse the situation. Attempts to intimidate the population can be countered by broadcasting and ultimately discrediting the insurgents' cause; protraction can be subverted by long-term government programmes in development and political engagement with local communities. Indeed, co-option, embracing opposition into the political process, encouraging the growth of civil society, highlighting the consequences of violence, and offering positive choices all assist in making insurgency less attractive. In short, out-governing the rebel forces is the most effective way of ending insurgency while at the same time effecting transition.

Martin Evans' chapter, on stopping the violence in Algeria after 1988 is a reminder that the real termination of civil war is when systems of reconciliation and conflict resolution are well established, so that government and justice are accepted and practised. Enemies can be reconciled to a government through subjugation, co-option, and accommodation, but governments may also be forced into appeasement and capitulation by insurgents and revolutionaries. It is important to understand this spectrum when considering the status of individuals in terms of their attitude towards the reconciliation process. At the tactical level of transition, it might be expedient for governments to focus efforts on accommodation and concession, while pursuing a more strategic policy of isolating rebel leaders from their grass roots, and suppressing cadres of diehards, the so-called 'unreconcilables'. Alternatively, timely reconciliation with the leadership of a rebellion can bring in the rank and file fighters. In the mid-1990s, this latter approach was used successfully by the government of Tajikistan, while, in contrast, the Uzbek regime of Islam Karimov attempted to hunt down and defeat Jihadist insurgents when early attempts to reconcile them failed. Thus reconciliation can be seen as a strategy to be deployed in concert with other initiatives which bring about the resolution of conflict.

The argument that there can be no negotiation with insurgents is unworkable. Local, coercive or mutually beneficial accommodations are common and relatively straightforward to implement compared with large national schemes. National, tier one programmes must inevitably satisfy more principled agendas which larger movements, and possibly foreign sponsors, have invested in. If a tactical to strategic level approach is adopted, the problem is aggregating the smaller accommodations into a patchwork that forms a sustainable interconnected structure acceptable to all sides at the national level. In Afghanistan it should be noted that, not only are the various regional, ethnic, and sectarian groups divided by their own interests, the segmentary aspect of southern Pashtun society results in additional disputes at the subclan and familial level that override allegiances to higher confederate groupings. Equally, local considerations in a given area, such as the desire to preserve a source of wealth, or obedience to a powerful and influential patron, can cut across any established forms of fidelity. Local elites will always give primacy to personal interests in negotiations, which might include the assurance they can control their own land, or that their position of authority can be preserved in the eyes of their peers.

Negotiation is an integral component of transition. All parties, including interventionist states, will have a vision for the post-transition dispensation, but interests and opinions will conflict. The role of security forces is often to assist in shaping the environment through which negotiations can take place. Negotiations will be part of a process, and stalling or setbacks are to be expected. All actors will seek to influence others in the process, and periodically violence is used to signal a view or increase the stakes. Success is more likely where a range of satisfactory outcomes are accepted rather than a determinist stance. It is often assumed that an inclusive approach is more likely to deliver an acceptable outcome, but historically the evidence is not so conclusive. Nevertheless, reconciliation programmes and guarantees for the protagonists are essential.

Reconciliation programmes are demanding at all levels and require significant government resources. The cost of bearing and assisting these activities during and after transition often needs to be incorporated within the mandate of 'successor operations' for the intervention forces and the national government. Reconciliation certainly requires incentives and confidence building measures, some of which elicit criticism in those that had remained loyal to the 'armed struggle', and all those who consider making peace with the enemy to be a betrayal. Wherever possible local cultural norms, traditions, and institutions related to conflict avoidance, resolution, and restorative relations should be used to facilitate wider reconciliation initiatives. On the insurgents' side, demonstrating access to and cooperation from government departments, especially the ability to acquire tangible benefits or resolution of grievances, is crucial.[36] The obvious route for this is political representation. In Afghanistan, the absence of any political wing to represent the major insurgent groups

[36] See Imitiaz H. Bokhari, 'Internal Negotiations Among Many Actors: Afghanistan', in *Elusive Peace: Negotiating an End to Civil Wars*, edited by I. William Zartman (Washington, DC: Brookings Institute, 1995), p. 261.

makes the reconciliation process more problematic. On the other hand, the more covert discussions and informal local accommodations avoid spoilers, rival groups, and the scrutiny of the media which could compromise steps towards a settlement. Moreover, repeated contact with representatives of the insurgent groups can provide interlocutors for a subsequent national, strategic compromise. Informal dialogue may go some way to reduce the 'insider–outsider' friction of government power. Reaching local accommodations offers another benefit: it adds incrementally to the reduction of violence and builds stability in stages. Nonetheless, local reconciliation efforts can break down and the process can easily be set back if one or more groups become dissatisfied, a situation not uncommon in conflicts in eastern Democratic Republic of Congo in the 2000s, but local accommodations, which aid agencies have sometimes secured in order to provide desperately needed support to people regardless of their allegiances, might create the conditions where the intensity of the conflict is reduced to the extent that insurgent groups see the value in national talks.

Reconciliation requires a great deal of flexibility in thinking and a willingness to jettison those shibboleths that have become obstacles to peace. In any long-term counter-insurgency, it is common to see boundaries become fixed, each one representing a mental framework of assumptions and expectations. Many borders dividing African nations were created to assist colonial rulers or to accommodate their local allies and it is well known that they cut across the boundaries of human geography, rendering some ethnically homogenous groups into smaller factions and perpetuating grievances and cross-border conflicts into the following century. In Afghanistan, the enlargement of the province of Daikundi, ostensibly to give Hazara Afghans better representation in the Maijlis (parliament), caused deep resentment amongst southern Pashtuns. For them, such gerrymandering indicated that the Karzai administration was on the side of the northerners and that ultimately all Pashtun lands would be seized and divided. For the duration of the conflict most provincial boundaries actually remained unaltered, but the fact that these were the divisions used by the government was rejected by the Jihadist insurgents. The Taliban argued for a united Emirate, and set out to eliminate all distinctions of clan identity. They established their own bounded areas governed in theory by a civilian representative but in practice run by a military 'mahez' (front) commander. To complicate matters further, military units of ISAF and the Afghan security forces had created operational boundaries that did not always align with human activities. These were zones where opponents of the government could challenge points of authority, but, more importantly, such complex overlays make the establishment of a peaceful settlement in any given area more difficult.

If insurgents depend on the sanctuary of broken terrain in neighbouring states, or where they receive the indirect support of a foreign government or its people, any peace settlement will require the engagement of that state. In the Afghanistan conflict, there was very little peripheral interference from Iran, but serious allegations were made against the government of Pakistan and its security forces for supporting the insurgents. It appeared to be against Pakistan's interests to see Pashtun insurgents reconciled to a regime in Kabul, particularly if that government failed to recognize Islamabad's security concerns. Border clashes between Pakistani and Afghan security forces were episodic but insurgents appeared to be able to cross the Durand Line with impunity, carrying out attacks in both countries. The bitter divisions associated with the international border, dating back to the colonial era, accusations of interference in the sovereignty of each country (including significant terrorist attacks on Kabul allegedly facilitated by Pakistani intelligence and an American Special Forces raid into Pakistan to assassinate Osama bin Laden) made it unlikely there could be much support for reconciliation efforts in Afghanistan. This is particularly significant for the period after transition and the Western withdrawal of its combat forces in 2014.

One of the striking aspects of the Western counter-insurgency and stabilization mission in Afghanistan, and the reconciliation strategy was the ambiguity and occasional changes in emphasis and direction. In the first phases of the intervention, Afghans believed that a list had been drawn up that identified those that had either been members of the Taliban or had assisted them, and that if one's name was on this unpublished list, it would almost certainly lead to incarceration in the American detention facility at Guantanamo Bay or death at the hands of the government's or Westerners' security forces. Although a list had been designed to identify Taliban leaders and members of Al Qaeda, the Afghans' conviction that all were implicated, reinforced by the evidence of fighting in the south from 2006 (which was widely regarded as an 'invasion') seriously hampered any faith in reconciliation or individual reintegration. Clearly reconciliation can only be built on a degree of trust and sincerity, even if the belligerents disagree on points of principle. There must be an unambiguous strategy underpinning the process and the agenda; the release of a roadmap for peace in 2012, while unrealistic in terms of deadlines, at least set out the plan clearly. Going forward, the importance and legitimacy of local accommodations should be recognized and these efforts need to be coordinated, which might require devolved responsibility to provincial administration. Nevertheless, where insurgents refuse to recognize the legitimacy of a government, at any level, or where they see no strategic advantage in committing to peace, then a reconciliation process cannot get underway.

Expectations need to be managed on all sides. Proposals as to what can be offered and when, can be broadcast before negotiations get underway.

Security forces can create the space for reconciliation to take place. At the more senior levels, governments and international actors might also try to incentivize credible interlocutors, such as reconciled former combatants. In the Northern Ireland peace process of the 1990s, significant demonstrations by courageous families who had been victims of terrorism but who still spoke out for peace, had a galvanizing effect, and, collectively, added momentum to the reconciliation effort. There are always spoilers, eager to incite by acts of provocation. Disinformation campaigns from regime insiders and loyalists should always be anticipated. At this point, statesmanlike adherence to the principles of reconciliation becomes essential. It is also possible to elevate the status of those that are engaged in negotiations, rehabilitating the leaders of resistance as potential political actors involved in a power struggle. In Afghanistan it is striking that many senior insurgent commanders and former warlord leaders consider themselves as peers or even as senior to their counterparts in government. Status, if recognized and accommodated, can close the gap between 'expectation' and 'position'.

There is little doubt that transition represents a significant risk for all intervention organizations, be they aid agencies or military formations. A timeline of withdrawal gradually reduces the ability to influence events. The dynamic effect of a military drawdown might also encourage increased resistance, collusion between the security forces, and insurgents, and unfavourable accommodations between a population and rebel groups. Furthermore, previously cooperative civilians may refuse to continue working for external agencies, believing they need to seek more guaranteed employment. Support, even from erstwhile loyal local military units, cannot be taken for granted, and in Afghanistan this includes the ANSF, some of whom were in communication with the insurgents. Antonio Giustozzi, in his chapter in this volume, shows that collusion and deal-making is a common occurrence. For military formations preparing to withdraw, in addition to the problems of insufficient manpower, loyalty of the security forces and loss of 'human intelligence', there is a risk of breakdown in government and control, or, its erosion and evaporation.

The morale of international peacekeeping troops cannot be taken for granted. Soldiers and their families need to know that their efforts have been worthwhile, even if a campaign has been tough and complicated. At the end of the combat mission in Afghanistan, the announcement in Great Britain that there would be redundancies had a detrimental effect on soldiers' spirits, although there was no appreciable degradation in their willingness to carry out their duties. In such circumstances, where peace is approaching, it must be possible to create new opportunities for personnel with skills and experience in internal security and reconstruction. This is particularly important for the local military forces that have been raised. A careful disarmament and demobilization programme, which avoids flooding the job market with thousands of veterans and which provides viable livelihoods, needs to be planned and resourced before the final transfer of power. In Afghanistan, the esteem accorded engineers, and the national shortage in skilled personnel for food processing and manufacturing, points to the opportunity to train many soldiers in light engineering skills through motorcycle and vehicle maintenance programmes. Such schemes, enacted in the short-term, would create a cadre of demobilized soldiers already equipped for the next phase of transition. In Afghanistan, almost every sector of the economy is plagued by a low skilled workforce. This idea of re-skilling, or redeploying military personnel to other tasks, is not new. It is striking that, during decolonization, European personnel were often 'recycled' to other theatres, and their numbers, if not absorbed into the fabric of the Cold War formations in Europe, only gradually reduced. In this volume, James Dunsby's chapter shows how private security contractors, if well managed, can be crucial in covering the gap between departing international organizations and the establishment of fully functioning local security systems.

Transitions carry both strategic and tactical risks. A rapid change of government policy can overturn carefully laid plans at the tactical level, and encourage local civilians and security forces to adopt an entirely independent line of action. Equally, the collapse of the newly established host nation government, or the assassination of key interlocutors, can wreck the process of transition entirely. One cannot rule out a *coup d'etat,* involving internal or proxy forces, nor can one be certain that there would not be an erosion of established policy and practice through increasing passive resistance by the population. Popular unrest that can only be contained by significant force, including rioting, might become serious, particularly if local government officials refused to take responsibility for the consequences. In Afghanistan's transition, there were periodic 'strategic shock' events, that is, incidents which, whilst relatively small, had significant effects on the country or internationally. These included the inadvertent burning of a Qur'an by American forces, prisoner abuse, and the killing of civilians, either deliberately by individual soldiers or accidentally in airstrikes. Mass casualty events, including those of peacekeepers, can prompt an accelerated exit as governments face criticism at home, especially if the operation had already been of a protracted and costly nature.

In Afghanistan, there were specific strategic risk factors which could upset timetabled transition plans. One concern was that Pakistan might lose faith in the roadmap to peace and increase its support to selected Afghan resistance factions. The fact that Pakistan's Khyber Pathunkwa province had provided a safe haven for insurgent operations against the West, and Pakistan's decision to close the ground lines of communication on which ISAF partly depended for months in 2012, meant that Islamabad's stance on transition was strategically significant.[37] There was no guarantee that Iran might be tempted to increase its efforts as Western withdrawal became manifest and the risk of retaliation declined. Nevertheless, Western states could also not rule out entirely the risk that the ANSF would divide on sectarian or ethnic lines and that the break-up of the Afghan Army could precipitate a civil war. Afghan society, which was rarely homogeneous historically, was riven by fissures that had only deepened with thirty years of civil unrest.

In addition to the strategic concerns about transition there were a number of tactical risk factors for ISAF. One was that local deals could be struck between ANSF and the insurgents which would jeopardize the Afghan government and make the security of ISAF personnel much more hazardous. Infiltration and the increase of 'green on blue' insider attacks had demonstrated the effect on physical and operational security with increasing frequency from 2010. In terms of logistics, there was also a risk of premature contract termination by the large numbers of civilians working in support of the ISAF presence. This risk can be offset by the duplication of contracts which encourages competition, but the breakdown of a chain of haulage companies, for example, can have a significant impact. In the early 2000s, Afghanistan had suffered a prolonged drought. The overall regional decline in precipitation, coupled with food insecurity and a population at greater risk of shocks, meant that there was a chance of famine leading to civil unrest, perhaps with looting and rioting in urban spaces on a large scale. Even where food security is guaranteed, there has often been a risk of faction and clan infighting astride routes and urban spaces which would increase levels of violence.

There were further risks that insurgents skilled in the use of improvised explosive devices could be released from the Afghan criminal justice system in time to disrupt ISAF withdrawal, or that the insurgents, assisted by the Pakistan Taliban (Terikh-i Taliban Pakistan, or TTP), would launch their own 'surge' at the most vulnerable period of transition. There was a risk that incomplete and piecemeal transition could open up greater freedom of activity for insurgents. While it was expected that small-scale skirmishing against the ISAF withdrawal would necessitate extra security along routes, there could be no guarantees about the rest of the transition process and therefore about security. Students of Mao would recognize that what seems to be a successful effort to reconcile or restore relations can be merely a tactic to deceive while consolidating strength for a new phase in the conflict.[38] Consequently the

[37] 'Pakistan to Reopen NATO Supply Route', *Al Jazeera*, 4 July 2012, <http://www.aljazeera.com/news/asia/2012/07/20127317715654310.html>.

[38] Francis Grice, 'The Insurgent Myth of Mao: A Critical Reappraisal of the Chinese Guerrilla Legend' (PhD Dissertation, King's College London, 2014).

assassination of provincial and local government figures, the centre of gravity in tying the local government to population, could presage a more determined effort against the national government post-transition. Historically, Afghan governments that had become dependent on external funding and military forces did their best to keep their donors fixed, raising the possibility that the Afghan government could initiate fresh operations in the hope of retaining ISAF's support. But changes in Western governments also bring out significant changes in policy towards Afghanistan. As new agendas are asserted after transition, there have been real concerns that Afghanistan's fragile recovery might be abandoned. A policy impasse in one of the ISAF partner states could precipitate withdrawal earlier than anticipated, and run the risk of a scramble for the exit.

During the campaign in Afghanistan, interventionist forces were required to apply counter-insurgency techniques, and to understand the balance between political and military solutions. Transition is the final phase of a counter-insurgency where the tilt is almost entirely political in character. Underpinning transition is the sovereignty of the government as the legitimate authority of that country. The transfer of executive functions during transition necessitates a deliberate effort on the part of ISAF to reduce its control over affairs for which they previously had responsibility, including provincial reconstruction teams. It is easy for military and civilian advisors to overlook their potential to distort activities and dominate relationships, thereby undermining the transfer of responsibility.

At the tactical and operational levels, transition involves working to bridge the gap between the interventionist forces and the capability of the local authorities and their own security forces. Where the early phases of a counter-insurgency invariably require a significant amount of fighting and military effort, transition is about transferring what has been won to the local and national government. The 'lines of effort' of transition should therefore be pursued with appreciation that they are conducted with the elimination of any reliance on interventionist forces and resources in mind; that the objectives of the interventionist forces should be achieved through the success of local government and its security forces; that ISAF must work to promote in the perceptions of local people the effectiveness of the capabilities of the Afghan government; that one would expect control will be lost gradually in the fulfilment of the transition plan; and an understanding that local history and culture has made Afghan civilians hesitant to commit themselves until it is evident what new dispensation has emerged.

Political solutions which determine the success of transition require the government and its international backers to show the population, and the insurgents, there is more to gain by peace. Every agency should enable district and provincial governors to govern. There must be an effective and functioning legal system, with higher profile trials and swift justice, which obey the fundamental principles of the law but which respect and, where possible, incorporate local systems. The political dialogue of negotiation must be incentivized by the chance of material and moral gain for individuals and communities. The process must be universal and inclusive, engaging as many leaders and communities as possible in case of failure in one part of the network or system, and, wherever possible, sustaining the momentum of peacemaking. Tony King, in his chapter in this volume, suggests an alternative approach to a sustainable peace in societies, like Afghanistan, where the centre has always had difficulties influencing and imposing on the peripheries. He examines the possibility of accepting the continuation of a traditional patrimonial system rather than a Weberian state model.

At the end, whatever the final political system, the remaining military elements need to focus on limited operations to create time and space for solutions to be worked out, dampening violence and suppressing extremists. Pressure can be maintained by the continued capture, killing, and discrediting of insurgent leaders in order to show they are enemies of peace who jeopardize transition opportunities. The key is to erode the legitimacy of violence while maintaining the idea that insurgents are citizens who can be rehabilitated. Depriving the insurgents of resources with which to continue their struggle, while rewarding those civilians who cooperate with the local security forces, are also legitimate operations. Even while negotiations are underway, counter-insurgents can inflict heavy losses on rebel groups in order to demoralize them. The doctrinal objectives are to convince them that the path of resistance leads to death and harm whilst peace holds out the prospect of improvement. The population can be persuaded by a vision of a better future. The insurgents of the 2010s in Afghanistan were plagued by the problems insurgents had always faced: a shortage of skilled advisors and facilitators, disloyalty and disunity, vulnerability to detection and betrayal; logistical weaknesses and heavy casualties amongst commanders and dedicated cadre personnel. The emphasis though of the interventionist forces must be to identify and defeat the insurgents' strategy, and this requires an analysis of their vulnerabilities, weaknesses in their strategic narrative, and loopholes in their legitimacy as well exploitation of their tactical weaknesses. Above all, the purpose of military forces in transition is to gradually transfer their responsibilities to their local counterparts in order to ensure national and local structures are resilient and sustainable. The temptation is always to assume control. Lawrence of Arabia's oft-quoted advice to those assisting and supporting local forces is still extant: 'Do not try to do too much with your own hands.... Better the Arabs do it tolerably than that you do it perfectly.... It is their war, and you are to help them, not to win it for them'.[39]

International forces and institutions have a vital role to play in restoring peace and stability, but Afghanistan, like any state at the end of an intervention, will need to go through its own process of determining who holds political power and what level of security it will provide.[40] For the Afghans, this is likely to vary across the country, and may remain precarious in parts of the south and east. Predictions are impossible to make with certainty, but any forecast in the short-term can be aided by identifying individuals and groups that have most to lose and those that are aggrieved with the current dispensation, those that wish to retain what gains they and their communities have made, and what level of international assistance might be sustainable over the long-term.

In the final analysis, transition, handover and withdrawal require a clear strategy which prioritizes politics over military action; the development of local institutions including security forces; a gradualist approach with milestones that incentivize, test, and inoculate; long-term programmes for economic and political transition; credible and robust systems of reconciliation and conflict resolution supported by wise statesmanship; and the realistic management of expectations, morale, and risk. Long after an intervention, when immediate interests have faded away, and with reflection, it may become apparent what benefits were achieved. To those who so often asked: 'what was the purpose of the war in Afghanistan?', and, with implied disillusionment, 'was it worth it?', the answer may be found in a better understanding of the real, strategic purpose of transition, namely: to create opportunities for local people, and to establish the foundations of a new nation. That, surely, will be the epitaph of those who laid down their lives in the struggle for a better peace.

References

'Afghanistan: Mortality rate', accessed 8 March 2014, <http://www.indexmundi.com/facts/afghanistan/mortality-rate>.

'Afghanistan Statistics', *Unicef Website*, accessed 8 March 2014, <http://www.unicef.org/infobycountry/afghanistan_statistics.html>.

[39] T. E. Lawrence, 'Twenty-Seven Articles', *The Arab Bulletin*, 20 August 1917.

[40] Barbara F. Walter, *Committing to Peace: The Successful Settlement of Civil Wars* (Princeton, NJ: Princeton University Press, 2002), p. 3; Mediators and the 'Good Offices' of the UN were critical to the success of the Geneva Accords which led to the Soviet withdrawal from Afghanistan in 1989. David Axelrod notes that these third parties can establish an agenda which keeps the belligerents on track, in spite of deteriorating ground conditions and a return to violence: cited in Walter, *Committing to Peace*, p. 3.

Allawi, Ali A., *The Occupation of Iraq: Winning the War, Losing the Peace* (New Haven, CT: Yale University Press, 2007).

Ashdown, Paddy, *Swords into Ploughshares: Bringing Peace to the Twenty-First Century* (London: Orion, 2007).

Azarbaijani-Moghaddam, Sippi, Mirwais Wardak, Idrees Zaman, and Annabel Taylor, *Afghan Hearts, Afghan Minds: Exploring Afghan perceptions of civil–military relations* (British and Irish Afghan Assistance Group, 2008).

Bokhari, Imitiaz H., 'Internal Negotiations Among Many Actors: Afghanistan', in *Elusive Peace: Negotiating an End to Civil Wars*, edited by I. William Zartman (Washington, DC: Brookings Institute, 1995), pp. 231–64.

Caplan, Richard, ed., *Exit Strategies and State Building* (Oxford: Oxford University Press, 2012).

Collier, Paul, *Breaking the Conflict Trap: Civil War and Development Policy* (Washington, DC: Oxford University Press, 2003).

Cramer, Christopher, *Civil War is not a Stupid Thing* (London: Hurst and Co., 2006).

Diamond, Larry, *Squandered Victory: The American Occupation and the Bungled Effort to Bring Democracy to Iraq* (New York: Times Books, 2005).

Diamond, Larry, *The Spirit of Democracy: The Struggle to Build Free Societies Throughout the World* (New York: Henry Holt and Company, 2008).

Ferguson, Niall, *The Rise and Fall of the American Empire* (New York: Penguin, 2004).

Galula, David, *Counterinsurgency Warfare: Theory and Practice* (London: Praeger Security International, 2006).

Grice, Francis, 'The Insurgent Myth of Mao: A Critical Reappraisal of the Chinese Guerrilla Legend' (PhD Dissertation, King's College London, 2014).

Hart, Basil H. Liddell, *Strategy* (New York: Praeger Publishers, Inc., 1967).

Johnson, Rob, '*Mizh der beitabora khalqi-i*': A Comparative Study of Afghan-Pashtun Perspectives on Negotiating with the British and the Soviets, 1839–1989', *Journal of Imperial and Commonwealth History*, Special Edition, 39, no. 4 (November 2011): pp. 551–70.

Joint Doctrine Publication (JDP) 6/10 *Security Transitions* (2010).

Kilcullen, David, 'The Twenty-Eight Articles', in *Counterinsurgency* (London: Hurst, 2010), pp. 29–49.

Lamb, Robert D., *Ungoverned Areas and Threats from Safe Havens: Final report of the Ungoverned Areas Project* (Office of the Under Secretary of Defense for Policy, Department of Defense, 2008).

Lapping, Brian, *End of Empire* (New York: St. Martin's Press, 1990).

Lawrence, T. E., 'Twenty-Seven Articles', *The Arab Bulletin*, 20 August 1917.

Layne, Christopher, 'The Unipolar Illusion: Why New Great Powers Will Rise', in *The Cold War and After: Prospects for Peace*, edited by Sean M. Lynn-Jones and Steven E. Miller (Cambridge, MA: MIT Press, 1993), pp. 242–90.

Layne, Christopher, 'The Unipolar Illusion Revisited: The Coming End of the United States' Unipolar Moment', *International Security* 31, no. 2 (2006): pp. 7–41.

Ledwidge, Frank, *Losing Small Wars* (New Haven, CT: Yale University Press, 2012).

'Let's face it: We didn't win in Afghanistan', *The Chronicle Herald*, 10 February 2013, <http://thechronicleherald.ca/novascotia/677174-let-s-face-it-we-didn-t-win-inafghanistan>.

Luttwak, Edward, *Coup D'Etat* (London: Penguin Press, 1968).

Martin, Mike, 'War on its Head: An Oral History of the Helmandi Conflict, 1978–2012' (PhD Dissertation, King's College London, 2013).

Nagl, John, *Counterinsurgency Field Manual FM3-24* (Chicago: University of Chicago Press, 2007).

OECD-DAC, *The State's Legitimacy in Fragile Situations*, January 2010, <www.oecd.org/dataoecd/45/6/44794487.pdf>.

'Pakistan to Reopen NATO Supply Route', *Al Jazeera*, 4 July 2012, <http://www.aljazeera.com/news/asia/2012/07/20127317715654310.html>.

Paley, Julia, *Democracy: Anthropological Approaches* (Santa Fe, CA: School for Advanced Research Press, 2008).

Putzel, James and Jonathan Di John, *Meeting the Challenge of Crisis States* (Crisis States Research Centre, London School of Economics, 2012).

Ricks, Thomas E., *Fiasco: The American Military Adventure in Iraq* (New York: Penguin Books, 2007).

Soares de Oliveira, Ricardo, 'Illiberal Peacebuilding in Angola', *Journal of Modern African Studies* 49, no. 2 (2011): pp. 287–314.

Strachan, Hew, Jonathan Bailey, and Richard Iron, eds, *Blair's Wars and Britain's Generals* (Oxford: Oxford University Press, 2013).

Suhrke, Astri, 'Reconstruction as Modernisation: The "Post-Conflict" Project in Afghanistan', *Third World Quarterly* 28, no. 7 (2007): pp. 1291–308.

Suhrke, Astri, 'The Dangers of a Tight Embrace: Externally Assisted Statebuilding in Afghanistan', in *The Dilemmas of Statebuilding*, edited by Roland Paris and Timothy Sisk (New York: Routledge, 2009), pp. 227–51.

Synot, Hilary, *Bad Days in Basra* (London: I.B. Tauris, 2008).

Walt, Stephen, 'Lessons of two wars: we will lose in Iraq and Afghanistan', *Foreign Policy*, 16 August 2011, <http://walt.foreignpolicy.com/posts/2011/08/16/lessons_of_two_wars_we_will_lose_in_iraq_and_afghanistan>.

Walter, Barbara F., *Committing to Peace: The Successful Settlement of Civil Wars* (Princeton, NJ: Princeton University Press, 2002).

Part I

Historical and theoretical exits

1

Transition and the end of empire

John Darwin

This short contribution offers what is necessarily a somewhat schematic account of decolonization and the end of empire, with some emphasis on the British example. The intention is to suggest some parallels with those wider concerns about transition in the recent past and, indeed, the present.

The simplest way to capture the significance of decolonization and the end of empire is to note that, between 1945 and the 1990s, the number of sovereign states in the world grew from a little over 50 to just short of 200. Evidently, we live in a world that has been created by decolonization and by the end of, or, in some cases, the collapse of empires. There was a stage when historians and others (indeed perhaps not so much historians as 'others'), wrote about decolonization as an analogy of becoming a property-owning adult: first receiving a key to the door (sovereignty), then taking out a mortgage (the necessary burden of foreign investment for economic development), and owning a house (a diversified economy): in short, entering the 'adult' world of work and responsibility. The shift from colonial dependency to sovereign statehood would, on this model, be orderly, swift, and rewarding. In most cases, however, the actual experience of decolonization has turned out to be far more prolonged and much more in the nature of a 'transition' of the kind featured in this volume. Perhaps it would be helpful to think about transition *from* what, transition *through* what, transition *how*, and lastly perhaps, transition *to* what.

We start with the first of those questions: *transition from what*. If one tries to imagine the world before decolonization, before the crash of empires, one must consider a world that was dominated by a Europe-centred colonial world order. There were perhaps four preconditions which made it possible for such a large part of the world's surface to be governed, or in some cases overawed, by the European great powers. It might be worth bearing in mind their connection with our main concerns in this volume. The first of these was legitimacy. The colonial world order and empire itself were underpinned by a sense of their legal, ideological, and cultural justification. First, legal, because international lawyers proclaimed that it was perfectly licit for powers, that is the Great Powers, to intervene in other parts of the world, to protect the interests of their own citizens and subjects, and especially in that other part of the world where there was no effective or recognizable government that would protect those interests. The capacity to protect foreigners was treated as a fundamental criterion of governmental capacity, and its absence as evidence of 'barbarism'.

Secondly, ideological—because the notion that material and cultural progress was the greatest good that could be given to a particular society or people, and that only parts of Europe (not even all Europe) were capable of delivering progress—was deeply entrenched in the nineteenth century and survived into the 1950s and 1960s. The annual reports of the (British) government of India were titled 'The Moral and Material Progress of India', with, in parenthesis, 'under our guidance'. We might acknowledge that many elements of that view are with us today.

Thirdly, cultural, because there was a presumption that although many parts of the world possessed beautiful artefacts, and espoused beautiful ideas, what their cultures lacked was what one of the great protagonists of the imperial idea, the Social Darwinist Benjamin Kidd, called 'social efficiency': the capacity to translate culture into material progress. The criterion of 'social efficiency' meant that the cultures of the non-Western world were beautiful but useless. The world was imagined in terms of a cultural hierarchy in which only the cultures of European societies combined beauty and usefulness, and only they were fit for dissemination world-wide.

The second great precondition, after legitimacy, was geopolitics. Two things really ensured that empire was a sustainable burden up until the point when it ceased to be. The first of these was a broad consensus amongst the European great powers that empire was justifiable, morally defensible and that, by and large, it was better for European powers to divide the world amicably between them than to fight over the bits that each was going to receive. Thus empire was a 'good thing' and a partition of the world was both practicable and desirable. The scramble for Africa was perhaps the greatest demonstration of this view. For although historians are often tempted to write as though this was imperialism 'red in tooth and claw', the reality was that partition came by agreement and that only African blood was spilt. Indeed, in what is sometimes described as the age of imperialism from 1880 to 1914, no two European powers went to war over a colonial dispute. The second factor was the way in which a power balance existed across Eurasia in which most of those parts of Eurasia which later came to be powerful contenders for predominance in the world (China and Japan especially) were in the nineteenth and early twentieth century in a relatively passive (China) or less powerful (Japan before *c.*1930) state. Power therefore was concentrated within Europe. American self-preoccupation (partly a consequence of its ferocious internal conflicts) remained almost unbroken before 1898 and recurrent thereafter.

The third precondition for a colonial world order was the willingness of domestic populations (in Britain, France, Belgium, the Netherlands, Spain, Portugal, and Germany) to accept the burden of Empire. They had to accept first of all that the price of empire was a bearable one in terms of the fiscal burden and opportunity costs in welfare terms. Secondly, domestic opinion had to believe—or be persuaded—that the benefits that empire conferred outweighed its costs (usually those arising from its defence). Finally, domestic opinion had to accept the premises of an ideology of imperial power, or at least to see no conflict between them and the political values of their own society. Although there were always domestic critics of empire, they rarely commanded more than a marginal influence before the period of imperial decline. After that, of course, they were remarkably vocal.

There was a fourth precondition worth thinking about in terms of our current concerns. All empire depended upon the cooperation of key elements in the society over which colonial rule was being imposed. This has been a truism amongst imperial historians for 60 or 70 years. The prime reason for this was that in very few cases were even the most enthusiastic of imperialists willing or able to deploy either the physical force (in the shape of an army) or the large-scale administrative infrastructure to rule by coercion. Empire existed by and large as a deal between the imperial power, its rulers and agents, and indigenous elites on the ground who commanded real social power. The deal usually embodied an acceptance by the outside power that it would not interfere with the vital interests of that local elite in return for their willingness to acknowledge the over-rule of the outside power. In reality, the deal was subject to more or less constant renegotiation, as the needs and interests of the different parties evolved. But as most shrewder colonial officials understood, an attack on its ruling principles would place the colonial regime in jeopardy.

Secondly *transition through what.* From today's vantage point we can see that it was the Second World War which really marked the last moment at which this colonial world order was globally sustainable. One of the key factors at work was the way in which the European powers themselves were over-shadowed by the two emerging super-powers, and in particular, the way in which the main European colonial powers, Britain perhaps most strikingly, had been exhausted financially and in other ways by the Second World War and were no longer capable of sustaining these global burdens. But of course the strange thing was that despite what might seem the obvious logic of abandoning empire in 1945, especially for Britain and France, that was not the course that was chosen. In some cases, certainly, *force majeure* resulted in an early departure: from India and Palestine in the British case; from the Netherlands East Indies (Indonesia), in the case of the Dutch. But what is striking is the determination of British and French and other governments (including, for example, Portugal's) to stay on wherever they could. For them, empire had not become useless. First, because in the special circumstances of the post-war years, it had become *economically* more useful and valuable than ever. It was the need to exploit their empire more ruthlessly than before because of the impoverishment of the home society that drove the greater intrusion by British colonial power into territories it had previously ruled rather loosely (through what was called 'indirect rule') and on a shoestring. Secondly, there was a strong strategic or geo-strategic motive seen most vividly in the case of the Middle East, where there was in 1945 every reason for an early British departure on all kinds of prudential grounds. The geo-strategic imperative was based upon the new facts of the Cold War and the realization that the only feasible way to defend Britain and Western Europe against Soviet aggression was by taking advantage of the great arm of British power created during the Second World War: its air force. But since the Soviet Union was too far away to be bombed from Britain itself, it was vital to have bases in the Middle East from which the great industrial cities of the Ukraine and southern Russia could be attacked, or at least credibly threatened, as the best deterrent against a Soviet onslaught in Europe.

Given this commitment to stay on, the question then arose: how to hang on in the circumstances obtaining after 1945? Here there were two answers. The first was by being willing to inject greater power, not least military power and financial resources, into their colonial operations; and the other was by enlisting the support of one (at least) of the superpowers: it had to be the United States. What was crucial here was that the United States had acknowledged by the end of the Second World War that much as it might wish to see the erosion or removal of the British and the French empires, it would be disastrous if they were to be replaced by an enlargement of Soviet power or by the emergence of communist political movements. This prospect was enough to ensure that, at least for the time being, the United States would be willing to lend diplomatic, military, and financial support to the maintenance of British and French imperial power.

But if support was forthcoming at the geo-political level, it was much less clear that it would be available at the local level in colonial politics. Here, nevertheless, a great delusion was to flourish—one whose influence can still be detected in much more recent pronouncements about the political attitudes of 'sturdy country folk'. This was the belief that while political resistance was likely in some parts of the colonial population, especially in towns and among the ambitious literate elite, drawing encouragement from the democratic rhetoric of the Second World War and the United Nations Charter, it would nevertheless be spotty, spasmodic, and manageable. For amongst the great mass of the rural population, or so it was argued, a shrewd commonsense attitude would prevail and the gradual modification of colonial rule, coupled with the promise of eventual self-government, would be enough to keep them moderately loyal to or at least acquiescent in imperial power for a lengthy phase of transition. That turned out to be a great delusion indeed.

Thirdly—*transition how*. As it turned out the *added* burdens of post-war empire were only briefly sustainable. It was clear by the middle of the 1950s that in Britain certainly, and in France perhaps partly by the force of circumstances in Southeast Asia, a timetable had to be constructed for the reduction of colonial authority and the transfer of power to successor regimes. But in the British case certainly, this was undertaken in the belief that by doling out doses of self-government, the British government, or its colonial agents and authorities, could control the timetable of political change. They assumed that slowly increasing the amount of power given to local political actors and movements would allow the colonial government to constrain their behaviour and shape their political values. This would help to ensure that progress towards independence could be carefully staged, partly as a reassurance to opinion at home, partly to uphold local order. It would also make it more likely that the successor regime would adopt the democratic ideals which the post-war version of the imperial mission proclaimed as its objective.

Nevertheless it turned out that this attempt to control the timetable was another delusion. As soon as the British began to give some power to a political movement, or a group of political leaders, they demanded more. The reason that they demanded more was not because they were insatiable power addicts searching for total control, but because this response was built-in to the logic of the situation. Those political leaders, to whom doses of power were being doled out, knew that if they did not get most of the political loaf (if not the whole loaf) as quickly as possible, others would come forward to challenge their place. They might lose control over the political process and the pattern of 'nation-building'—and lose it once and for all. That was their fear, and, in many cases, not an unreasonable one. They were also acutely aware that they could not hope to build up a position of political power without being able to offer a large quantity of patronage and reward to those whose support they wished to draw towards their new regime. Consequently, the pressure they brought to bear on their colonial masters was for a swift and complete declension of power. Faced with the threat of a political breakdown at the most delicate moment of the political transition, the colonial authorities invariably lost their nerve. The demand for complete independence became all but irresistible.

The second grand illusion was that by creating regimes that were led gradually towards independence and then rewarded with support of various kinds (technical assistance, development aid, promises of strategic protection) the happy outcome would be the emergence of new nation-states that would continue to look to the old 'mother country' as their sponsor, their father figure, their big brother. Empire might have vanished, but much of the influence it had conferred in the past would be preserved for the future despite the change of constitutional regime. In the case of the European countries Britain, France, and Belgium, the reality, except in a few (but not unimportant) cases, turned out to be different. This was partly because the capacity to provide such a quantity of aid or support or military protection or any of the other things that might have turned such independent states into something like client states was not available. The British High Commissioner in what became Ghana bewailed the fact that compared with what was on offer from other countries in the world what the British Government had to offer to secure the enthusiastic attachment of the Ghanaian government was trivial. In other words to preserve influence *after* colonial rule was demitted, it was necessary to inject as much if not more resources than were deployed while it was still actually being governed. A salutary thought.

The third element of this *transition how* was that it was not always the case that it was possible to hand power to clear-cut legitimate successor regimes. On the contrary, in large parts of the world the collapse of empire did not lead to the emergence of a new regime smoothly and clearly inheriting the old colonial borders. In the Middle East, South Asia, Southeast Asia, Korea, and East Africa, the colonial empires left behind not a set of 'nations-in-making' but zones over which there was to be bitter conflict between rival claimants to the colonial legacy. Where it did work the transfer of power was able to exploit something, which may perhaps be a factor in the kinds of contemporary concerns with which we are concerned here: that is the extent to which it was possible for the imperial power and its agents to offer something which local political actors valued highly. Very often those political actors were themselves deeply conscious of the fact that across much of the territory—the colonial territory about to become a new nation-state—their own authority and influence was comparatively limited, if not actually contested. What the colonial power could give them was the legitimacy of being the rightful inheritors. That was something (once the political battle was won) for which it was worthwhile for even the sturdiest nationalist to play the part of the obsequious receiver of the sceptre of rule from a courtly representative of the old oppressor. The promise of international legitimacy (the last great gift of the imperialists) was a powerful motive for observing at least the appearance of a dignified handover.

The last issue which arises under the heading of *transition how* is the question of to whom liberation in a colonial setting was actually to go. It was convenient usually to think in terms of liberating a 'nation'; liberating a national community represented by a political movement, a national party, or a nationalist party. What soon became apparent in case after case was that the idea of liberation was not something that could be hermetically sealed around one particular party or regime. Other peoples within what were usually multi-ethnic political units (most colonies were multi-ethnic political units, most states today are multi-ethnic political units), other ethnic groups within these units, began to ask: 'What are we to get out of the process of liberation?' Quite rapidly, the post-independence arguments within the 'national' elite over the division of the spoils spilt over to include a much wider group of ethnic communities. Once they began to mobilize on the old anti-colonial model, they usually drew down on their heads the repressive machinery inherited from the colonial regime, now under new management. The political diasporas soon to be found in most Western capitals were the melancholy product.

The last scene is *transition to what*. We might say that the aim of the decolonization process was to create a world of nations—that was the kind of language often used in the 1950s and 1960s. As we have seen, a world of nations remains perhaps an ideal rather than anything remotely resembling a reality—certainly a world of nation-states. The task has been complicated in recent times by the effects of globalization which has often undermined the significance of national borders almost before they have actually become really embedded in many parts of the world. The growth of ethnic consciousness at a sub-national level often expressing itself in diaspora movements that themselves feed back to increase the sense of ethnic identity in the original starting point has also accentuated that sense that the creation of nation-states has been a much more uphill task than was originally imagined by the architects of decolonization. We might therefore conclude that decolonization, far from being a completed process, far from being something which has fashioned a stable or carefully 'demarcated' world of nation-states, remains very much a work in progress, and that it has become a journey toward what one might call an unknown destination.

References

Brown, Judith and Wm R. Louis, eds, *The Oxford History of the British Empire IV—The Twentieth Century* (Oxford: Oxford University Press, 1999).

Darwin, John, *Britain and Decolonisation: The Retreat from Empire in the Post-War World* (London: Macmillan, 1988).

Darwin, John, *The End of the British Empire: The Historical Debate* (London: Blackwell, 1991).

Eddy, J. and Deryck Schreuder, eds, *The Rise of Colonial Nationalism* (Sydney: Allen & Unwin, 1988).

Gallagher, John, *The Decline, Revival and Fall of the British Empire* (Cambridge: Cambridge University Press, 1982).

Johnson, Robert, *British Imperialism* (London and New York: Palgrave, 2003).

Louis, Wm R., *Imperialism at Bay, 1941–45: The United States and the Decolonization of the British Empire* (Oxford: Clarendon, 1977).

Mansergh, Nicholas, *The Commonwealth Experience, vol II, From British to Multiracial Commonwealth* (London: Macmillan, 1982).

2

Tropical transitions in colonial counter-insurgency

From Malayan Emergency to post-colonial partnership

Karl Hack

Introduction

To understand how 'transition' was managed for the Malayan Emergency, we must understand the nature and decolonizing background of the campaign.

The Emergency officially lasted from mid-June 1948 until 31 July 1960, with small numbers of communist insurgents fighting on from the Malaysian-Thai border area until a peace agreement in December 1989. It commenced with both sides ill-prepared, the communists having anticipated ratcheting up to full 'people's war' over several months, and the colonial authorities having a modest police force of 9,000, and a military of 10 battalions (plus two Malay Regiment battalions and a Royal Artillery Regiment unit organized as infantry). Except for the Malay Regiment, the military had been intended to act mainly as a strategic reserve to support British power throughout the east.[1]

The Malayan Communist Party (MCP) failed to establish main rural bases in 1948–49, before switching emphasis to economic sabotage and ambushes. Starting with around 2–3,000 poorly organized men, they reached a peak estimated yearly average of 7,294 in 1951, falling to 5,765 for 1952, and 2,798 in 1955. By independence on 31 August 1957 less than 1,800 MLA

[1] I describe British plans for a strategic reserve (and Malayan forces) in my *Defence and Decolonisation in Southeast Asia: Britain, Malaya and Singapore 1941–1968* (Richmond: Curzon, 2001).

remained, of whom about 200 were fighters. Most were located in southern Thailand, to which the MNLA (Malayan National Liberation Army) command had retreated in 1953–54, leaving weakening clusters of fighters in Malaya.[2]

In short, the Emergency spluttered into life in 1948, peaked in 1951, saw dramatic falls in incidents in 1952, and continuing improvement thereafter, but demanded sustained pressure versus pockets of insurgents into 1957–58.

The MNLA fighters[3]—about 90 per cent Chinese, plus Malays and Indians—were supported by a 'Mass Organization' (*Min Yuen*), in turn succoured by up to a million sympathizers: from a Malayan population growing from around 5–6 million over 1948–57. This was split between Malays (around 46 per cent, 1948), Chinese (37 per cent), and Indians. The Chinese were mostly first to third generation immigrant stock speaking a cacophony of dialects, most immigrants having come to work at docks, on plantations, and in mines.

The canvas on which the campaign played out was a long stretch of land about the size of England without Wales, jutting southwards from the Southeast Asian land mass. This was bisected by a 'main range' of jungle-covered mountain and forest, from which communist controlled insurgents had fought the Japanese during the Pacific War. Jungle edge eased into smallholdings, rubber plantations, and tin mines, and then more heavily populated coastal strips. The western coast was more highly developed, with a higher Chinese percentage, the eastern more sparsely populated and Malay dominated.

The government context was so thoroughly 'colonial' that some might dismiss any chance of adapting lessons from Malaya to non-colonial situations. An alternative, however, is to confront that 'colonial' nature, and ask which of its 'colonial' characteristics are *sui generis*, and which might contain valuable hints for how transitions might be improved in non-colonial contexts. Are some distinctive but positive aspects of 'colonial' counter-insurgency replicable in modern conflicts? After all, assisting a colonial state's counter-insurgency does share characteristics with assisting a non-colonial state: inherent tension between local sovereignty and assisting power desires to reshape that state and society; and likely claims that intervening forces are exercising alien, illegitimate power. In both cases it is also likely that conflict will be more than the binary one of state versus insurgent. In Malaya the underlying struggle by multiple groups was to define a post-colonial state. British success did not come, therefore, so much by reshaping a 'nation' and politics strictly in its preferred image, as by recognizing the grain of local politics, working with that,

[2] Director of Operations (R. H. Bowen), 'Review of Emergency in Malaya, June 1948–August 1957', 12 September 1957, Air 20/10377, The National Archives (TNA). Henceforth referred to as DOO Review 1957.

[3] MNLA was the official name from February 1949, sometimes rendered MRLA (Malayan Races Liberation Army.) This comes down to different interpretations of *Min tsu*, Special Branch using 'Races' in the 1940s–50s, and Secretary General Chin Peng preferring 'National'.

and transiting power along it even when it contradicted key parts of post-war British decolonization fantasies.

What was Britain's wider, post-war decolonization vision? A weakened Britain emerged from war determined to unite micro-colonies into Dominion-scale states and federations, large enough to sustain major institutions such as universities, and to support rather than sap British world power. These would be guided, slowly, towards self-government within the Commonwealth, and their elites from trusteeship under costly British protection to Commonwealth partnership. Hence 1940s–50s plans for massaging into life federations (and where possible new identities to match) in the Caribbean, West, Central, and possibly East Africa, and an eventual merger of Malaya and Singapore if not a wider 'Dominion of Southeast Asia' to include Britain's Borneo territories. The preferred route was a gradual introduction of elections from the local level upwards, and tutorship in governance by slowly expanding the number of elected members on Legislative Councils (LegCos), and then the number of the elected majorities' chosen representatives on Executive Councils (ExCos). Some of the latter would then be allowed to act as trainee ministers (in Malaya as minority unofficial 'Members' of government) before a locally elected Chief Minister could eventually form his own government. This last stage would leave Britain's Governor/High Commissioner, and a small knot of officials in the ExCo, with residual security and financial powers, before the final handover of untrammelled control.

The plan that emerged for Southeast Asia by 1945 fitted this pattern, with nine sovereign Malay States (five formerly loosely federated) and two port Settlements (formerly united with Singapore in the Straits Settlements Colony) cobbled into the Malayan Union in 1946. In addition, the new post-war colonies of Singapore, Sarawak (taken over from the Brooke Rajas), and North Borneo (ceded by the British North Borneo Company) were to facilitate modernization and political progress. A regional Governor-General (from 1948 Commissioner-General) was tasked to coax these territories into closer association, and the locally raised military forces for Malaya and Singapore were divided between the territories. Malaya got the infantry, Singapore got the navy, and they shared auxiliary air force flights.[4]

This, it was hoped, would provide time for parties and coalitions to emerge which could bridge racial divides and foster a 'Malayan nation'. New states, new nations, and ultimately new partners in a thriving Commonwealth—in

[4] See Karl Hack, 'Theories and Approaches to British Decolonization in Southeast Asia', in *The Transformation of Southeast Asia: International Perspectives on Decolonization*, edited by Marc Frey, Ronald W. Pruessen, and T. T. Yong (London: M.E. Sharpe, 2003), pp. 105–26, and Hack, *Defence and Decolonisation*.

which post-colonial allies would buttress Britain's world power—would result.[5]

In reality, local groups saw 'decolonization' as much as a civil struggle (if not civil war) to define the post-colonial state, as an exercise in attaining stability and transferring power. Many Malays, represented by the United Malays National Organisation (UMNO), wished above all to wrest back Malay control, challenging Chinese economic dominance and the retreat of the Malay language. The MCP, meanwhile, wished to secure a communist state, if necessary via temporary cooperation with bourgeois nationalists. Its members' motivations varied from unadulterated anti-colonialism, through belief in communist ideology, to semi-educated individuals seeking an effective path to modernity. The British hoped to find allies for their notion of a new 'Malayan nation', meanwhile, that would bridge ethnic and cultural chasms.[6] In reality that vision would win insufficient support. British officials knew as early as 1946–47 that their vision was in peril, when UMNO was formed to defeat the abortive Malayan Union of 1946–48. The Malayan Union had promised equality of citizenship for Chinese, and an end to Malay sovereignty of the Sultans in their States. This raised the ire of Malays who were already nervous following mainly Chinese guerrilla activity in 1942–45. From 1948, Britain would wage a quiet struggle to resuscitate the 'Malayan' ideals of the Union, which on 1 February 1948 was replaced by the Federation of Malaya or—in Malay—*Persekutuan Tanah Melayu* (Federation of Malay Lands), with more limited Chinese citizenship. Britain had retreated from forcing multiracial equality on Malays, to trying to gradually bring them round voluntarily to partnership with Chinese and Indians.

Technically, the state in which these aims played out—the 'Federation of Malaya'—was not a colony, but a protectorate. The Federation grouped nine technically sovereign Malay states each under its Sultan, together with the two urban port 'Settlements' of Malacca and Penang.

The 11 State and Settlement Governments, each under its Sultan or Resident Commissioner and Malay Mentri Besar (Chief Minister) retained control in areas such as land policy, and jealously guarded powers the British had tried to strip from them in 1946–48. In some states, notably on the east coast, most of the State Government and many District Officers (DOs) had always remained Malay. In others, notably most West Coast States, a higher percentage of DOs were British, and there had been limited centralization in the Federation Malay States (FMS) established in 1895–96. In both cases, local Sultans were

[5] See Hack, *Defence and Decolonisation*, for the Southeast Asian aspect of this.

[6] For the emerging notion of the 'Malayan nation' as the British aim, with some local support, but overcome by communal orientations, see Karl Hack, 'The Malayan Trajectory in Singapore's History', in *Singapore from Temasek to the 21st Century*, edited by Karl Hack and Jean-Louis Margolin (with Karine Delaye), (Singapore: NUS Press, 2010), pp. 43–291; and Tim Harper, *The End of Empire and the Making of Malaya* (Cambridge: Cambridge University Press, 1999).

theoretically obliged to accept the advice of British residents on all matters excepting Malay religion and custom, but after 1948 they were in a defensive mood.

At the federal centre, however, British colonial power was more solidly cemented from 1946, continuing into the Federation. In the latter the High Commissioner was advised by an ExCo filled with officials and nominees, below which sat a LegCo of officials and nominated unofficials. The first LegCo elections would be held as late as 1955. The idea in 1948 had been to hold elections for some LegCo seats more quickly (Singapore held LegCo elections for a minority of seats in 1948), but this was delayed due to the Emergency conditions. Instead, elections started at New Village and municipal level from December 1951 up to 1953, then at State level from 1954 to 1955, with these confirming the 'Alliance' as the predominant political party.

The Alliance was not Britain's preferred model of politics, which would have been one of multi-communal, issue-driven parties on a British model.[7] The Alliance was first formed in February 1952, to fight Malaya's second municipal elections, in Kuala Lumpur. It was set up to defeat the IMP (Independence of Malaya Party), which under charismatic former UMNO founder-leader Dato Onn was then espousing multi-communalism. As late as 1951 it had been IMP members combined with some Malayan Chinese Association (MCA) members (the MCA formed in 1949 from traditional and business Chinese elites to help in the Emergency), who held most appointed posts on government bodies.

During 1952–54 the colonial government gradually accepted that the Alliance was triumphing. The Alliance consisted of the communal United Malays National Organisation (UMNO), the communal MCA and from 1954 the Malayan Indian Congress (MIC). The MCA itself was partly divided over this shift into 1952 with some members retaining additional dual IMP and MCA membership. It only came down unequivocally on the side of the Alliance as the latter's victories multiplied in 1952–53.[8]

So from 1952 to 1955 'transitioning' of Emergency matters to local control increasingly meant the association of more Alliance representatives (together with smaller numbers representing planters, mining, royalty, and others), with government and Emergency machinery, as well as accelerating elections.

For the purpose of discussing such transitions in more detail, we now divide the Emergency into rough 'phases', namely:

[7] Hack, *Defence and Decolonisation*, p. 135.

[8] In Singapore, the Institute of Southeast Asian Studies (ISEAS) holds the Tan Cheng Lock papers (Tan was the first MCA leader), and these show Tan still toying with the IMP into 1952–53, and reluctant to totally drop the possibility of a non-communal option, even as colleagues such as Colonel H. S. Lee (whose papers are also at ISEAS) pressed ahead with changing the Kuala Lumpur Alliance into a national one through 1952–53. See letter from Tan Cheng Lock to H. S. Lee, 22 February 1952, H. S. Lee 1.80, ISEAS, *passim*.

1. Terror and counter-terror, 1948–49.
2. Population control, 1950–52.
3. Optimization, 1952–55.
4. Mopping up, peacemaking, and normalization, 1953–60.[9]

These periods overlap, reflecting the reality that *campaigns may exhibit different characteristics or stages of operation at the same time in different geographical areas,*[10] and that different 'stages' will also overlap in the same area as one phase winds down and another gears up.

Campaign phases and transitioning

Terror and counter-terror of 1948–49

In this period insurgents attempted to seize rural bases, and mounted large operations and ambushes utilizing up to a few hundred guerrillas.

The army were tasked with aiding the civil power, with the police coordinating operations. But with only 9,000 police personnel—often lacking radios—they were unable to give adequate guidance. Insurgents enjoyed support in Chinese jungle fringe settlements, inhabited by 'squatters', with whom the government had limited contact. As a result the army often acted on its own initiative, occasionally shooting villagers who ran. In one of the worst incidents at Batang Kali in December 1948, Scots Guards shot 24 unarmed Chinese villagers.[11] Nevertheless, Security Force (SF) sweeps, combined with large-scale detention and the deportation of non-citizen Chinese, prevented insurgents from establishing main bases, and broke them into smaller units.

By mid-1949 incidents slumped as military action broke up larger insurgent groups and prevented them from simply wandering into remote villages. The MCP now reduced activity as it reorganized their MNLA, and the *Min Yuen* into a cell structure able to support the MNLA despite security force action. Once reorganized, the MNLA increased operations into 1950, creating a sense

[9] For a fuller discussion of periodization in relation to historiographical controversies see my 'The Malayan Emergency as Counter-Insurgency Paradigm', *Journal of Strategic Studies* 32, no. 3 (June 2009): pp. 383–414, further developed in my 'Using and Abusing the Past: The Malayan Emergency as Counter- Insurgency Paradigm', in *The British Counterinsurgency Approach: From Malaya to Iraq and Afghanistan*, edited by Paul Dixon (London: Palgrave Macmillan, 2012), pp. 207–42.

[10] Ignoring this point can result in naïve assumptions, such as that Malaya had changed to an overwhelmingly positive, 'winning hearts and minds' mode as a whole (rather than such methods being part of a blend and variable by district) by 1952–53.

[11] See 'Judgment in the case of Keyu [Chong Nyok Keyu] et al. versus Secretaries of States for Foreign and Commonwealth Affairs and of Defence', 4 September 2012, <http://www.judiciary.gov.uk/Resources/JCO/Documents/Judgments/keyu-sec-state-foreign-commonwealth-affairs-judg ment-04092012.pdf>. This was the case brought for judicial review of the British decision not to hold an inquiry into the Batang Kali massacre, and at the time of writing the decision was subject to appeal.

of crisis as the government realized it had previously been lulled into a false sense of optimism.

In this period there were no elections. Malays alone were recruited to the expanding Malay Regiment (which the Sultans insisted remain Malay only). Malays also formed the bulk of the expanding police. Chinese assistance came through the MCA raising welfare funds, and giving ad hoc advice on which detainees were safe to release.

Population Control of 1950–52

This period began with incidents soaring as the MNLA, relying on its reorganized *Min Yuen* to provide support from rural settlements despite increased SF patrols, stressed sabotage, ambushes, attacks on isolated police posts, and increased some attacking forces to platoon size (100–200) once again. The iconic moment was an MNLA attack on the isolated police post of Bukit Kepong in Johore on 23 February 1950, which killed 21 Malay police.[12]

Bukit Kepong was the high water mark for such larger-scale attacks. The government used the sense of crisis to transform counter-insurgency. A soldier—Lieutenant General Briggs—was appointed Director of Operations (DOO) in a civil capacity to direct all SF from April 1950. He could call on an expanding Special Branch (SB) using small numbers of SEP (Surrendered Enemy Personnel) with increasing skill.

Even better, State opposition to ceding the direction of population movements (States controlled land) was overcome. Previously individual States had moved small numbers of Chinese 'squatters', sometimes simply dispersing them, on only a limited scale moving them to new settlements. This was due to commercial and Malay reluctance to surrender good land, limited finance, and the ease of deportation of non-citizen Chinese up to 1950, of whom more than 12,000 were deported by March 1953 (others being voluntarily repatriated).[13]

In early 1950, Briggs formulated a comprehensive plan—the 'Briggs Plan'—with the support of High Commissioner Sir Henry Gurney. This included the centrally coordinated resettlement of up to 500,000 'squatters', and was launched from June 1950. As this is the basis from which 'transition' would take place, this process will be considered here in further detail. The Briggs Plan comprised three elements:

[12] Special Branch interrogations (including those of Mat Indera, Marie bin Kadir, and excerpts from that of Tan Guat) released for Utusan Malaysia versus Mohamad Sabu trial, Penang High Court, 8–9 October 2012, and in the author's possession.

[13] Detention and Deportation, CO1022/132, TNA. Under the Federation Agreement a proportion of Chinese gained citizenship, based on birth combined with long uninterrupted residence.

1. population movement and spatial control;
2. operational control;
3. a military framework;
4. strike forces.

POPULATION MOVEMENT AND SPATIAL CONTROL

This element involved the resettlement of 'squatters' (including some longer-settled farmers) and (from 1951) a concentration of around 600,000 labourers. The latter involved moving dwellings small distances into defensible clusters. More than three-quarters of squatters were moved by December 1951, by which time planning was beginning for greater security and aftercare. In 1952 the resettlements were rebranded 'New Villages', with clinics, schools, halls, and other facilities gradually added to wired perimeters, search posts, curfews, and food controls. Following such developments, the vast majority of 'New Villages' would persist into independence.[14]

OPERATIONAL CONTROL

A unified civilian-military committee structure was established, from a Federal War Executive Committee (FWEC) under Gurney, through to State War Executive Committees (SWECs) under State Mentri Besars, then to DWECs under District Officer (DO) chairmanship, and ad hoc WECs when operations spanned multiple civilian districts. The leading local civilian chaired these committees, with senior police and military officers present, and others such as Special Branch and Chinese advisers attending as required

DWECs identified areas where opportunities for concentrated operations existed (due to SEP or informants) and coordinated resource allocations. They made fine judgements, for instance on when a Home Guard (which soared to more than 250,000 in 1951–52)[15] could be armed, or how far to increase or ease restrictions (curfews, restrictions on food). They also identified New Villages for special attention, with concentrated visits from dignitaries, tightened curfews, and demands for more information coupled with requests for

[14] The nature and persistence of resettlements and 'New Villages' is discussed in my 'Malaya—Between Two Terrors: "People's History" and the Malayan Emergency', in *A People's History of Counterinsurgency*, edited by Hannah Gurman (New York: Free Press, 2013), pp. 17–49. Arguments that such rural areas grew slightly slower than Malaya overall at some times miss the obvious points that (a) in a few cases people preferred to return to older abodes once restrictions were lifted; (b) as an urbanizing society a move of younger Chinese to larger towns cities was both inevitable and possibly desirable; and (c) deportation and deaths had removed a small but significant fraction of men who were candidates to be fathers.

[15] I am including Malay Kampong guard and other smaller analogous figures in this total, all such forces later being amalgamated into one command.

villagers to say how they could be helped. SWECs and DWECs were the nerve and command system.[16]

In terms of 'transitions' one issue is how this WEC network—which integrated kinetic, 'war-fighting' army patrols and operations into population control—was adjusted to allow increasing Malayan influence. Bearing in mind the colonial context, we should note two key aspects. First, British officials who helped to direct counter-insurgency were integrated into the local security forces and WEC machinery. The Chair of any committee was the senior local official, from High Commissioner (FWEC, from 1952 Federal ExCo), through the Mentri Besar or in his absence the British Adviser (SWEC) to DO (DWEC). From the abolishment of the FWEC in 1952 there were several Malayan 'Members' present at the Federal ExCo when it discussed Emergency matters. The Mentri Besars were Malays. So too were some DOs, more so on the east coast. Overall though, most WEC personnel were initially British, due to the British presence as state officials, police officers, and military commanders. At SWEC and below, local political representatives were initially mainly absent. Instead, there were some 'Advisory Committees' at SWEC and DWEC level. The various state bodies were also encouraged to vote block grants to WECs, and to limit their own sittings.[17] Democratic oversight was therefore made more remote in the critical 1950–52 period, and the colonial or 'assisting' power's officials were imbricated into the local administrative structure.[18]

MILITARY FRAMEWORK

Particular units were associated with each area, allowing regular patrols and a build-up of intelligence. The police concentrated within this framework on normal policing as well as limited paramilitary activity. This raises additional issues, namely: when and how the command of framework units shifted to Malayan control, how the operational control of groups of units shifted, and the way that the control of the police changed. Until 1950–52 almost all police commanders from the District level up were British, and Malay Regiment higher officers tended to be seconded British officers. Again, rather than being outside advisers, assisting-country personnel were integrated into local command structures as expatriates. In the case of the police, despite the importation of some 'Palestine Sergeants' in 1948–49, some British commanders had joined as cadets in the 1930s, had passed examinations in Malay, or even spoke Chinese dialects.[19] They knew the land and the people, and below

[16] See for instance H. S. Lee Papers File 79/2, ISEAS, *passim* for several examples of such treatment by Selangor's SWEC in 1952–53.

[17] DOO Review 1957, p. 14, para. 48.

[18] DOO Review 1957, p. 14, para. 51.

[19] Two excellent examples where we have comprehensive archival collections covering recruitment to senior Emergency positions in the 1940s–50s are John Davis (Davis Papers, Documents 16593, Imperial War Museum (IWM)) and John Harrison (National Library of Australia

them the local rank and file had been imbued with a partly British (and British colonial) policing ethos—down to an emphasis on competitive games.[20]

STRIKE FORCES

Security force assets outside of framework forces, including some Special Branch (SB) personnel, were to be concentrated for larger operations. The initial plan was to 'roll up' insurgents, from the south (Johore, now spelt Johor)[21] to the north. Given that Johore was one of the strongest insurgent redoubts, this floundered. Over the period 1951–52 an alternative emerged, of deploying greater forces to areas of opportunity, where local SWECs/DWECs and SB confirmed that a nearby MCP committee/s had become targets due to losses and/or additional flows of information. The preferred targets, however, became not MNLA units per se, but directing area committees. This started to involve WEC-directed police–SB–army operations, featuring increasing food control and patrols, arresting hardcore supporters so less committed recruits would take their place and be identified and 'turned', and using the resulting intelligence to create killing zones around one or more of the New Villages. The return to targeting much larger areas would have to wait until 1953.

The period of 1950–51, meanwhile, saw a peak in activity, as insurgent supporters fled resettlement. These flights increased the size of the MNLA. With the MCP's August 1950 orders also stipulating all-out opposition to resettlement, the Emergency reached its height.

By October 1951 both the MCP and SF felt themselves to be at crisis point, as incidents peaked, and the cumulative pressure of resettlement put a rapidly expanded, under-trained police force under severe stress. Police numbers had reached more than 67,000 full- and part-time officers, with an additional 250,000 Home and Kampong Guard and 23 battalions, in 1951–52. Expansion, not training, had been the priority. Then, on 6 October 1951, insurgents ambushed and killed Sir Henry Gurney, setting in motion a major leadership renewal. By February 1952 Sir Gerald Templer had been appointed as both DOO and High Commissioner, with Colonel Arthur Young from London as his new Commissioner of Police.

Simultaneously, the MCP concluded that it could not sustain its current tactics, and issued orders which programmed reductions in the MNLA and in

(NLA): Papers of John Noel Douglas Harrison MS 8756). Both went to Guangzhou (Canton) in the 1930s to learn Chinese.

20 We are lucky to have good collections of police officers' papers which cover careers from recruitment to retirement, notably those of John Davies (Imperial War Museum) and John Harrison (National Library of Australia). For the imbrication of aspects of British policing see the latter for Pieces 30–2 and for copies of the *Malayan Police* magazine from the 1930s–60s.

21 For the sake of consistency and ease of reference I have retained the Malay spellings common at the time throughout, e.g. Johore not Johor, Trengganu not Terengganu, etc.

incidents, and a shift to increase planting, stockpiling, and political work. Its October 1951 Resolutions (or 'Directives') radically changed the short- to medium-term campaign trajectory (just before the British leadership changes). Future activity involved downsizing units and changing their operational emphasis and strengthening political foundations.[22]

MNLA DOWNSIZING OF UNITS AND CHANGE OF OPERATIONAL EMPHASIS

Unit sizes were reduced, some men transferred to small armed groups to support the *Min Yuen*, and an increased emphasis put on deep jungle planting and stockpiling to counter the resettlement's effects on logistics. A previous emphasis on sabotage (for instance attacking buses, trains, and slashing rubber trees) was severely curtailed to avoid alienating local support, as were activities such as shooting at crowds to kill 'running dogs'. These orders reached proximate units almost immediately, then trickled through the jungle to reach the last units up to a year later. That implied a gradual decline in incidents from the end of 1951 until late 1952.

MCP STRENGTHENING OF POLITICAL FOUNDATIONS

Strengthening the MNLA's political foundations involved greater penetration of political parties, unions, and schools and courting the 'medium national bourgeoisie'. As in 1949, the 1951–52 reorganization would sacrifice the immediate scale of attack in order to enable a later upsurge based on greater political and logistical support. In reality, incidents plummeted throughout 1952, in some categories by half in that year, but in fact they never recovered. The SF under Templer's dynamic leadership took advantage of the lull to consolidate an ongoing 'optimization' of resettlement, and of wider measures built on the foundation of population control.

In 1952 the physical population movement was largely completed (with aftercare just picking up), incidents were falling, SF-initiated contacts were holding up, and Templer was injecting new ideas, intelligence efficiencies, and energy into the improving situation. Hence from late 1952 onwards there was increasing scope to re-train, and to increase the association of Malays with the campaign.

[22] CO1022/187, TNA. I have analysed these at greater length in my '"Iron claws on Malaya": The Historiography of the Malayan Emergency', *Journal of Southeast Asian Studies* 30, no. 1 (1999): pp. 99–125; and 'British Intelligence and counter-insurgency in the Era of Decolonisation', *Intelligence and National Security* 14, no. 2 (1999): pp. 124–55. Chin Peng—MCP Secretary General—has broadly confirmed these interpretations in C. C. Chin and Karl Hack, eds, *Dialogues with Chin Peng: New Light on the Malayan Communist Party* (Singapore: NUS Press, 2004), pp. 143–68; and Chin Peng, *My Side of History* (Singapore: Media Masters, 2003), pp. 270, 299–300.

The optimization of 1952–55

'Optimization' was characterized by incremental improvements in operations around clusters of New Villages,[23] and increasing elections, accompanied by more association of local representatives with the WEC system. At the federal level the FWEC roles were merged into the regular Federal ExCo in 1952, meaning that local ministers—first appointees and then selected by the Chief Minister from those elected in 1955—were automatically associated with top-level Emergency decision-making.

A separate DOO sub-Committee of the Federal ExCo, with relevant military and police commanders, now met separately and weekly, to advise on operational planning. As the pattern of the Alliance winning elections became undeniable, it was decided to associate politicians with this Operations sub-Committee as well. In October 1954 five political leaders—two Malay, one Chinese, one Indian, and one European—became full members of the Federal DOO sub-Committee. In January 1955 'wider racial representation was provided on SWECs and DWECs as well, from which Operations sub-Committees were then formed to handle advice on day to day conduct of operations'.[24] Such integration was intended to have political capital as well as being useful in refining the 'hearts and minds' side of the campaign. But it left the detailed direction of operations mainly with military officers on various operational sub-committees.

In short, there was a move from having 'Advisory Committees' to WECs in 1950–52—of local politicians and communal representatives—to directly including Malayan politicians on WECs in 1952–55, while spinning off operational sub-committees beneath these. This also reflected the fact that some advisory committees had reduced their activity into 1953, partly due to frustration at being asked to help (and take risks by offering information) without having any real influence.[25] It meant that gradually the WECs had more unofficial Malayan representation, even if Malayans were scarcely starting to rise to positions (such as State Secretary for Chinese Affairs, Home Guard Officer, or DO) which would secure WEC membership in an official capacity.[26]

[23] These operations typically involved increasing food control and patrols, arresting hardcore suppliers to force reliance on softer supporters, turning some of the latter, and generating live intelligence on insurgent intentions to facilitate ambushes and captures, leading to local MCP committee dissemination or elimination. For a summary see Hack, 'The Malayan Emergency as Counter-Insurgency paradigm'. DOO Instruction no. 36 of 26 June 1954 described food controls as 'The main weapons of DWEC against the CT' going forward. See H. S. Lee Papers 7.44/1–19, ISEAS.

[24] DOO Review 1957, p. 14, para. 51.

[25] See H. S. Lee Papers 74/8, 1–36, ISEAS, for meetings of the Selangor States Chinese Consultative Committee and its various problems and declining frequency in 1952–53.

[26] Arkib Negara Malaysia 2005/0018549, Minutes of Meeting of Negri Sembilan SWEC, Monday 3 October 1955, for instance. The chair was Honourable Enche Shamsuddin bin Nain as Mentri Besar, and also in attendance were the British Adviser, Acting Chief Police Officer (Enche Mohd.

With incidents at less than one-seventh of peak levels by mid-1954, the path also seemed open to faster decolonization. The posts of DOO and High Commissioner were separated by June 1954.[27] It was accepted that this might reduce the focus on making all appointments serve the Emergency. Nevertheless, British officials remained in key security positions, in charge of most of the higher echelon army, police, SB, DWEC, and other posts, even as political direction started to pass to Malayans.

Optimization also meant that the numbers of SF fell from the peak levels necessary to achieve effective population control in 1950–52. Police retraining began in late 1952. By 1953 numbers were falling. The 23 battalions and 250,000 Home Guard were also gradually reduced, and in select cases wire fences were allowed to decay as areas around some New Villages improved. Resources were reduced overall and concentrated at the points of greatest need. By 1953 the MNLA was decayed enough to risk concentrating some larger strike forces in particular states again. Colonel Young was also able to launch 'Operation Service' which saw the police going out of their way to find ways of helping the public.[28]

Mopping up, peacemaking, and normalization 1955–60

Here the artificiality of hard periodization becomes apparent. The first 'White Area' was created before this period, in September 1953, in Malacca. A 'White Area' was one where insurgent activity was deemed very low, and where consequently most Emergency restrictions were lifted. This was aimed at appeasing local opinion, and as an inducement for further areas. Yet while one area became 'white', another might experience tightened food-intelligence operations, central cooking of rice, and increased curfews and arrests. The nature of such combined food–Special Branch–military operations—intended to fuel intelligence-led ambushes and kills as the SF closed in on local MCP committees—were tightened over time. As late as April 1956—as 'White Areas' started to cover most of the country—the DOO wrote that 'screwing the people down in the strongest and most determined manner' remained vital in 'bad' areas. One of the responsibilities of the new Emergency Operations Council

Salleh bin Ismail), Commander Gurkha 26 Brigade, British Secretary for Chinese Affairs, Planters' Rep., two more Europeans, Yap Mau Tatt, and Honourable Enche Idris bin Matsil.

[27] DOO Review 1957, p. 8.

[28] The sharper-eyed reader will note that the same Colonel Young then went to Kenya in 1954 only to resign after months saying that local cover-ups of abuses and lack of support made a similar 'Operation Service' and reforms there ineffective. See Papers of Sir Arthur Edwin Young, GB 0162 MSS. Brit. Emp. S. 486, Bodleian Library of Commonwealth and African Studies at the Weston Library (formerly Rhodes House), Oxford.

(EOC) from March 1956 was to take decisions on which 'Uncooperative Areas' required such 'strong and positive action'.[29]

Notwithstanding the variegated nature of the campaign, by 1955 a qualitatively different situation had coalesced. Militarily, the back of the insurgency was broken and remaining MNLA forces were becoming isolated. Politically, the Alliance had swept municipal and State elections, and its representatives were functioning as nominated 'Members' (trainee ministers) on the Federal ExCo with limited functions (this started in 1951). The Alliance also demanded that Federal elections take place before the end of 1954, with a move towards full self government soon afterwards. Federal elections were finally set for July 1955, with the winner to form a government.

Alliance leader Tunku Abdul Rahman announced, in early January 1955 that, if elected, his ministers would seek an amnesty for insurgents, perhaps allowing communists to join the constitutional process. Previous 'surrender terms' only promised 'good treatment', and left the possibility of prosecution if a person had civilian blood on their hands. What followed was 'behind-closed-doors' jostling. The Tunku and MCA colleague Tan Cheng Lock already sat on the DOO Operations sub-Committee. They joined in its 17 January discussion which concluded that there should be no changes in surrender terms at this point in time. Instead, it quietly appointed a committee to examine the possibility of a wider amnesty. British representatives emphasized that they did not want any move that recognized the MCP, or allowed it to convert declining insurgency into greater subversion. The Tunku acknowledged that direct 'negotiation' was impossible, as was recognition of the MCP as a legal party. The holding position was that the colonial government made public, in March 1955, the *de facto* policy of not generally prosecuting 'Surrendered Enemy Personnel' (SEP).

The MCP subsequently sent letters to Alliance ministers from May 1955, offering to negotiate. In July 1955 the Alliance won 54 out of 55 elected seats on the LegCo. Tunku Abdul Rahman became Chief Minister, appointing a number of ministers except those for key functions such as security and finance. Britain quickly agreed that it would hold a Constitutional Conference in London in 1956 (January–February), with the Alliance clear that it would seek a date for full self-government.

The Tunku also made clear in August 1955 that he should offer to meet Chin Peng in person, even if only to explain the new amnesty terms which were due

[29] Arkib Negara Malaysia, 2005/0018534, Conference of Executive Secretaries [of SWECS], Held on 3 May 1956, Item 6. DOO to Templer, 15 March 1956, WO216/901, TNA. For instance, a near riot and accusations of women being visible semi-naked in search tents led to the Report on food operations at Semenyih in 1956, see *Report on the Conduct of Food Searches at Semenyih in the Kajang district of Selangor* (Kuala Lumpur: Government Press, 1956). FCO141/7475, 'Commission of Enquiry into the Semenyih incident', TNA.

in September 1955. Various statements also indicated that he would not be bound on what he could say. The Amnesty terms he was to discuss stipulated that all AMSEP (Amnesty SEP) could surrender to public, safe areas from which the SF would retire to (later suspended due to 'abuse') military 'shout before you shoot' orders, and that after 'investigations' those AMSEP demonstrating loyalty would be helped to reintegrate into society. Others would be offered the chance to leave for China. Above all, for the Amnesty period they would not be prosecuted for *any crime* committed under communist direction before Amnesty day.[30] The effects of these terms were largely nullified, however, by repeated MCP offers to negotiate in September and October, and the Alliance's desire to agree to negotiate.[31] Preliminary meetings in October to November hammered out the terms for a formal meeting at Baling on 28 and 29 December 1955.

A number of aspects about the path to Baling are fascinating. First, the switch from a British to an Alliance initiative in 1955, with Alliance politicians needing to do everything possible to facilitate peace and reduce irksome Emergency restrictions. Secondly, the British response was fearful of allowing Federation ministers to 'negotiate', lest they throw away a winning hand in an attempt to accelerate improvement, and so unblock the way to independence. The British felt the dangers of letting the MCP back into society—like 'maggots to a pile of bread'—were acute.[32]

Yet the British could not block the Alliance without risking the withdrawal of its members from WECs and other bodies (something they briefly did in 1954), and a serious loss of confidence and efficiency. The British solution was to work behind the scenes on bodies such as the DOO Operations sub-Committee. They encouraged ministers, if they must go to Baling, to do so only to explain amnesty terms, and to take Singapore's fiercely anti-communist Chief Minister David Marshall. The High Commissioner also announced on 30 November that a continuation of the Emergency at present levels would not impede further constitutional advance. That followed a mock 'Baling meeting' at which 'Chin Peng' (local information officer C.C. Too) cornered the 'Tunku' (Major General Lindsay Smith) by making a final offer of ending the fighting if the MCP could be legally recognized and his men walk free. The Major-General was stumped, and the British determined to remove any danger that the Tunku would feel he needed concessions to accelerate independence.

[30] Arkib Negara Malaysia (The Malaysian National Archives, henceforth, ANM), File 1957/0569642, SEP. See also Karl Hack, 'Negotiating with the Malayan Communist Party, 1948–89', *Journal of Imperial and Commonwealth History* 39, no. 4 (2011): pp. 607–32.

[31] Kumar Ramakrishna, *Emergency Propaganda* (Richmond: Curzon, 2002), p. 195.

[32] 'End of Empire' transcripts, research notes with Guy Madoc (Head of Special Branch in 1955), MSS. Brit. Emp. S. 527, Bodleian Library of Commonwealth and African Studies at the Weston Library, Oxford.

From 28 to 29 December 1955, the Tunku, David Marshall, and Tan Cheng Lock for the MCA faced MCP Secretary-General Chin Peng and two colleagues in a school house at the border town of Baling. The British were not active participants. The Tunku insisted anyone surrendering could choose between going to China, or undergoing investigation prior to reintegration: Chin Peng could not accept investigations or anything smacking of 'surrender'. The Tunku refused to budge on that or MCP recognition. Chin Peng then offered that if the Tunku gained a subsequent British promise of independence and local control of security forces, his men would 'lay down' arms. Without agreement, a visibly deflated Chin Peng returned to the jungle.

The British breathed a sigh of relief. The Amnesty ended on 8 February 1956 (leaving normal surrender terms) having netted just 74 AMSEPs. The January–February 1956 Constitutional Conference easily agreed to accelerate Malayan decolonization.[33] The Conference agreed 31 August 1957 as the target date, providing that local parties agreed on details including the new constitution. In terms of 'transition', and with a view to Chin Peng's Baling concession, it also agreed an early transfer of internal security. The key to this and the subsequent post-colonial defence agreement was the division of political direction from actual 'control' of military units, and that the Emergency was 'War by Committee'.[34] Some WECs continued into the independence period, concentrating on declining areas of threat, notably closer to the border.[35] An additional factor was that the British trusted Alliance ministers' anti-communist instincts after Baling, recognized they were the only viable successors, and were loathe to risk any Alliance obstruction or alienation.

In these circumstances the Constitutional Conference agreed that in the period before independence Emergency direction would transfer to a Minister for Internal Defence and Security, reporting to the Federal ExCo. This happened in March 1956. Tunku Abdul Rahman was Minister for Internal Defence and Security as well as Chief Minister. As such, he chaired a new 'Emergency Operations Council' (EOC), consisting of: himself; the DOO (British and also GOC Malaya); the British AOC Malaya; three ministers representing Malay, Indian, and Chinese communities; and the British Commissioner of Police. Below this EOC, SWECs had long been chaired by the Malay Mentri Besar, with their European 'Executive Secretaries' acting as the link between the DOO Staff in Kuala Lumpur and the SWECs, to communicate policies

[33] Kumar, *Emergency Propaganda*, p. 197.

[34] The phrase 'our system of war by committee', was the Principal Staff Officer's as used at a March 1955 meeting, see ANM 2005/0018534, 'Ministers of a Meeting of SWEC and Assistant Controllers of Supplies... 17 and 18 March 1955'.

[35] ANM 2005/0018533, War Executive Committees, for Operation Bamboo and various Perak and border committees in 1962.

downwards.[36] As late as July 1957 seven of the eleven Executive Secretaries were still European.[37]

The DOO became responsible to the EOC for day to day operations, and retained operational command of all SF allotted to them. The EOC was assisted by a Working Party of professional advisers, including the Directors of Intelligence and Information.[38] Furthermore, in the words of the DOO Report of 1957, 'actual control of British military units remained the ultimate responsibility of the British GOC Malaya' and unit commanders. When the Anglo-Malayan Defence Agreement was signed in October 1957, this remained the case. By that point most British and Commonwealth troops had been concentrated in particular areas, reducing visibility. North Johore and Perak initially remained under the operational control of HQ 17 Gurkha Division, the rest of the country now coming under control of the independent Malaya's HQ Federation Army, which assumed control of all Federation Army units.[39]

GOC Malaya also ceased to be the DOO from September 1957, though the new DOO for 1957–59 was Indian-born British officer Lieutenant General James Cassels.[40] Below these higher levels, in the SWECs and DWECs, things were changing rapidly by 1957–58, as Malayans replaced retiring British officials, DOs, and higher-ranked police officers.

The increase in unofficial members—mainly Alliance representatives—on these committees had already caused some concerns. In 1956 Tunku Abdul Rahman was asked to emphasize to DWEC unofficial members that they must avoid compromising security—following breaches—and 'accept responsibility for decisions taken' by their DWEC.[41]

As for officials on the WECS, Geoffrey Bourne noted in September 1957, in his final annual DOO's Report, that expatriate departures were only now becoming problematic. He was not so concerned with the rundown of British Army numbers in 1958, as 'by the exodus of experienced expatriate

[36] ANM 2005/0018534, 'Note of a meeting of the Conference of Chairmen and Deputy Chairmen of State War Executive Committees.... 28 November 1955'. Chaired by the DOO, this consisted mainly of the Mentri Besars, all Malay, the Resident Commissioner of Penang and Malacca who were both European, and the British Advisers, who were all European.

[37] ANM 2005/0018533, War Executive Committees, List of Exec Secs of SWECs as of 1 July 1957 dated 12 July 1957. The others were three Malays (for Kelantan, Trengganu and tiny Perlis) and one Chinese (for Penang).

[38] DOO Review 1957, p. 14, para. 52.

[39] *Federation of Malaya Annual Report 1957* (Kuala Lumpur: Government Press), p. 4. The delay in signing was partly a Malayan device to demonstrate the reality of their control, partly about finessing details on how far, and how, Britain could use forces to support Commonwealth countries (it could) or SEATO (in effect, only after first withdrawing forces from Malaya to another territory, such as Singapore).

[40] *Federation of Malaya Annual Report 1957*, p. 4.

[41] ANM 2005/0018534, 'Conference of Executive Secretaries [to SWECs] Held on 3 May 1956, Item 4. Everyone at this conference—e.g. military commanders and the State Secretaries—was European.

officers, particularly from the Police, Civil Service, Medical and Public works departments. The continuance of adequate administration and the effective Chairmanship of SWECs and DWECs is already being threatened. Nothing can replace the experience of the officers who are leaving. . . '.[42]

This exodus had been gathering pace from 1955 and 1956, when the percentage of Asian gazetted police officers rose from 33.6 per cent to 50.8 per cent.[43] The departing DOO wanted the maintenance of the SB prioritized, adding that, 'The demands must all be met in the face of the departure during 1957 of about a third of the experienced expatriate officers . . . '. Even within the SB the rapid promotion of local staff, especially of Chinese SB Inspectors, threatened the efficiency of the vital base level of personnel who dealt with the public and informants. Fortunately the Alliance, through the EOC, prioritized SB recruitment, and the British Army posted additional Military Intelligence Officers (MIOs) to help the SB work. The MIOs core work since their introduction in 1952 had been to link the police and army. In addition, a significant number of expatriate SB officers stayed after independence. One, Tim Hatton, was acting Director on occasions before retiring in 1967.[44]

As Commonwealth forces concentrated on fewer black spots from 1955, this also meant senior British commanders withdrawing from some DWECs, though at least one senior British officer remained on each SWEC.[45] By 1955 there were just three brigade commanders, mainly around the States of Perak and Johore.[46]

Counter-insurgency campaigning, meanwhile, progressed seamlessly across independence. There was a renewal of the 1955 Amnesty terms in the form of the *Merdeka* (Independence) Amnesty of September 1957–58. The October 1957 Anglo-Malayan Defence Agreement (AMDA) allowed the 1955-formed 'Commonwealth Strategic Reserve' (28 Commonwealth Infantry Brigade) of British Gurkha units plus a small Australian and New Zealand presence to

[42] DOO Review 1957, p. 23, paras 85–6.

[43] Leon Comber, *Malaya's Secret Police 1945–60: The Role of the Special Branch in the Malayan Emergency* (Singapore: ISEAS, 2008), p. 272. The Colonial Office ceased to employ expatriate officers on pensionable, permanent terms as early as 1953, though exceptions were made for special needs such as policing jungle forts.

[44] DOO Review 1957, p. 23, paras 85–6; Comber, *Malaya's Secret Police*, p. 273.

[45] From 1950 following British military dispositions—the 'framework'—had tended to parallel police organization. So, a Brigade HQ with a number of battalions was located at each Police Contingent (State) HQ, with the Brigade Commander operationally responsible to the SWEC, which he attended. Below the Brigade and SWEC levels each battalion headquarters generally corresponded to a Police Circle HQ, being operationally responsible to the DWEC with the battalion commander sitting on the latter. Company HQ would then be associated with a Police District HQ, the company commander working in association with the OC Police district.

[46] DOO Review 1957, p. 19, para. 72. In Perak by 1955 there were two Brigade commanders, both on SWEC. In Johore by 1955 there was the GOC 17 Gurkha Division, who sat on the SWEC. Elsewhere one Brigade commander and his battalion commanders shared SWEC membership.

continue until 1971.[47] AMDA preserved the option of using CSR and air assets in support of 'Commonwealth and international obligations', though technically requiring Britain to seek Malayan agreement for use of its bases in support of non-British territories. That allowed Malaya to deny any SEATO link, while still allowing Britain to withdraw and deploy Malayan-based forces by routing them via Singapore.[48]

AMDA was palatable to the Malayans because they needed to preserve resources to develop amenities for Malays if they were to keep their multi-communal Alliance successful. British military help came with £33 million in grants and loans over the years 1957–61.[49] In addition, they did not have resources sufficient for external defence. The British had earlier hoped that Malaya and Singapore would proceed towards self-government as a unit. Hence defence forces were distributed, Singapore funding the Malayan Naval Reserve, Malaya the Malay Regiment (and later Federation Regiment). The Malayan Auxiliary Air Force's three flights of obsolescent aircraft were distributed across both territories. The new country's Royal Malayan Air Force (RMAF) was only constituted in 1958, receiving just one light Pioneer aircraft that year. It could do little more than assist Emergency transport and jungle fort provisioning until 1960.[50] The small Royal Malayan Navy (RMN) was also transferred from Singapore to Malayan control after independence, both forces relying heavily on seconded British officers for many years.[51]

Much reduced Commonwealth forces, meanwhile, continued to assist counter-insurgency. 3 Royal Australian Regiment arrived in September 1957 as part of 28 Commonwealth Infantry Brigade, and in 1958–59 helped clear Perak in Operation Ginger.[52] Assisted by such intense operations, the Emergency narrowed towards a border focus. The Emergency formally ended in

[47] It was organized as 28 Commonwealth Infantry Brigade from 1955, and continuing from then until 1971 based near Malacca in Malaya, and from 1971 to 1974 in Singapore as 28 ANZUK Infantry Brigade. AMDA negotiations were held up in 1957 first because the Malayans preferred to sign as an independent state, and secondly as there was British sensitivity about losing the British right to use nuclear weapons, which it wanted to have theoretically as a contribution to SEATO.

[48] Hack, *Defence and Decolonisation*, pp. 226–31 summarizes the debates, and the British desire to be able to tell SEATO it could use Malayan-based aircraft as a nuclear armed contribution to that organization's deterrent, alongside Tunku Abdul Rahman's need to tell some UMNO supporters there was no direct SEATO link following August 1957 press reports that nuclear weapons might be sent. British High Commissioner G. Tory reassured Malaya in September 1957 that Britain would not introduce nuclear weapons to Malaya or deliver them from Malayan bases without its prior agreement.

[49] Hack, *Defence and Decolonisation*, p. 231.

[50] Hack, *Defence and Decolonisation*, pp. 146, 261. Malcolm Postgate, *Operation Firedog: Air Support in the Malayan Emergency, 1948–1960* (London: HMSO, 1992), pp. 137–8.

[51] Hack, *Defence and Decolonisation*, pp. 146, 244.

[52] Colin Bannister, *An Inch of Bravery: 3RAR in the Malayan Emergency, 1957–59* (Canberra: Directorate of Public Affairs, 1994); Peter Dennis and Jeffrey Grey, *Emergency and Confrontation: Australian military operations in Malaya and Borneo 1959–66* (St Leonards: Allen & Unwin with the Australian War Memorial, 1996).

July 1960, but Emergency regulations, WECs, and operations continued as needed along the border area. The communists would re-launch their campaign in a much reduced form from about 1968 to 1989, mainly as small flying columns from the border and assassinations.

Conclusions

Malayan 'transitioning' was strongly coloured by its 'colonial' aspect. Some British personnel started Malayan careers in the 1930s, and some held positions into independence. Claude Fenner joined the police in the 1930s, rising to be Commissioner of Police from 1958. John Davis served the police and Malayan Civil Service before finishing as Deputy Chairman of Kedah SWEC in 1960.[53] One simplistic response might be to say that Malaya is therefore irrelevant to non-colonial situations. My response, however, has been to detail the case study and key aspects of 'colonial transitioning', so others can use this in thinking about the nature, scope, and limits of its significance, and about whether even some peculiarly 'colonial' aspects might provide useful hints for non-colonial situations.

With the above aims in mind, the characteristics of Malayan colonial counter-insurgency transitioning I wish to emphasize are:

1. 'Foreign' or assisting personnel were embedded in host country administration and armed forces, in the first case as 'expatriate' members of administrative and police services, and later as seconded officers. Changes in local structures and processes were in this way embedded and programmed in over time, rather than being extraneous and temporary. This is radically different to having advisory personnel regarded as extraneous, whose influence might therefore be less, and might completely disappear with their removal. Small but significant numbers stayed on for some time after independence.
2. Committee by War was crucial to counter-insurgency and transitioning. The embedded nature of assisting personnel in the military-civilian WECs facilitated a slow transition as local personnel rose to senior administrative posts, and as more political and community representatives were brought onto WECs as unofficial members. This model left key processes in place while personnel transited out. It provided institutions that could be gently localized. It should also be noted that it was these

[53] Margaret Sheenan, *Our Man in Malaya: John Davis* (Stroud: Sutton Publishing, 2007), pp. 234–48. Both also served as officers of the wartime Force 136—the local arm of the SOE—which liaised with the communists when they were wartime anti-Japanese jungle fighters.

WECs that from 1950 tightly integrated army war-fighting functions into the core strategy of population and spatial control, fitting them into wider combined intelligence-administrative-military operations that put pressure on particular MCP committees. An individual patrol or battalion might *experience* ambush action that was in fact tightly directed by DOO, DOO sub-committee, and WECs towards particular integrated operations, or towards sustaining the protective 'framework'. Operations therefore remained *both* population-centric and enemy-centric in a blended, coordinated way. The Malayan WEC model tightly related these different types of activity, and gentle transitioning to local personnel in the WECs was the key to transitioning control of this coordination.

3. The British had an overarching conception of colonial transitioning (decolonization) which patterned counter-insurgency transitioning. This did not envisage working towards an exit strategy, so much as a movement from one type of persistent relationship to another. For colonies this meant from trusteeship—where British leadership and forces provided protection and directed locally enlisted forces—towards British partnership in a post-colonial period. This meant that British forces could gain time for viable local political forces to emerge, and provide a graduated local-to-federal level set of elections, but could not guarantee the outcomes. The Alliance was not Britain's preferred political solution. The British recognized that providing space meant genuinely allowing local politics to find a viable local foothold, and then working with them. 'Nation-building' could be tempered but not radically designed or redirected. During 1952–57 the British accepted that the local forces represented by the Alliance were commanding local loyalty, and worked with them.
4. Although this creating of political space and working with the grassroots of local society worked in Malaya (and Kenya and arguably Northern Ireland to some extent), it could also fail spectacularly (Palestine and Aden). Finding a way of formulating the limits of the mission to create political space is an issue, since by its nature end states cannot be guaranteed. Although the process involved a well-disposed, efficient, stable Alliance in Malaya, in other situation there could be an inefficient, corrupt, or even stable but hostile government, or simply one that opposes particular core assisting power ideas about governance and democracy.
5. The emphasis on transitioning to new types of relationship by an incremental process meant that 'independence' (perhaps for a non-colonial conflict, main force exit) was not an ending so much as a symbol of longer-term shifts. Hence withdrawal of the final, highest level British

officers in the police happened across independence to post-colonial periods with a final expatriate British Commissioner of Police appointed in September 1958. In the military, seconded British officers remained crucial in building embryonic post-colonial air and naval forces. British forces also remained committed by a new defence treaty to assist in counter-insurgency, in return being allowed to play a partially circumscribed 'Commonwealth Strategic Reserve' role.

6. Negotiations and concessions as a part of transition process involved ceding real initiative to local partners, with particular rapidity from 1955 (Federal elections, the Baling talks). The emphasis in the latter was on strengthening local resolve to avoid what Britain saw as potentially disastrous concessions, such as MCP recognition.
7. The Malayan example suggests that to see 'transitioning' as merely an endgame or late-stage element may be unhelpful. Key 'transitioning' episodes happened across multiple campaign phases. A key police change came in 1952–54 when numbers were reduced and retrained by Colonel Young, and an Operation Service was instituted.[54] The development of a Home Guard was also organized into Phases I–III (with further subdivisions) early on, ranging from an unarmed Home Guard where the population could sustain rotas, through lending some weapons during patrol, to allowing weapons to be kept in members' own houses. WECs decided when an HG would transition. Likewise, WEC transitioning was a gradual process of increasing local officials, and associating more local political representatives, which was continuous across 1951–56. In the same way, the transition from temporarily having one military man as DOO and High Commissioner (Templer, 1952–54) came early on. The British insisted throughout on formal civilian primacy, and maintained unity of command only for as long as they felt strictly necessary.[55] In short, the Malayan model was one of multiple transitions in different phases and areas.
8. The creation of a force ethos was also embedded in long-term development and in-campaign transitions. Police transition towards a service ethos from 1952 has been noted. From its inception in 1933–34 the 'Malay Regiment' had a 'traditional' Malay-style dress uniform, was encouraged to view the Sultans as figureheads, and to see itself in the tradition of legendary Malay warrior Hang Tuah. By the time of independence the British left

[54] Papers of Sir Arthur Edwin Young, GB 0162 MSS. Brit. Emp. S. 486, Bodleian Library of Commonwealth and African Studies at the Weston Library, Oxford, contrast those on Malaya which record success and changes, with Kenya, which culminate in his resignation saying he could not in Kenyan conditions succeed in an equivalent manner to Malaya's Operation Service, and had been obstructed by senior administrators from investigating accusations of brutality.

[55] DOO Review 1957, p. 26, paras 94–5.

an army of seven Malay Regiment battalions, and a mixed race battalion and supporting units, all with an entrenched identity and loyal to the Federation.[56] British administrators meanwhile sought to develop a multiracial 'Malayan' identity, drawing on the traditions of various race, that could overlay differences between States and races, before ultimately accepting a Malay predominance over the new mix.

Together, the eight characteristics listed above achieved what could be called *deep transitioning*, imbricated into the longer campaign. Beyond the above points, it is fitting to finish with the assessment of Lieutenant General Geoffrey Bourne as DOO in 1957 on successful Malayan transitioning. In his opinion, 'The Malayan statesmen who took over control from the British Government possessed integrity and ability, and enjoyed the support of the majority of the population.'[57] As suggested above, this was partly the result of a long, complex, tropical and colonial relationship, but also of the British bending to the tropical wind like bamboo.

Acknowledgements

This chapter has benefited from research in the Arkib Negara of Malaysia, and the National Library of Australia, for both of which I am grateful for British Academy funding.

References

Bannister, Colin, *An Inch of Bravery: 3RAR in the Malayan Emergency, 1957–59* (Canberra: Directorate of Public Affairs, 1994).

Blackburn, Kevin, 'Colonial forces as postcolonial memories: the commemoration of the Malay Regiment in modern Malaysia and Singapore', in *Colonial Armies in*

[56] The first experimental Malay Regiment company was raised in 1933–4, there were two by the Emergency commencement, and seven by independence. Britain from 1945 periodically hoped to introduce mixed race units, being persuaded that the Sultans and UMNO would not tolerate the Malay Regiment being diluted. It therefore introduced mixed race units into the Federation Army from 1953. Hack, *Defence and Decolonisation*, pp. 110–12, 144–6. To be fair, the Chinese proved more difficult to recruit anyway. For the origins and nature of the Malay Regiment and other colonial forces in the region, see Karl Hack, 'Imperialism and decolonisation in Southeast Asia: colonial forces and British world power', and Kevin Blackburn, 'Colonial forces as postcolonial memories: the commemoration of the Malay Regiment in modern Malaysia and Singapore', both in *Colonial Armies in Southeast Asia*, edited by Karl Hack and Tobias Rettig (London: Routledge, 2006), respectively pp. 239–66 and 302–26. See also Kevin Blackburn and Karl Hack, *War Memory and the Making of Modern Malaysia and Singapore* (Singapore: NUS Press, 2012), pp. 207–21, 227–36.

[57] DOO Review 1957, p. 25, para. 90 (d).

Southeast Asia, edited by Karl Hack and Tobias Rettig (London: Routledge, 2006), pp. 302–26.

Blackburn, Kevin and Karl Hack, *War Memory and the Making of Modern Malaysia and Singapore* (Singapore: NUS Press, 2012).

Chin, C.C. and Karl Hack, eds, *Dialogues with Chin Peng: New Light on the Malayan Communist Party* (Singapore: NUS Press, 2004).

Chin, Peng, *My Side of History* (Singapore: Media Masters, 2003).

Comber, Leon, *Malaya's Secret Police 1945–60: The Role of the Special Branch in the Malayan Emergency* (Singapore: ISEAS, 2008).

Dennis, Peter and Jeffrey Grey, *Emergency and Confrontation: Australian military operations in Malaya and Borneo 1959–66* (St Leonards: Allen & Unwin with the Australian War Memorial, 1996).

Federation of Malaya Annual Report 1957 (Kuala Lumpur: Government Press).

Hack, Karl, 'British Intelligence and counter-insurgency in the Era of Decolonisation', *Intelligence and National Security* 14, no. 2 (1999): pp. 124–55.

Hack, Karl, *Defence and Decolonisation in Southeast Asia: Britain, Malaya and Singapore 1941–1968* (Richmond: Curzon, 2001).

Hack, Karl, 'Imperialism and decolonisation in Southeast Asia: colonial forces and British world power', in *Colonial Armies in Southeast Asia*, edited by Karl Hack and Tobias Rettig (London: Routledge, 2006), pp. 239–66.

Hack, Karl, '"Iron claws on Malaya": The Historiography of the Malayan Emergency', *Journal of Southeast Asian Studies* 30, no. 1 (1999): pp. 99–125.

Hack, Karl, 'Malaya—Between Two Terrors: "People's History" and the Malayan Emergency', in *A People's History of Counterinsurgency*, edited by Hannah Gurman (New York: Free Press, 2013), pp. 17–49.

Hack, Karl, 'The Malayan Emergency as Counter-Insurgency Paradigm', *Journal of Strategic Studies* 32, no. 3 (June 2009): pp. 383–414.

Hack, Karl, 'The Malayan Trajectory in Singapore's History', in *Singapore from Temasek to the 21st Century*, edited by Karl Hack and J.-L. Margolin (with K. Delaye), (Singapore: NUS Press, 2010), pp. 43–291.

Hack, Karl, 'Negotiating with the Malayan Communist Party, 1948–89', *Journal of Imperial and Commonwealth History* 39, no. 4 (2011): pp. 607–32.

Hack, Karl, 'Theories and Approaches to British Decolonization in Southeast Asia', in *The Transformation of Southeast Asia: International Perspectives on Decolonization*, edited by Marc Frey, Ronald W. Pruessen, and T. T. Yong (London: M.E. Sharpe, 2003), pp. 105–26.

Hack, Karl, 'Using and Abusing the Past: The Malayan Emergency as Counterinsurgency Paradigm', in *The British Counterinsurgency Approach: From Malaya to Iraq and Afghanistan*, edited by Paul Dixon (London: Palgrave Macmillan, 2012), pp. 207–42.

Harper, Tim, *The End of Empire and the Making of Malaya* (Cambridge: Cambridge University Press, 1999).

'Judgment in the case of Keyu [Chong Nyok Keyu] et al. versus Secretaries of States for Foreign and Commonwealth Affairs and of Defence', 4 September 2012, <http://www.judiciary.gov.uk/Resources/JCO/Documents/Judgments/keyu-sec-state-foreign-commonwealth-affairs-judgment-04092012.pdf>.

Postgate, Malcolm, *Operation Firedog: Air support in the Malayan Emergency, 1948–1960* (London: HMSO, 1992).
Ramakrishna, Kumar, *Emergency Propaganda* (Richmond: Curzon, 2002).
Report on the Conduct of Food Searches at Semenyih in the Kajang district of Selangor (Kuala Lumpur: Government Press, 1956).
Sheenan, Margaret, *Our Man in Malaya: John Davis* (Stroud: Sutton Publishing, 2007).

3

Transitions

Britain's decolonization of India and Pakistan

Robert Johnson

There is still considerable controversy surrounding Britain's exit from South Asia, despite the publication of official documents concerned with the transfer of power, the best collection edited by Nicholas Mansergh in 12 volumes, and an almost continuous and uninterrupted series of publications about the process, its origins, and its outcomes since 1947.[1] Although difficult to select the very best scholarship amongst a glittering array of academic work, one is drawn to the works of two of the most cited individuals in particular, both from Oxford, namely Professor Judith Brown and Dr John Darwin.[2] While Brown traced the Indian nationalist drive towards independence, Darwin highlighted how domestic British democratization, new post-war agendas of welfare and economic stabilization, and the diminished relative importance of India to the UK economy pushed the government of Clement Attlee towards the conclusion that India must go. Some have chosen to see the transfer of power as either a nationalist triumph, forcing the British out, while others focus on decolonization, that is to say, a process led by the metropolitan centre in London. Yet, this is an artificial and selective reading of the sources. Brown's and Darwin's works are in fact complimentary, since it was the combined effect of unrest in India and new priorities for the British at home that led to India's independence.

[1] Nicholas Mansergh, ed., *Constitutional Relations between Britain and India: The Transfer of Power, 1942–47*, 12 vols, (London: Her Majesty's Stationery Office, 1970–83).

[2] Judith M. Brown, *Modern India: The Origins of an Asian Democracy* (Oxford: Oxford University Press, 1985); John Darwin, *Britain and Decolonization: The Retreat from Empire in the Post-War World* (London: Macmillan, 1987).

Lord Ismay, the Viceroy's Chief of Staff, and Hugh Dalton, then Chancellor of the Exchequer, summed up the dual effect of domestic priorities and local pressure. On 24 February 1947, Dalton noted: 'when you are in a place where you are not wanted, and where you have not got the force, or perhaps the will, to squash those who don't want you, the only thing to do is to come out.... I don't believe that one person in a hundred thousand in this country cares tuppence about it, as long as British people are not being mauled about out there'.[3] Lord Ismay recorded:

> Before I left England on 18th March, I was doubtful whether a mistake had not been made in fixing the date for the transfer of power to Indian hands as early as June 1948. I had been in India for a week before it was borne in on me that so far from being too early, it was too late. I got the impression that in a very short time we should find ourselves still saddled with tremendous responsibilities, but equipped with no power wherewith to discharge them. The few British officials that were still in service were at the end of their tether...British arms were represented by little more than token forces.[4]

Both of these accounts underscore some of the factors common to other transitions, such as domestic public opinion, the effect of one's own casualties on that opinion, the limitations of force and the concerns about published timetables for withdrawal.

In recent interventions involving military force, Western political leaders have been eager to emphasize the short-term nature of occupation, in part to avoid the deeply unpopular idea of colonialism. The inherent contradiction of a *short-term* military intervention for the purpose of stabilization is that stabilization can take years, even decades. Moreover, the history of early colonial interventions, including those in India, also revealed that, in the short-term, the use of military force can sometimes create further destabilization. Indeed, the British conquest of India was conducted in stages, with the British presence, coterminous with unstable polities, seemingly making further military interventions more likely, despite the disapproval of Parliament.[5] British liberals nevertheless came to believe that British rule, based on the rule of law and public accountability, was preferable to the rule of corrupt and abusive Indian princes. James Mill, scholar and author of the *History of India*, in giving evidence to the Commons' Select Committee on 16 February 1832 argued: 'In my opinion the best thing for the happiness of the people is that our government should be nominally, as well as really, extended over those territories; that our own modes of governing should be adopted and our own

[3] Hugh Dalton, *High Tide and After: Memoirs, 1945–60* (London: F. Muller, 1962), p. 211.

[4] Cited in Robin J. Moore, *Escape from Empire: The Attlee Government and the Indian Problem* (Oxford: Oxford University Press, 1983), p. 238.

[5] 28 May 1782, *Journals of the House of Commons*, vol. Xxxviii (1780–82), p. 1032.

people put in charge of government.'[6] In 1839, Thomas Babington Macaulay, the Law member of the Governor-General's Council, advocated a British educational system for India in order to create a cadre of Indians able to assist the British in this enlightened and Western style of government.[7] He envisaged that: 'it may be that the public mind of India may expand under our system 'til it has outgrown that system, that by good government we may educate our subjects into a capacity for good government; that having been instructed in European knowledge, they may in some future date, demand European institutions.'[8] Such sentiments were later used to support the idea that the British had always been moving India towards self-government, although Indian nationalists suggested that the British had long been engaged in 'constitution-mongering' in order to delay genuine autonomy and independence. Even at the time, there were critics from within the British establishment in India. Sir John Malcolm, the Governor of Bombay (1826–30), believed:

> Our greatest error in India appears to have been a desire to establish systems founded on general principles.... In our precipitate attempts to improve the condition of the people, we have often proceeded without sufficient knowledge.... I have been led, by what I have seen, to apprehend as much danger from *political* as well as religious zealots.[9]

Many scholars have sought to trace the origins of transition in India and it was often asserted that the transfer of power was part of Britain's overall 'decline'. Bernard Porter, historian of the British Empire, was not alone in arguing that this decline set in from the 1870s, and Peter Cain and Anthony Hopkins posited that Britain became an ageing and defensive power, increasingly reliant on the City to stave off the inevitable shrivelling of British global influence.[10] Undoubtedly, the shift in global power at the end of the Second World War, and the onset of the Cold War, had its impact. The scholarly debate has been fully explored by John Darwin, and it is clear that what shaped the government's decisions was a combination of structural changes in strategic relationships, and shifts in economic and military power. There was pragmatic decision making about the best way to manage change and yet

[6] James Mill, cited in Frederick Madden and David Fieldhouse, eds, *Imperial Reconstruction, 1740–1840: The Evolution of Alternative Systems of Government* (New York: Greenwood, 1987), p. 246.

[7] John Keay, *India: A History* (London: Harper Collins, 2000), pp. 429–30.

[8] Eric Stokes, *The English Utilitarians and India* (Oxford: Oxford University Press, 1959), p. 45.

[9] Select Committee of Enquiry into the Affairs of the East India Company, 17 April 1832, *Parliamentary Papers*, XIV, 1831–32, p. 36.

[10] Bernard Porter, *The Lion's Share: A Short History of British Imperialism*, 2nd edn (London: Longmans, 1984); Peter J. Cain and Anthony G. Hopkins, *British Imperialism: Crisis and Deconstruction, 1914–1990* (London: Longmans, 1993).

maintain influence, and thus uphold Britain's national interests.[11] While Britain was sometimes confronted with fait accompli, it attempted to control the processes of drawdown and decolonization: it did so with mixed success.

Among the central strands of the British government's approach to transition was a desire to maintain the country's reputation and prestige. For a nation whose wealth had been founded on global trade, the British were eager to preserve their business links. Where formal empire and expensive physical possession could be transferred into a partnership with economic benefits for both, then this was the option pursued. Yet the process was not smooth or applied consistently. In the 1950s there was still hope that Southeast Asian and African colonies could be developed as components of a Sterling Bloc. Nevertheless the concern to maintain Britain's international reputation, as a state that would honour international agreements and uphold international law, was significant.[12] Government correspondence about the establishing of Pakistan in 1948 reveals that relations with the Superpowers, but also with the Arab-Muslim world, influenced thinking about future support for the new Pakistan. Complimenting this first principle was the desire to maintain good relations with the newly independent state, for which the Commonwealth provided a useful constitutional and diplomatic mechanism. Again, membership was not without its own problems, particularly as India and Pakistan insisted on the status of republics, and Burma, part of the Indian Empire, refused to join; but solutions were found. Despite the success of the Commonwealth, after 1945 Britain's priorities had shifted towards closer relations with the United States and Europe. Relinquishing India made the process of alignment with the 1949 NATO pact far easier.

In practical terms, the British favoured a gradual transfer of power which gave them the opportunity to train and develop a new political elite with whom they could conduct business and cordial diplomacy in the future. In essence this meant that peaceful transfers of power were essential, but faith in gradualism periodically threatened to sour relations. Attempts to introduce local governance in India in the Inter-War Years, the so-called Montagu-Chelmsford reforms and the subsequent 1935 Government of India Act, which together established 'dyarchy' and self-government in the provinces under British central guardianship, was seen by Indian nationalist leaders as a deliberate attempt to avoid granting dominion status and progressing to full national devolution. The failure to grant dominion status in 1931 left Indians as 'second class' imperial citizens, despite a significant contribution to the British war effort in 1914–18. Consequently, there was widespread civil

[11] John Darwin, *The End of the British Empire: The Historical Debate* (London: Blackwell, 1991).

[12] Ronald Hyam, ed., *The Labour Government and the End of Empire, 1945–51* (London: Her Majesty's Stationery Office, 1994).

unrest. Nevertheless, there was success in bringing Indians into the Indian Civil Service, the development of civil society, professional training in the medical professions, the appointment of Indian officers as part of the 'Indianisation' of the Indian Army, and expansion of the Indian service sector in the economy.

The outbreak of the Second World War interrupted and threatened to jeopardize the process of transition. Despite the sentiments of the Atlantic Charter of 1941, which stressed that the democracies were fighting for the freedom of occupied peoples, the British government initially ignored the Indian National Congress and then, through the Cripps Mission of March 1942, offered places in the Viceroy's Council, with promises of representative government and dominion status after the war. The British also insisted on the protection of minorities' interests and the freedom for individual provinces to elect to join an Indian Union, which was a way of preserving the Princely States. Incensed by the lack of progress, fearful that Muslims would stay outside a united India, and inspired by Mohandas Gandhi's campaign of non-cooperation, the Indian National Congress launched a 'Quit India' movement on 8 August 1942.[13]

The Quit India campaign was supposed to be a mass movement of non-violence, where the retraction of cooperation with the British would force the Raj to collapse. Brutality would be met with *satyagraha* which assumed the self-sacrifice of Gandhi and his supporters would shame the British into halting their operations. Fully informed by their comprehensive intelligence, the British swooped on the ringleaders before the campaign had even begun, and eventually some 66,000 were incarcerated. Using wartime legislation, the press was banned from reporting the campaign, Congress Committees were temporarily outlawed and its offices and papers seized.[14] The radical wing of the movement advocated a campaign of sabotage, but Congress leaders knew that, while the Indian Army remained loyal to the British, there was no chance

[13] British Library, Asia, Pacific and Africa Collections, formerly the India Office Records, hereafter IOR. Coll. 117/C27/QA: Gandhi, 'Quit India' movement and disturbances: statistics supplied by Central and Provincial Governments, Sep 1942–Jul 1944, L/PJ/8/630, IOR; Coll. 117/C27/Q Pt 1: Gandhi, 'Quit India' movement and disturbances: calendars of events, narratives, reports and other information compiled in India to assist Secretary of State in replying to Parliamentary Questions, Sep 1942–Apr 1943, L/PJ/8/627, IOR; Coll. 117/C27/Q Pt 2: Gandhi, 'Quit India' movement and disturbances: calendars of events, narratives, reports and other information compiled in India to assist Secretary of State in replying to Parliamentary Questions, 1942–Nov 1945, L/PJ/8/628, IOR.

[14] Warnings of unrest preceded the campaign and Cabinet had approved stronger measures to safeguard the war effort and the defence of India. War Cabinet 91 (42), secret, 13 July 1942, and enclosures Governor General to Sec. State India, 11 July 1942 and Government of India Home Department to Sec State India, 11 July 1942, CAB 65/27/7, The National Archives (TNA). See also War Cabinet, secret, 'Policy to be Adopted towards Mr Gandhi', 27 June 1942, CAB 66/26/1, TNA which showed a willingness to take a stronger line with Reuters and the media.

of a violent campaign succeeding.[15] Nevertheless, Gandhi and the Congress leaders were unable to persuade all their followers to adopt an entirely non-violent path. News of Gandhi's arrest sparked two weeks of rioting whilst *hartals* (boycotting) and civil disobedience spread. Disruptions to food supply caused acute shortages in some areas. Telephone lines, post offices, courts, revenue offices, and even police stations were the targets for attack and arson. In extreme cases, railway tracks were torn up. At its height, the Quit India campaign required an entire British division to be diverted to Bombay to quash the unrest. But the vulnerability of the strategic railways really alarmed the British authorities, and the Viceroy, Lord Linlithgow, authorized the RAF to fly sorties over crowds to keep them off railway lines running across the Eastern Provinces and Bihar which led to the precarious front lines against the Japanese.[16] Pilots were instructed to fly low, fire Verey light flares and warning shots. Congress accused the British of machine gunning the demonstrators.[17] The British authorities were prepared to take every measure necessary to crush the unrest in order to release the 35,000 troops that they might need as a strategic reserve to confront a Japanese offensive. The calculation was that they had a window of opportunity of just six weeks before that attack came. Linlithgow informed Churchill that he was:

> engaged here in meeting by far the most serious rebellion since that of 1857, the gravity and extent of which we have so far concealed for reasons of military security.... Mob violence remains rampant over large tracts of the countryside and I am by no means confident that we may not see in September a formidable effort to renew this widespread sabotage of our war effort.[18]

When the idea of strafing saboteurs from the air was raised in the House of Commons on 8 October 1942, there was support for a firm line.[19] Eventually, with the Indian Army and its British units at full stretch, the campaign was brought to manageable levels of violence.

[15] An assessment of the unrest by Congress was intercepted by Military Intelligence. WO 208/819A, 25C, TNA. The British Central Intelligence Department was very well informed about INC plans, having intercepted mail and penetrated the organization at various levels. CID briefings were held daily or every two days at the height of the crisis. See Home Department: History of the Congress Rebellion, Part 1, 1942–3, *Gandhi's Independence Campaign: Statistics to assist the S[ecretary of] S[tate] to reply to P[arliamentary] Questions]* L/PJ/8/628, IOR.

[16] Interestingly, the General Staff and Home Department had already discussed the possibility of creating a paramilitary force for internal security police in 1941, especially for strategic railway protection, 174/44/41, *Gandhi's Independence Campaign: Statistics to assist the S[ecretary of] S[tate] to reply to P[arliamentary] Questions]* L/PJ/8/628, IOR.

[17] Lawrence James, *Raj: The Making and Unmaking of British India* (London: Little Brown and Company, 1997), p. 566; P. N. Chopra, '"Quit India" Movement of 1942', *Journal of Indian History* 49, no. 145/147 (1971): pp. 39–40 and P. N. Chopra, *Quit India: British Secret Documents* (New Delhi: Interprint, 1986). The crew of one of these aircraft that crash landed was murdered by a mob.

[18] N. M. Mansergh, E. W. R. Lumby and P. Moon, eds, *Constitutional Relations between Britain and India: The Transfer of Power: 1942–47*, II (London: Allen and Unwin, 1970), pp. 853–4.

[19] Hansard, 5th Series, 383, p. 1342.

Nevertheless, the Government of India remained concerned about the potentially disastrous effect of Congress and Japanese propaganda, as revealed by the correspondence surrounding the Special Powers Ordinance for the Military Operational Area passed in 1943.[20] The Ordinance provided for the setting up of measures to deal with fifth column activity in the zone behind the front line. This Ordinance was seen as preferable to full martial law which ran the risk of the army acting in an unrestrained and heavy handed way. The Viceroy was concerned that, in previous episodes of martial law, the army in Bihar had established special courts 'untrammelled by the usual controls', which tended to be 'hasty in decision and inadequate in record of summaries of evidence', adding 'I fear the same results if the army is given *carte blanche*'.[21] General Molesworth, responsible for the area close to the Japanese lines, wanted careful drafting of what the limits of military authority and jurisdiction were.[22] It seems that both the army and the government were eager to maintain the primacy of political leadership and to ensure close civil–military cooperation. Yet, from 1943, it was clear that British authority now rested on less secure foundations. The authorities anticipated that the end of the war would mean a return to widespread violence that the army would be unwilling and perhaps unable to contain. Army Headquarters informed the Military Secretary: 'It is fair to say that, as the war draws to its close . . . the general I[nternal] S[ecurity] position is bound to deteriorate, as interested parties begin to prepare (as they are now preparing) for the eventual struggle for power'.[23] In 1945, plans drawn up to deal with political agitation and violence showed that everything depended on the loyalty of the Indian troops, but this could not be taken for granted.[24] The additional pressure was that thousands of Indian soldiers were being demobilized after the war and were in need of work.

The issue of greatest sensitivity was the fate of Indian troops who had either defected to the Japanese as Indian National Army (INA) personnel, or the Indian sailors who had mutinied for better conditions at the end of the war. While there was sympathy for those who had rioted because of their eagerness

[20] On Indian Army morale see, for example, 'Secret Appreciation of Indian Morale', Overseas Planning Committee, Ministry of Information, 1942, INF 1/556, TNA. The situation was assessed by Brig. W. J. Cawthorn, DMI, in 'Reactions in Indian units to Japanese Propaganda', Most Secret, Weekly Intelligence Survey, India Internal, 31 Mar 1944, L/WS/1433, IOR and 'The Future of the Internal Security Situation in India', 31 Aug 1942, L/WS/1/1337, IOR. Measures had already been designed from the outbreak of the war, see J. A. Thorne, *Confidential report on the control during the war of the press, broadcasting and films, and on publicity of the purpose of the war*, Delhi, 1939, L/I/1/1136, IOR.

[21] Viceroy to Secretary of State for India, telegram, Secret 36616, 23 Sep 1943, L/PJ/8/566, IOR.

[22] Note by Under Secretary of State, 29 Sep 1943, L/PJ/8/566, IOR.

[23] GHQ (India) to the Military Secretary, India Office, Most Secret, 20 Dec 1942, L/WS/1/1337, IOR.

[24] Defence HQ Outline Plan, Operation Asylum, Most Secret, 9 Dec 1945, L/WS/2/65, IOR; Chiefs of Staff Committee, Indian Army, 'Subversive attempts on the loyalty of the Indian Army', Secret, 10 May 1943, L/WS/1/707, IOR.

to demobilize, many Indian 'regulars' believed the former INA men should be punished as traitors. During the war, they had fought them in Burma and were often unimpressed by their allegiances or their fighting ability. At its height, the INA had mustered 43,000 personnel, a not insignificant number, although it could not sustain this size throughout the war and many of the INA subsequently rejoined the British-led war effort. Nevertheless, Indian civilians were more anxious, especially when the war ended. When Lieutenant General Sir Francis Tuker, commanding IVth Indian Corps, suggested deporting the former INA men to Japan or perhaps use 'the wall and the firing squad', Indian politicians feared that the British might attempt a reign of terror. Jawarhalal Nehru and Congress seized the opportunity to turn the INA into a national cause, arguing that the INA had fought for India's freedom. Attempts to have INA men tried under the Indian Penal Code gave the nationalists the public platform they needed to promote the cause of independence.

Wavell, as Viceroy (1943–7), attempted to work out a solution with each of the factions in Indian politics, but, for all his charm, empathy, and intellectual ability, he was simply unable to get agreement. Wavell summed up the squabbling by borrowing from Lewis Carroll's 'Jabberwocky': 'Twas brillig; and the Congreelites / Did harge and shobble in the swope, / All jinsy were the Pakistanites, / and the spruft Sikhs outscrope'.[25] Mohammed Ali Jinnah, leading the Muslim League, eventually tired of the talks and declared a Direct Action Day on 16 August 1946. Designed to assert that Muslims' interests had to be respected, the demonstrations merely deepened existing communal antagonism with Hindus. Some 4,000 were killed in the fighting. The increasing violence around India put an additional burden on the Indian Army which was now much diminished in size and strength since the end of the war.[26]

On 7 September 1946, Wavell drew up a secret plan for the withdrawal from India 'in the event of a political breakdown'.[27] Only a select handful were party to the plan, and there was agreement that such a plan was needed as the 'best solution to our difficulties if we cannot get the parties to co-operate in producing a solution'. Wavell admitted that whatever the decision in London, there was 'an administrative limitation to the continuance of our control', noting that he assumed the government at home was 'not about to announce a decision to continue to rule in India for another fifteen or twenty years'. One is given the impression that this would have been the preference of the secret committee as the means to 'rally support to our side and... involve the

[25] Cited in Trevor Royle, *The Last Days of the Raj* (London: Hodder and Stoughton, 1989), p. 150.

[26] Auchinleck felt the army, reduced to 800,000 with plans for a reduction to 340,000 by mid-1947, was too small to manage the internal security burdens placed upon it. Political Intelligence, 1946, L/WS/1/1009, IOR.

[27] Lord Wavell, 'A Policy for India', Top Secret, Sep 1946, L/PO/6/116, IOR.

immediate reinforcement of the [armed] services'. Wavell believed that, such was the atmosphere in India, 'one must either rule firmly or not at all'. Coloured by his experiences through the war, he observed that: 'With a largely uneducated and highly excitable people, easily moved to violence, it is essential that agitation and incitement to unbridled riot should be stopped at once'.[28]

Nevertheless, Wavell was concerned not only with physical security, but the capacity to actually administer the country. He noted: 'the machinery on which our control in India has depended is rapidly running down . . . [the Indian Civil Service] have always been few in number and their effect has depended on their prestige, their confidence that they can rely on the support of the government, and their solidarity', but now Wavell felt that Indianization had eroded the service and made it susceptible to communal preferences. The situation was similar for the Provincial and subordinate services, especially the police:

> These have been diluted during the war; and service traditions have been weakened. Communal or sectional interests are now powerful and loyalty to the government has been undermined . . . partly by the knowledge that British control will soon terminate and that the services must look for the prospects to new masters. It is, therefore, no longer possible to rely implicitly upon them to carry out the orders of a British Government. Similar considerations apply to the Army, though, at present in a much less degree.

Wavell warned his colleagues that 'law and order in the country depends almost entirely on the reliability and cohesion of the Indian Army' but 'one cannot expect to maintain indefinitely the integrity of the Army while both the main political parties are preaching communal war and when it is known that the British officers, who alone hold the army together, are leaving soon'.[29] Wavell advised that in the provinces, a governor could no longer afford to over-rule his Indian ministry on an issue on which they had threatened to resign, since he would be able to call on no one else. He cautioned that a Governor could only really enforce his decisions 'to a limited degree by persuasion and bluff'. Wavell estimated that Britain would only be able to enforce its will for one and a half years longer at best.

In London, the government was soon brought to the same judgement. The Cabinet concluded on 10 December 1946:

[28] For this, the morale of the Indian Army was critical. Morale Reports, September 1946, L/WS/1/1637, IOR.

[29] Similar views were expressed by General Tucker, see: M. D. Wainwright, 'Keeping the Peace in India, 1946–7: The Role of Lt General Sir Francis Tuker in Eastern Command', in *The Partition of India: Policies and Perspectives, 1935–1947*, edited by C. H. Philips and M. D. Wainwright (London: George Allen and Unwin, 1970), pp. 127–47.

> The strength of British forces in India was not great. And the Indian Army, though the Commander in Chief had great personal influence with it, could not fairly be expected to prove a reliable instrument for maintaining public order in conditions tantamount to civil war. One thing was quite certain viz., that we could not put back the clock and introduce a period of firm British rule. Neither the military nor the administrative machine in India was any longer capable of this.[30]

During 1946, the Indian Army staged a military exercise to practise internal security duties, including the use of minimum force, the rules for the use of lethal force and the anticipated moments to assume martial law and when to relinquish it to civilian authorities. Although it was a long established practice, civilian administrators seemed unfamiliar with their duties and reluctant to use their powers.[31] At the end of the year, Wavell wrote in his journal on 31 December 1946:

> The administration has declined, and the machine at the Centre is hardly working at all now, my [Indian] ministers are too busy with politics. And while the British are still legally and morally responsible for what happens in India, we have lost nearly all power to control events; we are simply running on the momentum of our previous prestige. The loyalty of the Police is doubtful in some of the Provinces, they are tinged with communalism; fortunately the Indian Army seems unaffected so far, but it can hardly remain so indefinitely, if communal tension continues'.[32]

Attlee believed that Wavell had lost confidence in the ability to make the transfer at all and he appointed Viscount Mountbatten, the former commander in chief of forces in Southeast Asia, as his replacement in February 1947. The British government had decided that Indian independence must be fixed for June 1948 at the latest. Attlee instructed Mountbatten that the 'definite objective' of the government was 'to obtain a unitary Government for British India and the Indian States, if possible within the British Commonwealth, through the medium of a Constituent Assembly'.[33] He was to use his powers of persuasion to get all parties to work together for this end. Yet, despite a relentless charm offensive, Mountbatten was unable to get any agreement. The Cabinet reported in May 1947 that: 'the refusal of the Muslim League to participate in the work of the Constituent assembly destroyed any

[30] 'India: Constitutional Position, Cabinet Conclusions', 10 Dec 1946, CAB 128/8, TNA.

[31] Rob Johnson, 'Military Aid to the Civil Power: The Army in India and Internal Security', in *The Indian Army, 1939–1947*, edited by Alan Jefferies and Patrick Rose (London: Ashgate, 2012), pp. 215–39.

[32] Penderel Moon, ed., *Wavell: The Viceroy's Journal* (Oxford: Oxford University Press, 1973), p. 402.

[33] Clement Attlee's Minute to the Secretary of State for India, 18 March 1947, L/PJ/10/79, IOR. See also the Prime Minister's plan in January 1947 emphasizing the need to have a Constituent Assembly decide on the basis of self-determination the character of the new government of India. Cabinet, Indian Policy, Memorandum by the Prime Minister, Top Secret, 4 January 1947, CAB 129/16, TNA.

possibility that the Cabinet Mission Plan [outlined above] could be successfully put into effect'.[34] There was 'no prospect of a Union of India'. Nevertheless, Attlee drew attention to 'the difficulties and dangers necessarily inherent in any scheme of partition [since] the situation in many parts of India was already highly inflammable'. The Cabinet was aware that there was a significant risk of bloodshed in the Punjab, and the Sikh community would be divided, although it was hoped their participation in the Boundary Commission would reduce the unrest. The Prime Minister also acknowledged the logistical and administrative complexity of dividing the Indian Army between the successor states, as well as partition of trade, finance, and industry. The government was concerned that India would choose to leave the Commonwealth, although Pakistan would likely stay within it. Nevertheless, the government would go ahead and grant India dominion status in the short-term as the means to transfer power legitimately and constitutionally into the hands of the Indian leadership.

Transition also required a degree of continuity, and it was the request of all Indian parties that the British leave European officers within the new armies of India and Pakistan 'to assist in carrying out the division of the army between the new States and building up effective military organisations on a fresh basis'. The government noted that this would be impossible if the two countries became republics. Granting dominion status in the short-term to an interim government could solve the problem, since full independence could come *after* the transfer of power to this interim authority. At the same time, the India office would cease to be and the King would divest himself of the title 'Emperor of India'.

The Prime Minister told the Cabinet that 'communal feeling in India was now intense' and that serious disorders could break out as soon as the plan to partition India was announced. Attlee relayed Mountbatten's view that 'the only hope of checking widespread communal warfare was to suppress the first signs of it promptly and ruthlessly, using for this purpose all the force required, including tanks and aircraft, and giving full publicity throughout India to the action taken and the reasons for it'. The Cabinet approved the judgement, assuring the Viceroy that he 'had the support of His Majesty's Government'.[35] The Prime Minister drew up a memorandum detailing that, in the event that Mountbatten's final attempt at getting agreement on an Indian Union failing, he was to announce to the Indian party leaders the government's intention to accept partition.[36] The intention was to 'thrust upon the Indians the responsibility for deciding whether or not India shall be divided

[34] Cabinet 50 (47), 23 May 1947, CAB/128/10, TNA.
[35] Cabinet 50 (47), 23 May 1947, CAB/128/10, TNA.
[36] Cabinet, Indian Policy, Memorandum by the Prime Minister, 22 May 1947, CAB 129/19, TNA.

and in what way. Based on self-determination, it was fully expected that a bifurcated Muslim state, split between the northwest and Bengal, would be the result. In common with other parts of the British Empire, many in government hoped that the economic demands for cooperation between the new states would force them to work towards some sort of federation.

Nevertheless, in June, Mountbatten announced that the date of the transfer of power would be brought forward from June 1948 to August 1947, barely three months away. He made a public appeal for 'a reasonable measure of goodwill between the communities'.[37] Admitting that he had failed to get agreement for the Cabinet Mission Plan of 1946, he believed the only alternative to coercing Indians into a single state was partition. He stressed his desire to avoid worsening the plight of the Sikhs of the Punjab by involving them in the boundary commission and expressed his view that he could not wait until the Constituent assemblies had completed their work on the details of the transfer. Instead, everything was to be 'transferred many months earlier than the most optimistic of us thought possible, and at the same time leave it to the people of British India to decide for themselves on their future'.[38]

The communist left took a keen interest in the partition, popular protest, and particularly the fate of the Indian Army. In a classic conspiracy theory, the Soviet *Red Star* paper reported that: 'the new British plan is nothing but an attempt to retain India as an important integral part of the British Empire. The chief economic positions still remain in British hands—the railways, marine transport, the port economy, irrigation systems, finances, the basic part of the jute industry, almost the whole mining industry'. In a deft reversal of Marxist theory, the author asserted: 'the defence of economic positions and interests is not possible without political power', but added, in order to show the British were exercising continuity in their imperialism, 'That power will be secured in the person of the capitalists, landowners and businessmen who are dependent upon British capital'.[39] There was in fact little chance that Britain would remain in control of Indian infrastructure or industry, and while the proportion of trade between the new states and Britain remained healthy for several years, South Asian countries gradually shifted their share increasingly towards other countries. If there was an accusation of bad faith to be answered, it was over the British desire to protect minority interests. The accelerated timetable for withdrawal meant the hasty abandonment of these sections, including the Sikhs of the Punjab. Furthermore, the Princely States were advised to choose either the new India or Pakistan. Those that delayed their decision, such as Kashmir and Hyderabad were unceremoniously invaded in 1948.

[37] Cabinet, Broadcast by Viceroy, CAB 21/2038/2, TNA.
[38] Cabinet, Broadcast by Viceroy, CAB 21/2038/2, TNA.
[39] *Red Star*, 31 July 1947, FO 371/63567, TNA.

By far the most depressing episode of the entire transfer was the severe loss of life in the Punjab and Bengal. Increased rivalry between the Indian National Congress and the Muslim League had fuelled communalism to a pathological degree in some provinces. Fears and rumours stoked the antagonism, and when the partition was implemented in the autumn 1947, panic caused a flight by communities who realized they would be on the wrong side of the border. Gangs rushed in to seize land or to avenge themselves against the rival community, and news of deaths inflicted by one side merely encouraged the other to take reprisals. Most scholars assert that around half a million were killed during the widespread violence of partition. Five million refugees passed into India and approximately the same number fled to Pakistan, with some twelve million left homeless. Alan Flack of the Indian Civil Service wrote: 'Lots of people here are depressed and miserable about the transfer of power. The whole show is now so utterly corrupt that the educated classes feel that it can't go on. The Punjab is an absolute inferno and is still going strong. Thousands have been murdered... '.[40] V. P. Menon, a former member of the Viceroy's Council, took it upon himself to ask Mountbatten to return to Delhi and become Chairman of an Emergency Committee.[41] Mountbatten was energy personified: organizing guards of local politicians, deploying units to the worst affected areas, sending out medical units, and attaching security forces to trains and refugee convoys. Indeed, the crisis meant that Mountbatten ignored constitutional arrangements and issued instructions as a quasi-military commander. He also established and tactfully chaired a Joint Defence Committee between India and Pakistan, which did much to allay fears on both sides, and ultimately prevented a war breaking out.

While the Indian Army was tasked to provide security as best it could across the country, in the Punjab, where the worst unrest was anticipated, the Indian government set up the Punjab Boundary Force (PBF) in May 1947. Its personnel were drawn from Hindu, Muslim, and Sikh backgrounds, led by Asian and European officers. Daniel Marston, who researched this force, believes that the PBF managed to remain impartial in the majority of cases where communal violence had broken out.[42] There were, admittedly, a few incidents in Lahore and Amritsar, where the violence was at its worst, but, on the whole, soldiers and officers from the different communities remained cohesive and focused on their mission.[43] The press at the time was highly critical of the PBF because

[40] Cited in Royle, *Last Days of the Raj*, p. 245.

[41] Royle, *Last Days of the Raj*, p. 256.

[42] Daniel Marston, 'The Indian Army, Partition and the Punjab Boundary Force, 1945–47', *War in History* 16, no. 4 (2009): pp. 469–505.

[43] Urvashi Butalia, *The Other Side of Silence: Voices from the Partition of India* (London: Viking, 2000); Yasmin Khan, *The Great Partition: The Making of India and Pakistan* (New Haven: Yale University Press, 2007); Ian Talbot, *Divided Cities: Partition and Its Aftermath in Lahore and Amritsar, 1947–1957* (New York: Oxford University Press, 2007).

it seemed they did nothing to prevent the shocking and large-scale massacres taking place, but such a small force was overwhelmed by the extent of the fighting. Furthermore, Marston argues that the collapse of the police force and civil administration in the province deprived the PBF of the intelligence about the problems and likely conflicts in specific districts. PBF units were therefore often operating 'blind', unable to prevent conflict between the most militant parts of each community, and forced to react, which meant supporting the evacuation of the many refugees. General Sir Frank Messervy, General Officer Commanding Northern Command, advised military units to gather their own intelligence: 'civil intelligence... breaks down completely in the rural areas where the trouble starts. The military intelligence net is now being established.... [T]he details are not yet fully worked out but it is ideal to have one reliable agent on every patrol.... [T]roops must also gather intelligence.'[44]

One Indian officer, Brigadier Candeth, attributed the problem to a simple lack of manpower. He recalled:

> Our job mainly was to see that these attacks [on columns of refugees] didn't take place and, by and large, once we got sufficient troops into the Punjab we were able to control it and to some extent we stopped or minimized the number of incidents that took place. You couldn't stop it entirely because the trains were easy targets.[45]

Most Indian units were undergoing reorganization, that is dividing up or disbanding, at precisely the moment the violence broke out. Some units were simply unable to get to areas of disorder because they had no transport or insufficient fuel. The fact that the Punjab had been the preferred recruiting ground of the Indian Army for generations, and especially during the war, meant that a large number of men conducting the killings had military experience.[46]

The British succeeded in stage-managing the final phase of their departure, both in India and in Pakistan, with dignified parades, but while Britain fulfilled its national interests, the massacres of transition meant they had not achieved the lasting goodwill they had hoped for. Moreover, having to divide the Indian Army, including the Gurkhas (half of which remained in British service), was felt to be tantamount to betrayal. British military and civilian personnel had mixed feelings about the transition from India, summed up as bewilderment at the speed of the process, weariness, fatalism and professional

[44] Major General Pete Rees, [Commander Punjab Boundary Force] 'Some Remarks on the Disturbances in the Punjab', March 1947, Rees papers, file 50, IOR cited in Marston, 'The Indian Army, Partition and the Punjab Boundary Force', p. 487.

[45] Cited in Royle, *Last Days of the Raj*, p. 249.

[46] Robin Jeffrey, 'The Punjab Boundary Force and the Problem of Order, August 1947', *Modern Asian Studies* 8, no. 4 (1974): pp. 491–520; Swarna Aiyar, 'August Anarchy: The Partition Massacres in Punjab, 1947', *South Asia* 18, no. 1 (1995): pp. 13–36.

indifference, a sense of abandonment of Indian personnel, but also affection, and pride.

Surprise at the suddenness of the ending was a typical, almost universal feeling. Olaf Caroe, a former army officer and the last Governor of the North-West Frontier Province (NWFP), felt the handover had been 'much too hurried. We were at the centre of a vast typhoon which was going on all around us, but of which we [in the relatively peaceful NWFP] were curiously unaware at the time'.[47] Most British military personnel were busy and there was little time for reflection until much later—and by then it was all over. Robin Latimer, a civilian administrator, stated: 'One didn't have much time to brood about independence... some said "Don't go!"... Even allowing for being polite, they seemed really not to want us to leave'.[48] Part of the reason for this was Indian anxiety about their personal safety, since the British had provided the security forces. To accord with the directive that India was approaching independence and had responsibility for security, and to avoid unnecessary casualties, some British units were confined to their barracks where, depending on their location, they unofficially sheltered Hindu or Muslim fugitives. All expressed a sense of shock at the scale and ferocity of the communal massacres taking place around them. Lieutenant D. J. McCaskill, 1st Battalion, Lancashire Fusiliers, at Lucknow came to believe the British Army had been 'not so much holding the Empire together as keeping the Muslims and Hindus apart'. He felt compelled to add a justification, which was phrased as an imperial achievement:

> I don't feel Britain has too much to be ashamed of. There were so many different cultures and religions in India that only a third party could keep any peace between them. The British have their faults—who hasn't—but we must have had something going for us since the huge sub-continent remained a single unit while we were there, and only splintered into fragments of its once glorious self after we left....

Many of the British personnel expressed a sense of exhaustion, the result of the high tempo of the war years and then the preparation for the handover of power which began almost immediately. Lieutenant General Reginald Savory, the Adjutant-General of the Indian Army, felt frustration that: 'we were leaving a job half finished. Our intention in India was to hand over a running show and I believe that if we could have held on for another ten years that would have been the case. But the will was lacking.'[49] Auchinleck had

[47] Charles Allen, *Plain Tales* (London: Andre Deutsch, 1975), p. 255.

[48] Robin Neillands, *Fighting Retreat: The British Empire, 1947–97* (London: Hodder and Stoughton, 1996), pp. 105–6.

[49] General Savory, letter, 28 June 1947, Savory Papers, National Army Museum (NAM); Allen, *Plain Tales*, p. 257.

informed Mountbatten that the task of dividing up the army would take three years, but it was not until June 1947 that a committee for the 'Reconstitution of the Armed Forces of India' was set up, and Mountbatten wanted the division of the army complete by August.[50] Ian Stephens, whose father and grandfather had been military men and who lived in India, believed that a sense of disillusionment was widespread because: 'much of what they'd served for seemed to be breaking up, and they pulled out, fatigued, [to] rebuild their lives'. David Symington, a civilian, also noted the soldiers were 'very tired and pretty browned off with the political failure'.[51] Although many of the officers wanted to stay, they felt they couldn't choose between a Hindu-led or a Muslim-led government. Leaving was accepted with fatalism: some were glad to go home to see friends and families again and 'get some rest', some left without any feelings at all—just looking forward to another posting, whilst others subsequently became nostalgic for the environment.

The sense of abandonment of Indian soldiers was particularly difficult for British officers of the Indian Army to bear since it impinged directly on their sense of honour and loyalty. Rupert Mayne, of Mayne's Horse, drove past great columns of refugees passing in opposite directions between Amritsar and Lahore. A former soldier of 4th Indian Division stepped out of the line, stood to attention and explained that he had fought through North Africa and Italy, and then asked for help. Mayne was unable to help him. He replied: 'Your politicians asked for *swaraj* [self-rule], and this is *swaraj*'.[52] Yet, senior officers were aware that some former soldiers were leading the murder gangs and General Messervy advised that pensioners should be informed their pensions would be stopped if they were found participating in the violence.

Lieutenant J. P. Cross, 1st/1st Gurkha Rifles, was angry that his unit had received no instructions on the handover 'until the last minute'. Despite promises that the battalion would transfer into British Army service, it transpired that it would not: 'The Gurkhas could not understand it; nor could we. We were left without positive directions and therefore could give none. Pressures of events obscured the heartbreak,... there was no properly planned handover to the Indian officers. They never came until after the bitter end. And [referring to the massacres] the end was bitter.' He continued:

> However fine the motive behind the act of pulling out, where men meant more than ciphers and numbers, it hurt. Those who have never served in a tight knit community like a Gurkha battalion can have little idea of the wealth of camaraderie and warmth of human relationship that exists between officers and men. Nothing really made sense and it was a heartless and painful experience ... on parting, tears were shed and the sorrow was genuine and hard to bear.... [I was]

[50] Marston, 'The Indian Army, Partition, and the Punjab Boundary Force', p. 485.
[51] Allen, *Plain Tales*, p. 258. [52] Allen, *Plain Tales*, p. 257.

> indignant at the unseemly haste of having to meet an unrealistic political deadline. We were abandoning our men, we had broken trust and, by God, it hurt.

One officer believed the breaking up of the Indian Army ruined all that had been achieved and gave an equally emotional response:

> to us it was the heartbreak of heartbreaks. We felt it beyond credence. We had united these dozens of different castes, creeds, colours, and beliefs under one flag. We had united them under one regimental colour. It took us two hundred years to build that up, and for that to go literally at the stroke of a pen—it was something that one will never get over.[53]

Field Marshall Claude Auchinleck, the Commander in Chief in India, wrote:

> All Indian Army officers hated the idea but we did as we were told. They had to be split... which meant that regiments like my own, half Hindu and half Moslem, were just torn in half—and they wept on each others' shoulders when it happened... you felt your life's work would be finished when what you had been working at all along was just torn in two pieces.[54]

This feeling that partition was a disaster and 'horrifying' was reinforced by the communal killing and the sense that the unification of India, which the British regarded as one of their key achievements, had been destroyed.

The assessment of scholars is that the British faced an impossible dilemma, and that they lacked the means or the authority to enforce their will in the final years of the Raj. Robert Holland believes that Mountbatten recognized the inevitability of withdrawal and got the task finished.[55] After years of 'constitution-mongering', his achievement was to implement the transfer of power. Where he failed was in persuading Jinnah and Nehru to avoid partition, and there is a widespread belief that he rushed the whole process, leaving too little time for negotiations which had the effect of increasing the urgency, desperation, and violence. The view was widespread at the time. Sir George Cunningham, the Governor of the North-West Frontier Province, wrote: 'the opinion of most sensible people out here [is] that the trouble was enormously aggravated by the speed at which everything was done'.[56] An alternative view is that Britain achieved its national interests. John Darwin concludes that Mountbatten kept the new states in the Commonwealth, satisfied American demands and thus preserved much needed financial support, ameliorated the criticisms of the Muslim world which kept them aligned against the Soviet Union, and prevented both the new states of India and Pakistan falling to communism.[57] Moreover, Britain managed to ensure India continued with its

[53] Allen, *Plain Tales*, p. 252. [54] Allen, *Plain Tales*, p. 252.
[55] R. F. Holland, *European Decolonization: An Introductory Survey* (London: Macmillan, 1985).
[56] Royle, *Last Days of the Raj*, pp. 245–6. [57] Darwin, *Britain and Decolonization*.

loan repayments although, as noted above, India no longer represented a large share of Britain's trade. Indian commentators believed the British were responsible for partition, and had deliberately set Muslims against Hindus. However, while the Cabinet records and the correspondence of Mountbatten suggest the British felt responsible for the breakdown of law and order, they no longer had the power to prevent it. After the failure of the Cripps Mission (1942–45) and the Cabinet Plan of 1946, they had nothing left to offer, and, other than seizing the initiative with the idea of partition and the date of the final transfer of power, could only react to events.

Almost all the testimonies of military personnel reflect with pride their service in India. The Somerset Light Infantry was the last regiment to leave India and they did so with dignity in a final parade on the quayside at Bombay. Major Freddie de Butts commanded the Guard of Honour at the end and wrote that whilst the Indians cheered, some also wept. He felt the parade had somehow encapsulated: 'the affection and admiration of India, not only for the British soldier, but for the whole British race and tradition of empire'. This might appear to be a bold, even outrageous claim but for his final remark, which seems curiously apt: 'never can an occupying army have had such a send off'.[58] Auchinleck was more critical, believing those in Britain, in contrast to those who had *served* in the subcontinent, had *used* India: 'The English never cared, the politicians especially. I don't think they ever took any interest at all'.[59] Ed Brown, a soldier of the Royal Warwickshire Regiment, captured a mood about the British Empire that was more typical of attitudes at home. He felt that at the back of the 'Jewel in the Crown' there was 'squalor, hunger, filth, disease and beggary. Only when I came out of the army could I see what a terrible thing it was that a country had been allowed to exist like this. Such snobbery, so many riches, so much starvation'.[60]

The process of British transition out of India and Pakistan consisted of setting clear objectives in line with national interests but was very much tempered by what was practical and realistic. When it was evident that Britain could no longer broker agreement between the Indian factions, nor expect to assert its authority over the Indian leaders, Mountbatten got approval to accelerate the timetable for withdrawal. The perception of British administrators and military officers working in India at the time and many others since has been that the speed of transfer was too rapid and created its own dynamic of instability. Some scholars nevertheless assert that British leaders had no choice and that, in order to preserve their own national strategic interests, they had to bring forward the transfer of power, partition, and the division of the Indian Army. While criticized for permitting the violence of Calcutta, the

[58] Neillands, *Fighting Retreat*, p. 113. [59] Allen, *Plain Tales*, p. 260.
[60] Allen, *Plain Tales*, p. 260.

Punjab, and Bengal, the range and scale of problems were beyond the capacity of the British to tackle them. At the tactical level, Brigadier R. C. B. Bristow, who took part in the operations to quell unrest in the Punjab in August 1947, believed the army had the aspiration to fulfil its duty of aid to the civil power, but was faced by a situation beyond its control. He concluded: 'the normal internal security role of the army was to support the civil power in maintaining law and order, but we faced a crisis in which the civil power was ineffective, law and order had completely broken down, and the reliability of the troops varied'.[61] The collusion of many police units in the communal violence in 1947 meant the army was deprived of crucial intelligence and found itself reacting to events. Insufficient manpower meant it was spread too thin and communications were often inadequate. Despite this, and on-going reorganization which created widespread uncertainty, the cohesion of the Indian Army remained intact. Many British officers praised the Indian troops for their impartiality and professionalism in the face of severe provocation, including ambushes and attacks by armed police.

The role of armies in countering insurgency is to destroy and isolate insurgent groups, create the political space and time for conflict resolution negotiations to succeed, and de-escalate the violence in order to return as efficiently as possible to civilian control. One Foreign and Commonwealth Office official recently described the approach of the joint military–civil effort as: 'Fight, Build, Talk, and Commit'. The 'fight' component reinforces the idea that every state must possess a monopoly of violence, control its borders and territorial space, and have the ability to impose sanctions to ensure compliance with the law. States need also to ensure they enjoy the consent of the population, that there is a viable economy and that they can 'build' and sustain local institutions. States need to ensure, through 'talks', that they offer a more attractive benefit than the insurgents, that they understand the needs of the people and they offer representation, equality before the law, equality of opportunity, and both civil and legal rights that protect the individual. State authorities need to 'commit' to long-term projects, to the maintenance of good government and the welfare of the people as part of the 'social contract' between citizen and state. In the event of insurgency, states also have to take account of the dynamics of local 'agency', including the experiences, perceptions, beliefs, and values amongst the aggrieved population. In the case of the transition of India, the British government knew which of these criteria it could and could not ensure. When the balance of consent tipped against them, they chose not to engage in a protracted counter-insurgency, but they sanctioned a robust 'fight' component to prevent civil war, inter-state war, and further mass

[61] Bristow, *Memories*, p. 164 cited in Marston, 'The Indian Army, Partition and the Punjab Boundary Force', p. 505.

murders. They attempted to 'build' new institutions, having trained leaders in the public services, they engaged in 'talks' to find the best and most acceptable solutions and they committed to a timetable for withdrawal, the enduring partnership of the Commonwealth, on-going commercial and financial links, and even permitted British officers to stay on and assist in the early development of the new Indian Army and the Pakistan Army. They refused to take a partisan position and remained even-handed to both states, upheld the international legal standards of the day and withdrew as they had pledged to do.

References

Aiyar, Swarna, 'August Anarchy: The Partition Massacres in Punjab, 1947', *South Asia* 18, no. 1 (1995): pp. 13–36.

Allen, Charles, *Plain Tales* (London: Andre Deutsch, 1975).

Brown, Judith M., *Modern India: The Origins of an Asian Democracy* (Oxford: Oxford University Press, 1985).

Butalia, Urvashi, *The Other Side of Silence: Voices from the Partition of India* (London: Viking, 2000).

Cain, Peter J. and Anthony G. Hopkins, *British Imperialism: Crisis and Deconstruction, 1914–1990* (London: Longmans, 1993).

Chopra, P. N., *Quit India: British Secret Documents* (New Delhi: Interprint, 1986).

Chopra, P. N., '"Quit India" Movement of 1942', *Journal of Indian History* 49, no. 145/147 (1971): pp. 1–56.

Dalton, Hugh, *High Tide and After: Memoirs, 1945–60* (London: F. Muller, 1962).

Darwin, John, *Britain and Decolonization: The Retreat from Empire in the Post-War World* (London: Macmillan, 1987).

Darwin, John, *The End of the British Empire: The Historical Debate* (London: Blackwell, 1991).

Holland, R. F., *European Decolonization: An Introductory Survey* (London: Macmillan, 1985).

Hyam, Ronald, ed., *The Labour Government and the End of Empire, 1945–51* (London: Her Majesty's Stationery Office, 1994).

James, Lawrence, *Raj: The Making and Unmaking of British India* (London: Little Brown and Company, 1997).

Jeffrey, Robin, 'The Punjab Boundary Force and the Problem of Order, August 1947', *Modern Asian Studies* 8, no. 4 (1974): pp. 491–520.

Johnson, Rob, 'Military Aid to the Civil Power: The Army in India and Internal Security', in *The Indian Army, 1939–1947*, edited by Alan Jefferies and Patrick Rose (London: Ashgate, 2012), pp. 215–39.

Keay, John, *India: A History* (London: Harper Collins, 2000).

Khan, Yasmin, *The Great Partition: The Making of India and Pakistan* (New Haven: Yale University Press, 2007).

Madden, Frederick and David Fieldhouse, eds, *Imperial Reconstruction, 1740–1840: The Evolution of Alternative Systems of Government* (New York: Greenwood, 1987).

Mansergh, Nicholas, ed., *Constitutional Relations between Britain and India: The Transfer of Power, 1942–47*, 12 vols, (London: Her Majesty's Stationery Office, 1970–83).

Marston, Daniel, 'The Indian Army, Partition and the Punjab Boundary Force, 1945–47', *War in History* 16, no. 4 (2009): pp. 469–505.

Moon, Penderel, ed., *Wavell: The Viceroy's Journal* (Oxford: Oxford University Press, 1973).

Moore, Robin J., *Escape from Empire: The Attlee Government and the Indian Problem* (Oxford: Oxford University Press, 1983).

Neillands, Robin, *Fighting Retreat: The British Empire, 1947–97* (London: Hodder and Stoughton, 1996).

Porter, Bernard, *The Lion's Share: A Short History of British Imperialism*, 2nd edn (London: Longmans, 1984).

Royle, Trevor, *The Last Days of the Raj* (London: Hodder and Stoughton, 1989).

Select Committee of Enquiry into the Affairs of the East India Company, 17 April 1832, *Parliamentary Papers*, XIV, 1831–32.

Stokes, Eric, *The English Utilitarians and India* (Oxford: Oxford University Press, 1959).

Talbot, Ian, *Divided Cities: Partition and Its Aftermath in Lahore and Amritsar, 1947–1957* (New York: Oxford University Press, 2007).

Wainwright, M. D., 'Keeping the Peace in India, 1946–7: The Role of Lt General Sir Francis Tuker in Eastern Command', in *The Partition of India: Policies and Perspectives, 1935–1947*, edited by C. H. Philips and M. D. Wainwright (London: George Allen and Unwin, 1970), pp. 127–47.

4

Exit from empire

Counter-insurgency and decolonization in Kenya, 1952–1963

David M. Anderson

The 'exit' from Kenya began in the summer of 1959. From then until the British flag was lowered from its perch above the manicured lawns of Nairobi's Government House for the final time, in December 1963, the colonial administration was energetically engaged in the end game of empire. The catalytic event that started the clock ticking on this four-and-a-half-year exit was the beating to death of eleven prisoners at the Hola Detention Camp, on 3 March 1959, an event that provoked a rapid reassessment of British interests and obligations in Kenya.[1] This calamitously embarrassing incident was the culmination of a prolonged struggle to dampen down the last embers of the Mau Mau Rebellion, but at no time before the Hola incident, and despite the many other scandals of a dirty campaign against the insurgents, did the British contemplate a precipitous scuttle from Kenya. Up until Hola, despite the proximate decolonization of other African territories, British rule in Kenya was planned to extend well into the 1970s, and even beyond if Kenya's white minority played their cards right. This vociferous and politically acute white population, numbering over 60,000 by 1961, had grand hopes to engineer a 'Rhodesian' solution, that would see white political (and economic) supremacy

[1] Government of the United Kingdom, *Documents Relating to the Death of Eleven Mau Mau Detainees at Hola Camp in Kenya*, PP, Cmd 778 (London: HMSO, 1959); Government of the United Kingdom, *Further Documents Relating to the Death of Eleven Mau Mau Detainees at Hola Camp in Kenya*, PP, Cmd 816 (London: HMSO, 1959); Government of the United Kingdom, *Record of Proceedings and Evidence in the Enquiry into the Deaths of Eleven Mau Mau Detainees at Hola Camp in Kenya*, PP, Cmd 795 (London: HMSO, 1959).

maintained in an East African federation lasting long into the future.[2] At the time that Kenya's Emergency began, in October 1952, the white settler minority dominated every aspect of the politics and the economy of the colony, presiding over an immigrant South Asian community of 180,000, and 8.6 million Africans, including 1.4 million Kikuyu amongst whom the Mau Mau rising had by then emerged.[3]

If the end game and exit came as a shock to this dominant white community, it was carried through with determination and grit by a Conservative government in London that had set its mind to be rid of the nuisance that Kenya had become. Only narrowly avoiding the Opposition's call for a full parliamentary enquiry into the conduct of the counter-insurgency in Kenya following the Hola incident, an investigation that the Colonial Office by then knew only too well would potentially reveal a devastating catalogue of excess and abuse,[4] Harold Macmillan gave his Secretary of State for the Colonies, Iain MacLeod, the job of managing the politics of Kenya's exit.[5] The military campaign was by then already over, having been successfully completed before the end of 1956.[6] The task from 1959 for the Colonial Secretary was therefore a political one: to bring the State of Emergency to an end, to reactivate and energize local politics in Kenya in a manner that would generate a stable and, if possible, 'friendly' successor regime, and to protect Britain's economic and strategic interest in the process.

To understand how successfully these goals were achieved we must first consider the context of the conflict that had ultimately brought about this accelerated decolonization. Though the war against the Mau Mau had been won, its shadow hung darkly over the plans for exit. The opening section of this chapter will accordingly consider the character of that war and its 'unfinished business'—essentially, a discussion of how this war was won between 1952 and 1956, and at what cost. A second, much briefer section, will describe how the British sought to 'make the peace' in Kenya between 1956 and 1959. This set in motion several processes that could not easily be put aside when the decision was taken to accelerate toward decolonization, these 'reconstruction'

[2] Keith Kyle, *The Politics of the Independence of Kenya* (Basingstoke: Macmillan, 1999).

[3] Bethwell A. Ogot, 'The decisive years, 1956–63', in *Decolonization and Independence in Kenya, 1940–93*, edited by Bethwell A. Ogot and William Robert Ochieng' (London: James Currey, 1995), pp. 48–82; Michael McWilliam, 'The managed economy: agricultural change, development, and finance in Kenya 1945–1963', in *History of East Africa, vol. III*, edited by D. A. Low and Alison Smith (Oxford: Clarendon Press, 1976), pp. 251–89, remains an indispensable survey of Kenya's political economy in the final years of empire.

[4] Caroline Elkins, *Britain's Gulag: The Brutal End of Empire in Kenya* (London: Jonathan Cape, 2005), pp. 349–53.

[5] David M. Anderson, *Histories of the Hanged: Britain's Dirty War in Kenya and the End of Empire* (London: Weidenfeld and Nicolson, 2005), pp. 328–30.

[6] Huw Bennett, *Fighting the Mau Mau: The British Army and Counter-insurgency in the Kenya Emergency* (Cambridge: Cambridge University Press, 2013), pp. 12–29.

factors impacting directly upon the management of the exit. The third section will examine the period of exit, from June 1959, when the clock began ticking, to the departure in December 1963. In this phase, compromise and containment were the key themes, as pragmatism trumped principle at every critical moment. The final discussion will elucidate the implications for other 'exits' that might be drawn from the Kenya case.

Winning the war, 1952–1956

The colonial war that arose from the rebellion of Kenya's Mau Mau movement in the 1950s was an asymmetric conflict, pitting the British Army against a poorly-armed, untrained, and ill-disciplined, irregular African militia. The first British military regiment, the Lancashire Fusiliers, arrived in Kenya on 20 October 1952, to act 'in aid of civil authority' under Emergency regulations declared by Governor Baring. The State of Emergency gave wide-ranging powers to Baring, who moved swiftly to bring in new legislation that made it easier to apprehend and detain suspects without trial; to reform judicial practice by greatly extending the death penalty and by creating special courts to hear Mau Mau cases; and to introduce collective punishments of recalcitrant communities and the imposition of curfews on government orders. Referral to London was obligatory, but in practice the Governor's local authority invariably held sway.[7] It is undoubtedly the case that London gave too little scrutiny to some of the powers first requested by Baring, and then struggled to get a grip on an administration in Nairobi that became increasingly belligerent and hawkish as the rebellion dragged on.

Reactions to rebellion

Always under pressure from an aggressive and fearful white settler population, Baring and most of his senior staff at first adopted the view that swift and firm suppression would nip things in the bud: 'it'll be over by Christmas' was the common assumption in the first weeks of the Emergency. This proved deeply complacent. A surge of successful and bloody Mau Mau attacks in the first quarter of 1953 indicated the inadequacy of the government response.[8] Between March and June 1953, a new and more effective structure emerged for the management of the counter-insurgency. A small War Council was now formed, comprising the Governor and his Deputy, the Chief of Staff (from

[7] Anderson, *Histories of the Hanged*, pp. 62, 70–2, 97–8.

[8] Anthony Clayton, *Counter-Insurgency in Kenya: A Study in Military Operations Against Mau Mau* (London: Frank Cass, 1976), pp. 3–6; Anderson, *Histories of the Hanged*, pp. 68–72.

June 1953 this was General Erskine), and a single representative of the white settlers (Michael Blundell), while a number of coordinating committees were established in the Secretariat and at provincial and district levels to implement policies.[9]

It took the British a little time longer to get the measure of their enemy. The rounding-up and arrest of political suspects at the outset of the Emergency provoked a flight to the forest by rebel sympathizers, whose force eventually numbered more than 20,000.[10] Although automatic weapons and ammunition were stolen from British forces and from settler farms and residences, the rebel forces were never well-armed and depended largely on the crude manufacture of their own weapons. The forest fighters split into two territorial wings, one in the Mount Kenya area; the other in the Aberdares to the west. Liaison between the command structures in these two areas was never strong, but weakened considerably from the second half of 1954, as the British forced the insurgents away from the forest fringes and into the higher mountains, where gangs became isolated.[11] This retreat into the high mountains broke the links between the forest fighters and their 'passive wing' supporters living in the rural areas of Central Province and in the capital city of Nairobi. Food and medical supplies were readily carried into the forests by couriers among the passive wing during the early phase of the conflict, but by May 1954 the supply lines had been fractured—a crucial factor in the weakening and ultimate defeat of the Mau Mau forces.[12]

The rebellion had initially grown out of the frustrations of the African nationalist movement in the years immediately following the Second World War. The requirements of war-time planning had drawn a European settler minority into the heart of government between 1942 and 1945, a fact that hampered post-war constitutional reform. Making slow progress in efforts to gain political rights for Africans, and amid growing land hunger among poorer Africans resentful of the tracts of land in central Kenya held by European settlers, some within the nationalist movement formed a radical wing that by 1950 was covertly organizing for armed struggle.[13] By 1952, violent attacks were regularly being mounted against influential moderate Africans in government employment,

[9] Bennett, *Fighting the Mau Mau*, pp. 23–4; R. W. Heather 'Counter-insurgency and intelligence in Kenya, 1952–56' (PhD thesis: Cambridge University, 1993).

[10] Anderson, *Histories of the Hanged*, pp. 235–8; Wunyabari O. Maloba, *Mau Mau and Kenya: An Analysis of a Peasant Revolt* (Nairobi: East African Educational Publishers, 1993), pp. 131–3.

[11] Donald L. Barnett and Karari Njama, *Mau Mau from Within: Autobiography and Analysis of Kenya's Peasant Revolt* (Letchworth: MacGibbon & Kee, 1966), pp. 455–6.

[12] David M. Anderson, 'The battle of Dandora swamp: reconstructing Mau Mau's Land and Freedom Army', in *Mau Mau and Nationhood: Arms, Authority and Memory*, edited by E. S. Atieno Odhiambo and John M. Lonsdale (Oxford: James Currey, 2002), pp. 155–77.

[13] D. W. Throup, *Economic and Social Origins of Mau Mau 1945–53* (London: James Currey, 1987).

these assassinations culminating in the murder of Senior Chief Waruhiu in October 1952, and the declaration of Emergency.[14]

Among the leaders of these militants were several ex-British Army veterans from the Burma campaign, who had served there with the King's African Rifles.[15] The raw recruits who flocked to join them in the forests when the Emergency was declared were predominantly young men aged between 15 and 30, mostly unmarried, and without access to or prospects of achieving landed property. Land hunger was one of the principal driving forces of the rebellion, as was poverty. Not all Mau Mau recruits came from poorer families, but the majority certainly did: as the leading historian of the causes of the rebellion, David Throup, has expressed it, this was a revolt of 'the have-nots'.[16] Socio-economic factors lay at the heart of Kikuyu discontent. Not everyone advocated violence, but there were few among the Kikuyu who did not understand what motivated the rebels and drove them to the forest.

The young militants who formed the rebel forces of the Mau Mau armies were largely confined to one ethnic group, the Kikuyu of Kenya's central highlands, occupying the Kikuyu Reserves of Kiambu, Murang'a (Fort Hall), and Nyeri, and the more northerly districts of Embu and Meru. The circumscribed ethnic and geographic character of the rebellion had two consequences. First, the British were able to contain the rising within the Central Province and parts of the Rift Valley Province where Kikuyu-speakers were predominant, never having to contend with a colony-wide insurrection. Second, the Kikuyu militants were opposed by the more politically moderate among their kinsmen, allowing the British to cultivate a 'Loyalist' militia, the Kikuyu Home Guard, that could be deployed against the rebels from within their own communities.[17] The recruitment and strategic deployment of the Home Guard became a critical feature in the counter-insurgency campaign. At the peak of recruitment, in March 1954, at 25,600 the Home Guard in Central Province outnumbered the Mau Mau fighters. The British were thus able to argue that the rebellion was never a truly nationalist rising, and that it had even given rise to what amounted to a civil war among Kikuyu.[18] Both points would have significance for the way in which the exit from Kenya was managed, even though the Home Guard was wound down during 1955 and many of its members transferred to the Tribal Police and other arms of government service.[19]

[14] Anderson, *Histories of the Hanged*, pp. 55–61.
[15] Waruhiu Itote, *Mau Mau General* (Nairobi: East African Publishing House, 1967).
[16] Throup, *Economic and Social Origins*.
[17] See Daniel Branch, *Defeating Mau Mau, Creating Kenya: Counter-Insurgency, Civil War and Decolonization* (Cambridge: Cambridge University Press, 2009), for the history of the Loyalists.
[18] Branch, *Defeating Mau Mau*, p. 72.
[19] Branch, *Defeating Mau Mau*, p. 111.

Militarization and the civil administration

The Home Guard were but one among a variety of forces assembled by the British to fight Kenya's counter-insurgency. By May 1953, the military deployment comprised 39 Brigade (made up of three battalions of British troops, each of 500 men), and 70 Brigade (usually five battalions of the King's African Rifles, each of around 600 men), augmented by the Kenya Regiment, an armoured car squadron, and an artillery battery.[20] More than 60 per cent of the British troops serving in Kenya were conscripts. The African rank-and-file of the King's African Rifles were led by British officers seconded from regular regiments, some of these also being conscripts.[21] The Kenya Regiment, recruited from among the white settler population, was deployed mostly in intelligence duties and in supervisory roles with the Home Guard.[22] Among the civilian security forces there were three branches of police. The Kenya Police was greatly expanded during the Emergency, increasing from 7,135 personnel in October 1952 to 11,166 by the end of 1953, the number of European officers tripling in this period. The Police Reserve was also mobilized to take up routine duties, its numbers swelling from a pre-Emergency establishment of 2,982 to 8,547 by December 1953. The Tribal Police, working under the authority of the district administration and the African chiefs, almost doubled in size, climbing to 2,195 men. An additional 2,009 African Special Police were recruited for guard duties under the supervision of Police Reservists.[23] Finally, the prison service, hugely expanded to run more than 50 new detention camps, employed 14,000 warders and other staff by 1954, the vast majority of them virtually untrained.[24] This massive increase in manpower led to grave inexperience and lack of training at junior levels in both the police and prison services, factors that would present significant problems as Britain devised its exit strategy between 1959 and 1963.

The militarization of the civil administration in the African areas of Kenya was a key feature of the Emergency. More than 200 Home Guards posts were constructed in the Central Province by 1954, these fortified garrisons dominating the landscape.[25] Home Guard posts were nothing less than military

[20] Clayton, *Counter-insurgency in Kenya*, pp. 23–5.

[21] For KAR history, see Timothy H. Parsons, *The African Rank-and File: Social Implications of Colonial Military Service in the King's African Rifles, 1902–1964* (Oxford: James Currey, 1999).

[22] Guy Campbell, *The Charging Buffalo: A History of the Kenya Regiment* (London: Leo Cooper, 1986); L. Weaver, 'The Kenya Regiment', in *A History of the King's African Rifles and East African Forces*, edited by Malcolm Page (London: Leo Cooper, 1998), pp. 239–49. Both authors are former members of the regiment. There is no independent history yet available.

[23] Figures from *Kenya Police Annual Reports, 1952 and 1953* (Nairobi: Government Printer, 1952 and 1953); for discussion, see D. W. Throup, 'Crime, politics and the police in colonial Kenya, 1939–63', in *Policing and Decolonisation; Nationalism, Politics and the Police, 1917–65*, edited by David M. Anderson and David Killingray (Manchester: Manchester University Press, 1992), p. 141.

[24] Clayton, *Counter-insurgency in Kenya*, p. 18.

[25] Branch, *Defeating Mau Mau*, pp. 66–72.

camps, staffed by an armed civilian militia, under the loose supervision of African headmen and European District Officers and Kenya Regiment. There was also a rapid creation of many new police stations: while there had been only four police stations in the Kikuyu Reserves in October 1952, by the end of the year 27 new posts had been built. One year later, each of Kikuyuland's administration locations had at least one police station—over 70 in all.[26]

In the first eighteen months of the Emergency, British Army units and the King's African Rifles (KAR) were deployed throughout the Kikuyu Reserves, alongside the police and Home Guard, but after Operation Anvil in May 1954 had 'cleared' Mau Mau supporters from Nairobi, the Army confined their activities to the forest and mountain regions in pursuit of the Mau Mau gangs, leaving the police and Home Guard, assisted by the Kenya Regiment, to keep the peace in the populated rural areas. The forested areas where the Army would operate were declared as 'free fire' zones.[27] As the Army left the Kikuyu Reserves, the police and Home Guard numbers were ramped up and their capacity strengthened: having initially been armed with spears, machetes, and bows, 90 per cent of all Home Guard had been issued with rifles by December 1953.[28] This reinforced the sense over the critical years of 1954 and 1955 that the civilian administration of the Kikuyu areas had been militarized by the requirements of the counter-insurgency.

Indiscipline and the 'rule of fear'

The conduct of the counter-insurgency campaign suffered from poor discipline and a lack of strategic direction from the outset. There was no clear military strategy until Erskine's arrival, and in the first nine months of the Emergency the behaviour of the security forces had already deteriorated badly. Military patrols through the Kikuyu Reserves by the KAR were accompanied by the 'roughing up' of suspects, and British regiments were found to have kept score-sheets and awarded prizes for 'kills'. Rumours were widespread of the torture of suspects in interrogations, and even of the routine shooting of prisoners.[29] Retaliations for Mau Mau attacks were the norm, most notably at Lari in March 1953, where the reprisals resulted in a second massacre of suspects by the security forces.[30] Erskine was appalled by what he encountered on his arrival in Kenya, and immediately issued a warning to his troops as to their future conduct, announced the courts martial of an officer involved in a particularly notorious case of murderous brutality, had two commanding

[26] Throup, 'Crime, politics and the police', pp. 141–2.
[27] Bennett, *Fighting the Mau Mau*, pp. 19–24; Clayton, *Counter-insurgency in Kenya*, p. 13.
[28] Clayton, *Counter-insurgency in Kenya*, pp. 29–30.
[29] Bennett, *Fighting the Mau Mau*, pp. 165–70.
[30] Anderson, *Histories of the Hanged*, pp. 125–38.

officers of one KAR regiment dismissed from their posts and sent home to the UK, and arranged for a formal enquiry to be held on the conduct of the military in an effort to 'clear the air'.[31] Erskine also speedily came to the view that while he could stamp out the worst excesses in the two Brigades under his command, the real problems lay elsewhere: in the Kenya Regiment, the various arms of the police, and the Home Guard. This gave rise to the commander's determination to separate his military units from working directly with civil formations at the earliest opportunity. As Erskine's conduct in the War Council would indicate, he understood that excesses and abuses were likely to happen in a counter-insurgency campaign that involved poorly trained police and local militia units: in what must of necessity be a 'dirty war', his concern was to protect the reputation of the British Army.[32]

That 'dirty war' was largely fought between the police and the colonial administration, and Mau Mau's passive wing among the Kikuyu civilian population. Alongside Erskine, Arthur Young was appointed as Commissioner of Police, coming out to Kenya in September 1953. With experience from Malaya, Young was a policeman who knew what a counter-insurgency campaign looked like, and he was keenly aware of the need to protect the civil capacity of the police from excessive militarization.[33] Like Erskine, he was horrified by what he found in Kenya. The rapid expansion of the police force to cope with the Emergency had seen a lowering of standards and a dearth of training. The police had become alienated from local communities and were viewed as but one element in a regime of surveillance and control. Brutality and excess had also become norms in the daily practice of policing in central Kenya. Pointing out that the police should be the guardians of the rule of law, what Young observed in the Kikuyu districts of Kenya in 1954 he described as 'the rule of fear'.[34]

Young did his best to purge the police, Home Guard, and colonial administration of the abuses of power that he saw, setting up an internal investigation unit within Special Branch to mount prosecutions. But officers in this unit found that their work was actively obstructed, and that members of the civilian administration refused to cooperate in their enquiries. Young's inability to effectively challenge the culture of impunity that had grown among the police and the colonial administration, the body responsible for the Home Guard, ultimately led to his resignation in December 1954, after only just over a year in his post.[35]

[31] Bennett, *Fighting the Mau Mau*, pp. 111, 114, 117–18, 195, 211–13, for Erskine's actions, and for the McLean Court of Enquiry see, pp. 118–23.

[32] Clayton, *Counter-insurgency in Kenya*, pp. 6–7, 37–41.

[33] Anderson, *Histories of the Hanged*, pp. 299–300.

[34] Young to Baring, 14 December 1954, Papers of Sir Arthur Edwin Young, GB 0162 MSS. Brit Emp. S. 486, Bodleian Library of Commonwealth and African Studies at the Weston Library, Oxford.

[35] Anderson, *Histories of the Hanged*, pp. 305–7.

The investigations promoted by Young primarily focused on the activities of the Kikuyu Home Guard and the British district officers supervising them. The Home Guard were at the sharp end of the counter-insurgency, extensively used in civilian actions to identify and root out Mau Mau supporters, and so regularly targeted for Mau Mau attack. Although officials were loathe to admit as much in public, it was clear that Home Guard deployments and the positioning of posts were used in an effort to draw Mau Mau into combat. In effect, the Home Guard was a surrogate force, used to do the things the British, and especially Erskine and the British Army, did not wish to do for themselves. Described by one senior official as 'an undisciplined rabble', the Home Guard were nonetheless allowed to rule the Kikuyu districts with a fist of iron by 1954, given the freedom to solve local problems by whatever means seemed necessary.[36] In the best cases, the Home Guard held the ring over an uneasy peace with local rebel sympathizers: in the worst cases, as at Ruthagathi in Nyeri, Home Guard posts were the centre of extortion and terror over the local population.[37] Efforts to build a 'hearts and minds' campaign in the Kikuyu areas fell foul of the tit-for-tat character of the struggle between the rebels and Home Guard that had become entrenched by 1954. Having created a militia to divide the Kikuyu, the British could not then control it. It was the implications of this failure that Erskine continually referred to when insisting that the rebellion needed a political, not a solely military solution.

'Screening' and detention without trial

While Home Guard excesses appear to have been considered a price worth paying in order to keep control of the rural areas, it was in the detention camps that the worst aspects of the 'dirty war' finally emerged. The system of detention without trial was imposed from an early stage in the Emergency, then massively expanded during Operation Anvil in May 1954. This proved to be the most intractable and damaging aspect of the counter-insurgency. Detention emerged out of the perceived need to identify rebel sympathizers among civilian Kikuyu and segregate them from the rest of the population. This was at first seen as an effective and practical means to protect white settlers from attack by their African employees. By November 1952, white farmers were organizing their own 'screening' of labourers. The government soon formalized the task, setting up screening teams to tour the white farms and the main towns. Anyone who was believed to have taken a Mau Mau 'oath' was liable to detention, even

[36] Branch, *Defeating Mau Mau*, pp. 72–88.

[37] David M. Anderson, 'Surrogates of the State: Collaboration and Atrocity in Kenya's Mau Mau War', in *The Barbarisation of Warfare*, edited by George Kassimeris (London: Hurst & Co, 2006), pp. 178–81.

if the acceptance of the oath had been due to coercion or fear. And many were committed to detention simply on the basis of information provided by other Kikuyu, usually Head-men and Home Guard, without any investigation to substantiate or refute allegations. It was an invidious, random, and often brutal process.[38] Some observers at the time argued that this wholesale 'roughing up' of the civilian population did more to drive Kikuyu into the arms of the rebels than any Mau Mau recruiter could ever have accomplished.[39] But despite the obvious and well-publicized problems, screening expanded in scope to become a central tactic in the colonial government's response to the rebellion.

Kikuyu found to have associations with Mau Mau in the screening process were issued with Detention Orders and placed in hastily constructed prison camps. During 1953, this was formalized into a system of permanent camps, and then a method for categorizing detainees was introduced. Conditions in the camps varied, but rations were inadequate, sanitation dreadful, and the health of inmates notoriously bad. Most camps were grossly overcrowded. After reaching a peak of more than 70,000 detainees in 1955, the camps were segregated to separate 'hard core' detainees from those thought to be less dangerous. Most detention orders were issued for a period of not less than 3 years, and many for between 5 and 7 years.[40] Worse still, the efforts to 'break' detainees through repeated interrogations intended to draw 'confessions' amounted to widespread abuse and torture. By 1955, the administration of the detention camps had become a major logistical challenge—being both expensive and challenging, as detainees increasingly displayed patterns of organized resistance within the camps. By herding men into detention and mistreating them, the British radicalized many Kikuyu who had not previously been of a militant persuasion.

The systematic use of 'compelling force' in camps housing 'hard core' Mau Mau was formally sanctioned at a meeting in London between Governor Baring and the Secretary of State for the Colonies, Alan Lennox-Boyd, in 1957. The policy was unquestionably abusive, and in practice it amounted to torture. The implementation of 'compelling force' led directly to the deaths of detainees in the Hola Camp massacre.[41] The whole system of detention without trial was a gross and deeply damaging mistake.

[38] David M. Anderson, 'British abuse and torture in Kenya's counter-insurgency, 1952–60', *Small Wars & Insurgencies* 23, no. 4/5 (2012): pp. 700–19.

[39] See the complaints regarding screening described in Anderson, 'British abuse', pp. 703–9; and for the wider implications, Huw Bennett, 'The British Army and Controlling Barbarisation During the Kenya Emergency', in *The Warrior's Dishonour: Barbarity, Morality and Torture in Modern Warfare*, edited by George Kassimeris (Aldershot: Ashgate, 2006), pp. 132–54; Huw Bennett, 'The Other Side of the COIN: Minimum and Exemplary Force in British Army Counter-insurgency in Kenya', *Small Wars & Insurgencies* 18, no. 4 (2007): pp. 638–64.

[40] Elkins, *Britain's Gulag*, pp. 131, 217–19.

[41] This argument is set out in Anderson, 'British abuse'.

The war fought behind the wire of the detention camps would go on to 1959, but by 1956 the rebel forces in the forests had diminished to a remnant of only a few hundred hardy souls. The capture of rebel leader Dedan Kimathi in October 1956, and his execution on 18 February 1957, effectively marked the end of the forest war.[42] Official estimates indicated that only 10,000 insurgents had been killed in action,[43] although the actual figures were certainly above 25,000.[44] More than 1,000 convicted terrorists were hanged. But among the bulk of the Kikuyu civilian population, support for the rebels remained formidably strong despite the military successes of the British counter-insurgency. The British commander, Erskine, believed that 90 per cent of adult Kikuyu were rebel sympathizers.[45]

Imposing the peace, 1956–1959

The military wind-down after December 1956 was thought by many to bring an end to the counter-insurgency, but this left the detention camps and the 'rehabilitation' and release of the detainees as the key issue in imposing the peace. Between 1956 and 1959, that peace was imposed not by the military, but by the colonial administration.[46] This was accomplished in three parts. First, a form of order was re-established in the Kikuyu areas through the rewarding of allies with the economic gains of victory. Second, local politics was reconstituted to allow those same allies to dominate all positions of authority. Thirdly, the detainees were released from the camps back into society, but only on the condition that they admitted their guilt and accepted 'rehabilitation'. The last of these was to be the sticking point. Let us consider each in turn.

Rewarding allies: a victor's peace

Throughout the Emergency, Kenya's white settlers had argued that Mau Mau rebels should be treated as traitors. On this basis, the Forfeiture of Lands Act, passed as Emergency legislation in December 1953, allowed the government

[42] Anderson, *Histories of the Hanged*, pp. 288–90.

[43] Government of the United Kingdom, *Historical Survey of the Origins and Growth of Mau Mau (Corfield Report)*, Cmnd 1030 (London: HMSO, 1960), statistical appendix.

[44] John Blacker, 'The Demography of Mau Mau: Fertility and Mortality in Kenya in the 1950s, a Demographer's Viewpoint', *African Affairs* 106, no. 423 (2007): pp. 205–27.

[45] Clayton, *Counter-insurgency in Kenya*, p. 7.

[46] Ogot, 'The decisive years', gives the best account of this period, but see also George Bennett and Alison Smith, 'Kenya: from "White Man's Country" to Kenyatta's state, 1945–1963', in *History of East Africa, vol. III*, Low and Smith, eds, pp. 109–56; and McWilliam, 'The managed economy'.

to seize the landed property and chattels of convicted terrorists. Some 3,510 legal orders for seizure had been issued under the Act by the end of 1956.[47] The existence of this law, widely publicized by the government, made it seem as if convicts and detainees were 'fair game' to the predations of their Loyalist neighbours, and even where no legal order existed many returned from incarceration to their villages to find their animals and furniture stolen, even the window frames and doors removed from their dwellings.[48] With Loyalists holding every position of authority, and with the law so literally on their side, there seemed little point in complaining about such things.

Several policy reforms introduced explicitly to 'make the peace' were applied in Central Kenya to the benefit of Loyalists. Land consolidation, and the forced villagization that was its necessary precursor, were by far the most important. Forced villagization had begun as a counter-insurgency tactic during 1954. Rural Kikuyu were removed from their traditional smallholdings scattered along the ridges of Kiambu, Murang'a, and Nyeri, and placed in newly constructed villages. Between May 1954 and the end of 1956 over 1 million Kikuyu had already been forcibly resettled in 854 purpose-built villages.[49] Each village was home to not less than 500 people, and was placed under the surveillance of a nearby Home Guard post. Some villages were styled as 'punitive', where families believed to be Mau Mau sympathizers were kept under close scrutiny and where strict curfews were imposed, while others were 'protective' villages where the families of Loyalists were gathered together. Forced labour was used to construct these new settlements, with Loyalist chiefs and Home Guard overseeing the work. This amounted to an effective segregation of the countryside around the affiliations of the warring factions.[50]

Land consolidation, begun in earnest in early 1956, took this resettlement programme a step further and confirmed the exclusion of the rebels. The opportunity for this radical reform was brought about by the Swynnerton Plan of late 1953, which had recommended that Africans be permitted to grow cash crops and that their agriculture be commercialized, through the consolidation of existing scattered land holdings into economic farm units with clear legal tenure. This scheme implied the creation of fewer, larger farms, each better able to sustain a prosperous family—a landed rural elite—and also to employ wage labourers—a rural proletariat. This was exactly the development that many of those who had initiated the Mau Mau movement had feared—a colonial scheme that would deny them the right to inherit land

[47] Ogot, 'The decisive years', p. 50.

[48] Marshall Clough, *Mau Mau Memoirs; History, Memory and Politics* (Boulder, CO: Lynne Reiner Publishers, 1999), pp. 215–18.

[49] Ogot, 'The decisive years', p. 50.

[50] Branch, *Defeating Mau Mau*, pp. 107–8.

through lineage in the traditional way. The adoption of Swynnerton's ideas for the introduction of land consolidation was therefore no concession to the rebels, but rather an opportunistic push toward the 'modernization' that Mau Mau had opposed.

The political utility of this measure in bringing benefits to the wealthier Loyalists was made explicit. In January 1956, the district commissioner of Nyeri urged his colleagues to push ahead, stating that 'consolidation should be used as a reward while the Emergency continues'.[51] The colonial administration openly rejoiced in the opportunity this initiative brought. To ensure the reward went to the right people, Loyalists were put in charge of the entire process on the ground, beginning with the measurement and recording of existing fragmented land-holdings, then the choice of plot for re-allocation, and finally in the issuing of private land title deeds. Mau Mau supporters were disadvantaged in every aspect of this, many returning from detention in later years to find that they were simply excluded from re-allocation and title, and their lands given to others. But so too were those who had been tenants of Loyalists, many of whom now found themselves declared landless in the push to create a waged rural labouring class.

The gains in land for the Loyalist elite were matched by rewards in the labour market that benefited the less wealthy among Britain's Kikuyu allies. In 1955 two separate government commissions reported on aspects of African employment, each making recommendations for improvements in pay and opportunities. The Carpenter Commission proposed a minimum wage for urban African workers, and encouraged the growth of collective bargaining as a means to securing better working conditions.[52] Kikuyu were excluded from the labour market in Nairobi following May 1954, but by the end of 1955 there was a steady flow of Loyalist labour re-entering the city. By 1957, as movement restrictions on Loyalists were gradually lifted, this turned into a flood. Ex-detainees, and others suspected of Mau Mau sympathies, simply could not obtain the permits required to look for work in the city. Nairobi's improved working conditions and pay thus became a Loyalist monopoly.[53] The same was true for the enlargement of African employment in the colonial civil service and improvements in conditions that came about after 1955 as a consequence of the Lidbury Commission. This report recommended the opening of new levels of employment to Africans, and advocated equal pay with other races for work of the same type. This marked the beginnings of the 'Africanization' of the civil service that would accelerate greatly as

[51] Hughes, DC Nyeri, 'Directive on Land Consolidation and Farm planning', 3 January 1956, VP/1/27, Kenya National Archives (KNA).

[52] Colony and Protectorate of Kenya, *Report of the Committee on African Wages (Carpenter Commission)* (Nairobi: Government Printer, 1954).

[53] Branch, *Defeating Mau Mau*, pp. 126–30.

independence came closer, and it opened the door to a surge of Loyalists seeking government employment at all levels.[54] In economic terms, the war had brought many, though not all, of the Loyalist victors their reward.

The keys to the kingdom: power politics

African political parties were banned under Emergency regulations in June 1953, but the introduction of the Lyttelton Constitution in 1954 had opened the way for future African participation in an electoral system once the rebellion was over. With the military victory won, the decision was taken in June 1955 to allow African political parties again, but only at district level and with the discretion of colonial officers who approved parties for registration. National parties were not permitted in what amounted to a colonial 'micro-management' of re-emergent political activism. A plethora of state-sponsored local parties soon sprang up. As Ogot has tersely noted, this policy aimed 'to create a base upon which a collaborative African leadership could emerge and to undermine the support of Mau Mau freedom fighters'.[55]

To minimize Kikuyu influence, the registration of political parties was not at first permitted in Central Province, while in the non-Kikuyu areas, notably in Rift Valley Province and Coast Province, the British gave backing to those politicians who had most vocally opposed the rebellion. By the time that a legal framework was in place for African elections in 1956, it was decided to allow only those individual Kikuyu who held a Loyalty Certificate issued by the government to vote. Rebels and their supporters were purposefully excluded from participation. The criteria used to determine the franchise allowed for multiple votes to those who qualified on more than one basis. To qualify, it was necessary to have a school education to intermediary level; an income of £120 per annum or property to a value of £500; or five years or more service in government or a distinguished record of public service. Those who met all three criteria thus got three votes. Local committees, usually comprising chiefs, head-men, and the most fervent Home Guard commanders, advised District Commissioners on the issuing of Loyalty Certificates and the arbitration of claims to voting rights under each of the three criteria. Senior Kikuyu Loyalists jealously guarded the privilege that political participation implied, and many junior members of the Home Guard were in fact refused registration as voters. Voting was not intended for the poor, and, not surprisingly, hardly any women were registered as voters.[56]

[54] Colony and Protectorate of Kenya, *Report of the Commission on the Civil Services of the East African Territories and East African High Commission 1953–54 (Lidbury Commission)* (Nairobi: Government Printer, 1954).

[55] Ogot, 'The decisive years', p. 48.

[56] Branch, *Defeating Mau Mau*, pp. 157–9.

When finally compiled, the electoral roll in Central Province for 1957 listed 35,644 voters, representing only 7.4 per cent of the adult population of the province. Because of multiple qualification criteria, this amounted to 50,363 votes. More than half of these votes were held in the Meru district, where support for the British had been strongest, while Nyeri, where the rebellion had been most fervent, had only 3,627 votes.[57] Not surprisingly, a Meru Loyalist, Bernard Mate, was duly elected at the first poll in 1957. He sat in the Legislative Council, as one of eight elected members representing Kenya's African peoples. Over the entire country, at the 1957 elections only 126,508 Africans had been registered to vote, all of them deemed 'loyal' to the government.[58] Thereafter, Kikuyu political participation was slowly broadened up to 1960, but at no point were rebels permitted any access to authority or power through the ballot. Electoral politics, and the benefits it brought, was a reward kept for elite Loyalists, who would go on to 'become the gate-keepers of the post-colonial state'.[59]

Rehabilitation and release

Prisoners convicted of Mau Mau crimes served long sentences in Kenya's gaols, their status unaltered by the ending of the war in the forests. But those in the detention camps, who had been convicted of no crime, now presented the colonial authorities with a dilemma: to bring the war to an end they should be released, but how rapidly, and on what terms? The problem was immense, as the camps still held 45,423 detainees at the end of 1955.[60]

Attention focused on this question as the shooting war in the forest drew to a close in the late summer of 1955. The Kenya administration had already begun to release those who had confessed of their crimes (mostly oath-taking) and accepted rehabilitation, but they remained intransigent that those considered to be leaders of the movement, and the worst criminals among the 'hard core' detainees who were refusing to make confessions, should *never* be released: plans were in place in 1955 to put some 12,000 such people into permanent 'exile' in prison camps in the remote northern areas of Kenya.[61] Although London expressed grave concerns about this, for Baring's senior staff it had become a matter of principle: full release of all detainees without confessions would be a denial of the entire policy of detention and rehabilitation. Politically, the dilemma over release was deepened by the fact that many had been interned on the accusation of Loyalists in their home

57 Branch, *Defeating Mau Mau*, pp. 154–5.

58 Ogot, 'The decisive years', p. 54.

59 Branch, *Defeating Mau Mau*, p. 151.

60 'Daily average numbers of Mau Mau detainees and convicts, 1954–59', AH/6/4-9, KNA.

61 For a wider discussion of this see, Maloba, *Mau Mau and Kenya*, pp. 138–47.

villages—British allies who feared that retribution might be meted out if detained men were now allowed to return. Loyalists had been repeatedly assured that the Mau Mau 'hard core' would never return, and Baring feared huge political difficulties if this commitment was broken. By early 1957, a compromise was reached with London, and it was decided to retain a smaller number of the most dangerous detainees, two or three thousand perhaps, while rapidly releasing the remainder.[62]

The release of detainees was first accelerated from early 1956, to a rate of around 2,000 per month. By the end of the year, however, more than 30,000 detainees had still not confessed,[63] and the accelerated release programme was threatened by the inability to generate confessions. The author of the initial strategy for rehabilitation, Tom Askwith in the Ministry for African Affairs, saw the process as being both a religious experience and educational—a mixture of the confessional and the school, purging detainees of the 'curse' of Mau Mau while also fostering in them a renewed sense of citizenship.[64] Under less benign leadership from 1956, rehabilitation became a battleground over which colonial officials desperately sought to impose their will on recalcitrant and irreconcilable Mau Mau supporters within the camps. Hard labour was now increasingly imposed upon detainees to wear down their resistance, with groups of 'hard core' being separated out and subjected to what became known as the 'dilution technique'.[65] The term was a euphemism for the use of brutal force against small groups of detainees in order to break their will: systematic and purposeful physical torture. In the Mwea camps, where this technique was first tried, it achieved encouraging results, increasing the numbers of confessions from 'hard core' detainees. From June 1957, formal authority was granted from London to use this violence, 'compelling force', against detainees who refused to obey orders. This was how the British proposed to gain the confessions that would allow them to continue with the accelerated release of detainees.

For three years, from 1956 until April 1959, the war fought behind the wire of the detention camps was as intensive as it had been at any time during the struggle in the forests. But this confrontational violence held dangerous risks. The 'compelling force' of the 'dilution technique' left many detainees badly injured, and there were deaths. By 1958, several cases of murder of detainees

62 See Elkins, *Britain's Gulag*, pp. 314–16, for a discussion of this.

63 Elkins, *Britain's Gulag*, p. 315.

64 Robert B. Edgerton, *Mau Mau: An African Crucible* (London: I.B.Tauris, 1990), p. 179. For more on Askwith see: Joanna Lewis, *Empire State-Building: War and Welfare in Kenya 1925–52* (Oxford: James Currey, 2000), pp. 287–9; Tom Askwith, *From Mau Mau to Harambee: Memoirs and Memoranda of Colonial Kenya* (Cambridge: African Studies Centre Monographs, 1995).

65 Elkins, *Britain's Gulag*, pp. 319–21.

by camp warders were put before the courts, and there were other 'unexplained deaths' being reported.[66] In response to the violent regime, the detainees had developed more coherent and effective patterns of collective resistance. A cascade of letters now poured out from some of the camps, complaining of the mistreatment and detailing accusations of abuse and torture, smuggled to sympathizers and then on to London where opposition MPs used the information provided to ask awkward questions in the British parliament.[67] This publicity was already generating wide criticism of the Kenya administration, in March 1959, when the Hola Camp massacre was reported in London. In an incident provoked by the decision to use 'compelling force' against a group of 85 'hard core' detainees at Hola, eleven men were murdered, beaten to death by African warders under the direction of the European camp commandant.[68]

Hola proved to be the straw that broke the camel's back for the British government regarding Kenya. There had been many other deaths caused by brutality in the camps, but this was the largest reported incident of its kind. A lame attempt to cover-up the cause of the deaths, and to suggest that the detainees had died from drinking contaminated water, was quickly exposed and only served to deepen political embarrassment. When the incident was first discussed in the House of Commons, on 16 June 1959, the usual critics from the opposition benches were joined by members of the government in their condemnation of the colonial administration. Lennox-Boyd teetered on the verge of resignation as Colonial Secretary, and Prime Minister Macmillan's diary entries from the time show that he feared a split in his Cabinet over the Hola affair.[69]

Behind the scenes, Macmillan's government was already engaged in a reassessment of its imperial commitments, and the prospective economic and political costs of retaining Kenya now seemed considerable. Many in the Conservative Party, including Iain MacLeod, who soon replaced Lennox-Boyd as Secretary of State for the Colonies, feared that the legacy of Hola and the mishandling of the detention camps in general increased the likelihood of further violence in Kenya should the British, and especially white settlers, seek to re-establish control over the long-term.[70] MacLeod thought it was time to go, and even among Conservatives most agreed with him. Plans were hastily assembled for Britain's exit from Kenya. In November 1959 it was announced that 2,500 detainees would be immediately released, and that the State of

[66] Anderson, 'British abuse and torture', *passim*.
[67] Elkins, *Britain's Gulag*, ch. 10.
[68] Government of the United Kingdom, *Record of Proceedings and Evidence in the Enquiry into the Deaths of Eleven Mau Mau Detainees at Hola Camp in Kenya*.
[69] Kyle, *The Politics of the Independence*, pp. 96–7.
[70] See Gary Wasserman, *Politics of Decolonization: Kenya Europeans and the Land Issue 1960–1965* (Cambridge: Cambridge University Press, 1976), pp. 9–10, for discussion of MacLeod's motives.

Emergency would be lifted. Even before MacLeod departed for Nairobi to see things for himself, the date for the first constitutional conference in London at which the path toward Kenya's decolonization would be mapped out had been set for January 1960.[71] The clock on exit had started to tick.

The ticking clock, 1959–1963

In January 1959, Lennox-Boyd had hosted a meeting at Chequers to discuss the future of Britain's East African territories, attended by Baring and the other Governors. The initial proposal on the table stated that East Africans were not ready for self-government, and that British rule must last another 15–20 years.[72] It was a position that the Colonial Secretary fully endorsed. Lennox-Boyd refused to be committed to a firm date for the transfer of power in Kenya, but even in the weeks immediately following news of the Hola debacle, although before the parliamentary debates, he stated that he did 'not see any prospect in the foreseeable future of HMG [Her Majesty's Government] relinquishing control'.[73] Within a few weeks his Cabinet and parliamentary colleagues no longer shared confidence in this judgement.

The impact of MacLeod's fresh approach to Kenya's problems therefore cannot be overstated. He remained as Colonial Secretary only until 8 October 1961, but over these two years it seemed that everything in Kenya had changed. Whereas Lennox-Boyd, an imperialist of the old school, had been prepared to muddle along, fixing things to allow settler influence to remain in place, MacLeod looked forward to a post-imperial world in which British influence took other forms. Structural issues, such as the impact of Cold War politics on Britain's role in Kenya, the problems of defence planning and the ending of military conscription, or the effect of Britain's failure at Suez in 1956, and the emerging crisis in the Congo and in the Central African Federation, were a backcloth to all of Britain's exits from empire at this time,[74] but they made no substantive difference to MacLeod's decision-making with direct regard to Kenya. Local contingencies, damage limitation, and the calculation of how those could be managed looking ahead were the crucial determinants. Kenya would have African majority rule: MacLeod merely needed to work out how to bring it about.

Before visiting Kenya in December 1959, MacLeod made it clear to officials in the Colonial Office that the presence of settlers in Kenya should make no

[71] Kyle, *The Politics of the Independence*, pp. 99–102.

[72] Minute by Gorell-Barnes, 31 December 1958, CO 822/1819, The National Archives (TNA).

[73] Memorandum by Lennox-Boyd, 10 April 1959, CAB 134/1558 CPC(59)2, TNA.

[74] David A. Percox, *Britain, Kenya and the Cold War: Imperial Defence, Colonial Security and Decolonisation* (London: Tauris Academic Studies, 2004), *passim*.

difference to the speed and progress of exit, and that there was no need to tie the three East African territories (Kenya, Uganda, Tanganyika) to the same timetable.[75] For those still believing that Kenya's decolonization lay two decades or more away, this was radical thinking. To emphasize the change, MacLeod also announced that steps would rapidly be taken to make it possible for Africans to own land in the area previously reserved as the 'White Highlands'. This caused a near panic among white landowners in Kenya, and lurched the economy briefly into crisis, but it rallied African politicians and others of a more liberal persuasion to MacLeod's side.[76]

In effect, MacLeod had taken the big decision on Kenya's future by December 1959: what remained was to find a *modus operandi* by which this might be implemented. Three constitutional conferences at London's Lancaster House, in January 1960, February to April 1962, and October 1963, devised and redevised the architecture of Kenya's constitutional settlement.[77] Changes were made even in the last of these meetings that fundamentally altered the internal political dynamics of the post-colonial settlement, but at no point did the British seriously countenance a delay. Up to the end of 1962, the emphasis was on the need to establish structures for internal self-rule for a majority African government, but without full independence. Duncan Sandys, who followed Reginald Maudling as Colonial Secretary, still thought at the beginning of 1963 that full independence might be delayed, although by then Kenya's new governor, Malcolm MacDonald, had decided that it was the accelerator, and not the brake, that needed to be applied—and it was he who now set the pace.[78] Although the process toward full independence steadily gathered momentum from late 1959 onwards, it was not until June 1963 that the date was finally set for *Uhuru*—freedom: 12 December 1963.[79]

Over these four years and more, three different Conservative Colonial Secretaries skilfully avoided fixing a firm date as they knew this might inflame opposition in their own party. With tricky local problems, such as the definitions of constituency and regional boundaries, or the position of the Somali community in Kenya's north, in time-honoured bureaucratic fashion the British adopted a strategy of controlled deflection, setting up commissions of enquiry that would investigate and report at a point when there would be less time for prevarication over difficult decisions. As time slipped away, decisions became increasingly pragmatic and compromises were more easily broached. In this process, power gradually moved from the British to Kenya's

[75] Kyle, *The Politics of the Independence*, pp. 99–100.
[76] McWilliam, 'The managed economy', especially p. 286.
[77] Kyle, *The Politics of the Independence*, pp. 102–8, 143–50, 189–93.
[78] MacDonald to Sandys, 14 January 1963, and Duncan Sandys, 'Points for discussion with Governor of Kenya', n.d., folio 20, both CO 822/3099, TNA.
[79] Kyle, *The Politics of the Independence*, p. 182.

African political leaders, who were eventually able to strike political bargains that may have seemed unlikely at earlier stages of the process.

Pragmatism and compromise can be seen in relation to each of the four central questions that needed to be resolved in order to implement the exit. The first was the shape of the independence constitution. The constitutional debate came down to a quarrel between federalists, represented by the Kenya African Democratic Union (KADU), and centralists, represented by the Kenya African National Union (KANU). Up until the eleventh hour, at the final Lancaster House conference of October 1963, the British clung on to the federal model, believing that it better protected the interests of minority groups.[80] This also brought the advantage of rewarding Britain's long-term allies in Kenya, especially the non-Kikuyu groups who had stood firm during the Mau Mau revolt, but it was recognized all along that this would create an extraordinarily expensive form of government. The centralists were against any notion of reserved seats for minorities, or devolved powers, and could point toward the cost advantages of a simpler constitutional arrangement: and they argued that it was easier to implement because it reflected the existing political divisions of provinces, districts and constituencies, without creating new political bodies. If efficiency and functionality could not win this argument, what eventually persuaded the British to retreat from the federalist model was simply the evidence of the ballot box: by 1963 it was clear that the centralists gathered in the KANU party, essentially a coalition of Kikuyu and Luo political interests, held overwhelming support and seemed sure to secure a sweeping victory in the final independence elections.[81] In the final settlement, elements of the federal structure were left in place, but its implementation required the assent and active participation of the central government—something that KANU's leaders had made clear they would not condone.[82] But after December 1963, that would no longer be a British problem. Political pragmatism therefore trumped principle, despite the dues owed to allies and loyal friends, and disregarding British anxieties about a government led by Jomo Kenyatta coming to power.

Kenyatta's personal position, and the political transfer of power he represented, is our second central question. Having arrested him in October 1952, placed him on trial as the leader of the Mau Mau movement, convicted him, sentenced him to indefinite detention, and then portrayed him as the incarnation of the rebellion's evil beliefs and practices, Kenyatta's personal 'rehabilitation' was one of the more remarkable events of Kenya's late colonial

[80] See Blundell's two memoirs for his views of this, Michael Blundell, *So Rough a Wind* (London: Weidenfeld & Nicolson, 1964), pp. 261–308; Michael Blundell, *Love Affair with the Sun: A Memoir of Seventy Years in Kenya* (Nairobi: Kenway Publications, 1994), pp. 106–24.

[81] Ogot, 'The decisive years', pp. 69–76.

[82] Kyle, *The Politics of the Independence*, pp. 143–9.

history.[83] The decision first to allow Kenyatta's release in 1960, then to allow him to become politically active, and then to accept his leadership of KANU, were steps the British took in response to negotiations with Kenya's other African political leaders.[84] Kenyatta's restoration to legitimate politics was made a condition of African participation in the negotiations, even raised at MacLeod's initial meetings in Nairobi in December 1959, and was broadly supported by all sides.[85] Although many British officials were deeply uncomfortable at Kenyatta's re-emergence, they had little choice but to accept it if they wished to stick with the timetable for exit. However, as Kenyatta slowly played himself back into Kenya's politics as the moderate he always was, even the more conservative amongst the British and the white settlers gained confidence that he was not likely to inaugurate a Mau Mau government: far from it, as Kenyatta's heavily pro-Loyalist first Cabinet would vividly demonstrate.

The bureaucratic transfer of power was in many ways more challenging than the political transfer, and it poses our third central question. The Africanization of the colonial administration in Kenya had hardly made any progress at all before 1952, and although the Emergency saw a rapid expansion of employment in all areas of government service, there remained legal barriers to the advancement of Africans in the police and army, as well as in the civil service. Substantive skilled and semi-skilled posts in the Kenya Civil Service amounted to 16,200 in 1950, a figure that had climbed to over 40,000 by 1960. The abolition of racialized salary scales announced in the Lidbury Report of 1955 had relatively little impact on African advancement until the decision on exit was made, and then, from 1960, Africanization suddenly moved at a dramatic tempo. The neglect of earlier years was quickly and deeply regretted, as Michael McWilliam has noted: 'The result was a sudden exodus of expatriate officers who had to be not only compensated, but replaced at short-notice by expensive temporary officials working on contract.'[86] It proved costly, too, as this rapid transformation coincided with a substantial rise in civil service pay rates. The new rates of pay immediately benefited those Africans to be rapidly promoted through the system, but the churn of experienced staff leaving the Colony created instability and uncertainty that made the transfer of knowledge and skills a significant challenge. Over 1960–62, Britain paid out an additional £9.2 million in grant-in-aid in order to balance Kenya's books.[87]

[83] For a personal account see, Jomo Kenyatta, *Suffering Without Bitterness: The Founding of the Kenya Nation* (Nairobi: East African Publishing House, 1968).
[84] Kyle, *The Politics of the Independence*, gives a full account of this over chapters 8 and 9.
[85] Kyle, *The Politics of the Independence*, pp. 100–1.
[86] McWilliam, 'The managed economy', pp. 287–8.
[87] McWilliam, 'The managed economy', p. 288.

Africanization was at first referred to by the less overt term 'localization'. The man appointed in 1960 as 'Localization and Training Officer', and charged with immediately Africanizing the top civil service posts in the country was Terence Gavaghan,[88] the same officer who had enforced the 'dilution technique' in the Mwea camps that led directly to the precipitous events at Hola in March 1959. According to Gavaghan's own account, of the top 10,000 posts in the civil service 'only a sprinkling were African'. An arbitrary target was set of 3,000 Africans to be placed in these top posts before independence. Under his firm direction, the Kenya Institute of Administration was set up in 1961, following a syllabus broadly similar to that offered to British Colonial Office cadets.[89] At that time, African officers held only 21 of the 228 officer positions in the Provincial Administration, and only 9 of 93 posts in the Ministries from Assistant Secretary to Permanent Secretary.[90] The change was rapid and dramatic. The first African District Commissioners came into post in September 1962. By the time of exit, in December 1963, Africans held more than one-third of the senior civil service posts, and by the end of 1965 all but a handful of the remaining Europeans had departed.[91] For Kenyans who had been educated to degree level abroad, and for those graduating from the new universities of the East African region, the civil service remained a highly professional and well-regarded employer throughout the 1960s.[92]

In the security domain, Africanization of the police proved an easier task than the army. The police had been disarmed at the end of 1956, and steps were then taken to restore the force to its purely civilian role. Kikuyu had been purged from the force at the beginning of the Emergency, and there was now a rush to increase their numbers with the recruitment of trusted Loyalists. From January 1960 onwards, steps were taken to improve the quality of African applicants and to accelerate their promotion within the force, but as the Chief Commissioner conceded, the speed of decolonization meant that the police were 'overtaken by events and had to scramble'. The best recruits found themselves rapidly moved up the ranks—one officer attended three training courses in the 18 months leading up to independence, was promoted three times, and managed only six weeks of police work in this period.[93] Ben Gethi,

[88] C. Chenevix Trench, *Men Who Ruled Kenya: The Kenya Administration, 1892–1963* (London: The Radcliffe Press, 1993), p. 294; Terence Gavaghan, *Of Lions and Dung Beetles: A Man in the Middle of Colonial Administration in Kenya* (Ilfracombe: Arthur H. Stockwell, 1990), pp. 285–95.

[89] Terence Gavaghan, 'White to black 1', in *Colony to Nation: British Administration in Kenya 1940–63*, edited by John Johnson (Banham, Norfolk: The Erskine Press, 2002), pp. 230–5, and for the further work of the KIA, C. Fuller, 'Training the new administration', in Johnson, ed., *Colony to Nation*, pp. 230–5.

[90] Fuller, 'Training the new administration', p. 239.

[91] Trench, *Men Who Ruled Kenya*, pp. 294–5. For an account of Africanization between 1962 and 1965, see Patrick Crichton, 'White to black 2', in Johnson, ed., *Colony to Nation*, pp. 235–9.

[92] Crichton, 'White to black 2', p. 237.

[93] Throup, 'Crime, politics and the police', p. 152.

who would go on to be Commissioner of Police in 1978, and his deputy, Michael Arrum, were both among the first Africans promoted to gazetted rank in 1961.[94] The Africanization of the Special Branch proved the most challenging task, the first training course having to be scrapped and a less bureaucratic version put in its place. Some still wanted a Rolls Royce of a Special Branch, as one senior British officer commented, but they 'settled for a Ford'.[95] At Kenyatta's insistence, in October 1963, the post of Director of Intelligence in Special Branch was Africanized before independence, but otherwise the efforts of other African politicians to politicize the police were firmly resisted. And once installed as Kenya's first President, Kenyatta drew his personal bodyguard not from the military, but from a wholly Kikuyu detachment of police from the General Service Unit.

Because the King's African Rifles was a regional regiment, arrangements for its transfer were complicated. The general need to Africanize the officer corps was under discussion well before 1960, in preparation for the independence of Tanganyika and Uganda, although in neither country was the process a great success. In Kenya there was more time, but while Britain accepted that it had done too little in the past, and worried that without British officers that Kenya's three battalions (3, 5, and 11 KAR) would be little more than 'an armed rabble', there was reluctance to pay the likely costs of additional training. Britain's keenness to maintain a defence presence in the region beyond independence brought considerable political controversy, however, and although this was at first used as a gambit in negotiations over Africanization and training, the Kenyans were simply not prepared to sacrifice sovereignty in any way. A local training programme was eventually developed in Kenya before independence under the British East Africa Command, with accelerated promotions for African officers. Standards on promotion exams were 'quietly relaxed'; all the African Captains who took the exam for Major in December 1963 passed, 'even though they had not been warned to prepare for the test'.[96] Meanwhile, the British continued to pay for the retention of essential expatriate personnel in Kenya, many of whom might be directly involved in the continued training of the new officer corps after independence.[97] The simple fact was that the Kenya battalions depended upon the British for all their logistical support, and, as Parsons has trenchantly noted, 'the Kenyan army would have collapsed if British forces had withdrawn immediately after independence'.[98]

[94] Throup, 'Crime, politics and the police', p. 154.
[95] Throup, 'Crime, politics and the police', p. 153, quoting Deputy Commissioner Manby.
[96] Timothy H. Parsons, *The 1964 Army Mutinies and the Making of Modern East Africa* (Westport CT: Praeger, 2003), pp. 82–3.
[97] Percox, *Britain, Kenya and the Cold War*, pp. 204–5.
[98] Parsons, *The 1964 Army Mutinies*, p. 80.

The importance of the military transition became clear only six weeks after Kenya's independence, when around 100 men of the Kenya Rifles (11 KAR) mutinied in their barracks at Lanet. This incident followed similar mutinies, but larger, in the Uganda and Tanganyika forces, all in the final week of January 1964. Although complaints about low pay and harsh discipline lay behind the mutiny, the African soldiers were in large part provoked by the continued presence of British officers in their midst. It was a British military contingent of the Royal Horse Artillery, based at nearby Nakuru, who first halted the mutiny—fighting their way into the barracks and killing one mutineer. After a stand-off lasting into a second day, a battalion of Gordon Highlanders then swept into the camp behind a Ferret armoured car and affected the surrender of the mutineers.[99] Kenyatta had no wish to be dependent upon the British military, but their presence at Lanet had saved and ultimately strengthened his government.

Our final central question concerns the fate of the minority communities, and we will take the white settlers and the Somalis as our examples. When Michael Blundell returned from the Lancaster House talks at which the buy-out of settler farms was confirmed, a bag of coins was thrown at him and he was branded a Judas for having betrayed his fellows.[100] Feelings ran high, but, again, pragmatism triumphed. The Million Acre Scheme, through which white farms were transferred to African ownership on a willing-buyer-willing–seller basis, offered guaranteed prices to white landowners fixed at market rates pertaining before the announcement of the exit. Settlers who chose to leave therefore did as well out of the deal as they could have expected.[101]

White settlers may not have been happy, but at least they did not feel cheated. The same could not be said of the Somali minority. Kenya's Northern Frontier District, where the vast majority of Kenya's Somalis lived, had been held under military administration for virtually the entire period of colonial rule and had suffered from a lack of development and only limited integration in the wider political economy. Even before the independence of British Somaliland and Italian Somalia, and their unification into one independent state on 1 July 1960, in response to the first Lancaster House talks on Kenya's independence a political party, the Northern Province Peoples Progressive Party (NPPPP) had been formed in the town of Wajir to campaign for the unification of the Northern Frontier district with the new state of Somalia.[102] By the time that Reginald Maudling, MacLeod's successor as Colonial Secretary, made it to Nairobi in November 1961, there were four more Somali

[99] Parsons, *The 1964 Army Mutinies*, pp. 117–23, 128–30.
[100] Interview with Sir Michael Blundell, Nairobi, February 1981.
[101] Wasserman, *Politics of Decolonization*, pp. 135–63.
[102] Kyle, *The Politics of the Independence*, p. 157.

parties all advocating secession. At the second Lancaster House conference, Kenya's increasingly strident African politicians in both KADU and KANU objected strongly to any idea of secession, arguing forcefully for the maintenance of full Kenyan sovereignty over all lands within the borders of the Colony. In an effort to conciliate, the British set up a commission 'to discover the views of the people of the Northern Frontier district'. This proved an embarrassing mistake. When the referendum held in 1962 showed a huge majority in favour of secession to the new Somalia, the British had to square up to the problem of disappointing the Somali minority of the north by rejecting the result, or risking derailing the entire constitutional process at a critical point in the negotiations with KADU and KANU. The British capitulated to the needs of the greater goal, and Somali aspirations were rejected. When Kenya's independence elections came in 1963, the polls were boycotted in the north.

The decision made little difference to British interests at the time, but for the Kenyans it was to have immediate consequences. In the weeks leading up to Kenya's independence celebrations, the first armed attacks on government installations in the Northern Frontier District began. Within one year of Kenya's independence, the defence forces of the new nation were fighting a low-key insurrection in the north. The Shifta War would last for the next 25 years.[103]

Implications

No two exits from empire were ever identical, least of all when they flowed from a counter-insurgency, so it would be facile to propose that general lessons might be drawn from the Kenyan case. However, several critical aspects of the Kenya experience may have important implications for other exits.

With hindsight, it is starkly clear that Kenya's Emergency Powers were implemented in too indiscriminate a manner, were too draconian, and were kept in place far too long. The militarization of the general administration, and the incarceration of such large numbers of people did not contribute to the winning of 'hearts and minds', but instead deeply divided the local population. The violence of the counter-insurgency, especially in the detention camps, was the catalyst for exit. But in the wind-down the vexed politics of the Kikuyu civil war seemed to play far less a role in the exit than might have been expected. The rebels were excluded from the process, and Kenya's African politicians of all other persuasions focused their attention on the

[103] Daniel Branch, *Kenya: Between Hope and Despair, 1963–2012* (New Haven & London: Yale University Press, 2012), pp. 28–35.

immediate goal of being rid of the British, saving their internecine squabbles over the legacies of counter-insurgency violence for later. Claims and counter-claims for the restitution of property and the righting of counter-insurgency wrongs would be petitioned to the Kenyan courts, and elsewhere, after 1963, but these were not issues that were allowed to hinder the exit.

Britain's exit from Kenya held within its orbit a fundamental contradiction. In restoring stability first through the counter-insurgency, and then through the manner in which the peace was made, the state invigorated and endorsed a robust governance structure that was authoritarian and purposefully not consensual. Rebels and those who sympathized with them were at no point reconciled in this process, and indeed some specific policies within the constitution excluded and alienated them—the initial denial of a voting franchize, and the confiscation of property, including land, are the most obvious examples. The authoritarianism of local government allies of the state, once set in place, frequently took on coercive and exploitative forms that were not easy to limit, running through the exit period and beyond. This 'reward' of allies and the exclusion of enemies did not build any sense of a shared future, but rather deepened existing division. When the driver shifted, therefore, towards building capacity through Africanization and developing a strong constitutional base, it again could only draw upon allies of the state. Although never overtly made a matter for discussion, the character of the counter-insurgency had a very direct impact upon the exit in many covert ways.

If the past mattered in shaping the exit, the future was also crucially important. Exits are about planning for a different future—managing damage limitation, and protecting longer-term interests for the British, building social and economic aspirations and gaining political freedom and sovereignty for the Kenyans. As the exit drew nearer, British interests—economic, political, and strategic—loomed ever larger in their deliberations with Kenya's African leaders. Even with their 'loyal' friends from the Emergency, the British were in the end ruthlessly pragmatic; even though the British asked for and listened to African views on all aspects of the exit, their own interests invariably remained paramount; and even when Britain was forced into unwelcome concessions and changes of policy in the later stages of the exit, these were skilfully presented as political victories for compromise and good sense. In short, the exit was managed in Britain's best future interests.

Africanization was often presented as a nation-building task, but Britain's goal in exit was not to build a nation, or even a state, but merely to hand over to a stable regime. The ticking clock severely constrained what could be done to consolidate that stability, however, and in the end Britain was forced to rely upon the capacity of the in-coming regime to hold the ring. As Kenya went on to become the West's strongest Cold War ally in the region over the next 30 years, this calculated gamble paid dividends.

Can Britain be said then to have had an exit strategy in Kenya? By the end, or near the end, yes there was a strategy. But it emerged organically, out of responses to political events: it was not formed systemically as a set of goals or targets. And, as a consequence, there was a great deal of 'unfinished business' when the British left. The alliances forged as being necessary for exit left a legacy of political factionalisms, but no tradition of political opposition. The rapid indigenization of the administration left weak institutions staffed by young and inexperienced civil servants. The legacy of state violence created by the Emergency remained as a very persistent characteristic of the security arms of Kenya's government through and beyond the transition. All of these features of the exit marked the kind of state that independent Kenya would become.

Acknowledgements

John Lonsdale and Daniel Branch by no means share my views on everything in this chapter, but I am grateful to them both for their comments on the draft.

References

Anderson, David M., 'The battle of Dandora swamp: reconstructing Mau Mau's Land & Freedom Army', in *Mau Mau and Nationhood: Arms, Authority and Memory*, edited by E. S. Atieno Odhiambo and John M. Lonsdale (Oxford: James Currey, 2002), pp. 155–77.

Anderson, David M., 'British abuse and torture in Kenya's counter-insurgency, 1952–60', *Small Wars & Insurgencies* 23, no. 4/5 (2012): pp. 700–19.

Anderson, David M., *Histories of the Hanged: Britain's Dirty War in Kenya and the End of Empire* (London: Weidenfeld and Nicolson, 2005).

Anderson, David M., 'Surrogates of the State: Collaboration and Atrocity in Kenya's Mau Mau War', in *The Barbarisation of Warfare*, edited by George Kassimeris (London, Hurst & Co, 2006), pp. 172–88.

Askwith, Tom, *From Mau Mau to Harambee: Memoirs and Memoranda of Colonial Kenya* (Cambridge: African Studies Centre Monographs, 1995).

Barnett, Donald L. and Karari Njama, *Mau Mau from Within: Autobiography and Analysis of Kenya's Peasant Revolt* (Letchworth: MacGibbon & Kee, 1966).

Bennett, George and Alison Smith, 'Kenya: from "White Man's Country" to Kenyatta's state, 1945–1963', in *History of East Africa, vol. III*, edited by D. A. Low and Alison Smith (Oxford: Clarendon Press, 1976), pp. 109–56.

Bennett, Huw, 'The British Army and Controlling Barbarisation During the Kenya Emergency', in *The Warrior's Dishonour: Barbarity, Morality and Torture in Modern Warfare*, edited by George Kassimeris (Aldershot: Ashgate, 2006), pp. 132–54.

Bennett, Huw, *Fighting the Mau Mau: The British Army and Counter-insurgency in the Kenya Emergency* (Cambridge: Cambridge University Press, 2013).

Bennett, Huw, 'The Other Side of the COIN: Minimum and Exemplary Force in British Army Counter-insurgency in Kenya', *Small Wars & Insurgencies* 18, no. 4 (2007): pp. 638–64.

Blacker, John, 'The Demography of Mau Mau: Fertility and Mortality in Kenya in the 1950s, a Demographer's Viewpoint', *African Affairs* 106, no. 423 (2007): pp. 205–27.

Blundell, Michael, *Love Affair with the Sun: A Memoir of Seventy Years in Kenya* (Nairobi: Kenway Publications, 1994).

Blundell, Michael, *So Rough a Wind* (London: Weidenfeld & Nicolson, 1964).

Branch, Daniel, *Defeating Mau Mau, Creating Kenya: Counter-Insurgency, Civil War and Decolonization* (Cambridge: Cambridge University Press, 2009).

Branch, Daniel, *Kenya: Between Hope and Despair, 1963–2012* (New Haven & London: Yale University Press, 2012).

Campbell, Guy, *The Charging Buffalo: A History of the Kenya Regiment* (London: Leo Cooper, 1986).

Chenevix Trench, C., *Men Who Ruled Kenya: The Kenya Administration, 1892–1963* (London: Radcliffe Press, 1993).

Clayton, Anthony, *Counter-Insurgency in Kenya: A Study in Military Operations Against Mau Mau* (London: Frank Cass, 1976).

Clough, Marshall, *Mau Mau Memoirs; History, Memory and Politics* (Boulder, CO: Lynne Reiner Publishers, 1998).

Colony and Protectorate of Kenya, *Kenya Police Annual Reports, 1952 and 1953* (Nairobi: Government Printer, 1952 and 1953).

Colony and Protectorate of Kenya, *Report of the Commission on the Civil Services of the East African Territories and East African High Commission 1953–54 (Lidbury Commission)* (Nairobi: Government Printer, 1954).

Colony and Protectorate of Kenya, *Report of the Committee on African Wages (Carpenter Commission)* (Nairobi: Government Printer, 1954).

Crichton, Patrick, 'White to black 2', in *Colony to Nation: British Administration in Kenya 1940–63*, edited by John Johnson (Banham, Norfolk: The Erskine Press, 2002), pp. 235–9.

Edgerton, Robert B., *Mau Mau: An African Crucible* (London: I.B.Tauris, 1990).

Elkins, Caroline, *Britain's Gulag: The Brutal End of Empire in Kenya* (London: Jonathan Cape, 2005).

Fuller, C., 'Training the new administration', in *Colony to Nation: British Administration in Kenya 1940–63*, edited by John Johnson (Banham, Norfolk: The Erskine Press, 2002), pp. 239–43.

Gavaghan, Terence, *Corridors of Wire: A Saga of Colonial Power and Preventive Detention in Kenya*, privately published by the author, 1994.

Gavaghan, Terence, *Of Lions and Dung Beetles: A Man in the Middle of Colonial Administration in Kenya* (Ilfracombe: Arthur H. Stockwell, 1999).

Gavaghan, Terence, 'White to black 1', in *Colony to Nation: British Administration in Kenya 1940–63*, edited by John Johnson (Banham, Norfolk: The Erskine Press, 2002), pp. 230–5.

Government of Kenya, *Report on the General Administration of Prisons and Detention Camps in Kenya [Heaton Report]* (Nairobi: Government Printer, 1959).

Government of the United Kingdom, *Documents Relating to the Death of Eleven Mau Mau Detainees at Hola Camp in Kenya*, PP, Cmd 778 (London: HMSO, 1959).

Government of the United Kingdom, *Further Documents Relating to the Death of Eleven Mau Mau Detainees at Hola Camp in Kenya*, PP, Cmd 816 (London: HMSO, 1959).

Government of the United Kingdom, *Historical Survey of the Origins and Growth of Mau Mau (Corfield Report)*, Cmnd 1030 (London: HMSO, 1960).

Government of the United Kingdom, *Record of Proceedings and Evidence in the Enquiry into the Deaths of Eleven Mau Mau Detainees at Hola Camp in Kenya*, PP, Cmd 795 (London: HMSO, 1959).

Government of the United Kingdom, *Report by the Parliamentary Delegation to Kenya, January 1954*, PP, Cmd 9081 (London: HMSO, 1954).

Heather, R. W., 'Counterinsurgency and intelligence in Kenya, 1952–56' (PhD thesis, Cambridge University, 1993).

Itote, Waruhiu, *Mau Mau General* (Nairobi: East African Publishing House, 1967).

Kenyatta, Jomo, *Suffering Without Bitterness: The Founding of the Kenya Nation* (Nairobi: East African Publishing House, 1968).

Kyle, Keith, *The Politics of the Independence of Kenya* (Basingstoke: Macmillan, 1999).

Lewis, Joanna, *Empire State-Building: War and Welfare in Kenya 1925–52* (Oxford: James Currey, 2000).

Maloba, Wunyabari O., *Mau Mau and Kenya: An Analysis of a Peasant Revolt* (Nairobi: East African Educational Publishers, 1993).

McWilliam, Michael, 'The managed economy: agricultural change, development, and finance in Kenya 1945–1963', in *History of East Africa, vol. III*, edited by D. A. Low and Alison Smith (Oxford: Clarendon Press, 1976), pp. 251–89.

Ogot, Bethwell A., 'The decisive years, 1956–63', in *Decolonization and Independence in Kenya, 1940–93*, edited by Bethwell A. Ogot and W. R. Ochieng' (London: James Currey, 1995), pp. 48–71.

Parsons, Timothy H., *The African Rank-and File: Social Implications of Colonial Military Service in the King's African Rifles, 1902–1964* (Oxford: James Currey, 1999).

Parsons, Timothy H., *The 1964 Army Mutinies and the Making of Modern East Africa* (Westport CN: Praeger, 2003).

Percox, David A., *Britain, Kenya and the Cold War: Imperial Defence, Colonial Security and Decolonisation* (London: Tauris Academic Studies, 2004).

Sorrenson, M. P. K., *Land Reform in Kikuyu Country: A Study in Government Policy* (Nairobi & London: Oxford University Press, 1967).

Throup, D. W., 'Crime, politics and the police in colonial Kenya, 1939–63', in *Policing and Decolonisation; Nationalism, Politics and the Police, 1917–65*, edited by David M. Anderson and David Killingray (Manchester: Manchester University Press, 1992), pp. 127–57.

Throup, D. W., *Economic and Social Origins of Mau Mau 1945–53* (London: James Currey, 1987).

Wasserman, Gary, *Politics of Decolonization: Kenya Europeans and the Land Issue 1960–1965* (Cambridge: Cambridge University Press, 1976).

Weaver, L., 'The Kenya Regiment', in *A History of the King's African Rifles and East African Forces*, edited by Malcolm Page (London: Leo Cooper, 1998), pp. 239–49.

5

'A graveyard for the British'? Tactics, military operations, and the paucity of strategy in Aden, 1964–1967

Aaron Edwards

Introduction: Aden, 1967

On 20 June 1967, 23 British soldiers and one civil servant were killed in a spate of violence across the colony of Aden.[1] What made these events significant was not merely the high loss of life, but that events had taken place as a direct result of a paucity of strategy in both Aden and in Whitehall on the policy of withdrawal. For the preceding months Britain had been moving to a position where it could hand over responsibility for the governance and security of Aden—and other states in the Federation of South Arabia—to local tribal rulers according to a hastily conceived and executed plan.

The plan, which would see a process of 'Arabization' take root across the civil service and security forces, was more ad hoc and opportunistic than admitted at the time. As a result, the violent incidents on 20 June, in what became known in the press as 'Black Tuesday', were all the more shocking because they were perpetrated by locally-recruited Arabs who had hitherto been judged integral to the decolonization process. In a sequence of events not seen since the Indian Mutiny of 1857, British forces and local Arabs were drawn into a violent conflict that would decide the future of this part of the Middle East.

[1] This chapter draws on research from Aaron Edwards, *Defending the Realm? The Politics of Britain's Small Wars since 1945* (Manchester: Manchester University Press, 2012), ch. 5; and Aaron Edwards, *Mad Mitch's Tribal Law: Aden and the End of Empire* (Edinburgh: Mainstream, 2014).

However, this is not the entire story. While Arabization certainly became a hook upon which to hang the transfer of power, the Labour government in London continued to hedge its bets on who might emerge as the strongest group in the region. Up until June 1967, British Labour politicians claimed to be adopting a 'realistic' policy on Aden, which, in practice, meant that they were still largely unsure who they should transfer power to in the last days of Empire. The traditional rulers of the 24 states making up the Federation were initially judged to be the *heirs apparent*, yet they came under increasing pressure from their opponents in a range of extremist groups, from the National Liberation Front (NLF), a Marxist inspired terrorist group that specialized in targeted assassination and lobbing grenades in the general direction of anything symbolic of colonial authority, and the Front for the Liberation of Occupied South Yemen (FLOSY), a broad-fronted nationalist organization with links to the Aden Trades Union Council (ATUC) and a predilection for mass demonstrations. Both groups led interdependent campaigns of subversion, intimidation and terrorism against the British and their Federation allies.

Meanwhile, on the ground, British troops were caught in the middle of a fluid conflict with no coherent direction emanating from either their own chain of command in Middle East Command, or, for that matter, from the High Commissioner situated at Government House in Steamer Point. The latter, as the proverbial 'man on the spot', was supposed to channel strategic guidance from London that would, ultimately, produce a coherent civil–military approach to withdrawal and the transfer of power. However, his tendency to placate Federation Ministers while satisfying the appetite within the Federal Regular Army (FRA) for accelerated Arabization meant that he was performing a political high-wire balancing act on a daily basis. Consequently, as this chapter shows, there was a tendency to backfill this paucity of strategy with an over-reliance on accomplishing operational and tactical priorities in conjunction with local tribal rulers dependent on British rule and patronage. The result has often been characterized as 'a scuttle', which left a vacuum in the Middle East that was quickly filled by the Soviet Union.

From colonization to Arabization: the paucity of strategy?

Aden had been seized by the East India Company in 1839 and was administered thereafter by the Indian government until it became an official British colony in 1937. It lies at the heart of the Gulf of Aden and is a key pinch-point in a vital trade route through the Suez Canal (opened in the late nineteenth century). Indeed, its strategic position at the time linked South Arabia to other parts of the British Empire and became an important staging post prior to the independence of India in 1947. Post-independence the focus shifted, at first to

Egypt, then to the colony of Kenya, where Britain held bases in Nairobi and Mombasa, and to Cyprus until 1960, when operational headquarters in the Middle East shifted to Aden. Its strategic position was complimented by the economic advantage given to Britain by retaining a foothold in this part of the world, which revolved around the assets provided by the port, the BP oil refinery, and Middle East Command.[2]

In 1962 the British government announced that Aden would become the seventeenth state to join the newly created Federation of South Arabia.[3] The news was greeted with a toxic mix of enthusiasm and suspicion by Arabs, with the leader of the ATUC, Abdullah Al-Asnag, bringing people onto the streets to protest against what he perceived to be a continuation of British colonization by proxy. Protests soon turned violent in the wake of the revolution in Yemen in September 1962, which became, in historian Spencer Mawby's view, 'perhaps the most significant event in the twentieth century history of southwest Arabia'.[4] The revolution gave sustenance to the forces of Arab nationalism in Aden and saw many migrant workers from North Yemen and Somalia take to the streets in protest at the planned merger. Police were promptly dispatched to quell the disturbances, promptly firing on a crowd that had attempted to burn down a shop in the Crater district. One man was killed and several wounded and the police made arrests after a mob tried to burn down the Aden Immigration Department.[5] The Federal government reacted decisively by threatening the protestors with imprisonment if they continued to loot and destroy government buildings. It even attempted to ban the demonstrations. But its calls for calm fell on deaf ears and over 3,000 people were now engaged in pitched battles with the police.

The colonial governor (later High Commissioner), who had responsibility for dealing with internal security matters,[6] stubbornly refused to be moved by these disturbances; shortly after midday, three platoons of British troops were

[2] Gillian King, *Imperial Outpost—Aden: Its Place in British Strategic Policy* (London: Oxford University Press, 1964), p. 41.

[3] Previously, South Arabia had constituted the colony of Aden and the 24 states of the Aden Protectorate.

[4] Spencer Mawby, *British Policy in Aden and the Protectorates 1955–67: Last Outpost of a Middle East Empire* (London: Routledge, 2005), p. 90.

[5] Telegram from Sir C. Johnston to the Secretary of State for the Colonies, 24 and 25 September 1962, CO 1015/2596, The National Archives (TNA).

[6] Under the Treaty between the UK and Federation: 'The United Kingdom shall take such steps as may at any time in the opinion of the United Kingdom be necessary or desirable for the defence of the Federation and after consultation with the Federation for its internal security'. Interestingly the Treaty also called for the maintenance of a Federal Army under the command of 'a person appointed by the Federation with the agreement of the United Kingdom'. See HMG, *Treaty of Friendship and Protection between the United Kingdom of Great Britain and Northern Ireland and the Federation of South Arabia and Supplementary Treaty providing for the accession of Aden to the Federation, September 1964* (London: HMSO, 1964), Cmnd. 2451. The title of the Federation of Arab Emirates of the South was changed to the Federation of South Arabia on 3 May 1962.

deployed in aid of the civil power.[7] Within a few months street protestors gave way to gunmen and bombers. Perhaps the most serious incident to date took place on 10 December 1963 when a grenade attack on High Commissioner, Sir Kennedy Trevaskis, succeeded in killing two and wounding 50 others.[8] The assassination bid forced Trevaskis' hand and shortly afterwards he declared a state of emergency, which was complemented by legislation enacted by the Federal Supreme Council.

Trouble soon spread to the interior of South Arabia. And the first real test for British troops came in 1964, when dissidents from the Dhanbaris and Absaris tribes, two of the six major tribes 'upcountry' in the Radfan, threatened to cut off access between key commercial centres by mining the Dhala road, the principal arterial route connecting the port to the interior. Military operations were launched with the initial aim of restoring freedom of movement and the flow of free trade—and they initially had considerable success. The advantage given to the military, who now dominated the high ground, allowed Middle East Command to report on the progress of handing over responsibility to the FRA, despite them playing only a supporting role in the suppression of dissidents from the rural-based NLF:

> Within the last year, great advances have been made towards the Arabisation of the Federal Regular Army at all levels, and, in conformity with a similar process currently taking place throughout the Federation, this will continue in accordance with a carefully planned programme.[9]

But what was this 'carefully planned programme', and why did it not eliminate the trouble caused by the tribes who, despite surrendering in July 1964,[10] continued to create problems for British officials until withdrawal?

It is clear that the military believed they had a longer time-frame in order to implement the Arabization programme. Commander of the FRA, Brigadier James Lunt, anticipated that by 'the middle of 1966, if present plans work out,

[7] C. H. Johnston, *The View from Steamer Point: Being an Account of Three Years in Aden* (London: Collins, 1964), p. 192.

[8] Recent evidence in the official Aden archives suggests that Al Asnag was behind the attack, though it was initially thought to be the work of Egyptian agents. That different conclusions were drawn about who ordered the attack is indicative of the misunderstanding of the origins, course, and consequences of the violence.

[9] HQ Middle East Land Forces, *Operations in Radfan, 14 April–30 June 1964* (Aden: HQ MEC, 1 August 1964).

[10] Final Surrender Documents of Radfan Tribes 1964 campaign, 22nd July 1964, R?20/C/2583, British Library, India Office Records (IOR). The surrender documents were worded along similar lines. Thumb prints and signatures were taken from the tribal leaders, who admitted that 'some of our fellowmates have gone to Yemen and obtained some aide of arms, ammunitions, money, etc, on conditions that they would assault the people of the Federation. We perceived now that what has been given to us of arms was designed to cause subversion in our country and trouble the peace of our people, and we, therefore, have returned to our Amir and our Government admitting our guilt'.

the situation in Headquarters FRA will be that all the second grade and third grade staff officers will be Arab'. In his professional judgement, the Chief of Staff (a full Colonel or Qaid) and the Brigade Commander (a Brigadier or Zaim) would be British.[11] In the last days of the Conservative government during 1964, British policy was committed to providing military aid to the Federation, a position shared by Harold Wilson in opposition, who was telling political allies in private that 'Aden must be held as an important base, both for communications and as a centre for peace-keeping operations. Whatever measures are necessary to this end must be taken'.[12] It is clear that within a year of winning the general election in October 1964, Wilson had changed his mind, abandoning previous British assurances to maintain even a token level of military training.[13]

While the Labour government had given a commitment to contain terrorism in Aden, it lacked the stomach for a fight and, in strategic terms, it no longer possessed the economic resources either. By 1966 the game was up, as one after another British officials began to consolidate the new direction in policy, one that did not see either a British military presence in South Arabia or, at the very least, a commitment to provide continuing military assistance in the form of training, equipment, or advice. It was unfortunate for the Federation authorities that the forthcoming Westminster election coincided with Denis Healey's Defence Review, the stated purpose of which was to 'relate expenditure on defence to the nation's resources'. As the party's own internal papers reveal, it was continuing with a policy previously initiated by the Attlee government in the immediate post-war period:

> In the past Britain has attempted too much. As a result we have wasted fantastic sums and scarce resources on unrealistic projects, our economy has been subjected to an increasingly unbearable strain and in the past some of our forces, performing key roles in Britain's peace keeping and Commonwealth commitments, were left undermanned and underequipped.[14]

Almost every administration criticized the last one. Labour's policy material in the mid-1960s was no different, laying the blame for the poor health of the defence budget squarely at the door of the previous Conservative government. This was re-affirmed by Wilson in 'Prime Minister's Questions' several months

[11] Arabisation of Federal Army Commission of Enquiry, Letter from JD Lunt to Colonel JB Chaplin, Permanent Secretary, Federation MoD, 23 January 1964, R/20/D/189, IOR. Copies were also sent to the GOC and the Acting Assistant High Commissioner.

[12] Rt. Hon. Harold Wilson MP speaking to a meeting of European Socialist Leaders held at Transport House on 12 May 1964, Aden, Labour History Archive and Study Centre, Manchester (LHASC).

[13] Harold Wilson speaking in response to a question by a Conservative MP on the issue of Aden and South Arabia, *House of Commons Debates* (Hansard), 10 May 1966, Vol. 728, Col. 219.

[14] Peter Shore Papers, 5/97, Papers on Foreign Affairs, Labour Research Department, accompanying letter dated 10 February 1966, London School of Economics (LSE).

after Healey published his Defence Review, when responding to a Conservative charge that the British government was now abandoning their Federation allies. The Prime Minister told the House: 'we simply cannot go on a basis of accepting these unilateral military commitments which are far beyond the economic, military and financial capacity of this country'.[15]

Yet, the lack of choreography in these remarks did little except to expose the vulnerabilities placed on those who had previously bought British assurances that they would maintain a base in Aden for its own protection, even after independence.[16] Nevertheless, the retreat from Britain's only Middle Eastern colony was now becoming a reality. As the former Governor made perfectly clear in his memoirs, 'the safest way of determining our aims in South Arabia will be by a hard-headed calculation of the two interests involved—those of Britain, and of the indigenous inhabitants'.[17] Imperial interests, principally, what was good for the Metropolis, would always trump local feelings.

Denis Healey first mooted the government's decision to move away from the original Conservative policy in 1965, and his Defence Review gave a date for withdrawal no later than 1970. Shortly after its publication in January, the goalposts were again moved back to January 1968 and, finally, brought forward to November 1967. The reasons for the shifting of the date for withdrawal were partly party political, partly strategic, and partly, as this chapter demonstrates, because of the increasing opposition from the NLF in Aden, who soon established themselves, like the Jewish insurgents had done almost two decades previously, as a government in waiting. The ruling tribal elite and Adeni 'moderates' were abandoned and Aden rapidly descended into chaos. Seizing the opportunity to both eliminate their opponents and 'to show the Arab world and international observers that they were evicting the British by force', the NLF succeeded in demonstrating that 'it was they, and not the British, who were determining events'.[18] With the benefit of hindsight, we now know the consequences of South Arabia's descent into chaos. What is not as well known is why the process of transition ultimately failed.[19]

[15] *House of Commons Debates* (Hansard), 10 May 1966, Vol. 728, Col. 219. Aden was costing the British taxpayer approximately £20 million per annum to maintain.

[16] See comments by Duncan Sandys, Minister for Commonwealth Relations and the Colonies, *House of Commons Debates* (Hansard), 7 July 1964, Vol. 698, Col. 216; and those made by Denis Healey, Defence Minister, in *House of Commons Debates* (Hansard), 27 October 1967, Vol. 751, Col. 576; see also Mawby, *British Policy in Aden and the Protectorates*, p. 152, for commentary on Labour's retreat on these assurances.

[17] Johnston, *The View from Steamer Point*, p. 194.

[18] Jonathan Walker, 'Red Wolves and British Lions: The Conflict in Aden', in *Counterinsurgency in Modern Warfare*, edited by Daniel Marston and Carter Malkasian (Oxford: Osprey, 2010), p. 153.

[19] It is perhaps no accident that the current President of Yemen, Abd Rabu Mansur Al-Hadi, who was born in Aden in 1945 joined the Federation's South Arabian Army in 1964, attending military training college in Britain just prior to independence, and later rose to prominence as Minister of Defence and Vice-President.

The failure to think through the implications of this fundamental shift in policy meant that the process of Arabization suffered. Decisions such as the proposed merger of the Federal Army and the Armed Police, to constitute a unified South Arabian Army (SAA), caused considerable friction between competing tribal dynamics within the Security Forces. As the next section demonstrates, the armed opposition groups knew only too well the weaknesses in British plans to hand over power to local Arabs and they set about appealing directly to the self-interest of these groups in the wake of Britain's announcement that it would withdraw from South Arabia.

The failure of Arabization?

Although it would be entirely convenient to criticize the paucity of strategic guidance emanating from London on the transition from colonial rule to South Arabian independence, by itself, this cannot explain the very real operational and tactical weaknesses that permeated military planning and decision-making. Those who take a more dispassionate view of military operations in Aden after 1964 point to the fact that senior military commanders saw Aden as a 'quaint backwater'.[20] It was this culture of complacency in underestimating the serious threat being posed to the security of the colony that ensured a Brigadier, with little recent operational experience and close to retirement, was appointed as Aden's garrison commander. Nothing was done to rectify this, nor was anything done to effect a thorough re-assessment of the intelligence mechanism in Aden until 1966 either.[21] The policemen and soldiers, at least those from a British background, were fighting blind. Compounding matters was the fact that British security forces did not really understand the tribal dynamics underpinning relations between the Arabs themselves or between Adeni's, immigrants, and tribes from elsewhere in the Federation. Nor did anyone seem to have a clear picture of the threat they were facing from the Egyptian Intelligence Service who continued to arm NLF and FLOSY militants from across the border in Yemen.

Recent research has also pointed to the tendency of British troops to underestimate their enemies, while sticking too rigidly to doctrine in undertaking counter-insurgency and internal security operations.[22] Nowhere was this better illustrated than by events on 20 June 1967 and the Argyll's re-occupation of Crater, a fortnight later.

[20] Interview with Lieutenant General Sir Robert Richardson, September 2012.

[21] For more on the intelligence reorganization and effectiveness of the NLF see Edwards, *Mad Mitch's Tribal Law*.

[22] See Edwards, *Defending the Realm?*, ch. 5.

Events on 20 June sounded the death-knell for Britain's makeshift strategy of Arabization. On the morning of 20 June a three-tonne Bedford truck ferrying soldiers from the Royal Corps of Transport was fired on at an entrance to Khormaksar military base. Nine troops and one civilian passing at the time were killed in the attack. It was quickly followed up just after midday when militants armed with assault rifles and Blindicide rocket-launchers ambushed two Land Rovers carrying soldiers from the Royal Northumberland Fusiliers and the Argyll and Sutherland Highlanders. Ironically, the Fusiliers were at the end of their six-month tour. The ensuing exchange of fire resulted in the deaths of 23 soldiers, one British civil servant and over 200 Arabs.[23]

Arguably, the precarious trust that had been built up between the British and their Arab allies had been dealt a body blow 12 months earlier in 1966, with the announcement of the intent to withdraw. Nonetheless, events on Black Tuesday deepened the mistrust that had continued to build between the Arabs and British troops to a level from which relations never recovered. The delicate political manoeuvring by elements inside the High Commission and at Middle East Command was indicative of how civil–military relations had deteriorated. It was amidst such an atmosphere that Lieutenant Colonel Colin Mitchell and others were beginning to perceive a weakness in the decision-making process at the strategic–operational interface.

Giving the order for a limited reconnaissance mission into Crater a fortnight after Black Tuesday (in the absence of his General Officer Commanding), Brigadier Charles Dunbar was taking a huge risk, though it was one that ultimately played well with the troops and with many people back home in the UK.

At 7 p.m. on the evening of 3 July 1967 the Argylls massed on the edge of Crater. Soon they would be piped into Crater to the tune of their Regimental charge 'Monymusk', even though the NLF threatened to turn the town into 'a graveyard for the British'.[24] The reality was somewhat different with one company commander admitting privately to the new Brigade Major, Bob Richardson, that the enemy 'didn't even have thunder flashes' at their disposal.[25] The implication, of course, was that opposition simply evaporated in the face of a robust military response. And the Argylls certainly planned on taking casualties, with Colonel Mitchell informing his men that their main objective was '[t]o kill genuine terrorists while conducting a military occupation of Crater aimed at establishing good relations between 1 A&SH [Argyll

[23] Casualties included 1 Lancashire Rifleman, 9 Royal Northumberland Fusiliers, 8 troopers from the Royal Corps of Transport, 1 from the King's Own Borderers, and 3 Argyll and Sutherland Highlanders, giving a total of 22 killed and 31 wounded.

[24] Dunbar Papers, 2/3, NLF, 'The Blazing Hills', Daily Bulletin published by the NLF in Crater, No. 2, 3 July 1967, Liddell Hart Centre for Military Archives (LHCMA).

[25] Interview with Lieutenant General Sir Robert Richardson, 20 July 2013.

and Sutherland Highlanders] and the local nationals'.[26] In little over an hour the Argylls had re-entered Crater, killing only one Arab who resisted and six others unfortunate enough to go up against a battalion of well-trained and highly motivated soldiers. Mitchell's Second-in-Command, Major Nigel Crowe, confided in a letter to his friend Lord Chalfont, a Minister in the Foreign Office, of his frustrations at the Argylls being effectively muzzled from unleashing the kind of robust plan that had been drawn up by their Commanding Officer just two weeks earlier.[27]

Having served for the majority of his career in the Middle East Crowe was also aware that the lack of a robust entrance and pursuit of those responsible for the murders on 20 June would have signalled to the Arabs that the soldiers did not have the full backing of the government. 'I fear we are now never going to see anyone brought to justice for the massacre, and this will only be taken as a sign of weakness by the Arabs',[28] he duly informed Chalfont. Crowe's observations were correct and no one was ever apprehended for the killings.[29] It could easily be inferred that the reasons why the killers escaped justice was because of the collusion of Armed Policemen with the NLF gunmen, something increasingly borne out as the Argylls bedded into the town until the final withdrawal. As one officer wrote in the regimental journal *The Thin Red Line* at the time:

> We live in Crater cheek-by-jowl with the local population. A Company hold the Northern part of Crater, from a line just north of the Chartered Bank Building. B Company hold the Western and Southern part, including the main residential area alongside Holkat Bay, and the line south of Aidrus Road. Their section now includes the Aidrus Mosque, a source of trouble on several occasions which was until recently D Company's task. D Company dominates the very heart of Crater.[30]

This was an integral component in Colonel Mitchell's decision not only to retake Crater but to hold it and clear it of any residual NLF activity by placing his men on high-points overlooking the town:

> Platoons and Sections live in a variety of buildings which dominate each particular area of responsibility. Occupied buildings vary from schools to the Treasury Building, from the clinic to ordinary private flats. Each position is chosen for its ability to dominate its particular area, and the Argylls are masters of the rooftops. Foot,

[26] Dunbar Papers, 2/1, Extract from *The Thin Red Line*, September 1967, LHCMA.

[27] Wigg Papers, 3/45, Letter from Major N.D.L. Crowe, 13 July 1967, LSE.

[28] Wigg Papers, 3/45, Letter from Major N.D.L. Crowe, 13 July 1967, LSE.

[29] See the comments of Brigadier Dunbar in Dunbar Papers, 2/4, 'Staff in Confidence: Commissioner of Police—P.G. Owen, Esq, CMG', document written by Dunbar examining the shortcomings of the Commissioner, 8 March 1967, LHCMA.

[30] Dunbar Papers, 2/1, Extract from *The Thin Red Line*, September 1967, LHCMA.

mobile, and armoured car patrols police the streets at frequent and varying intervals.[31]

Often to be found in the thick of it, either challenging locals about their movements or standing aloft high-rise buildings relating his maps to the ground, Mitchell was extremely frustrated by the lack of firm direction from his superiors. He made no secret of the fact that he thought that British prestige was badly damaged by the murder of the soldiers and the imposition of terrorist rule over the Crater district on Black Tuesday. Yet he could do little about it. As he later noted in his memoirs, he 'had spent long enough in Whitehall to know the stultifying effects of rule by committee'.[32] His position was clear. 'I was not prepared,' he said, 'to see my men killed by being forbidden to defend themselves simply to avoid upsetting Arab leaders of politicians remote from the fighting back home'.[33]

Aden's Chief Justice was quickly ordered to undertake an inquiry into the events of 20 June 1967. He blamed the outbreak of violence on a 'spur of the moment decision' taken in the heady atmosphere created by the Arab-Israeli Six-Day War.[34] According to his report, there were significant rumours to the effect that the British were prepared to abandon their allies. As a result discipline within the ranks of the police broke down. An ensuing gun battle broke out and, according to the report, things just 'got out of hand'. In the Chief Justice's opinion:

> It is noted that the behaviour of the Armed Police on 20 of June was entirely out of character, that it is a force which has enjoyed the highest reputation in the past, that throughout the emergency it has proved its worth time and again in the control of disturbances of all kinds, and that it clearly has a vital role to play in the future.[35]

Although forensic in its detailing of the events of Black Tuesday, the report conveniently side-stepped the fundamental problem of a hasty withdrawal and overriding paucity of strategic thought on how it should be managed.

It was in this strategic vacuum that Colonel Mitchell's imposition of 'Argyll law' in Crater could have only a temporary effect. Ironically, the clampdown

[31] Dunbar Papers, 2/1, Extract from *The Thin Red Line*, September 1967, LHCMA.

[32] Lieutenant Colonel C. Mitchell, *Having Been a Soldier* (London: Hamish Hamilton, 1969), p. 169.

[33] *Daily Express*, 17 July 1968.

[34] Trevaskis knew differently, arguing that: 'The crisis came like a thunder storm in June out of the sultry atmosphere of injured Arab pride which had followed Israel's victory in the Six Day War. Tribalism reacted according to its own rules and, for all their British parade-ground look, some of the sympathisers with the aggrieved did what any indigo-daubed warrior would have done. They shot down the first group of British soldiers to come within range of their weapons'. Sir Kennedy Trevaskis, *Shades of Amber: A South Arabian Episode* (London: Hutchinson, 1968), p. 247.

[35] Summary of the Chief Justice's Report on the events of 20 June in Crater, 14 August 1967, Ministry of Defence (DEFE): 24/1793, TNA.

on terrorism in Crater only pushed the NLF into stepping up its terrorist attacks against the tribal rulers elsewhere in South Arabia and concentrated their efforts on soft targets in other parts of the Aden urban area. In a bellicose statement to its rank and file the NLF urged a pragmatic response to British obduracy and vowed to continue its armed struggle:

> The entry of British troops into the town of Crater after the siege cannot be considered an act for regaining a lost dignity, but a foolish act. Our bullets and grenades will continue to cause fear in the hearts of the Scottish 'red rats'. When will Britain understand that the solution does not lie in continuing along the wrong path but in correcting the mistakes... When will Britain learn this?[36]

The NLF then reiterated its strong belief that 'the use of force and violence, [will] achieve what political methods have failed to achieve'.[37] The scene was set for a violent confrontation between British troops and the violent custodians of extreme forms of Arab nationalism.

In neighbouring Sheikh Othman violence continued. The 1st Battalion of the Parachute Regiment (Paras) had moved into the town in the early hours of 1 June and had held a number of key points as a means of keeping open the main arterial route upcountry. The soldiers met with stiff opposition in the form of terrorist attacks from FLOSY who were by now engaged in internecine warfare with their rivals in the NLF. In practical terms the Paras were caught in a three-way fight for much of the summer months that would culminate in a violent confrontation as both nationalist groupings fought for supremacy. As 1 Para pulled out of the area and fell back to a defensive position around Khormaksar Airbase in September they could only spectate as the NLF and FLOSY fought each other for control of Sheikh Othman. By early November the NLF had emerged victorious, having annihilated its opponents with the 75mm guns of the SAA's armoured cars. Britain's plan to ensure the SAA backed the Federation in the transition towards independence lay in tatters.

While still clinging to somewhat nominal control over the rebellious Crater district in the summer months, Britain followed no overall strategic-level plan. Arabization had been all but abandoned. Although the focus had now switched to ensuring that withdrawal took place in an orderly fashion, the politicians turned to the soldiers to shoulder the burden. In his interviews with the media, Mitchell alleged that the events of 20 June personified a 'national malaise', precipitated locally just as 'the British civil and military authorities thrust their ostrich necks deeper and deeper into the Arabian sands in the hope that, by pretending there was no emergency, this wish could become fact'.[38]

[36] Dunbar Papers, 2/3, 'The Blazing Hills', No. 4, 5 July 1967, LHCMA.
[37] Dunbar Papers, 2/3, 'The Blazing Hills', No. 4, 5 July 1967, LHCMA.
[38] Lieutenant Colonel Colin Mitchell, 'The truth about Aden by the one man who can tell it... MAD MITCH', *Sunday Express*, 13 October 1968.

Meanwhile, soldiers had been following Internal Security doctrine, which emphasized the use of CS gas to curtail rioting,[39] internment, vehicle checkpoints, house raids, cordon and search, and the use of lethal force when judgement deemed necessary.[40] The guidelines were mainly coercive and aimed at conflict prevention. However, they were interpreted by Mitchell in a way that augmented his policy of 'tolerant toughness'. For instance, many Arabs who came up against Argyll checkpoints and who tried to run away, for example, were shot in the back. This did little to endear the local population to what many now came to see as British duplicity and a determination to put the lives of its own troops ahead of local nationals. In the end the military could do little to backfill the paucity of strategy.[41] Arabization soon gave way to damage limitation as Britain set its sights on abandoning its last Middle East outpost.

Conclusion

Undoubtedly, there was a disconnection in civil–military relations both on the ground in Aden and in Whitehall, which permitted the military to perceive a lack of will amongst the civilian authorities. Distrust permeated relations between the military and the police, with Brigadier Charles Dunbar observing how there is 'still good material to build on in the police force but this will not last long under the present leadership'.[42] In an interview he gave to a London-based newspaper, Colin Mitchell added fuel to the fire by disclosing how he had already 'displeased my superiors when, on arrival, a few days before, I was interviewed for Aden Forces Radio and, when asked what I thought of the security situation, had replied that Aden was "the least buttoned-up place I had ever known"'.[43]

Yet, politicians gave a mixed reception to Mitchell's military operations in Crater. While Denis Healey and much of the top-level ministers and civil servants approved of the re-occupation, even they could not shield the Colonel from the perception that the operation came about in the main because

[39] Interestingly, Denis Healey boasted in the House of Commons that the use of CS gas was in many ways 'more humane' than the employment of lethal force. 'I think that on reflection my hon. Friend would agree that it was far more humane for British forces and police to be able to use this gas in the Hong Kong riots last year and in some of the civil disturbances in Aden than to be confined to the use of, for example, rifles and machine guns, as was the case at Amritsar, for example', *House of Commons Debates* (Hansard), 17 July 1968, Vol. 768, Col. 1420.

[40] See War Office, *Keeping the Peace: Part 1—Doctrine*, WO Code No. 9800 (London: The War Office, 7 January 1963); War Office, *Keeping the Peace: Part 2—Tactics and Training*, WO Code No. 9801 (London: The War Office, 16 January 1963).

[41] For more on this point see Edwards, *Mad Mitch's Tribal Law*.

[42] Dunbar Papers, 2/4, 'Staff in Confidence: Commissioner of Police—P.G. Owen', LHCMA.

[43] Mitchell, 'The truth about Aden', *Sunday Express*, 13 October 1968.

of a contravention of orders, a view advanced in the House of Commons by Labour backbench MP Tam Dalyell. Mitchell dismissed Dalyell's criticism, stating: 'Mr. Dalyell was not in Aden and has extremely limited military experience. He is a professional politician. I am a professional soldier in a professional regiment.'[44] What Mitchell and his men did not know at the time was that the phased operation had to be tightly controlled by Middle East Command because of assurances British representatives had given to senior members of the NLF in a secret meeting in the fortnight leading up to the re-occupation.

This was part of a wider plan by the Labour government to seek out other potential partners in the eventuality that the tribal rulers could not secure the overwhelming support of the SAA. This hedging of bets was to culminate in November 1967, when Wilson's government authorized a delegation (led by Lord Eddie Shackleton) to meet NLF leaders in Geneva, Switzerland. It was with a certain amount of confidence that Foreign Secretary George Brown could inform the House of Commons in mid-November:

> I believe that when the dust has died down, not only this country, not only Arabia and the Middle East, but also hon. Members opposite, will realise that, given the situation from which we started, we have done a tremendous job in getting it sorted out.[45]

It was a difficult speech for Brown, having to contend with a number of MPs shouting him down with calls of 'absolutely disgraceful' in light of his break from previous policy. While Labour's suspicion of power politics, its anti-colonial impulse, and the use of force as a last resort may well have loomed large in the minds of Labour ministers, it was nonetheless the commitment to their 1966 electoral manifesto that dominated much of their decision-making at this time.[46]

However, what political and military leaders continually under-estimated was the local political and tribal dynamics that made the process of Arabization unworkable. There is evidence to suggest that British authorities walked a tight rope, particularly since the delay in establishing a joint command for the FRA and the Federal Guard. As the Aden Governor revealed in a telegram to

[44] *Daily Express*, 17 July 1968.

[45] *House of Commons Debates* (Hansard), 14 November 1967, Vol. 754, Col. 231.

[46] Labour's manifesto claimed that 'Britain's security and influence in the world depend no less on the strength of her economy than on her military power. Excessive and mis-directed defence expenditure by Conservative Governments has weakened our economy without providing forces sufficient to carry out the tasks imposed on them without dangerous overstrain'. The 1966 Defence Review therefore had three objectives: to bring the runaway growth in defence expenditure under control, to decide on military objectives according to the limits of resources and to carry out these tasks with 'the full range of weapons needed for the job', *Labour Party Manifesto: Time for Decision* (1966).

the Secretary of State for the Colonies as early as February 1963, there was a 'fear among Federal Ministers that this would lead to the union of the two forces and so eventually open the door to a military coup d'état'.[47] By staving off amalgamation until the formal announcement of withdrawal, and then failing to secure a defence treaty guarantee from the British beyond independence, the Federation essentially prepared the conditions for its own demise.

References

Edwards, Aaron, *Defending the Realm? The Politics of Britain's Small Wars since 1945* (Manchester: Manchester University Press, 2012).

Edwards, Aaron, *Mad Mitch's Tribal Law: Aden and the End of Empire* (Edinburgh: Mainstream Publishing, 2014).

HMG, *Treaty of Friendship and Protection between the United Kingdom of Great Britain and Northern Ireland and the Federation of South Arabia and Supplementary Treaty providing for the accession of Aden to the Federation, September 1964* (London: HMSO, 1964).

HQ Middle East Land Forces, *Operations in Radfan, 14 April–30 June 1964* (Aden: HQ MEC, 1 August 1964).

Johnston, C. H., *The View from Steamer Point: Being an Account of Three Years in Aden* (London: Collins, 1964).

King, Gillian, *Imperial Outpost—Aden: Its Place in British Strategic Policy* (London: Oxford University Press, 1964).

Mawby, Spencer, *British Policy in Aden and the Protectorates 1955–67: Last Outpost of a Middle East Empire* (London: Routledge, 2005).

Mitchell, Lieutenant Colonel C., 'The truth about Aden by the one man who can tell it...MAD MITCH', *Sunday Express*, 13 October 1968.

Mitchell, Lieutenant Colonel C., *Having Been a Soldier* (London: Hamish Hamilton, 1969).

Trevaskis, Sir Kennedy, *Shades of Amber: A South Arabia Episode* (London: Hutchinson, 1968).

Walker, Jonathan, 'Red Wolves and British Lions: The Conflict in Aden', in *Counter-insurgency in Modern Warfare*, edited by Daniel Marston and Carter Malkasian (Oxford: Osprey, 2010), pp. 137–56.

War Office, *Keeping the Peace: Part 1—Doctrine*, WO Code No. 9800 (London: The War Office, 7 January 1963).

War Office, *Keeping the Peace: Part 2—Tactics and Training*, WO Code No. 9801 (London: The War Office, 16 January 1963).

[47] Arabisation of Federal Army Commission of Enquiry, Telegram from High Commissioner to Secretary of State for the Colonies, 15 February 1963, R/20/D/189, IOR.

6

Transitioning in and out of COIN

Efficiency, legitimacy, and power in Oman

James Worrall

Introduction: a unique but encouraging case

Given the successful nature of the counter-insurgency campaign in Oman, which in its most focused phase lasted from 1970 to 1976, it is surprising that so little attention has been paid to the study of this surprising victory. Especially when compared to the attention that other operations, *viz* Malaya, have received, Oman's defeat of a communist insurgency and its transition from medieval space to modernity has received scant academic attention and analysis. While direct comparisons with more recent campaigns such as Afghanistan can be misleading, it does seem somewhat odd that a successful counter-insurgency (COIN) campaign in a Middle Eastern, Muslim, desert state has been largely ignored in favour of learning lessons from the jungles of Southeast Asia.[1]

This chapter's focus is on the British role in Oman, specifically from the start of its deepening involvement in the COIN campaign in 1970 until the withdrawal of most of its military assets in 1976. It examines the series of transitions made across this period and beyond in order to support Oman in its battle against a Marxist insurgency which in 1970 threatened to overwhelm the Sultanate and menaced the whole of the Gulf region. Much of the literature on this particular counter-insurgency campaign has focused on tactical elements or has given a brief overview of the overall strategy of the campaign; what it has failed to examine is both the policy-making and the series of transitions that Britain went through not just in the campaign itself but also in its wider relations with the Sultanate.

[1] For example Field Manual-3.24 has just one reference to Oman which is under further reading.

This chapter identifies a series of key transitions during the campaign from 1970 to 1976 exploring how decisions were made to pursue these changes and how they were both responsive to conditions on the ground and wider interests and constraints operating on Britain at that time. It also attempts to place the critical counter-insurgency period from 1970 to 1976 into a wider context in order to show how transitions are best conducted through a relationship which has a longer-term perspective. Ultimately, this chapter argues that by seeing the Anglo-Omani relationship in its historical context and over a longer period (rather than just being focused on the study of one part of a COIN campaign), useful insights can be derived from how a clear strategy can assist in the creation of a state through an ongoing partnership which is ever evolving, but which at its heart retains a core bond of trust and respect.

Despite the central lessons which can be learnt from the Anglo-Omani relationship, it is important to be aware that some of the specifics of the approach to counter-insurgency may not be applicable in all situations. One should also bear in mind that the events in Oman represent a specific type of campaign which is categorized in the British Army's latest Field Manual as being 'indirect', meaning that: 'The military contribution... is likely to be small and based on specific capabilities such as Special Forces and intelligence. The role will be to provide expert advice and assistance to the host nation's security forces. The principal contribution to the counter-insurgency effort will be through the provision of political advice and economic and development assistance to the host government.'[2]

It can be argued that in reality Britain's role in Oman was far from being truly 'indirect'. There were a number of significant assets deployed across the period and Britain also maintained two airbases in Oman, RAF Salalah and RAF Masirah. Indeed, at one point in the campaign, the former came under direct daily attack and was protected by a contingent of the Royal Air Force Regiment.[3] For the Omanis too, Britain's role was not seen as being 'indirect'; it was recognized as being crucial to the success of the entire campaign. In addition, there were contingency plans in place should a sudden downturn in the situation have led to an imminent Marxist takeover of the state.[4] This would have necessitated the deployment of significant British military assets, clearly indicating that this was not a peripheral campaign but one of vital national importance that just happened to have been conducted in an indirect manner.

[2] British Army Field Manual, *Countering Insurgency*, Vol. 1, Part 10 (Warminster: Ministry of Defence, October 2009), p. 15.

[3] For an impression of the fuller scale of direct British military commitment see: *Britain's Small Wars Website*, 26 September 2013, <http://www.britains-smallwars.com/Desert_song/omanunits.html>.

[4] J. E. Worrall, *Statebuilding and Counterinsurgency in Oman: Political, Military and Diplomatic Relations at the End of Empire* (London: I.B. Tauris, 2014), pp. 100–1.

Needless to say then, for campaigns in which significant numbers of troops have already been committed, the approach of cautious transition into COIN is less useful, however, there are still lessons to be learnt from the overall approach taken in terms of building capacity, the focus on development, and planning for withdrawal.

In order to examine the British role in Oman and its transition processes this chapter proceeds by first providing some historical background of the Anglo-Omani relationship and the origins and nature of the insurgency. It then examines the deliberate process by which Britain became increasingly involved in the counter-insurgency campaign and the wider process of building capacity in the Omani government. Next it explores the progress of the COIN campaign and the series of transitions which took place over time, with an increasing focus on how British forces were drawn down as the campaign success became clear and political imperatives at home were changing. This drawdown would not have been possible without the success of the COIN campaign and, more importantly perhaps, the wider statebuilding programme supported by Britain which is explored next. This is then followed by an assessment of the nature of the withdrawal and an examination of the post-transition continuities in the Anglo-Omani relationship, before a conclusion attempts to extract some of the key lessons of the Omani case for transitions out of COIN and for the longer term assistance of state-building.

Ultimately, for Britain, the success in Oman can be ascribed to a number of factors including good strategic direction from the politicians, strong region-specific knowledge, clear commitment from officials, and a good operational plan. When these factors were combined with the specific conditions of both regional dynamics and the nature of the insurgency (plus a degree of good fortune), the case of Oman demonstrates that transitioning out of COIN can be relatively straightforward, particularly if there is a strong relationship and a clear long-term commitment between the parties involved.

Historical background

Britain has had a long and cordial relationship with Oman which can be traced back to 1646 and the signature of an agreement between Imam al-Yarubi (then the political and spiritual leader of Oman) and the East India Company.[5] A full commercial treaty was signed between the two powers in 1798 which was only superseded in 1951 by a Treaty of Friendship, Commerce

[5] J. E. Worrall, 'The British Historical View of Oman and Ibadism', in *Oman and Overseas*, edited by Michaela Hoffman-ruf and Abdulrahman Al Salimi (New York/Zurich: Olms, 2013), pp. 299–312.

and Navigation. In the interim a number of other agreements were signed which controlled the slave trade (1839 and 1844), restricted Oman's ability to cede or sell territory without British permission (1891), and which gave Britain a say in the awarding of oil concessions (1923), as well as an agreement giving extraterritorial rights to British citizens in Oman (1939).[6] Despite the restrictive nature of these additional treaties Oman remained an independent state and was never a British protectorate. This would remain important in the way in which Britain generally saw Oman as a partner rather than an area to control, and was especially evident during the COIN campaign in Dhofar where it is clear that there were surprisingly few holdovers of a colonial mentality given the fact that the bulk of decolonization had only occurred the previous decade.[7]

The extended nature of the Anglo-Omani relationship provides important context, and indeed, any study of the patterns of interaction demonstrates a series of British engagements to defend the Sultanic system of rule.[8] For the purposes of this chapter it is not necessary to delve further into history than the 1950s in order to demonstrate that a series of transitions have occurred within a broader relationship, and to show how the policy which was cemented in the 1950s underpinned the approach taken during the Dhofar War in the 1970s.

The 1950s witnessed a series of changes in Arabia driven by a mixture of the demands of modernization, new ideologies and nationalisms, and the hunt for oil. For Oman under its then Sultan, Sa'id bin Taimour who had acceded to the throne in 1932, major challenges of state formation and consolidation remained, along with a persistent cash flow crisis and a debt overhang which only after 20 years was finally coming under control.[9] Given the weaknesses of the Omani state and the longstanding division between the interior and the coastal regions of the country, which remained relatively calm due to the British brokered Treaty of Sib of 1920, the situation in this corner of Arabia remained tense, especially when an expansionist Saudi Arabia was actively looking for new territories and oil supplies.

The Saudis had first laid claim in 1949 to a vast swathe of territory in present-day Abu Dhabi and in 1952 sent forces to occupy the key border oasis at al-Buraimi which was shared between Oman and Abu Dhabi. Britain persuaded the Sultan not to immediately remove the Saudi party and

[6] Joseph A. Kéchichian, *Oman and the World: The Emergence of an Independent Foreign Policy* (California: Rand, 1995), pp. 123–9.

[7] Worrall, *Statebuilding and Counterinsurgency in Oman*, chapters 5 & 6.

[8] For more detail on Anglo-Omani relations over the longer term see: Worrall, 'The British Historical View of Oman and Ibadism'.

[9] Uzi Rabi, *The Emergence of States in a Tribal Society: Oman under Sa'id Bin Taymur, 1932–1970* (Brighton: Sussex Academic Press, 2006).

arbitration was entered into in July 1954. This soon collapsed as it became evident that the Saudis were trying to bribe tribes to change their allegiance to Saudi Arabia. Soon after, the Trucial Scouts and Sultanate forces removed the Saudis from the oasis.[10]

Given this situation it is little surprise that when the Ibadi Imam, Muhammed al-Khalili, who was both the spiritual and temporal leader of Inner Oman, died in 1954 and was replaced by the much younger Imam Ghalib bin Ali al-Hinai, whose brother Talib had clear designs on independence, tensions should come to the surface between the Sultan and the interior. The spark for a conflict, which would last from 1954 to 1959, was oil exploration licences granted by the Sultan which impinged upon the Imam's territory, thus exposing differing interpretations of the Treaty of Sib. This disagreement led to conflict when the Imam rebelled against a Sultan determined to gain control over all of his territory. The initial focus of the revolt was placed upon attacking the British officered Muscat Field Force which had remained near Buraimi after expelling the Saudis.

For the duration of their occupation of Buraimi the Saudis had been providing money and arms to Omani tribes, support which was stepped up after the Saudis had been expelled from Buraimi and were looking for revenge. What became known as the Imamate Rebellion appeared to have fizzled out quite rapidly as the Sultan's forces occupied a series of key towns in the interior. The Imam eventually abdicated his position at the end of 1955 and declared his allegiance to the Sultan while his brother Talib escaped to Saudi Arabia where he set about establishing a 'liberation army'. The insurrection soared back to life in 1957 when Talib returned from Saudi Arabia with around 300 fighters. This time it was much harder to extinguish as other tribal groupings joined this new force and a more general uprising began. Eventually, with much difficulty and considerable British assistance in the form of three companies of the 1st Battalion of the Cameronians and a troop of the 15/19 Hussars along with RAF jets and a squadron of ferret armoured cars, the rebellion was driven into the mountains. Although continuing guerilla attacks still caused problems on the plain, the rebellion had been contained but had not been eliminated. The rebellion was only formally ended in 1959 after a daring Special Air Service (SAS) raid on the mountainous refuge of the rebels.[11]

As a result of Sultan Sa'id's request for formal British assistance in putting down the rebellion and because in the post-Suez world Britain wanted to take a less visible role in defending Oman in the future, in 1958 an Exchange of

[10] Tore T. Petersen, 'Anglo-American Rivalry in the Middle East: The Struggle for the Buraimi Oasis, 1952–1957', *The International History Review* 14, no. 1 (1992): pp. 71–91.

[11] For detailed accounts of the Imamate Rebellion see: David Smiley, *Arabian Assignment* (London: Leo Cooper, 1975); and John E. Peterson, *Oman's Insurgencies—The Sultanate's Struggle for Supremacy* (London: Saqi Books, 2007).

Letters was arranged which set Britain's relations with Oman on a course which would endure. The letters, signed on 25 July, were primarily designed to strengthen the Sultan's Armed Forces (SAF) so that they would be in a better position to deal with any future rebellions, but also contained provision for assistance in economic development. This agreement therefore set policy on a twin track of encouraging development, through British funding initially, and also in offering considerable indirect support for the SAF.[12]

The most significant aspect was the use of Loan Service Personnel (LSP) who were British officers and NCOs who would be attached to the Sultan's forces to offer training and direction. This went beyond the 'advisory' capacity usually associated with indirect assistance and meant that the British LSP, supplemented by Contract Officers (former British and Commonwealth troops), served as an integral part of the SAF and not only filled technical and specialized roles but also led small units into combat and headed up the Armed Forces as a whole. To some extent a comparison can be made with the Gurkhas as a British officered force, except in this instance the British officers took their orders from the Sultan.

As part of the stiffening of the sinews of the SAF under the Exchange of Letters, a new Sultan of Oman's Air Force (SOAF) was also established and staffed with British pilots and ground crew. This intertwining of the British and Omani forces strengthened the Sultanate's capabilities and formed the basis of a closer partnership which has endured. Despite this British assistance there were too few revenues, until after the export of commercial quantities of oil after 1967, to support anything other than a very small armed forces establishment and much effort was expended to now firmly tie in the territories of the Imamate more formally into the structures of the Sultanate. Indeed, Britain was so preoccupied with the potential of the revival of the Imamate Rebellion during the early 1960s that the rumblings of insurrection in Oman's southern province of Dhofar were either ignored or downplayed for far too long.

The scene was set for a rebellion which would be on a much greater scale and represent a larger threat to the Sultanate and to Britain's interests in the region that the Imamate Rebellion ever had. What began as demands for more autonomy and more resources in the southern province of Dhofar soon became a war for independence caught up in the wave of anti-imperialism and Arab nationalism that was sweeping the region. An insurrection began in earnest in 1965 after the formation of the Dhofar Liberation Front (DLF). The rebellion began quite slowly and almost served the knockout blow when in

[12] Muscat and Oman (Exchange of Letters) *House of Commons Debates*, 16 November 1960, Vol. 630 c36W, <http://hansard.millbanksystems.com/written_answers/1960/nov/16/muscat-%20and-oman-exchange-of-letters>.

1966 some of Sultan Sa'id's Dhofar Force attempted to assassinate him during an inspection and then defected to the rebels in the mountains.[13] The rebellion steadily grew while the SAF never had the strength or the tactics to deal it a knockout blow. Sultan Sa'id was so angry at the attempted assassination and the disloyalty of the Dhofaris that he wanted to punish them rather than understand and accommodate some of their demands.

After Britain's disastrous retreat from Aden at the end of 1967 and with the Marxist National Liberation front forces winning a brief but vicious civil war against their rivals the scene was set for a transformation of the Dhofar insurgency. With a friendly, anti-British force in control of South Yemen the rebels had a secure base area and a new source of supplies. In 1968 the DLF morphed into the PFLOAG (Popular Front for the Liberation of the Occupied Arabian Gulf) as the organization became openly Marxist and secured support from around the Communist world. This led to a further transformation in the insurgency as attacks continued and the balance which had enabled the SAF to hold on was destroyed. From then on, as the situation continued to deteriorate, it looked increasingly likely that Britain was going to be drawn in to a potentially open-ended commitment to save the Sultan once more. By early 1970 the situation in Dhofar looked grave as the loss of the western town of Raykyut left only the capital Salalah in government hands. An SAS appreciation of the situation in early 1970 stated that:

> [T]he SAF are overstretched and tired . . . the methods used by the rebels, so far, are effective and they have seized the initiative and are dominating the *jebal* [mountains]. There is a feeling of abandonment among the uncommitted *jebali* and the operations by the SAF are hampered by interference from the Sultan, no clear long-term aim, no overall direction and poor intelligence.[14]

In June 1970, for the first time, attacks were made outside of Dhofar on SAF camps at Izki and Nizwa in the north of Oman, the fear was that the rebellion would spread outside of Dhofar and/or that there would also be a re-ignition of the Imamate Rebellion.

It is with this context, whereby Britain was already committed to Oman that the situation was at, or near to, crisis point. Britain had declared in 1968 that all of its forces would leave the Gulf by the end of 1971, and so policy-makers faced some difficult choices about what support they could offer the Sultanate. When one also factors in the serious economic problems and sterling crisis of

[13] John E. Peterson, 'Oman: The 1966 Assassination Attempt on Sultan Sa'id Bin Taymur', Arabian Peninsula Background Note, No. APBN-004, August 2004, <http://www.jepeterson.net/sitebuildercontent/sitebuilderfiles/APBN-%20004_Oman_1966_Assassination_Attempt_on_Sultan_Said.pdf>.

[14] Foreign and Commonwealth Office (FCO): 8/1437, Doc. 72, An Outline Plan To Restore The Situation In Dhofar Using Special Air Service Regiment Troops, 7 April 1970.

1967–69,[15] severe defence cuts[16] and the knowledge that another debacle like that at Aden could see communist influence surging into the soon to be vacated Gulf States, this left those in Whitehall with a series of dilemmas and yet ultimately no real choice about intervention; the question was really on what scale.

Transition into COIN: parsimony and caution

As 1970 began there was a real sense of rising concern in the FCO (Foreign and Commonwealth Office) and in the Gulf about the situation in Dhofar. Given the not inconsiderable assets Britain maintained in the region, totalling some 8,000 men based in Bahrain and Sharjah and including a sizeable naval and RAF presence,[17] it was not inconceivable that a full-scale British involvement to put down the rebellion in Dhofar could have been ordered. Yet this was precisely what Britain had hoped to avoid ever having to do again after the Imamate Rebellion and flew in the face of the policy established under the 1958 Exchange of Letters. Not to mention the fact that Britain was supposed to be withdrawing militarily from the region rather than getting sucked into a war. The assets were there and could be drawn upon in limited ways until they left the region[18] but committing significant British troops to the Dhofar war as a first resort was clearly a non-starter from the very beginning.

This meant that from the outset another option was required which was more indirect but which could potentially be both less politically and economically costly, and militarily as successful, while also being more sustainable for the longer term. Attempting to devise such a strategy given the embarrassment of Aden, the need for stability in Oman for military withdrawal to go ahead, and a Labour government not keen to engage in fresh commitments, led to the government taking the approach outlined under the Exchange of Letters, yet with more vigour. Throughout 1969, as the gravity of the situation became clearer, officials at the FCO worked hard to find ways of persuading Sultan Sa'id to spend more money and to adopt a less hard-line approach towards those rebels who may be amenable to a regime with a different outlook.

[15] Michael D. Bordo, Ronald MacDonald, and Michael J. Oliver, *Sterling In Crisis: 1964–1969*, accessed 14 September 2013, <http://www.cepr.org/meets/wkcn/1/1671/papers/Bordo_Mac_Oliver.pdf>.

[16] John Baylis, ed., *British Defence Policy in a Changing World* (London: Croom Helm, 1976), pp. 107–10.

[17] John E. Peterson, *Defending Arabia* (London: Croom Helm, 1986), p. 79.

[18] Worrall, *Statebuilding and Counterinsurgency in Oman*, ch. 3.

The debt-averse Sultan was unwilling to rush things, especially on the development front and while oil revenues remained relatively modest. By early 1970 there was a full-scale FCO effort to try to convince him of the need to expand the SAF, adopt a different approach to the campaign, and to accelerate the development programmes which were moving forward at a very slow pace. Lieutenant Colonel Watts of the SAS had visited Dhofar and had devised a comprehensive plan for a reinvigorated approach to the counter-insurgency campaign which would require a modest number of SAS troops to be deployed. Despite the gravity of the situation, when British proposals were put to him in April 1970, Sultan Sa'id remained opposed to the new COIN approach and to an acceleration of the development programme, however, he did acquiesce to the expansion and modernization of the SAF, including purchasing modern FN rifles, artillery, more skyvan transport planes and establishing a navy, as well as creating a fourth battalion of the SAF. Britain at this stage was willing to commit some forces to helping Sa'id hold the line until the SAF modernization and expansion was complete but this depended on the Sultan accepting the whole package proposed. When he refused, the whole approach was thrown into confusion.[19]

Britain remained, from April 1970, in a very difficult position—not willing to contribute forces unless there was a wholesale change of approach, yet facing a rapidly deteriorating situation and an interlocutor who refused to listen to advice or moderate his position. Perhaps Sa'id was hoping that Britain would eventually be forced to intervene as it had in the 1950s. Nevertheless, though, Britain was not in this dilemma for long as events changed quickly. On 23 July a coup, led by Sa'id's son Qaboos, deposed Sa'id and brought the Sandhurst trained Qaboos to power.[20] This led to a rapid transformation in the approach to the campaign and the swift implementation of Watts' counter-insurgency strategy, as well as the opening of the taps on development flows and the further expansion of SAF capabilities. By September 1970, after receiving the formal request for British assistance, the SAS were already in Oman. Although their numbers were small, with only around 40 in the initial deployment, four had been deployed very soon after the coup to offer 'training' to the new Sultan's bodyguards. This rapid British approach was further facilitated by the election of a Conservative government in June 1970 which was more willing to countenance interventions and had a greater determination to salvage as much as possible of Britain's 'East of Suez' role.

[19] Worrall, *Statebuilding and Counterinsurgency in Oman*, pp. 65–70.

[20] For more on the coup, which was welcomed by Britain but for which there is no evidence of a direct British government role, see Worrall, *Statebuilding and Counterinsurgency in Oman*, pp. 72–5.

COIN progress and drawdown

Once the commitment to assistance for Oman had been made, it was kept under review every six months, and a close eye was kept on progress by officials in the Gulf and Whitehall in the interim. In addition, the British LSP were now able to run the campaign much more effectively under the new political regime in the Sultanate. Qaboos, while deeply interested in the campaign and eager to get involved, was not a micro-manager and he recognized the professionalism of both contract officers and LSP.

For much of the initial period of transition, from around August 1970 until the end of 1971, much effort was focused on making sure that the commitment to providing support for the Sultanate in all fields was met: this meant identifying and strengthening those particular areas where British support could have the most effect. One of the most important of these areas was getting LSP into the right positions in order to support and add real value to the SAF expansion programme; the requests and authorizations of increasing numbers of LSP was seen by both sides as being of vital importance. Proper leadership at all levels of the SAF was clearly key to the campaign and provided the backbone of resistance to the PFLOAG challenge. Over this initial period of transition into COIN there was also a gradual expansion of SAS numbers and their role in turning surrendered enemy personnel (SEPs) into some kind of useful additional fighting force, although SAS numbers remained very limited overall and were only authorized to hit a ceiling of 65 in mid-1971. There were even attempts to try to limit the mandate for the SAS operation to expire at the end of 1971, so cautious was the overall approach, although this particular decision was over-ruled by the Prime Minister himself. Similarly, in August 1971 the deployment of a second squadron of SAS was authorizsed for six months. In this initial phase, decisions were also taken that would strengthen the defences of RAF Salalah with more RAF Regiment troops deployed, as well as a Royal Artillery unit which came to be known as 'Cracker Battery'; this had a sophisticated radar and was able to hit targets on the *jebal*, thus trying to push rebels back from the Salalah Plain and offering fire support to the SAF. As well as this, a field Surgical Team was dispatched which would be able to offer services to the British units that had been deployed and was, in addition, a major morale boost for the SAF. On the development front, a small force of Royal Engineers arrived and operated across the country to try to aid in accelerating development and in planning for future developments which would be put out to tender with private companies.[21]

[21] Worrall, *Statebuilding and Counterinsurgency in Oman*, pp. 98–101.

The second phase, which lasted from the end of 1971 until mid-1973, was focused on tinkering with the existing package of support and fine tuning it. Support was provided in the establishment of the new Navy, technical services for the SOAF and with the loan of helicopters in particular. In addition, there continued to be authorizations on new LSP deployments in order to cope with the rapid growth of the SAF and to cover certain technical requirements. Meanwhile, the previous reinforcements had seen the SAF finally begin to take the offensive over the course of 1971, although they were by no means strong enough to have a significant impact. Towards the end of 1971 a new strategy was implemented. By focusing on re-establishing themselves on the *jebal* and clearing the eastern sector where PFLOAG were furthest from their supply lines, coupled with the first attempt to at least disrupt supply lines from Yemen with the establishment of the Sarfait line in the west near the border with South Yemen, progress began to be made. During this transition into a much more active phase of COIN campaigning, Britain's focus switched from expanding direct military contributions to beginning to find ways to help Oman's financial difficulties. The rapid expansion of the SAF and the development programme, coupled with Britain demanding repayment for many of the aspects of its assistance and particularly supplies and the LSP, had led to a cash flow crisis despite increasing receipts from oil sales. The recognition of the crucial role of the LSP, in particular, led to extensive debates about the best way to take some of the cost burden of the LSP onto Britain's shoulders and away from the Omanis. Thus the second phase of Britain's transition into COIN in Dhofar worked to reinforce the first phase. Overall, despite the somewhat more activist position of the Conservative government which was further driven by the commitment of officials, there remained a deeply cautious approach, especially after the first phase, to weighing the costs and benefits of additional British assistance.

The third phase, which to some extent began as early as 1971, in reality lasted from the end of 1972 until the end of the war. It was built on a recognition that with British forces having left the Gulf at the end of 1971 there was no longer any 'over the horizon' backup. It also recognized that the position in Dhofar was still fragile despite advances being made, and that Britain could not send, and the Sultanate could not afford, the resources required to totally dominate the battle space and separate the insurgents from the population. A surge was required to break the deadlock which was re-emerging. Given the fact that the troops and finance needed to enable final success could not come from Britain or Oman, London needed to find ways of getting other countries to assist. This is connected to wider attempts at legitimization of the Sultanate detailed in the next section, but took on the form of a diplomatic campaign to solicit troops, in particular from Jordan and Iran, and financial and in-kind contributions from Abu Dhabi, Saudi Arabia,

Pakistan, India, and Qatar. As these diplomatic overtures became more successful, a slow trickle of support quickly became a flood and Britain increasingly took on the role of managing these contributions and trying to integrate them into the conduct of the campaign. This was a major transition which somewhat paradoxically both diluted and strengthened Britain's military role in the counter-insurgency campaign. It also enabled the campaign to begin to make much more rapid progress as lines of control defended by large numbers of Iranian troops, who were useful in static positions but much less so in patrolling the *jebal*, were able to break up Dhofar into segments which could then be cleared by the SAF and the SAS and their *firqat* protégées.

The fourth phase sought to capitalize on the successes of the transitions seen in the previous phases and, coupled with the re-election of the Labour party to office in 1974, accommodate an administration which was not eager to see any expansion of the direct British commitment to Oman (although a loan of further helicopters was approved). Given the backdrop of economic crisis in Britain, defence reviews and elements of the Labour party which were questioning the probity of upholding an undemocratic regime, this transition into a new era of gradual drawdown was somewhat inevitable and was facilitated by the successes that the previous transitions had brought about. Oman's importance initially meant that unlike the previous government which had always tried to find ways to cautiously improve and increase its assistance to the Sultanate, there was a freeze in terms of the support which was offered in both military and financial aspects. In many ways, given the nature of the debates in Whitehall about cost cutting, this was a very good outcome for the Sultanate. As the Defence Review began in earnest in 1975, opportunities began to be taken to start to find ways of taking advantage of the rapidly improving situation on the ground in Dhofar to withdraw aspects of the direct British support while maintaining key elements, especially the LSP which were considered to be completely separate from other assistance. This process, of course, also did not affect the continuing flow of advice, consultation, and expertise which was offered by London for both the COIN campaign and the state-building process. One of the first opportunities to begin to start the process of gradual transition out of the counter-insurgency campaign came as early as 1975 when the Chiefs of Staff took the decision that, since RAF Salalah was no longer coming under attack, part of the RAF Regiment detachment would be withdrawn in the first week of April 1975, as would the Royal Artillery detachment, the 'Cracker Battery'.[22] A decision was also taken

[22] J. E. Worrall, 'Britain's Last Bastion in Arabia: The End of the Dhofar War, The Labour Government and the Withdrawal from RAF Salalah and Masirah, 1974–1977', in *Challenging Retrenchment in the Middle East*, edited by Tore T. Petersen (Trondheim: Tapir Academic Press, 2010), pp. 165–6.

just a short while later not to replace the rest of the RAF Regiment when their tour ended in June 1975. This was the first actual reduction in British military support and signalled the start of a gradual process which would lead to most British units leaving Oman by the end of 1976.

Alongside this transition was a need not only to drawdown the units which were deployed in Dhofar but to also rethink the long-term need for Britain's remaining bases in the Gulf. While throughout its period in office RAF Masirah was seen as a critical asset by the Conservative government and by FCO officials, as early as November 1972 officials began to try to find ways to enable the RAF to hand back Salalah (which had always been less desirable for Britain and indeed was only established as a *quid pro quo* for Masirah under the 1958 Exchange of Letters). It is interesting that the beginning of the transition process to withdraw from RAF Salalah was taken at the height of the insurgency with a view to a handover as soon as practicable after the successful completion of the counter-insurgency campaign.[23]

The campaign was going so well with the surge of extra troops and resources that by September 1975 the situation on the ground was improving at a faster rate than predicted by operational plans. Indeed, in December 1975 it was declared that 'Dhofar is safe for Development'[24] and the campaign moved into containment of the remaining rebels. However, due to the threat posed, the nature of the terrain, and the presence of a secure rear area in South Yemen, it was not until 1980 that the danger had been completely eliminated.

Even before the declaration of victory in late 1975, FCO and MoD (Ministry of Defence) officials were quick to seize on the improving conditions and the withdrawal of the RAF Regiment to raise the issue of RAF Salalah, with the MoD pushing for a withdrawal timetable which was rather more accelerated than that proposed by the FCO. As early as June 1975 negotiations were opened with Sultan Qaboos for withdrawal from Salalah, albeit with a planned 'residual British deterrent presence' but a six-month withdrawal timetable. Qaboos was very unhappy about this proposal and it was only after protracted negotiations that a withdrawal date was set for 31 March 1977, with the Sultan agreeing to pay for the continuing RAF presence at a cost of £465,000 after the end of October 1976. Britain's presence at Masirah which had earlier been called a 'vital' national interest was subject to the cuts imposed under the Labour Defence Review, and after further negotiations a withdrawal date of April 1977 was eventually set to coincide with that at Salalah.[25]

[23] Worrall, 'Britain's Last Bastion in Arabia', p. 155.
[24] Worrall, 'Britain's Last Bastion in Arabia', p. 168.
[25] Worrall, 'Britain's Last Bastion in Arabia', p. 170.

Statebuilding: efficiency, legitimacy and power

While the rebellion was confined to one corner of the country, the need to construct a proper functioning state and to embark on a full development and modernization programme was a requirement for the whole nation. This process continued along three main tracks: a rapid process of development with the construction of roads, schools, hospitals, and other key infrastructure; a process of legitimacy building—both internally and externally, which would in turn aid in obtaining external assistance in both the development and counter-insurgency programmes; and finally the construction of an efficient and effective centralized administration which could eventually administer the development programme, maintain legitimacy, and also govern the Sultanate.

This three pronged approach to state-building was designed to build legitimacy at all levels. By demonstrating a clear ability and commitment to deliver goods and services and to bring the benefits of modernity to the Omani people as a whole, a process which was initially targeted at both Dhofar and the key population centres in the north, the state could build a rapid amount of internal legitimacy. It did not matter who provided the development on the ground, it simply needed to be efficiently delivered, in order to prove to the population that their government could deliver on the promise of a new era. Since Oman lacked the capacity and trained workforce to build modern infrastructure this could only come from external foreign contractors, often of course British. Linked to this, was the construction and building of Omani capacity in central government. Here again, there was a need to supervise this process through a system of embedding a small number of British civilian experts in the ministries and wider guidance from FCO officials for Qaboos and his Uncle, Tariq bin Taimour, who had been appointed Prime Minister. At the same time as this new government was slowly built, with a great many bumps along the way, a further track emerged which was aimed at cementing legitimacy and calming the disruption which would inevitably be caused for a tribal society which was modernizing and developing rapidly.[26] This was the creation of a new narrative of 'rebirth' for the nation which emphasized the balancing of the introduction of a more compassionate and responsive ruler with the protection of traditions, the continuance of the Sultanic system of rule and a whole panoply of symbols and invented or re-invented traditions.[27] These three aspects added greatly to the creation of the fourth key aspect: the creation of the belief in the people's minds that the state was not only legitimate

[26] Worrall, *Statebuilding and Counterinsurgency in Oman*, ch. 4.

[27] Dawn Chatty, 'Rituals of Royalty and the Elaboration of Ceremony in Oman: View from the Edge', *International Journal of Middle East Studies* 41, no. 1 (2009): pp. 39–58.

but also powerful. The symbols, newly emerging governance structures and the sudden state presence and wealth which was displayed by the development programme was also backed up by the public display of the armed forces at every opportunity, and the creation for the first time of policing systems which were able to apply force where needed across the country.[28]

Ultimately, this statebuilding approach underpinned the counter-insurgency campaign and ensured that the insurgency could not spread to the rest of the country. This approach was also key to the series of successful transitions which took place not just in the COIN campaign itself, enabling Britain to confine itself more and more into an advisory rather than an active role.

Withdrawal or realignment: post-transition continuities

The ability of Britain to transition out of COIN was in large part down to the cautious way that Whitehall had allowed Britain to enter the campaign in the first place, and the wider strategies in terms of the counter-insurgency effort and the state-building programme that were put in place and supported. The key thing to note here is that in reality the transition out of COIN for Britain was not a withdrawal but merely a realignment in a wider relationship. Britain's overall policy towards Oman remained exactly the same—to offer support wherever requested and to give advice and guidance but to encourage the pursuit of the same policy expressed under the Exchange of Letters with slightly greater focus on state-building and development and less on military capacity-building. Indeed, the next phase continued to be underpinned by these policies and the role of British advisors in the ministries, although their number gradually shrank, remained important to further consolidate the efficiency of the state. In addition, British LSP remained critical to the functioning of the armed forces. The next transition would begin from the end of the 1970s as a process of 'Omanization' began at all levels. This transition was however, quite slow and as late as 1987 the heads of all three branches of the Omani armed forces remained British, whether LSP or contract officers. By the early 1990s commanders were all Omani and had British advisors, and thus the next transition began to take place in earnest.[29]

Out of this process of Omanization, and based on the wider relationship, a fully fledged partnership between the two states began to emerge and grow throughout the 1990s. The relationship is based on continuing Omani need

[28] J. E. Worrall, *Policing Oman: From the Oman Gendarmerie to the Royal Oman Police, Britain's Role in the Creation of Internal Security Structures*, Unpublished Conference Paper, 2009.

[29] For an interesting viewpoint from a British Contract Officer see: Alan Hoskins, *A Contract Officer in the Oman* (Tunbridge Wells: Costello, 1988).

for training in all spheres with a strong tradition of Omani students studying for higher degrees in Britain, as well as regular exchanges between many personnel from Omani government services. This is all underpinned by close cooperation between the British and Omani armed forces and the continuing tradition of sending LSP[30] to Oman, meaning that training and relationships are maintained.[31]

We can see therefore that there were, and remain, far more continuities in terms of Britain's commitment to Oman, and that the policies pursued in the aftermath of the COIN campaign itself have continuing resonance to the present day.

Conclusion and lessons

There are a wide range of lessons that can be learnt about the British approach to counter-insurgency and state-building in Oman that have ongoing utility for stabilization efforts and COIN campaigns both now and in the future.

A key element of our thinking about transition is based on conceptions of success, what it is and how it can be measured. Britain's experience of transition in the case of Oman demonstrates that the best approach is to plan ahead, and be cautious but committed. The simple goal in Oman was to create a state which could function in the modern world, and while the COIN campaign itself was clearly vitally important, it was the state-building process which was seen as the real priority. The focus was largely on results for the Omani people, and this is most clearly seen in terms of development. Accounts of the short period from 1969 to 1974, often express shock and amazement at the rapid progress in terms of development and modernization that was made during this five-year period. This was how Britain measured its success, by real changes on the ground, which impacted on people's lives. This approach was also applied to the counter-insurgency campaign itself, and in turn allowed transitions to flow from changes on the ground. One of the critical factors which enabled these successes, and a further key lesson for transition, is the power of relationships and their ability to build trust, capacity, and understanding. This applies at all levels, from the personal bonds of LSP to the highest level of government. By taking an approach which embedded British personnel into Omani structures where they could build trust, capacity, and offer leadership, Britain was able to make small numbers have a

[30] Currently there are around 100 LSP in Oman. See: British Embassy in Muscat, <https://www.gov.uk/government/world/oman#priorities,%20accessed%2014%20September%202013>.

[31] For just one recent example see: *Paras Join Forces with Omani Soldiers*, 22 June 2012, <http://www.army.mod.uk/news/24216.aspx,%20accessed%2014%20September%202013>.

disproportionate impact and this in turn made transitioning easier. This was because it was built on the delivery of success, left clear capacity in its wake, and on a practical level withdrawing hundreds of troops is much easier than withdrawing thousands. But perhaps the most important lesson from the Omani case, and the focus of this chapter, is that there are real benefits to thinking about transition differently.

One of the major issues we face when thinking about counter-insurgency today is that we tend to have a very 'Western' view, a binary view, which wants to categorize things very clearly and work to very short timescales. COIN, state-building, and transition should not be seen in such a way. Just as recent literature studying civil wars has come to see that there is in fact a complex continuum between peace and war,[32] so thinking about COIN should not be seen as a binary activity. Simply thinking about counter-insurgency as either 'on' or 'off' is unhelpful. By taking Westphalian state vs. state notions of warfare and using them to categorize an entirely different type of conflict, we not only misunderstand the full nature of the conflict itself, but we also think in the short term. What Oman teaches us then is not only that counter-insurgency and state-building go hand in hand during periods of insurgency, but that the process of state-building itself, in all its variations, is in fact the institutionalization of a COIN strategy for the *long term*. When we think of how we can best assist governments of the countries experiencing civil conflicts, a long-term view based on a good diplomatic relationship is crucial. We therefore need to see the idea of transition in similar terms, not just as a short-term 'exit strategy' but instead as a series of small changes in a wider relationship of friendship and support, rather than a rupture that enables us to withdraw and move on to the next crisis situation. The concept of a constant series of transitions along a continuum within a wider and ongoing relationship which is nourished by a strong awareness of previous bonds and a shared history is a much better way of conceptualizing transition, and is far more likely to lead to a successful outcome, as the case of Oman so clearly demonstrates.

References

Baylis, John, ed., *British Defence Policy in a Changing World* (London: Croom Helm, 1976).

Bordo, Michael D., Ronald MacDonald, and Michael J. Oliver, *Sterling in Crisis: 1964–1969*, CEPR Working Paper, accessed 14 September 2013, <http://www.cepr.org/meets/wkcn/1/1671/papers/Bordo_Mac_Oliver.pdf>.

[32] Paul Richards, ed., *No Peace, No War: An Anthropology of Armed Conflicts* (Athens, OH: Ohio University Press, 2004).

Britain's Small Wars Website, The Desert Song: Oman and Dhofar, accessed 14 September 2013, <http://www.britains-smallwars.com/Desert_song/omanunits.html>.

British Army Field Manual, *Countering Insurgency*, Vol. 1, Part 10 (Warminster: Ministry of Defence, October 2009).

Chatty, Dawn, 'Rituals of Royalty and the Elaboration of Ceremony in Oman: View from the Edge', *International Journal of Middle East Studies* 41, no. 1 (2009): pp. 39–58.

Hoskins, Alan, *A Contract Officer in the Oman* (Tunbridge Wells: Costello, 1988).

Kéchichian, Joseph A., *Oman and the World: The Emergence of an Independent Foreign Policy* (California: Rand, 1995).

Muscat and Oman (Exchange of Letters) *House of Commons Debates*, 16 November 1960, Vol. 630 c36W, <http://hansard.millbanksystems.com/written_answers/1960/nov/16/muscat-and-oman-exchange-of-letters>.

Petersen, Tore T., 'Anglo-American Rivalry in the Middle East: The Struggle for the Buraimi Oasis, 1952–1957', *The International History Review* 14, no. 1 (1992): pp. 71–91.

Peterson, John E., *Defending Arabia* (London: Croom Helm, 1986).

Peterson, John E., 'Oman: The 1966 Assassination Attempt on Sultan Sa'id Bin Taymur', Arabian Peninsula Background Note, No. APBN-004, August 2004, <http://www.jepeterson.net/sitebuildercontent/sitebuilderfiles/APBN-004_Oman_1966_Assassination_Attempt_on_Sultan_Said.pdf>.

Peterson, John E., *Oman's Insurgencies—The Sultanate's Struggle for Supremacy* (London: Saqi Books, 2007).

Rabi, Uzi, *The Emergence of States in a Tribal Society: Oman under Sa'id Bin Taymur, 1932–1970* (Brighton: Sussex Academic Press, 2006).

Richards, Paul, ed., *No Peace, No War: An Anthropology of Armed Conflicts* (Athens, OH: Ohio University Press, 2004).

Smiley, David, *Arabian Assignment* (London: Leo Cooper, 1975).

Worrall, J. E., 'Britain's Last Bastion in Arabia: The End of the Dhofar War, The Labour Government and the Withdrawal from RAF Salalah and Masirah, 1974–1977', in *Challenging Retrenchment in the Middle East*, edited by T. T. Petersen (Trondheim: Tapir Academic Press, 2010), pp. 115–40.

Worrall, J. E., 'The British Historical View of Oman and Ibadism', in *Oman and Overseas*, edited by Michaela Hoffman-ruf and Abdulrahman Al Salimi (New York/Zurich: Olms, 2013), pp. 299–312.

Worrall, J. E., *Policing Oman: From the Oman Gendarmerie to the Royal Oman Police, Britain's Role in the Creation of Internal Security Structures*, Unpublished Conference Paper, 2009.

Worrall, J. E., *Statebuilding and Counterinsurgency in Oman: Political, Military and Diplomatic Relations at the End of Empire* (London: I.B. Tauris, 2014).

7

Vanishing act

Britain's abandonment of Arabia and retreat from the Gulf

Saul Kelly

Introduction

With few exceptions, Britain's abandonment of Arabia and retreat from the Gulf has been presented by contemporary commentators and later historians, in an almost Whiggish or Marxist manner, as a seemingly inevitable result of the retreat of the British Empire in the face of the inexorable march of Arab nationalism.[1] Whereas contemporaries were intent on justifying this flight from Arabia, as a way of covering up their own less than glorious roles, historians have been concerned to chronicle it, sometimes by simply repeating the 'official' line. The last High Commissioner in South Arabia, Sir Humphrey Trevelyan, wrote soon after the event: 'We left without glory but without disaster. Nor was it a humiliation. For our withdrawal was the result not of military or political pressure but of our decision, right or wrong, to leave.... It might have been worse... whatever was to come after us, the time for us to be there was over. And, if we were to go, it was better not to linger on.'[2] Every line of Trevelyan's apologia can be challenged, as can the exculpatory conclusions of a prominent historian on Britain's exit from the Gulf: 'It all turned out... exactly as the British had hoped all along but could hardly

[1] For example, Gillian King, *Imperial Outpost—Aden: Its Place in British Strategic Policy* (Oxford: Oxford University Press, 1965); 'Britain East of Suez', Special Issue of *International Affairs* 42, no. 2 (1966); F. Halliday, *Arabia Without Sultans* (London: Penguin, 1974); Glen Balfour Paul, *The End of Empire in the Middle East* (Cambridge: Cambridge University Press, 1991). For the exception, see J. B. Kelly, *Arabia, the Gulf and the West* (London: Weidenfeld & Nicolson, 1980).

[2] Humphrey Trevelyan, *The Middle East in Revolution* (London: Macmillan, 1970), pp. 263–4.

dare to believe would happen: a new state on good terms with Britain, no sharp breaks or ruptures, and with the new union [of Arab Emirates] still informally within the British imperial system.'[3] Above all, what contemporaries and historians have in common is a desire to present a picture of the British having done 'the right thing' by leaving the inhabitants of southern and eastern Arabia to attend to their own affairs. This attitude is embodied in Trevelyan's remark that '[t]he local boys had made good', a reference to the murderous thugs of the National Liberation Front having seized power in Aden and the hinterland.[4] It is designed to still any qualms about the manner of Britain leaving South Arabia and the Gulf. For, far from being an orderly 'transfer of power', or 'transition' from Britain to the successor states, the British fled Arabia in a mood of panic and confusion. It is not an edifying story, but it needs to be told.

The scuttle: the abandonment of Aden

> Sir Humphrey Trevelyan said... he would not want to be associated with a scuttle on Palestine lines... in no circumstances should we just abdicate.[5]

> Not since the scuttle from the Mandate in Palestine in 1948 had a British attempt at measured and deliberate decolonization ended so abjectly and unceremoniously.[6]

On 27 November 1947 the United Nations (UN) Organisation voted to partition Palestine, and Britain counted down the days to her departure in May 1948, when Arabs and Jews were left to fight it out for the territorial spoils of war, or wars, since the struggle continues to this day as one of the running sores in the Middle East. Twenty years later, on 27 November 1967, Britain left her colony of Aden, in a similar manner, which destabilized Arabia, the Persian Gulf, and the wider region for many decades. There was no proper 'transition' process between the outgoing colonial administration and the new successor government. There was just a hurried evacuation of British personnel and perfunctory

[3] Wm. Roger Louis, 'The British Withdrawal from the Persian Gulf, 1967–71', *The Journal of Imperial and Commonwealth History* 31, no. 1 (2003): pp. 83–108.

[4] Trevelyan, *The Middle East in Revolution*, p. 263.

[5] S. R. Ashton and Wm. Roger Louis, eds, *British Documents on the End of Empire (BDEEP), Series A, Vol. 5, East of Suez and the Commonwealth, 1964–1971, Part 1, East of Suez* (London: The Stationery Office, 2004), p. 239; [Aden]: 'FO record of a meeting between Mr Brown and Sir H. Trevelyan and officials on the conditions under which the UK will withdraw', 6 May 1967, FCO 8/250, no 1, The National Archives (TNA).

[6] Peter Hinchcliffe, *Without Glory in Arabia: The British Retreat from Aden* (London: I.B. Tauris, 2006), p. 1. Peter Hinchcliffe served in Aden and the Federation of South Arabia and was later British Ambassador to Kuwait, High Commissioner to Zambia and Ambassador to Jordan.

arrangements made in Geneva for a hand-over. The departing British High Commissioner, Trevelyan, had never met, let alone negotiated with his successors, the National Liberation Front (NLF), though he did know that they were a violent terrorist group. Britain had only recognized the NLF ten days before it left Aden for ever. Lord Shackleton's delegation to the last-minute hand-over talks in Switzerland (which included discussion of a grant-in-aid) had been surprised to recognize some familiar faces in the NLF delegation, since they had been unaware of the various changes of allegiance during the dying days of the British administration. All this shows that the British government had no real idea who was to succeed them in Aden and South Arabia. It was as if an important landed family had decided it could no longer afford the upkeep on their estate and had decided to abandon it, along with the well-appointed house and the loyal tenant-farmers to the depredations of a roving band of bandits, left the keys in a safe-deposit box in a Swiss bank, and promised to pay protection money! The NLF took up residence in Aden and the hinterland, drove out and often tortured and killed the faithful old British retainers, set up a cult-like Marxist-Leninist regime, became a menace to the neighbourhood and invited in the leaders of the cult, the Chinese and Russian communists, to help spread mayhem in Arabia, the Persian Gulf, the Horn of Africa, and the Indian Ocean. How had this lamentable state of affairs come to pass? Why had the British government allowed itself to be intimidated out of Aden? Why had they simply abandoned their supporters, who had placed faith in Britain's oft reiterated pledges, to their often grisly fate at the hands of these new Jacobins of South Arabia, in what some Britons who had served there called the 'Great Betrayal'?[7] Why had the British government left a strategic vacuum in South Arabia which affected the entire region? It was a major foreign policy reversal for Britain, and yet senior Foreign Office officials had been aware in 1965 of the difficulty of fixing a date for Britain's departure from Aden 'without leaving chaos behind... that we might therefore end up with two power vacuums, one in Aden and one in the Gulf.'[8] Does the reason offered by Trevelyan, quoted above, that it was time for Britain to leave South Arabia stand up to scrutiny? Certainly, the British left 'without glory', but is it true to say that it was 'without disaster' for Britain and the people it left behind? As for it being 'without humiliation', it looks uncannily like those other national humiliations over Palestine and at Suez. In reassessing Britain's abandonment of Aden one can see that it is a story of missed opportunities and of a transition deferred, until final disaster struck. What were the reasons for this catastrophe?

Aden's importance derived from its strategic position at the south-western tip of Arabia, commanding the southern entrance to the Red Sea and the

[7] Hinchcliffe, *Without Glory in Arabia*, p. 6.
[8] Hinchcliffe, *Without Glory in Arabia*, p. 205.

sea-routes to India and the Far East. As such, it served as a bunkering port for commercial shipping and the Royal Navy, as well as an entrepot for the trade of Yemen, South Arabia, Ethiopia, and the Horn of Africa. By 1959, following the Suez debacle and the Cyprus Emergency, it also served as the main British army, naval, and air base in the Middle East. As such, it was the lynch-pin in British strategy east of Suez, as was demonstrated in the deployments to Kuwait in 1961, East Africa in 1964, and to Malaysia and Borneo in the Confrontation with Indonesia between 1961 and 1966. The hinterland of Aden was a harsh, unforgiving land of broken mountains, plateaux, wadis, and deserts. It was inhabited by wild and highly disputatious tribes who, when not scratching a living from the wretched earth were preoccupied with their running feuds. They gave their often perfunctory allegiance to a motley collection of shaikhs, amirs, saiyyids, and sultans. With a rifle in his hands, the tribesman of South Arabia was a natural-born democrat, who believed in the power of the bullet rather than the ballot-box. It was for reasons of the sheer ungovernability of the hinterland that the Government of India, which had annexed Aden in 1839, had shied away from any involvement with the tribes of the interior. In the late nineteenth century, however, the encroachment of the Ottoman Turks from their fastnesses in the High Yemen had led to a modification of India's policy, with a series of treaties being drawn up with the rulers of South Arabia, requiring them to place the conduct of their foreign relations in British India's hands and not to cede any of their territory without prior permission. Responsibility for the observance of these treaties passed from the Government of India and the India Office (its representative department in London) to the British government and the Colonial Office in 1921 as part of the general assumption of control by that department over Middle Eastern affairs after the First World War. It was not until 1937, however, that the Colonial Office forced India to concede control over Aden itself, which became a Crown Colony (although it was an integral 'barbican' and 'sallyport' for the defence of India, and had a large population of Indian merchants), on the grounds that its future lay in integration with the hinterland. In order to achieve this, and to ward off the unwanted territorial claims of the Imam of Yemen and the newly-minted King of Saudi Arabia, the Colonial Office continued its policy of pacifying the hinterland, dividing the protectorate into its western and eastern regions, concluding advisory treaties with the rulers and appointing British political officers as advisers, and raising tribal levies to keep the peace in their districts (such as the Aden Protectorate Levies and the Hadrami Bedouin Legion).

The tribal rulers became increasingly dependent upon advice and subventions from their British advisers to keep their recalcitrant subjects in check. This, and the reform of their tribal councils, the *daulahs*, when combined with the growing, though limited, development aid to the rulers in the 1950s and

1960s, had the unintended effect of undermining the authority and influence of the tribal rulers. It was a critical flaw in Colonial Office policy, which helps explain the collapse of British authority in the protectorates in 1967. This is a point which has been overlooked by most writers on this subject. If anything they argue the exact opposite: that the lack of development in the protectorates had the effect of undermining the shaikhs, and therefore, British rule.[9] But this is to interpret events from a strictly western perspective, which sees development aid as a benevolent act and therefore to be welcomed by the recipient. In fact, it was rejected by the tribesmen as unwarranted interference in their traditional way of life and their desire to use the only political institution open to them, the *daulah*, to arbitrate their disputes over their often hereditary rights and entitlements. By undermining the *daulah* as the only truly functioning instrument of government in the interior, the Colonial Office had made a rod for their own backs.

It was the unwanted attentions of the Colonial Office, rather than the meddling of the Imam of Yemen and the new Egyptian leader, Nasser, which led to the tribal disturbances in the western Protectorate in 1954 and the rejection by the rulers of a proposal for federation. The Colonial Office took the hint and rowed back on its interventionist policy. Federation raised the thorny question of the future of the Aden colony and its relationship with the protected states. Any alteration of Aden's status depended upon its place in Britain's strategic calculations east of Suez, but it was deemed too important in 1956 for the British government to relinquish control for the foreseeable future. This attempt to delay the constitutional advance of Aden was an error since it drove the Sultan of Lahej, in the Western Protectorate, and the South Arabian League into the arms of Nasser and the Yemenis. Despite much that has been written on the subject, there was no great opposition in the colony and the Western Protectorate to a merger, only to its terms.[10] Whereas the protectorate rulers and the leading merchants of Aden wanted a loose grouping, backed by a British defence guarantee, this was rejected by the radical nationalists of the Aden Trade Union Congress (TUC), who wanted to kick the British out, overthrow the rulers and the Imam of Yemen and forge a union with their radical compatriots to the north. The result of this was the separate political development of Aden and the protectorates. Whereas the Federation of the Arab Emirates of the South came into being in 1959, under British treaty guarantees of advice, protection, external and internal defence, and financial, economic, and social aid, the radical nationalists of Aden boycotted the 1959

[9] See: Thomas Mockaitis, *British Counter-Insurgency in the post-imperial era* (Manchester: Manchester University Press, 1995), pp. 45 and 50; Jonathan Walker, *Aden Insurgency: The Savage War in South Arabia, 1962–1967* (Staplehurst: Spellmount, 2005), pp. 286–7.

[10] Hinchcliffe, *Without Glory in Arabia*, pp. 14–15.

elections to the legislative council on the grounds that they were unrepresentative, since their supporters, the migrant Yemeni and Protectorate Arab workers, could not vote (though they had no such right back home). The Governor of Aden, Sir William Luce, put forward a bold plan in the late 1950s for the Colonial Office to grant Aden self-rule and allow it to seek admittance to the Federation. The perceived strategic importance of Aden meant the Macmillan government missed a golden opportunity to establish a federated state in South Arabia, under British protection and influence and with base facilities.[11] Consequently, the task was to devise a formula which would still meet all these requirements and to do so before the local, regional, and international dimensions changed to the detriment of both Britain and South Arabia.

It was not until 26 September 1962 that the Aden legislature voted for the colony's accession to the Federation, despite the violent street protests of the Aden TUC and its political offshoot, the People's Socialist Party (PSP). That very night, an Egyptian-backed army coup in Sana overthrew the new Imam of Yemen and declared a republic. Four of the leaders of the PSP immediately went north to become ministers in the new republican government, to be followed by others after preferment and support for their planned revolution in the south. If the vote had occurred one day later, it is very likely that it would have gone against the merger. It was now a straight fight between the British, to put the federation on its own two feet, and the Yemeni-Adeni nationalists, backed by the Egyptians, to cut it off at the knees. The solution was for the British to give sufficient financial aid and to protect the federation from its enemies. A complacent Colonial Office did neither while, unknown to it, the Adeni adepts of the Arab Nationalist Movement, in exile in Sana, created the National Liberation Front of South Yemen (NLF), dedicated to the destruction of the Federation and British rule, and its replacement by a revolutionary new state. The NLF, with Egyptian backing, chose the tribes of the Radfan, a mountainous area in the amirate of Dhala, on the border with Yemen, to kick off their insurgency on 14 October 1963, a day celebrated ever after as the date of the 'South Yemeni Revolution'.[12]

What was significant about the Radfan uprising was not that the tribes had engaged in their age-old method of airing their grievances, but that the Egyptians were so prepared, through their provision of arms, money, and guidance, to stir up disaffection in the protectorates in order to undermine

[11] On this see: Spencer Mawby, *British Policy in Aden and the Protectorates, 1955–67* (London: Routledge, 2005); Hinchcliffe, *Without Glory in Arabia*, pp. 13–23; David Goldsworthy, ed., *BDEEP, Series A, Vol. 3, The Conservative Government and the End of Empire, 1951–1957, Part 1* (London: The Stationery Office, 1994), p. 143; Ronald Hyam and Wm. Roger Louis, eds, *BDEEP, Series A, Vol. 4, The Conservative Government and the End of Empire, 1957–1964, Part 1* (London: The Stationery Office, 2000), pp. lvi–lvii, 17, 557–98.

[12] Noel Brehony, *Yemen Divided: The Story of a Failed State in South Arabia* (London: I.B. Tauris, 2011), p. 19.

the British position in South Arabia. Behind the Egyptians were the Soviets, who had provided the military hardware and air transport for Nasser's foray into the Yemen.[13]

The new Governor of Aden and High Commissioner of the protectorates, Sir Kennedy Trevaskis, was aware from his long service in the Western Protectorate that the battle for South Arabia would be won or lost in the protectorates. It was for this reason that he persuaded Duncan Sandys, the Colonial Secretary, that if Nasser's subversive campaign was to be defeated, then Britain would have to cede sovereignty over Aden (except the base areas) and confer independence upon South Arabia. If the Adeni nationalists had truly believed in independence per se, they would have welcomed the decision. But they were not free agents. The leader of the PSP, Abdullah al-Asnag, had been instructed on his frequent trips to Cairo in 1963 to continue the campaign to drive the British out of South Arabia, a campaign given vocal support by Britain's enemies in the United Nations and Europe. Sandys's offer was greeted with a general strike in Aden and, in December, by an assassination attempt on the life of Trevaskis as he was about to board an aircraft at Khormaksar airport, en route to London for the constitutional conference to fix the date of South Arabia's independence. Trevaskis and his wife cheated death but his deputy, George Henderson, and an Indian woman bystander were not so lucky. The result of this grenade attack was the imposition of a state of emergency in Aden and the suspension of the Trevaskis/Sandys plan. The transition had been deferred yet again.

Nevertheless, the Egyptian-inspired Radfan uprising had been fought to a standstill in June 1964 by British and federal troops, despite the attempt by the NLF, and some historians, to argue otherwise.[14] Moreover, Trevaskis was hopeful of the ultimate success of his secret campaign against the Egyptians and the Republicans in Yemen through cross-border sabotage and subversion. In the summer of 1964 the delayed constitutional conference meeting in London set the date of 1968 for independence for South Arabia. It was now a race against time to strengthen the federation so that it could survive as a new state. Any chance that this would happen vanished with the Labour Party coming to power in Britain in October 1964.[15]

The Labour government of Harold Wilson was ideologically predisposed to favour the nationalist and socialist aspirations of the radical politicians and trade unionists of Aden over the interests of the hereditary rulers of the

[13] See: Jesse Ferris, 'Soviet support for Egypt's intervention in Yemen, 1962–1963', *Journal of Cold War Studies* 10, no. 4 (2008): pp. 5–36.

[14] Mockaitis, *British Counter-Insurgency in the Post-Imperial Era*, pp. 54–5; David French, *Army, Empire and Cold War* (Oxford: Oxford University Press, 2012), p. 289; David French, *The British Way in Counter-Insurgency, 1945–67* (Oxford: Oxford University Press, 2001), pp. 239–41.

[15] Hyam and Louis, *The Conservative Government and the End of Empire*, pp. lvii–lviii, 596–646.

protectorates. Labour politicians had made this clear, not only in their protests in Parliament against the detainment of nationalists during the state of emergency, but in their various visits to Aden while in opposition at the invitation of the PSP (in particular, George Thomson, later Minister of State at the Foreign Office and subsequently Secretary of State for Commonwealth Affairs, became the party's trouble-shooter on Aden).[16] The day before the British general election, a grimly farcical election had taken place in Aden which, despite the nationalist boycott, had led to the election as an 'independent' of the incarcerated Khalifah Abdullah Hasan al-Khalifah, the would-be assassin of Trevaskis and the actual murderer of George Henderson. Understandably Trevaskis refused to bow to the nationalist clamour for al-Khalifah's release, but the new Colonial Secretary, Arthur Greenwood had no such qualms and, as an act of goodwill, allowed al-Khalifah to go free and take up his seat on the legislative council. This slap in the face for Trevaskis was followed by his sacking in late 1964 when he refused, on the grounds that it would lead to anarchy in South Arabia, to carry out Greenwood's new policy of courting the radical nationalists of the Aden TUC and the PSP. In order to achieve this, the Labour Cabinet ministers, Greenwood, Healey, Stewart, and Gordon-Walker were prepared to promise a military withdrawal from the Aden base and a unitary state.[17] This was a repeat of the mistake that Attlee's government had made in 1946 of promising the withdrawal of military forces from the Suez Canal Zone base, which became the default position of the Egyptians in all subsequent negotiations over a defence treaty.

The futility of such a policy of surrender was amply demonstrated during the course of 1965 as the PSP committed itself to a terrorist strategy in Aden and the Federation, in order not only to put pressure on the British but to compete with the NLF for the shifting allegiance of the Adeni 'street' and the tribesmen of the interior. As Nasser sought an exit strategy from his disastrous foray into the Yemen, and at the same time to maintain control over the terrorist campaign against the British in South Arabia, he presided over the amalgamation of the PSP with the South Arabian League (SAL) in May 1965 to form the Organisation for the Liberation of the Occupied South (OLOS). A disappointed Greenwood sought to win back the PSP by inviting Asnag and his high command to a constitutional conference in London in August 1965, only for Asnag to stage a walk-out and return to Cairo to direct OLOS's terror operations in Aden, leading to the murder of the speaker of the legislative assembly and the superintendent of police. The British government responded by suspending Aden's constitution and restoring direct rule, much to the regret

[16] Mawby, *British Policy in Aden and the Protectorates, 1955–67*, p. 93.

[17] Mawby, *British Policy in Aden and the Protectorates, 1955–67*, pp. 129–30; Ashton and Louis, *East of Suez and the Commonwealth, 1964–1971*, pp. xlvi–xlvii and cxxvi–cxxvii.

of Greenwood, the delight of the nationalists, and the dismay of the federal rulers. In effect, the Wilson government had declared war on the nationalists, whom they had been courting for the past year. The question now was whether they had the will to see it through.

The answer came swiftly on 22 February 1966 in the form of the announcement in the British Parliament by the Secretary of State for Defence, Denis Healey, as part of a sweeping defence review of the position east of Suez, that Britain would withdraw from Aden colony and base by the end of 1968. This had been under serious consideration in Whitehall for the previous year. The killer blow, however, was that Britain would not defend the South Arabian Federation after independence. This was not only in direct contravention of the public statements made by Lord Beswick (a junior minister at the Colonial Office) in November 1965, and Healey himself in January 1966, but the pledges made by the British government in 1959, when the Federation came into being, which were reiterated following the constitutional conference in London in July–August 1964. When Duncan Sandys drew this to the attention of the House of Commons, Healey tried to brush it aside, only to have to apologise the next day for having misled the House.[18] Healey's announcement effectively destroyed the last vestiges of British authority in South Arabia. Terrorist incidents multiplied at a time when the British security forces found themselves hampered by a lack of intelligence on the competing terrorist bands run by OLOS and the NLF, as well as concern by international bodies such as the Red Cross over internment procedures. Nasser reversed his pull-out from the Yemen, realizing that he had only to maintain a footprint there to claim the credit for the British withdrawal from South Arabia. As if to celebrate the moment he presided over the merger of Asnag's OLOS with Qahtan al-Shaabi's NLF into the deceivingly harmless FLOSY, the Front for the Liberation of South Yemen (though the Marxist-Leninist wing of the NLF was to split away later in the year). Seeing the writing on the wall, King Faisal of Saudi Arabia refrained from giving material and financial help to the now stricken South Arabian state.[19]

Having signalled its intention to abandon the Federation to its fate, the Labour government was without any policy worthy of the name. All it could do was to impose strictures on the operation of the security forces in Aden and the hinterland. Its weakness was reflected in its desperate diplomacy: the appeasement by the new Foreign Secretary, George Brown, of his 'great friend' Nasser; Thomson's fruitless pursuit of the Adeni nationalists; the British government's acceptance in May 1966, as the Foreign Office assumed responsibility for South Arabia from the Colonial Office (which became the Commonwealth Office), of a UN resolution calling for UN supervised elections, always a sign of

[18] Hinchcliffe, *Without Glory in Arabia*, pp. 207–11.
[19] Ashton and Louis, *East of Suez and the Commonwealth, 1964–1971*, pp. xlvi–xlvii, 185–9.

Britain losing her grip (as over Palestine and Cyprus); the UN mission to South Arabia in April 1967 (which ended in farce when the FLOSY refused to have anything to do with them); the Foreign Office's despatch of the Labour MP, and KGB-MI5 double-agent Tom Driberg, to the Yemen and the Sudan to win over FLOSY 'moderates'; Lord Shackleton's visit to Aden the same month which betrayed the Federal rulers by advancing the date of withdrawal to January 1968; and Trevelyan's appointment in May as the last High Commissioner, on the understanding of no 'scuttle', as in Palestine, and an orderly withdrawal of British military and civil personnel.[20] Trevelyan made his task harder by lifting the ban on the NLF, which unsurprisingly led to a spike in the incidence of murder and robbery in Aden to fund their terror campaign.

The British government did not have the will to grab the opportunity offered by Nasser's catastrophic defeat at the hands of Israel in the June 1967 War to reverse course and restore order and security in South Arabia. As a sop to King Faisal, however, who had warned Prime Minister Wilson of the dire consequences for Arabia and the Gulf of the British withdrawal from Aden, Brown announced on 20 June a series of defence measures for the 'transition' period which were intended to still the concerns of the Federal rulers and the Saudis, and at the same time secure a lucrative new defence contract with the desert kingdom.[21] Brown's proposed measures, based on Trevelyan's withdrawal plan, were rendered more or less irrelevant on the very day they were made by the mutiny of elements of the South Arabian Army, the South Arabian Police, and the Aden Police in the colony which led to the deaths of 22 British soldiers and the wounding of 31 more. Trevelyan refused to allow either the South Arabian Federal forces, who were eager to reclaim their tarnished honour but whom he did not trust, or the Argyll and Sutherland Highlanders, who had lost men to ambush, to restore civil order in Crater, the most affected area in Aden. Trevelyan and his advisers feared a massacre of British personnel not only in Aden but up-country. That his fears were unfounded was shown by the easy re-entry into Crater on 3 July of the Argylls, accompanied by their intrepid commander Colonel Colin, 'Mad Mitch', Mitchell, to the skirl of the bagpipes, and their keeping the peace there for the next four and a half months. Labour's revenge for Mad Mitch's initiative was to indulge in carping criticism of the methods employed by the Argylls and to threaten the regiment with disbandment in 1968.[22] Trevelyan

[20] See George Brown, *In My Way: The Political Memoirs of Lord George-Brown* (London: Gollancz, 1971), p. 14; Christopher Andrew and Oleg Gordievsky, *KGB: The Inside Story* (London: Hodder & Stoughton, 1990), p. 434; Mawby, *British Policy in Aden and the Protectorates, 1955–67*, pp. 154–7; Ashton and Louis, *East of Suez and the Commonwealth, 1964–1971*, pp. xlvii, 211–27.

[21] Hinchcliffe, *Without Glory in Arabia*, pp. 56–74; Mawby, *British Policy in Aden and the Protectorates, 1955–67*, pp. 157–8.

[22] See: Mawby, *British Policy in Aden and the Protectorates, 1955–67*, p. 169.

later justified his inaction in Crater by coming up with a novel doctrine whereby diplomats were expected to protect British forces from harm, rather than the other way around. It is a doctrine which has been used by subsequent generations of British diplomats to justify British military withdrawal from a theatre of operations, the latest example being during the Iraq War in 2009.

At the end of June 1967 an increasingly terrified Trevelyan quietly advanced the date of the British evacuation from South Arabia to 20 November 1967.[23] On cue, the NLF opened their final offensive to topple the Federal rulers. With the collapse of the Federal government by 5 September, Trevelyan recognized the NLF (with only a few thousand fighters) and FLOSY (with not many more) as the 'representatives' of the people of South Arabia and indicated his willingness to discuss with them the transfer of sovereignty. Ignoring Trevelyan as an irrelevance to the outcome, the NLF, now with the support of the South Arabian Army whom it had successfully subverted, fought and beat FLOSY for the prize of being the successor to the *ancien regime*. The tangle that Trevelyan had got himself into, and the depths to which he had sunk, was shown by his threat to launch RAF bombing runs against the Shaikh of Beihan if he sought to regain his patrimony from the NLF, which had seized it with the aid of the South Arabian Army. Trevelyan's logic also led him to sanction RAF strikes against a FLOSY raiding party crossing the Yemen border. Well might the Sharif of Beihan ruefully remark that: 'In any dealing with the British it is better to be their enemy than their friend. If you are their friend, they will sell you. If you are their enemy there is a good chance they will buy you.'[24] The final act was announced by Brown in the House of Commons on 2 November 1967, when he relayed the Cabinet's decision to evacuate British personnel from Aden that month and to enter into negotiations with the NLF (in Geneva) for the transfer of power. The strange nature of those final proceedings has been remarked upon earlier in this chapter, as was also shown in the manner of Trevelyan's departure on 28 November and his birthday review of a fleet the size of the one assembled for the Suez operation in 1956. The irony of this was not lost on the Royal Marines bandsmen as they played out Trevelyan to the tune of 'Things Ain't What they Used to Be'.[25] *Sic transit imperium.*

It is understandable, if hardly laudable, that Trevelyan should have wanted, writing shortly after the event, to put the best spin possible on the inglorious end to British rule in South Arabia. But the reasons he gave for the abruptness of that leave-taking do not stand up to scrutiny. In short, it was a disaster, not only for Britain's loyal supporters in South Arabia but for Britain and her

[23] Ashton and Louis, *East of Suez and the Commonwealth, 1964–1971*, pp. li, 255–66.
[24] Brehony, *Yemen Divided*, p. 221, n.7.
[25] A song from a popular musical of the day. The Argylls preferred 'the Barren Rocks of Aden'. It is worth noting, as if in riposte to the Trevelyan 'doctrine', that the last British forces (Royal Marine Commandos) were the last to leave Aden, the next day.

Western allies. It was not only the Federal rulers who had to flee for their lives from the NLF to Saudi Arabia and other countries, but some 200,000 of their subjects (out of a population of 700,000 in the old protectorates). Moreover, it says much about the nature the new regime of the People's Republic of South Yemen (PRSY) that nearly two-thirds of the population of Aden (some 140,000 out of 220,000) felt the need to take flight as well, leaving the port a shell of its former self, coinciding as it did with the closure of the Suez Canal as a result of the 1967 War. This did not dissuade the Soviet Union from sending a flotilla of warships to Aden in June 1968 (and again in January 1969) and signing a technical and military agreement with the new regime, which provided for the supply of Soviet arms and advisors. Both the Soviets and the Communist Chinese were quick to encourage the PRSY in their support of the Dhofari rebels in their insurgency against the Sultan of Oman. Britain's precipitate departure, or scuttle, from South Arabia, had provided the West's Cold War enemies with a golden strategic opportunity to control one of the world's great choke-points, the entrance to the Red Sea. They were quick to take advantage of it in the coming decades, from Oman and the Gulf, to the Horn of Africa and the Indian Ocean. It was a strategic reversal and humiliation, for Britain and her Western allies, especially the United States, no matter how much Trevelyan and other apologists might have tried to cover it up. The Foreign and Commonwealth Office were aware of the serious consequences of leaving Aden, and that it would leave a strategic vacuum in both South Arabia and the Gulf. Britain and her allies, both in Arabia, the Gulf and further afield, were to pay dearly for this, as will be shown in the next section.

The double-cross: the retreat from the Gulf

> Britain will stay in the Persian Gulf as long as necessary to maintain peace and stability, and the states on both sides of the Gulf understand and appreciate this policy.[26]

> We have decided to withdraw our forces from the Persian Gulf... [by the end of 1971][27]

On the very day, 30 October 1967, that the Labour Cabinet confirmed that Britain would leave Aden the following month, it despatched its Minister of State for Foreign Affairs, Goronwy Roberts, to the Gulf to convey this decision

[26] Goronwy Roberts, Minister of State for Foreign Affairs, 13 November 1967, as quoted in Kelly, *Arabia, the Gulf and the West*, p. 48.

[27] Harold Wilson, Prime Minister, 16 January 1968, *Parliamentary Debates (Hansard): House of Commons Official Report, 5th Series* (London: Her Majesty's Stationery Office), vol. 756, col. 1580.

to the local Rulers and to reassure them that this did not mean a similar abandonment of Britain's responsibilities there, namely the protection of her large oil interests and her treaty commitments. The last entailed British responsibility for the defence and foreign affairs of the protected states of the Sultanate of Muscat and Oman, the seven shaikhdoms of the Trucial Coast (so-named after their agreement to the truces enforced by Britain against piracy and maritime warfare in the nineteenth century), Bahrain, and Qatar.[28] Roberts visited the Gulf shaikhdoms and Iran, and gave a press conference on 13 November at which he stated: 'Britain will stay in the Persian Gulf as long as is necessary to maintain peace and stability, and the states on both sides of the Gulf understand and appreciate this policy.'[29] Other Labour ministers had made similar statements during the course of 1967.[30] Yet just over two months later, on Tuesday, 16 January 1968, Prime Minister Wilson, stood up in the House of Commons and announced that the British government had 'decided to withdraw our forces from the Persian Gulf', as well as the Far East (with the exception of Hong Kong) by the end of 1971.[31] Why had the Labour government decided to go back on its promises so soon after giving them? And what were the effects in the Gulf of such a momentous decision on what has been called 'Black Tuesday', which the Permanent Under-Secretary at the Foreign and Commonwealth Office (FCO), Sir Paul Gore-Booth, regarded as tantamount to 'the abandonment of our claim to be a world *power*...'?[32] Others in the Office, responsible for Gulf affairs, referred to it as 'the double-cross'.[33]

The answer to the conundrum about the Labour government reneging on its successive promises to stay in the Gulf lies in the very statements made by ministers from April to December 1967. They were all intended to conceal the fact that the government was preparing to withdraw from the Gulf all along. After the Cabinet approved on 11 April Denis Healey's radical ideas for the rundown of British forces east of Suez, especially in the Far East, Denis Healey had stated in the House of Commons that: 'The Gulf is an area of such vital importance not only to Western Europe as a whole but also to world peace that it would be totally irresponsible for us to withdraw our forces from the

[28] Kuwait achieved independence in 1961 but the instrument abrogating the 1899 and 1914 protectorate agreements with Britain contained a stipulation that the latter would extend a helping hand if necessary (i.e. in the event of an irredentist threat from Iraq, as indeed happened in 1961).

[29] Kelly, *Arabia, the Gulf and the West*, p. 48.

[30] Healey in April, Brown in July, and Wilson in December 1967. See Kelly, *Arabia, the Gulf and the West*, pp. 47–8.

[31] *Parliamentary Debates*, vol. 756, col. 1580.

[32] Cited in Jeffrey Pickering, 'Politics and "Black Tuesday": Shifting Power in the Cabinet and the decision to Withdraw from East of Suez, November 1967–January 1968', *Twentieth Century British History* 13, no. 2 (2002): p. 168.

[33] Louis, 'The British Withdrawal from the Persian Gulf, 1967–71', p. 88.

area.'[34] Despite such platitudes, withdrawal was under active consideration by the government at this time. The only difference of opinion was over when this should occur. The Political Resident in the Persian Gulf, Sir Stewart Crawford, favoured a slow hand-over in the Gulf and 'a smooth transition from one security system to another'. He was against fixing a date for withdrawal because it would 'frighten the Rulers and reduce their readiness to co-operate with us in developing their States to the point where they no longer needed our protection'. He believed that it would also spark Arab nationalist propaganda and subversion and remove any chance of settling the outstanding territorial disputes between the Gulf states, leaving a legacy of instability.[35] In contrast, the Defence Review Working Party for the Official Defence and Overseas Policy Committee of the Cabinet, in a report of 7 June (largely drafted by the FCO), talked about a British withdrawal by the mid-1970s:

> After our decision to withdraw militarily as well as politically from Aden by 1968, no one really believes that we shall be able (or even wish) to stay indefinitely in the Gulf. By the mid-1970s we must expect a world where almost all colonial and quasi-colonial traces have disappeared and the overseas deployment of British power has contracted further than at present. If we have not gone from the Gulf, the pressures on us to go are likely to be very severe indeed.[36]

The imminent loss of the Aden base was already beginning to have an effect on attitudes towards the military viability of Britain's long-term future in the Gulf. This played into the hands of the Treasury which, since 1960, had been sceptical about the need for a continued defence commitment in the Gulf, believing that ordinary commercial rules would protect Britain's large oil interests there (they were to be rudely disabused of this notion during the oil price shocks of the 1970s).[37] But there was no mention of withdrawal from the Gulf in the Supplementary Defence White Paper of 18 July, which announced the 'rebalancing' of forces in Malaysia and Singapore.[38] Yet such left-wing stalwarts of the Labour Cabinet as Tony Benn, Richard Crossman, and Barbara Castle regarded this as the moment when the tocsin sounded for the death of 'the British Empire east of Suez'.[39] Still, the Foreign Secretary,

[34] As quoted in Kelly, *Arabia, the Gulf and the West*, p. 47.

[35] Simon C. Smith, *Britain's Revival and Fall in the Gulf* (London: Routledge, 2004), pp. 69–70.

[36] Smith, *Britain's Revival and Fall in the Gulf*, p. 27; for a later version of this report, incorporating this wording and also reflecting Crawford's views, see: Ashton and Louis, *East of Suez and the Commonwealth, 1964–1971*, doc. 118, pp. 403–19.

[37] Smith, *Britain's Revival and Fall in the Gulf*, p. 28; and Gill Bennett, *Six Moments of Crisis: Inside Foreign Policy* (Oxford: Oxford University Press, 2013), p. 97.

[38] This White Paper is seen as critical for pointing towards the withdrawal east of Suez by Saki Dockrill in *Britain's Retreat from East of Suez* (Basingstoke: Palgrave Macmillan, 2002), pp. 193–9; Smith, *Britain's Revival and Fall in the Gulf*, pp. 51ff; and John W. Young, *The Labour Governments, 1964–1970: International Policy*, vol. 2 (Manchester: Manchester University Press, 2003), pp. 55–6.

[39] As quoted in Young, *The Labour Governments, 1964–1970*, p. 49.

George Brown, could state in a debate in the House of Commons on 20 July that: 'In the present disturbed situation in the Middle East we must be particularly concerned about the stability and security of the Gulf area, for which we still have treaty responsibilities. . . . Our forces are not in the Persian Gulf simply to protect our oil interests as such, but to maintain stability in the area.'[40] This was the reassuring message that Roberts took to the Gulf in November, even though the FCO knew that it and the Ministry of Defence (MOD) were working towards a simultaneous military and political withdrawal from the Gulf by the mid-1970s at the latest, and earlier 'if the course of events permits'. Any public announcement to this effect, however, was adjudged to be:

> politically disastrous. Coming so soon after our assurances at the time of the Defence Review that we were determined to uphold our Gulf commitments it would destroy the Rulers' confidence in Her Majesty's Government and reduce their readiness to co-operate with us in developing their states to the point where we can disengage in good order.[41]

What precipitated the actual decision, publicly announced by Wilson on 16 January 1968, to bring forward the withdrawal from the Gulf from the mid-1970s to the end of 1971, was of course the currency crisis in the autumn of 1967 which led to the devaluation of the pound on 18 November and cuts in public expenditure in order to secure a loan from the International Monetary Fund. The financial crisis had been caused, in part, by the reduction of oil supplies from the Gulf during the June 1967 Arab-Israeli War. This fact, which emphasized the need for security of supply, seems to have eluded the mandarins of the Treasury. The crisis gave the Treasury primacy in the determination of the timing, nature, and 'narrative' on the withdrawal from the Gulf. The actual cost of the British military presence in the Gulf was minor (some £12 million in foreign exchange costs and £25 million in budgetary costs) when compared with the envisaged cuts in social expenditure of some £606 million. In order to persuade the Parliamentary Labour Party and the electorate of the need for swingeing cuts in social expenditure, however, the officials at the Treasury as well as the Labour Cabinet, coaxed along by Wilson and his new Chancellor of the Exchequer, Roy Jenkins, dressed up the fairly minor cuts in defence expenditure in the next few financial years as bigger than they were (especially if the projected £400 million cost of the F-111 strike aircraft was included), describing it in dramatic terms of the withdrawal from 'east of Suez'. This meant, in the main, the pull-out from Malaysia and Singapore. The Gulf was thrown in for good measure, almost as an afterthought! (It should be

[40] As quoted in Kelly, *Arabia, the Gulf and the West*, pp. 47–8.
[41] Ashton and Louis, *East of Suez and the Commonwealth, 1964–1971*, doc. 118, pp. 413–15.

noted, however, that the Cabinet was quite prepared to subsidize the new Marxist-Leninist regime in South Yemen to the tune of £12 million, though it is not clear how much of this was eventually forthcoming).[42] The date fixed for the withdrawal from the Gulf, namely the end of 1971, represented a compromise between the Treasury, who wanted to go by April 1971, and the FCO and MOD, who attempted to hold out for a March 1972 departure. The actual decision to leave the Gulf by the end of 1971 was made, therefore, for domestic political reasons, which destroys the long-lasting myth that it was primarily due to financial and economic considerations.[43] Although the Labour Cabinet was constitutionally responsible for this momentous decision, it is clear that certain Treasury, FCO, and MOD permanent officials were not only behind it but believed in its necessity and provided the necessary policy justifications to their political masters for public consumption.

The Americans were appalled by the British decision, about which they had not been consulted. The fait accompli by Brown, on a flying visit to Washington in January 1968 was too much for the US Secretary of State, Dean Rusk, who had feared such a decision for several years, yet urged Brown: 'For God's sake, act like Britain.' For President Johnson this was 'tantamount to British withdrawal from world affairs'.[44] His Administration had no intention of replacing Britain in the Gulf, although they were aware that the Soviets might take advantage of any opportunities to increase their influence in the region. The State Department impressed upon the British Embassy in Washington the importance of maintaining its political and economic, if not military, presence in the Gulf. American concerns may have delayed Britain's departure by a few months, but they did not alter the decision or its implementation. Neither Wilson, his Cabinet, nor the FCO, seemed to be especially concerned at the reaction from Washington, and the latter's downgrading of the Anglo-American 'special relationship'. There was even a detectable trace of exuberant defiance by Wilson that Britain was now free to seek a new role in the world, one that centred on Europe rather than east of Suez.

That was not a prospect that appealed to Lee Kuan Yew, the Prime Minister of Singapore, who flew to London to berate the Wilson government for their failure of will in an unsuccessful attempt to have them reverse the decision. The rulers of the Gulf were stunned by it, conveyed as it was by Roberts who seems to have flown back to the Gulf to perform this invidious task as a matter

[42] Brehony, *Yemen Divided*, pp. 29, 33, 43; Bennett, *Six Moments of Crisis*, p. 115.

[43] See: Shohei Sato, 'Britain's decision to withdraw from the Persian Gulf, 1964–68: A pattern and a puzzle', *The Journal of Imperial and Commonwealth History* 37, no. 1 (2009): pp. 107–8. I well remember, in answer to my enquiry about the decision on withdrawal from the Gulf, this hoary old myth being trotted out in the mid-1990s by a distant relative by marriage, Lord ('Jack') Diamond, the former Chief Secretary to the Treasury, who was present at the relevant series of Cabinet meetings held in January 1968.

[44] Smith, *Britain's Revival and Fall in the Gulf*, pp. 132–7.

of 'honour'. The Political Agent in Bahrain, Anthony Parsons, thought Roberts did not understand the magnitude of his new message to the al-Khalifah, as to other rulers in the Gulf: 'The Ruler and his brothers consider that they have been betrayed by an unvarnished volte face only two months after the reassurance of November 1967; and that they are being faced with the sudden and unilateral termination of 150 years of mutual relationship with no warning or genuine consultation'. They accurately predicted the fall-out from this decision, being 'highly sceptical of the chances of the Gulf States getting together to form a meaningful unity or of Iran allowing Bahrain to be included in any Gulf-wide mutual security system'. The Gulf rulers thought the precipitate departure date provided a 'derisory period' in which to resolve the long-standing territorial disputes and claims and to set up any sort of defensive system, given that none of the states concerned could defend themselves.[45] Shaikh Sabah of Kuwait was concerned that the British withdrawal would 'make way for Soviet influence, which was already spreading fast in the Yemeni Republic and South Yemen'.[46] Yet when the Gulf Rulers offered to subsidize the costs of the continued British military presence in the Gulf, the proposal was dismissed by Denis Healey on the grounds that: 'I don't very much like the idea of being a sort of white slaver for Arab sheikhs.... I think it would be a great mistake if we allowed ourselves to become mercenaries for people who like to have a few British troops around.' Ironically, he did not have the same qualms about taking local money to maintain the garrisons in West Germany and Hong Kong. But Healey's boorish, and offensive remarks, for which he was forced to apologise, reflected a wider feeling within Whitehall (in the FCO, the MOD, and especially the Treasury) that 'it was a mistake to get ourselves into a position of dependence on the Rulers which acceptance of the offer would imply'.[47]

The effect of the announcement of Britain's decision to withdraw from its military bases in the Gulf was to lift the lid on the endemic rivalries in the region which made British disengagement, in terms of a military and political transition, all the harder. First, there was the question of whether Britain was also intending to terminate its treaties of protection with the Gulf shaikhdoms, which underwrote these statelets, and if so what would replace them? The head of the FCO's Arabian Department, M. S. Weir, thought there was 'no question of trying, or even being thought to be trying, to promote another "Whitehall Federation" on the lines of South Arabia', but the shock of the announcement of Britain's withdrawal did have the effect of persuading the rulers to look again at the idea of a Federation of Arab Emirates, which came

[45] Smith, *Britain's Revival and Fall in the Gulf*, p. 73.
[46] Smith, *Britain's Revival and Fall in the Gulf*, p. 74.
[47] Smith, *Britain's Revival and Fall in the Gulf*, p. 76.

into being in name only on 30 March 1968.[48] It immediately evoked a reaction from Iran, which restated its dubious historical claim to Bahrain.[49] This second factor was to impede the progress of the Gulf shaikhdoms towards federation since Qatar and the Trucial shaikhs were loathe to enter into any association with Bahrain which might require them to support the al-Khalifah family against Iran. They also feared that Bahrain would dominate such a federation, given its greater population, and its educated and wealthy merchant class. Thirdly, there were the old quarrels and enmities which divided the shaikhdoms and made the chances of political union seem remote. These antipathies centred on territorial disputes, between Bahrain and Qatar over the Hawar Islands and Zubarah; between Qatar and Abu Dhabi over the Khaur al-Udaid; between Abu Dhabi and Dubai over the alignment of their border; over the Buraimi Oasis divided between Abu Dhabi and Muscat/Oman but claimed by Saudi Arabia. For their part, both Bahrain and Qatar were reluctant to support Abu Dhabi against Saudi Arabia. These rivalries determined the dynamics of the meetings held in 1968 to try and hammer out the future shape of the Federation (later Union) of Arab Emirates (UAE). Fourthly, there was the declaration by the opposition Conservative Party in Britain that, if it won the next general election, it would reverse the Labour government's decision on military withdrawal from the Gulf. This led the Gulf rulers to expect continued British protection and to drag their feet on federation. The former High Commissioner in Aden, Trevaskis, on a fact-finding tour for the Conservatives in the Gulf in November 1968 did not conceal his doubts about the future of the UAE from Shaikh Rashid of Dubai, comparing it to the ill-starred South Arabian Federation. The Political Agent in Bahrain, Parsons, thought it likely that Trevaskis, in his report to the Conservative leadership, would 'probably be anti-UAE, pro a pattern of mini-states and... encouraging as regards a reversal of the decision to withdraw if the Conservatives win the next general election'.[50] Not to be outdone, Trevaskis told Shaikh Isa of Bahrain that Parsons was 'a slave of the Labour Party, and cannot speak his own mind... '.[51] Whatever Trevaskis may have told the Conservatives on his return, the FCO diplomats in the Gulf gave the Leader of the Opposition, Edward Heath, a rough ride when he toured the Gulf in March 1969, accompanied by his private secretary (and later a Conservative Foreign Secretary),

48 Smith, *Britain's Revival and Fall in the Gulf*, p. 77.

49 On this see: S. B. Kelly, ed., *Fighting the Retreat from Arabia and the Gulf: The Collected Essays and Reviews of J.B. Kelly*, vol. 1 (London: New English Review Press, 2013), chapters 3 and 7.

50 Smith, *Britain's Revival and Fall in the Gulf*, p. 34.

51 Louis, 'The British Withdrawal from the Persian Gulf, 1967–71', p. 104, n.16. It is clear from his memoir, *They Say the Lion: Britain's Legacy to the Arabs* (London: J. Cape, 1986), p. 107, that Parsons was against Britain's continued 'imperial' presence in the Gulf.

Douglas Hurd.[52] The diplomats were worried that any pledge by Heath to reverse, when in government, the decision to withdraw would remove the incentive of the rulers towards federation, arouse Arab nationalist, Saudi, and Iranian opposition and lead to 'an Aden-type situation'.[53]

The FCO were not the only ones to be worried that Britain might not leave the Gulf on time. The Shah, encouraged by the British Ambassador in Tehran, Denis Wright, broke the deadlock resulting from his reassertion of the Iranian claim to Bahrain, which in turn impeded progress on federation, by agreeing on 9 March 1970 to the implementation of the Anglo-Iranian accord of December 1969 calling for an UN-supervised referendum to be held on the future of Bahrain. This resulted, in April, in an overwhelming vote in favour of independence, which was endorsed by the UN Security Council the following month. Although the FCO had successfully removed one obstacle to Britain's exit from the Gulf, others remained. One lay in the Saudi threat to the Shaikh Zayid of Abu Dhabi in May 1970 to refuse to recognize the federation unless the latter met Saudi territorial claims to a great swathe of Abu Dhabi, from Khaur al-Udaid in the west, to the Batin-Liwa tract in the south (where lay the newly-discovered al-Shaiba/Zarrara oil structure), to the Buraimi Oasis in the northeast.[54] The FCO proceeded to bring pressure on Shaikh Zayid to accede to Saudi claims, even though in doing so Britain was contravening the terms of her own, still existing, treaty rights and obligations to Abu Dhabi.

Whatever Heath and the Conservative Party might think about the future of Britain's position in the Gulf, the FCO had plotted its exit strategy and intended to adhere to it. This became a live question when the Conservatives unexpectedly won the June 1970 election and came to power. They had pledged both in their election manifesto and their address in reply to the Queen's Speech on 6 July not to shirk Britain's responsibilities in the Gulf. Yet it is clear that the new Foreign Secretary, Sir Alec Douglas-Home, did not know at first how best to proceed. He turned for answers to an old Gulf hand, the former Political Resident, Sir William Luce, whom he sent to consult the Rulers in the summer of 1970. Both Luce and his former colleagues in the 'Office' presented a united front to Home, arguing against a reversal of the decision on withdrawal, or even a postponement, as it would remove the incentive of the Rulers to look to organize their own futures. It would also run contrary to the opinions of the

[52] Hurd, a former diplomat, seems to have been bruised by this encounter with the denizens of the Office, and seems to have rowed back on his initial support for Heath's inclination to reverse Labour's decision to withdraw from the Gulf. For his ex-post-facto, and mildly defeatist justification of withdrawal, as being in 'the spirit of the age', see: Douglas Hurd, *An End to Promises: A Sketch of Government* (London: Collins, 1979), p. 46.

[53] As expressed by Roberts. See Hurd, *An End to Promises*, p. 34.

[54] It is hard to agree, therefore, with Louis ('The British Withdrawal from the Persian Gulf, 1967–71', p. 101) that the British calculation that the Saudis would remain 'inert' over Buraimi proved to be correct.

Shah of Iran, the King of Saudi Arabia, and Colonel Nasser of Egypt, whom the FCO were anxious to appease in the expectation, unwarranted as it proved, that these regional powers would guarantee the future stability of the Gulf. This convenient illusion led Luce and the FCO (who, at heart, knew better) to make another leap of faith, arguing against any specific new British defence commitment in the Gulf after the military withdrawal and the termination of the exclusive agreements (of protection) by the end of 1971. Luce went so far as to predict that 'there is very unlikely to be any identifiable threat of external aggression (including support by a contiguous territory of internal revolt) against which it could be in HMG's interest to undertake a defence commitment to the Union [UAE]'.[55] That this prediction did not even survive contact with reality before Britain left the Gulf, let alone after it, did not dissuade the FCO from its chosen course. It succeeded, given Luce's stature, in convincing Heath that his government should force the Rulers to unite and 'make it clear to them that we could not remain in the Gulf on the present footing'.[56] Announcing this decision to the House of Commons on 1 March 1971, Douglas-Home stated that the Conservative government would offer a Treaty of Friendship to the UAE and, as a fig-leaf to cover the absence of a new defence agreement, would turn over the Trucial Oman Scouts to form the nucleus of the new Union Army, provide training teams, and engage in joint exercises and naval port visits (all of which continue to this day).[57] It is with some justification that Denis Healey mocked the Conservatives for their own about-face on the Gulf.

It now remained for Luce and the FCO to tie off the loose ends of Britain's remaining involvement in the Gulf to ensure a swift exit by the end of 1971. In order to achieve this they resorted to the tactics of the *suq*. It was made clear to Shaikh Zayid that if he failed to satisfy the territorial demands of King Faisal and conclude a settlement with him by the end of 1971 (which would form the boundaries of the UAE), then he would have to face the wrath of the Saudi ruler on his own, for Britain would not come to his aid. Abandoned by Britain, Zayid had no real choice but to bow to Saudi demands, ceding territory to the west (Khaur al-Udaid, which gave the Saudis territorial access to the Lower Gulf for the first time) and to the south (among the oilfields of the al-Shaiba/Zarrara structure). Luce used the same tactic with regard to the two Qawasim shaikhdoms of Sharjah and Ras al-Khaimah, whose islands, respectively, of Abu Musa and the Greater and Lesser Tunbs, equidistant between the Persian and Arabian shores, were claimed by the Shah as his reward for waiving his dubious claim to Bahrain. Luce made it clear in June 1971 to Shaikh Khalid ibn

[55] Smith, *Britain's Revival and Fall in the Gulf*, p. 36.
[56] Smith, *Britain's Revival and Fall in the Gulf*, p. 37.
[57] See: Saul Kelly and Gareth Stansfield, 'Britain, the United Arab Emirates and the defence of the Gulf revisited', *International Affairs* 89, no. 5 (2013): pp. 1203–19.

Muhammad of Sharjah and Shaikh Saqr ibn Muhammad of Ras al-Khaimah that Britain would not defend them if the Shah decided to take the islands by force, so they had best come to an agreement with the Shah. Short of money, and tempted by prospective oil royalties, Shaikh Khalid, succumbed to Persian persuasion and an accommodation was reached in November. Shaikh Saqr, the 'Napoleon of the Gulf', held out with the support of the Iraqi government, so was debarred from joining the UAE when it was proclaimed on 18 July. Bahrain declared its independence on 14 August and Qatar followed suit on 1 September, both becoming members of the Arab League and the UN. Luce agreed with Iran that the British government would not oppose the Iranian occupation of the Tunbs (owned by Ras al-Khaimah) after the formal inauguration of the UAE on 2 December, and the commencement of the Treaty of Friendship with Britain since there was no obligation on Britain to defend Ras al-Khaimah. Anxious to claim a cheap victory at Britain's expense, to compensate for his 'concession' over Bahrain, the Shah appeared to break the agreement by seizing Abu Musa and the Tunbs on 30 November. The Royal Navy's carrier group, on station just outside the Strait of Hormuz, did nothing to stop him. It has been said that there was no collusion between Britain and Iran over the Iranian occupation of the islands on the eve of the British withdrawal.[58] The documents show otherwise. Luce connived, through secret discussions with the Shah, over the timing of the Iranian takeover of the islands on 30 November, three days before the official British withdrawal from the Gulf.[59] In colluding with the Shah, Luce had betrayed his principles and his erstwhile protégés as one of the last guardians of the Gulf. This shows how the process of disengagement, or transition, in the Gulf had corrupted the integrity of the individuals involved.

The hasty nature of Britain's exit from the Gulf is symbolized in the farcical way in which it was wound up. What should have been a solemn ceremony in Dubai on 1 December between the outgoing Political Resident, Sir Geoffrey Arthur, and the Rulers of the six emirates, involving the cancellation of the British treaties of protection, became mixed up with the drafting of a proclamation banning unlicensed demonstrations in Dubai, Sharjah, and Ras al-Khaimah, which had broken out as a result of the Iranian seizure of the islands. Shaikh Khalid of Sharjah put Arthur on the spot by demanding an explanation of the Iranian fait accompli. The chaos continued into the next day, as Arthur signed the new agreements between Britain and the UAE while pressmen and photographers stood on the tables and blocked the doorways. Arthur thought 'it was little short of a miracle that nobody was injured and that the documents were retrieved intact'. Julian Walker, the Political Agent in

[58] Louis, 'The British Withdrawal from the Persian Gulf, 1967–71', p. 107, n. 91.
[59] Smith, *Britain's Revival and Fall in the Gulf*, p. 107.

Dubai, described how: 'Along with the UAE rulers, we literally had to climb out of the window on to the beach side of the villa in order to see the raising of the flag', and the 21-gun salute.[60] So came to an end 150 years of the British presence in the Gulf.

Actions have consequences, and the British withdrawal from the Gulf is no exception. Despite what has been claimed, it resulted in the very instability that the FCO had trumpeted as the main reason why Britain should leave the Gulf by the end of 1971.[61] In the early months of 1972 the Lower Gulf was rocked by coups, first in Sharjah, where Shaikh Khalid was killed by the former ruler Shaikh Saqr, aided and abetted by Iraq and Ras al-Khaimah, for 'giving away' Abu Musa to the Iranians. Order was soon restored by the ruling family but it was part of the backwash from Britain's exit from the Gulf. The Amir of Qatar soon followed, overthrown by his family and the army, but since his father-in-law was Shaikh Rashid of Dubai, it poisoned relations with the UAE from the start. The new Amir of Qatar, Shaikh Khalifah bin Hamad, accused the UAE of being 'no Union at all'. Even the new British Ambassador to the UAE, and former Political Agent in Abu Dhabi, C. J. Treadwell, admitted that: 'The UAE is a federation of seven disparate states controlled by ruling families whose one common characteristic is an inability to comprehend the meaning of modern political government'.[62] Since Shaikh Zayid and Shaikh Rashid were 'the cornerstone of the Union', he thought it would collapse if they ever fell out.

In their rush to leave the Gulf, the FCO did not explore the real option of a 'Greater Oman', a more natural political arrangement for the Trucial Shaikhdoms, in federation with the Sultanate of Oman, than the failed attempt to merge them with Qatar and Bahrain. Such an arrangement would have aroused the opposition of Saudi Arabia and Iran, however, thus undermining the FCO's attempt to encourage these traditional territorial poachers in the Gulf to become its new gamekeepers of Western interests in the Gulf, in line with the new 'Twin-Pillars' policy of the Nixon Administration. It was a comforting illusion, as the next decade was to show, helpfully fostered by the glittering prospect of further lucrative arms contracts, following the securing in 1970, as Britain negotiated with Iran on the Gulf, of a £100 million contract for the supply of the new Chieftain tank to the Shah's army (for which the middleman received a knighthood).

Luce and the FCO had been anxious to ensure at all stages that their plans for withdrawing from the Gulf met with the approval of the self-proclaimed

[60] Loveday Morris, 'A Day of Chaos and Jubilation', *The National*, 11 November 2011, <www.thenational.ae/news/uae-news/a-day-of-chaos-and-jubilation>.

[61] Louis, 'The British Withdrawal from the Persian Gulf, 1967–71', p. 102.

[62] Smith, *Britain's Revival and Fall in the Gulf*, p. 108.

'Godfather' of Arab nationalism, Nasser in Cairo. His death in 1970 led others, especially Colonel Gaddafi in Tripoli and Saddam Hussein in Baghdad, to squabble over his mantle. Britain's handing over of Abu Musa and the Tunbs to Iran provided the new generation of Arab nationalist leaders with the perfect opportunity to retaliate for this 'rape of Arab soil'. While Gaddafi nationalized British Petroleum's concession and assets in Libya, the Iraqi government severed diplomatic relations with Britain, expelled 60,000 Iranians from Iraq, and six months later nationalized Iraq Petroleum Company's surviving assets in the country. This was yet more evidence that the Western oil companies and governments were losing control over the supply and price of vital oil supplies in the Gulf and the wider Middle East, which was to become a chronic threat to Western economic stability in the 1970s. Yet the British Treasury had ruled that ordinary commercial considerations would govern the supply of oil from the Persian Gulf, and this mantra had been repeated by the FCO and politicians of both the Labour and Conservative parties as one of the primary justifications for the British political and military withdrawal. It was a misjudgement of monumental proportions by the British policy-making elite. Britain had abdicated its responsibility for safeguarding the West's oil supplies, an attractive dowry which she could have brought with her as she contemplated entering into a state of wedded bliss with the European Economic Community. There was a certain historical symmetry, however, to Britain's exit from the Gulf. She left it in the same mercenary spirit as she had first entered it in 1622, when the ships of the East India Company had helped Shah Abbas I's army defeat the Portuguese at Hormuz and were rewarded with lucrative commercial links with Persia.[63]

Conclusion: vanishing act

The British position in Arabia and the Gulf was built up over 150 years; it was liquidated in six, between 1965 and 1971. Moreover, Britain simply abandoned their former subjects and protégés to their respective fates, and did not really care what followed or made adequate provision for it. Why did Britain simply vanish from Arabia, in a cloud of fear and confusion, leaving a strategic vacuum in her place, into which her regional and great power enemies stepped? It was a catastrophic failure of British foreign policy and yet it was hardly remarked upon at the time or has been since. Then, as now, there has been little inclination to question the inevitability of the end of empire and of

[63] See: Saul Kelly, 'The Gamekeeper versus the Mercenary Spirit: The Pax Britannica in the Gulf', in *Imperial Crossroads: The Great Powers and the Persian Gulf*, edited by J. Macris and S. Kelly (Annapolis: Naval Institute Press, 2012), pp. 49–60.

the triumph of Afro-Asian nationalism. It is within this, historically determinist, context, that both Liberal and Marxist historians have sought to explain the British abandonment of Aden and the retreat from the Gulf. Yet neither the Rulers of South Arabia and the Gulf, let alone most of their peoples, asked the British to leave. If anything they wanted them to stay, and were willing in the case of the Gulf Rulers to pay for their continued protection by Britain. Even that great advocate and friend of Arab nationalism and its leaders, Sir Humphrey Trevelyan, admitted that the British scuttle from Aden was 'the result not of military pressure but of our decision, right or wrong to leave'.[64] As for the retreat from the Gulf, his boss back in London, Sir Paul Gore-Booth, the Permanent Under-Secretary, recorded in his memoirs that: 'In the Office there had been some anxiety about an indefinite prolongation in the Gulf of a "special position" which might involve us in internal struggles in the Arab world.'[65] Here you have a clue as to the real, underlying reason for Britain's flight from Arabia. The Foreign Office had never been comfortable with its imperial inheritance of the Gulf from the India Office in 1947 and Aden from the Colonial Office in 1967. This was not only due to the lack of administrative training of the diplomats, compared to the Indian Political Officers or the Colonial Service, but to a fundamental difference in philosophy between the services. Whereas the 'Colonials' and the 'Indians' had an ingrained sense of responsibility for the fate of the peoples they governed, the 'Diplomats' regarded their charges as temporary and tradeable, as commodities to be haggled over in the international marketplace, or the *suq*, as part of a grand bargain to reconcile relations between Britain and foreign powers. This helps explain the sacrifice of the South Arabian Federation to Nasser and the Yemeni nationalists and the negotiations with Saudi Arabia and Iran over the establishment of the UAE. The Foreign Office (or Foreign and Commonwealth Office from 1968, when it accumulated to itself primary control for the conduct of Britain's overseas relations) regarded Britain's relations with Egypt, Saudi Arabia, and Iran to be of far more importance than her solemn responsibilities for the shaikhs, sayyids, sultans, and amirs of south and eastern Arabia. The latter were, in this view, an obstacle, even an embarrassment, to the cultivation of better relations with the regional powers in the Middle East, and so could be sacrificed to the wider British interest. The Office managed to convince their political masters of this for the simple reason that they controlled the flow of information, and could craft their briefs to appeal to political prejudices and the *zeitgeist* of the age. The trouble with this view is that it flew in the face of all the evidence to the contrary about the intentions of the regional powers, who were the traditional rivals

[64] Trevelyan, *The Middle East in Revolution*, p. 263.
[65] Paul Gore-Booth, *With Great Truth and Respect* (London: Constable, 1974), p. 377.

and even the enemies of British interests in Aden and the Gulf, let alone the Middle East. By trying, and singularly failing, to appease these powers through facilitating their territorial aggrandisement in Arabia and the Gulf in 1967–71, Britain laid herself open to blackmail, threats, and intimidation in the next decade. While those 'twin-pillars' of Western security, the Shah of Iran and the King of Saudi Arabia, competed with each other to see who could push the OPEC oil price higher to fund their struggle for paramountcy in the Gulf, something which put the Western world into economic recession, Iraq and South Yemen sought Soviet backing to destabilize the new order in the Gulf and Oman. The Gulf became a cockpit of tension in the 1970s which was to explode into three large-scale and bloody wars in the ensuing decades. It is a fitting irony that it drew first Britain, in Oman and with the Armilla Patrol, and then the United States, back into the Gulf as the reluctant maritime policemen, again safeguarding Western interests and the security of the Gulf Arab states through defence agreements.[66] At the very least these should have been concluded as Britain moved out of Aden and the Gulf between 1967 and 1971. The failure to do so was due to a lethal combination of illusion, political prejudice, and lack of will by the British policy-making elite which ended in disaster not only for Britain but her erstwhile friends in Arabia and the Gulf. It proved to be a bitter, and unnecessary, legacy.[67]

References

Andrew, Christopher and Oleg Gordievsky, *KGB: The Inside Story* (London: Hodder & Stoughton, 1990).

Ashton, S. R. and Wm. Roger Louis, eds, *British Documents on the End of Empire (BDEEP), Series A, Vol. 5, East of Suez and the Commonwealth, 1964–1971, Part 1, East of Suez* (London: The Stationery Office, 2004).

Bennett, Gill, *Six Moments of Crisis: Inside Foreign Policy* (Oxford: Oxford University Press, 2013).

Brehony, Noel, *Yemen Divided: The Story of a Failed State in South Arabia* (London: I.B. Tauris, 2011).

'Britain East of Suez', Special Issue, *International Affairs* 42, no. 2 (1966).

Brown, George, *In My Way: The Political Memoirs of Lord George-Brown* (London: Gollancz, 1971).

[66] See Kelly and Stansfield, 'Britain, the United Arab Emirates and the defence of the Gulf revisited', *passim*.

[67] The retired diplomat, Oliver Miles, who had been private secretary to Trevelyan in 1967, admitted to me in 2005 that 'we should not have left the Gulf', though he defended the decision to abandon Aden. Given the advanced state of collapse in South Arabia when he arrived, that is not a surprising conclusion.

Dockrill, Saki, *Britain's Retreat from East of Suez* (Basingstoke: Palgrave Macmillan, 2002).

Ferris, Jesse, 'Soviet support for Egypt's intervention in Yemen, 1962–1963', *Journal of Cold War Studies* 10, no. 4 (2008): pp. 5–36.

French, David, *Army, Empire and Cold War* (Oxford: Oxford University Press, 2012).

French, David, *The British Way in Counter-Insurgency, 1945–67* (Oxford: Oxford University Press, 2001), pp. 239–41.

Goldsworthy, David, ed., *BDEEP, Series A, Vol. 3, The Conservative Government and the End of Empire, 1951–1957, Part 1* (London: The Stationery Office, 1994).

Gore-Booth, Paul, *With Great Truth and Respect* (London: Constable, 1974).

Halliday, F., *Arabia Without Sultans* (London: Penguin, 1974).

Hinchcliffe, Peter, *Without Glory in Arabia: The British Retreat from Aden* (London: I.B. Tauris, 2006).

Hurd, Douglas, *An End to Promises: A Sketch of Government* (London: Collins, 1979).

Hyam, Ronald and Wm. Roger Louis, eds, *BDEEP, Series A, Vol. 4, The Conservative Government and the End of Empire, 1957–1964, Part 1* (London: The Stationery Office, 2000).

Kelly, J. B., *Arabia, the Gulf and the West* (London: Weidenfeld & Nicolson, 1980).

Kelly, S. B., ed., *Fighting the Retreat from Arabia and the Gulf: The Collected Essays and Reviews of J.B. Kelly*, vol. 1 (London: New English Review Press, 2013).

Kelly, Saul, 'The Gamekeeper versus the Mercenary Spirit: The Pax Britannica in the Gulf', in *Imperial Crossroads: The Great Powers and the Persian Gulf*, edited by J. Macris and S. Kelly (Annapolis: Naval Institute Press, 2012), pp. 49–60.

Kelly, Saul and Gareth Stansfield, 'Britain, the United Arab Emirates and the defence of the Gulf revisited', *International Affairs* 89, no. 5 (2013): pp. 1203–19.

King, Gillian, *Imperial Outpost–Aden: Its Place in British Strategic Policy* (Oxford: Oxford University Press, 1965).

Louis, Wm. Roger, 'The British Withdrawal from the Persian Gulf, 1967–71', *The Journal of Imperial and Commonwealth History* 31, no. 1 (2003): pp. 83–108.

Mawby, Spencer, *British Policy in Aden and the Protectorates, 1955–67* (London: Routledge, 2005).

Mockaitis, Thomas, *British Counter-Insurgency in the Post-Imperial Era* (Manchester: Manchester University Press, 1995).

Morris, Loveday, 'A Day of Chaos and Jubilation', *The National*, 11 November 2011, <www.thenational.ae/news/uae-news/a-day-of-chaos-and-jubilation>.

Parliamentary Debates (Hansard): House of Commons Official Report, 5th Series (London: Her Majesty's Stationery Office).

Parsons, Anthony, *They Say the Lion: Britain's Legacy to the Arabs* (London: J. Cape, 1986).

Paul, Glen Balfour, *The End of Empire in the Middle East* (Cambridge: Cambridge University Press, 1991).

Pickering, Jeffrey, 'Politics and "Black Tuesday": Shifting Power in the Cabinet and the decision to Withdraw from East of Suez, November 1967–January 1968', *Twentieth Century British History* 13, no. 2 (2002): pp. 144–70.

Sato, Shohei, 'Britain's decision to withdraw from the Persian Gulf, 1964–68: A pattern and a puzzle', *The Journal of Imperial and Commonwealth History* 37, no. 1 (2009): pp. 99–117.

Smith, Simon C., *Britain's Revival and Fall in the Gulf* (London: Routledge, 2004).
Trevelyan, Humphrey, *The Middle East in Revolution* (London: Macmillan, 1970).
Walker, Jonathan, *Aden Insurgency: The Savage War in South Arabia, 1962–1967* (Staplehurst: Spellmount, 2005).
Young, John W., *The Labour Governments, 1964–1970: International Policy*, vol. 2 (Manchester: Manchester University Press, 2003).

8

The Soviet withdrawal from Afghanistan

Rodric Braithwaite

> You have brought an army into the country. But how do you propose to take it out again?
>
> *Mehrab Khan to Alexander Burnes, 1839*

> [A] system, though excellent in itself, may not be good as applied to this country, nor may it be such as to meet appreciation.
>
> *William Macnaughten, British representative in Kabul, to Lord Auckland, Governor General of India, 1840*[1]

Introduction: the Soviet invasion

The Soviets invaded Afghanistan in order to put their own man in charge of the Communist regime, train its security forces to defend him, and then leave. The story that they intended to threaten the West's oil supplies, go for a warm water port, or incorporate Afghanistan into the Soviet Union was Western propaganda. For the Russians, Afghanistan was a strategically important country on their vulnerable southern border. Their relations with Afghanistan had been friendly since the British had relinquished their grip on Afghan foreign policy in 1919. Trade and aid had grown, and from the 1950s onwards the Russians had brought increasing numbers of Afghan military officers and technical experts to the Soviet Union for training. This relationship was not based on ideology. The Russians worked equally well with King Zahir and with his successor President Daud, who replaced the King in a coup in 1973. They

[1] Mohan Lal, *Life of Dost Mohamed*, Vol. II, p. 198, quoted in William Dalrymple, *Return of a King: The Battle for Afghanistan* (London: Bloomsbury, 2012), pp. 160 and 235.

had little time for the tiny Afghan Communist Party, a quarrelsome and unruly bunch of inexperienced intellectuals, who regularly rejected their advice—although they naturally kept in touch with them through their intelligence agents.

But then, partly thanks to their sympathizers in the Afghan armed forces, the Communists seized power in April 1978 in a bloody coup, murdering Daud and his family in the process. The Russians had no choice but to recognize them. But they were rejected by the Afghan people. Insurgency spread in the countryside and mutiny in the armed forces. In March 1979 insurgency and mutiny combined in the city and province of Herat. The 17th Division went over to the rebels, and the Kabul government lost control. They panicked, and asked the Russians to send troops to restore order. The Russian leadership refused: they feared getting mixed up in someone else's civil war, and they had no desire to support a regime which could only survive with Russian bayonets. They told the Kabul governments to sort things out with their own forces. They did, however, promise military and economic supplies, and the General Staff began some discreet planning in case the situation worsened.

Although the Kabul government successfully suppressed the Herat rising, revolts and mutinies continued to break out all over the country, and dissension rose within the Afghan Communist Party. In September 1979, Prime Minister Amin had President Taraki murdered, took sole control, and stepped up the terror against his opponents both inside and outside the Party. For the Russians, the situation in Afghanistan seemed to be disintegrating in a welter of internecine bloodshed and insurgency. Moreover, the Russians feared that the Americans would take advantage of the disorder. Amin had studied in New York, and the KGB claimed to have evidence that he was in contact with the Americans, perhaps even an agent of the CIA. They claimed too that the Americans were looking to move to Afghanistan some of their electronic intelligence posts that had been thrown out of Iran by the revolutionaries who had come to power there. There is little evidence to support these claims, which may simply reflect Soviet paranoia. But they were not wholly implausible. In any case during the Cold War each side naturally expected the worst of the other, and neither could afford to plan except on the basis of a worst case scenario.

The Russians reluctantly decided to intervene. The process by which they reached their final decision is not well documented, however it is known that the decision was taken by the politicians against the advice of the military. When the then Chief of Staff, Ogarkov, warned the Minister of Defence of the risks, Ustinov told him sharply that his job was not to teach the Politburo its business but to carry out its orders.[2]

[2] Aleksandr Lyakhovski, *Tragedia i Doblest Afgana* (Tragedy and Valour of Afghanistan) (Moscow: Eksmo, 2004), p. 208. Lyakhovski's massive history was also published in 1995 and 2009, in

Initially the Soviet intervention was seen as a success. A brilliant special forces operation killed Amin on 27 December, and replaced him with a Soviet puppet, Babrak Karmal. The operation was backed by the 40th Army, initially consisting of about 80,000 troops, or four divisions, which entered Afghanistan at the same time. It was an improvised force, put together in the last weeks before the invasion, its cadre divisions filled out with reservists, and its transport commandeered from the civilian sector. Over the next few months the reservists were replaced with professional officers and serving conscript soldiers, and the civilian vehicles were sent home. Although the Russians had made a successful entry into Afghanistan, they also made an understandable but strategic error: they decided that the best way of stabilizing Afghanistan in the long run was to re-engineer its political and social system on Soviet socialist lines; to bring Afghanistan, as they said, from the fourteenth into the twentieth century. It was a very ambitious idea, but not wholly absurd. After all they had brought law and order (Soviet style), economic and agricultural development, higher education (including education for women) to their Central Asian republics, which were similar to Afghanistan in many ways—ethnically, culturally, economically. Why should similar methods not also succeed in Afghanistan?

The difficulty was that the Afghan people proved unwilling to accept an atheist Communist regime backed by foreign troops. The Russians soon became stuck in a quagmire over the next nine years: like the British 130 years earlier, it did indeed prove much harder to get the army out than it had been to bring it in.

The decision to withdraw

Gorbachev came to power in March 1985 determined to cut through the Gordian knot and disentangle the Soviet Union from Afghanistan. He spent the first few months consolidating his position, tackling (unsuccessfully) the country's increasingly dire economic situation, beginning to reform its political system, and starting to dismantle the Cold War. Some Western accounts claim that he gave his generals a year to settle the Afghan imbroglio by military means, and that it was only thereafter that he seriously tackled the problem himself. No convincing evidence has yet emerged to back this story; Gorbachev denies it, the timings are wrong, and senior generals seem to have

somewhat inconsistent editions. It is not always easy to use, and has not been translated into English. Apart from Lyakhovski's account, the Russians have not yet settled down to writing about the war in a systematic and scholarly way, no doubt because the subject is still too sensitive and too raw. That will change as time passes and more information continues to arise. A great deal more research needs to be done before we have a full view of that war.

been no more keen on the war after five years of fighting than Ogarkov had been before it started.[3] General Valentin Varennikov, who for most of the second part of the war was the senior general in Afghanistan, claims in his memoirs that he had been convinced from 1984 onward that only a political solution would be viable.[4]

But once Gorbachev had settled in, Afghanistan became the subject of intensive (and well documented) discussion within the Politburo. He set out the dilemma in words that still resonate: 'We could leave quickly, without worrying about the consequences, and blame everything on our predecessors. But that we cannot do. We have not given an account of ourselves to the people. A million of our soldiers have passed through Afghanistan [he was exaggerating: the figure was nearer 700,000]. And it looks as if they did so in vain. So why did those people die?'[5] His arguments were supported not only by political colleagues, but by his generals as well. Akhromeev, the Chief of Staff, said Soviet troops could go where they liked, but as soon as they withdrew the Mujahedeen moved straight back in. He concluded firmly that 'we have lost this war'.[6]

In October 1985, Gorbachev summoned Babrak Karmal to Moscow to tell him that the 40th Army would leave in a year or eighteen months. Karmal was already proving a broken reed. In November 1986 Gorbachev replaced him with Mohammad Najibullah, a far more effective operator who had been running the Afghan secret police. They agreed that the Afghan government should now pursue a 'Policy of Reconciliation', by abandoning the aim of building socialism, seeking the support of religious leaders, and reaching out to the opposition. The policy had only limited success, not least because

[3] This story appears to be based on Western press reports which sometimes refer to Western intelligence analyses. Steven R. Galster, 'Rivalry and Reconciliation in Afghanistan: What Prospects for the Accords?', *Third World Quarterly* 10, no. 1 (1988) cites a *Washington Post* report of 17 April 1988. Barnett Rubin, *The Fragmentation of Afghanistan* (New Haven: Yale University Press, 1995), p. 146, gives no source. Some Western commentators argue that Gorbachev's first year saw a surge in military activity and the highest rate of Soviet casualties of the whole war. In fact, Soviet casualties decreased, though Afghan military casualties rose. There were indeed some major operations in the course of the year. Two SpetsNaz (Special Forces) brigades were introduced into Afghanistan in mid-1985 as part of the Soviet strategy of switching from Soviet-led ground operations to greater reliance on the Afghan Army, but I have seen nothing even in the Western accounts which demonstrates that all this happened as a result of a specific directive from Gorbachev. Lyakhovski, *Tragedia i Doblest Afgana* (p. 585) refers to the Galster article, but rejects the story. The Soviet generals hated Gorbachev, and used any stick to beat him. But the story does not appear in those of their memoirs I have consulted, nor in other Russian sources I have seen. Gorbachev denied the story to me in an interview on 10 March 2010. I am most grateful to Colonel David Fivecoat, US Army, for clarifying the military aspects.

[4] V. Varennikov, *Nepovtorimoe* (Unrepeatable), vol. 4 (Moscow: Sovetskii Pisatel', 2001), p. 37.

[5] Politburo meeting of 22 February 1987, in: A. Chernyaev et al., *V Politburo TsK KPSS* (In the Politburo of the Central Committee of the CPSU) (Moscow: Alpina Business Books, 2006), p. 149.

[6] Politburo meeting of 13 November 1986, in Chernyaev, *V Politburo TsK KPSS*, p. 109.

Najibullah was unwilling to relinquish any significant part of his personal power, and the opposition still hoped for victory.

There is another persistent story, popularized by the film *Charlie Wilson's War* (2007), that it was Stinger anti-aircraft missiles provided to the rebels by the CIA that forced the Russians out of Afghanistan. Once again the timings are wrong. The first Stingers were fired outside Jalalabad eleven months after Babrak visited Moscow. They thus had no influence at all on the Soviet political decision to withdraw. They did have an effect on the ground. The Soviet Air Force had to modify its tactics. Its aircraft bombed from greater heights and more inaccurately, and took off and landed in tight spirals. Helicopters flew closer to the ground and remained for shorter periods over their targets. But otherwise the air force continued to fly and fight as before. Even before the appearance of the Stingers, the Mujahedeen had made effective use against Soviet aircraft of heavy machine guns, surface to air missiles, and small arms fire. The change of tactics meant that the Soviet rate of loss continued at much the same rate after the Stingers were introduced.

Even with the pressure Gorbachev was now exerting, it took three years for the negotiations to come to fruition. The Americans were still determined to keep the Russians' feet to the fire, partly for general Cold War reasons, partly as payback for Vietnam. The Afghan rebels and influential people in Pakistan were determined that the war should not end until an Islamist government had been installed in Kabul. However, by the spring of 1988 the Russians had got the minimum of what they needed: international agreement in Geneva that the 40th Army should leave in good order, and that Najibullah would continue—at least for the time being—to run the regime in Kabul, backed by his fairly competent Afghan Army. This was the opposite of what the Americans and their allies had wanted. To that extent it was a negotiating success for the Russians.

Withdrawal: the plan

The Geneva Agreements provided that half the 40th Army should leave between 15 May and mid-August 1988, and the other half between November and 15 February 1989. Their departure would be monitored by UN observers. The Russians allowed foreign journalists to follow the withdrawal as well.

The Soviet general staff had started to plan for the withdrawal in February 1988. The formal directive was issued by the Soviet Defence Minister in April before the Agreements had been signed, and some small garrisons were pulled out straight away. At that stage there were about 110,000 Soviet troops in Afghanistan, consisting of 509 formations, units, and other bodies. They were equipped with 672 tanks, 1,594 armoured fighting vehicles, 2,862 armoured personnel carriers, 2,136 guns and mortars, 326 helicopters, 160 aircraft, and 18,153 vehicles. They were deployed in 25 garrisons and 45 barracks ('military townships').

The overall plan was that the Soviet forces would leave Afghanistan by air and by two ground routes, in the west through Kushka and in the east through Termez, and that they would be prepared to fight if necessary. As a first stage, the troops were to be brought in from the outlying garrisons especially in the south and east, and concentrated at the main bases on the eastern and western routes. To safeguard the ground routes, additional guard posts were to be manned by airborne and other units along the roads. Great care was to be taken to protect the troops as they withdrew. Based in part on experience gained during the withdrawal of several regiments of the 40th Army in mid-1986, pre-emptive air and artillery strikes were to be mounted against rebel concentrations.[7] At night troop positions along the withdrawal routes were to be illuminated by aircraft. The guard posts were to fold in behind as the last column passed through. Intelligence surveillance was to be provided throughout, from the air, by electronic means, and through the local assets of the KGB and military intelligence. Arrangements were made for medical support, vehicle maintenance, and fuel along the way. The soldiers themselves were to go home by road and by air, carrying only their personal weapons and equipment and their kitbags. The 40th Army's equipment and stores were to be brought home, handed over to the Afghans, or destroyed. Arrangements were negotiated with the Afghans for the formal transfer of buildings and of the stores and equipment that were to be left behind.[8]

Withdrawal: the reality

On the whole this plan worked as intended.[9] By August the garrisons of Jalalabad, Gardez, Ghazni, Kandahar, Lashkar Gah, Herat, Faisabad, and Shindand had

[7] Oleg Vladimirovich Krivopalov, *Vyvod voisk iz Afganistana, mai 1988-fevral 1989* (The withdrawal of forces from Afghanistan, May 1988–February 1989), accessed 18 September 2013, <http://www.rsva-ural.ru/library/mbook.php?id=976>. The 40th Army had its own substantial air element, with fighter-bombers, fighters, helicopters, transport aircraft, and specialized reconnaissance aircraft for close support of military operations on the ground, to move troops around the battlefield, and to interdict Mujahedeen supply routes. They used missiles, bombs, cassette bombs, air-laid mines, and a few laser guided weapons. Long-range bombers supported the campaign from bases in the Soviet Union. At the time the Russians were accused of following a deliberate policy of destroying crops and villages in order to drive the population into exile. I know of no documentary evidence for this. However, their bombing was often indiscriminate, and they often razed recalcitrant villages to the ground. In this, their air campaign resembled the American campaign in Vietnam. Unlike the Americans, however, they did not use chemical weapons to destroy crops and tree cover and—collaterally—people.

[8] Equipment figures for the 40th Army and substantial details of the withdrawal plan are in V. Bogdanov, *Afganskaya Voina* (Moscow: np., 2005), pp. 280–98.

[9] This was the opinion of Lyakhovski and his senior military colleagues such as General Gromov, the last commander of the 40th Army. See: Lyakhovski, *Tragedia i Doblest Afgana*, p. 585.

been evacuated in an uninterrupted stream. The first to go were four columns from Jalalabad. Among them was the 15th Independent Special Forces Brigade, whose deputy commander was Oleg Krivopalov.[10] He was with the brigade when it was withdrawn in April 1988 from Asadabad, where it had been under continuous bombardment, to Jalalabad, which was itself under increasing attack. In Jalalabad the brigade repaired its worn-out vehicles, helped prepare the buildings and stores that were to be handed over to the Afghans, and under protest built a bomb-proof shelter, which the soldiers grimly nicknamed 'The Sarcophagus', for the Soviet advisers who were to remain behind. By then Jalalabad had been heavily reinforced by well-equipped units of the Afghan Army to defend the city against the Mujahedeen attacks that were expected once the Soviets had left. But the position of the Soviet advisers rapidly became untenable, and they were withdrawn in August 1989.

Krivopalov fondly remembered the farewell ceremony organized in Jalalabad by the local authorities, and the crowds in the streets who saw the Soviet columns off with flowers. Other observers, such as the British journalist Helen Womack who accompanied the column, were less convinced that the popular mood was so friendly.[11] The column was attacked by the odd sniper, but reached Kabul safely. With other units it departed for the Soviet Union the following day, after another elaborate farewell ceremony addressed by President Najibullah himself. This time the column came under fire a couple of times, but the fire was suppressed by Soviet aircraft and artillery. After travelling 500 miles from Jalalabad, Krivopalov's unit crossed the Amur Darya without having suffered any casualties.

This first phase was completed strictly according to the timetable. In practice only the withdrawal of the 860th Independent Motor-Rifle Regiment from Faisabad encountered problems when the guard posts along its route came under fairly heavy fire. But the columns themselves were not attacked.

Thereafter Soviet forces were present in only six provinces (Kabul, Herat, Parwan, Samangan, Balkh, Baghlan) and their numbers were down to 50,000. The plan was that the remaining forces should prepare for their withdrawal, and leave in an orderly fashion between November 1988 and February 1989.

The timetable was, however, disrupted as a result of pressure from the Najibullah government, which was not at all happy to see the Russians depart. During the late summer, the Afghan Army mounted several provocative attacks on the Mujahedeen in an attempt to draw the Russians into the fighting. These attempts were unsuccessful. But the net result was that the Soviet government agreed that the final phase of the withdrawal should be

[10] Krivopalov, *Vyvod voisk iz Afganistana.*

[11] Rodric Braithwaite, *Afgantsy: The Russians in Afghanistan 1979–89* (London: Profile Books, 2011), p. 283.

conducted not in three months, but in one, from 15 January to 15 February. At this late stage, Najibullah also lobbied hard with the Russians, both in Kabul and among his sympathizers in Moscow (who included both the KGB head, Vladimir Kryuchkov, and the liberal Foreign Minister Eduard Shevardnadze), for the Russians to launch an operation against Ahmad Shah Masud, the most formidable resistance leader, and his stronghold in the Pandshir Valley. The Soviet generals in Afghanistan were thoroughly opposed to an action that had no military purpose, but they were over-ruled from Moscow. Towards the end of January they mounted brief but intensive air and artillery strikes against Masud: Operation Typhoon. They claimed to have killed 600 insurgents; there were few Soviet casualties.

In addition Najibullah requested that Soviet troops should be left behind in significant numbers to guard the route over the Salang Pass between Kabul and the Soviet Union, and that aircraft based inside the Soviet Union should continue to support his forces after the 40th Army had left. Both requests were rejected by Gorbachev, who insisted that the Geneva Agreements should be observed to the letter.

The second stage of the withdrawal was therefore conducted under much less favourable conditions than the first. The rebels made little attempt to interfere but bitter winter conditions impeded movement, especially over the Salang Pass on the eastern route: there were 34 avalanches in the Pass on 3 and 4 January alone. Nevertheless the engineers cleared the routes, and the final phase of the withdrawal was completed on time. The planning had paid off. The withdrawal of the 40th Army was conducted rapidly, according to the timetable, and in good order—Soviet-style. It was observed throughout by teams from the UN and by hundreds of Soviet and Western journalists. Even so, things were quite disordered in places.

Soviet logistics

The Russians have, on the whole, been very good at logistics. The campaigns of 1812 and 1814, which took the Russians from Moscow all the way to Paris, were among other things, a logistical triumph.[12] In the Soviet period the Russians proved, time and again, that they were very good at moving large bodies of people and equipment. In the 1930s they carted millions of people off to the Gulag. In 1941 they evacuated whole industries to Siberia in the face of the advancing Germans. Throughout the Second World War

[12] Dominic Lieven, *Russia Against Napoleon: The Battle for Europe, 1807 to 1814* (London: Penguin, 2009).

they successfully moved very large numbers of troops and equipment over large distances: Operation Bagration in the summer of 1944 was the largest offensive operation launched by any of the combatants during the war. In the summer of 1968 they moved eighteen divisions into Czechoslovakia, backed by eight Warsaw Pact divisions, and moved them out again in a matter of months.

One reason that the Soviets were able to move such large forces so quickly was that they did not worry too much about the welfare of the people or the goods they were moving. They provided only the very minimum of food and comfort. There are documented cases of soldiers dying of cold or starvation as they were being moved around the wartime Soviet Union. For example, a trainload of more than 3,000 men set out from Tbilisi in January 1942. The temperature was minus 50 degrees. The train was unheated and there was neither food nor medical assistance. It arrived at its destination 20 days late. By then nearly 200 men had gone missing, 21 had suffered frostbite, and two had died.[13]

The Russians used the same crudely effective methods to get their people into Afghanistan. The 40th Army consisted at first mainly of understrength cadre units from the military districts bordering on Afghanistan, which had to be brought up to strength with local reservists: some were untraceable, others went into hiding. About 8,000 vehicles were commandeered from local factories and farms. But the formidable administrative and logistical difficulties were overcome, and the army deployed into Afghanistan on time. Once again some soldiers went hungry, however this time none of them seem to have died.

The creation and deployment of the 40th Army was thus another triumph of Soviet-style improvisation. The many serious shortcomings which later emerged might not have mattered so much if the army had been able to leave, as it had originally hoped, without much fighting and after little more than a year. Yet throughout much of the war the soldiers suffered from inadequate food, clothing, and accommodation, and primitive sanitary arrangements. Funds allocated to improve conditions were never forthcoming. The army's health system nearly collapsed as a result.[14] The generals may have had longer to prepare the withdrawal from Afghanistan than they had to prepare the invasion, however they once again stuck to the old ways and ignored some of the finer points of detail. And the Afghans—both those allied to the Soviets and their enemies—did not make it any easier for them.

[13] Rodric Braithwaite, *Moscow 1941: A City and its People at War* (London: Profile Books, 2006), p. 323.

[14] Braithwaite, *Afgantsy*, p. 121.

A fighting withdrawal?

The Western press suggested at the time that the Soviets had to conduct a 'fighting withdrawal' against a determined and organized effort to stop them. There is no evidence of that. The Mujahedeen had refused to participate in the Geneva negotiations, so there was no grand agreement with them on the modalities of withdrawal. But at the beginning of December 1988 a very senior Soviet diplomat met several of the most senior Mujahedeen leaders in Saudi Arabia. They told him in effect: 'If you really leave, then we won't shoot at you.'[15] The Mujahedeen were in any case neither organized nor motivated to mount a coherent campaign against the withdrawal. Once the foreign infidels were clearly leaving, they had no reason to stop them. Many simply went home and others joined the government militias. The main field commanders positioned themselves for the power struggle to come.

Furthermore the Russians paved the way with the inhabitants along the routes. The lines of communication were already open. Throughout the war the Russians maintained covert contacts with the insurgents at all levels. In 1982 they negotiated a ceasefire with Masud, the commander in the Pandshir Valley. There were understandings at other levels as well. Indeed some of the small Soviet units guarding block posts and gas pipelines could hardly have survived if they had not negotiated local deals—often involving the provision of simple medical services and supplies—with the villagers around them. Of course these deals broke down frequently but they helped to mitigate the rigours of the war for both sides.

That is not to suggest that no fighting went on during the Soviet withdrawal. The Russians used artillery and air strikes freely to suppress potential threats. There were misunderstandings, skirmishes, IEDs, and random shelling by both sides. Village elders and field commanders could not always prevent independent action by hotheads. During the last year of the war Soviet casualties were still running at an average of 87 a month, and in the last two weeks alone the Russians lost 32 people. But the precautionary measures they took ensured that the withdrawal went off as planned.[16]

An eyewitness, Vasili Starodymov, describes a last minute operation in Kandahar, which had already been evacuated by the main Soviet force.[17] The Afghan garrison was defending itself successfully against successive attacks by the rebels, but it was running short of munitions. The Russians flew in supplies and a contingent of reconnaissance troops to secure the

[15] Y. Vorontsov, Interview, *Rossiiskie Vesti*, no. 18 (May 2007): pp. 23–30.

[16] G. Krivosheev, *Rossia I SSSR v voinakh XX veka* (Moscow: OLMA-Press, 2001), p. 539.

[17] Vasili Starodymov, 'Art of War', accessed 18 September 2013, <http://artofwar.ru/s/starodymow_n_a/text_0160.shtml>; Krivopalov, *Vyvod voisk iz Afganistana*.

airport which was under constant rocket and mortar fire.[18] The Russians delivered over a thousand tons in the course of the month. The troops flew out of Kandahar and crossed back into the Soviet Union on the final day, 15 February.

At the end of January 1989, again according to Starodymov, two Soviet political officers met the elders of Shindand district, in order to persuade the local civilians and, if possible, the local rebel leaders, that the Soviet troops were leaving and that the rebels should not provoke clashes. The meeting took place in a peaceful enough atmosphere. The elders listened carefully to the Soviet officers, and their Mullah said that they would send word into the mountains that the Russians should be allowed to pass. He concluded: 'For nine years they did us harm. But at the last stage, we will behave well, we will not touch them, and we will commend them to Allah.'[19]

But the elders' efforts were not always sufficient to prevent trouble. Starodymov reports a steady trickle of casualties throughout the withdrawal. North of Herat the road to Iran turns westwards, while the main road continues towards Kushka. A Soviet guard post, reinforced by artillery, remained to protect the junction as the troops withdrew, and the departing columns would concentrate there to check their vehicles before beginning the difficult part of the road through the mountains. A week before the final deadline a waiting column came under heavy fire. The fire was returned by the Soviet gunners, and the column disentangled itself without loss, but the artillery commander was wounded in the exchange. In mid-January an armoured personnel carrier checking the guard posts around Shindand hit an IED, and an officer and three soldiers were killed. An experienced sergeant was wounded at the end of the month during the shelling of the air base in Kandahar. Both men had already served their time, but had been held back to help in the withdrawal. A few days later another officer was killed in Shindand itself when his armoured vehicle was hit by a shell.[20]

Vasili Kopashin described what happened to the garrison of a small guard post on the eastern route. They first had to find someone to hand their surplus equipment to: mortars, heavy machine guns, and tons of ammunition. The local gendarmerie (Tsarandoi) post was deserted except for a lone Afghan. After some serious physical persuasion he agreed to sign for the equipment in exchange for a few television sets. The soldiers then set off for the nearby air base:

[18] The reconnaissance troops (*razvedchiki*) were experienced soldiers organized in sub-units in the motor rifle units. They prided themselves on their toughness and independence, but were looked down upon by the special forces of the KGB and GRU.

[19] Starodymov, 'Art of War'.

[20] Starodymov, 'Art of War'.

> After a few kilometres the lorry was met by a large group of insurgents who were standing along the road on both sides. The road was blocked by a Toyota with a heavy machine gun mounted on it. The soldier-interpreter said to the insurgents in Tajik: 'Get the car off the road' and added in Russian 'all the documents have been signed'. An agreement had been reached with the field commanders before the withdrawal, the essence of which was that the Soviet forces would move along strictly defined routes, without looting or oppressing the local population, on [the] condition that the insurgents would not fire on our columns. 'What the hell are you up to, you're not shooting, we're not shooting, what else do you want?!' 'Okay', came the answer from the crowd, the Toyota was moved aside, the lorry continued on its way, and the insurgents went off happily to take over our guard post.[21]

Kopashin was at the battalion headquarters when the little group arrived:

> It was I who opened the door to the lorry...and the first thing I noticed was the face of the battery commander: it was whiter than paper and in his right hand he held a grenade, with the index finger of his left hand in the firing ring.... Only the driver of the lorry was absolutely calm: he was a middle-aged civilian [there were very many civilian drivers on the transporters and heavy lorries] and simply didn't understand what might happen to him if he met the insurgents.[22]

Kopashin then drove with the others from the battalion headquarters to the air base. He described the flight home: 'The aircraft landed just long enough to take people on board, and then took off again. There was some confusion during the loading, and our battalion was loaded onto two separate aircraft. There were so many people in the plane that we flew standing up, as if we were in a bus during the rush hour.'[23]

Disposing of the equipment

The Russians took home the vehicles, weapons, and equipment that were organic to the departing units. Their attempts to hand over the remainder to the Afghans did not go smoothly. Kopashin explained why:

> The plan was that the transfer of equipment, weapons and other goods was to be carried out by joint commissions, with a final act of agreement signed in Kabul by the Soviet and Afghan sides. That is what happened where units were actually

[21] This and other references to Kopashin's account are from V. Kopashin, *The Withdrawal of Soviet Forces from Afghanistan: what the Media did not say*, accessed 18 September 2013, <http://artofwar.ru/k/kopashin_w_w/wywodsowetskihwojskizafganistanaochemneweshalismi.shtml>. I have slightly altered the order of some of the paragraphs in Kopashin's account for the sake of clarity.

[22] Kopashin, *The Withdrawal of Soviet Forces from Afghanistan.*

[23] Kopashin, *The Withdrawal of Soviet Forces from Afghanistan.*

stationed in proper bases, but in addition there were dozens if not hundreds of guard posts scattered for tens of kilometres around. In the course of the years, goods and munitions had piled up at these guard posts, and when the moment came to withdraw there was simply no one to take them over. In my case the weapons, vehicles, ammunition and every other kind of property which we handed over to the Afghans found its way to the insurgents not only that same day, but within an hour of being handed over. . . .

[I]n the ravine next to our unit we were using dynamite to destroy unusable military equipment which even the Afghans would not take over (they demanded that equipment should be in good repair and fit for battle). . . . In the medical centre [at battalion headquarters] all the rooms were ideally clean, the beds had new bed linen on them, there were flowers on the pillows, the ventilators were humming quietly, the refrigerators were working, everything was in its place and—there was not a single person in the huge building, the medical staff had already left, it looked like a Spielberg fantasy film. 'We're dumping all that stuff: it would have been enough to equip two or three local hospitals', I thought. A big crowd of Afghans some 200–300 strong was on its way from the local village. 'In twenty minutes they will begin to loot and smash everything, the first building will go up in an hour, and by morning everything will have been burned down.'[24]

And indeed, as Kopashin looked back as he drove to the air base: 'In the area of our barracks a huge column of flame wound into the sky. It was the building of the medical centre. The Afghans were getting their revenge on us for all they had suffered over many years.' This was not an exception. Similar scenes took place elsewhere. And in at least one place the Soviet soldiers, furious at having to withdraw, trashed their own base to prevent it falling into Afghan hands.[25]

For Kopashin the last bitter straw came two decades later: 'Of course the Afghans were given equipment and weapons which were obsolete at that period, but I was amazed when I saw on the television what kind of vehicles our contemporary Russian army was using during the recent war in Georgia. It was the same obsolete equipment which we handed over to the Afghans in 1988 as useless scrap metal!'[26]

The Russians withdrew the whole of the 40th Army except for some military advisers and specialist troops to operate the Afghan Army's SCUD missiles—all of whom were withdrawn fairly soon—and KGB frontier forces in the areas bordering on the Soviet Union. However, Afghanistan had been heavily dependent on foreign aid even before the war began, and the Russians committed themselves to continue supplying Najibullah with fuel, food, military equipment, and munitions. The columns of lorries went on trundling down the eastern route from the Soviet Union with essential supplies. An air bridge

[24] Kopashin, *The Withdrawal of Soviet Forces from Afghanistan.*
[25] Braithwaite, *Afgantsy*, p. 284.
[26] Kopashin, *The Withdrawal of Soviet Forces from Afghanistan.*

to Kabul was established a month after the Russian departure and flew an average of 24–25 flights a day in 1989 and 14–15 flights a day in 1990. From 1989 to 1991 Soviet aid ran at about 30 million roubles a year, considerably down from previous years, but just about enough to keep Najibullah's head above water.[27]

Then and now: settling for second best

General Gromov, the last commander of the 40th Army, led the final small contingent of troops across the Amu Darya River into the Soviet Union on 15 February 1989. Their vehicles were newly painted, their flags were flying. But they left Afghanistan with heavy hearts. Like his fellow veterans, Gromov remembered with great bitterness, that no senior politician came down from Moscow to greet the returning troops. The 40th Army had not been defeated on the battlefield, but their departure was not celebrated as a victory.

There are of course great differences between the Soviet war in Afghanistan and the war that the American-led Coalition was fighting two decades later. The armies were quite different in their methods and traditions. The weapons were very different too: neither the Russians in Afghanistan—nor indeed the Americans in Vietnam—had much in the way of smart weapons, and those wars were inevitably much more bloody. And when it comes to the withdrawal, there are important differences too. The Russians had only a few hundred miles to go, and when they had crossed the Soviet frontier they were back home. Coalition routes home—whether through Pakistan to the south or through the former Soviet Union to the north—are longer, more complicated, and beset with political difficulties.

But there are some major similarities. Both the Soviets and the Coalition greatly underestimated the difficulties they would face. Both achieved stunning initial victories, but became mired in a long-term fight that they could not win by any conventional military definition. Both believed that the key to success was to stabilize Afghanistan by winning 'hearts and minds', and re-engineering Afghan politics and society in their own image, a task entirely beyond their ability. And so both had to scale back their objectives to something much more modest. Both abandoned their aim of introducing their own systems into Afghanistan, which the Afghans had failed to appreciate. Both

[27] G. Gareev, 'Afgantsy i My: Sovietskaya Voennaya Pomoshch Afganistanu' in *Moya Poslednaya Voina* (The Afghans and US: Soviet Military Help to Afghanistan in My Last War), accessed 18 September 2013, <http://www.rsva.ru/biblio/prose_af/last_war/foreword.shtml>; Paul Robinson and Jay Dixon, *Aiding Afghanistan: A History of Soviet Assistance to a Developing Country* (London: Hurst and Company, 2013), p. 175, quoting Valeri Ivanov, a senior economic official in the Soviet embassy at the time.

settled instead for withdrawing their armies in good order, leaving behind a friendly government capable of defending itself and led by a man of their choice.

As the Coalition's civilian and military spokesmen have continually stressed, the key to such a reduced definition of success lies in the stability of the government in Kabul and the ability and willingness of the Afghan security forces to support it. The Coalition currently intends to continue to give substantial aid to the Kabul government after its main force has withdrawn at the end of 2014. Unlike the Russians, it proposes to leave behind an unspecified number of troops to continue training the new Afghan Army and to engage in Special Forces operations against terrorist groups. It has the capacity to do both. How long it will retain the necessary political will, and whether the forces it leaves behind will simply prove a continuing provocation to Afghans who want to see the last of foreign troops in their country, are open questions. NATO has described these modest but difficult tasks as a 'strategy': an inflated and cavalier use of a good word.

Two Afghan armies: The Afghan Army during the Soviet war

The Afghan Army which fought alongside the Russians was fully equipped with aircraft, helicopters, artillery, and armour. Many of the officers spoke Russian and had been well trained in the Soviet Union in the use of sophisticated equipment. There were about 1,800 Soviet military advisers in Afghanistan: three or four in each Afghan battalion, four or five in each regiment, eleven or twelve in each division. It was a dangerous business: many were killed in combat, but few of them fell to 'green on blue' attacks by their Afghan comrades. Almost all left before or during the Soviet military withdrawal. By the end of the war the Afghan Army had grown to twelve divisions, and a number of specialized brigades and smaller units. It was armed with modern—if not the most modern—Soviet weapons: aircraft, helicopters, tanks, and artillery.

Between them the Afghan security forces—the army, the secret police (the KhAD), and the Tsarandoi (the police/gendarmerie)—were almost 300,000 strong when the Russians left. Many of these were former insurgents bought over by the regime. Others were local forces, of dubious loyalty, raised by regional warlords such as General Dostum in the Uzbek North of the country. Of course these Afghan forces suffered from serious weaknesses. Afghan officers were often unwilling to take decisions: their sense of initiative was sapped by the presence of their Soviet advisers. Units were often reluctant to fight, although they did better if they were backed by Soviet units. Most were well-below their nominal strength: an Afghan division might consist of no more than a thousand men, a tenth of what it should have been. Desertion was always a major problem.[28] Despite its weaknesses this army was able to mount quite complex independent operations after the Russians left. In March 1989 it successfully saw off a major attempt by the Mujahedeen to capture Jalalabad, and in 1990 it expelled the Mujahedeen from their heavily fortified positions in Paghman near Kabul.

The Afghan Army in 2013

Unlike the Russians, the Coalition did not inherit coherent Afghan security forces when they invaded Afghanistan: all had disintegrated under the stress of civil war. It was a major plank of NATO policy to rebuild the Afghans' capacity to defend themselves. Figures currently given by NATO spokesmen for the size of the Afghan security forces available to President Karzai vary from 250,000 to 350,000.[29]

These forces are therefore similar in number to those which fought alongside the Soviets. They suffer from some of the same weaknesses: high rates of desertion, ethnic and local rivalries, and divided loyalties. A Pentagon assessment released in November 2012 found that only one of the Afghan Army's 23 brigades was able to operate independently without air or other military support from the United States or its NATO partners.[30] This new model Afghan Army will have fewer heavy weapons and less battle experience than its Soviet-trained predecessor. It is unlikely to prove more capable.

Conclusion: politics decide

Arguably, the size and competence of the Afghan Army is not the main issue. After the Russians left, Najibullah's army began to fall apart. This was not because it could not fight, but rather because both the army and the regime disintegrated in a welter of intrigue. The end came after three years when the Russians went bankrupt at the end of 1991. They cut off the supplies of fuel, food, equipment, and munitions without which neither the army nor the

[28] The rule of thumb was that if the desertion rate was no more than about 30 per cent a year you were all right. If it went much above that you were in trouble; 60 per cent was bad news.

[29] Thom Shanker, 'NATO Plan Tries to Avoid Sweeping Cuts in Afghan Troops', *New York Times*, 21 February 2013, <http://www.nytimes.com/2013/02/22/us/philip-m-breedlove-is-likely-candidate-for-top-nato-post.html?ref=johnrallen&_r=0>.

[30] Elisabeth Bumiller, 'Pentagon Says Afghan Forces Still Need Assistance', *New York Times*, 10 December 2012, <http://www.nytimes.com/2012/12/11/world/asia/afghan-army-weak-as-transition-nears-pentagon-says.html>; *Report on Progress Toward Security and Stability in Afghanistan* (US Department of Defence: Washington, December 2012), p. 93.

regime could function. The consequence was civil war and the victory of the Taliban.

Once the NATO Coalition leaves in 2014 there is no obvious guarantee that things will be much different, or that the new model Afghan Army will remain any more united or loyal to the regime in Kabul. Events will probably be decided, as they were after 1989, by the convolutions of Afghan politics, rather than the proficiency or otherwise of Afghan soldiers. This time, too, the army could split and take different sides in a civil war. Some hope that a regional agreement can be reached among Afghanistan's neighbours which would give a guarantee against foreign interference in the future. It is an optimistic thought. India, Iran, China, Pakistan, and indeed the former Soviet republics to the north, all have conflicting interests. The chances that they will agree on a deal over Afghanistan are thin. Pakistan in particular is unlikely to accept that its freedom of manoeuvre should be constrained.

Thirty years of invasion and civil war may have destroyed much of Afghanistan's economy and many of its traditional social and political relationships, yet when foreign troops finally depart, the war-weary Afghans will at last have the opportunity to set up a viable state of their own. This will be a slow, painful, and unpredictable process, though one thing seems certain: the Afghans' new state will bear little resemblance to the centralized 'socialist' or 'democratic' regimes which successive waves of foreigners have attempted to create in their name.

References

Bogdanov, V., *Afganskaya Voina* (Moscow: np., 2005).

Braithwaite, Rodric, *Afgantsy: The Russians in Afghanistan 1979–89* (London: Profile Books, 2011).

Braithwaite, Rodric, *Moscow 1941: A City and its People at War* (London: Profile Books, 2006).

Bumiller, Elisabeth, 'Pentagon Says Afghan Forces Still Need Assistance', *New York Times*, 10 December 2012, <http://www.nytimes.com/2012/12/11/world/asia/afghan-army-weak-as-transition-nears-pentagon-says.html>.

Chernyaev, A. et al., *V Politburo TsK KPSS* (In the Politburo of the Central Committee of the CPSU) (Moscow: Alpina Business Books, 2006).

Dalrymple, William, *Return of a King: The Battle for Afghanistan* (London: Bloomsbury, 2012).

Galster, Steven R., 'Rivalry and reconciliation in Afghanistan: What prospects for the Accords?' *Third World Quarterly* 10, no. 1 (1988): pp. 1505–41.

Gareev, G., 'Afgantsy i My: Sovietskaya Voennaya Pomoshch Afganistanu', in *Moya Poslednaya Voina* (The Afghans and US: Soviet Military Help to Afghanistan in My

Last War), accessed 18 September 2013, <http://www.rsva.ru/biblio/prose_af/last_war/foreword.shtml>.

Kopashin, V., *The Withdrawal of Soviet Forces from Afghanistan: what the Media did not say*, accessed 18 September 2013, <http://artofwar.ru/k/kopashin_w_w/wywodsowetskihwojskizafganistanaochemnew eshalismi.shtml>.

Krivopalov, Oleg Vladimirovich, *Vyvod voisk iz Afganistana, mai 1988-fevral 1989* (The withdrawal of forces from Afghanistan, May 1988–February 1989), accessed 18 September 2013, <http://www.rsva-ural.ru/library/mbook.php?id=976>.

Krivosheev, G., *Rossia I SSSR v voinakh XX veka* (Moscow: OLMA-Press, 2001).

Lieven, Dominic, *Russia Against Napoleon: The Battle for Europe, 1807 to 1814* (London: Penguin, 2009).

Lyakhovski, Aleksandr, *Tragedia i Doblest Afgana* (Tragedy and Valour of Afghanistan), (Moscow: Eksmo, 2004).

Report on Progress Toward Security and Stability in Afghanistan (US Department of Defence: Washington, December 2012).

Robinson, Paul and Jay Dixon, *Aiding Afghanistan: A History of Soviet Assistance to a Developing Country* (London: Hurst and Company, 2013).

Rubin, Barnett, *The Fragmentation of Afghanistan* (New Haven: Yale University Press, 1995).

Shanker, Thom, 'NATO plan tries to avoid sweeping cuts in Afghan troops', *New York Times*, 21 February 2013, <http://www.nytimes.com/2013/02/22/us/philip-m-breedlove-is-likely-candidate-for-top-nato-post.html?ref=johnrallen&_r=0>.

Starodymov, Vasili, 'Art of War', accessed 18 September 2013, <http://artofwar.ru/s/starodymow_n_a/text_0160.shtml>.

Varennikov, V., *Nepovtorimoe* (Unrepeatable), vol. 4 (Moscow: Sovetskii Pisatel', 2001).

Vorontsov, Y., 'Interview', *Rossiiskie Vesti*, no. 18 (May 2007): pp. 23–30.

9

Stopping the cycles of violence

Political transition in Algeria since 1988 in a comparative perspective

Martin Evans

On 15 April 1999 Abdelaziz Bouteflika was elected president of Algeria at the age of 62. A veteran of the national liberation struggle, part of the military clique led by Houari Boumidiène that took power in 1962, and Minister of Foreign Affairs from 1963 to 1978, Bouteflika was the official candidate in all but name.[1] His campaign was given blanket coverage by state radio and television while the six other candidates were ignored. Then in the contest itself the media claimed a 60 per cent electoral turn out, with Bouteflika winning 70 per cent of the vote. However, the fact that all the rival candidates stood down in protest on the eve of the ballot, claiming massive fraud, meant that from the beginning his tenure was dogged with controversy.[2]

Bouteflika brushed aside reservations about his legitimacy, ploughing ahead with his programme that mixed nationalism with promises of honesty in government and economic recovery. Above all Bouteflika pledged to extinguish the violence that had gripped the country since 1992 and led to the deaths of 200,000 people. In this way Bouteflika was grappling with a dilemma that has confronted politicians from Argentina to Northern Ireland: how to

[1] Bouteflika lost out to Chadli Bendjedid in the in-fighting over who should succeed Boumediène as president after the latter's death in 1978. Thereafter Bouteflika went into exile, returning to Algeria in the late 1980s. The impetus for Bouteflika's candidature came from inside the military during the autumn of 1998.

[2] The other five candidates were Hocine Aït Ahmed, leader of the *Front des Forces Socialistes* (FFS); Mouloud Hamrouche, reformist Prime Minister from 1989 to 1991; Abdallah Djaballah, candidate from a new Islamist party; Mokdad Sifi, Prime Minister between 1993 and 1995; and Youcef Khatib, a veteran from the war of liberation against the French.

stop cycles of violence. He wished to bring about a process of national reconciliation. Capitalizing upon a ceasefire in place with some of the Islamist guerrillas since September 1997, Bouteflika wanted to enact a permanent transition to peace and stability.

This chapter will explore the contours of this transition process, analysing the specificities of the Algerian case. In doing so, the chapter will draw out differences between what will be termed 'external transition' between a state and a state in the making, as with India in 1947 or Algeria winning independence from France in 1962, and 'internal transition' within a state where that state is trying to stop cycles of violence between itself and parts of the domestic population. External transition and internal transition are two ends of a spectrum across which exists a range of differing scenarios. Within each scenario the symmetry between external and internal factors will vary according to each historical example. In Algeria in the 1990s, it will be argued that the internal dynamics were dominant, even if these internal factors were still contingent on the international context.

The Algerian example

If the 'Arab Spring' is about political transition, it is wrong to conceptualize this process as a new phenomenon. In reality the region has been engaging with constitutional democracy for over a hundred years. In 1908 the Ottoman Arab provinces witnessed an upsurge in political participation following the re-introduction of the Ottoman Constitution that allowed elections, freedom of speech and a relaxation of censorship.[3] In Egypt the 1923 Constitution introduced pluralism, full male suffrage, and regular elections which Eugene Rogan has described as 'the highest degree of multiparty democracy in the modern history of the Arab world'.[4] More recently huge riots in Algeria in October 1988, the result of mass disaffection, led the regime to usher in multiparty elections that seemingly set the country on the road from an authoritarian one-party system to a democratic one.

This transformation was the pivotal moment in post-independence history. But the main beneficiary was the Islamist party formed in 1989: the Islamic Salvation Front or FIS (*Front Islamique de Salut*). The FIS expressed anger at the system and won local elections in June 1990. Yet, when the FIS was poised to

[3] The Ottoman Constitution was first introduced in 1876 but suspended two years later. In 1908 the Arab provinces enfranchisement was limited to a male, urban, bourgeois population. Although this was 8 per cent of the population, it was analogous to the enfranchisement in Italy. On this see: Michelle Campos, *Ottoman Brothers: Muslims, Christians and Jews in Early-Twentieth Century Palestine* (Stanford: Stanford University Press, 2010).

[4] Eugene Rogan, *The Arabs: A History* (London: Allen Lane, 2009), p. 192.

win national elections in January 1992, the army, the real power broker in Algerian politics, moved in and cancelled the process.[5] It was a thinly disguised *coup d'état* where under a state of emergency the FIS was banned and rule was carried out by an interim council. What followed was a tense standoff between the army and angry FIS supporters. However, full-scale violence did not erupt until early 1993 when small terrorist groups, determined to bring the regime to its knees, launched terrorist attacks in and around the capital Algiers.[6] Very quickly the country was plunged into an ever worsening cycle of conflict as the army confronted these armed groups head on.[7]

By the mid-1990s the violence in Algeria was a major international issue. On 9 April 1997 Amnesty International sent a letter to the United Nations (UN) Commission on Human Rights identifying Algeria as one of five countries 'where the Commission needs to give urgent attention to serious human rights violations.'[8] Five months later Mary Robinson, newly appointed as UN High Commissioner for Human Rights, made a public plea for an end to the bloodshed, while Amnesty International, in conjunction with three other human rights organizations—Human Rights Watch, the International Federation of the Leagues of the Rights of Man, and Reporters Without Borders—called for a special United Nations session on Algeria, a demand that was backed up by the US on 5 January 1998. How countries or international organizations could or should intervene was unclear, however, especially given that the Algerian authorities rejected all help in the name of national sovereignty. Moreover, the situation on the ground was very confused as the then French Prime Minister, Lionel Jospin, underlined on French television on 30 September 1997:

> The great difficulty is that we do not have much idea about what is really going on in Algeria.... It is not like Chile under Pinochet with democrats fighting a dictatorial regime. We are confronted with a fanatical and violent opposition fighting against a regime which...has recourse to violence and power of the state, so we have to be careful.[9]

[5] On the complexities of the coup see Martin Evans and John Phillips, *Algeria: Anger of the Dispossessed* (London: Yale University Press, 2007), pp. 166–76. See also Lounis Aggoun and Jean-Baptiste Rivoire, *Françalgérie, crimes et mensonges d'États* (Paris: La Découverte, 2004), pp. 240–58.

[6] On the exact nature of the violence see Evans and Phillips, *Algeria*, pp. 185–210. See also Aggoun and Rivoire, *Françalgérie, crimes et mensonges d'États*, pp. 294–332.

[7] On the violence of the 1990s see: Abed Charef, *Algérie, le grand dérapage* (La Tour d'Aigues: L'Aube, 1994); Reporters sans frontières, *Le Drame Algérien. Un peuple en otage* (Paris: La Découverte, 1994); Djallal Malti, *La Nouvelle Guerre d'Algérie* (Paris: La Découverte, 1999).

[8] 'Amnesty International Statement to the 53rd UN Commission on Human Rights', 9 April 1997, <http://www.amnesty.org/en/library/asset/IOR41/008/1997/en/e56e02c5-ea78-11dd-b05d-65164b228191/ior410081997en.pdf>. The other five countries were Colombia, Indonesia, East Timor, Nigeria, and Turkey.

[9] Evans and Phillips, *Algeria*, p. 245.

Truth and the Algerian violence

At an official level this violence is interpreted in terms of a simple narrative: Islamist violence against Algerian society. Understood in this way, Algerians were the victims of terrorism who were saved by the army; an image that places Algeria on the front line of the global struggle against Islamist terrorism. As such this narrative presents recent history as one of heroes and villains. It carefully avoids complications to construct a straightforward story of 'civilization' versus 'barbarism'.

Unravelling this narrative is difficult, largely because during the 1990s Algeria was off-limits. Journalists were targeted.[10] Reporting was tightly controlled by the authorities. This made differentiating truth from untruth difficult, especially because all sides became adept at manipulating events for their own political end. Consequently, it has taken time to discern the exact contours of the violence.

In this respect it needs to be noted that this violence did not begin in January 1992 with the cancellation of elections. Already in early 1982 a few hundred guerrillas had taken to the mountains just south of Algiers, led by Mustapha Bouyali, a disenchanted National Liberation Front (*Front de Libération Nationale*, FLN) veteran who had gravitated towards Islamist circles during the late 1970s.[11] Calling themselves the Armed Islamic Movement (*Mouvement Islamique Armé*—MIA), this group launched a series of attacks against the police and army which, although never reaching the levels of the 1990s Islamist violence, still represented a thorn in the side of the government. Bouyali was eventually killed in the Algiers Casbah in January 1987, followed by the arrest and trial of some 202 MIA militants. Despite these reverses, though, a nucleus hung on throughout the late 1980s and early 1990s who continued to see themselves in a state of war against the government. At this point armed opposition also came from another direction: the returning Algerians who had fought in Afghanistan against the Soviet Union.[12] Estimates vary as to how many had travelled to Afghanistan, with

[10] On 17 May 1993 Omar Belhouchet, editor of the daily *El Watan*, narrowly missed assassination in Algiers. In the face of the violence many hundreds of journalists went into exile, while those who remained lived in a specially guarded residence to the west of Algiers.

[11] On this see: Ahmed Rouadjia, *Les Frères et la mosquée: Énquête sur le Mouvement Islamiste en Algérie* (Paris: Karthala, 1990) and Michael Willis, *The Islamist Challenge in Algeria: A Political History* (Reading: Ithica Press, 1996).

[12] It is estimated that about 25,000 Arabs fought in Afghanistan. On the international dimensions of the conflict and its impact upon the Arab world see: Jason Burke, *Al-Qaeda* (London: Penguin, 2003).

numbers ranging from 300 to 2,800.[13] However, in 1989 they were a real presence on the streets appearing at demonstrations in Afghan combat fatigues. Fired up by the defeat of the Red Army, which was interpreted as an act of God, they wanted to wage war on the Algerian government which was seen to be, like so many other Muslim governments, mired in corruption and anti-Islamic values. By the summer of 1991 small groups of Afghan veterans were operating in the mountains to the southeast of Algiers and calling for a *jihad* against the regime.[14]

Nor was the 1990s violence a civil war, although the international media interpreted it as such. Yes, Algerian was killing Algerian, but this was not like the American Civil War or the Spanish Civil War where two clearly delineated sides confronted each other. There were no clear boundaries. Furthermore, even if the armed groups did enjoy some support at the beginning, the shape of the conflict quickly changed to one where the population was caught in between the violence. Seen through this lens, it is possible to identify six strands to this violence.

The first strand was a war of terrorism and counter-terrorism which pitted the various armed Islamist groups against the army. By 1993 it was estimated that there were 22,000 armed men across the country, but this terrorism was not centrally controlled. It was a diffuse phenomenon where each group operated independently with their own localities, leaders, and agendas.[15] As the country reeled from this violence, the government responded with the establishment of a specialist force of 15,000 men in April 1993 that operated outside the law and matched terrorist violence blow for blow.[16] It was a ruthless strategy that was backed up by the establishment of special military courts which, according to Amnesty International, violated many of the international fair trial standards.[17]

The second, most overwhelming strand of violence was against the ordinary population trapped between terrorism and counter-terrorism. A large part of

[13] Saïd Makhloufi, Kamareddin Kherbane, and Abdallah Anas were three Algerians who fought in Afghanistan and who each played a pivotal role in Islamist violence during the 1990s.

[14] On 28 November 1991 a 60-strong Afghan group attacked a police station close to the Tunisia frontier, killing three reservists and stealing an arsenal of weapons, including several rocket launchers.

[15] On this see: Amine Touati, *Algérie, les islamistes à l'assaut au pouvoir* (Paris: L'Harmattan, 1995) and Benjamin Stora, *La Guerre Invisible, Algérie, Années 90* (Paris: Presses de Sciences Po, 2001).

[16] Garbed in black balaclavas, these special forces became known as the 'ninjas' because of their resemblance to the ninja cartoon characters.

[17] On 2 March 1993 Amnesty International published a report that documented the deterioration of human rights since the state of emergency. In particular Amnesty underlined the widespread use of torture by the regime including sexual abuse with bottles, beatings with sticks, and suffocating with a cloth soaked in dirty water.

this was indiscriminate terrorism that reached a highpoint in the two years after 1993. Large numbers too died in the spate of massacres that took place in 1997 and 1998 in the hinterland of Algiers. Certain social groups were particularly vulnerable. So, Islamists specifically targeted those journalists, academics, and writers who were seen to be mouthpieces of French influence. Venom was particularly reserved for women, especially professionally successful women, who were judged to be too 'French' in their manners and style of dress.[18]

From the beginning much of this violence was murky. In particular, searching questions were asked about the role of the army in this violence and why it was failing in its basic duty to protect citizens. Journalists such as Séverine Labat pondered whether the regime was letting high profile intellectuals be murdered as a way of providing the West with a stark choice: back the army in the face of Islamist terrorism.[19] These questions arose yet again during the massacres of 1997 and 1998 when a series of eye-witness accounts claimed that the violence was being manipulated by the army to turn the population against the Islamists.[20]

The third strand of violence was the targeting of foreigners. This aimed to bring Algeria to the world's attention on the cold calculation that the death of a foreigner would have more international impact than that of an Algerian. However, this became a source of tension within Islamist groups which leads to the fourth strand of violence: fighting between Islamists. Collectively the groups that launched the wave of terrorist violence in 1993 became known as the Armed Islamic Group (*Groupe Islamique Armé*—GIA), many of whom accused the FIS of selling out because of rumours of negotiations with the regime. Conversely pro-FIS groups were perturbed by the impact of GIA tactics which were seen to be alienating large parts of the population through indiscriminate violence.[21] To counter the GIA, judged to be out of control and infiltrated by the secret services, the Islamic Salvation Army

[18] For example, the Algerian feminist activist Khalida Messaoudi was repeatedly targeted by Islamists because of her anti-Islamist stance. On this see: Khalida Messaoudi, *Une Algérienne Debout* (Paris: Flammarion, 1995).

[19] Severine Labat, 'Les Islamistes, Nouvelle Barbarie', in Reporters sans frontières, *Le Drame Algérien*, p. 180.

[20] A number of witness accounts have posed questions about the role of the army. These include: Nesroulah Yous, *Qui a tué à Bentalha? Algérie, chronique d'un massacre annoncé* (Paris: La Découverte, 2000); Habib Saouïdia, *La Sale Guerre* (Paris: La Découverte, 2001); Mohammed Samraoui, *Chronique des années de sang. Algérie: comment les services secrets ont manipulé les groupes islamistes* (Paris: Denoël, 2003).

[21] The FIS was also worried about being left behind by the GIA, particularly when Mohammed Said and Aderrazak Redjam, two members of the FIS executive, defected to the GIA in February 1994.

(*Armée Islamique de Salut*—AIS) was formed in July 1994—the 'official' wing of the FIS and subject to its political control. The AIS explicitly condemned the killing of foreigners.[22] Equally the army encouraged these divisions between the GIA and the AIS, hoping that GIA excesses would force the AIS to accept a ceasefire.

The fifth strand of violence is within the regime. Algerian politics is difficult to decipher. Ordinary Algerians talk of *le pouvoir* (the power), a shadowy military mafia that operates behind the scenes and is considered to be the real power, but it would be misleading to think of *le pouvoir* as a unified structure. In truth the levers of power are dominated by a small number of rival groups who used the violence as a smokescreen to settle accounts and to stop anyone threatening their economic interests. Thus, in January 1992, shortly after the military coup which stopped the electoral process, Mohammed Boudiaf returned from exile to become the president of the interim council. As one of the historic leaders of the FLN, the military leaders hoped that Boudiaf would give the coup a veneer of legitimacy.[23] Immediately though he announced an anti-corruption drive that, by threatening the highest echelons of the military, aimed to win over the population. For this reason, when Boudiaf was assassinated in June 1992, most commentators believed that is was by insiders who wanted to protect their economic interests, rather than a lone Islamist terrorist as the authorities claimed.[24] Equally, many were sceptical when Islamist terrorists were blamed for the murder of Kasdi Merbah, former Head of the Secret Services and Prime Minister from 5 November 1988 to 10 September 1990, on 21 August 1993.[25] Why? Because Merbah had been one of the key figures behind Boudiaf 's anti-corruption drive who had urged the authorities to enter into negotiations with the FIS, and in an open letter, published on 13 July 1993, he had called upon insurgents to lay down their weapons.[26] In this manner the killing of Merbah pointed towards another

[22] In a communiqué issued in Bonn on 25 July 1994 and signed by two AIS leaders, Madani Mezraq and Ahmed Ben Aicham, it called on all factions to unite around the imprisoned leadership. The communiqué was explicitly critical of the GIA violence on the grounds that it was needless and was turning the population against the Islamist cause.

[23] Mohammed Boudiaf was the principal architect of the co-ordinated FLN attacks launched on 1 November 1954. Boudiaf was one of the five FLN leaders who were captured by the French on 22 October 1956 when their aeroplane, bound from Morocco to Tunisia, was forced down when it crossed over into Algerian airspace. On the internal history of the FLN see: Mohammed Harbi, *Le FLN, mirage et réalité. Des origins à la prise du pouvoir* (Paris: Jeune Afrique, 1980); Gilbert Meynier, *Histoire intérieure du FLN, 1954–1962* (Paris: Fayar, 2002).

[24] On the context of the Boudiaf assassination see Aggoun and Rivoire, *Françalgérie, crimes et mensonges d'États*, pp. 281–93.

[25] He was killed in a car ambush close to his home on 21 August 1993, 28 miles to the east of Algiers. On the context for the killing see: Aggoun and Rivoire, *Françalgérie, crimes et mensonges d'États*, pp. 326–30.

[26] Merbah was also part of a cell of high ranking army officers who were determined to clean up corruption. These officers subsequently published revelations about high ranking corruption in

pattern: the liquidation of third force figures by part of *le pouvoir* who saw any compromise with the Islamists as a threat to their own interests.[27]

This question of economic interests leads into the sixth strand of the violence, namely extortion by guerrillas and pro-government militias. Very quickly GIA violence blended into extortion and racketeering as leaders on the ground used intimidation to extract monetary support from the local population, a pattern that has clear parallels with terrorist activity in Northern Ireland.[28] The same was also true of pro-government militias who used that anti-terrorist struggle as a cover for corruption and black market activity.[29] This issue of criminality then raises a general argument about the violence as outlined by Luis Martinez.[30] For him the activities of the radical Islamists and their government opponents have to be interpreted as rationally calculated attempts to gain wealth and social prestige within parameters set by the post-colonial state. So, the political and ideological content of the 1992 electoral contest gave way to a new phase after 1993 where all sides used ruthless methods to maximize their own power. Controversially, Martinez contended that the purposeful accumulation of wealth and status by violence is deeply ingrained in Algeria's national culture. In resorting to war, the contending parties were simply replicating in their own time the 'banditry' of the Ottoman era.[31] In short, for Martinez, violence was about exacting the maximum political and social leverage.

Stemming the violence

By 1994 the Algerian regime was isolated. There was no end in sight to the violence, but at every point the Algerian government refused outside mediation. Consequently, when a coalition of political parties, including the FIS, unveiled a common solution in early 1995 this was rejected out of hand by the Algerian government.[32] The new head of state, the military officer Liamine

Algeria on the internet under the title *Mouvement algérien des officers libres* (MAOL). On this see: Aggoun and Rivoire, *Françalgérie, crimes et mensonges d'États*, pp. 548–50.

[27] The intention was to keep wanted politics in Algeria. Other figures of potential reconciliation who were killed in murky circumstances were Abdelhak Benhamouda in 1997 and later Abdelkader Hachani in 1999.

[28] On this see: Hugh Roberts, *Battlefield Algeria* (London: Verso, 2002).

[29] In April 1998 a dozen people from Relizane, including two mayors, were arrested on charges of extortion and murder.

[30] Luis Martinez, *The Algerian Civil War 1990–1998* (London: Hurst & Company, 2000).

[31] The Ottoman period in Algeria lasted from 1517, when Muslims in the region looked to the Ottoman Empire to protect them against Spain, until 1830, the moment of the French invasion.

[32] The Sant'Egidio community in Rome was a Catholic liberal movement that emerged from May 1968 protests and was dedicated to promoting cooperation among religions and conflict resolution. Within this initiative the community invited all parties and the government to a peace conference on 21 and 22 November 1994. The government refused to participate, while

Zeroual, denounced the platform as an attack on national sovereignty, partly because the other parties had allied themselves with the FIS, a banned political entity, but also because the negotiations had been held in Rome under non-Algerian auspices.

Determined to find his own solution, Zeroual submitted himself to a presidential electoral contest in November 1995.[33] The election was a foregone conclusion, but even so it was clear from the contest that ordinary people wanted a return to normality.[34] Strengthened by this legitimacy, Zeroual introduced a new constitution, endorsed by a referendum in November 1996, followed by national elections in June 1997 which were won by a new pro-regime party, the RND (*Rassemblement National Démocratique*). Despite accusations of electoral fraud, Western governments ignored any irregularities on the grounds that Zeroual was bringing the country out of an impasse. At the same time Zeroual put out feelers to the AIS. The AIS wanted to differentiate themselves from the GIA violence, which it saw as out of control, and on this basis negotiated a ceasefire in September 1997.[35] It was a victory for Zeroual. Nevertheless he was under pressure from hardliners within the regime, unhappy at any compromise with terrorism, and on 11 September 1998 Zeroual was forced to stand down.

By this point the AIS ceasefire had endured. Thus, when Bouteflika took power he set out to capitalize on this. From a position of military strength, he sought to transform the ceasefire into a permanent settlement; a transition to a peaceful society, or at least one where violence was minimized. The summer of 1999 saw behind the scenes contacts between government emissaries and the AIS because both sides realized that they had a mutual interest in ending the conflict. On 1 June 1999 the AIS announced that it was ready to formalize a truce. Three days later Bouteflika signalled his desire to enshrine this process in a legal framework. On 6 June the AIS took up the offer and announced an immediate cessation of military activity.[36] The Presidential Office then issued a statement outlining the 'law on civil concord'.

six major opposition parties, including the FIS, agreed to negotiate a common platform. The resultant Rome Platform underlined the rejection of violence; respect for human rights as outlined by the UN; and the need to remove the army from politics. It called for fresh elections and the re-legalization of the FIS: a significant event because this meant that the FIS recognized the principle of political pluralism for the first time.

[33] The other three candidates were Mahfoud Nahnah whose Islamist party, the *Mouvement de la société pour la paix*—MSP, rejected violence; Saïd Sadi, whose party, the *Rassemblement pour la culture et la démocratie*—RCD, was a secular party whose power base was in Kablyia; and Noureddine Boukrouh.

[34] Zeroual won 61 per cent of the vote.

[35] The Algerian public were given no precise details on the ceasefire.

[36] The FIS leaders gave their blessing apart from the still imprisoned Ali Belhadj who was always the most hard-line of the FIS leadership.

Many Algerians, ground down by the violence, were hopeful. However, two of the 1999 presidential candidates, Hocine Aït Ahmed and Taleb Ibrahimi, were critical. For them the process was flawed because it was silent on three key issues: the problem of the 'disappeared'; the ending of the state of emergency; and the future legal status of the FIS. Bouteflika ignored this criticism. His model of transition was one tightly controlled from above. The population was not involved in shaping the process. The civil concord was simply put to them. They had to reply 'for' or 'against' to the referendum question: 'Are you for or against the initiative of the President of the Republic to establish peace and civil concord?' In this manner Bouteflika did not want to be constrained. By leaving the wording vague, he wanted to give himself the widest possible room for manoeuvre. Algerians, aware of the ambiguity but desperate for hope, approved at a level of 98.6 per cent on a turnout of 85 per cent. The result was a huge boost for Bouteflika. He had fulfilled his electoral promise to 'extinguish the fire' and proclaimed the concord as a massive step forward on the way to a renewed Algeria.

As such the Algerian process differed sharply from political transitions elsewhere where the dominant model was that of the truth commissions.[37] This model was particularly prevalent in Latin America, although the most influential was the South African Truth and Reconciliation Commission that was set up in 1995.[38] In the South African case the defining figure was Archbishop Desmond Tutu and under his guidance the model developed was one based on Christian values of truth and forgiveness.[39] Within this process, victims and perpetrators were brought together in an attempt to bring about a healing process, no matter how raw and painful. Truth, Tutu argued, was the key because this would allow the people and society to move on. In acting so, the Commission was avoiding vengeance. It was not like the Nuremberg Trials in 1945 and 1946 when the issue was a legal cleansing process aimed at prosecution and de-Nazification.[40] Instead the purpose was to establish the human rights abuses; to give victims a voice; and to construct an impartial account of the past. As the Promotion of Truth and Reconciliation Act outlined in 1995:

[37] On this see Priscilla B. Hayner, 'Fifteen Truth Commissions—1974 1994: A Comparative Study', *Human Rights Quarterly* 16, no. 4 (1994): pp. 597–655.

[38] On this see Priscilla B. Hayner, *Unspeakable Truths: Facing the Challenge of Truth Commissions* (London: Routledge, 2001). See also the South African Truth and Reconciliation Website at: <www.justice.gov.za/tra/>.

[39] Desmond Tutu, *No Future Without Forgiveness: A Personal Overview of South Africa's Truth and Reconciliation Commission* (London: Rider, 1999).

[40] On this see Guenael Mettraux, ed., *Perspectives on the Nuremberg Trial* (Oxford: Oxford University Press, 2008).

> A commission is necessary to enable South Africans to come to terms with their past on a morally accepted basis and to advance the cause of reconciliation.[41]

Inevitably, Tutu's blueprint for reconciliation did have opponents who argued that this process allowed perpetrators to escape retribution while marginalizing larger and much more problematic issues such as how to address the economic injustices of apartheid.[42] But what is undeniable is the international impact of the Tutu framework. He created a model which has shaped conflict resolution and political transition across the globe.

This global impact is recognized by Herbert Adam who, in analysing how countries have moved on from repressive pasts since 1945, sees South Africa as one of six models of transition which are: amnesia (post-Franco Spain); trial and justice (Nuremberg trials); lustrative (the punishment of collaborators by excluding them from public office); negotiated restitution (reparations and compensation); political re-education; and truth commissions.[43] To these six I would add a further model: political expediency, namely the moment when a country's ruling elite, often due to outside pressure, confronts a difficult past because it is deemed to be in that country's political interests. This has been the case with the expansion of the European Union since the end of the Cold War where honesty about past abuses became a litmus test of democratic transition.[44] In the case of Latvia, which joined the EU in 2004, the run-up to membership involved an official recognition of Latvians' involvement in the Holocaust, while with Croatia, which became a member in 2013, one of the sticking points over membership was the way in which the Croatian government was reluctant to supply evidence in relation to the prosecution of Croat officers accused of war crimes during the wars in the former Yugoslavia.[45]

Of course these models must be seen as both inter-connected and open to variegation. For example, the Moroccan Equity and Reconciliation Commission, established by Royal Decree in January 2004 to investigate human rights abuses between 1956, the year of independence from the French, and 1999, the accession to the throne of Mohammed VI, blended aspects of truth

[41] The Truth and Reconciliation Commission was based upon the Promotion of National Unity and Reconciliation Act, 1995 which can be accessed at: <www.justice.za/trc>.

[42] For a critical perspective see Audrey R. Chapman and Hugo van der Merwe, eds, *Truth and Reconciliation in South Africa: Did the TRC Deliver* (Pennsylvania: University of Pennsylvania Press, 2008).

[43] Herbert Adam, 'Divided Memories: Reckoning with a Criminal Regime', in *Justice and the Politics of Memory*, edited by Gabriel R. Ricci (Somerset, NJ: Transaction Publishers, 2003), pp. 1–20.

[44] On this see: Martin Evans, 'Rethinking Memories, Monuments, Histories: The Memory of World War Two since the end of the Cold War', *National Identities* 8, no. 4 (2006): pp. 317–46.

[45] The United Kingdom and the Netherlands made the surrender of Ante Gotovina, accused of war crimes committed in 1995, a precondition for Croatia's accession to the European Union.

commission and restitution with amnesia and political expediency.[46] So, although there was an investigative process, this process was tightly prescribed. It displayed nothing like the openness of the South African model because the Moroccan Commission could not reveal the names of perpetrators.[47] Furthermore, although the Moroccan Commission sought to financially compensate victims, the process could neither implicate the previous King, Hassan II, in any abuses nor investigate those committed since 1999 under Mohammed VI.[48] While, finally, there was an aspect of political expediency, Mohammed VI knew that in a post-Cold War era, where the West was less willing to ignore human rights violations in the name of anti-communism, he had to turn the page on this period in Moroccan history. He had to appease critics at home and abroad by facing up to past abuses.

Ultimately Mohammed VI was trying to carry out a policy that, by projecting change, would preserve the status-quo. Bouteflika was involved in the same balancing act, but one that carefully avoided any enactment of Tutu's Truth and Reconciliation framework, however superficial. Instead Bouteflika's process was firmly anchored at the amnesia end of Adam's spectrum, in effect bearing all the hallmarks of the Spanish model of transition following the death of Franco in November 1975. There in 1977 a cross-party pact brought together actors from across the divide—from conservatives through to socialists and communists—who all agreed to avoid confrontation in the interest of building new democratic structures.[49] Central to Spanish transition was a 'pact of silence' where all sides agreed not to return to the past because this would be too divisive. By re-opening the wounds of the Spanish Civil War it would make it impossible to establish the lasting structures for a democracy.

Bouteflika made a similar calculation in 1999. Both sides agreed to move on by forgetting their murderous divisions and focusing on the future. There was no talk of victory. There was no talk of surrender. Rather, armed Islamists were allowed to return with their heads held high. Indeed Bouteflika held out the possibility of legalizing the FIS while, given immunity from prosecution, they had the right to hang on to booty extracted from racketeering.

As part of this pact of silence the suffering of civilians was ignored, despite the fact that they had been the primary victims of the violence. They had to accept that thousands of unrepentant terrorists were being let back into society. The civil concord was in effect a common pardon. Nobody—the

[46] On the Moroccan case see: Pierre Vermeren, *Le Maroc de Mohammed VI: la transition inachevée* (Paris: La Découverte, 2009).

[47] This was justified on the grounds that such disclosures would threaten the process of reconciliation.

[48] Nevertheless this was the first of its kind in North Africa and the Middle East. On this see: Human Rights Watch, *Morocco's Truth Commission*, Report 17:11 (Human Rights Watch, November 2005).

[49] On the case of Spain see Paloma Aguilar, *Memory and Amnesia: The Role of the Spanish Civil War in the Transition to Democracy* (Oxford: Berghahn, 2002).

army or the armed groups—was brought to account. On this basis in January 2000 the civil concord led to an amnesty for 6,000 AIS militants. The transition process, therefore, was deliberately opaque and this opaqueness continued when Bouteflika, re-elected in April 2004 in spite of accusations of fraud, sought to bring a final closure to the reconciliation process with a peace charter that was put to a referendum on 29 September 2005. This charter enshrined a broad amnesty for past abuses that covered members of the state security forces and armed groups who were in prison or about to surrender. In theory this did not extend to those who had committed 'acts of collective massacre, rape or the use of explosives in public places', but given the lack of any serious investigation into these crimes, the Algerian public knew that such promises were disingenuous.[50] This meant that voting took place in a cynical atmosphere where large numbers of Algerians had disengaged from the process and, although the charter was approved, in parts of the country there was a 50 per cent abstention rate.[51] Nevertheless Bouteflika pressed ahead and on 1 November 2005, 6,778 prisoners were amnestied.

Repressing criticism

For Bouteflika truth was a necessary sacrifice. Without an amnesty, he claimed, it would have been impossible to coax the guerrillas into the peace process. Many Algerians did not agree, however. They were angry at a transition predicated upon denial. It shut out the majority in the interests of the warring groups as Djamel Berrabah, President of the Coordination Committee for Truth and Justice, argued on 13 April 2000 in an interview with *L'Express*:

> The ruling class has made a deal with the Islamists: 'Be quiet, we know what you have done, you know what we have done—leave us in power and you will get your share.'[52]

Berrabah's comments were a measure of how, with so many unanswered questions, Algeria experienced an upsurge in grass roots activist groups. Modelling themselves on the grieving mothers of Chile who campaigned for justice for the disappeared during the years following the military coup in 1973, 1998 saw the establishment of the National Association of the Families of the Disappeared (*Association National des Familles de Disparus*—ANFD) and SOS-Disappeared (*SOS Disparus*—SOS-D) led by Nacéra Dutour and Lila Ighil,

[50] This is partly because the authorities wanted double agents to disappear into obscurity.

[51] Officials claimed that the charter was approved by 97 per cent on a 79 per cent turnout. These figures were challenged by *Le Soir d'Algérie* which claimed that the turnout was 50 per cent in eastern parts of the country.

[52] Evans and Phillips, *Algeria*, p. 264.

respectively. Their campaign, supported by Louisa Hanoune, leader of the Trotskyist Workers Party (*Parti des Travailleurs*—PT) and the Hocine Aït Ahmed's (*Front des Forces Socialistes*—FFS), tried to break down official silence through regular vigils outside the National Assembly and the Justice Ministry, holding photographs and banners aloft, and the lobbying of international human rights organizations.[53] They accused the government of a whitewash by refusing to examine the role of security forces in disappearances and it was on these grounds that they called for a boycott of the 29 September 1995 referendum. In their view the peace charter glorified violence, inscribed immunity from prosecution, and represented a denial of truth and justice to hundreds of thousands of victims and their families.[54] Allied to this the government faced a steady stream of criticism from abroad in the form of eye-witness accounts, television documentaries, newspaper articles, human rights reports, and critical websites on the internet.[55]

Bouteflika was able to shrug off this opposition largely because on one fundamental level his transition process delivered: the levels of violence rescinded significantly and the overwhelming majority of Algerians were grateful for this fact, even if they were unhappy at aspects of the process. On top of this Bouteflika, in a bid to suffocate criticism, introduced censorship laws and denounced opponents as supporters of 'terrorists and throat cutters', while exploiting the threat of terrorism as a way to instil fear and conformity amongst the population. Finally, Algeria's diplomatic isolation was done away with in the aftermath of 9/11. Now the US wanted allies in the 'war on terror' and immediately courted Algeria as a country with vital inside knowledge on Islamist terrorism.

If Bouteflika's transition was about ending the violence while preserving the status-quo, then the external legitimacy derived from the US was a vital boost. However, the predominant factor for why this transition has endured is internal. Although there is still a huge gulf between rulers and the ruled, very few Algerians want a return to the violence of the 1990s and the result has been a very cautious atmosphere—sceptical about the Arab revolutions and sceptical about those who sought to emulate them in Algeria—which explains

[53] The ANFD filed 2,500 cases to the United Nations Working Group on Forced Disappearances.

[54] The official Office National des Droits de l'Homme (ONDH) a state organization established in 1992 to monitor human rights abuses, outlined 4,185 cases by the end of 1999. However no attempt was made to examine the role of the security forces. These findings were attacked by civilian groups who claimed that 4,185 was just the tip of the iceberg.

[55] There were critical documentaries broadcast on French television and Al-Jazeera. For example, the French station, Canal Plus, broadcast *Algérie, la grande manipulation* on 31 October 2000. Also the British newspaper, *The Independent*, contained a steady stream of articles that challenged the Algerian authorities by Robert Fisk. On this see: Robert Fisk, *The Great War for Civilisation: The Conquest of the Middle East* (London: Harper Perennial, 2006).

why the country has remained relatively calm in comparison with Egypt, Libya, Tunisia, or Syria since early 2011.[56]

Conclusion

In the case of British withdrawal from India the transition to independence was a combination of push and pull factors.[57] The push was mass support for Indian nationalism while the pull was a mixture of British public opinion, largely indifferent or unconvinced of the case for continued imperial rule in India; the new priorities of the Labour government, which recognized that it was not in Britain's interests to maintain domination; and the fact that Britain did not have the financial or military resources to maintain rule. Together these factors produced a logic of decolonization in 1947.

A similar scenario transpired with Algerian independence in 1962. When the FLN launched its war of national liberation in November 1954, the French government argued that the UN had no legal right to intervene because Algeria was sovereign territory.[58] By 1962 the international landscape had been transformed. In September 1958 the FLN established a Provisional Government and in 1961 the French government had no alternative but to enter into negotiations with this Provisional Government, in effect a state in waiting that had been recognized by the Arab states and the Asian communist states. So, like India, there was a logic of decolonization where independence would lead to accession to the UN as a new nation state.[59]

What drove this process was a combination of push and pull factors. Charles de Gaulle returned to power in 1958 to resolve the Algerian War. Initially he tried to follow the Fourth Republic strategy that sought to defeat the FLN while winning over Arab 'hearts and minds' to achieve a solution that kept French sovereignty intact. But by December 1960 de Gaulle had come to the conclusion that the push factor was too strong: most Algerians wanted national independence. Moreover, by this point French public opinion was weary of the whole conflict. It wanted de Gaulle to finish the war and bring the

[56] On the Algerian case see: Martin Evans, 'The 2012 National Elections: Why Algeria remains the exception in North Africa', 11 July 2012, <http://www.opendemocracy.net/martin-evans/2012-national-elections-why-algeria-remains-exception-in-north-africa>. For a comparative perspective see: Michael Willis, *Power and Politics in the Maghreb* (New York: Columbia University Press, 2012).

[57] On India see: John Darwin, *Britain and Decolonization: The Retreat from Empire in the Post-War World* (London: Macmillan, 1987).

[58] On the international context see: Matthew Connelley, *A Diplomatic Revolution: Algeria's Fight for Independence and the Origins of the Cold War* (Oxford: Oxford University Press, 2002).

[59] On this see: Martin Evans, *Algeria: France's Undeclared War* (Oxford: Oxford University Press, 2012), pp. 339–48.

conscripts home. And finally there was the international context. The US was putting pressure on de Gaulle to end the Algerian crisis because in Africa and Asia it was stirring up anti-Western feeling and pushing opinion towards to the Soviet Union. Thus, on all fronts de Gaulle was boxed in. He had no option but to negotiate independence with the FLN, although, as a master politician, de Gaulle made a virtue out of this necessity. To domestic and international opinion he constructed decolonization as a victory of modernization that allowed France to marry the twentieth century.[60]

Algeria in the 1990s was not the same as Algeria in 1962 and India in 1947. In the 1990s the Algerian military was never boxed in like Britain in 1947 or de Gaulle by 1962. It was determined to resist international pressure, while at the same time there were no decolonization pull factors. The Algerian military was not an external force that had to consider domestic public opinion. Unlike decolonization there was never going to be a tipping point where it had no alternative but to withdraw. Equally, in contrast to Algerian and Indian anti-colonial nationalists, Islamist guerrillas had no precise political aim or any real international support and this meant that, eventually, their struggle just came to a dead end.

On one level the situation in Algeria in the 1990s is more akin to the 'dirty wars' in Latin America between 1960s and 1990s when military governments used death squads, torture, and repression to defeat leftist guerrillas—hence the name 'dirty wars'.[61] But in those cases external factors were eventually crucial in framing transitions to democracy because, once the Cold War was over it was no longer in the interests of the US to ignore human rights in the name of anti-communism. In contrast, 9/11 allowed Algeria to draw a veil over human rights abuses because the US did not want to ask difficult questions that could destabilize the regime. Of course US support did not prevent the overthrow of Ben Ali in Tunisia or Mubarak in Egypt, but in the Algerian case there is the predominance of specific internal factors, namely the psychological legacy of the 1990s violence that has produced a highly circumspect atmosphere at a popular level. However, if the model for understanding Algeria is post Franco-Spain, it is significant to note that even there society has eventually returned to the unanswered questions of the Spanish Civil War.[62] With that example in mind, it is interesting to ponder at what point, and under what circumstances Algeria and Algerians, will confront the blank spots of Bouteflika's transition process.

[60] This aspect is explored by Todd Shepherd in *The Invention of Decolonization: The Algerian War and the Remaking of France* (Ithica: Cornell University Press, 2006).

[61] On the process in Latin America see: Hayner, *Unspeakable Truths*.

[62] Aguilar, *Memory and Amnesia*.

References

Adam, Herbert, 'Divided Memories: Reckoning with a Criminal Regime', in *Justice and the Politics of Memory*, edited by Gabriel R. Ricci (Somerset, NJ: Transaction Publishers, 2003), pp. 1–20.

Aggoun, Lounis and Jean-Baptiste Rivoire, *Françalgérie, crimes et mensonges d'États* (Paris: La Découverte, 2004).

Aguilar, Paloma, *Memory and Amnesia: The Role of the Spanish Civil War in the Transition to Democracy* (Oxford: Berghahn, 2002).

'Amnesty International Statement to the 53rd UN Commission on Human Rights', 9 April 1997, <http://www.amnesty.org/en/library/asset/IOR41/008/1997/en/e56e02c5-ea78-11dd-b05d-65164b228191en.pdf>.

Burke, Jason, *Al-Qaeda* (London: Penguin, 2003).

Campos, Michelle, *Ottoman Brothers: Muslims, Christians and Jews in Early-Twentieth Century Palestine* (Stanford: Stanford University Press, 2010).

Chapman, Audrey R. and Hugo van der Merwe, eds, *Truth and Reconciliation in South Africa: Did the TRC Deliver* (Pennsylvania: University of Pennsylvania Press, 2008).

Charef, Abed, *Algérie, le grand dérapage* (La Tour d'Aigues: L'Aube, 1994).

Connelley, Matthew, *A Diplomatic Revolution: Algeria's Fight for Independence and the Origins of the Cold War* (Oxford: Oxford University Press, 2002).

Darwin, John, *Britain and Decolonization: The Retreat from Empire in the Post-War World* (London: Macmillan, 1987).

Evans, Martin, *Algeria: France's Undeclared War* (Oxford: Oxford University Press, 2012).

Evans, Martin, 'Rethinking memories, monuments, histories: The memory of World War Two since the end of the Cold War', *National Identities* 8, no. 4 (2006): pp. 317–46.

Evans, Martin, 'The 2012 National Elections: Why Algeria remains the exception in North Africa', 11 July 2012, <http://www.opendemocracy.net/martin-evans/2012-national-elections-why-algeria-remains-exception-in-north-africa>.

Evans, Martin and John Phillips, *Algeria: Anger of the Dispossessed* (London: Yale University Press, 2007).

Fisk, Robert, *The Great War for Civilisation: The Conquest of the Middle East* (London: Harper Perennial, 2006).

Harbi, Mohammed, *Le FLN, mirage et réalité. Des origins à la prise du pouvoir* (Paris: Jeune Afrique, 1980).

Hayner, Priscilla B., 'Fifteen Truth Commissions—1974–1994: A Comparative Study', *Human Rights Quarterly* 16, no. 4 (1994): pp. 597–655.

Hayner, Priscilla B., *Unspeakable Truths: Facing the Challenge of Truth Commissions* (London: Routledge, 2001).

Human Rights Watch, *Morocco's Truth Commission,* Report 17:11 (Human Rights Watch, November 2005).

Malti, Djallal, *La Nouvelle Guerre d'Algérie* (Paris: La Découverte, 1999).

Martinez, Luis, *The Algerian Civil War 1990–1998* (London: Hurst & Company, 2000).

Messaoudi, Khalida, *Une Algérienne Debout* (Paris: Flammarion, 1995).

Mettraux, Guenael, ed., *Perspectives on the Nuremberg Trial* (Oxford: Oxford University Press, 2008).

Meynier, Gilbert, *Histoire intérieure du FLN, 1954–1962* (Paris: Fayar, 2002).

Reporters sans frontières, *Le Drame Algérien. Un peuple en otage* (Paris: La Découverte, 1994).

Roberts, Hugh, *Battlefield Algeria* (London: Verso, 2002).

Rogan, Eugene, *The Arabs: A History* (London: Allen Lane, 2009).

Rouadjia, Ahmed, *Les Frères et la mosquée: Énquête sur le Mouvement Islamiste en Algérie* (Paris: Karthala, 1990).

Samraoui, Mohammed, *Chronique des années de sang. Algérie: comment les services secrets ont manipulé les groupes islamistes* (Paris: Denoël, 2003).

Saouïdia, Habib, *La Sale Guerre* (Paris: La Découverte, 2001).

Shepherd Todd, *The Invention of Decolonization: The Algerian War and the Remaking of France* (Ithica: Cornell University Press, 2006).

South African Truth and Reconciliation Website: www.justice.gov.za/tra/.

Stora, Benjamin, *La Guerre Invisible, Algérie, Années 90* (Paris: Presses de Sciences Po, 2001).

Touati, Amine, *Algérie, les islamistes à l'assaut au pouvoir* (Paris: L'Harmattan, 1995).

Tutu, Desmond, *No Future Without Forgiveness: A Personal Overview of South Africa's Truth and Reconciliation Commission* (London: Rider, 1999).

Vermeren, Pierre, *Le Maroc de Mohammed VI: la transition inachevée* (Paris: La Découverte, 2009).

Willis, Michael, *The Islamist Challenge in Algeria: A Political History* (Reading: Ithaca Press, 1996).

Willis, Michael, *Power and Politics in the Maghreb* (New York: Columbia University Press, 2012).

Yous, Nesroulah, *Qui a tué à Bentalha? Algérie, chronique d'un massacre annoncé* (Paris: La Découverte, 2000).

10

The end of Operation New Dawn

The Tropic Lightning Division in Iraq

Mark Battjes

> We ultimately set the conditions to go to zero through built in flexibility of the major bases we were occupying.... We continued down the path as if we were going to zero. So for us, it didn't really affect us too much. We had thought through those possibilities from the very beginning.
>
> Senior Leader of the 25th Infantry Division,
> Schofield Barracks, Hawaii, July 2012

On 18 December 2011 the last elements of the United States (US) Army remaining in Iraq crossed the border into Kuwait, ending Operation New Dawn. This did not, however, end the involvement of the United States in Iraq. The United States and Iraq continue to cooperate as partners under the guidelines laid out in the 'Strategic Framework Agreement for a Relationship of Friendship and Cooperation between the United States of America and the Republic of Iraq', signed on 17 November 2008.[1] The Department of State (DOS), supported by the Department of Defense (DOD) through the Office of Security Cooperation—Iraq (OSC-I), is charged with implementing the Strategic Framework Agreement for the United States Government. Before it could do so, responsibility for operations, security, property, and equipment had to be transitioned from the US military. This chapter will examine that transition through the experience of the US Army's 25th Infantry Division[2] (25ID), the last US Army

[1] Hereafter referred to as the Strategic Framework Agreement.

[2] The Commanding General of the 25th Infantry Division throughout its time in Iraq was Major General Bernard S. Champoux. At the time of writing, Lieutenant General Champoux is serving as the Chief of Staff for US Forces, Korea.

division headquarters in Iraq.[3] The experience of the 25ID in closing the Iraq theatre illustrates well the themes discussed throughout this volume. The chapter begins with a brief review of the situation in Iraq in the fall of 2011 and then discusses how the division organized its staff to confront the complexity of the transition and used that unique organization to address the dynamic nature of the transition, the increased risk associated with the loss of control, and the difficulty of executing a contested transition.

Situation in October 2011

In early October 2011 the situation in Iraq presented unique challenges to 25ID. The division had been in Iraq since December 2010 serving as the headquarters for United States Division—Center (USD-C) under the command of United States Forces—Iraq (USF-I).[4] At the time that the division assumed responsibility as USD-C the area of operations encompassed just two provinces, Baghdad and Anbar, and the US Army had two other division headquarters operating in the country.[5] However, by October 2011, the 25ID had assumed responsibility for the nine provinces south of Baghdad and was preparing to assume responsibility for all US forces north of Baghdad when the US 4th Infantry Division departed later in the month.[6] This change alone represented a significant challenge, but the situation was even more complex.

The Strategic Framework Agreement signed in November 2008 required the United States and Iraq to 'continue to foster close cooperation concerning defense and security arrangements without prejudice to Iraqi sovereignty over its land, sea, and air territory. Such security and defense cooperation shall be undertaken pursuant to the *Agreement Between the United States of America and the Republic of Iraq on the Withdrawal of United States forces from Iraq and the Organization of Their Activities during Their Temporary Presence in Iraq*.'[7] The terms of the Security Agreement imposed a deadline of 31 December 2011 for

[3] The author served as the Division Battle Major with the 25th Infantry Division during its final days in Iraq from 17 July 2011 until the departure of the division headquarters on 17 December 2011. Information and insights drawn from the author's personal experience will be identified as such.

[4] Previously known as Multinational Forces—Iraq (MNF-I).

[5] The US Army's 4th Infantry Division served as United States Division—North (USD-N), and the US Army National Guard's 36th Infantry Division served as United States Division—South (USD-S).

[6] United States Division—Center and 25th Infantry Division Command History Report, Chronology of Key Events, December 2011.

[7] Strategic Framework Agreement, Section III. The document referred to in Section III of the Strategic Framework Agreement was generally referred to as the 'Security Agreement'. It was also referred to as a Status of Forces Agreement (SOFA) in the popular press, but it was not actually a SOFA.

the withdrawal of all US Forces from the territory of Iraq.[8] This was not, however, considered a definitive withdrawal date.

Throughout 2011 the United States Government negotiated with the Government of Iraq (GOI) to extend the presence of US forces in the country. In his opening statement to the Senate Foreign Relations Committee on 1 February 2011, Senator Richard Lugar opined that 'although the United States should continue preparations for winding down the military mission, withdrawal from Iraq cannot be the sole driver of our policy there'.[9] This remained true throughout most of 2011. In a visit to Iraq in August 2011, Admiral Michael Mullen, the Chairman of the Joint Chiefs of Staff, emphasized that any request from the GOI to retain some US forces in the country had to be made quickly; two days later the Iraqi Parliament authorized Prime Minister Nouri al-Maliki to begin negotiations on extending the Security Agreement.[10]

As a result of the strategic uncertainty, planners in Iraq and the Pentagon had to maintain flexibility in order to accommodate the potential for some US forces to remain in the country. In testimony before the National Security, Homeland Defense and Foreign Operations Subcommittee of the House of Representatives Committee on Oversight and Government Reform regarding the status of the transition to a civilian-led mission in Iraq on 12 October 2011, Alan F. Estevez, Assistant Secretary of Defense for Logistics and Materiel Readiness, reported that as of 1 October 2011 there were still over 43,000 US military personnel and 53,000 DOD contractors in Iraq.[11] Under later questioning, Mr Estevez stated that the current requirement to withdraw all personnel from Iraq remained feasible and that 'should there be successful negotiations, turning some of that around is also complicated but absolutely executable'.[12] In other words, there were still an enormous number of people in Iraq with plans and operations ongoing to ensure their complete withdrawal, but it was also possible that some of those personnel could be authorized to remain if the administration's negotiations with the GOI were successful.

The negotiations were not successful and President Obama announced on 21 October 2011 that all US forces would be withdrawn in accordance with the

[8] 'Agreement Between the United States of America and the Republic of Iraq on the Withdrawal of United States forces from Iraq and the Organization of Their Activities during Their Temporary Presence in Iraq', Article 24, Subsection 1. Hereafter, this will be cited as Security Agreement.

[9] Richard Lugar, *Opening Statement before the Senate Foreign Relations Committee*, 1 February 2011, <http://www.foreign.senate.gov/imo/media/doc/LugarStatement020111a.pdf>.

[10] Kenneth Katzman, *Iraq: Politics, Governance, and Human Rights, Congressional Research Service Report*, 10 November 2011, p. 31, <http://www.fas.org/sgp/crs/mideast/RS21968.pdf>.

[11] Alan F. Estevez, *Testimony before the National Security, Homeland Defense and Foreign Operations Subcommittee of the House of Representatives Committee on Oversight and Government Reform*, 12 October 2011, pp. 24–9, <http://www.gpo.gov/fdsys/pkg/CHRG-112hhrg73166/pdf/CHRG-112hhrg73166.pdf>.

[12] Estevez, *Testimony*, pp. 46–7.

Security Agreement.[13] As a result, Operation New Dawn would end and the US military would have to execute a full transition of responsibility.

The situation in Iraq in the late fall of 2011 demonstrates well the complex and dynamic environment that confronted the 25ID throughout its time in Iraq, and as the division received orders directing it to conduct the full transition this complex and dynamic environment had created several critical obstacles to overcome with just over two months remaining before the final transition had to be completed. The division needed to close or transfer all of the remaining bases in the country, some of which had remained open far longer than was ideal in order to accommodate the possibility of a large residual force remaining in Iraq. This required the division to move personnel and equipment, account for real property being transferred to the GOI or to the DOS, and in some cases remove sensitive or classified infrastructure while continuing to secure the base and protect all US personnel.

Protection was also a major challenge as a result of the changing situation. Protecting US forces as the division withdrew personnel required maintaining a delicate balance between ground combat personnel, such as infantry and armour, and enabling forces, such as aviation, medical evacuation, and intelligence. Additionally, the fact that US forces were withdrawing was known to terrorist, militia, and insurgent elements and this presented them with an opportunity to attack US forces during vulnerable transition periods. Successful attacks, especially those resulting in a lot of US casualties immediately prior to the closure of a US base could be used to demonstrate to the enemy's audiences at home and abroad that the US mission in Iraq was a failure and that they were responsible for that failure. The reduced number of US military personnel required the division to partner more closely with Iraqi Security Forces (ISF) to provide additional security during operations, which represented a not insubstantial increase in risk. Finally, the protection of US forces was complicated by the Security Agreement which required that 'all such military operations that are carried out pursuant to this Agreement shall be conducted with the agreement of the Government of Iraq'.[14] The US military retained the inherent right to self-defence,[15] but some operations were limited due to this requirement.

Finally, the division had to assist in the transition of responsibility for many key functions, including protection, to the DOS. Although much of this work was done through the division's higher headquarters, the division retained responsibility for a portion of the transition.[16] According to Congressional

[13] Katzman, *Iraq: Politics, Governance, and Human Rights*, p. 31.
[14] Security Agreement, Article 4, Subsection 2.
[15] Security Agreement, Article 4, Subsection 5.
[16] Interview with senior member of 25ID Transition Staff, Baghdad, Iraq, 13 April 2011.

testimony in October 2011 the DOS presence would consist of some 17,000 personnel, more than 14,000 of whom would be contractors.[17] The contractors would provide life support, conduct logistical operations, and 7,500 of them would provide security which would include operating UAVs, protecting compounds, securing embassy personnel and convoys, disposing of unexploded ordnance or bombs, and recovering downed aircraft.[18] The DOS presence was intended to be fully operational by October.[19] When the division received orders to execute a full withdrawal, however, this was not the truth on the ground.

The situation as described above was not ideal for the execution of a military transition. The final composition and disposition of US forces inside Iraq had fluctuated from upwards of 12,000 personnel to zero. The number of bases to remain open and the amount of life support required continually changed as a result. As units left Iraq the remaining US headquarters were unable to influence operations as effectively as they had previously because they had both fewer forces at their disposal and a reduced ability to partner with ISF in those areas where the US military had already departed. Finally, the enemy continued to contest the transition and sought to ensure that the US's mission in Iraq was perceived as ending in failure.

The 25ID had prepared itself well to confront these difficulties, beginning long before its deployment to Iraq. As will be shown in this chapter, the division took a unique approach to organizing its staff in order to optimize its effectiveness. The staff reorganization enabled the division to be flexible in its operational approach. Furthermore, the division maintained a sharp focus on protecting the transition and US forces throughout the entirety of the process, which ensured that it was able to deny enemy forces the ability to negatively impact upon the transition and affect the strategic narrative.

Organizing to execute the transition

As noted throughout this volume, the difficulty and importance of the transition from military operations has often been overlooked by military planners. The 25ID, however, was able to counter this trend because of the timing and circumstances of its deployment to Iraq. The division was scheduled to

[17] Jason Chaffetz, *Opening Statement before the National Security, Homeland Defense and Foreign Operations Subcommittee of the House of Representatives Committee on Oversight and Government Reform*, 12 October 2011, <http://www.gpo.gov/fdsys/pkg/CHRG-112hhrg73166/pdf/CHRG-112hhrg73166.pdf>.

[18] Chaffetz, *Opening Statement*, p. 2.

[19] John F. Kerry, *Opening Statement before the Senate Foreign Relations Committee*, 1 February 2011, <http://www.state.gov/secretary/remarks/2013/09/212603.htm>.

deploy to Iraq in December 2010 and the two other divisions in place upon its arrival were not programmed to be replaced. Moreover, the Security Agreement directing full withdrawal in December 2011 had been in place for several years. Therefore, the division knew that it was possible that it would be the final division headquarters to serve in Iraq and that it might have to execute a complete withdrawal of US forces and a full transition of the military mission. A senior leader of the division stated that as a result the division's 'approach was a lot a different. Whereas everyone else was handing off their piece of terrain to another unit, we didn't have that luxury. We were there to conclude operations and pull all troops and material out of the country.'[20]

This knowledge enabled the division to anticipate the difficulty and complexity associated with the transition and take action during its training and preparation period to counter it. The Commanding General, Major General Bernard Champoux, recognized the unique nature of the problem and directed his Deputy Commanding Generals to closely examine the staff and its organization to determine if it was optimized to solve the problems the division might encounter.[21] The US Army organizes its division staffs into several groups: personal staff, coordinating staff, and special staff.[22] Each component staff group is based on providing support to the Commanding General in a single function, be it operations, logistics, fire support, intelligence, etc. Although this model is tested and generally flexible, the division senior leadership determined that it was not optimized to support execution of the tasks the 25ID expected to have to accomplish during its tour.[23] Therefore, the division staff partially reorganized itself by creating standing staff organizations aligned against lines of effort (LOE) that operated alongside of and in conjunction with the traditional general staff sections.

The LOEs and their corresponding standing staff organizations were named Reposture,[24] Transition, Protection, Effective Communications,[25] and

[20] Interview with 25ID Senior Leader, Schofield Barracks, HI, 6 July 2012.

[21] Interview with 25ID Senior Leader, Baghdad, Iraq, 21 September 2011.

[22] US Department of the Army, Field Manual 6-0, Mission Command: Command and Control of Army Forces (Washington, DC: Government Printing Office, 2003). The current generation of Army doctrine, based on the Army Doctrinal Publications (ADPs) does not specify the organization of the division staff. However, the US Army's divisions continue to align their staffs using the personal, coordinating, and special staff structure. The coordinating staff contains the familiar numbered staff sections—G-1 is Adjutant/Human Resources, G-2 is Intelligence, and so on—that is often referred to as the Napoleonic staff model.

[23] Interview with 25ID Staff Primary, Schofield Barracks, HI, 5 June 2012.

[24] The term reposture is not a US military doctrinal term. The division used this term to refer to all actions that were necessary in order to reposition or withdraw US military forces to include the closure or transfer to GOI control of US bases, the tactical movement of US forces out of Iraq, the termination of contract services, and the transfer or removal of US military equipment.

[25] The Effective Communications LOE operated in support of all the other LOEs and the division's operations as a whole. Discussion of its efforts is outside the scope of this chapter.

Strengthen the Iraqi Security Forces (SISF). The general and special staff sections provided personnel, leaders, and resources to the LOE staffs on a full- and part-time basis. Each of the LOEs was led by a division staff member in the rank of Lieutenant Colonel who in some cases was a primary division staff officer.[26] The LOE staffs developed a mission statement derived from guidance received from the Commanding General and their anticipated tasks, and organized themselves internally to meet their mission requirements. The hybrid staff organization was tested and refined during the division's Mission Rehearsal Exercise (MRX) in August and September 2010.[27] Three of the LOEs—Reposture, Protection, and Transition—are particularly relevant to illustrate the challenges associated with a military transition and their mission and organization will be described here.

The Reposture LOE's mission was to provide 'staff oversight and coordination for the transition, return, and closure of all USD-C property and facilities to the GOI and USM-I [United States Mission—Iraq]'.[28] This mission was directly tied to accomplishing the withdrawal set forth in the Security Agreement and also required the division to enable the DOS to establish and begin operating its enduring footprint in the country.[29] An infantry officer served as the LOE chief and he was supported by officers, non-commissioned officers, warrant officers, and Department of the Army (DA) civilians from across the entire division staff, to include engineers, logisticians, human resources specialists, and medical, contracting, and information technology personnel.[30] The unique requirements of the group's mission required them to attend several training courses prior to and after arrival in the theatre, including an Operational Contract Support course and Base Transition training provided by USF-I.[31]

The Reposture LOE enabled the division to develop specialists in base closure, something that no member of the standard coordinating or special staff is specifically trained to do. The hybrid organization created a dedicated, cross-functional team to be those specialists. Furthermore, the LOE staff members maintained their connections to their general or special staff sections, amplifying their capabilities.[32] They also operated in close coordination with the other LOE staffs, particularly Protection.[33]

[26] The organization of specific LOE staffs will be discussed further in the subsequent paragraphs.
[27] United States Division—Center and 25th Infantry Division, Command History Feeder Report, Protection LOE, 29 April 2011, p. 3.
[28] United States Division—Center and 25th Infantry Division, Command History Feeder Report, Reposture LOE, 13 April 2011, p. 2.
[29] Reposture LOE, 13 April 2011, pp. 2–4.
[30] Reposture LOE, 13 April 2011, p. 3.
[31] Reposture LOE, 13 April 2011, p. 3.
[32] Interview with member of the 25ID Reposture staff, Baghdad, Iraq, 30 January 2011.
[33] Reposture LOE, 13 April 2011, p. 5.

The US Army recognizes protection as one of the seven warfighting functions. Protection is not, however, a single, cohesive personal, coordinating, or special staff section under the current divisional model. However, protecting the force was critical to the division's success, particularly because of its impact on the perceived success or failure of US operations in Iraq if the transition was contested by enemy forces. If the division suffered significant casualties and it appeared to audiences in Iraq and around the world that the US was being forced out, then that could be interpreted as a strategic failure for the United States.[34]

The Protection LOE staff section was formed during the division's Mission Rehearsal Exercise in response to the Commanding General's stated intent and the operational approach the division developed to accomplish that intent.[35] The Division Engineer served as the Protection LOE chief and the Division Chemical, Biological, Radiological, Nuclear, and Explosive (CBRNE) Officer served as his deputy.[36] They were supported by a relatively large staff that included officers, non-commissioned officers, and DA civilians with specialties in engineering, military policing, explosive ordnance disposal, electronic warfare, information operations, medical operations, and safety.[37]

The Protection cell's purpose was to identify and mitigate threats to US and Iraqi forces in order to ensure mission accomplishment.[38] They further organized themselves into three sub-cells: Identify the Threat, Mitigate the Threat, and Respond to Incidents.[39] Each member of the Protection staff served in one of those cells and participated in working groups and staff assistance visits. The Protection line of effort and its staff integrated, coordinated, and synchronized all of their efforts with the other division staff sections and functional cells, to include Operations, Intelligence, Reposture, SISF, and Transition.[40]

The Transition LOE was much smaller than the two discussed previously. The Transition LOE staff was formed using the division's G9[41] section and was composed primarily of civil affairs officers and non-commissioned officers, including the primary staff officer who was serving as the G9 officer in charge.[42] The Transition LOE's mission was to ensure 'that USD-C enabling activities are transferred to enduring organizations including USM-I and the Iraqi Government in order to ensure the preconditions for ISF success'.[43] In an

[34] Interview with 25ID Senior Leader, Baghdad, Iraq, 22 July 2011.
[35] Protection LOE, 29 April 2011, p. 3.
[36] Protection LOE, 29 April 2011, p. 4.
[37] Protection LOE, 29 April 2011, p. 4.
[38] Protection LOE, 29 April 2011, p. 5.
[39] Protection LOE, 29 April 2011, p. 5.
[40] Protection LOE, 29 April 2011, p. 6.
[41] On the US Army division staff, the G9 is the civil affairs staff section.
[42] United States Division—Center and 25th Infantry Division, Command History Feeder Report, Transition LOE, 5 October 2011, p. 1.
[43] Transition LOE, 5 October 2011, p. 1.

interview, a senior member of the Transition staff indicated that for the division this consisted of four main components.[44]

First, the Transition staff monitored the completion and closure of all remaining Commander's Emergency Relief Program (CERP) projects that were ongoing in the division's area of operations. Although the number and type of CERP projects had dwindled continuously since the beginning of Operation New Dawn, the Transition cell still had to close out projects totalling $22 million during July, August, and September of 2011.[45] The Transition team also assisted in the closure and withdrawal from Iraq of the Provincial Reconstruction Teams (PRTs) that were operating in Anbar and Baghdad.[46] This included helping them complete open projects that were not funded through CERP and transitioning key relationships and programmes to the Department of State where required.

The other two components of the Transition staff's mission consisted of liaison and monitoring functions. The first of these was support to the Reconciliation and Engagement Cell (REC) operating out of the International Zone.[47] This standalone cell reported directly to the Commanding General, 25ID, and had established over many years an invaluable number of contacts and relationships with key Iraqi tribal leaders and other local power brokers. It was critical to the success of the transition to pass these contacts and relationships to the Department of State which was establishing a similar cell within the embassy's Political-Military section.[48] The second such effort was to monitor the establishment of the Department of Defense's Office of Security Cooperation-Iraq (OSC-I) and the International Narcotics and Law (INL) bureau of the Department of State. This effort did not involve assistance but was instead utilized to provide the division's command group with a regular assessment of the new agencies' progress so that the division's senior leaders could address any concerns with USF-I leadership.

The division's partial reorganization of its staff enabled it to address the complex and dynamic problem sets that it would encounter while executing the military transition. It also optimized portions of the division staff that may not otherwise have been fully utilized. As a division staff primary recalled after returning to Schofield Barracks 'you have all kinds of talent in the division headquarters that might not be fully utilized in Operation New Dawn if we didn't establish these lines of effort'.[49] The reorganization also enabled the division to focus effort on specific problem sets by empowering the officers in

[44] Interview with member of Transition Staff, Baghdad, Iraq, 13 April 2011.
[45] Transition LOE, 5 October 2011, p. 2.
[46] Interview with member of Transition Staff, Baghdad, Iraq, 13 April 2011.
[47] Interview with member of Transition Staff, Baghdad, Iraq, 13 April 2011.
[48] Interview with member of Transition Staff, Baghdad, Iraq, 13 April 2011.
[49] Interview with 25ID staff primary, Schofield Barracks, HI, 5 June 2012.

charge of the LOEs, rather than potentially diluting the effort by requiring it all to flow through a single staff section, such as the G3 (Operations).[50]

Finally, it is also important to note while discussing the organization for transition that the division's subordinate forces were US Army Brigade Combat Teams (BCTs), Combat Aviation Brigades, and other battalion and brigade-sized units. Although the BCTs were augmented by US military personnel to serve in a Security Force Assistance capacity, they retained the vast majority of their subordinate battalions, and resultant combat power, and were therefore capable of operating as a BCT. This is in contrast with the organization of forces during the ongoing transition in Afghanistan where planners are meeting the requirements imposed by the force cap and a diverse multinational force by creating ad-hoc formations that are built utilizing the components of a BCT, but lack the cohesion and robust capabilities provided by a full BCT. During the closing days of Operation New Dawn, the ability to call on the capabilities of a full BCT was a significant advantage for the division and enabled it to adapt its responses to the facts on the ground.

Flexibly responding to a dynamic situation

The flexibility that the division possessed as a result of its internal reorganization enabled it to accomplish its mission to complete the military transition during the final two months. One of the major challenges that remained with such little time left was the closure and transfer of US military bases throughout the country. On the day that President Obama announced the complete withdrawal of US forces 12 bases remained in the division's footprint that needed to be closed or transferred to GOI control, including the massive Victory Base Complex (VBC) at Baghdad International Airport. This could have been an impossible mission to accomplish, but as a senior leader of the division noted 'we ultimately set the conditions to go to zero[51] through built in flexibility of the major bases we were occupying... we continued down the path as if we were going to zero. So for us, it [the complete withdrawal] didn't really affect us too much. We had thought through those possibilities from the very beginning and went to the worst case. The worst case being all US personnel and equipment leaving the country by December 31st.'[52]

Although the division was preparing for complete withdrawal as the Security Agreement negotiations were ongoing, it could not execute the complete

[50] Interview with 25ID staff primary, Schofield Barracks, HI, 5 June 2012.

[51] The term 'go to zero' was used colloquially by military personnel in Iraq to refer to a complete withdrawal of US forces.

[52] Interview with 25ID Senior Leader, Schofield Barracks, HI, 6 July 2012.

withdrawal without impacting current operations. The main effort of US military operations in Iraq from the time the division arrived until September 2011 was to advise, train, and assist the ISF. However, as a senior leader of the division stated in a command history interview, 'from a physics standpoint, I realized that we couldn't wait until September to begin reposturing or, just physically, we weren't going to be able to get it done'.[53] In order to overcome this challenge, the Reposture staff closely examined the largest bases in Iraq to identify portions of each base that could be closed early without a significant impact on operations. These areas were then closed or transferred as a series of so-called partial transfers.[54]

The Reposture LOE conducted such a transfer involving the US base at Taji.[55] The group's command history report from July 2011 noted that 'Stakeholder Conferences were scheduled once a month to synchronize the efforts to transfer Taji to OSC-I [Office of Security Cooperation—Iraq[56]]. The Taji footprint changed many times and ultimately included 4 partial transfers and the requirement to continue services outside USF controlled boundaries.'[57] Partial transfers required the Reposture staff to develop plans to handover responsibility for small portions of larger bases to the GOI or to USM-I while maintaining the overall capability of the base to support US military operations from and within them. While this increased the complexity, oversight, and management required to close these bases it enabled the division to simultaneously begin to close a base and utilize it. As a result, once the final withdrawal was announced, the division had a much smaller problem to confront in order to complete the largest closures.

The negotiations to extend the Security Agreement throughout the division's time in Iraq also impacted on its ability to prepare some bases for closure. For example, if the negotiations were successful and the US military was able to retain a sizeable force in the country then it would need a suitable control headquarters location for USF-I while reducing the overt military presence in Iraq, particularly in Baghdad. In April 2011, Al Asad Air Base in western Iraq was designated as the location for the future USF-I headquarters and the USF-I staff and infrastructure moved to the base in the fall of 2011.[58] The Base Command Group at Al Asad and the Reposture staff created and

[53] Interview with 25ID Senior Leader, 21 September 2011, Baghdad, Iraq.

[54] Interview with 25ID Senior Leader, 21 September 2011, Baghdad, Iraq.

[55] Taji is a base on the northwest side of Baghdad, just outside of what would be considered the Baghdad city limits. It served as a major US base throughout operations in Iraq. Its primary function was to host US Army helicopter forces that supported operations in and around Baghdad.

[56] OSC-I is the residual US military mission in Iraq. It operates under the United States Mission—Iraq led by the US ambassador. The OSC-I's several hundred personnel are responsible for continued training with Iraqi Security Forces as well as supporting foreign military sales.

[57] United States Division—Center and 25th Infantry Division, Command History Feeder Report, Reposture LOE, 28 July 2011, p. 15.

[58] Reposture LOE, 28 July 2011, p. 17.

executed multiple plans in order to close Al Asad as a result of this decision. The first plan had been developed in order to close the base without repositioning the USF-I headquarters there. Another plan was created to partially close Al Asad but retain the USF-I footprint.[59] Ultimately, the division executed the complete closure, including the withdrawal of all USF-I personnel and equipment from the base after they had been repositioned there from VBC. However, because the division staff maintained its flexibility it was able to respond to this challenge and Al Asad was successfully closed on 8 December 2011, less than seven weeks after the President's announcement.

Closing out the service contracts associated with each base added another layer of complexity to the closure process.[60] The Reposture staff identified approximately 100 contracts that were funded by USD-C and more than 1,000 contracts that were funded and in force throughout the division's area of operations.[61] The staff had difficulty accounting for all of the personnel, equipment, and property associated with each contract. Moreover, they determined that some contracts were being managed by units that were headquartered outside of Iraq.[62] The Reposture staff's planning for each base closure had to account for the time required to notify the contractors, contract managers, and contracted employees of the closure plans and then follow-up to ensure that the appropriate actions were being taken to end the contract. In order for the base to close on schedule, this process had to occur simultaneously with the other steps and potentially be completed out of sequence.

The effort to transfer key functional responsibilities to the Department of State also demonstrated the division's flexible execution of the transition process. As discussed above, much of the planning for and execution of the transition of responsibilities to the DOS occurred at USF-I headquarters.[63] But, because the division was responsible for Baghdad and the handover of major bases within the Iraqi capital, the division had an intense interest in ensuring that the transition process was completed. Complicating matters was the fact that the military, and the division especially, was not able to direct the DOS to take action, nor could it enforce the military's preferred timeline for DOS actions. As a senior member of the division staff noted in an interview conducted in July 2011, 'as our timeline proceeded we found that everyone else's timelines were moving to the right and impacting our ability to hand off processes'.[64]

The lack of responsibility for most transition operations was not the only challenge the division encountered as it tried to shepherd the transition

[59] Reposture LOE, 28 July 2011, p. 17.
[60] Interview with member of the 25ID Reposture staff, 30 January 2011.
[61] Reposture LOE, 28 July 2011, pp. 22–3. [62] Reposture LOE, 28 July 2011, p. 23.
[63] Interview with member of Transition Staff, Baghdad, Iraq, 13 April 2011.
[64] Interview with senior member of the 25ID staff, Baghdad, Iraq, 9 July 2011.

process to completion. One senior leader noted that 'a big inhibitor in the transition process for us was the assumption that all of us made all along... that there would be full and immediate US government funding of the proposed transition processes and mechanisms'.[65] When this funding was not immediately forthcoming, it required the DOS to delay implementation of programmes and denied them the ability to assume some functions as early as the military desired. The problem was exacerbated during the summer of 2011 when a large portion of the staff at the US Embassy rotated out of Iraq, a problem the division's Transition staff identified during the spring but were not able to affect.[66] In some sections of the Embassy the changeover exceeded 90 per cent of the staff.[67]

The transition process also crossed several staff and LOE boundaries. This was particularly true for Protection and Reposture. As noted above regarding Taji, it was not always clear which bases or portions of bases DOS or OSC-I needed to remain operational following the withdrawal of US forces. The lack of funding compounded the problem because it prevented necessary construction and other improvements from beginning on schedule.[68] Without knowing exactly which areas were going to be operational, the Protection staff could only provide its best guess about what kinds of assets would be required and begin the process of transferring them.[69] This flexible response facilitated the division's ability to complete the transition on time while also enabling some decisions, such as which portions of Taji to retain or what protection assets to utilize, to be delayed until the final disposition of US forces was determined.

Despite all of these challenges, the Transition cell had largely completed its work by September 2011 and the Reposture and Protection staffs were able to develop and implement feasible plans that ensured that DOS and OSC-I had the necessary facilities and equipment to assume full control of operations upon the division's departure in December. The ability to retain flexibility in execution, and conduct some portions of the base closure process non-sequentially, ensured that the division was able to close 12 bases and move more than 43,000 military personnel out of the country in slightly more than eight weeks time. Moreover, it did all of this while providing a high level of protection to all portions of the transition process.

[65] Interview with senior member of the 25ID staff, Baghdad, Iraq, 9 July 2011.
[66] Interview with member of Transition Staff, Baghdad, Iraq, 13 April 2011.
[67] Interview with senior member of the 25ID staff, Baghdad, Iraq, 9 July 2011.
[68] Interview with member of the 25ID Reposture staff, Baghdad, Iraq, 30 January 2011.
[69] Interview with member of the 25ID Protection staff, Baghdad, Iraq, 13 March 2011.

Mitigating risk and protecting the transition

The complete withdrawal of US military forces necessarily required the full relinquishment of control for all military operations in the country. While this is an obvious statement, it is important to highlight this fact because of the challenges that doing so presented to the division. It particularly tested the division's ability to protect the transition process itself and ensure that when enemy forces in Iraq contested the transition and withdrawal, as expected, they did not significantly impact the perceived success or failure of the US mission in Iraq solely as a result of what happened during the final transition process. As a senior leader of the division recalled in an interview, 'we always knew that protecting the force was going to have to be a constant effort. Partly, because we've never done this before.... What does success look like on December 31st?... If it's a bunch of US casualties and the US limping out of here then it is probably strategic failure.'[70]

During the division's first 90 days in theatre, the Protection LOE staff identified that there were no existing plans to protect the transition of the military mission to the DOS and no plans to transition the protection functions and assets[71] to DOS security contractors.[72] This was a striking observation considering the scope of DOS responsibilities that were supposed to be operational by October of 2011, as discussed in the earlier section 'Situation in October 2011'. Moreover, there were no existing plans to protect US forces as they either repositioned within or withdrew from the theatre.[73] Determining how best to protect the force during the repositioning and withdrawal was critical because as the number of US forces and bases were reduced it provided fewer locations at which terrorist or insurgent attacks could be directed. It also meant that there were fewer US military forces to respond to any attack that did occur and, because of the restrictions imposed by the Security Agreement, US forces were not able to conduct unilateral operations to provide their own security. Lastly, smaller bases often had concentrated life support areas, with many soldiers and civilians living in a condensed footprint, which meant that the effects of a successful attack could be amplified.

As a result of these observations, the Protection staff began to build deliberate plans to accomplish all three objectives: protect the transition, transition protection assets and functions, and protect forces as they repostured. In

[70] Interview with 25ID Senior Leader, Baghdad, Iraq, 22 July 2011.

[71] This chapter will not discuss specific protection assets or capabilities that are still in use in order to protect US military and civilian personnel who continue to rely on them.

[72] Protection LOE, 29 April 2011, p. 13.

[73] Protection LOE, 29 April 2011, p. 14.

coordination with the Operations and Intelligence staffs,[74] Protection analysed friendly operations against enemy attack patterns in order to improve the effectiveness of USF and ISF operations and reduce the risk to both. They also provided Staff Assistance Visits (SAVs) to the subordinate BCTs and base tenant units to help them design and implement security measures to mitigate the effects of attacks on smaller life support area footprints and reduce the threat of attacks as bases were closed. Following the SAVs, the Protection staff issued guidance and directives on the layout, utilization, and specific protection measures for living areas to mitigate risks from enemy attacks and accidents such as fires.[75]

Protecting bases as they closed proved to be a particularly daunting challenge. From October 2011 until the final departure from Iraq, several US bases were subjected to significant attacks during the final days of closure.[76] It is difficult to conceal the fact that a base is closing from the civilian population in the local area. Traffic patterns change as equipment is removed from the base; the number of personnel residing at and working in the base, to include US military personnel, contractors, and local civilian employees, must be reduced. The commanders of local Iraqi police and military units had to be informed of the plan so that they could receive transferred equipment, sign for the property, and potentially occupy the base. All of these provided indicators to enemy forces that the closure of a base was imminent, therefore giving them the opportunity to conduct an attack designed to counter the US's strategic narrative and burnish their own credibility.

The Protection, Reposture, and SISF cells worked together to counter this problem.[77] They identified specific protection measures and equipment to remain in position for as long as possible. The Reposture cell ensured that property and equipment transfers and the official transfer paperwork were complete in advance of the planned closure date in order to provide the departing unit a window of time to close the base instead of a single, specific day. SISF and the subordinate unit at the base coordinated with the ISF in the area to provide protection for US convoy operations and final closure of the base. This worked best in locations where US units had developed close working relationships with their Iraqi partners. In those situations the ISF commanders' reputations were on the line and they would often do their utmost to ensure that the transfer or closure of the base and the movement

[74] The Operations and Intelligence staffs also supported the division's overall protection mission through the conduct of targeted offensive operations which remain classified and will not be discussed in this chapter.

[75] United States Division—Center and 25th Infantry Division, Command History Feeder Report, Protection LOE, 3 October 2011, p. 20.

[76] Author's personal experience. Details of the attacks remain classified.

[77] Protection LOE, 3 October 2011, pp. 2–3.

of US forces was completely unimpeded by attacks. The division Protection staff coordinated all of these efforts and ensured that they remained synchronized with other current operations. Although some bases were targeted with serious attacks during their final days, the efforts taken by the Protection and Reposture staffs ensured that these were largely unsuccessful.

Another of the division's key responsibilities during the final months of Operation New Dawn, particularly after the departure of USD-S and USD-N, was to synchronize, coordinate, and protect operational manoeuvre—the movement of US forces by ground from their bases inside of Iraq, through the entirety of the USD-C battlespace, and into Kuwait.[78] This was a large undertaking. As noted above, on 1 October 2011 there were still more than 43,000 US military personnel in Iraq which meant that nearly 500 soldiers had to leave Iraq each day in order to achieve full withdrawal in accordance with the Security Agreement.[79] Most US military and contractor personnel departed Iraq via air transport. However, some pieces of equipment still had to be moved out of Iraq by ground. The ground movements were referred to as Tactical Road Marches (TRMs).

The US military was fortunate that the Iraqi theatre had a relatively mature and pervasive road network to use to execute operational manoeuvre. Nonetheless, there were only a few main arteries from north to south that were suitable for the large scale convoys required to complete the TRMs. This limited the number of possible routes that the TRMs could utilize, particularly from isolated bases in the west and southeast of the country. As a result, detailed planning and synchronization of assets was required to ensure that TRMs were conducted with the least amount of risk possible. This also ensured that operations conformed to the 25ID Commanding General's force protection guidance to 'mitigate risks to the force by balancing exposure of troops with our capability to support them in contact'.[80]

In order to accomplish such detailed planning, the division Operations, Intelligence, and Protection staffs synchronized the movement of TRMs and the provision of combat enablers by hour for the 24–72 hours that a TRM would be conducting its movement. Subordinate unit planners were advised on the location of high threat areas and times to avoid travelling through them; if a unit was delayed for any reason, the TRM might be directed to remain in place at an open US base to avoid such risks. The staff coordinated intelligence, surveillance, and reconnaissance assets to conduct operations in advance of a unit's arrival in high threat areas and along other areas of the

[78] The discussion of operational manoeuvre, and particularly the execution of the TRMs, is drawn primarily from the author's personal experience. One of his key duties was to synchronize the movement of all TRMs and allocate combat enablers for the next 72 hours of operations. Additionally, the author was responsible for recommending changes to TRMs and combat enabler allocations during execution.

[79] Estevez, *Testimony*, pp. 24–9.

[80] Protection LOE, 29 April 2011, p. 5.

route. Subordinate units planned, coordinated, and executed operations with their ISF counterparts[81] to defeat threats to operational manoeuvre. Attack and reconnaissance helicopters were allocated to these subordinate unit operations and in such a manner that they would be in position to respond to any attack against a specific TRM. Finally, division planners ensured that all TRMs, even those conducted during the final 72 hours of Operation New Dawn, were fully supported by medical evacuation assets and forward surgical teams capable of providing life saving care within one hour of an injury occurring.

The dedicated effort by the division staff, subordinate unit planners, and the ISF units that supported them produced resounding success. From early September 2011 to 12 November 2011 the division supported 19 operational manoeuvre TRMs consisting of 843 vehicles and more than 3,500 personnel.[82] Not a single attack was recorded against any TRM during that time period or subsequently.[83] This occurred despite the fact that some TRMs traversed nearly the entire length of the Iraqi theatre of operations, including high threat areas in and around Baghdad. It also included the most vulnerable portion of the withdrawal: the final 72 hours as the division collapsed the remaining US military footprint from Baghdad all the way to Kuwait.

Division planners divided the final 72 hours into half hour increments and carefully orchestrated the movement of TRMs, helicopters, medical evacuation and surgical teams, and the closure of bases and their support areas over that time period. It is impossible to say exactly how many versions of the plan were produced as conditions continued to change, but the basic plan remained remarkably intact and the division executed the final withdrawal in the 72 hours as envisioned, to include closing four major bases and ensuring the safe movement of the final TRMs.

The division executed all of the functions just described—closing bases, protecting the transition, and managing operational manoeuvre—while also reducing its own presence to zero. This was not a trivial problem. The division staff normally consists of over 800 personnel, a substantial force that requires a great deal of equipment and life support to sustain. The division recognized that it could not simply keep its full staff operational throughout the final withdrawal. It took action to mitigate this problem even before departing Schofield Barracks in 2010. The division deployed only the personnel it

[81] It should also be noted that in many locations ISF units conducted operations to protect US operational manoeuvre without a US force partner. Several US units established such good working relationships with their ISF partners that the ISF units provided additional security during their TRMs.

[82] United States Division—Center and 25th Infantry Division, Command History, USD-C Accomplishments Report, 12 November 2011, p. 1.

[83] USD-C Accomplishments Report, 12 November 2011, p. 1. This is also derived from the author's personal experience. He received reports on every enemy contact across the entirety of the battlespace as a result of his duty position.

required to conduct operations in Iraq; the remainder of the division staff stayed in Hawaii to support ongoing operations at Schofield Barracks, while simultaneously supporting operations in Iraq through telecommunications reach-back capability.

Moreover, the division staff managed its own withdrawal from Iraq just as carefully as it managed the withdrawal of its subordinate elements. As early as the spring of 2011 division planners analysed the staff's daily, weekly, and monthly requirements to determine how best to reduce the staff as the withdrawal proceeded.[84] The result was a plan that reduced the division staff in stages. The first stage occurred when the division main command post relocated to Camp Adder in November 2011. At this time approximately one-third of the division staff remained in Baghdad to remove key equipment from the headquarters building and then returned directly to Schofield Barracks. Two more major reductions occurred during the next few weeks until approximately 70 personnel remained to support the execution of the operation's final 72 hours. This group departed Iraq on a single US Air Force C-17 just prior to the closure of the last base, Camp Adder, while a small cell in Kuwait provided mission command for the final TRM.

The division's constant focus on protection, a focus that began during its preparations for deployment at Schofield Barracks in 2010, enabled it to secure the most vulnerable portions of the transition throughout its final execution and deny any of the enemy forces that contested the transition a spectacularly successful attack. The division not only organized itself to do so, it also constantly evaluated and assessed the threat in order to adjust its own operations. These adjustments were then utilized to reallocate enabling assets to best support both the closure of bases and the operational manoeuvre that accompanied them. This continued from the beginning of operational manoeuvre in September 2011 all the way until the very last vehicle crossed the border into Kuwait without a single security incident during the final TRM on 18 December 2011.

Conclusion

When President Obama announced on 21 October 2011 that all US forces were being withdrawn from Iraq it could have been a cataclysmic moment for the Tropic Lightning Division because of the immense scope of such an operation. That it was not demonstrates the importance that military planners must accord to the planning of the transition. The 25ID began planning to

[84] Interview with 25ID Senior Leader, Schofield Barracks, Hawaii, 6 July 2012.

execute and control the transition from the moment it received its deployment order in 2010 and never relinquished that focus despite the changing circumstances that accompanied the final negotiations on an extension of the Security Agreement. Following the President's announcement, the division oversaw the closure of 12 bases, including the largest in Iraq, the movement of tens of thousands of US military personnel, civilians, and contractors out of the country, and the final withdrawal of US forces by ground out of Iraq, while simultaneously reducing its own headquarter's footprint and redeploying its own personnel. Moreover, it did so nearly two weeks earlier than required.

Much of the division's success can be traced to its decision to re-organize its staff to maximize the talent available to solve the innumerable problems that are inherent to such a complex operation. The lines of effort and their standing staff organizations were able to draw on expertise from across the division staff and focus effort on specific issues while the rest of the division staff continued to perform all of its standard functions. These LOEs proved so successful that two of them, SISF and Transition, completed their operations well ahead of the division's withdrawal.[85]

The other main component of the 25ID's success was the effort it dedicated to protecting the transition. This required the division to conducted detailed staff analysis in order to allocate enabling assets and combat power to the most vulnerable operations and counter the enemy threat to the mission. The closure of bases and the ground movement of forces out of Iraq were extremely vulnerable operations and a significant, successful attack against them could have been severely detrimental to the US's strategic narrative. The division's ability to synchronize the closure of bases and the movement of the TRMs to ensure their support with all available intelligence, protection, medical support, and other assets was essential to its success at protecting the transition.

Although the 25ID's operations during the final days of Operation New Dawn should not be considered a template for future theatre closures, the way the division conducted the operation can provide key insights to planners at the strategic, operational, and tactical level on the conduct of future transitions.

References

Interviews

Member of the Reposture Staff 25ID, interview by CPT Pedro Tehaji, 30th Military History Detachment, Baghdad, Iraq, 31 January 2011.

Member of the Protection Staff 25ID, interview by CPT Pedro Tehaji, 30th Military History Detachment, Baghdad, Iraq, 13 March 2011.

[85] Interview with 25ID Senior Leader, Schofield Barracks, Hawaii, 6 July 2012.

Member of the Transition Staff 25ID, interview by CPT Pedro Tehaji, 30th Military History Detachment, Baghdad, Iraq, 13 April 2011.

Primary Staff Officer, 25ID, interview by Mr Adam Elia, 25ID Command Historian, Schofield Barracks, HI, 5 June 2012.

Senior Leader, 25ID, interview by Mr Adam Elia, 25 ID Command Historian, and CPT Pedro Tehaji, 30th Military History Detachment, Baghdad, Iraq, 9 July 2011.

Senior Leader, 25ID, interview by Mr Adam Elia, 25 ID Command Historian, and CPT Pedro Tehaji, 30th Military History Detachment, Baghdad, Iraq, 22 July 2011.

Senior Leader, 25ID, interview by Mr Adam Elia, 25 ID Command Historian, and CPT Pedro Tehaji, 30th Military History Detachment, Baghdad, Iraq, 21 September 2011.

Senior Leader, 25ID, interview by Mr Adam Elia, 25 ID Command Historian, Schofield Barracks, HI, 6 July 2012.

US Government Documents

'Agreement Between the United States of America and the Republic of Iraq on the Withdrawal of United States forces from Iraq and the Organization of Their Activities during Their Temporary Presence in Iraq', 17 November 2008.

'Strategic Framework Agreement for a Relationship of Friendship and Cooperation between the United States of America and the Republic of Iraq', 17 November 2008.

Chaffetz, Jason, *Opening Statement before the National Security, Homeland Defense and Foreign Operations Subcommittee of the House of Representatives Committee on Oversight and Government Reform,* 12 October 2011, <http://www.gpo.gov/fdsys/pkg/CHRG-112hhrg73166/pdf/CHRG-112hhrg73166.pdf>.

Estevez, Alan F., *Testimony before the National Security, Homeland Defense and Foreign Operations Subcommittee of the House of Representatives Committee on Oversight and Government Reform,* 12 October 2011, <http://www.gpo.gov/fdsys/pkg/CHRG-112hhrg73166/pdf/CHRG-112hhrg73166.pdf>.

Headquarters, Department of the Army, Field Manual 6-0, Mission Command: Command and Control of Army Forces, August 2003, C-4, <http://www.bits.de/NRANEU/others/amd-us-archive/fm6%2803%29.pdf>.

Katzman, Kenneth, *Iraq: Politics, Governance, and Human Rights, Congressional Research Service Report,* 10 November 2011, <http://www.fas.org/sgp/crs/mideast/RS21968.pdf>.

Kerry, John F., *Opening Statement before the Senate Foreign Relations Committee,* 1 February 2011, <http://www.state.gov/secretary/remarks/2013/09/212603.htm>.

Lugar, Richard, *Opening Statement before the Senate Foreign Relations Committee,* 1 February 2011, <http://www.foreign.senate.gov/imo/media/doc/LugarStatement020111a.pdf>.

US Congress, House of Representatives, National Security, Homeland Defense and Foreign Operations Subcommittee of the House of Representatives Committee on Oversight and Government Reform, 'Status Report on the Transition to a Civilian-Led Mission in Iraq', 112th Cong., 1st sess., 12 October 2011.

US Congress, Senate, Committee on Foreign Relations, 'Iraq: The Challenging Transition to a Civilian Mission', 112th Cong., 1st sess., 1 February 2011.

US Department of the Army, Field Manual 6-0, *Mission Command: Command and Control of Army Forces* (Washington, DC: Government Printing Office, 2003).

US Division—Center and 25th Infantry Division, Command History Feeder Report, Protection LOE, 29 April 2011.

US Division—Center and 25th Infantry Division, Command History Feeder Report, Protection LOE, 3 October 2011.

US Division—Center and 25th Infantry Division, Command History Feeder Report, Reposture LOE, 13 April 2011.

US Division—Center and 25th Infantry Division, Command History Feeder Report, Reposture LOE, 28 July 2011.

US Division—Center and 25th Infantry Division, Command History Feeder Report, Transition LOE, 5 October 2011.

US Division—Center and 25th Infantry Division, USD-C Accomplishments Report, 12 November 2011.

11

Transitions and hybrid political orders

Roger Mac Ginty

Introduction

This chapter recommends the lens of hybridity as a way of understanding the interaction between top-down and bottom-up actors and dynamics in contexts of transition. Traditional ways of examining transitions and peace-support interventions tend to be limiting. They often constrain how we think about conflict situations and point us towards equally constrained policy prescriptions.

This chapter begins with a short section that asks: why do we, and the organizations that we work for, think the way that we do? This fundamental first question is often overlooked in the rush to implement policy and fulfil mandates. Yet how we define and conceptualize issues shapes how we deal with them. The chapter then introduces the concept of 'hybridity' and outlines a four-part model of hybridization to help illustrate the hybrid political orders and processes that develop when different cultures, norms, and practices interact with one another. These hybrid political orders are the fusion of indigenous and traditional practices with externally derived practices often associated with state-building and peace enforcement programmes. By accepting the hybrid nature of institutions, societies, and practices, we can transcend orthodox approaches to peacemaking and state-building that are often intolerant of deviation from Western state-centric models. Rather than thinking of neat organizational charts in which there are vertical silos of power and responsibility (international community > national government > local government > local communities), it is more prudent to conceive of a more jumbled picture in which there are multiple cross-cutting types of power and practices. To use the analogy of modern art, it is more useful to think of societies experiencing peace-support interventions as a paint-splattered

Jackson Pollock mess rather than a piece of hyperrealist art that is so perfect it looks like a photograph.

The problem, however, is that many Western governments, militaries, and INGOs are patterned to think along straight lines. It is not the case that we have to 'unlearn' our existing ways of understanding the world around us. Instead, this chapter argues that we augment our existing ways of interpreting the world with an additional analytical approach, namely that provided by the concept of hybridity. If we review peace-support interventions in the post-Cold War era then the picture is decidedly mixed. There have been some unmitigated disasters—expensive in terms of blood, treasure, and legitimacy. It is the contention of this chapter that some of the blame for this lies in a rigid adherence, among leading Western states and the international organizations that they influence, to a worldview that is seriously outmoded. This worldview is based on the orthodoxy of the Weberian state as the ideal political unit, and is imbued with a firm belief that Western, rational, technocratic liberal 'solutions' can act as a salve against conflict recidivism. This worldview is at the head of a juggernaut of thinking and practices that, taken together, can be called 'the liberal peace'. The lens offered by hybridity, the chapter argues, encourages us to step back from a strict adherence to the legal-rationalist-institutionalist approach and instead see societies and polities as hybrids that are comprised of a complex of indigenous and exogenous ideas and practices. A more finely grained understanding of the nature of hybrid political orders can help us navigate through the complexities of societies undergoing post-war transitions.

Why do we think the way that we do?

It is rare for us to ask this question. Often individuals, institutions, and societies rationalize and act in particular ways because of tradition or because a particular route is socially or economically sanctioned. Frequently 'off the shelf' ways of thinking and acting are available to us and we do not need to make individual decisions.[1] So, for example, a business or a public service might have protocols on how to deal with certain queries or deliver certain services. The employee merely has to follow the protocol rather than think up original ways of acting. Usually the customer will expect such routinized responses and so employee and customer are engaged in a mutual bargain of shared expectation and behaviour. This bargain is often unspoken, although it is reciprocal.

[1] Erving Goffman, *The Presentation of Self in Everyday Life* (New York: Anchor Books, 1959), p. 8.

But it is worth stepping back from the routinized ways of thinking and acting to consider what shapes how we think. Clearly multiple factors contribute to this—many of them beyond the scope of this chapter. But given our interest in international peace-support interventions, three linked factors are worth identifying: rationality, liberalism, and technocracy. In combination, they have shaped much contemporary intervention policy and have provided a framework of legitimation through which particular intervention strategies are justified. They have also led to a situation of epistemic closure, or a mutually reinforcing situation in which the problem, the frame of inquiry, and the 'solution' become one. In such circumstances, alternative ways of approaching problems are regarded as unusual or even deviant. The story of how these three factors have come together is complex and took place over many centuries, so an abbreviated version is set out here.

Rationality stems from the belief that all phenomena can be understood; that with enough resources and mental capacity we can find an explanation for social and natural phenomena. In its modern incarnation, this view stretches from the Scottish Enlightenment to the development of scientific and social scientific inquiries. There is little doubting that scientists have made enormous progress in understanding the world we live in and the ways in which humans interact with it and each other. The danger is that rationalists have convinced themselves that *everything* is open to rational inquiry and explanation.[2] In this mindset, all conflicts and the behaviour of local populations can be explained if the right resources are directed at them. This is very probably true, but rationalists make a fundamental mistake: they assume that *their* way of seeing the world can explain everything. Certainly it can, and has, explained much. But it does not have universal powers. Instead, the brand of rationality adopted by many governments, international organizations, and academic disciplines is peculiarly Western. It was fashioned in the specific context of Western societies, governments, and institutions over the past 200 years. Fundamentally, given our interest in contemporary international intervention, this brand of rationality does not always extend to other societies and contexts, especially those that operate in non-Western ways.

In the modern Western mindset (and it is important not to over-homogenize categories or slip into essentialism), individuals are rational actors who seek to maximize the benefits for themselves and their families. Individuals tend to be secular, or if they are religious, this aspect of their lives resides in the private

[2] Good critiques of the limitations of orthodox ways of thinking can be found in Patrick Chabal, *The End of Conceit: Western rationality and postcolonialism* (London: Zed Books, 2012); and Pankaj Mishra, *From the Ruins of Empire: The revolt against the west and the remaking of Asia* (London: Allen Lane, 2012).

realm. They live in modern states and express their political desires through routinized mechanisms like elections or through broad-based political parties. Yet this way of conceiving the world only applies so far. It has difficulty in explaining societies that operate along different lines. For example, in many contexts, and particularly those experiencing conflict and transitions, the state is weak, remote, or absent.[3] Kinship or ethnic identity, rather than the individual, provide a basic organizing bloc for society. Religion or even mysticism may be treated seriously.[4] Resources may be shared via clientelism and patronage rather than according to a transparent and justifiable rubric set down by the state. All of these aspects can be explained using rational thought, but they are not at all obvious if one is used to conceiving of a world in which there are functional states, individuals rather than clans, and a publicly legitimated rule of law.

Problems arise when we transfer our Western modes of thinking to non-Western contexts. Donors, militaries, and international organizations have sought to 'localize' their thinking through the adoption of conflict sensitive methodologies, or the use of ethnographic techniques. But it is very difficult, having been patterned by one mode of thinking to adopt another way of thinking. If notions of statehood, the rule of law, a written constitution, and secularism have been hardwired into the ways that individuals and institutions see the world around them, it is very difficult to unlearn that. Post-colonial authors have been very helpful in alerting us to the pitfalls of self-styled Western rationalism, but many rationalist thought processes have become structurally embedded in how organizations gather and disseminate information. As a result, it is very difficult to leave behind completely the assumptions that shape how we seek to understand the world.

Liberalism, the second factor that shapes how we think about the world, is very much linked with rationality. It is the guiding intellectual tradition that has been deployed (rhetorically at any rate) to justify peace-support interventions on behalf of the international community.[5] Although it has had a complex history, and is capable of displaying many 'faces', ideas linked with liberalism crop up with frequency in the discourses that justify intervention. Speeches by Tony Blair and George W. Bush, for example, were laden with references to liberal ideas.[6] Tropes running through the liberal discourse

[3] An excellent account of the irrelevance of statehood in some contexts can be found in P. Kabama, '"Heart of Darkness": Current images of DRC and their theoretical underpinnings', *Anthropological Theory* 10, no. 3 (2010): pp. 265–301.

[4] Jeffrey Haynes, *Religious Transnational Actors and Soft Power* (London: Ashgate, 2012).

[5] Michael W. Doyle, 'Liberalism and world politics', *American Political Science Review* 80, no. 4 (1986): pp. 1151–69.

[6] Tony Blair, 'PM's world affairs speech to Lord Mayor's Banquet', 13 November 2006, <http://www.number10.gov.uk/Page10409>; George W. Bush, 'State of the Union Address, 2002', accessed 30 March 2013, <www.whitehouse.gov/stateoftheunion2002>.

include the recognition of the individual as a sovereign actor, an emphasis on tolerance, diversity, and equal opportunity, the pursuit of freedom, an optimism in people's ability to reform themselves and institutions, the rationality of individuals and collectives, and the importance of individual property and the law.[7] The precise combination and emphasis of these elements changes with time and context.

The regularity with which liberal ideas and rhetoric have been used to justify international peace-support interventions in the post-Cold War era has led interventions to be called 'the liberal peace' or 'liberal interventionism'.[8] Proponents of the liberal peace have been leading Western states and their militaries, international organizations, and international financial institutions. What is interesting, from the point of view of this chapter, is how liberal ideas have conditioned how conflict is defined and approached. Liberalism amounts to a set of mutually reinforcing ideas that believe that liberal forms of institutional organization are superior to alternatives because they result in peace. Thus, in the liberal mindset, rational, empowered citizens will guide their properly constituted governments towards pacific policies. In other words, liberals believe that liberal forms of governance and institutions predispose states towards peace. As is often noted, liberal democracies rarely go to war with one another, therefore, if liberal forms of governance can be propagated internationally, the chances of war will be diminished. Such thinking regards alternative forms of governance as inferior.[9] Importantly, liberalism is not just a set of ideas and prescriptions: it also conditions how its advocates think. By privileging individuals, rationality, and by believing that individuals and institutions can be reformed, it is prone to regard societies based on kinship and tradition as being anti-modern. Moreover, liberal optimism (the belief in the reformability of people and institutions) points proponents of liberal internationalism towards intervention: if people and systems can be changed, then we must do so. In other words, at the heart of liberalism lies an obligation to intervene, or at least a script that justifies intervention.

The third factor that shapes how we think in relation to international intervention is technocracy or the prioritization of bureaucracy. Technocracy

[7] Roger Mac Ginty, *International Peacebuilding and Local Resistance: Hybrid forms of peace* (Basingstoke: Palgrave, 2011), p. 26.

[8] There is a voluminous literature unpacking the liberal peace. See, for example, Oliver P. Richmond, *The Transformation of Peace* (Basingstoke: Palgrave, 2007); David Chandler, 'Responsibility to Protect? Imposing the "liberal peace"', *International Peacekeeping* 11, no. 1 (2004): pp. 59–81; Edward Newman, Roland Paris, and Oliver P. Richmond, eds, *New Perspectives on Liberal Peacebuilding* (Tokyo: United Nations University Press, 2010). A counter critique comes in the form of Roland Paris, 'Saving Liberal Peacebuilding', *Review of International Studies* 36, no. 2 (2010): pp. 337–65.

[9] Roger Mac Ginty, 'Indigenous peacemaking versus the liberal peace', *Cooperation and Conflict* 43, no. 2 (2008): pp. 139–63.

is by no means new. Empires, after all, depended on remarkable feats of gathering and managing information. But the influence of technocracy has accelerated in recent decades, with ideas, norms, and practices from the world of business management finding their way into the third sector, INGOs, and peacebuilding and development policy.[10] Thus, for example, practices associated with total quality management, benchmarking, and audit trails play a significant role in how peace, reconstruction, and development are organized.[11]

Technocracy in itself is not problematic, especially as it offers the possibility of the cost-effective and efficient delivery of services. This can be especially attractive in deeply divided societies or societies affected by violent conflict in which resources may be distributed according to ethnic or religious discrimination. Technocracy and bureaucracy offer routine and transparency. Problems arise, however, when technocratic systems become un-reflexive and operate according to routine regardless of local circumstances.[12]

The peacebuilding and reconstruction sectors have experienced a 'technocratic turn' in recent years. This has been manifest in the state-building and good governance programmes that have formed a core part of international interventions, the standardization of conflict analysis frameworks, and the professionalization of an international cadre of peacebuilding and intervention 'experts'. Of course, each of these developments is not necessarily harmful. Yet they do point to a trend in which selected, often external, actors are privileged and local actors find themselves marginalized. Consider one example: the standardization of conflict analysis models used by international organizations, donors states, and their militaries.[13] These models, whether from the United Nations (UN) or International Non-Governmental Organizations (INGOs), are all rather similar. They consider the same factors to be important in explaining conflict and often recommend the same prescriptions (frequently associated with state-building, good governance reform, and enhancing a preferred version of civil society). But what these standardized conflict analysis models often fail to do is to take into account local analyses of the conflict. Local analyses may be highly contextualized and include issues that seem an anathema to Western observers, for example, blood revenge,

[10] Roger Mac Ginty, 'Routine Peace: Technocracy and peacebuilding', *Cooperation and Conflict* 47, no. 3 (2012): pp. 287–308.

[11] Richard Box, 'Running government like a business: implications for public administration theory and practice', *The American Review of Public Administration* 29, no. 1 (1999): pp. 19–43.

[12] Laurent Goetschel and Tobias Hagmann, 'Civilian Peacebuilding: Peace by bureaucratic means?' *Conflict, Security and Development* 9, no. 1 (2009): pp. 55–73; Timothy Donais, 'Empowerment of Imposition? Dilemmas of local ownership in post-conflict peacebuilding processes', *Peace and Change* 34, no. 1 (2009): pp. 3–26.

[13] See, for example, Conflict Sensitivity Consortium, 'Conflict Sensitivity Consortium Benchmarking Paper', Draft, 29 April 2009, <http://www.conflictsensitivity.org/sites/default/files/CSA%20Benchmarking%20paper-full.pdf>.

family honour, and religious observance. Such issues tend to be dismissed by many orthodox approaches to conflict analysis. As a result, standardized Western conflict analysis models tend to write the local out of the conflict story and impose a Western narrative onto the conflict. This has profound consequences for the development of state-building and peace-support policy.

This triumvirate of ideas (rationality, liberalism, and technocracy) will operate in different combinations according to circumstance. They have been foundational in shaping how conflicts are interpreted by intervening institutions and the subsequent policy responses that are developed. Crucially, the triumvirate of ideas and practices are often intolerant of alternatives. Deviation from these ideas, and the Western-influenced state-building and governance policies that stem from them, is often regarded as policy 'failure'. As will be argued below, if we accept the notion of hybridity as a way of interpreting the interaction between top-down and bottom-up forces in peace-support interventions, then it becomes very difficult to sustain absolutist categories such as 'success' or 'failure'.

Hybridity and hybridization

Hybridity is the mixing of ideas, norms, and practices.[14] It is common in all societies and institutions and reveals a human capacity for adaptation and accommodation. It manifests itself in social negotiation as individuals and groups attempt to find a *modus vivendi*. Hybridity is not the simple mixing of two groups or practices to form a discrete third group or institution. Instead it refers to a more complex process in which actors and norms are 'prior hybridized'; that is, they are the result of previous processes of hybridization.[15] Britain's history of successive invasions by Angles, Celts, Romans, Normans, Vikings, and many more is instructive of the long-term historical lens required to conceptualize hybridity.[16] It also reminds us that some of the melding of ideas and practices was the result of violence and imposition, while some was the result of marriage, economic activity, and the passage of time as various groups reached an accommodation with one another.

[14] This section draws on Roger Mac Ginty, *International Peacebuilding and Local Resistance*; and Roger Mac Ginty, 'Hybrid Peace: The interaction between top down and bottom up peace', *Security Dialogue* 41, no. 4 (2010): pp. 391–412. See also, Volker Boege, Anne Brown, Kevin Clements, and Anna Nolan, 'Building Peace and Political Communities in Hybrid Political Orders', *International Peacekeeping* 16, no. 5 (2009): pp. 599–614.

[15] Nestor G. Canclini, *Hybrid Cultures: Strategies for entering and leaving modernity* (Minnesota: University of Minnesota Press, 2005).

[16] Alistair Moffat, *Sea Kingdoms: The History of Celtic Britain and Ireland* (Edinburgh: Birlinn, 2001).

While many processes of hybridization take place over the long-term, it is worth noting that these processes are accelerated in peace-support intervention contexts. In such cases, we often see the massive influx of ideas, practices, and personnel from outside. Often this influx is concentrated over a relatively compressed time period. State-building, good governance, reconstruction, and security programmes often involve the rapid and large-scale importation of working practices, language, equipment, and people. This confronts the host society with a challenge. While some actors and institutions will welcome the new ideas and practices, others will reject them or perhaps take a more circumspect view. For example, national elites and those who find employment with a state-building programme may welcome the importation of new ideas and practices. Others might find these threatening to traditional power structures. The result is a complex process of hybridization that contains conflict, cooperation, coalescence, and the possibility of re-conflict and re-cooperation, etc. There should be no expectation of consistency on behalf of actors: they may welcome one aspect of the externally-driven state-building and security programme but resent another.

Crucially, hybridity is not a one-way street in which external agents bring in new ideas and practices and force local actors to react to these. Instead of an exclusively top-down transmission chain whereby external practices and personnel are introduced to the host country, it is prudent to conceive of the top-down, bottom-up, and horizontal mixing of ideas and practices. External actors, whether peacekeepers, good governance programme managers, or political officers are not immune to influences from the local context. This might mean changing the pace of work or deviating from a programme to take local cultural norms into account (for example, working through tribal leaders to agree on a local peace accord). The important point is that no actor, even ostensibly powerful international actors such as the North Atlantic Treaty Organization (NATO), is able to set and maintain a unilateral course of action. Instead, they experience blowback, mimicry, and a host of other pressures as local actors seek to exploit, subvert, negotiate with, delay, and implement internationally mandated policies.[17] The result is often something of a mess (perhaps here is it useful to visualize the work of artist Jackson Pollock) and this explains why orthodox Western modes of thinking, that draw on rationality, liberalism, and technocracy, are often inadequate for helping us to deal with the reality of societies undergoing transition.

There are four reasons why this chapter recommends the notion of hybridity as a way of understanding the complex contexts of state-building and peace-support interventions. First, it reminds us of the agency of local actors.

[17] Homi K. Bhabha, 'Of mimicry and man: The ambivalence of colonial discourse', *October* 28 (1984): pp. 125–33.

Many accounts of international peace-support operations concentrate overwhelmingly on international actors, their policies and woes. Local actors are essentially written out of the story or subjectified into cartoon-like caricatures: willing collaborators or wily resisters. In such a perspective, the agency of local actors is restricted to reaction; they have little power of initiation or independence from the dynamics introduced by international actors. The reality, of course, is much more complex, with local actors capable of adopting multiple stances and changing over time. Moreover, while local actors may have limited material power (e.g. military or monetary resources) they may also have access to non-material forms of power such as legitimacy.

Secondly, the concept of hybridity encourages us to look within categories and see diversity, dissent, and change. It is common for narratives of conflict to use, as a shorthand, very broad categorizations as though they are fixed. So, for example, media and policy commentary on Afghanistan uses the terms 'Taliban', 'international community', and 'NATO' in the sense that these are homogenous units. As we know, the true picture is much more complex, yet we persist with these labels along with others such as 'local', 'international', 'external', or 'internal'. Clearly we need to use terms like this to be comprehensible (and this chapter uses all of these terms) but it is sensible to use them in the knowledge that categories are malleable. The lens of hybridity accepts that actors are rarely homogenous. Instead they are the site of change and debate, albeit sometimes well-concealed.

Thirdly, the concept of hybridity encourages us to look at the interface between categories and to move away from notions of discrete actors that have little interaction with each other. Hybridity involves much subtle social negotiation, assimilation, and reaction. Often this occurs over long periods of time and is perhaps imperceptible to those involved. The interaction may be indirect. Fundamentally, the notion of hybridity encourages us to see the relational character of political, economic, and social processes whereby our actions and reactions are shaped by a complex social interactionism.

The final reason to recommend the lens of hybridity is that it encourages us to step back from top-down analyses that privilege formal actors such as states, international organizations, and international financial institutions. It encourages us to see the totality of actors and does not privilege one set of actors above another. Many accounts of conflict and peace-support interventions emphasize international actors but, in doing so, reproduce partial accounts of the context. Hybridity thus encourages us to transcend state-centric, realistic accounts of conflict-affected contexts and to consider the totality of actors.

Having conceptualized hybridity and recommended it as a tool for interpreting the interaction between exogenous and indigenous actors, this chapter now moves on to outline a four-part model of hybridization. Like all models, this is an abstraction that simplifies a more complex reality. However, it does present us with a way of understanding the multiple and continuous interactions that characterize contemporary peace-support intervention contexts.

The four-part model is comprised of:

1. the ability of international actors to impose their preferred norms, practices, and institutions;
2. the ability of international actors to incentivize the use of their preferred norms, practices, and institutions;
3. the ability of local actors to resist, subvert, negotiate with, delay, and exploit internationally-preferred norms, practices, and institutions;
4. the ability of local actors to present and maintain alternatives to internationally-preferred norms, practices, and institutions.

All four parts of the model may operate simultaneously, resulting in a confusing hybrid political landscape. It is depicted in Figure 11.1. The four parts of the model require some elucidation.

The first part, the ability of international actors to impose their preferred version of peace, governance, and order, refers to both the direct and indirect forms of persuasion. At one end of the spectrum we have regime change and military support for a preferred political order, with the interventions in Iraq and Afghanistan providing examples of militarized intervention. But away

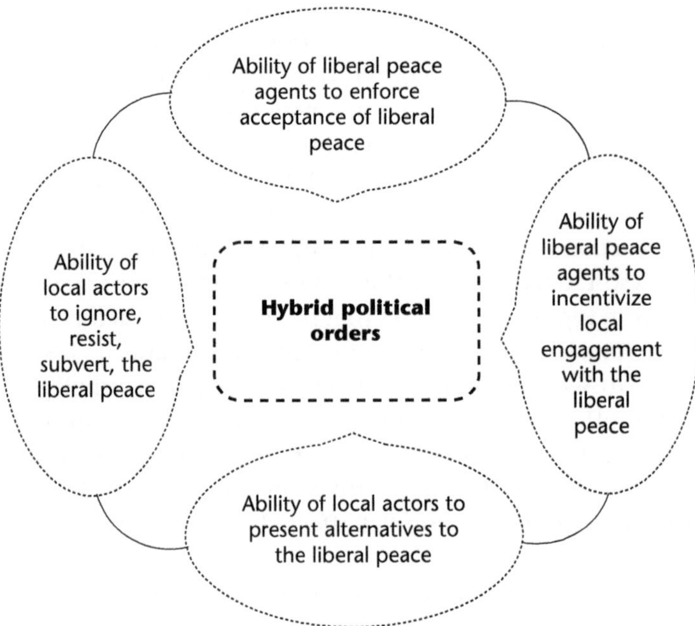

Figure 11.1. Hybrid political orders (Crown copyright)

from direct violence, leading states, international organizations, and international financial institutions can call on a range of coercive instruments that help discipline other states, communities, and movements. These coercive instruments involve the conditionality linked with International Monetary Fund assistance or the assistance that follows donors' conferences. It also involves the ability of leading states and international organizations to confer or withhold legitimacy towards aspirant and non-state bodies, and to political leaders. In a number of cases, international actors have been 'kingmakers', validating the leadership of transitional governments and their premiers. Conceived in this light, the dominant international, political, and economic system becomes a series of obligations that discipline member states into acting in particular ways. States are disciplined through (non)-recognition of their statehood, the granting of membership to international bodies, and access to the material and non-material resources disbursed by international organizations and financial institutions.

But alongside this coercive aspect of dominant international actors, there is incentivization in the form of the resources on offer to local actors, whether national elites or those at lower political levels. These incentives are both material and non-material, and internal actors may compete to gain access to these resources and deny access to their local rivals. As mentioned above, these resources may be tied to conditionalities, for example, the introduction of good governance reforms may be linked to reconstruction funding in a bid to tackle corruption. In keeping with the conceptual discussion of hybridity in the last section, it is worth noting that the situation is usually much more complex than a simple economic transaction between well-funded international actors and cash-hungry local actors. Certainly economic inducements play a part. But both sides have agency and are capable of shaping the nature of the bargain. International actors, despite having material and coercive resources, are often anxious to secure something in return such as access, security, or legitimacy.

The third part of the model refers to the agency of local actors to adapt, subvert, negotiate with, and delay the preferences of international actors. This is likely to be a complex and uneven process, as some local actors will have more agency than others. Some will also have more motivation to use their agency than others. Proponents of the liberal peace are unlikely to be able to impose their technologies and norms unchanged onto local contexts. The extent of the changes will depend on the outcome of the combined agencies of local and international actors. It is also worth noting that peace-support and state-building interventions are frequently shaped by temporal considerations: they are often time-limited with international actors focused on an exit strategy or forced to divert their attentions to new challenges.

The final part of the model again highlights the agency of local actors, and the extent to which they can construct or maintain alternatives to international state-building or stability efforts. This will differ from context to context, and will be connected to the extent to which local actors have been able to conserve social capital during and after a conflict. In a number of cases, we have seen that while external actors, and their proxies and clients in national government are able to exercise material power, they struggle to command affective and non-material power.[18] In other words, while international actors can provide military security, oversee a state-building process, and fund infrastructure projects, they are less well-equipped to meet local cultural expectations.

The four-part model is simply a way to try to understand the complex interactionism between the multiple actors involved in a conflict-affected society. The model seeks to illustrate the constant movement as different actors try to position themselves to meet a series of tactical and strategic goals. It is worth restating that hybridity is a condition of human life—all societies are hybrids and are the result of long processes of adaptation and social navigation. But the peculiar circumstances of a peace-support transition means that the processes of hybridization become intensified. External actors, together with their local proxies and clients, often have a highly normative and prescriptive agenda, most obviously state-building or stabilization. This agenda may synchronise, conflict or run parallel with multiple local agendas. The result will be a fusion, indeed a confusion, as the local and international evolve and mix to produce hybrid political orders, practices, and norms.

Hybridity can help illustrate the texture and fluidity of societies under-going transition. It adds to the suite of analytical tools that we have available to us. Consider, for example, the case of economic reform in post-Saddam Iraq.[19] The US-led interim administration introduced a raft of changes aimed at opening the Iraqi economy up to foreign direct investment, and sweeping away the centrist and nationalizing ethos of the Saddam regime. In quick succession there were a range of banking and financial services reforms, a programme of privatization, and the introduction of laws allowing foreign

[18] Roland Bleiker and Emma Hutchison, 'Fear No More: Emotions and world politics', *Review of International Studies* 34, no. 1 (2008): pp. 115–35.

[19] Roger Mac Ginty, *International Peacebuilding and Local Resistance*, pp. 115–33. See also, Justin Alexander and Colin Rowat, 'A clean slate in Iraq: From debt to development', *Middle East Report* 228 (2003): pp. 32–6; Simon Bromley, 'Blood for Oil?', *New Political Economy* 11, no. 3 (2006): pp. 419–34; Rajiv Chandrasekaran, *Imperial Life in the Emerald City: Inside Baghdad's Green Zone* (London: Bloomsbury, 2007); Toby Dodge, 'Iraqi Transitions: From regime change to state collapse', *Third World Quarterly* 26, no. 4/5 (2005): pp. 705–21; Eric Herring, 'Neoliberalism versus Peacebuilding in Iraq', in *Whose Peace? Critical Perspectives on the Political Economy of Peacebuilding*, edited by Michael Pugh, Neil Cooper, and Mandy Turner (Basingstoke: Palgrave Macmillan, 2008), pp. 47–64.

ownership of business and the repatriation of profits out of Iraq. The interim administration was very open about its aim to create a market economy in Iraq based on a regulated private sector. Yet, by looking only at this top-down account of economic change we would see only a skewed picture. The programme of privatization was a failure, and many sectors of the licit economy stagnated. A hybrid approach encourages us to see the top-down and the bottom-up. So as well as examining top-down measures to change the economy, it is also important to look at the economies of survival, thrift, and opportunity that were bottom-up and accounted for the bulk of economic activity for most Iraqis. Iraq, like all other societies has a hybrid economy (public and private sectors, licit and illicit sectors, etc.) and so it makes sense that we adopt a hybrid approach in trying to capture it.

A similar argument can be made in relation to security in Afghanistan.[20] The country has a highly hybridized form of security (provided by both state and non-state armed actors) and many traditional policy and academic tools that assume that the state has a monopoly of violence lack explanatory power. The hybridized nature of Afghanistan's security means that we have to free ourselves from static models to analyse Afghanistan (models rooted in the Weberian model of statehood or in the state as the principal referent of our analyses). Instead, security in Afghanistan is highly contested, with warlords and tribes empowered by Kabul, NATO, the CIA, and others providing some form of security in some areas. The result is a fluid assortment of security actors, some backed by a NATO force that is transitioning out of Afghanistan. By recognizing the hybrid nature of security in Afghanistan we are confronted by the existence of multiple forms of agency. We immediately see that Western and formal actors have limited power, and need to see them in the context of other actors (many of which are organized very differently compared to Western military and political institutions).

Whether we think of governance and accountability systems in Liberia, civil society in Burundi, or justice systems in Timor Leste, we are confronted with hybrid orders. These represent a melding of indigenous and exogenous norms and practices. They are likely to be fluid and so demand analytical frames that are deft enough to cope with transient and inconsistent relationships between actors and practices.

[20] Roger Mac Ginty, *International Peacebuilding and local resistance*, pp. 91–114; Antonio Giustozzi, 'Bureaucratic Façade and Political Realities of Disarmament and Demobilisation in Afghanistan', *Conflict, Security and Development* 8, no. 2 (2008): pp. 169–82; Anatol Lieven, 'The war in Afghanistan: Its background and future prospects', *Conflict, Security and Development* 9, no. 3 (2009): pp. 333–59.

Implications

So what are the implications of the notion of hybridity given the focus of this volume on transitions and internationally-supported peace-support interventions? The first is that the notion of hybridity encourages us to think about our own epistemologies or the tools that we use (as social scientists, military planners, development specialists, or journalists, etc.) to understand the world around us. Hybridity reminds us of the agency of all actors, and encourages us to look beyond accounts of interventions and transitions that concentrate most of their attention of the top-down aspect of interventions. Certainly, the top-down aspects are important and can often be seen in the provision of security and the spread of technologies of governance. But without taking into account how these externally introduced goods and practices are accepted, rejected, and used by local populations and institutions, we risk having a partial picture. The epistemologies, research methods, and reporting mechanisms that we tend to use are biased towards a top-down and Western perspective. So, for example, the UN, donor organizations, and militaries usually gather information in particular ways, report it in particular ways, and focus on specific types of information. These methods are often linked with bureaucratic convenience and can be routine rather than reflexive and adaptable. They often suffer from an urban bias and gather the low-hanging data fruit rather than hard to access, yet important, information. By encouraging us to take account of the agency of *all* actors, the notion of hybridity encourages us to think of research methodologies that can capture the hidden or non-obvious 'transcript' of society as well as the public transcript of government statements and official statistics.[21] So there is a built-in guard against the 'orientalism' that bedevils many dominant approaches to research and information gathering.

In a similar vein, hybridity encourages us to recognize the fluid and 'messy' nature of societies undergoing transition. Thus, it reminds us that rendering the political, economic, or cultural landscapes into neat organizational charts or 'silos' risks producing inaccurate depictions of the society. It is, of course, tempting to make social phenomena as comprehensible as possible. Yet we should be careful in relation to overly-neat depictions of contexts that are anything but neat. This is not to say that social scientific inquiry is futile. Instead, it is to encourage a more humble epistemology that is not premised on the assumption that everything can be explained with the tools at our fingertips.

[21] Roger Mac Ginty, 'The transcripts of peace: Public, hidden or non-obvious?', *Journal of Intervention and Statebuilding* 7, no. 4 (2013): pp. 423–30; J. C. Scott, *Weapons of the Weak: Everyday forms of peasant resistance* (Yale: Yale University Press, 1987).

A second implication of thinking about hybridity in relation to transitions and peace-support interventions is the need to move away from the very limiting categories of 'success' and 'failure'. For complex political, economic, and technocratic reasons, the military and policy worlds often judge their progress against the rigid dyad of success or failure. In this world, policies are either successful or not. Programmes and projects are often measured in very instrumentalized ways. For example, the success or failure of a project may be measured in terms of hitting deadlines or training a required number of personnel. While one can argue for the necessity of mission- or project-specific indicators in terms of financial management and efficiency, it is difficult to justify such a rigid way of measurement given the complexity of transition contexts. The notions of 'success' or 'failure' seem destined to reduce a very complex context into cartoon-like simplicity. Hybridity reminds us of the multiple dynamics that are simultaneously at work. Some of this may be in tune with a mission or project goals. Others may work against it. Thus orthodox indicators may be poorly suited to such dynamic environments.

The technocratic rigidity of many Western international interveners means that deviation from mission or project goals may be seen as 'failure'. This reflects a basic intolerance often seen in top-down interventions: that there is basically a right and a wrong way for the society under transition to develop. Deviation from published mission goals may be explained in terms of the resistance, corruption, or traditionalism of local actors. These local actors may be depicted as 'not ready' for good governance reforms, democracy, and the Weberian state. They are subjectified as anti-modern or somehow undeveloped. Yet this wholly negative view of deviation from top-down mission goals is very revealing about the intolerance of worldviews within Western-led organizations. The technocratic reporting culture within many militaries, INGOs, bilateral donors, and international organizations means that only 'good news' is reported, or a positive spin is put on narratives that deviate from the preferred script.

There is, however, another way of seeing deviation. Instead of seeing it as 'failure' or the thwarting of 'success', much deviation of preferred Western outcomes can be seen in terms of local agency, participation, and ownership. This requires a move away from the success/failure rubric. Of course, some local agency may be harmful or be antithetical to Western notions of gender rights or legitimacy. But not all deviations from mission goals should be seen in such a negative light. If oft mentioned terms like 'local participation' and 'local ownership' are to be meaningful, then they must be tolerant of the agency of local actors to hybridize and engage with top-down policies and resources. This might take policies to places unanticipated by programme designers. As already alluded to, this will raise a series of ethical and practical quandaries for Western actors who are charged with the implementation of programmes. To brand all deviation as 'failure' reveals a need to control at the heart of top-down programmes of stabilization and international intervention. Hybridity reminds us that no actor is able to chart and maintain a unilateral course of action. Instead, all actors must be seen in a relational context in which other actors have a capacity to influence how they act and react.

A third implication of hybridity in relation to transitions and international interventions is that it contains the capacity to change actors themselves. This applies to both local and international actors, and all actors in between. So not only do actors change their strategies and policies, interaction with other actors will prompt changes in their own identity. Consider, for example, institutional actors like the British Army and NATO who have been involved in the stabilization of post-Taliban Afghanistan. The long-term nature of the engagement has had an impact on the culture of these organizations and how they define themselves. This ranges from the fall-out from 'green on blue' incidents to structural changes in these organizations necessitated by the war in Afghanistan. This is despite the enormous material power that both organizations have at their disposal. So what post-colonial scholars call 'mimicry' is not just something that happens to local actors when they interact with international actors. Instead, these changes in behaviour occur to all actors. In a sense, they become hybrid actors; hybridized by their interaction with others.

Concluding discussion

A common critique of the concept of hybridity is to dismiss it as a vapid or overly loose category because everything is hybrid. If everything can be placed into the hybrid category, then what use is the category? The main use is that it encourages us to stretch the conventional ways that we use to describe and conceive of conflict and transitions. The traditional categories that we deploy tend to depict a world of straight lines and discreet categories. By recognizing the hybrid nature of political orders and processes, we are liberated from limiting paradigms. We are encouraged to look within and between categories to the extent that we question the very categories themselves. Moreover, it is not the case that all actors are similarly hybrid all of the time. Instead, some actors and processes are able to resist hybridity to some extent and force their will on others.

A further criticism of the concept of hybridity is that if we question all categories then we become intellectually paralysed—unable to interrogate concepts and hold a comprehensible dialogue with others. Yet if we accept the hybrid and changing nature of actors and processes, then we should be able to construct more accurate accounts of transitions and better understand the dynamics within them. As has been argued in this chapter, neatly categorized accounts of transition risk inaccuracy, and policy based on overly simplified analyses risks being irrelevant or harmful. So rather than intellectual paralysis, this chapter argues that hybridity offers an enhanced ability to comprehend the dynamics of complex environments. The four-part model outlined in this chapter is an abstract way of simplifying the variable geometry of multiple processes simultaneously interacting with one another.

While the chapter advocates the adoption of hybridity as a conceptual lens, it does not necessarily advocate that hybrid political orders are purposively manufactured. Instead, hybridity is a condition that evolves as different actors interact with one another. The precise nature of the hybrid order will ultimately depend on the power relations between the actors and dynamics. While a hybrid political order may be created (for example, through the deliberate bringing together of indigenous and international justice practices) it is difficult to foresee how people will interact with and use new political, economic, and cultural spaces. Hybrid political orders and practice emerge and develop over time. Elements of this development are likely to be unanticipated, and may involve practices and stances that conflict with preferred Western notions of political and cultural activity. To automatically brand hybrid political orders and practices as 'failure' or policy deviation seems shortsighted and reveals the limits of our own thinking. 'Failure' and policy deviation may actually be local participation, ownership, and autonomy. In certain circumstances, such hybridity is to be encouraged, even celebrated.

References

Alexander, Justin and Colin Rowat, 'A clean slate in Iraq: From debt to development', *Middle East Report* 228 (2003): pp. 32–6.

Bhabha, Homi K., 'Of mimicry and man: The ambivalence of colonial discourse', *October* 28 (1984): pp. 125–33.

Blair, Tony, 'PM's world affairs speech to Lord Mayor's Banquet', 13 November 2006, <http://www.number10.gov.uk/Page10409>.

Bleiker, Roland and Emma Hutchison, 'Fear no more: Emotions and world politics', *Review of International Studies* 34, no. 1 (2008): pp. 115–35.

Boege, Volker, Anne Brown, Kevin Clements, and Anna Nolan, 'Building peace and political communities in hybrid political orders', *International Peacekeeping* 16, no. 5 (2009): pp. 599–614.

Box, Richard, 'Running government like a business: Implications for public administration theory and practice', *The American Review of Public Administration* 29, no. 1 (1999): pp. 19–43.

Bromley, Simon, 'Blood for oil?', *New Political Economy* 11, no. 3 (2006): pp. 419–34.

Bush, George W., 'State of the Union Address, 2002', accessed 30 March 2013, <www.whitehouse.gov/stateoftheunion2002>.

Canclini, Nestor G., *Hybrid Cultures: Strategies for entering and leaving modernity* (Minnesota: University of Minnesota Press, 2005).

Chabal, Patrick, *The End of Conceit: Western rationality and postcolonialism* (London: Zed Books, 2012).

Chandler, David, 'Responsibility to Protect? Imposing the "liberal peace"', *International Peacekeeping* 11, no. 1 (2004): pp. 59–81.

Chandrasekaran, Rajiv, *Imperial Life in the Emerald City: Inside Baghdad's Green Zone* (London: Bloomsbury, 2007).

Conflict Sensitivity Consortium, 'Conflict Sensitivity Consortium Benchmarking Paper', Draft, 29 April 2009, <http://www.conflictsensitivity.org/sites/default/files/CSA%20Benchmarking%20paper-full.pdf>.

Dodge, Toby, 'Iraqi Transitions: From regime change to state collapse', *Third World Quarterly* 26, no. 4/5 (2005): pp. 705–21.

Donais, Timothy, 'Empowerment or imposition? Dilemmas of local ownership in post-conflict peacebuilding processes', *Peace and Change* 34, no. 1 (2009): pp. 3–26.

Doyle, Michael W., 'Liberalism and world politics', *American Political Science Review* 80, no. 4 (1986): pp. 1151–69.

Goetschel, Laurent and Tobias Hagmann, 'Civilian peacebuilding: Peace by bureaucratic means?' *Conflict, Security and Development* 9, no. 1 (2009): pp. 55–73.

Goffman, Erving, *The Presentation of Self in Everyday Life* (New York: Anchor Books, 1959).

Haynes, Jeffrey, *Religious Transnational Actors and Soft Power* (London: Ashgate, 2012).

Herring, Eric, 'Neoliberalism versus Peacebuilding in Iraq', in *Whose Peace? Critical Perspectives on the Political Economy of Peacebuilding*, edited by Michael Pugh, Neil Cooper, and Mandy Turner (Basingstoke: Palgrave Macmillan, 2008), pp. 47–64.

Kabama, P., '"Heart of Darkness": Current images of DRC and their theoretical underpinnings', *Anthropological Theory* 10, no. 3 (2010): pp. 265–301.

Mac Ginty, Roger, 'Hybrid peace: The interaction between top down and bottom up peace', *Security Dialogue* 41, no. 4 (2010): pp. 391–412.

Mac Ginty, Roger, 'Indigenous peacemaking versus the liberal peace', *Cooperation and Conflict* 43, no. 2 (2008): pp. 139–63.

Mac Ginty, Roger, *International Peacebuilding and Local Resistance: Hybrid forms of peace* (Basingstoke: Palgrave, 2011).

Mac Ginty, Roger, 'Routine Peace: Technocracy and peacebuilding', *Cooperation and Conflict* 47, no. 3 (2012): pp. 287–308.

Mac Ginty, Roger, 'The transcripts of peace: Public, hidden or non-obvious?', *Journal of Intervention and Statebuilding* 7, no. 4 (2013): pp. 423–30.

Mishra, Pankaj, *From the Ruins of Empire: The revolt against the west and the remaking of Asia* (London: Allen Lane, 2012).

Moffat, Alistair, *Sea Kingdoms: The History of Celtic Britain and Ireland* (Edinburgh: Birlinn, 2001).

Newman, Edward, Roland Paris, and Oliver Richmond, eds, *New Perspectives on Liberal Peacebuilding* (Tokyo: United Nations University Press, 2010).

Paris, Roland, 'Saving liberal peacebuilding', *Review of International Studies* 36, no. 2 (2010): pp. 337–65.

Richmond, Oliver P., *The Transformation of Peace* (Basingstoke: Palgrave, 2007).

Scott, J. C., *Weapons of the Weak: Everyday forms of peasant resistance* (Yale: Yale University Press, 1987).

12

News media, communications, and the limits of perception management and propaganda during military operations

Piers Robinson

Overview

Conflict defined the twentieth century with the two World Wars and the Cold War shaping the geo-political context for almost the entire century. The twenty-first century has seen no let-up, with the two major US-led wars in Iraq and Afghanistan dominating the foreign policy agendas of Western governments and the militarized response, the so-called 'war on terror', to terrorist groups such as Al Qaeda. At the same time, the last 100 years have witnessed the rapid emergence of new forms of mass communication, including wireless radio, newsreels and cinema, mass circulation newspapers, television, and the Internet. Right from the start, the power of communication in wartime was fully recognized: From the deployment of Nazi propaganda, masterminded by Goebbels, through to the creation of the Ministry of Information in Britain, tasked with the 'maintenance of morale', communications media became an integral part of national war efforts. Today, governments devote significant resources in order to shape the *information environment* in their favour and, in doing so, win the battle for 'hearts and minds'.[1]

But to what extent can the information environment be controlled and influenced in wartime?[2] To what extent can the *perceptions* of domestic

[1] Philip M. Taylor, *Munitions of the Mind: A History of Propaganda* (Manchester: Manchester University Press, 2003).

[2] Throughout this chapter my discussion should be understood to refer to 'limited wars' of 'national interest' whereby military force is deployed in the context of perceived national interests being at stake (e.g. Vietnam War, Iraq War). As such, this category of war is distinct from so-called

publics, global audiences, and people within conflict zones be *managed*? If, as US General Petraeus is reported to have stated, information war is '60 percent of the fight',[3] what is the extent, and what is the limit, of strategies aimed at influencing military outcomes by shaping the non-material information environment? By drawing upon the body of academic knowledge that has been generated over the last thirty years, this chapter aims to provide an informed answer to this question. But first, understanding how we got to where we are now is important, and so this chapter begins with a brief overview of media operations since the Vietnam conflict, a war which has in many ways defined military and political thinking regarding media and publics. This chapter then proceeds in two parts. The first part evaluates scholarly debate with regard to the interaction between media, domestic audiences, and war, paying particular attention to the recent research findings of major studies.[4] Here it is noted that, along with many other aspects of 'tactical transition', perception-management activities during the end phase of a conflict have received scant attention from both academics and practitioners. The second part evaluates media operations with respect to both global audiences and populations within conflict zones, the so-called battle for 'hearts and minds'. Highlighting the reduced influence that inevitably accompanies the exit and transition phases of a conflict, the chapter concludes with a frank discussion about the limits of media operations within the context of low-intensity and long-term counter-insurgency wars as has been witnessed over the last 12 years in Iraq and Afghanistan. First, however, it is necessary to introduce some definitions and clarifications related to two issues.

Perception management/propaganda and 'tactical transitions'

First, this chapter is concerned primarily with *perception management*. As a form of organized political communication designed to influence attitudes, 'perception management' is, to all intent and purpose, identical to activities

humanitarian interventions (e.g. *Operation Restore Hope* in Somalia 1992–93) and 'total wars' of national survival (e.g. the Second World War). Public opinion, propaganda, and media dynamics during 'limited wars' of 'national interest' are different from those that occur during humanitarian interventions and 'total wars' of national survival. Briefly, and crudely, public tolerance for casualties, elite influence over media and public attitudes, and public support for war, are all much higher during 'total wars' of national survival, and relatively lower during humanitarian interventions, when compared with 'limited wars' of 'national interest'.

[3] Thomas M. Cioppa, 'Operation Iraqi Freedom Strategic Communication Analysis and Assessment', *Media, War and Conflict* 10, no. 1 (2009): p. 27.

[4] In particular Christopher Gelpi, Peter D. Feaver, and Jason Reifler, *Paying the Human Costs of War: American Public Opinion and Casualties in Military Conflicts* (Princeton: Princeton University Press, 2009); Matthew Baum and Tim J. Groeling, *War Stories: The causes and consequences of public views of war* (Princeton: Princeton University Press, 2010).

that have historically been described as 'propaganda'. Such activities can involve both truth-telling and deception. Throughout the chapter both terms will be used but they should be understood as relating to the same activities.[5] Perception management, or propaganda, is one component of *information warfare* (or information operations), which, in turn, refers to a wide range of activities, including battlefield communication, public communication, and intelligence gathering. As a subset of *information warfare*, the objective of perception management is the shaping of the attitudes of people, whether domestic publics, the 'global' public, or audiences within conflict zones. Different names have been used to describe 'perception management', including *strategic communication* and, more recently, *public diplomacy* and *global engagement*. Perception management can also be a major part of psychological operations (PSYOPS) and information operations during counter-insurgency (COIN) operations.[6] Other terms and categorizations in circulation include *media operations, media management, public relations*, and *information operations*. Indeed, there are a number of categorizations and definitions available,[7] and terminology shifts between the US and UK contexts. For succinctness, this chapter places together under the label 'perception management' and 'propaganda' all activities that are aimed at shaping the information space according to one's needs and, in doing so, influencing attitudes in your favour.

Second, the bulk of academic research into media and war has rarely focused upon the withdrawal or 'tactical transition' phases of armed conflicts. Rather, scholars have tended to stay focused on exploring the high- and low-intensity-phases of a conflict, as well as media–state dynamics during the build-up to a war. The interaction between the military, the media, and the end phase of a conflict has, in contrast, received sparse attention. This is also the case with respect to practitioners involved in perception management and propaganda activities amongst whom there is little sustained attention to the issue of how to approach the battle for 'hearts and minds' when transition and withdrawal are underway. This is perhaps surprising given the significance of 'closing moments', the way they are mediated, and their impact on a country's collective memory of a war. Images of US personnel being airlifted by helicopter from the US Embassy roof in Saigon as communist forces advanced have

[5] For further discussion of definitional issues pertaining to propaganda and contemporary organized political communication see Philip M. Taylor, *War and the Media: Propaganda and Persuasion in the Gulf War* (Manchester: Manchester University Press, 1992); Philip M. Taylor, 'Perception management and the "War" Against Terrorism', *Journal of Information Warfare* 1, no. 3 (2002): p. 20; Garth S. Jowett and Victoria O'Donnell, *Propaganda and Persuasion*, 5th edn (London: Sage, 2012).

[6] See for example Joint Publication 3-24, *Counter Insurgency Operations*, 9 October 2009, <http://www.dtic.mil/doctrine/new_pubs/jp3_24.pdf>.

[7] For one set of categorizations see Douglas H. Dearth, 'Shaping the "Information Space"', *Journal of Information Warfare* 1, no. 3 (2002): p. 1.

become a defining image of US defeat in Vietnam. In Somalia, US withdrawal was epitomized by the television images of a downed Black Hawk helicopter and one of its killed crew members being dragged through the streets of Mogadishu. Such 'closing images' undoubtedly play a part in how a society remembers past conflicts, although even here their importance should not be overstated; probably most Americans alive today have not caught anything more than a fleeting glimpse of these images, let alone fully understood what they were seeing. Such images also undoubtedly influence, on some level, policy decisions with regard to current and future conflicts. But, again, this should perhaps not be overstated; policy-makers and politicians tend to recall and invoke images to suit their purpose, rather than being haunted by images from wars gone wrong. In short, interest in how and why some events come to symbolize a war, from a historical perspective, is less relevant to immediate and current concerns over perception management during an ongoing conflict. Perhaps more pointedly, and from the perspective of those seeking to manage perceptions in wartime, it is questionable whether any kind of meaningful influence and control can be exerted over how a conflict is ultimately remembered both by the media and society at large. These qualifications aside, the scholarly research and thinking conducted into media-state dynamics during war discussed in this chapter is also applicable to withdrawal or 'tactical transition' phases, even if the express goal of this scholarship does not lie in exploring these end phases of a war, and the substantive arguments that emerge in this chapter are also logically applicable to the closing stages of a war.

A brief history of perception management and propaganda

The American experience in Vietnam serves as a defining moment in the history of contemporary perception-management activities. At the time of the final US defeat and withdrawal in 1975, a rapidly emerging argument amongst many military and political officials was that domestic dissent and adversarial news media coverage had denied victory to the US. More precise analysis of these claims revolved around, for example, US coverage of the 1968 Tet offensive and how overly pessimistic coverage of this uprising fuelled the context in which President Johnson decided to place the US on the path of withdrawal from the war in South East Asia.[8] However, at the time, a more general feeling emerged that US political and military leaders had been on the

[8] David Culbert, 'Television's visual impact on decision-making in the USA, 1968: The Tet Offensive and Chicago's Democratic National Convention', *Journal of Contemporary History* 33, no. 3 (1998): pp. 419–49; Peter Braestrup, *Big Story: How the American Press and Television Reported and Interpreted the Crisis of Tet 1968 in Vietnam and Washington* (Novati, CA: Presidio Press, 1994).

receiving end of an oppositional news media[9] and a casualty-phobic US public, the combination of which led, at least in part, to US defeat. As Richard Nixon stated in his memoirs:

> The Vietnam War was complicated by factors that never before occurred in America's conduct of war.... More than ever before, television showed the terrible human suffering and sacrifice of war. Whatever the intention behind such relentless and literal reporting of war, the result was a serious demoralization of the home front, raising the question whether America would ever again be able to fight an enemy abroad with unity and strength of purpose at home.[10]

And thus was born the *Vietnam syndrome*, the belief that rising casualties, adversarial media and declining public support could be enough to lose a war.

Armed with the belief that wars can be lost through failure to maintain media and public support, increasing attention has been paid to perception management since the Vietnam War. It was during the Falklands conflict in 1982 that the British government (re)learned[11] the utility of placing journalists alongside combatants as a means to foster sympathetic reporting.[12] Haunted by the *Vietnam syndrome* and influenced in part by the British experience,[13] the US military adopted the *pool system* in the 1991 Gulf War, allowing selected journalists to accompany frontline units while others were channelled towards the memorable set-piece press briefings delivered at hotels in Saudi Arabia. Indeed, it was largely the use of dramatic images of 'smart' bombs and sanitized language (such as the use of the terms 'collateral damage' and 'surgical strikes') during these briefings which ensured the media coverage did not relay too much of the grim reality of war.[14] Since the 1999 Kosovo conflict, attempts to manage the information environment during wars and crises have been further strengthened. Coalition military operations in Kosovo, Afghanistan, and Iraq have been accompanied by sustained and highly organized attempts to influence media agendas by promoting coverage of some issues rather than others, and by encouraging the framing of stories in ways that support the government's cause.[15] As Robin Brown has described, at

[9] Daniel C. Hallin, 'The Media, the War in Vietnam, and Political Support: A Critique of the Thesis of an Oppositional Media', *Journal of Politics* 46, no. 1 (1984): pp. 2–24.

[10] Richard M. Nixon, *Memoirs* (New York: Grossett and Dunlap, 1978), p. 350.

[11] I write '(re)learned' because this insight was established during the First World War. See Susan Carruthers, *The Media at War: Communication and Conflict in the Twentieth Century*, 2nd edn (Basingstoke: Macmillan, 2011).

[12] Glasgow University Media Group, *War and Peace News* (Milton Keynes: Open University Press, 1985).

[13] Carruthers, *The Media at War.*

[14] Taylor, *War and the Media*; W. Lance Bennett and David L. Paletz, eds, *Taken by Storm: The Media, Public Opinion, and US Foreign Policy in the Gulf War* (Chicago: University of Chicago Press, 1994).

[15] Steve Tatham, *Losing Arab Hearts and Minds: The Coalition, Al Jazeera and Muslim Public Opinion* (London: C. Hurst and Co. Publishers, 2006).

least some of the impetus for these attempts during the initial intervention in Afghanistan came from the UK government's Director of Communications and Strategy, Alastair Campbell, whose:

> solution was to create Coalition Information Centres (CICs) in Washington, London and Islamabad that would coordinate the release of information, attempt to control the news agenda and rebut opposition claims in exactly the way that the Clinton–Blair 'war room' model operated in domestic politics.[16]

Other activities inherent in the 'war room' model include the coordinated use of press releases, news media appearances, press conferences, and speeches. In strategic terms, these activities seek to encourage the development of common news media frames over time. In tactical terms, they serve to minimize coverage of damaging or hostile stories and to discredit oppositional counter-narratives. Another important component of coalition propaganda during the period around the Iraq invasion in 2003 was the US Office of Global Diplomacy (previously known as the US CIC and then later as the Office of Global Communications). This group included senior diplomats, military personnel, and PR experts such as Victoria (Torie) Clarke who coordinated with Campbell's Iraq Information Group (IIG) in the UK.[17]

The importance of perception management activities to the current generation of politicians is also profound. In the US political context, Bennett et al. describe how, for the Bush administration, perception management (with respect to public affairs) became firmly established as a new form of governing: the 'malleable and subordinate nature of reality, the elastic human capacity to perceive it, and the mechanisms used to shape it' mean that 'narratives matter more than material reality'.[18] In turn, narratives shape perceptions of reality that then 'open the way to the use of power to create those realities'.[19] In the UK context, in part flowing from the Labour Party's bitter experience with a hostile right-wing British press, the Blair government was also focused on perception management (via public relations or 'spin'). Indeed, the reputation of the Blair government for spin has been widely documented and discussed.[20] Most recently, Blair's Chief of Staff Jonathan Powell published his memoirs, titled

[16] Robin Brown, 'Spinning the War: Political communications, information operations and public diplomacy in the War on Terrorism', in *War and the Media: Reporting Conflict 24/7*, edited by Daya K. Thussu and Des Freedman (London: Sage, 2003), pp. 87–101.

[17] Piers Robinson et al., *Pockets of Resistance: British News Media, War and Theory in the 2003 Invasion of Iraq* (Manchester: Manchester University Press, 2010).

[18] W. Lance Bennett, Regina G. Lawrence, and Steven Livingston, *When the Press Fails: Political Power and the News Media from Iraq to Katrina* (Chicago: University of Chicago Press, 2007), pp. 136–7.

[19] Bennett et al., *When the Press Fails*, p. 137.

[20] For example: B. Franklin, 'The Hand of History: New Labour, News Management and Governance', in *The New Labour Reader*, edited by Andrew Chadwick and Richard Heffernan (Cambridge: Polity Press, 2003), pp. 304–8.

The New Machiavelli: How to wield power in the modern world, in which he devotes an entire chapter to detailing the Blair government's approach to dealing with the media.[21] With Campbell in charge, Powell states, 'we needed a proactive media operation that not just responded to stories, but created them'.[22] Finally, an MI6/Secret Intelligence Service (SIS) officer has provided an important insight into the extent to which concern over public affairs had increased in the years running up to the 2003 invasion of Iraq. When asked about the presence of Campbell, the communications director, during secret briefings from MI6, he notes that '[p]ost 1997, the culture, disciplines, attitudes of HMG went through phases of profound change. It wouldn't have happened before, closer to the Cold War... I think it's difficult for the Chief to say, "[c]an I have a private word, Prime Minister. I can't do it in front of Campbell"'.[23]

Since Vietnam, then, perception-management and propaganda activities have become evermore entrenched within the institutions of both government and the military. The employment of PR experts, or spin doctors,[24] the development of strategies such as embedding and pooling, the careful crafting of media messages, and systematic, coordinated, and extensive approaches to managing the media environment have all become central features of how contemporary governments and militaries function. Perhaps more significantly, at least for some, perception management has become vital not only for fending off the loss of morale on the home front, but also an integral part of actively shaping the information environment both globally and locally, as well as a central component of COIN operations. Indeed, it is the perception that US and UK militaries have simply not been getting their communication strategy right, which in turn has prevented military success in Iraq and Afghanistan, that has influenced recent work by British military practitioners Steven Tatham and Andrew Mackay in *Losing Arab Hearts and Minds* and *Behavioural Conflict*.[25] But to what extent are these convictions accurate? To what extent can perception management really win wars, and under what circumstances are these activities successful? I shall deal first with perception management and domestic audiences, the so-called home front, and then discuss perception management with regard to audiences within conflict zones.

[21] Jonathan Powell, *The New Machiavelli: How to wield power in the modern world* (London: Random House Books, 2010), pp. 189–210.

[22] Powell, *The New Machiavelli*, p. 193.

[23] SIS4, *Chilcot Inquiry*, Transcript page 63, accessed 14 January 2014, <http://www.iraqinquiry.org.uk/media/50700/SIS4-part-1.pdf>.

[24] For example, the employment of former journalists Alastair Campbell as the Strategy and Communications Director for the Blair Government from 1997 to 2003, Mark Laity (former BBC Defence correspondent) as NATO Chief of Strategic Communication, and communications consultant Victoria (Torie) Clarke in senior positions in the Bush administration.

[25] Tatham, *Losing Arab Hearts and Minds*; Andrew Mackay and Steve Tatham, *Behavioural Conflict: Why understanding people and their motivations will prove decisive in future conflict* (Saffron Waldon: Military Studies Press, 2011).

Managing the home front

Academic analysis of public opinion in wartime has been dominated by US-based research and, consistent with the earlier discussion, pre-occupied with the notion that losing public and media support can mean losing a war, the *Vietnam syndrome.* Although there has always been a good deal of scholarly disagreement, there is one area in which there is a reasonable degree of consensus, and that concerns the dynamics of media and public opinion during the early stages of a war.

Early stages: pre-war and the high-intensity conflict 'rally round the flag' phase

During the early stages of a conflict, both media and public support tends to remain at a comfortably high level. Connected with this observation is the logical implication that short wars tend to garner reasonably high levels of media and public support. In the UK context, the 1982 Falklands War is a good example of a short and successful conflict, one which was also dangerous and costly, but that also enjoyed widespread support throughout British society.[26] There are three major reasons frequently invoked for what has come to be known as 'the rally effect'.[27]

First, and at a basic level, international crises and the fear that they generate tend to cause publics and media to rally behind their leaders; this is in part due to a basic human desire for leadership and protection in times of fear and, also, in part due to the innate patriotism that most publics feel.[28] For example, as Aday describes with regard to the US context, 9/11 'propelled President George W. Bush from a controversial leader with tepid and declining popularity into one with stratospheric approval ratings, making it relatively easy for him to lead the country into war against the Taliban regime'.[29] Secondly, political elites, including the government and opposition parties, tend to rally in support of a war, for many of the same reasons that publics do. But the political elite rally is critical because it also exerts a powerful influence upon news media coverage of a crisis. Because news media rely heavily upon elite sources when deciding what to cover and how,[30] elite political consensus, as

[26] Glasgow Media Group, *War and Peace News.*

[27] John Mueller, *War, Presidents and Public Opinion* (New York: John Wiley, 1973).

[28] Robinson et al., *Pockets of Resistance*, pp. 36–7 and 100–2.

[29] Sean Aday, 'Leading the charge: Media, elites, and the use of emotion in stimulating rally effects in wartime', *Journal of Communication* 60, no. 3 (2010): p. 441.

[30] There is a long, empirically and theoretically supported, literature documenting the propensity of mainstream news to follow and reflect elite cues. For an overview see Piers Robinson, 'News Media and War', in *The Sage Handbook of Political Communication*, edited by Holli Semetko and Margaret Scammell (Thousand Oaks: Sage, 2012), pp. 342–55. For classic expositions of this

occurs when there is a rally, tends to be substantially reflected in media coverage. That media coverage in turn, to the extent that it influences public perceptions, serves merely to reinforce the political consensus behind the war. Thirdly, and finally, the informational context at the start of a conflict has also been identified as a critical variable. Early in a conflict, as Baum and Groeling describe,[31] a government enjoys a significant information advantage over its public, media, and other political elites. In short, governments know far more about a crisis than their media and their publics. As a result, public perceptions of reality are highly 'elastic' with government rhetoric and perception-management activities being able to shape media and public understanding about a crisis. The run-up to the 2003 Iraq war, when 'patchy' and 'sporadic' intelligence was drawn upon in order to persuade British and American publics that Iraq was a credible WMD (weapons of mass destruction) threat,[32] is a good example of just how elastic public perceptions of reality can be.

The combination of these factors provides ideal circumstances for successful perception management. All three factors work to reinforce the emergence of an information environment that is conducive to government and military war objectives. Indeed, the vast bulk of academic analysis of media and public opinion during these rally-phases highlights this dynamic.[33] Regarding the recent Iraq conflict, for example, Aday et al. document how US TV news media coverage of the invasion phase was largely sanitized with relatively small amounts of substantial criticism of coalition operations.[34] Again, Robinson et al., analysing UK press and television coverage of the Iraq invasion, show how the majority of media outlets were largely supportive both of coalition military efforts and the official justifications for war revolving around the WMD claim and moral arguments concerning the humanitarian rationale for action.[35] In the US public opinion support was solid for the invasion of

observation, see Daniel C. Hallin, *The Uncensored War: The Media and Vietnam* (Berkeley: University of California Press, 1986); and W. Lance Bennett, 'Toward a theory of press–state relations in the United States', *Journal of Communication* 40, no. 2 (1990): pp. 103–27.

[31] Baum and Groeling, *War Stories*.

[32] Joshua Rovner, *Fixing the Facts: National Security and the Politics of Intelligence* (Ithaca, NY: Cornell University Press, 2011); Brian Jones, *Failing Intelligence: The True Story of How We Were Fooled Into Going to War in Iraq* (London: Biteback, 2010); E. Herring and P. Robinson, 'Report X marks the spot: the British Government's deceptive dossier on Iraq and WMD', *Political Science Quarterly* (forthcoming 2014).

[33] For major works see Hallin, *The Uncensored War*; Glasgow Media Group, *War and Peace News*; Bennett and Paletz, *Taken by Storm*. For an overview, see Robinson, 'News Media and War'.

[34] Sean Aday, Steven Livingston, and Maeve Herbert, 'Embedding the truth: A cross-cultural analysis of objectivity and television coverage of the Iraq War', *The Harvard International Journal of Press/Politics* 10, no. 3 (2005): pp. 3–21.

[35] Robinson et al., *Pockets of Resistance*. See also Howard Tumber and Jerry Palmer, *Media at War: The Iraq Crisis* (London: Sage, 2004) and Justin Lewis, Rod Brooks, Nick Mosdell, and Terry Threadgold, *Shoot First and Ask Questions Later: Media Coverage of the 2003 Iraq War* (New York: Peter Lang, 2006).

Iraq and, even in Britain, majority support for the war emerged as troops went into action.[36] The ideal conditions for propaganda do not, however, remain indefinitely.

The long haul: low-intensity conflict and rising military casualties

As a conflict progresses, however, the environment for perception management starts to become sub-optimal. This is in part due to the inevitable rise in military casualties associated with a longer-term military campaign, in part to the emergence of elite divisions, and also due to the increasing influence of events on the ground. I shall discuss each in turn.

In his seminal work, *War, Presidents and Public Opinion*,[37] John Mueller examined opinion polls and casualty counts during the Korean and Vietnam Wars, and found that public support for these wars declined at first rapidly, and then more slowly, as US casualties mounted. Overall, he argued that public support declined inexorably as the death toll of US soldiers increased. For Mueller, this dynamic reflects a simple and rational response of US citizens to the rising cost of a war. The more lives that are lost, the more an individual is likely to calculate that a war is not worth fighting and, therefore, the more likely he or she is to withdraw their support. In essence, Mueller's work underpins the *Vietnam syndrome*. For those concerned with perception management, Mueller argues that news media play little part in this fundamental dynamic. Publics become aware of casualty counts with or without extensive or critical media attention, and they form their opinions on whether a war is worthwhile from there.

The second key dynamic is the emergence of elite divisions and the subsequent reflection of these divisions within media reporting. Just as members of the public might seek to evaluate the utility of a war as it progresses, political elites will also reflect upon a war and, as that war continues, are increasingly likely to start to raise questions. Once this questioning occurs publicly, journalists begin to report the divisions, thus reinforcing the sense of dissensus over a war. For example, as Hallin describes in the case of the Vietnam War,[38] US mainstream media coverage started to become critical at the point at which Washington became divided over the course of the war. This was during the 1968 Tet offensive when a political and very public debate started to emerge between the 'hawks' and 'doves' in the US administration. Once this debate started, journalists, at least to a certain extent, began to feel more comfortable with questioning the wisdom and direction of the war in Vietnam. In short,

[36] Justin Lewis, 'Television, public opinion and the war in Iraq: The case of Britain', *International Journal of Public Opinion Research* 16, no. 3 (2004): pp. 295–310.

[37] Mueller, *War, Presidents and Public Opinion*.

[38] Hallin, *The Uncensored War*.

elite divisions reported through media can then fuel further public debate and questioning with regard to a war. An important derivative dynamic here is the potential for news media to focus upon 'bad news'. In the case of the Vietnam War, Robinson argued that following the Tet offensive, US media coverage appeared to take sides in the debate between hawks and doves, focusing upon the bad news coming out of Vietnam.[39] In *War Stories*, Baum and Groeling emphasize the propensity of journalists to seek out sources who are critical of an existing policy. In particular, they note that a politician who criticizes his or her own party during a war is both particularly news worthy (because of its comparative rarity) and particularly influential on public opinion (because of the credibility that such criticism possesses). In short, divisions start to emerge amongst elites, and news coverage reports the political debates, perhaps focusing on the negative, and thus making perception-management activities increasingly challenging.

The third critical dynamic concerns, quite simply, the reality which emerges on the ground. As Baum and Groeling describe,[40] 'events on the ground' start to become increasingly important the longer a conflict goes on and gradually reality starts to exert its influence upon public perceptions. Events that are inevitably associated with longer-term military engagements, such as military setbacks, lack of progress or slow progress, mistakes, civilian casualties, as well as military casualties, all contribute to an increasing stock of knowledge that citizens draw upon in order to evaluate a war. In short, the information advantage enjoyed by a government at the start of a conflict, described above, slowly diminishes and elite rhetoric (including perception management) becomes less influential than do the facts on the ground. In short, the 'elasticity of reality'[41] declines as a conflict goes on. As Aday pithily states:

> It seems to be the case that even the White House has an elastic framing window in which to operate, one that typically opens during the lead-up and in the initial stages of a conflict, when the public is willing to rally and events are still largely hypothetical, but which will close if progress stalls or reverses.[42]

It is also worth emphasizing that, whilst news media may be an important component of how publics are informed about events on the ground, this should not be taken to mean that better control or perception management aimed at the media might alter the fact that publics become more and more aware of the costs of a war as it drags on. Indeed, an interesting and informative comparison can be made here with the Soviet experience in Afghanistan

[39] Piers Robinson, 'Theorising the influence of media on world politics', *European Journal of Communication* 16, no. 4 (2001): pp. 523–44.

[40] Baum and Groeling, *War Stories*.

[41] Baum and Groeling, *War Stories*.

[42] Sean Aday, 'Chasing the bad news: An analysis of 2005 Iraq and Afghanistan war coverage on NBC and Fox News Channel', *Journal of Communication* 60, no. 1 (2010): pp. 144–64.

(1979–88). In a country with a state-controlled media, citizens of the USSR still became aware of the conflict and, as one CIA report stated,[43] domestic 'concern about the war' grew and eventually 'influenced Soviet leaderships deliberations'. Much of the public discussion was put down to returning veterans, '15 major demonstrations since mid-1984' whilst dissent amongst intellectuals and officials (i.e. political elites) was also observed. In short, news got back to the home front, with or without a free media.

The limits to managing the 'home front': reality bites

At its most extreme, military and political angst over the *Vietnam syndrome* posits a scenario whereby anti-war publics, fuelled by biased media coverage and elite dissent, compromise the ability of the executive and military to fight a war effectively. This in turn, affects events on the ground and military failure inevitably follows. None of the research discussed above suggests that this is the case. In fact, publics, media, and political elites are historically supportive of military campaigns and content to reward leaders who prosecute short and successful wars. It is only when a war becomes longer than expected, protracted, and with a rising casualty count, that problems start to emerge. The leverage of events on the ground, elite dissent, and rising casualties start to erode public support and fuel a more critical stance on the part of news media. Crucially, this dynamic is a consequence of, and not a cause of, military failure.

There is some evidence, as discussed above, that, once a war becomes more protracted, elite dissent, casualties, and events might interact with negative news coverage perhaps fuelling and furthering declines in support for a war. And, as Gelpi, Feaver, and Reifler have argued, publics are not so much *casualty*-phobic as they are *defeat*-phobic. As a result, so long as publics believe a war is worthwhile and winnable, their support can be retained.[44] But even here, their analysis provides no evidence to suggest that political rhetoric and attempts to frame a war as winnable or justified can overcome the material realities associated with a long, drawn-out, and difficult conflict. Indeed, they at least appear to accept the importance of actual progress on the ground when they state: 'But also like Korea and Vietnam, the data from Iraq suggest that the public's tolerance for casualties will drop when events on the ground do not suggest progress toward victory'.[45] Put bluntly, there is a limit to the

[43] 'USSR: Domestic Fallout From the Afghan War', Intelligence Assessment, CIA, February 1988, <http://www.foia.cia.gov/sites/default/files/document_conversions/89801/DOC_0000500659.pdf>.

[44] Gelpi et al., *Paying the Human Costs of War.*

[45] Gelpi et al., *Paying the Human Costs of War*, p. 53. In fact, a close reading of their study shows that, even though perceptions of likely military success can attenuate declining public support for an on-going and lengthy conflict, support levels do not return to those enjoyed at the early stages

extent to which political elites can frame a war as winnable when faced with an on-going and ambiguous military campaign. There is, in other words, a limit to the potential of perception-management and propaganda activities as a war drags on and becomes increasingly costly and this applies equally, if not more so, to the end phase of a conflict when tactical transition occurs. Indeed, given the rapid loss of control for the intervening power, which is an inevitable consequence of the transition and withdrawal phase, the declining ability to influence perceptions reflects the broader dynamics inherent to this stage of a conflict.

Managing the rest: perception management and populations within conflict zones

Whilst the dynamics and interactions of war, public opinion, and the media have received ample scholarly attention over the years, the role of media and perception management aimed at influencing attitudes and opinions within war zones has remained under-researched, at least by academics. And yet, as noted earlier, significant attention has come to be devoted to managing the information space within war zones and ways of persuading both civilians and armed opponents to support the military and political objectives being pursued by intervening forces. In the broadest sense, perception management in the conflict area 'focuses on influencing the population's perception of events and the host nation's legitimacy, as well as insurgent decisions and decision-making processes'.[46] Much of the basic strategy involves coordinating and maintaining consistent messages, or narratives, aimed at countering insurgent narratives and propaganda, and draws upon psychological operation (PSYOPS), military deception, electronic warfare, and other capabilities.[47] These activities include engagement with local and international news media and, beyond that, dissemination of print media such as the NATO newspaper *Sada-e Azadi* in Afghanistan, advertising (such as the billboard adverts aimed at deterring suicide bombers in Afghanistan), as well as close integration of information operations with counter-insurgency (COIN) operations. Regarding COIN operations, communication of key themes and messages is seen as an integral part of operations in which insurgents have been pushed out.

of a conflict and, if little actual progress is made, public support will continue to erode. Although they show that patterns of support for a war are more variable than suggested by Mueller (*War, Presidents and Public Opinion*), the long-term picture is still one of declining support the longer a conflict goes on.

[46] Joint Publication 3–24, *Counter Insurgency Operations*, 5 October 2009, VI-1.

[47] Joint Publication 3–24, *Counter Insurgency Operations*, 5 October 2009, VI-2.

The challenges: audiences and information environment

If perception management is a challenge when dealing with domestic (i.e. Western) audiences, it is even more so when dealing with populations within a war zone. Two issues stand out as worthy of consideration: the receptivity of the audience and the degree of control over the information environment. I shall deal with each in turn.

Some early communication scholarship worked with simplistic assumptions about the influence of media messages upon audiences. The so-called 'magic bullet' or 'Hypodermic Needle Theory', inspired by notable events such as Orson Welles' *War of the Worlds* radio broadcast which caused mass panic in 1938, postulated a direct and uncomplicated causal link between media messages and audiences. Audiences watched and listened, and then attitudes and behaviours were influenced accordingly. But such a simplistic understanding was quickly overtaken by accounts that emphasized both the importance of variation in attributes of the audience and differing propensities to be influenced by media messages. Not all people are equally influenced by media messages, and they draw upon pre-existing knowledge or information from other sources when evaluating what they see or hear in the media.[48] Most usefully for the discussion here is Stuart Hall's influential work on how audiences decode media messages.[49] He argued that, with respect to message reception, audiences could be separated into three categories. First, most members of an audience would decode media messages in line with the hegemonic or dominant message that was encoded in the media text. The second category would engage in a negotiated reading of the media text, accepting some parts of the message but reinterpreting or rejecting other aspects of the message. The third, and proportionally much smaller, category would read media text in an oppositional fashion, rejecting any dominant messages that might be encoded in the media text. Of course, Hall was working with Western audiences watching Western media output. Transplanted to, for example, the Afghanistan context, it is likely that most of the audience, rather than being influenced by the dominant message, will engage in an oppositional reading or, at best, a negotiated reading. Only a minority will simply absorb the message being communicated and be influenced accordingly. This is precisely the point that military practitioners Mackay and Tatham put forward in their recent critique of coalition perception management activities in both Iraq and Afghanistan:

[48] For an introduction, see J. Corner, 'Reappraising reception: Aims, concepts and methods', in *Mass Media and Society*, edited by James Curran and Michael Gurevitch (London: Arnold, 1996), pp. 280–304.

[49] Stuart Hall, 'Encoding and Decoding in the television discourse', CCCS stencilled paper series (Paper 7), (Birmingham: University of Birmingham, 1973).

> In Iraq and in Afghanistan the Coalition pushed out messages, on specific channels, and hoped to achieve attitudinal change. As we have already seen, in Iraq these messages were focused on supporting the establishment of a democracy whilst in Afghanistan they were designed to build support for the government of Hamid Karzai and the continued presence of NATO and ISAF forces.... [I]t did not take into consideration that the audience themselves may already have held preconceived views about Karzai, GIRoA and ISAF, views that might contextualise their attitudes and behaviours.... In short, the audience was not already buying into the coalition message—in Afghanistan it was not a straight binary decision between the Taliban (let's not forget they are someone's father, brother, son) and ISAF.... In Iraq, the same binary offer existed, and here too the Iraqis refused to accept it. For them it was not a straight choice between elements of Saddam's former Ba'ath party and a new Western-supported government. Many Iraqis were simply not convinced by either....[50]

The second limiting factor concerns the degree of control over the information environment. At least when it comes to domestic audiences in the West, there exists at least some degree of certainty as to the channels through which most of the public receive news and information about the world. Even in the Internet/Facebook/Twitter era we know that the majority of people continue to rely upon traditional news providers in order to become informed about the world. In this environment, messages can be communicated in a reasonably effective manner, with some degree of confidence that the intended audience will receive the message. But the situation in a war zone, such as Afghanistan, is that whatever media system there is in place, its reach and penetration is far less than is the case with the long-established news media outlets in the West. For example, and again drawing upon Mackay and Tatham's critique, attempts to introduce media that can be used to influence perceptions meet with an uphill struggle in terms of gaining interest, let alone legitimacy, amongst the population. For example, these authors describe how the NATO newspaper in Afghanistan involved the production of over 400,000 copies every fortnight but that 'anecdotally less than 10 per cent reach the intended audience' whilst many ended up being 'sold off to locals for wrapping shopping and food in the markets'.[51] More generally, in an environment such as Iraq or Afghanistan, local populations are likely to be far more reliant upon less formal modes of communication such as word-of-mouth and even via personal communication devices such as mobile phones. Indeed the penetration of mobile phones, according to the Asia Foundation Survey, in Afghanistan is quite extraordinary, with over 70 per cent of the population having

[50] Mackay and Tatham, *Behavioural Conflict*, pp. 106–7.
[51] Mackay and Tatham, *Behavioural Conflict*, pp. 106–7.

access to this means of communication.[52] And, in all of this, coalition efforts are up against insurgent perception-management activities which are, inevitably, carefully coordinated and aimed at countering the coalition's message. In short, compared with Western populations, the information environment is significantly less conducive for coalition perception-management activities. Of course, as a conflict moves towards a withdrawal or tactical transition phase, there is every reason to believe that the local population will become even more disinterested and distrusting of coalition messages. The issue of declining influence and power of the intervener during the withdrawal and transition phase is again an important issue here.

Reality bites (again)

This returns us to Baum's concept of the elasticity of reality. If reality becomes increasingly inelastic from the point of view of a Western audience 'observing' a conflict from afar, this is even more so in the case of audiences within a conflict zone. Populations who have immediate experience of the war underway, multiple means of communication available to them, and a comparatively weakly developed national media system, are going to form attitudes and judgements that are driven far more by the material reality of the world around them than they are by perception management, propaganda, or Western 'elite rhetoric'.[53] Indeed, whereas with domestic Western audiences elite rhetoric starts out as far more influential than reality, within a conflict zone reality is probably far more influential than any rhetoric coming from Western governments or coalition forces. Security, food, and electricity are the immediate imperatives concerning a civilian population, and any failure to make significant and rapid progress with respect to the provision of these basic goods will shape attitudes and behaviours. The now well-documented events following the fall of Saddam Hussein, when a loss of control and security led rapidly to a hostile population and increasingly active insurgency, is testament to this simple, but important observation. The importance of material reality within a conflict zone and how it trumps communications is also well recognized by Mackay and Tatham:

> ...in a conflict environment it [attitude] will have more to do with deeds matching actions than with a clever marketing campaign. For example, messages of peace and security will not resonate if the local government offices are corrupt and if Coalition air strikes accidently kill civilians.[54]

[52] The Asia Foundation, *Afghanistan in 2012: A Survey of the Afghan People*, accessed 16 September 2013, <http://asiafoundation.org/country/afghanistan/2012-poll.php>.
[53] Baum and Groeling, *War Stories*.
[54] Mackay and Tatham, *Behavioural Conflict*, p. 107.

Also, the most recent Asia Foundation survey of Afghanistan finds that Afghan civilians identified insecurity (28 per cent), unemployment (27 per cent), and corruption (25 per cent) as the 'biggest problems facing Afghanistan as a whole'.[55] Whilst it might be that some Afghans' perceptions of these issues may be shaped by what they see and read in the media, these are also issues that people experience through their everyday lives and, no doubt through immediate experience. Again, reality matters more than 'clever marketing'.

Conclusions: 'You can't put lipstick on a pig'

Torie Clarke, who served as Assistant Secretary of Defense for Public Affairs under US Defense Secretary Donald Rumsfeld, published her provocatively titled book *Lipstick on a Pig*,[56] arguing that spin, or as we have termed it here perception management, is not viable in an era when there exists increased transparency of information. Admitting that fact, according to Clarke, then leads to an uncomfortable truth regarding the need not to create a pig in the first place. The insight, put bluntly, is that it is the policy which is the problem, not the way one might be communicating it.

Before returning to Clarke's difficult and profoundly challenging argument, it is worth recapping the major conclusions emerging from this chapter. In matters of war, it is important to differentiate between Western audiences and audiences within conflict zones, as well as the stage a war has reached. Contrary to Clarke's thesis, the academic consensus is that Western publics will give considerable leeway to their political leaders and military when a war starts. In part this is because of the information advantage that governments have in a conflict, and partly because publics are, by and large, trusting of their leaders and supportive of their troops when a war starts. Under these circumstances, and unlike the later transition and withdrawal phases, perception-management activities, well understood by practitioners and well-researched by academics, are comparatively successful from the point of view of governments and militaries. As a war drags on, reality begins to bite. In wars which are costly and provide minimal progress/success, the material consequences of a war become ever more influential and, as this occurs, the ability of governments and the militaries to maintain support is inexorably diminished. Whatever the scope for renewed perception-management and propaganda efforts, it is unlikely that these can overcome the material realities of a war which has become protracted and sub-optimal in terms of its outcome. At this point,

[55] The Asia Foundation, *Afghanistan in 2012: A Survey of the Afghan People*.

[56] Torie Clarke, *Lipstick on a Pig: Winning in the No-Spin Era by Someone Who Knows the Game* (New York: Simon and Schuster, 2006).

consistent with Clarke's thesis, one really is confronted with the 'lipstick on a pig' problem and little can be done to reverse declines in public support that occur all the way through to the withdrawal/tactical-transition.

With respect to people within a conflict zone, the combination of minimal control over an information environment and an audience already predisposed to engage in an oppositional reading of official communications output, means that material reality is central to perceptions and attitudes right from the start. Unless security and legitimacy are quickly attained, popular support will rapidly be lost and, drawing upon the concept of the elasticity of reality, elite rhetoric and perception management will achieve little in the absence of material progress. Of course, at least in the case of Afghanistan, talk of new 'strategic narratives' or 'winning hearts and minds' have often become a frequent topic of conversation. Indeed, this author was involved in one military event at which a senior official promoted the idea that military victory in Afghanistan could be achieved with the writing and establishment of a new 'strategic narrative', a 'story' that was more persuasive than that of the Taliban. And it would perhaps be churlish or ungenerous to say that the host of perception-management and propaganda activities within conflict zones are pointless or irrelevant. They possibly do have some effect, although one that has never been empirically demonstrated. But the bottom line is that the effect is unlikely to be significant enough to make a substantive change to the military and political situation in a country such as Afghanistan. Moreover, the declining effectiveness of propaganda activities goes hand-in-hand with broader dynamics afflicting transition and withdrawal whereby there is a risky and progressive loss of control on the part of the intervening power. In short, perception management and propaganda cannot turn around a war that is faltering in its objectives. At the same time, wars that are proceeding according to plan will not be derailed simply because the perception management is badly executed. There is little evidence to suggest otherwise when one honestly appraises the three major protracted wars that the US has fought over the last 50 years (Vietnam, Iraq, and Afghanistan) and the scholarship that has analysed media and public opinion during these conflicts. In a nutshell, perception management throughout the low-intensity conflict and tactical transition phase will always be of marginal effectiveness.

With these conclusions in mind, it is worth closing with a number of broader thoughts concerning the contemporary interest that so many in the military and government have in perception management. At its most extreme, as the brief discussion of Bennett et al. in the section 'A brief history of perception management and propaganda' showed, this belief falls into a worldview that sees that 'narratives matter more than material reality'.[57] When this belief takes hold, it becomes logical to perceive military problems or failures as one of failure to get the narrative right, or failure to keep the media on side. It was, of course, this mindset that underpinned the *Vietnam syndrome*. But even here, it was a combination of elite dissent, public aversion to rising casualties, and the increasing imposition of the essential reality that the war was not going according to plan, that led to the collapse of support for the war. It was not the fault of the media and it was not because the narrative was wrong somehow. Of course, similar arguments have arisen in the context of the recent wars in Iraq and Afghanistan. At a point now in 2014 when there is some level of agreement regarding the early political and military failures in Iraq, it is easier to see the following comments from US Defense Secretary Donald Rumsfeld in 2005 for what they are: an attempt to blame the media for a failing policy:

> We've arrived at a strange time in this country where the worst about America and our military seems to so quickly be taken as the truth by the press, and reported and spread around that world, often with little context and little scrutiny, let alone correction or accountability after the fact.[58]

But the more recent discussion about finding a strategic narrative with which to win hearts and minds in Afghanistan, whilst understandable, is making the same mistake of blaming problems on the narrative, as opposed to the actual policy. But as has been set out in this chapter, once beyond the rally phase, it is the policy and not the narrative that is critical.

In the final analysis, there comes a point at which a focus on perception management, the media, and strategic narratives can end up serving either political interests by providing a scapegoat for problems and failure, or provide a form of self-deception whereby problems on the ground are put down to a failure to get your message across. The notion that 'they simply don't understand what we are trying to do' is an easy way, psychologically, to help you keep believing that you and your policies are right and that the problem lies elsewhere. But in doing so, critical reflection on the policy being executed can readily be obscured. Torie Clarke's 'you can't put lipstick on a pig' should be a mantra to all those engaged in prosecuting military and political campaigns during war, particularly those involved in perception management activities. Her follow-up advice as to the importance of focusing less on the message and more on not creating a pig in the first place should give everyone pause for thought and critical self-reflection.

[57] Bennett et al., *When the Press Fails*, pp. 136–7.

[58] Cited in David S. Cloud, 'The Struggle for Iraq: The Military; Rumsfeld Says the Media Focus Too Much on Negatives in Iraq', *The New York Times*, 6 December 2005, <http://query.nytimes.com/gst/fullpage.html?res=9F04E3DA1331F935A35751C1A9639C8B63>.

References

Aday, Sean, 'Chasing the bad news: An analysis of 2005 Iraq and Afghanistan war coverage on NBC and Fox News Channel', *Journal of Communication* 60, no. 1 (2010): pp. 144–64.

Aday, Sean, 'Leading the charge: Media, elites, and the use of emotion in stimulating rally effects in wartime', *Journal of Communication* 60, no. 3 (2010): pp. 440–65.

Aday, Sean, Steven Livingston, and Maeve Herbert, 'Embedding the truth: A cross-cultural analysis of objectivity and television coverage of the Iraq War', *The Harvard International Journal of Press/Politics* 10, no. 3 (2005): pp. 3–21.

Baum, Matthew and Tim Groeling, *War Stories: The causes and consequences of public views of war* (Princeton: Princeton University Press, 2010).

Bennett, W. Lance, 'Toward a theory of press–state relations in the United States', *Journal of Communication* 40, no. 2 (1990): pp. 103–27.

Bennett, W. Lance, Regina G. Lawrence, and Steven Livingston, *When the Press Fails: Political Power and the News Media from Iraq to Katrina* (Chicago: University of Chicago Press, 2007).

Bennett, W. Lance and David L. Paletz, eds, *Taken by Storm: The Media, Public Opinion, and US Foreign Policy in the Gulf War* (Chicago: University of Chicago Press, 1994).

Braestrup, Peter, *Big Story: How the American Press and Television Reported and Interpreted the Crisis of Tet 1968 in Vietnam and Washington* (Novati, CA: Presidio Press, 1994).

Brown, Robin, 'Spinning the war: Political communications, information operations and public diplomacy in the War on Terrorism', in *War and the Media: Reporting Conflict 24/7*, edited by Daya K. Thussu and Des Freedman (London: Sage, 2003), pp. 87–101.

Carruthers, Susan, *The Media at War: Communication and Conflict in the Twentieth Century*, 2nd edn (Basingstoke: Macmillan, 2011).

Cioppa, Thomas M., 'Operation Iraqi Freedom Strategic Communication Analysis and Assessment', *Media, War and Conflict* 10, no. 1 (2009): pp. 25–45.

Clarke, Torie, *Lipstick on a Pig: Winning in the No-Spin Era by Someone Who Knows the Game* (New York: Simon and Schuster, 2006).

Corner, J., 'Reappraising reception: Aims, concepts and methods', in *Mass Media and Society*, edited by James Curran and Michael Gurevitch (London: Arnold, 1996), pp. 280–304.

Culbert, David, 'Television's visual impact on decision-making in the USA, 1968: The Tet Offensive and Chicago's Democratic National Convention', *Journal of Contemporary History* 33, no. 3 (1998): pp. 419–49.

Dearth, Douglas H., 'Shaping the "Information Space"', *Journal of Information Warfare* 1, no. 3 (2002): pp. 1–15.

Franklin, B., 'The Hand of History: New Labour, News Management and Governance', in *The New Labour Reader*, edited by Andrew Chadwick and Richard Heffernan (Cambridge: Polity Press, 2003), pp. 304–8.

Gelpi, Christopher, Peter D. Feaver, and Jason Reifler, *Paying the Human Costs of War: American Public Opinion and Casualties in Military Conflicts* (Princeton: Princeton University Press, 2009).

Glasgow University Media Group, *War and Peace News* (Milton Keynes: Open University Press, 1985).

Hall, Stuart, 'Encoding and decoding in the television discourse', CCCS stencilled paper series (Paper 7), (Birmingham: University of Birmingham, 1973).

Hallin, Daniel C., 'The Media, the War in Vietnam, and Political Support: A Critique of the Thesis of an Oppositional Media', *Journal of Politics* 46, no. 1 (1984): pp. 2–24.

Hallin, Daniel C., *The Uncensored War: The Media and Vietnam* (Berkeley: University of California Press, 1986).

Herring, E. and P. Robinson, 'Report X marks the spot: the British Government's Deceptive dossier on Iraq and WMD', *Political Science Quarterly*, (forthcoming 2014).

Jones, Brian, *Failing Intelligence: The True Story of How We Were Fooled Into Going to War in Iraq* (London: Biteback, 2010).

Jowett, Garth S. and Victoria O'Donnell, *Propaganda and Persuasion*, 5th edn (London: Sage, 2012).

Lewis, Justin, 'Television, public opinion and the war in Iraq: The case of Britain', *International Journal of Public Opinion Research* 16, no. 3 (2004): pp. 295–310.

Lewis, Justin, Rod Brooks, Nick Mosdell, and Terry Threadgold, *Shoot First and Ask Questions Later: Media Coverage of the 2003 Iraq War* (New York: Peter Lang, 2006).

Mackay, Andrew and Steve Tatham, *Behavioural Conflict: Why understanding people and their motivations will prove decisive in future conflict* (Saffron Waldon: Military Studies Press, 2011).

Mueller, John E., *War, Presidents and Public Opinion* (New York: John Wiley, 1973).

Nixon, Richard M., *Memoirs* (New York: Grossett and Dunlap, 1978).

Powell, Jonathan, *The New Machiavelli: How to wield power in the modern world* (London: Random House Books, 2010).

Robinson, Piers, 'News Media and War', in *The Sage Handbook of Political Communication*, edited by Holli Semetko and Margaret Scammell (Thousand Oaks: Sage, 2012), pp. 342–55.

Robinson, Piers, 'Theorising the influence of media on world politics', *European Journal of Communication* 16, no. 4 (2001): pp. 523–44.

Robinson, Piers, et al., *Pockets of Resistance: British News Media, War and Theory in the 2003 Invasion of Iraq* (Manchester: Manchester University Press, 2010).

Rovner, Joshua, *Fixing the Facts: National Security and the Politics of Intelligence* (Ithaca: Cornell University Press, 2011).

Tatham, Steve, *Losing Arab Hearts and Minds: The Coalition, Al Jazeera and Muslim Public Opinion* (London: C. Hurst and Co. Publishers, 2006).

Taylor, Philip M., *Munitions of the Mind: A History of Propaganda* (Manchester: Manchester University Press, 2003).

Taylor, Philip M., 'Perception management and the "War" Against Terrorism', *Journal of Information Warfare* 1, no. 3 (2002): pp. 16–29.

Taylor, Philip M., *War and the Media: Propaganda and Persuasion in the Gulf War* (Manchester: Manchester University Press, 1992).

Tumber, Howard and Jerry Palmer, *Media at War: The Iraq Crisis* (London: Sage, 2004).

Part II

The practice of exit: Security and governance transitions in Afghanistan

13

Delivering and conceptualizing transition

Experiences and lessons from the Helmand Provincial Reconstruction Team, 2010–2012

Peter Rundell

Introduction and context

In the second half of 2012, the Helmand Provincial Reconstruction Team (PRT) produced a note on *Guidance for Transition*, and this short chapter describes its rationale and specific content. This contribution also reflects on the conditions and contexts inhibiting or encouraging innovation and change. The context is familiar to most. A heavy expenditure of 'blood and treasure' by coalition partners, be they Afghan, US, British, Danish, Estonian, and Georgian troops, contributed to the marked expansion of security in Helmand province. A recent review noted that: 'substantial improvements in government effectiveness as a result of improved security, delivered by increased ISAF capability and a significant increase in the capacity of Afghan National Security Forces (ANSF), . . . has allowed the expansion of government officials and service delivery, even to districts that had not been controlled by the government'.[1]

Alongside this military effort, the civilians also delivered important gains. Up to 2010, the focus was on delivering immediate effects that could win popular consent, demonstrate the benefits of government control of an area, and contribute to licit economic activity in a Province which grows over half of Afghanistan's opium. The effects are easiest to measure in tangible terms: particularly through the establishment of schools, clinics, and roads. Slightly

[1] N. Pounds and C. Dennys, *Joint Transition Review*, July 2012 (unpublished).

less measurable are the effects of training (including patrolmen, teachers, and nurses). Possibly more lasting than either, but considerably harder to quantify, are the effects of new systems, processes, and fresh mind-sets.

Physical construction was extensive. Between January 2010 and January 2013 the PRT and the international community built 276km of main national and regional asphalt roads (with a further 89km under construction at the end of 2012). They also restored 400km of primary canals and 45 major assets of the canal system, such as sluices and gates. The civilian component built two court houses and refurbished another, with two other justice sector building projects in hand at the end of 2012, and built a National Directorate of Security (NDS) detention facility.[2] They have also refurbished the Helmand Provincial Prison, building dedicated juvenile and female facilities and a rehabilitation centre. The PRT has built the Lashkar Gah Training Centre, and 10 Afghan Uniformed Police (AUP) stations/check points to provide enhanced security.[3] By 2013 it was also building 16 Afghan National Security Forces (ANSF) local stations using traditional materials, and had completed another 18.

In 2006, Helmand had one hospital, nine comprehensive health clinics, and 20 basic health clinics, with only 245 health workers. In 2012, this had risen to three district hospitals, 15 comprehensive health clinics, 28 basic health clinics, 11 sub-clinics, and 870 health workers. The PRT had built, refurbished, or improved 22 health facilities, ranging from a Medical Training Centre and a Maternity School to a new drug store in the Hazarjoft District Hospital and a wall surrounding the Mian Poshta basic health centre. Moreover, the PRT has built 85 schools, with 42 more in the planning stage; and refurbished 61 more. All this work was done in conjunction with the Ministry of Education and is reflected in the Ministry's plans.

Transition timeline

The announcement of transition in 2010, and the requirement to close PRTs by the end of 2014, created a shift of focus for the PRT. Its attention was now drawn to the preconditions for *sustainable* transition without international support. This would require a government able to sustain control, even in so highly contested a region as Helmand, without the presence of international military forces. The Helmand Plan 2011–14 set as the 'End-State' the successful transition of Helmand in accordance with the *Inteqal* framework. To guide the PRT, reference was made to the 2010 Department for International

[2] The National Directorate for Security is Afghanistan's intelligence agency.
[3] Afghan Uniformed Police, the largest of the components of the Afghan National Police (ANP).

Development (DfID) paper on building peaceful states (BPSS)[4] which identified key underpinnings for a sustainable transition. In supporting 'effective, legitimate states and durable, positive peace' it identifies four objectives: to address the causes and effects of conflict and fragility; support inclusive political settlements; develop core state functions; and finally, respond to public expectations. In the summary of conclusions on core state functions—identified as 'security, law and justice, and financial and macroeconomic management', the paper notes the 'focus on the importance of accountability within each function'.[5]

All this was at the back of the PRT leadership's minds when, in mid-2012, the PRT reviewed its headline priorities in the light of developments since its defining strategy, the Helmand Plan 2011–14, was written. That review also drew on a Conflict Analysis for Helmand,[6] and was brought together in a consolidated document which reflected the enduring strategic purpose of the Helmand Plan.

From the work of the Joint Transition Review team, the BPSS paper, and other review work, the Head of Mission of the PRT identified a simplified headline task for the PRT: to support government legitimacy and accountability. The goal became to leave Helmand resilient, stable, and sustainable enough to manage conflicts in a peaceful way, and with a Provincial and District administration that can respond to the needs of its people. To that end the Head of Mission, Catriona Laing, set three priority lines of effort: inclusive legitimate political settlements; accountable governance; and accountable rule of law.

The delivery of this, in line with the objectives of earlier Helmand Plans and Road Maps, required continual effort and appetite for revision and innovation. For an organization reporting to three civilian public administrations, with different expectations, this is not always the easiest of things to achieve. With a high public profile—inevitable when so many troops were at risk—and heavy public investment, we expected, quite rightly, significant public scrutiny. This is natural but adds a burden which 'expeditionary' missions of this sort are rarely staffed to service. Interestingly, such activity became an important role for HQ-based units; that is, to deal with the overheads of such reporting. In addition, the pressure of scrutiny has the potential to make innovation increasingly difficult, with the costs of failure magnified.

However, in such a fast-moving environment, the calibrations and alignments of intervention aspirations and field conditions will change irrespective

[4] Department for International Development, *Building Peaceful States and Societies*, 2010, accessed 17 September 2013, <https://www.gov.uk/government/uploads/system/uploads/attachment_data/file/67694/Building-peaceful-states-and-societies.pdf>.

[5] *Building Peaceful States and Societies*, p. 7.

[6] Lou Perrotta and Stuart Gordon, *Helmand Provincial Conflict Analysis*, July 2012 (unpublished).

of the freedom PRT staff may have wished to exercise to innovate. As a result there was always a variety of experience from which to learn. Despite the difficulties of innovation, there were some important examples in PRT programmes. One significant case was the PRT's support for sub-national governance structures.

Despite the difficulties of implementing new initiatives, support for sub-national governance structures was built around a careful assessment of the way to relate Constitutional provisions for sub-Provincial structures (which, so far, have not been implemented) and Kabul's sub-national governance policy, to the political economy of Helmand. The design developed by the PRT Governance team represented a possible approach that could apply to the whole national challenge. It reflected the understanding embodied in recent controversy about state-building and 'hybrid orders',[7] aiming to achieve many of the benefits of hybrid systems (that is, cultural familiarity, inclusion of locally powerful actors, local relevance) while still pointing towards the Constitutional state-building goals for the longer term. Since the Councils play roles both within the Constitutional order (for example, in the Budget process) and within the traditional community-based system, they may provide a bridge through which the Constitutional state-building project can negotiate with local power structures a way ahead. Success in this regard could broaden community access to state-based public services without entailing unacceptable threats to brokers too powerful to displace completely. This, in turn, allowed the expansion of representative bodies as government control expanded, and gave scope for bodies to form that combined planning and accountability functions (in keeping with the spirit of Constitutional provisions) with security and justice functions that reflect both Pashtu tradition and levels of violence. Councils started to hold officials to account for their actions, both in delivery of services ('where is the teacher you promised for that school?' or 'why does it take so long to get a *taskera*[8]?') and for the conduct of their staff ('why was my brother shouted at when he went to the clinic?' or 'why was my family harassed when they went through the police check-point?').

This combination gave the Councils real political weight—contributing, alongside the expanding security envelope from ANSF and ISAF enforcement, to the growing levels of voter engagement in the electoral college. The Nawa re-election in early 2013 involved over 6,000 elders in the electoral college, demonstrating the relevance of the Council to senior figures in the District as

[7] See: Volker Boege, Anne Brown, Kevin P. Clements, and Anna Nolan, 'On hybrid political orders and emerging states: What is failing—states in the global south or research politics in the West?', *Berghof Handbook for Conflict Transformation Dialogue Series*, no. 8 (2009): pp. 15–35.

[8] Government of Afghanistan identity document.

well as confirming the extent of government security control. Their continued survival depended and continues to depend, of course, on ANSF security control and on sufficient government service delivery to make their political and accountability roles credible. It also depends on national policy for District-level bodies, which risks being tied to familiar models for delivering small-scale development programmes (linked to the Ministry of Reconstruction and Rural Development's [MRRD] donor programmes). Helmand's District Community Councils point instead towards compliance with Constitutional provisions, and treat MRRD as one delivery Ministry among many.

Alongside support for this pilot of District-level representative bodies came significant innovation in sub-national finance. Unlike other 'on-budget' donor programmes operating through the capital budget, the Helmand Provincial financial mechanisms aimed to reflect Kabul government systems as closely as possible, and by 1392 (2013) had been brought fully into the normal recurrent budget process (apart from having a separate donor earmarking at revenue stage). These mechanisms bring together District-level planning (with political oversight by the representative Council) with transparent Provincial-level arbitrage between line Ministries' bids. The overall budget is 'signed off' by the (Constitutionally elected) Provincial Council. It is then procured, delivered, reported, and accounted through government systems—though with national government-compliant innovations like the public (and televised) announcement of the projects for the coming year to an audience including all the main companies in Helmand. It should be noted that all those registered for tax and cleared for propriety were invited.

The funds for this, which came from a UK- and Danish-funded programme called Supporting Provincial Administration and Delivery, or SPAD, are for hazard pay, Operations and Maintenance,[9] and new small projects (the latter capped at 25 per cent). For 1392, US$ 9 million was made available, and Health and Education captured about half in the inter-Ministerial trade-offs. This was more than double the discretionary funds available to the Provincial administration for recurrent costs.

In delivering money through government systems, this programme ensured that officials became accustomed to using normal government mechanisms to deliver services—essential if improvements to public financial management are to mean anything. It also made it realistic for Councils to hold officials accountable for their actions, since the resources were for the first time genuinely at their discretion. Moreover, it required Provincial officials to connect both down to Districts and up to parent Kabul Ministries, starting to develop

[9] Operations and Maintenance, a key and under-funded element of the recurrent budget.

the habits which will be required in future if the improvements in service delivery and performance legitimacy of the government are to be sustained.

While in the heat of early 'hot' stabilization, the PRT did not have either an explicit lessons function or a strong record-keeping system, by 2010 it had introduced a monitoring and evaluation programme (known formally as the Helmand Monitoring and Evaluation Programme, or HMEP) and a system of quarterly reviews which allowed staff to learn from experience. If the Head of Mission's new priorities constituted the 'what' for the civilian effort, a complementary piece of work focused on the 'how': what lessons the PRT had learnt about the ways of working that are calculated to deliver the newly refined direction. The attempt to distil the lessons that emerged from PRT experience became the *Guidance for Transition* note.

Legitimacy and lessons

The reflective undertaking of deriving lessons invited more detailed thinking about, for example, what 'legitimacy' might mean in Helmand—although admittedly without the scope for the kind of primary anthropological field research which would ideally support such a question. Instead, the conclusions needed to be based on secondary sources, plus the experiences of practitioners in the field at the time. These reflect *a priori* understanding from the literature, extensive anecdotal experience from practitioners, field work by Task Force Helmand (TFH) cultural advisers and reports from TFH patrols, and primary research in a small target area of Nahri Saraj District.[10] A much abbreviated summary of the conclusions makes up a couple of paragraphs in the resulting *Guidance on Transition* note.

The pace of events, and of International Combined Team (ICT, the combination of the military Regional Command (South-West), the PRT and the US Regional Platform, RP) interventions, undoubtedly meant that mistakes were made. Some of these formed 'raw material' for the *Guidance for Transition* note. For example, in retrospect it became clear and, in part thanks to another report from HMEP, that the range of infrastructure that had been built exceeded the maintenance capacity of the Provincial administration. There were excellent reasons for this investment, ranging from promoting economic growth by connecting farmers with markets, to generating support or compliance by meeting popular aspirations. 'Black-topping' roads (that is, building metalled roads) reduced the threat of IEDs, both for ISAF troops and for ordinary Helmandis. Refurbishing schools helped to demonstrate to communities the advantages of coming over to the government side.

[10] D. Bray, *Understanding Power and Authority*, forthcoming.

Nevertheless, the fact remained that the Provincial administration needed to increase operations and maintenance and reinvestment expenditure massively from its current levels to sustain the infrastructure portfolio present at the time. In stabilization terms, the risk comes from 'perceived decline' where legitimacy and stability are concerned. As the *Guidance for Transition* note puts it: 'decline from a moderate level [is] much more damaging than slight progress even if at a lower level (better to go from 1 to 2 than from 5 to 4)'. HMEP data suggested that a strong predictor of declines in perceived legitimacy of the government, and of a commensurate increased welcome for the return of the Taliban, was an expectation of declines in health care standards.

In parallel with this recognition has come growing evidence of dependency, among government officials in particular. Where the ICT has built infrastructure, or determined policies, driven decision-making, or even filled in spreadsheets and provided information for reports, Afghan counterparts have felt able—indeed, compelled—to sit back and leave it to the internationals. What this means, therefore, is that as 'Transition' becomes more of a reality, this dependency becomes more of a threat to sustained delivery of government functions. Moreover, it is a difficult habit to break, since dependency undermines both incentives and capacity to act independently.

An encouraging counter-example in the work of the PRT has been in education. Here the team leader was provided by Denmark, also the lead donor nationally. The Danish-led PRT education team was always careful to keep in close step with national policy, and to support education in Helmand only within that policy framework. Education was also an unusually effective Ministry—part of most pilots of public service reform—which always enjoyed closer links between field and capital than most Ministries. Nevertheless, Helmand posed specific challenges, and the PRT team's task was always to make realistic the delivery of the Ministry's policy and plans in Helmand's 'kinetic' context.

This situation led to some clashes with the apparent imperatives of stabilization. For example, in 2010 there was a widespread problem with teachers' pay. In at least one District the local ISAF commander decided to pay teachers directly to prevent their absence at the start of the school year for enrolment, and, unfortunately, not knowing Ministry pay scales, he hit on a level of remuneration which was higher than the District Governor's. The intention, to ensure the opportunity for all to enrol, was admirable. However, the resultant negative effects on teachers attending work in neighbouring Districts can be imagined. The PRT education team worked with HQ military colleagues to prevent such 'hot stabilization' decisions taking effect for long enough to undermine the patient work being done to train teachers centrally to government standards, agree their pay and conditions suitable for Helmand, and press ahead a sustainable programme of school staffing and resourcing. Such tasks as school-book distribution were handled through government channels at least from District centre onwards, ensuring that officials were visibly and practically responsible for the outcome. And increasingly, as capacity was developed by collaboration instead of being atrophied by substitution, supplies were delivered from further and further up the chain.

In addition to formal school-based schooling, communities in Helmand may need access to more informal community-based education. Helmand was able to draw on policy evolving at the national level to apply, in proximal contexts, an innovative and locally-attuned version of community-based outreach into areas where formal government schooling had not yet reached. While this may not have been as powerful a signal of community allegiance to the government as a school opened in a village, it provided a first foothold for public services—and gave a much more positive message than a torched and empty building, as happens if ambition over-reaches the security provision.

The *Guidance for Transition* note identified 'Seven Deadly Sins' of such stabilization–transition operations. In many ways they are all means of failing in the cardinal virtues demanded of a PRT: patience and humility. The 'sins' were identified from the PRT's experience, especially its awareness of its own and its partners' shortcomings:

- providing more (infrastructure, staff, money, political support);
- seeing Helmand in isolation;
- focusing on Districts in isolation;
- treating themes in isolation;
- seeing Helmand through Western spectacles;
- imposing our perspectives on the national government of Afghanistan; and
- neglecting unintended consequences.

The note remains a live document, being used both to guide the PRT's and the ICT's actions in their remaining time in Helmand and to inform planning for other missions. Its background in innovation, changing context, and trial and error, is designed to give it relevance and practicality. More refined academic analysis, and time, will tell whether it strikes the right balance.

Postscript

The *Guidance for Transition* note, like the rest of this chapter, was written in Helmand in 2013. Since then the author has moved from Afghanistan to Libya, and the PRT has moved from Lashkar Gah to Bastion. But many of the same messages apply. For example, the cardinal virtues of patience and humility are no less important in helping the Libyan authorities to shape their border management agencies amid the uncertainties of post-conflict Tripoli than they were in Helmand—and no easier. The pressure to achieve visible results quickly drives much 'hot stabilization' effort, but even in cooler settings the political heat may create pressures that few stabilization teams can resist. Yet that leads to exactly those sins—providing more, seeing themes in isolation, imposing our perspectives, neglecting unintended long-term consequences—which *Guidance for Transition* identified.

Another of the observations in *Guidance for Transition* was '[A] process of graduated response to improved alignment provides positive incentives for stability—unlike past programmes which gave perverse incentives for violence by directing resources to areas of greatest contest.'[11] The same care over the actual incentives—as opposed to the rhetorical intentions—of the international community is needed when we risk focusing our support on security forces that have made least progress rather than those that have shown the most development.

In mid-2014 it is too soon to say which of the competing narratives of Helmand will eventually triumph. The Taliban's threat that 'NATO have the watches, but we have the time' is matched against the evidence that Helmandis want the government to continue to deliver the services to which they have become accustomed. If the first Premier of the People's Republic of China, Chou En-Lai was right to say of the French Revolution's success 'it's too soon to tell', it is certainly too soon to tell how the expectations of officials answering to citizens through popular assembly will survive as ISAF completes its withdrawal and Afghans vote in national elections. But there is at least a chance that, as long as the national picture leaves space for local patterns to persist, Helmand's experience of local legitimacy within a national policy framework may provide an enduring bright spot.

References

Boege, Volker, Anne Brown, Kevin P. Clements, and Anna Nolan, 'On hybrid political orders and emerging states: What is failing—states in the global south or research politics in the West?', *Berghof Handbook for Conflict Transformation Dialogue Series*, no. 8 (2009): pp. 15–35.

Bray, D., *Understanding Power and Authority*, forthcoming.

Department for International Development, *Building Peaceful States and Societies*, 2010, accessed 17 September 2013, <https://www.gov.uk/government/uploads/system/uploads/attachment_data/file/67694/Building-peaceful-states-and-societies.pdf>.

Perrotta, Lou and Stuart Gordon, *Helmand Provincial Conflict Analysis*, July 2012 (unpublished).

Pounds, N. and C. Dennys, *Joint Transition Review*, July 2012 (unpublished).

[11] *Guidance for Transition*, §2.4.3.

14

Political analysis and understanding in Afghanistan

Beyond transition

Anthony King

Introduction

Since the announcement of the decision to withdraw International Security Assistance Force (ISAF) troops from Afghanistan by December 2014 and in stark contrast to the optimism of 2010, when military commanders, buoyed with the 'victory' in Iraq, were enjoying a surge in troops and resources, a mood of pessimism has increasingly prevailed; the main question has become how to demonstrate success in Afghanistan after over a decade of effort. The apparently anodyne and benign concept of 'transition' has become a critical reference point here; it has been a key element in the 'narrative' of withdrawal. Crucially, the term 'transition' has sought to obscure the strategic disappointments experienced by the international community in Afghanistan by representing a forced withdrawal—and therefore a course of action typically associated with defeat—as a success. Because Western forces have apparently voluntarily chosen to withdraw according to a plan, 'transition' seems to denote that the conditions for an exit have been met. Clearly, there has been much progress in Afghanistan and, at the tactical level, great success. Yet, decisive strategic success has been elusive. No clear strategic goal has been identified as the US-lead intervention has oscillated between counter-terrorism and stabilization (counter-insurgency). Indeed, even the concept of stabilization has been badly compromised by unclarity, misperception, idealism, and blind optimism. As a result of strategic confusion—the lack of a unifying and achievable political goal—the crucial political articulation between tactical military activity and the consolidation of the Afghan regime seems to be missing. In this context, the word 'transition' seems to have been, at best, a semantic means of making up for a failed strategy, perhaps even indicative of bad faith by ISAF.

Instead of resorting to invoking success semantically, this chapter tries to identify the most politically expedient means of maximizing success following the withdrawal of Western combat troops. It lays out a course of action whereby the great tactical gains made in the last decade might be transformed into actual political progress across the entire country. To this end, this chapter examines the ISAF campaign and its plans for transition to argue that the campaign has, despite impressive levels of accumulated knowledge about the social and political dynamics in the theatre, been informed by a reductive and inappropriately state-centric political concept. This concept and its implementation in the south especially in the period after 2009 are discussed and criticized. This chapter concludes by offering an alternative political concept for transition and withdrawal, which while avowedly controversial and unpalatable, may offer the only realistic opportunity for ISAF and the international community to stabilize Afghanistan in the medium term.

Operation Omid

In June 2009, General Stanley McChrystal was appointed Commander (COM) ISAF, replacing General McKiernan who had effectively been sacked from the post. As a result of his experiences in Iraq as Commander Joint Special Operations Command—colloquially known as the 'Death Star'—and the close relationship which he had developed with General David Petraeus in that role, McChrystal—unlike the possibly unlucky McKiernan—was trusted as an effective counter-insurgent by senior military and commanders in Centcom and Washington; he 'got it', as the phrase goes. Indeed, his appointment was greeted with widespread enthusiasm not only in the US but in ISAF generally and a number of commentators have pointed to his success in galvanizing ISAF from 2009. One senior British General who had worked closely with McChrystal in Baghdad not implausibly suggested that when McChrystal took over Afghanistan in 2009, he was given a campaign which was going nowhere. There was no unity of effort, no clear concept of operations and insufficient troops and resources to achieve the necessary effects. This General pointed to the single-handed efforts of McChrystal in generating a new campaign plan for Afghanistan which transformed a situation which had been if not declining since 2006, simply stagnating since that time. McChrystal's new strategy—his application of the counter-insurgency (COIN) principles which had been rediscovered and re-applied so successfully to Iraq—was articulated in his 'O Plan' which his new operational headquarters, ISAF Joint Command, developed and then issued on 1 November 2009: Operation Omid (Hope, in Dari).[1]

Operation Omid organized the Afghan campaign on five lines of operation and laid out a deliberately comprehensive list of 17 decisive conditions, which included political, economic, judicial, and military reforms which needed to be achieved, if the campaign in Afghanistan were to be successful. In early 2010, McChrystal issued his commander's planning guidance which amended Operation Omid and on 23 November 2009 extended it sensibly out to 2020 with the operation phased into military and developmental periods; it was clear that most of the decisive conditions would take years, not months, to achieve. There was much to be admired about the plan and it included some critical decisions. Above all and despite General Richards' attempts to create Afghan Development Zones in 2006 when he was COM ISAF, ISAF efforts had become notably dispersed and disjointed by 2009. One of the centerpieces of Operation Omid was the designation of 80 key terrain districts, predominately in the south and the east on which all efforts would be focused and in which success was vital. This concentration of effort accorded precisely with the logic of classic counter-insurgent works such as that of Robert Thompson who advocated as his fifth principle of counter-insurgency that counter-insurgents should secure their base areas first. In the south, Kandahar City and its environs—and especially the districts along the Arghandab Valley of Panjwai, Zhari (the heartland of the Taliban movement and birthplace of Mullah Omar), Damon, and Dand—was properly identified at the ISAF main effort during Operation Omid.

There was much to praise about Operation Omid then. However, the plan was informed by a distinctive political concept which McChrystal made very clear in his *Initial Commander's Assessment* of Afghanistan which was leaked to the press in August 2009. The *Initial Assessment* usefully communicated the central ideas which informed McChrystal's approach to the campaign and, of course, Operation Omid itself:

> Our strategy cannot be focused on seizing terrain or destroying insurgents; our objective must be the people.... Success will be achieved when [the government] has earned the support of the powerful Afghan people and effectively controls its own territory.[2]

The influence of Field Manual (FM) 3–24 (and, therefore, indirectly the classic counter-insurgency texts of especially David Galula but also Robert Thompson[3])

[1] The material for this chapter is principally taken from the author's research as a member of the RC (S) Prism Cell 2009–10.

[2] General McChrystal, *Initial Commander's Assessment*, 30 August 2009, pp. 1–1, 2–15.

[3] David Galula, *Counter-Insurgency Warfare: Theory and Practice* (Westport, CT: Praeger, 2006); Robert Thompson, *Defeating Communist Insurgency: Experiences from Malaya and Vietnam* (London: Chatto and Windus, 1974).

was evident through this statement and through Operation Omid itself. In light of these texts, counter-insurgency campaigns were understood to be political contests between the would-be government and the insurgents for the people. Successful counter-insurgency campaigns prioritized the people and, indeed, in both Iraq and Afghanistan it became almost automatic for many Americans to prefix the adjective 'population-centric' to the word counter-insurgency. Reflecting this population-centric approach, Operation Omid defined the 'people of Afghanistan' as the centre of gravity. There could be no more demonstrative a means of focusing military efforts on the population. The mission affirmed the point, instructing Afghan and ISAF forces to conduct population-centric counter-insurgency operations in order to protect the people through the extension of security, governance, and development. The people were therefore the central point of Operation Omid but in fact, as McChrystal's statement reveals they represented only one pole of the campaign. The other pole was, of course, the government. The central idea animating McChrystal's plan was that the campaign should seek to extend the power of the Government of the Islamic Republic of Afghanistan (GIRoA) by linking it to the people—especially the village elders—and generating consent among the people for this state; counter-insurgency generally and in Afghanistan in 2009 involved empowering a state and connecting it with a people in order to marginalize and finally suppress insurgent groups. Indeed, Operation Omid clearly identified the powerbrokers as malign actors, whose negative influence had to be neutralized. They were explicitly identified as a central target of the operation. The aim was to marginalize these leaders and exclude them from the political process. This would be achieved by linking central government with acceptable sub-national actors and above all the elders, identified as critical in Operation Omid: GIRoA representatives and traditional leaders at district and sub-district level were seen to be closest to the people and, therefore, decisive in defeating the insurgency.

McChrystal has been widely praised for unifying the notoriously factionalized ISAF campaign and, indeed, in terms of his operational concept, there is clear evidence that it did permeate down to the Regional Command and Task Force level. It was noticeable that this dualistic political vision of state and people, central to Operation Omid, also framed the UK Helmand Task Force's concept of operations from 2009. Thus, the intelligence branch of 16 Air Assault Brigade, which deployed to Helmand between October 2009 and March 2010, understood the theatre in terms of four categories: the state (GIRoA), traditional actors (village elders/the population), the shadow state (the Taliban), and the dark state (the power brokers). The state and specifically GIRoA officials like Governor Mangal (typically appointed or at least ratified by

ISAF) and traditional actors (the people) were regarded as the only two legitimate actors. As in McChrystal's concept, the politics of Helmand operated—or were seen to operate around two poles—which had to be reinforced: the state/government and the people. The aim was to deepen the link between Mangal and Helmandis, the state and the people, in order to eliminate the nefarious influence of both the Taliban and the power brokers, who were regarded as corrupt and corrosive of legitimate state authority. The idea that the Afghan counter-insurgency campaign involved the extension of centralized state power over the population, which ideally consented to its authority because of the benefits it provided, was then evident not just in headquarters in Kabul but among military commanders and soldiers in the south itself, though the Afghans did not seem to perceive the issue as a contract between a people and a state at all.

In principle, there is nothing fundamentally wrong with such a vision of counter-insurgency. Counter-insurgency is concerned with the extension of political power over a population. Moreover, historically and empirically, most counter-insurgency campaigns have involved the generation of a more or less centralized bureaucratic (and sometimes democratic) state and the extension of its sovereignty over a people. Finally, McChrystal's plan reflected an understanding of Afghanistan which had been dominant in the international community and ISAF since the initial decision to intervene in 2001 and 2002 in order to stabilize the country following the expulsion of the Taliban regime. The Bonn Conference was a critical moment here. The conference agreed to the appointment of Hamid Karzai as interim president of Afghanistan and the creation of ISAF to ensure security in Kabul. However, at the Bonn conference, the international community began to commit itself to the development of a centralized, bureaucratic, and democratic Afghan state, as an ideal; although Islamic culture was recognized, federal models of decentralized political authority and more traditional means of political representation were rejected. 'The re-establishment of permanent governmental institutions' was envisaged as a way of creating this new Afghan state around Karzai as the elected president the structures of which were ratified by the new Afghan Constitution. The Afghan Compact agreed after the London Conference in 2006 confirmed the state-centric orientation:

> Democratic governance and the protection of human rights constitute the cornerstone of sustainable political progress in Afghanistan. The Afghan Government will rapidly expand its ability to provide basic services to the population throughout the country. It will recruit competent and credible professionals to public service on the basis of merit; establish a more effective, accountable and transparent administration at all levels of Government.[4]

[4] North Atlantic Treaty Organization (NATO), *The Afghanistan Compact*, 2006, accessed 22 September 2013, <http://www.nato.int/isaf/docu/epub/pdf/afghanistan_compact.pdf>, p. 3.

Political leaders were explicit about their vision of the new Afghan polity which they wanted to create. Gordon Brown, for instance, claimed that 'there could only be one winner [in Afghanistan]: democracy and a strong Afghan state'.[5] Even though the Bush administration initially eschewed state-building, they too recognized the need for a strong state because of their belief that 'the manner in which a state orders its internal social, political and economic relations is inextricably linked to the degree of threat' it is likely to pose internationally.[6] In 2007, Ronald Neumann, US ambassador to Afghanistan between 2005 and 2007, affirmed the state-centric project. Western leaders unanimously rejected alternative non-state initiatives because 'even if militia forces backed-up by coalition troops and air strikes could win local victories, we would only be strengthening forces inimical to central government'.[7] Although wary, eventually Karzai and his government accepted the idea of an Afghan Local Police (effectively a militia), although this force was quickly compromised by political interests. It is not necessary to accept Rory Stewart's extreme position on Afghanistan that the intervention was bound to fail but he too notes that the Afghan mission was predicated on the idea that the Western aim is to build a centralized state in the Hindu Kush. He cites Barack Obama and Gordon Brown to illustrate this preference for centralization and he disparages this enterprise as 'the irresistible illusion'; critically it is an illusion which attracted the most diverse range of accidental counter-insurgents. Despite Stewart's scepticism, it would be dubious to question the objective desirability of the values articulated at Bonn and London and in the Afghan Constitution and Compact. They represent a progressive viewpoint which is compatible with anyone of a liberal or democratic persuasion. However, while philosophically admirable, politically attractive and perhaps implementable in the West, they represented a highly idealistic perspective on Afghanistan. Indeed, I will argue below that this concept of state-centric power fundamentally misrepresents the nature of the Afghan polity and actively undermines the possibility of stability.

Although promoted with the best of intentions, there seem to be some sociological reasons for this preference for a centralized state model for Afghanistan. The international community present at Bonn, Toyko, Berlin, and London constituted a group of nearly 100 countries and the Afghan mission itself quickly became a vastly complex undertaking involving not only eventually NATO and the United Nations (UN) but 42 nations in ISAF (and their respective civilian representatives) and a huge number of further NGOs. Any chance of

[5] Rory Stewart, 'The Irresistible Illusion', *London Review of Books*, 9 July 2009, p. 3.

[6] Tim Bird and Alex Marshall, *Afghanistan: How the West Lost Its Way* (New Haven, CT: Yale University Press, 2011), p. 160.

[7] Bird and Marshall, *Afghanistan: How the West Lost Its Way*, p. 162.

success required at least some unification among these different nations, and especially those who committed themselves to ISAF. One of the few factors which the orchestrating Western nations shared and in which they could believe was the value of democracy and legitimate (bureaucratic) state authority; the North Atlantic Treaty commits NATO to the defence of democracy and the rule of law, for instance. In effect, in formal agreements like the Afghan Compact and public statements (as well as presumably private diplomatic interactions), Western leaders seem to have become involved in a well-recognized process which Irving Janis would call 'group think'.[8] The creation and maintenance of themselves as a coherent group became unwittingly more important than necessarily addressing reality. As Andrew Dobbins has shown, the entire process was precipitate and solidarity was prioritized over performance and the achievement of strategic goals. The priority given to gender rights in the Afghan Compact—so important in the West—but not nearly so relevant to Islam and, however regrettably, almost entirely invisible in rural Afghanistan, demonstrated very clearly the way in which Western values—upon which all Western nations could agree strongly—were projected onto the Afghan theatre. Rory Stewart has usefully highlighted the attractiveness of the state model for a diversity of Western actors:

> It [the Afghan strategy] conjures nightmares of 'failed states' and 'global extremism', offers the remedies of 'state-building' and 'counter-insurgency', and promises a final dream of 'legitimate, accountable governance'. The path is broad enough to include Scandinavian humanitarians and American special forces; general enough to be applied to Botswana as easily as to Afghanistan; sinuous and sophisticated enough to draw in policymakers; suggestive enough of crude moral imperatives to attract the *Daily Mail*; and almost too abstract to be defined or refuted.[9]

In fact, the visceral—and not just intellectual—commitment of members of ISAF and supporting civilian workers and military practitioners to this concept was materially evident in 2009.

When McChrystal wrote Operation Omid, the two poles of centralized state power and people which form the essential conceptual pillars in the document were in no way invented by him or unique to him. On the contrary, although he may have applied these principles with a clarity not yet achieved by ISAF, these ideas had always been central to the Western international effort in Afghanistan and were inscribed deeply into the perspectives and sentiments of many military and civilian personnel in theatre. The Afghan intervention from 2001 onwards was predicated on a belief that stability could be achieved only through the institution of a centralized, democratically accountable

[8] Irving Janis, *Group Think: Psychological studies of policy decisions and fiascos* (Boston: Houghton Mifflin Company, 1982).

[9] Stewart, 'The Irresistible Illusion', pp. 3–6.

bureaucratic state. By providing universal services to the population, this state would earn the consent of the people as a whole, which (notwithstanding ethnic and tribal differences) would at last be united as a citizenry. Through the building of state-owned Afghan Security Forces and the empowerment of official GIRoA structures, Operation Omid aimed to create stability by eliminating the insurgency and ultimately displacing the power brokers.

Not only has the campaign up to this point been informed by a state-centric vision of political power in Afghanistan but this concept is central to the process of transition. Transition is envisaged simply as an accelerated transfer of responsibility for security to the state's security forces. The fundamental character of GIRoA is presumed. Effectively, transition involves seeking simply to sustain GIRoA power through its security forces with rapidly dwindling ISAF forces out to the end of 2014, at which point GIRoA, as a centralized state, must deliver its own security (with financial support and some mentoring from the West).

The patrimonial state

McChrystal's Operation Omid was a reflection of deeply held views in the West about the nature of the enterprise in Afghanistan, in which state-building was central. Yet, while McChrystal formally committed himself to this project from 2009, implicit within his analysis of Afghanistan was a quite different political order. Interestingly, in his commander's initial assessment, this alternative vision of political reality appeared briefly but very clearly in perhaps the most important sentences which McChrystal or indeed any Western military commander has written in Afghanistan:

> There are no clear lines separating insurgent groups, criminal networks (including the narcotics networks) and corrupt GIRoA officials. Malign actors within GIRoA support insurgent groups directly, support criminal networks that are linked to insurgents and support corruption that helps feed the insurgency.[10]

This phrase appears almost exactly in Operation Omid itself. It is worth contemplating this passage at length and especially the phrase 'malign actors within GIRoA support insurgent groups' for this phrase illustrates a profound contradiction in the Afghan polity (and therefore in Western understanding of the conflict). Bizarrely and paradoxically, on a state-centric definition, the regime (GIRoA) is the insurgency; it is both the source of political authority and the means of resistance to it. The regime is its own negation; this is a contradiction in terms. Accordingly, the phrase—and passage as a whole—demonstrates

[10] McChrystal, *Initial Commander's Assessment*, pp. 2-9–2-10.

that any simplified notion of the Afghan political system in which a centralized state rules over a sovereign territory, to be opposed at certain points by (external) insurgent groups who have separated themselves from the regime is an inaccurate and indeed quite false image of reality. McChrystal's initial assessment admits but does not acknowledge that in Afghanistan the West is not dealing with a centralized or centralizing state but on the contrary with a patrimonial regime. This patrimonial regime is not based on unified political authority which is exercised by disinterested and salaried state bureaucrats, the servants of politicians and ministers directly accountable to a unified population—a citizenry—by means of the ballot. Afghanistan operates much more like France under the Valois rulers in the fourteenth and fifteenth centuries during the Hundred Years War. It is a patrimonial regime. One of the purposes of Weber's *Economy and Society*[11] was to document the alternative political and social forms which had appeared historically in order to facilitate sociological investigation. At the same time, he wanted to highlight the signal difference between modern, rational forms of political authority and those which had pertained in the past in order to highlight the distinctiveness of Western modernity. To this end, Weber discusses patrimonial and prebendal systems at length. For him, patrimonial systems are defined by the giving (or purchasing) of offices to (or by) clients, related to a patron by personal, kinship, tribal, or ethnic ties. Having procured an office, clients are then able—and indeed expected—to exploit that position to harvest taxes and to increase their own personal power with the presumption that their activities will be broadly in line with the patron who endowed the office to them. It is precisely because offices were lucrative that they were known as 'benefices'; they were legitimately seen to benefit incumbents. Patrimonial regimes have many unpalatable aspects. They are dominated by a small elite group which is more or less unaccountable; they are arbitrary and often unstable, wracked by endemic violence between competing patrons and clients at each level. Weber plainly saw them as infinitely less efficient that the modern bureaucracy with its salaried officials, files, and rule-following. However, the patrimonial system, typical in most agrarian civilizations and therefore for the greater part of human history (if not pre-history), has a number of advantages; it is extremely cheap. It requires no or very few highly paid and trained bureaucrats and, notwithstanding the potential for internecine violence, the small self-referential elite at its heart with their close personal ties create political unity even though the system is highly decentralized in the execution of power. It is also durable and flexible because of the tight bonds between the patrimonial elite.

[11] Max Weber, *Economy and Society: An Outline of Interpretive Sociology* (New York: Bedminster Press, 1968).

In his article in the *London Review of Books*, Alex de Waal[12] has identified the existence of patrimonial regimes as a central problem for Western interventions in the Third World. Dominated by their experiences of their own political system, Westerners have consistently failed to understand the patrimonial mechanisms which sustain these weak states. They ignore the ways in which, in the absence of formal bureaucracy structure and an educated class of administrators, rulers sustain their power through the informal use of kin, tribal, and political networks, balancing rivals and enemies with bribes and payments. They insist on how governance ideally ought to function, rather than how it actually operates in weak and fragmented states. Indeed, the West utterly fails to see the way in which they are themselves implicated in this system as they pump money into a country, therefore buttressing certain leaders and providing them with precisely those resources which are essential to sustaining their patrimony. In these personalized and informal political orders, money becomes the crucial resource and symbol of political power; 'Symbolic rewards such as titles and ribbons are valued less—cash is what counts.'[13] Alex de Waal's chief example is Sudan and he asks: 'How has Omar al-Bashir managed to remain in power in Sudan for 20 years, despite several civil wars, economic crisis and international ostracism?' Yet, the problem is general and is plainly evident, as de Waal shows, in Afghanistan: 'as Hamid Karzai's travails illustrate, without these well-tested mechanisms [of vernacular politics] no ruler can be expected to run a turbulent country. Real politics in countries like Afghanistan, Congo and Sudan operate much like village politics, on the basis of personal affinity, loyalty and reward.'[14] One of the critical features of these patrimonial systems is the decentralization of power and specifically the balance of power between the ruler and patrimonial elites; indeed, this relation is one of complex and contested interdependence:

> The provincial elites want the highest price from the ruler for their allegiance. They covet positions in government as well as resources, including trading licences, local taxation powers and straight cash. In a system where violence in not normally a bargaining tool, provincial elites can use elections, demonstrations, boycotts and strikes to bring the ruler to the table. He will want to pay the lowest price for their allegiance and can threaten to withhold resources, letting them whither in the political wilderness.... In states where violence is an option [eg Afghanistan], it can be used by both the ruler and the elites.[15]

Patrons and clients, from the ruler to provincial elites and down to tribal, local, or village leaders, are locked into a complex system of personalized ties where mutual interest and allegiance is cross-cut by individual self-promotion

[12] Alex de Waal, 'Dollarised', *London Review of Books*, 24 June 2010, pp. 38–41.
[13] de Waal, 'Dollarised', p. 40. [14] de Waal, 'Dollarised', p. 38.
[15] de Waal, 'Dollarised', p. 39.

and self-interest to create a system that is certainly turbulent but which is sufficiently flexible and strong enough to endure the internal and external pressures of globalization. Indeed, de Waal notes that Western intervention is one of the central destabilizing forces for many patrimonial regimes: '[W]estern governments spend significant sums trying to establish functioning sovereignty amid the factional politics of "fragile" states, and civil, inclusive and affordable patronage systems are being swept away. For the unfortunate populations of these countries, this is a loss just as devastating as the weakening of state institutions, and one less recognised.'[16]

In southern Afghanistan, informed by a Western state-centric model, Governor Wesa and his District Governors have been identified as the means of reconnecting government with the people. However, the reality is that since 2001 politics in and around Kandahar has been dominated by a small number of magnates, including Ahmed Wali Karzai, Gul Agha Sherzai, Jan Mohammed Khan, Sher Mohammed Akhundzada, Arif Noorzai, and Colonel Razziq all of whom hold or have held (or while alive held) legitimate governmental positions but whose power extends far beyond the official structures of the state. These local patrons, drawing on their tribal power bases, monopolize political and economic opportunities in and around Kandahar for their own benefit, sometimes corrupting government, the judiciary and commerce. It is important to recognize the nature of these patrons. As de Waal predicted, these individuals desire—and indeed occupy—positions in the official GIRoA state. These positions are important to them since they furnish them with power and authority and crucially link them to the West. However, their networks extend well beyond the fragile and thin entity of GIRoA. Crucially, they have dense political associations which extend horizontally across the patron class to produce a power broker network secured together through personal ties of kinship, tribal, and business. For instance, Ahmed Wali Karzai, the half-brother of Hamid Karzai, was married to Arif Noorzai's sister. These networks also extend downwards through multiple and deep client relations into a popular base of support in the city of Kandahar and the surrounding regions; their power extends downwards into the villages themselves, through local tribal leaders and eventually to the village elders themselves.

There is little doubt that the power brokers are problematic figures; indeed, they have been widely reviled by Western actors since the intervention. They are all intimately associated with the narcotics trade and, therefore, ipso facto corrupt. However, since approximately 80 per cent of GDP of the south is illicit narcotic production and trafficking, it is impossible for any individual to hold a position of power without involvement in the prime and indeed

[16] de Waal, 'Dollarised', p. 41.

practically sole form of economic activity in this region. Secondly, as McChrystal's initial assessment suggested, tribal insurgency (often mis-interpreted as part of a unified Taliban campaign) is often precipitated much higher up the patrimonial system by powerbrokers who benefit from NATO contracts at one level but collude in localized NATO or Afghan National Security Forces reverses elsewhere.[17] Indeed in many cases, the activities of these power brokers have been a major cause of the insurgency. Power brokers have large militias often re-described as Private Security Companies which have been involved in extortion on the roads or which have subcontracted work out to other firms (militias) which have extorted 'taxes' from road users. In some cases, such as Akhundzada in Sangin, the power brokers have actively sponsored insurgents to fight ISAF troops in defence of their interests.

However, there are a number of factors which need to be considered in terms of the power brokers. Decisively, they have been created and empowered by Western intervention from 2001 onwards; it is Western intervention which has generated and supported the Karzai patrimony, crystallizing the networks which now dominate Afghanistan. For instance, in Kandahar, Gul Agha Sherzai's re-appropriation of power (he had been Governor from 1992 to 1994 until he was forced out by the Taliban) was supported and facilitated by the CIA who found him a useful partner in prosecuting Operation Enduring Freedom against Al Qaeda and the remnants of the Taliban. In addition to direct financial underwriting, Sherzai has set up a number of businesses, including a vehicle leasing enterprise, which loans Toyota pick-ups to ISAF and the international community; they are obvious by the Sherzai stickers on the rear bumper. One of the crucial agreements at this stage was the decision to lease the land on which Kandahar Airfield was located from Sherzai (who claimed to own it). The result was that NATO has since that time been paying millions of dollars to Sherzai a year. Indeed, in June 2010, Bacha Sherzai, Gul Agha's brother, lost US$3 million in one night gambling in Las Vegas; the money was principally derived from Western contracts. Even as individual patrons have been criticized, ostracized, or ignored, they have been continually relied upon and rewarded for their services to the West. As de Waal suggested, the international community in Afghanistan has generated a patrimonial regime even while denying it, and even while claiming to build a centralized state.

Moreover, despite the great difficulties which the patrons pose, they represent the only plausible bases of power and authority. For instance, while he was alive, Ahmed Wali Karzai was one of the main facilitators for the West in Kandahar city. The Kandahar Provinicial Reconstruction Team (KPRT) relied

[17] Antonio Giustozzi, *Koran, Kalashnikov and Laptop: The Neo-Taliban Insurgency in Afghanistan 2002–7* (London: C. Hurst and Company Publishers, 2007).

on him for development projects in relation to the Dand Dam and indeed for most works within the city. Power brokers are also the only independent actors who exert effective political power against the Taliban. Colonel Razziq—recently promoted to Brigadier General and also known as 'the general' or 'the godfather'—is a colourful and instructive example here. The subject of a recent critical exposé in the US media, he controls the border crossing at Spin Boldak with his Afghan Border Police (which are part of his larger personal militia).[18] Since his brother and uncle were killed by the Taliban, he has been their implacable opponent. He has been extremely effective if brutal in interdicting the Taliban but he is, like most political figures in the south, also implicated in drug-running and other forms of smuggling.

Early in his command of Regional Command South in 2009, General Nick Carter prioritized governance but rejected the option of engaging politically with Ahmed Wali Karzai. He regarded Governor Wesa, as this 'tip of the spear'. Yet, as his tour went on, he altered his strategy and indeed he forced General McChrystal into accepting engagement with Ahmed Wali Karzai and Colonel Razziq.[19] For instance, in July and August 2010, there were serious problems in one of the districts just south-west of Kandahar City where a surge of insurgent activity generated a vacuum of governance, when a district governor had been deposed, threatening serious instability.[20] This led to a 67-man ministerial task force from Kabul descending on Kandahar and ordering Governor Wesa, with nominal authority over his own security forces, to clear the area of hostiles. In the event, Wesa proved only residually effective. Action was ultimately authorized and taken by Ahmed Wali Karzai and Colonel Razziq, in particular, who dominated the scene. The latter, in particular, proved decisive. A successful Afghan security operation was launched within 48 hours spearheaded by Razziq's Afghan Border Police.[21] Crucially, Razziq was able to draw on his significant local political networks to secure the area with minimal recourse to force. The incident shows how for all the vitriol directed at them, power brokers represent the only credible political authority in the south. GIRoA and its offices are not irrelevant but the political regime in Afghanistan is not and will not in the conceivable future be a centralized state uniting a homogenous population. It is and will be a patrimonial regime, consisting of a small elite, ruling in a decentralized way over a highly fragmented population in which they have a base of genuine, if very localized popular support. It was noticeable that having been regarded as a criminal in November 2009, Nick Carter re-evaluated Wali Karzai by the time he came to

[18] Daphne Benoit, 'Colonel Razziq: "Godfather" of the Afghan border', *AFP*, accessed 22 September 2013, <http://www.google.com/hostednews/afp/article/ALeqM5j11nN95CI13947tIX835N_Ix37rA>.

[19] Rajiv Chandrasekaran, *Little America* (London: Bloomsbury, 2012), p. 262.

[20] British officer RC (S), personal communication, 1 September 2010.

[21] Chandrasekaran, *Little America*, pp. 265–7.

implement Operation Moshtarrak III and Hamkari in July 2010 so that he was designated Carter's centre of gravity, to the severe consternation of his political superiors in Whitehall.

Transition and the patrimonial state

The current plan for transition is predictably informed by the ideas of centralized state power which have been fundamental to Western intervention in Afghanistan since 2001. The idea behind transition is to hand over responsibility to Afghan governance and security to GIRoA and above all the Afghan National Security Forces (ANSF) by 2014. In terms of ISAF, the effort is to create a sufficiently competent security force which is capable of suppressing the insurgency without the help of approximately 100,000 ISAF troops. At the political level, learning from the experience of Najibullah, political leaders in NATO have committed themselves to support Karzai and his successor beyond 2014; ultimately they are prepared to pay for an ANSF which Afghanistan does not have anything like the economic base—or administrative means of tax collection—to support itself. The plan is predicated on a continuing affirmation of GIRoA as an (unproblematically) centralized state and a presumption that the connection between GIRoA and ANSF are straightforward. Political leaders and military commanders in ISAF have assumed that civil–military relations or governmental control of the ANSF beyond 2014 are self-evident. As long as the ANSF are operationally capable, then stability is most likely to be achieved. The power brokers are, of course, ignored in all of this.

However, the easy presumption that a competent ANSF constitutes a sufficient condition for longer-term stability and that civil–military relations in Afghanistan will accord with those which are typical in the West with ANSF coming under the centralized control of the ministry of interior and thereby the president, seem to be anything but obvious. The recent rise in 'green on blue' attacks seem to illustrate the potential problem, for, while these have often been dismissed as the acts of rogue individuals, the numbers of incidents now seem to have reached a level where they constitute a pattern. Certainly, it would be wrong to exaggerate their effect or importance here; they are small in number and in absolute terms very few ISAF troops have been killed by Afghan security partners. Yet, these murders have become regular, if sporadic, and especially their increasing frequency seems to indicate something potentially important about the possibilities for transition. Indeed, even as early as 2009, Operation Omid half-recognized the potential danger of these incidents. It noted that one of the most dangerous courses of insurgent action was that 'a significant portion of malign actors, criminal groups and narcotic traffickers align with the insurgents' to mount 'coordinated attack against planned targets'. It might have added that the malign actors—the power brokers—or the insurgents brought significant sections of the ANSF with them against what was left of GIRoA.

There is clear evidence that in some cases, the Taliban have infiltrated the security forces. For instance on 16 July 2011, Lance Corporal Paul Watkins was shot dead in Helmand by an Afghan soldier whom he was mentoring. The Afghan soldier was later apprehended—quite accidentally. He confessed to having been recruited by a Taliban sergeant in the Afghan National Army (ANA) who had instructed this soldier—and other colleagues—that it was their duty to try and murder a British soldier. However, the sergeant recommended that this act was not carried out immediately but at a moment of opportunity at some point in the future. On 16 July, this soldier was sitting in a Land Rover alone with Corporal Watkins on a firing range. He seized his opportunity, shooting Watkins in the face at point blank range in the vehicle. Corporal Watkins' death illustrates that the Taliban have infiltrated the ANSF, at least to some extent, with potentially serious repercussions post-transition. However, perhaps more serious are the political implications of Watkins' murder. Despite periodic efforts to centralize control, the Taliban movement remains diverse and disparate, heavily mediated by local conditions and local tribal politics. It is unlikely that rogue soldiers are immune from these countervailing pressures. Rather, just as local fighters join (i.e. 'become') the Taliban for immediate political reasons, it seems likely that the rise in 'green on blue' incidents reflects political turbulence at a deeper level. Specifically, it does not seem implausible to suggest that 'green on blues' may be precipitated by political pressures coursing through patrimonial networks as various patrons at different levels seek to position themselves with a view to Western withdrawal. These murders may speak to very great political influences at work in the ANSF which extend far beyond the acknowledged official chain of command and its connection to GIRoA; murdering Western soldiers may be a preemptive indication of the politicized allegiance of the ANSF not to GIRoA but to much more local political authority. It is widely known that even when ANSF and especially Afghan National Police (ANP) units act as their own private militias or are in their pay, power brokers have personal relations with commanders. For instance, in 2009–10, Wali Karzai was in regular contact with the commander of 215 Corps in Kandahar quite independently of ISAF or GIRoA. The danger is that as Afghanistan moves towards transition, the ANSF may fissure into a number of political factions around one or other of the power brokers or even go over to a resurgent Taliban. The rogue murder of ISAF soldiers may point to a profound political instability in the ANSF. Indeed, suggesting the possibility of factionalism with the ANSF, there has been a significant rise in the number of 'green on greens' in the ANSF with members murdering each other for a variety of reasons. Some might be purely individual but the trend seems to imply something potentially more serious and political.

At the same time, while the West have failed to acknowledge or engage with the power brokers, even while empowering and enriching them, the Taliban seem to have identified the patrimonial regime which crystallized around Wali Karzai in the Kandahar as a major political threat. It has been noticeable that since the surge one of their main strategies has been targeted assassinations of critical figures in Karzai's regime. Whether they have learnt this strategy from the assassination of Osama Bin Laden in April 2011 or whether the threat which the surge generally posed to the organization stimulated the new approach is difficult to ascertain without access to classified Taliban sources. However, in the summer of 2011, the Taliban initiated a campaign of political assassination, killing Ahmed Wali Karzai and Jan Mohammed Khan in July 2011, and Khan Mohammed Mujahid, the Kandahar Chief of Police (in April 2011), followed by Burhanuddin Rabbani in September, as well as an assault on the Ministry of Interior with the aim of killing the minister himself. The murder of Wali Karzai was complex since some have claimed it to have been a crime of passion perpetrated by his aggrieved chief bodyguard. Yet, others claim it to have been initiated by the Taliban who both claimed responsibility for the murder and could have sponsored the bodyguard to carry out the attack. It was noticeable that they mounted a suicide attack on Wali Karzai's funeral, at which Hamid Karzai was present, killing four civilians. In the vacuum following the murder of Wali Karzai, Colonel Razziq has emerged, although it is unlikely he will presume the position of preeminence enjoyed by his ally, Wali Karzai. Promoted to General, he has been appointed Kandahar Chief of Police. However, he is a potentially important figure in a reconstituted regime. It is noticeable in that, perhaps indicating the threat he posed to the Taliban, he was the victim of a bomb attack in the summer of 2012 which, although badly burnt, he survived. The patrimonial regime has been significantly eroded in the last 18 months not because GIRoA has replaced it as Operation Omid intended but on the contrary because, instructively, of insurgent action. While the West disparaged the power brokers, the Taliban have seen them as the centre of gravity for the regime and for the West's efforts. Perhaps the rise of 'green on blue' incidents is not unrelated to this increased political turbulence as remaining leaders jostle ever more urgently for power and security—and the allegiance of the ANSF—with a view to 2014 as they themselves fear imminent assassination.

Conclusion

As the West withdraws, it has a choice. It could affirm its current plan, informed by long-standing ideas of building GIRoA as a centralized state but with rapidly diminishing troops and resources. In the light of the relative weakness of official GIRoA structures and personnel (despite over a decade of effort) and especially the frail link between the civil powers and the security forces, this would seem to be an extremely risky course of action. While the operational performance of the ANSF may be improved during the transition, any significant development in the capacity of the Afghan state to govern would seem to be unlikely. More specifically, even if the ANSF are augmented sufficiently to counter the insurgency independently, there is no guarantee of their long-term loyalty to either the ANA or ANP within the existing fragile structure of the Afghan state. An Aden-like situation would seem possible in Afghanistan with mass defections of the ANSF if the political relations between the military and the real sources of political power in Afghanistan are not affirmed and consolidated.

There is a second option; an alternative transition plan founded on a pragmatic observation of the organic emergence of an Afghan regime since 2001. Unpalatable as it may be to many Western leaders and difficult as it may be to reform the central concept of the campaign—and to unite a diversity of international actors around it—it seems likely that with the dwindling resources and declining political interest of the West in Afghanistan, that the only plausible political order in the short term through the period of transition and out to 2020 will be a regime founded not on a centralized GIRoA, whose apparatus is still only thin, but on the power brokers. The regime most likely to be sustainable out to 2020 and to continue to suppress the Taliban and assert its autonomy from Islamabad is a patrimonial regime, exorcised of its malignant elements. Specifically, stability in the south through the era of transition is likely to be created most successfully by developing a new post-Ahmed Wali Karzai patrimonial regime around figures like General Razziq, Gul Agha Sherzai, and, of course, most controversially Sher Mohammed Akhundzada. Karzai's sacking of Gulab Mangal as Governor of Helmand in September 2012 seemed to be the first move in reconstituting such a regime in the south, potentially making room for the rehabilitation of Akhundzada. In order to mitigate against these individuals' worst features and the sometimes predatory and competitive nature of the patrimonial system and to legitimate them in the West, they will have to be incorporated more closely into GIRoA structures and to be intensely mentored and partnered by the CIA, SIS, and Western diplomats; genuine, consistent, and enduring political engagement will be required with them for the first time. One of the most important requirements is that they be seen to exercise power in a more open and less discriminatory way; they need to include dis-favoured or actively excluded tribes and groupings in the political process in order to reduce the points of entry for the Taliban into Afghanistan.

Ironically, it may be expedient to reappoint individuals like Akhundzada, Razziq, or Sherzai as Governors—or some other equivalent position—of Kandahar, Helmand, and Oruzgan in order to achieve these ends. At the same time, and in order to prevent structural defection, it may be wise to connect the ANSF directly and explicitly to these named power brokers; a connection which will be all the easier and more effective if they hold important posts like Governor. Western politicians are currently looking at the example of Najibullah on how to extend a regime beyond withdrawal. Certainly, his rule demonstrates that it is possible to rule Afghanistan with sufficient international support. However, Najibullah also demonstrates that long-term stability and a lasting regime requires not external support but an internal organic power-base. The West has a choice of artificially endorsing the frail formal structures of GIRoA and ignoring the power brokers or of engaging with the extant and actual bases of power in this society (which includes GIRoA but goes beyond it). In helping the international community make its choice—between idealism and pragmatism—it might be noted that the appropriate comparison is not the modern Western state but only the Taliban regime of 1996 to 2001 which ISAF has tried to replace. When compared with the Taliban, the level to which the power brokers would need to be brought to represent an advance for Afghanistan is not very high. Almost any sustained economic development within a relatively stable patrimonial political framework which did not actually exploit large segments of the population, be they women or rival tribal groupings, would represent a significant improvement. In short, the kinds of conditions which pertained in Afghanistan in the 1950s would constitute a considerable success. The greatest transition which may be required as the West withdraws from Afghanistan may be the reformation of its own self-perceptions and, consequently, understanding of Afghanistan: a state-centric vision may need to be replaced by a concept of a patrimonial political order.

References

Benoit, Daphne, 'Colonel Razziq: "Godfather" of the Afghan border', *AFP*, accessed 22 September 2013, <http://www.google.com/hostednews/afp/article/AleqM5j11nN-95CI13947tIX835N_Ix37rA>.

Bird, Tim and Alex Marshall, *Afghanistan: How the West Lost Its Way* (New Haven, CT: Yale University Press 2011).

Chandrasekaran, Rajiv, *Little America* (London: Bloomsbury, 2012).

de Waal, Alex, 'Dollarised', *London Review of Books*, 24 June 2010, pp. 38–41.

Galula, David, *Counter-Insurgency Warfare: Theory and Practice* (Westport, CT: Praeger, 2006).

Giustozzi, Antonio, *Koran, Kalashnikov and Laptop: The Neo-Taliban Insurgency in Afghanistan 2002–7* (London: C. Hurst and Company Publishers, 2007).

Janis, Irving, *Group Think: Psychological Studies of Policy Decisions and Fiascos* (Boston: Houghton Mifflin Company, 1982).

McChrystal, General, *Initial Commander's Assessment*, 30 August 2009.

North Atlantic Treaty Organization (NATO), *The Afghanistan Compact*, 2006, accessed 22 September 2013, <http://www.nato.int/isaf/docu/epub/pdf/afghanistan_compact.pdf>.

Stewart, Rory, 'The Irresistible Illusion', *London Review of Books*, 9 July 2009.

Thompson, Robert, *Defeating Communist Insurgency: Experiences from Malaya and Vietnam* (London: Chatto and Windus, 1974).

Weber, Max, *Economy and Society: An Outline of Interpretive Sociology* (New York: Bedminster Press, 1968).

15

Negotiated agreements in tactical transitions

The Sangin Accord 2011

Mark Beautement

Former American Defense Secretary Robert Gates described Sangin District, in Helmand Province, as 'the most dangerous not only in Afghanistan but maybe the whole world'.[1] The United Kingdom 'suffered its heaviest losses in Sangin'.[2] On 20 September 2010, as responsibility for Sangin passed from the United Kingdom to the United States, the BBC reported that 'of the 337 UK deaths since 2001, a third have happened there'.[3] As British forces did not deploy to Sangin permanently until 21 June 2006,[4] this number—and the many wounded—testify to the intense combat and complex threat from Improvised Explosive Devices (IEDs) facing British, American, and Afghan National Security Forces, and the civilian government and local population they were there to support. Despite this, Sangin's District Governor Mohammad Sharif received a written offer of peace from the principal local political grouping aligned to the Taliban on 29 May 2010,[5] preceding the Afghan government's national peace and reconciliation *jirga* (a decision-making

[1] Robert Gates, quoted in Euan MacAskill, 'US claims to have driven Taliban out of Sangin', *The Guardian*, 8 March 2011, <http://www.guardian.co.uk/world/2011/mar/08/us-afghanistan-sangin-taliban-claim>.

[2] Ian Pannell, 'UK troops leave Helmand's Sangin', *BBC News*, 20 September 2010, <http://www.bbc.co.uk/news/uk-11367931>.

[3] Pannell, 'UK troops leave Helmand's Sangin'.

[4] Patrick Bishop, *3 PARA* (London: HarperPress 2007), p. 107.

[5] Phil Weatherill, 'Note from the field: Targeting the centre of gravity—adapting stabilisation in Sangin', *RUSI Journal* 156, no. 4 (2011): p. 98.

meeting) on 4 June 2010,[6] NATO's military surge, and Sangin's transfer from British to US forces. This offer formed the basis of the agreement negotiated by the Afghan Government, known as the Sangin Accord, announced by Helmand's Provincial Governor Gulab Mangal on 4 January 2011.[7]

Was there any relationship between motivations to negotiate and international policy and actions, notably the uses of military power, stabilization activities, and approaches to the co-option and legitimation of enemies? What role could an agreement like the Sangin Accord play in future transitions, given the risks to security and local understanding as an international presence withdraws? This chapter considers these questions while outlining the context of the Sangin Accord. It compares some explanations for negotiated agreements outlined by academic theory and military doctrine, notably I. William Zartman's ripeness theory and its evolutions. It offers some suggestions for promoting negotiated agreement in other local reconciliation scenarios.

Actions, and reactions, taken at the tactical level can have local, but also very far-reaching social, political, and military consequences in the eyes of the enemy, the local population, allies, and for our domestic and international audiences.[8] There are three reasons to analyse the relationship between military action and political objectives at the local level, though always alongside higher-level strategy and planning.

1. Engagement with central authorities in weakened states struggles to address local conflict drivers.
2. Resource or policy constraints can diminish the impact of a theatre-wide military advantage on local dynamics.
3. Some future deployments may be small-scale and focused on subnational objectives.

These are important research priorities, since 'local agendas—at the level of the individual, the family, the clan, the municipality, the community, the district or the ethnic group—at least partly drive the continuation of violence'.[9]

Achieving 'long-term success in counterinsurgency depends on the people taking charge of their own affairs and consenting to the government's rule',

[6] 'Afghan peace jirga backs Karzai Taliban talks proposal', *BBC News,* 4 June 2010, <http://www.bbc.co.uk/news/10234823>.

[7] 'Afghanistan: Sangin insurgents agree to stand up to Taliban', *The Telegraph,* 4 January 2011, <http://www.telegraph.co.uk/news/worldnews/asia/afghanistan/8238031/Afghanistan-Sangin-insurgents-agree-to-stand-up-to-Taliban.html>.

[8] Here, 'local' follows the definition given by Séverine Autesserre meaning 'subprovincial', and refers 'to district- or village-specific issues'. See Séverine Autesserre, *The Trouble with the Congo: Local Violence and the Failure of International Peacebuilding* (New York: Cambridge University Press, 2010), p. 43.

[9] Autesserre, *The Trouble with the Congo*, p. 6.

and requires the government to eliminate as many causes of the insurgency as feasible.[10] In 1965, Bernard Fall concluded that a government losing to an insurgency is not being outfought, it is being out-governed.[11] So, for academic theory to be truly useful, it must account for the relationship between military power, stabilization activity, and the legitimacy—and capacity—of the supported government to govern. The implications are profound, since 'once we acknowledge that the people's political views matter to our own definition of success or failure, an exclusively military definition relative to the enemy in battle is insufficient'.[12] Local analysis becomes especially important where centralized governance structures are weak or disputed, since engagement with apparently key leaders at the top or centre of society does not necessarily address local issues, especially in rural or peripheral areas.

Since resources are always finite, some leaders within an area of operations may seek political progress without a local military advantage. I define these locations as 'fringe' areas, where there is no permanent, definitive military dominance, and no imminent prospect of one without a change in the overall number of deployed personnel. Here, a population's perception of their own *insecurity* can play a part in motivating political progress. At times, this was the case in Sangin District during the three years preceding the public announcement of the Sangin Accord. The agreement came about while the Kabul government did not secure all the population covered by the Accord. Neither NATO nor Afghan National Security Forces had 'a strong forward presence among that part of the population which insurgents seek to control'[13]—despite this being considered a 'vital step in neutralising insurgents'.[14] Since 'twenty counterinsurgents per 1000 residents is often considered the minimum troop density required for effective counter-insurgency operations',[15] areas of low population density are more likely to have low military force levels. There is an increased chance that a stalemate is present when conflict in these fringe areas is analysed locally, even though at higher levels international and national forces may have a clear position of strength. For some, this impasse precludes political progress. For ripeness theory, stalemate is one required condition for genuine negotiation to begin—alongside a shared perception of a political way out.

[10] US Army, *Field Manual 3–24: Counterinsurgency* (Washington, DC: Department of the Army, 2006), para. 1–4.

[11] Bernard Fall, 'The theory and practice of insurgency and counterinsurgency', *Naval War College Review* 17, no. 8 (1965): p. 55.

[12] Emile Simpson, *War From The Ground Up: Twenty-First-Century Combat As Politics* (London: Hurst, 2012), p. 23.

[13] US Army, *Field Manual 3–24*, para. 3–12.

[14] US Army, *Field Manual 3–24*, para. 3–12.

[15] US Army, *Field Manual 3–24*, para. 1–67.

In Sangin, kernels of local agreement were generated despite the complex local conflict drivers and lower military presence. This raises opportunities for future deployments to fringe areas, where political progress is required despite a weak or disputed central government, and only a small military force is available. In policy terms, this points to the evolving thinking in the United States towards 'minimalist stabilization' deployments,[16] defined as 'small-scale, lowcost operations combining military and civilian activities to influence the political authority structure of a state in or recovering from violent conflict'.[17]

Critics of smaller military deployments argue,

> a light footprint makes the success of an operation more than usually dependent on the political dynamic of local actors. Since the malevolence or collapse of that political dynamic is precisely the reason that power is arrogated to an international presence, the light footprint is unsustainable as a model for general application.[18]

This depends upon whether a smaller military force can foster the motivation to negotiate while providing only limited permanent population security (so without military dominance), but supported by carefully targeted coercive raids and non-military activities designed to improve governance and legitimacy, including dialogue, confidence-building, public services, and infrastructure delivery. It is essential here to recognize that different resource levels are required to nourish the conditions for genuine, informal (but usually private) dialogue about significant subjects and those that may be needed to activate, implement, and support a public, formal agreement, since a credible and enduring security guarantee is often essential to offset the risk to newly co-opted communities after a public shift in allegiance. I argue that the Sangin Accord case study shows that informal dialogue is possible in fringe areas and lays vital foundations of trust, credibility, and access that cannot always be bought or accelerated later by force, illustrating that even where military forces lack a clear monopoly of violence it is possible for 'politics to become the continuation of warfare by other means'.[19]

[16] Stephen Watts, Caroline Baxter, Molly Dunigan, and Christopher Rizzi, *The Uses and Limitations of Small-scale Military Interventions* (Santa Monica: RAND Corporation, 2012), p. 1.

[17] Watts et al., *The Uses and Limitations of Small-scale Military Interventions*, pp. 10–11.

[18] Simon Chesterman, 'Transitional administration, state-building and the United Nations', in *Making States Work: State failure and the crisis of government*, edited by Simon Chesterman, Michael Ignatieff, and Ramesh Thakur (New York: United Nations University Press, 2005), p. 344.

[19] UK Foreign Secretary (2007–10) David Miliband, quoted in British Army, *Field Manual Vol. 1. Part 10 Countering Insurgency* (London: The Stationery Office, October 2009), para. 3–3.

Sangin District 1700–2005: a history of conflict, negotiation, and transition

The Sangin area has been strategically important in southern Afghanistan for centuries. Elites, foreigners, traders, and local rivals struggled for control, employing conflict, negotiation, and multiple identities and allegiances. The local name for the valley and main communities north of Sangin town is *Sarawan Qalah*, meaning 'place [or fort, castle] of the caravans'. As is common in Afghanistan and elsewhere, names and labels have fluid definitions and relate to human groupings as much as physical geography.[20]

It seems almost certain that Sangin was given to the Alikozai clans before 1747, bestowing significant power and prestige and exemption from government taxation, as long as the holders provided warriors for national military service.[21] Given this, since the eighteenth century the Alikozai tribe is likely to have focused political strategy on preserving this prime ancestral territory. One might also consider the 2011 Sangin Accord in this light.[22]

Great Britain has a long history with Afghanistan, and Helmand Province. Sangin is a mere 30 miles over the Ghorak Pass from Maiwand, *en route* to Kandahar. Both hold a central place in Afghan lore about the British, and the foreigner. If Afghan victory at Maiwand in 1880 and then defeat at Kandahar later that year left scars 'etched in the national psyche, particularly in the northern reaches of Helmand',[23] do they really motivate modern actions? Perhaps—Rajiv Chandrasekaran is one who claims, 'memories of Maiwand fuelled hopes of another Afghan victory, while Kandahar sparked desire for revenge'.[24] The Soviet invasion, and an Afghan's personal response to it, can evoke polarizing views. Sangin town contains the wreckage of Soviet tanks where Russian ground forces were apparently stopped by largely Alikozai resistance fighters, usually labelled Mujahedeen. These same men recounted proudly that no Soviet force ever held the Upper Sangin Valley, resorting instead to strafing villages with helicopters.[25] Those who resisted drew great

[20] Participant observation from 2009–10 indicated that many different interview subjects used the name *Sarawan Qalah* to denote one or more of: a small collection of dwellings; a specific village; the lower part of the Sangin valley just north of the town; the whole upper Sangin valley; traditionally Alikozai tribal lands; or the area's people and community.

[21] Mike Martin, *A Brief History of Helmand* (Warminster: British Army, 2011); Thomas Barfield, *Afghanistan: A Cultural and Political History* (Oxford: Princeton University Press, 2010).

[22] Robert Johnson, '*Mizh der beitabora khalqi-i*': A comparative study of Afghan–Pashtun perspectives on negotiating with the British and the Soviets, 1839–1989', *Journal of Imperial and Commonwealth History* 39, no. 4 (November 2011): pp. 551–70.

[23] Rajiv Chandrasekaran, *Little America, The War Within The War For Afghanistan* (London: Bloomsbury, 2012), p. 49.

[24] Chandrasekaran, *Little America*, p. 49.

[25] Provincial Reconstruction Team (PRT) officials who served in Sangin recall a group of local Alikozai elders recounting this story, and re-enacting the operation of Mujahedeen anti-aircraft gun positions, during a *shura* (meeting) in 2009.

acclaim, perceiving this as a 'battle for national dignity and national liberation in which they were prepared—literally—to fight to the death'.[26] Conversely, some residents of the Helmand valley south of Sangin, predominantly Ishaqzai tribesfolk, were labelled collaborators since the Soviets are alleged to have conquered and held that territory and enlisted (or conscripted) locals into security forces and the political administration.

This history of Sangin offers four important themes. First, there is a long record of interaction between Afghan groups, with outsiders perceived frequently as partisan (either knowingly or unknowingly) in local disputes. Secondly, local land and water ownership, and access, remain contested. Thirdly, central government has been weak and disputed, and used its offices and administrative boundaries at times to favour or disenfranchise local Afghans, sometimes along tribal lines. Fourthly, the Soviet campaign, the civil war that followed it and, later, Taliban rule and its aftermath, left a multi-polar social and political system under threat from criminality, and new agents—including exiled and displaced groups—competing for respect and power. Addressing as many of these as possible and synchronizing solutions with wider NATO campaign objectives and resources, would form the basis of the Sangin Accord.

2001–2009: hearts and mindsets

The decision to send NATO forces to Sangin in 2006, and the campaign that followed, have been assessed widely.[27] While recognizing that military operations continued throughout the period covered by this case study, this section only assesses military action in relation to the Sangin Accord. Three vignettes illustrate the challenge of seeking to influence evolving local calculations about the legitimacy of the Afghan government relative to governance in areas outside its control: one, the violence between Alikozai leader Dad Mohammad Khan (DMK) and local rivals in 2006; two, the failed uprising against the Taliban in 2007 by Alikozai-led groups within the Upper Sangin Valley; three, the impact of the distribution of wheat seed conducted under Governor Mangal's Food Zone Programme in 2009.

NATO's military deployment interacted with existing disputes. An illustrative event is the June 2006 assassination (by marginalized local rivals mostly from the Ishaqzai tribe) of 'members of the family of Dad Mohammad Khan, known locally as 'Amir Dado', the most prominent figure in the Sangin area.

[26] Rodric Braithwaite, *Afghantsy: The Russians in Afghanistan 1979–1989* (London: Profile Books, 2011), p. 331.

[27] For example Michael Clarke, ed., *The Afghan Papers: Committing Britain to War in Helmand 2005–06*, Whitehall Paper 77 (London: RUSI, 2011), notably ch. 2: Valentina Soria, 'A Tale of Flawed "Comprehensiveness": The Joint Plan for Helmand'.

'Amir Dado' was the tribal leader of the Alakozai tribe[28] in Helmand, an Afghan MP, and the Helmand Intelligence Chief in the years between 2001 and 2005. One of the dead men was his brother, a former District Governor of Sangin named Juma Gul.[29] There were

> Ishaqzai figures in the highest echelons of the Taliban leadership. Maulawi Aktar Mohammad Osmani, second only to Mullah Omar in the entire Taliban leadership, was an Ishaqzai from the village of Josh Ali [Jushalay], near Sangin, where he ran a madrasa. So when the attack on Dad Mohammad's clan came in June 2006 it was, in one sense, a Taliban attack on the Afghan government. However, it was also, to a greater or lesser degree, an Ishaqzai tribal vendetta, a drugs war hit, and a popular uprising against a local potentate.[30]

Multi-layered identities complicated strategies to support, or undermine, the legitimacy and political significance of members of the Afghan government, or the Taliban. Judgements about legitimacy also affected organizations. The Afghan government, and perhaps by association, NATO, suffered from a legitimacy deficit in Sangin after an event in spring 2007. For the Alikozai, it was a catastrophe. A dispute about taxation turned violent in the Upper Sangin Valley, but it also involved narcotics, in which both pro- and anti-government groups often collaborated across political boundaries for economic gain. It is impossible to say if the tax collectors were Quetta Shura Taliban, or drugs barons allied with Taliban-aligned individuals. Perhaps they were local rivals, considered 'foreigners' by the Alikozai, where 'foreigners' meant anybody from outside their immediate community. The Alikozai—historically a pro-government group—organized a community resistance of around 200 people, refused the demands for tax, and resisted with force.[31] If true, it would have been exceptional for a community to have confronted Taliban elements in this timeframe, on this scale. Nevertheless, while the facts were hazy, people believed it.

Alikozai elders recounted that the District Governor, and through him, military forces, were asked for help. Forty-eight hours later, the Alikozai group had diminished, as the support they had anticipated had not arrived.[32] Some 200 fighters arrived from outside Helmand and inflicted swift punishment

[28] NATO staff used the spelling Alikozai from 2009 to 2011, in the author's experience.

[29] Tom Coghlan, 'The Taliban in Helmand: an oral history', in *Decoding the New Taliban*, edited by Antonio Giustozzi (London: Hurst, 2009), pp. 119–20.

[30] Coghlan, 'The Taliban in Helmand', pp. 119–20; 'Bomb explosion "kills Afghan MP"', *BBC News*, 19 March 2009, <http://news.bbc.co.uk/1/hi/world/americas/7952333.stm>.

[31] On community resistance see Mohammed O. Tariq, 'Tribal Security System (*Arbakai*) in Southeast Afghanistan', *Crisis States Occasional Paper No. 7* (London: Crisis States Research Centre, 2008) or Seth Jones and Arturo Munoz, 'Afghanistan's Local War: Building Local Defense Forces' (Santa Monica: RAND Corporation, 2010), <http://www.rand.org/pubs/monographs/MG1002.html>.

[32] This may be linked to events in neighbouring Musa Qalah. See for example: Michael Semple, *Reconciliation in Afghanistan* (Washington, DC: United States Institute of Peace, 2009), pp. 80–8.

on the dissenting leaders, killing them, or dispersing them to Kandahar, Lashkar Gah, or abroad. Some stayed behind and they re-negotiated with the 'foreigners' to retain some leadership in their hereditary lands.[33] From that point, many analysts considered those local elders, judges, and religious leaders from the Alikozai tribe who stayed in Sangin as 'Taliban', although many Afghans did not see things in such stark categories. This many-layered concept of identity left important opportunities for future disagreement between local groups and outsiders, typically aggregated together as one 'Taliban' opponent.

The Helmand Food Zone Program was 'designed to decrease poppy production in the province by providing wheat seed, high value vegetable seed and fertilizer... as an alternative to growing poppy'.[34] In Sangin, the distribution increased the relative legitimacy of the government, and political understanding. By November 2009, Sangin residents were nevertheless disappointed that the international mission had not carried out reconstruction as they had anticipated. People often mistrusted the central government anyway: the Pashto word *charwaki* 'is used synonymously for government official, tax collector, policeman, and bandit'.[35] Despite administrative challenges, the Food Zone Programme 'brought local Taliban leaders into direct confrontation with their out-of-area counterparts' and offered a catalyst for large groups of locals to assemble in Sangin town increasing political actions and understanding.[36] This friction increased because farmers travelled up to 30 miles from outside the area to pay around 700 Afghanis ($14) for 100kg of subsidised wheat seed, 300kg of fertilizer, and some insecticide.[37]

The Afghan government's wheat seed distribution generated three responses outside the territory it controlled, depending on whether the Taliban military commanders and civilian officials in charge of a given zone within the Upper Sangin Valley (termed the 'shadow government' by NATO) were 'foreigners', or local men from Sangin. Some allowed farmers to keep the materials, usually where there was a kinship or other close bond between the shadow officials and the population. Some applied an Islamic *zakat* tax, at 10 per cent. Others used violence and intimidation, punishing the farmers for engaging with the Afghan government. Sometimes commanders applied one rule for their own area of responsibility (usually to generate consent) and applied a harsher rule elsewhere; others were

[33] The exact political mechanism is unknown, and it remains unclear whether this type of local negotiation required approval from the highest echelons of the Taliban leadership, or not.

[34] USAID Afghanistan, 'Hilmand Food Zone Project', 2013, <http://afghanistan.usaid.gov/en/USAID/Activity/255/Hilmand_Food_Zone_Project_HFZP>.

[35] Martin, *A Brief History of Helmand*, p. 5.

[36] Weatherill, 'Note from the Field', p. 95.

[37] UK Provincial Reconstruction Team, 'Helmand Counter Narcotics Strategy 2009/2010, Local Nationals Press Briefing—Press Release' [Unclassified], 25 September 2009.

consistent.[38] Taliban senior leaders replaced Mullah Abdul Khaleq, their shadow governor in Sangin, on 19 November 2009—he had lost control after public anger at attacks on local farmers.[39] This friction allowed the District Governor to begin mapping which local Taliban leaders prioritized community welfare, and to use the possibility of future stabilization work—in return for concessions—to challenge their legitimacy in areas where there was no permanent NATO/Afghan National Army presence. However, as many local shadow government personnel were respected Alikozai, left from 2007's failed uprising, a higher calibre of Afghan government official was needed to exploit this friction over wheat seed.

2010–2011: spring floods and shrines

Local frictions continued into 2010, exacerbated by extreme flooding in February—anecdotally the worst in living memory. District Governor Faisal Haq's office was known to have communicated with Upper Sangin Valley leaders since 2008, including over irrigation and flood defences for the upper reaches of the Helmand River. Haq was an Alikozai, and trumpeted himself as a central figure in the 2007 uprising. President Karzai's half-brother, Ahmad Wali Karzai, agreed to a marriage between their families (Haq alleged). Haq's counterparts in Sangin's rural areas were largely Alikozai military, civil, and judicial officials who had refused exile in 2007 and continued their roles as part of the local administration co-opted into the Taliban shadow governance structure, supplemented by 'foreign' Taliban appointees (termed 'Out Of Area' by NATO). The legitimacy deficit between older, exiled 'Government' and respected, younger, local 'Taliban' included a generational shift and a rivalry within traditional Alikozai hierarchy, such as it still existed.[40] This political landscape blended concepts of 'government' and 'counterstate' usually considered as distinct and in opposition.[41] If the 'counterstate' (or locals co-opted into the shadow government) was an accepted governance mechanism in the Sangin area before the latest incarnation of central government reasserted itself, then the 'state' and the 'counterstate' were reversed in the eyes of the local population. Assessments of legitimacy depend on subjective

[38] Participant observation by District Stabilisation Team staff between November 2009 and January 2010.

[39] Weatherill, 'Note from the Field', p. 98, n. 23.

[40] Tribal unity was further weakened by the death of Mullah Naqib (the Alikozai patriarch from Kandahar's Argandhab Valley) from natural causes in late 2007, while DMK's killing in 2009 denied them a political patron in Kabul (he was an MP at the time of his death).

[41] 'A counterstate is a competing structure that a movement sets up to replace the government. It includes the administrative and bureaucratic trappings of political power and performs the normal functions of a government', US Army, *Field Manual 3–24*, para. 1–32.

judgements about the institutions, the people occupying key appointments, and whether actions taken confer credibility on personnel or the organization. Yet from a position of apparent advantage, a weak response to natural disaster in 2010 catalysed local communities to make a dramatic reappraisal of the Taliban shadow government's claim to be their legitimate protectors.

The spring flooding caused extensive damage, particularly in Alikozai lands on the upper reaches of the Helmand River. Local people asked the Taliban shadow administration for help. In theory, the Taliban code of conduct, or *Layeha*, issued in May 2009, determined the correct response.[42] Between 2009 and 2011, however, local support for Out-Of-Area shadow government appointees depended increasingly on these outsiders waging 'a guerrilla campaign in concert with a rudimentary population-centric strategy . . . sensitive to local perceptions'.[43] As community confidence grew, locals were prepared to request and then demand more moderate treatment, forcing the removal of two Taliban Shadow Governors for brutality in 2010.[44] Importantly, this more moderate governance is sanctioned in both the 2006 and 2009 *Layeha* documents. This offered potential common ground with the District Government, likely stemming from greater acceptance that harsh treatment of the population was 'a major bane to the Taliban's political capital',[45] and from problems of asserting control—likely accelerated by the effective military targeting, notably of Out-Of-Area commanders and narcotics traffickers. While military forces based permanently in the district were heavily committed to protecting developments in the urban centre, elite NATO and Afghan forces conducted a relentless tempo of night raids and other operations into Sangin's rural areas. The District Government, approved by Provincial Governor Mangal, sent messages offering dialogue about the conditions under which the heavy engineering support required to repair the waterways and flood defences—using technical expertise to which the Taliban did not have access—might be provided. The legitimacy calculation began to change.

On 1 March 2010, literate former science teacher Mohammad Sharif replaced Faisal Haq as District Governor of Sangin, reportedly after a delegation from Baghran in the far north of Helmand lobbied President Karzai directly. The number of local people coming to meet Sharif in his office outside the NATO base increased from 5–10 Alikozai under Haq to some

[42] Thomas H. Johnson and Matthew C. DuPee, 'Analysing the new Taliban Code of Conduct (Layeha): an assessment of changing perspectives and strategies of the Afghan Taliban', *Central Asian Survey* 31, no. 1 (2012): p. 78.

[43] Johnson and DuPee, 'Analysing', p. 78.

[44] Mike Williams, 'How the British presence in Sangin restored trust in government', *The Guardian*, 20 September 2010, <http://www.guardian.co.uk/commentisfree/2010/sep/20/british-forces-in-sangin>.

[45] Johnson and DuPee, 'Analysing', p. 81.

60–70 daily, from all local groups.[46] Based on two years of observation by the Provincial Reconstruction Team's Sangin-based District Stabilisation Team, this measurement best illustrated the District Governor's potential as a credible representative. Measures like the number of combat incidents were less useful, since a locally driven reduction in violence was likely to attract scrutiny and reprisals from hard-line senior Taliban before trust and confidence, and the substance of any negotiation, matured enough to trigger a public switch in allegiance and the corresponding security guarantee.[47] This new leader brought the office of District Governor far closer to the credibility conferred on Upper Sangin Valley leaders by the wider Alikozai-dominated population. Mohammad Sharif began confidence-building dialogue, under the scrutiny of Provincial Governor Mangal.

Academic theory defines these 'pre-negotiations' as 'the parts of the negotiating process that take place before around-the-table negotiation begins'.[48] No member of the local Afghan Government had yet admitted to meeting the key Alikozai leaders. How was it then that 'on 29 May 2010, a formal offer of peace with the Upper Sangin Valley was made by eight of the most influential leaders and was swiftly followed by overtures from tribal groups in the south', in the Upper Gereshk Valley?[49] It is illuminating to consider how local people saw the role of communication with opponents, defined concepts of power, and reacted to emerging opportunities to meet their interests. Afghan conflict 'includes regular contact with enemy leaders (via telephone, letter or face-to-face)',[50] often because of kinship and other ties. 'Most conflicts end when one group switches sides or agrees to surrender' and Afghan conflict parties expect direct communication on these subjects.[51] 'Thus, the mere fact that our local partners are in dialog with the enemy is not an indicator, in and of itself, of disloyalty to the government.'[52] This is challenging for some Westernized organizations, which typically handle such communications centrally, considering the opening or cessation of dialogue as significant indicators, perhaps of relative strength or perceived legitimacy.

There are also differences in the way power and influence were understood, especially in rural areas. 'European political ideas elevated the exclusive

[46] District Stabilisation Team staff in Sangin recorded this and other statistics throughout 2010 while attempting to quantify changing political legitimacy.

[47] For a review of similar themes, see David Kilcullen, 'Measuring Progress in Afghanistan', 2009, <http://literature-index.wikispaces.com/file/view/Kilcullen-COIN+Metrics.pdf>.

[48] Harold H. Saunders, 'We need a larger theory of negotiation: The importance of pre-negotiation phases', *Negotiation Journal* 1, no. 3 (1985): pp. 252–3.

[49] Weatherill, 'Note from the Field', p. 98, n. 24.

[50] Kilcullen, 'Measuring progress', p. 9.

[51] Kilcullen, 'Measuring progress', p. 9.

[52] Kilcullen, 'Measuring progress', p. 9.

control of territory as a constituent element of sovereignty.'[53] Local Afghan communities expected 'multiple tributary relationships as a fundamental part of the political order',[54] meaning that aspirants to political control should also 'focus on the visible bestowal of honour, visitation, and expressions of mutual, albeit hierarchical, obligation' rather than near-exclusively on land and its control.[55] The generation of the Sangin Accord attempted to boost the Afghan Government's position, as the first step towards being a legitimate broker in a wider tapestry of local obligations.

Identifying a negotiating opportunity does not require that it be taken, or signify it is more valid than other policy options. To be truly useful, a negotiated agreement needs to advance the wider campaign, reducing the resources required to achieve an objective, ideally while increasing future prospects by addressing conflict drivers through mechanisms that boost the legitimacy of the government. The rationale for the Sangin Accord was to provide one policy option to support strategies to reduce conflict and 'increase the country's overall electricity supply by building a national power grid', since improving the Kajaki Dam—at the top end of the Helmand Valley, to the immediate north of Sangin District—was a key element of USAID's $5 billion plan.[56] The greater priority given then, rightly, to the more populous areas in central Helmand and Kandahar when determining where to send military forces—including newly trained Afghan National Security Force units—increased the potential value of a political agreement at that time. Kabul's Deputy Minister of energy and water Gulham Faruq Qarizada recognized this opportunity, saying of the conflict around Sangin and Kajaki, 'this isn't al-Qaeda. These are tribes that don't like each other. I would sit down with these tribes and tell them you want to put another turbine in. Everyone will get richer, there will be no battle, and everyone will be happier.'[57] Sangin's District Governor, supported and directed by Provincial Governor Mangal, approached his political outreach against this backdrop.

The period from May to December 2010 focused on confidence building and discussion on the substance of a possible agreement: participation in District Government, cessation of hostilities, and free access to Kajaki, in return for irrigation and flood defences, security guarantees to protect against 2007-style repercussions, and improvements to schools and health services. Water issues also had an important impact on local political dynamics, between the Alikozai and Ishaqzai lands to the south. A network of vital

[53] Magnus Marsden and Benjamin D. Hopkins, *Fragments of the Afghan Frontier* (London: Hurst, 2012), p. 28.

[54] Marsden and Hopkins, *Fragments*, p. 28.

[55] Marsden and Hopkins, *Fragments*, p. 28.

[56] Chandrasekaran, *Little America*, p. 305–6.

[57] Chandrasekaran, *Little America*, p. 306.

irrigation canals began near the villages of Jushalay and Mian Rod in the Upper Sangin Valley, irrigating nearby Alikozai farmland. However, the canals eventually flowed past Sangin town, into the Ishaqzai-controlled Upper Gereshk Valley. Farm yields for the marginalized Ishaqzai therefore depended directly on their local rivals regulating the water flow fairly. They did not, and this triggered a constant rotation of largely Ishaqzai fighters, some Taliban-aligned, into the Sangin Valley, seeking control of the canal nexus, and attempting to disrupt the Alikozai, NATO forces, and the government. As part of the Sangin Accord, the District Governor arbitrated water issues between these rivals, with help from the *mirabs* (stewards of the waterways), showing intent to widen the agreement to include many tribal and political groups, rather than to ally with just one.

In late autumn 2010 US and UK forces operated in Sangin together, temporarily doubling the NATO presence (since the incoming US Marine unit was broadly the same size as the departing British one) supported by additional Afghan National Security Forces. British Commander Lieutenant Colonel Paul James was clear that '[h]aving a battalion of US Marine Corps, on top of a UK Commando battalion, is frankly decisive'.[58] The Provincial and District Governors led a complementary nuanced political approach. In early January 2011 representatives of the Afghan Government, Upper Sangin Valley Taliban leaders, and the local community witnessed the public announcement of the Sangin Accord.[59] 'Under the agreement, the tribal leaders vowed to expel foreign fighters, allow Afghan and U.S. forces to patrol the area, contain Taliban attacks and help identify deadly roadside bombs.... In exchange, American and Afghan leaders are supposed to pump more money into the area.'[60] This included upgrading Route 611, the key road for the Kajaki Dam project. While 'Afghan officials and U.S. diplomats hailed the deal as a sign of how the promised carrot of reconstruction aid could lead to reintegration... Marine officers saw in the change of heart the power of the stick.'[61]

It is perhaps unsurprising for commanders to consider military actions as the dominant motivation for political shifts. Behind the scenes, other complimentary forces were also at work. Since early 2010, the District Governor challenged self-proclaimed power brokers to demonstrate their control over local fighters and IED networks by reducing activity, to build confidence, and

[58] 'Britain stirs clan lords to fight the Taliban', *The Australian*, 14 August 2010, <http://www.theaustralian.com.au/news/world/britain-stirs-clan-lords-to-fight-taliban/story-e6frg6so-1225905055147>.

[59] Zainullah Stanikzai, 'Ceasefire agreed in Sangin', *Pajhwok Afghan News*, 2 January 2011, <http://www.pajhwok.com/en/2011/01/02/ceasefire-agreed-sangin>.

[60] Dion Nissenbaum and Hashim Shukoor, 'U.S. Marines report peace deal with tribe in Afghan hot spot', *McClatchy Newspapers Washington Bureau*, 3 January 2011, <http://www.mcclatchydc.com/2011/01/03/v-print/106135/us-marines-report-peace-deal-with.html>.

[61] Chandrasekaran, *Little America*, p. 283.

validate the credibility of the interlocutors.[62] 'We have been pushing for this for 12 months', said Colonel Paul James, commander of 40 Commando battlegroup, stationed in Sangin. 'The tribes have responded positively. They are certainly not fighting us.'[63] In March 2010 (long before surge forces reached Helmand), the BBC reported '[t]he Taliban Civil Commission, the Taliban's unofficial government in Sangin . . . apparently feels it is not in the movement's interest to attack the reinvigorated bazaar [market place].'[64] Indeed '[v]iolence had started to decline before Western and Afghan forces mounted offensives. . . . From up to 30 Taliban attacks a day at the end of June, there are now fewer than half a dozen raids daily. On July 29 [2010], there were no attacks.'[65] Daoud Ahmadi, a spokesman for the Helmand governor, said several other factors had also contributed to the political shift. 'One was the replacement of government officials in Sangin after a 20-day consultation with tribal leaders, another was growing revulsion with the Taliban's cruelty, such as the hanging in June [2010] of a seven-year-old child accused of spying for the Western forces.'[66] Alongside social and political avenues, combat power (including a blend of static and manoeuvre forces, partnered with Afghans), the impact of operations outside Sangin, and the knowledge of the impending military surge were undoubtedly vital factors.

It is a testament to the bravery and resolve of many Afghan and international personnel alike that some political common ground could be found amidst such an outwardly intractable and violent corner of the world. What evolutions to academic theories on negotiation does this case study suggest? Can it be replicated in future transitions or conflicts, and should it?

The Sangin Accord: a genuine negotiated agreement?

Theoretically, there are three main explanations for the motivation to resolve conflict through negotiation. The first, reconciliation theory, is that the desire to negotiate, and the process of doing so, have a direct impact on conflict. The decisive activities are largely separate from military action, such as contact and communication between the conflict parties or intervention by mediators.[67] The second, negotiation theory, is divided broadly into two schools of thought: one, holds that the key to a successful resolution of conflict lies in

[62] Participant observation by the author, March–July 2010.

[63] 'Britain stirs clan lords to fight the Taliban'.

[64] Mark Urban, 'Newsnight: ingredients making Sangin so lethal', *BBC News*, 8 March 2010, <http://news.bbc.co.uk/1/hi/programmes/newsnight/8555922.stm>.

[65] 'Britain stirs clan lords to fight the Taliban'.

[66] 'Britain stirs clan lords to fight the Taliban'.

[67] For a brief review of this line, see Dean Pruitt, *Whither Ripeness Theory? Working Paper No. 25* (George Mason University: Institute for Conflict Management and Resolution, 2005), p. 38.

the substance of the proposals for a solution; the other holds that the key lies in the timing of efforts for resolution.[68] Those that prioritize substance argue 'parties resolve their conflict by finding an acceptable agreement... through the search for positive sum solutions or encompassing formulas',[69] and so this aligns with reconciliation theory, as social interactions between conflict parties and the mechanisms that facilitate them drive the calculations about legitimacy and genuineness that underpin a negotiated agreement.

The timing debate is dominated by Zartman's ripeness theory, which explains 'why, and therefore when, parties to a conflict are susceptible to their own or others' efforts to turn the conflict toward resolution through negotiation'.[70] The language of ripeness was influential before Zartman developed his theory in 1985. His key article quotes John Campbell's conclusion from the 1954 Trieste treaty negotiations, that 'ripeness of time is one of the absolute essences of diplomacy' and Henry Kissinger, who recognized in 1976 that 'stalemate is the most propitious condition for settlement'.[71] Zartman's definition is time-specific: 'it is the onset of negotiations that are the subject of the theory'.[72] The core theory does not consider the conditions necessary for genuine negotiations to become an effective agreement that leads to future stability. Zartman himself, and others, have sought to address these weaknesses. Despite legitimate criticisms of ripeness theory, it is used here to analyse the Sangin Accord because it makes a direct link between military conditions and the onset of negotiations.

Zartman is clear about the characteristics that define the moment when a conflict is ripe for resolution through negotiation. It is when 'the parties to a conflict (a) perceive themselves to be in a hurting stalemate and (b) perceive the possibility of a negotiated solution (a way out)', simultaneously.[73] The stalemate is a military one specifically, felt when all parties have an 'inability to bear the costs of further escalation'.[74] 'Parties do not have to be able to identify a specific solution, only a sense that a negotiated solution is possible for the searching and that the other party shares that sense and

[68] I. William Zartman, 'Ripeness: the hurting stalemate and beyond', in *Conflict Resolution after the Cold War*, edited by D. Druckman and P. Stern (Washington, DC: National Academy Press, 2000), p. 225. A smaller school 'focuses on relationships between the parties rather than either the substance or the procedure of the issues in conflict' (p. 245).

[69] Zartman, 'Ripeness: the hurting stalemate and beyond', p. 225.

[70] Zartman, 'Ripeness: the hurting stalemate and beyond', p. 228.

[71] John Campbell, *Successful Negotiation: Trieste* (Princeton: Princeton University Press, 1976); M. Golan, *The Secret Conversations of Henry Kissinger* (New York: Bantam, 1974), quoted in I. William Zartman, 'The timing of peace initiatives: Hurting stalemates and ripe moments', *The Global Review of Ethnopolitics* 1, no. 1 (2001): p. 8.

[72] Zartman, 'Ripeness: the hurting stalemate and beyond', p. 227.

[73] Zartman, 'Ripeness: the hurting stalemate and beyond', pp. 228–9.

[74] Zartman, 'Ripeness: the hurting stalemate and beyond', p. 231.

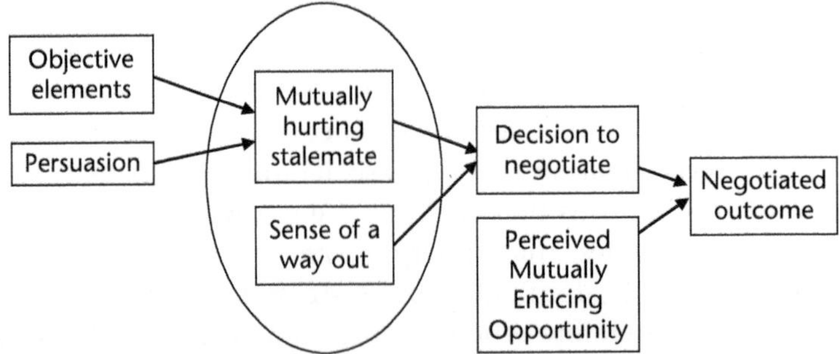

Figure 15.1. Constructing a Ripe Moment (circled) for genuine negotiation to open

the willingness to search too.'[75] Since 'the core of the negotiation process is the transformation of zero-sum attitudes and approaches into positive sum situations and approaches',[76] one of the main perceptual narratives underpinning the Way Out is 'the sense that concessions will be reciprocated, not just banked'.[77] These mutually perceived conditions provide the push into genuine negotiations.

Figure 15.1 shows how negotiation, politics, and military action might interact to create the core components of ripeness theory—the Mutually Hurting Stalemate (MHS) and the Way Out—that together constitute a ripe moment when genuine negotiations may begin.[78]

There are difficulties with Figure 15.1. It does not represent the different conflict parties, or any precursors to a Way Out. It implies there is no interaction between the desire for a political Way Out and perceptions of the factors that establish an MHS (notably the acceptance on all sides that further military escalation is too painful). This is problematic, for example, the conduct of one party's military forces may affect perceptions of their own negotiators, altering an opponents' willingness to consider them genuine partners in a shared Way Out. Nevertheless, the diagram captures Zartman's later formulation that 'negotiations completed under the shadow—or the push—of an MHS alone are likely to be unstable and unlikely to lead to a more enduring settlement. A negative shadow can begin the process but cannot provide for the change of mentalities to reconciliation.'[79] Perhaps stabilization activity could provide the Mutually Enhancing Opportunity (MEO) required to catalyse this necessary 'change of mentalities', balancing the

[75] Zartman, 'The timing of peace initiatives', p. 9.

[76] I. William Zartman and Maureen Berman, *The Practical Negotiator* (New Haven: Yale University Press, 1982), p. 12.

[77] Zartman, 'The Timing of Peace Initiatives', p. 9.

[78] The diagram combines two of Zartman's in 'Ripeness: the hurting stalemate and beyond', pp. 230, 242.

[79] Zartman, 'Ripeness: the hurting stalemate and beyond', p. 242.

coercion of a Mutually Hurting Stalemate. Further research is important, since 'when an MEO is not developed in the negotiations, the negotiations remain truncated and unstable, even if a conflict management agreement to suspend violence is reached'.[80]

Despite these drawbacks, the language of ripeness peppers commentary about the relationship between the military campaign and political progress in Afghanistan. At the time of writing, the status of dialogue involving the Taliban senior leadership remains unclear. In 2010, a source close to alleged talks between them and President Karzai's government indicated they 'are very, very serious about finding a way out'[81] and that 'Taliban representatives are fully authorised to speak for the Quetta Shura and its leader, Mohammad Omar'.[82] In the same year, the UK Parliament's Foreign Affairs Committee discussed Zartman's concepts, considering whether 'negotiations are more likely when you have a stalemate'.[83] It was considered time for 'that first step towards negotiations... trying to build trust between the parties',[84] although 'both sides believe that they can reach a position of greater strength or victory'.[85] These anticipated advantages would indicate the moment was not ripe for negotiation, according to Zartman's theory. This suggests Zartman's hypothesis has not been overtaken conclusively by another theory, and remains useful for explaining when and why genuine negotiation towards sustainable political agreement begins. Nevertheless, at the tactical level of transition, what can ripeness offer the practitioner aiming to promote both legitimacy and negotiated reconciliation, and monitor progress in real time? Druckman and Green's analysis matrix provides a useful starting point (Table 15.1).[86]

For them, 'the particular intersection of relative power and legitimacy defined in cells 6A and 6B (as well as those defined in cells 1A, 1B, 9A, and 9B) is a definition of a ripe moment', at which genuine negotiations could begin—if desired by all parties.[87] This offers a set of conditions for analysts to

[80] Zartman, 'Ripeness: the hurting stalemate and beyond', pp. 242–3.

[81] Karen DeYoung, 'U.S attempts to restart peace talks with the Taliban', *The Washington Post*, 3 February 2013, <http://articles.washingtonpost.com/2013-02-03/world/36728713_1_taliban-negotiators-taliban-office-taliban-leaders>.

[82] 'Time not ripe for peace talks: Pentagon', *Pajhwok Afghan News*, 6 October 2010, <http://www.pajhwok.com/en/2010/10/06/time-not-ripe-peace-talks-pentagon-0>.

[83] United Kingdom Parliament, 'Corrected transcript of oral evidence to the United Kingdom House of Commons Foreign Affairs Committee HC 514-i: The United Kingdom's Foreign Policy towards Afghanistan and Pakistan', 13 October 2010, <http://www.publications.parliament.uk/pa/cm201011/cmselect/cmfaff/514/514.pdf>, p. 216.

[84] United Kingdom Parliament, 'Corrected Transcript of Oral Evidence', p. 216.

[85] United Kingdom Parliament, 'Corrected Transcript of Oral Evidence', p. 216.

[86] Daniel Druckman and Justin Green, 'Playing Two Games: Internal Negotiations in the Philippines', in *Elusive Peace: Negotiating an End to Civil Wars*, edited by I.William Zartman (Washington, DC: The Brookings Institution, 1995), p. 307.

[87] Druckman and Green, 'Playing Two Games', p. 311.

Table 15.1. Relative power and legitimacy conditions under which insurgents and regimes would consider entering into negotiations

Insurgents' relative legitimacy	Relative power (insurgents versus regime)		
	Decreasing	Constant	Increasing
Decreasing	1A—Negotiate	2A—Do not negotiate	3A—Do not negotiate
Constant	4A—Do not negotiate	5A—Do not negotiate	6A—Negotiate
Increasing	7A—Do not negotiate	8A—Negotiate	9A—Negotiate
Insurgents' relative legitimacy	**Relative power (regime versus insurgents)**		
	Increasing	Constant	Decreasing
Increasing	1B—Negotiate	2B—Negotiate	3B—Negotiate
Constant	4B—Negotiate	5B—Negotiate	6B—Negotiate
Decreasing	7B—Do not negotiate	8B—Do not negotiate	9B—Negotiate
Ripe Moments when both sides seek genuine negotiated reconciliation = 1A+1B together, 6A+6B together, 9A+9B together.			

look for in case studies and in real time. Can these theories, developed initially from Cold War scenarios, explain a negotiated agreement brokered at the local level such as the Sangin Accord? Was there evidence of a Mutually Hurting Stalemate and a Way Out as the negotiations that led to the agreement began, including an inability to escalate the conflict? Did zero-sum attitudes evolve towards shared goals? Therefore, were the negotiations focused on genuine conflict resolution, or something else?

The Sangin Accord could not have been made without military force, nor activated without the prospect of a credible security guarantee. Within this framework, two specific strands played important supporting roles for the District Governor's political strategy. First, the overall NATO Commander, General McChrystal, determined key elements of the military approach in Sangin in the run up to the Accord, issuing guidance that 'emphasised the importance of avoiding civilian casualties'.[88] McChrystal's instructions

[88] Weatherill, 'Note from the Field', p. 93.

reduced the military impact on the population's daily life, improving ontological security; the trust people have in the existing social structure based on predictability and stability.[89] It is important to consider that predictability could also relate to life in areas outside NATO control, and so an absence of NATO-led security did not always hinder political evolution. A reduction in disturbance allowed a greater evaluation of life in contrast to Afghan Government controlled areas. Temporary patrols, if resulting in contested residential areas, could divert discussion to the conduct of the international forces rather than the calibre of the Taliban offer. That said, a high tempo of targeted raids 'against narcotic-trafficking and improvised explosive device laboratories impressed locals'[90] and showed that 'ISAF could strike, in a surgical manner, wherever it wanted'.[91] The two tactics in tandem supported political change, when targeted effectively.

Nevertheless, these approaches have little bearing on a theoretical assessment unless it can be shown that they brought about an MHS, perceived by all sides simultaneously. For Zartman, the MHS is founded upon perceptions of intolerable hurt—military casualties—and a belief that negotiation is possible because military escalation is unbearable. This requirement highlights an extreme challenge: practitioners and theoreticians must have sufficient access to determine the psychological perceptions held by all sides in near real time, and the resources to reassess them repeatedly. There is evidence—both objective and anecdotal—that combatants were inflicting hurt upon each other. Yet extensive data to support a retrospective assessment is not available at the time of writing—or perhaps impossible to construct at all—so we cannot say with any certainty that an MHS was present prior to the Sangin Accord announcement.

The same challenge exists for the Way Out. District and Provincial Government, supported by Provincial Reconstruction Team staff and others, were by early 2010 developing a framework of options around which any potential agreement could be structured. These formed the core of the Sangin Accord, conforming to Zartman's expectation that when the time is right, conflict parties 'grab on to proposals that usually have been in the air for a long time and that only now appear attractive'.[92] Developing possible topics for discussion is likely to support a Way Out by focusing minds on common objectives (such as improving public services), but again the theoretical assessment requires analysts to verify a mutually held perception that is virtually impossible to determine in hindsight.

[89] Anthony Giddens, *The Constitution of Society: Outline of the theory of Structuration* (Cambridge: Polity Press, 1986), pp. 50, 375.

[90] Weatherill, 'Note from the Field', p. 94.

[91] Weatherill, 'Note from the Field', p. 94.

[92] Zartman, 'Ripeness: the hurting stalemate and beyond', p. 225.

These challenges diminish the credibility of theory-driven conclusions. The issue is complicated further by opacity about when the negotiations opened, preventing a clear assessment of the presence, or not, of an MHS and a Way Out at that time. Is a community meeting the essential indicator, for example? That does not appear to have happened until December 2010, some seven months after a written offer was received. Assessments of the significance of silence, and indicators signposting transition from informal communication to formal negotiation needed to be tested against reality for 'in Afghanistan, warfare is normally accompanied by direct messaging'[93] occurring 'partly because people across all factions of the insurgency and the government side are related to each other, have common district or tribal ties and know each other well, because many families have members on both sides'.[94] This should allow comparison between a local timeline and the necessary conditions prescribed by ripeness theory.

The military situation in May 2010 had indications of a hurting stalemate for both government and insurgency, given the casualty figures and the resource constraints on escalation at that time. The District Governor had established confidence-building communication channels that could perhaps be termed a Way Out. It is hard to draw strong conclusions, but using the data presented here, ripeness theory would indicate that if formal negotiations opened around that time, they conform to a reasonable degree with Zartman's theoretical requirements. Referring to Table 15.2 (conditions under which insurgents and regimes would consider entering into negotiations), two possible scenarios are credible. First, a mutual boost to legitimacy through negotiation, with a constant power dynamic (8A and 2B), perhaps because of the intersection between Government stabilization offers and military coercion, Alikozai needs after the flooding, and a desire to reduce military pressure. Secondly, an increase in Afghan Government power and legitimacy at the direct expense of the Alikozai Taliban (1A and 1B). Only the latter case would be considered a ripe moment for genuine negotiated conflict resolution for theorists, although both scenarios are viable negotiating opportunities for policy-makers seeking less ambitious objectives through agreement.

Whether or not we can make a judgement about ripeness at the onset of talks, or the long-term significance of the Sangin Accord, it resonated sufficiently to merit a statement by the Taliban movement's spokesman Qārī' Yūsef Aḥmadī. He said,

> the Islamic Emirate of Afghanistan refutes these baseless claims of the enemy. Those media outlets which have published the report or are publishing it now, commit violation of journalistic code.... [The enemy] resorts to disseminating

[93] Kilcullen, 'Measuring progress in Afghanistan', p. 9.
[94] Kilcullen, 'Measuring progress in Afghanistan', p. 9.

> some fatuous and unbelievable reports every day and week, so our astute people and the Mujahideen should not allow the enemy to succeed in these schemes.[95]

If this indicates that the Sangin Accord created some desirable political impact, it is worthwhile to consider whether this case study offers any insights for future scenarios.

Conclusions—negotiated agreements in future tactical transitions

The Sangin Accord case study highlights eight considerations for practitioners and theoreticians considering if a negotiated agreement might support future transitions.

1. How do you, and your organization(s), understand the role negotiation plays in conflict strategy?
2. Why do you want an agreement at all?
3. With whom?
4. What outcome(s) do you seek?
5. Does academic theory support useful policy options (or not), and does your case study evolve academic understanding?
6. How will a negotiation be tracked, and handed over?
7. How can agreements be structured to promote stability, while anticipating turbulence?
8. Implementation matters as much as striking an agreement.

Audit how actors involved in conflict strategy understand negotiation, and address coordination challenges

Does negotiation as a practice (including its precursors, confidence-building communication or dialogue) have an evolutionary impact on conflict, or is a negotiating opportunity a consequence of the success or failure of other conflict strategies? If the former, tight restrictions on communication may inhibit progress (though it is essential to control formal bargaining more than exchanges of views). If the latter, debate focuses on the triggers that signify the time is right for dialogue. Conflict theorists observe that 'negotiation is only

[95] *Jihadology.net*, 'New statement from Qārī' Yūsef Aḥmadī, the spokesman of the Islamic Emirate of Afghanistan: Regarding the Rumors of Ceasefire in Sangin District', 5 January 2011, <http://jihadology.net/2011/01/05/new-statement-from-qari-yusef-a%E1%B8%A5madi-the-spokesman-of-the-islamic-emirate-of-afghanistan-regarding-the-rumors-of-ceasefire-in-sangin-district/>.

one of a family of approaches to the settlement of conflict; the others are domination, capitulation, inaction, withdrawal, and the intervention of third parties'.[96] Perhaps from a natural urge to preserve the reputation and deterrent value of military deployments, negotiated ends to conflicts are often described as Mixed Outcomes, rather than victories.[97] However, definitions of success should move beyond the domination or destruction of an opponent if a campaign is to be assessed by post-transition stability, where social cohesion is best assured by reconciliation through negotiated settlement. Some approaches may be counter-productive to longer-term social objectives if they generate new grievances (or exacerbate old ones) that the post-transition government cannot manage effectively. Economic issues (including those associated with stabilization projects) may affect the co-option of groups into a wider political tapestry as 'greed-based conflicts seek the continuation of war as an avenue to self-enrichment'.[98]

Determine why a negotiated agreement is desirable, and to whom

Not all offers of dialogue or negotiation are serious, or genuine. The desire for military objectives such as 'a tactical interlude, a breather for rest and rearmament'[99] may explain offers of dialogue. They may be 'a sop to external pressure, without any intent of opening a sincere search for a joint outcome'.[100] Questions over sincerity need not curtail negotiation, but perhaps should moderate the terms of discussion. Negotiated agreements based on unequal or one-sided concessions remain policy options for conflict management (but not, for theorists, conflict resolution), if the goal is the temporary 'elimination, neutralization, or control of the means of pursuing either the conflict or the crisis' rather than resolution of the underlying conflict drivers.[101] If ripeness theorists is correct, acting to bring about an MHS and a Way Out can transform motivations, since 'a sense of ripeness may . . . turn negotiations for side effects into negotiations to resolve conflict'.[102] Afghan

[96] Jeffrey Rubin, Dean Pruitt, and Sung H. Kim, *Social Conflict: Escalation, Stalemate, and Settlement*, 2nd edn (New York: McGraw-Hill, 1994), quoted in I. William Zartman, 'The Structuralist Dilemma in Negotiation', *Research Group in International Security*, January 1997, <http://id.cdint.org/content/documents/The_Structuralist_Dilemma_in_Negotiation.pdf>.

[97] For example, Ben Connable and Martin Libicki, *How Insurgencies End* (RAND National Defense Research Institute, 2010), <http://www.rand.org/content/dam/rand/pubs/monographs/2010/RAND_MG965.pdf>.

[98] Cynthian Arnson, 'The political economy of war' in *Rethinking the Economics of War: The Intersection of Need, Creed, and Greed*, edited by Cynthia Arnson and I. William Zartman (Baltimore: Johns Hopkins University Press, 2005), p. 11.

[99] Zartman, 'Ripeness: the hurting stalemate and beyond', p. 227.

[100] Zartman, 'Ripeness: the hurting stalemate and beyond', p. 227.

[101] I. William Zartman, *Ripe for resolution: Conflict resolution in* Africa, 2nd edn (New York: Oxford University Press, 1989), p. 8.

[102] Zartman, 'Ripeness: the hurting stalemate and beyond', p. 227.

efforts to build the relationships that led to the Sangin Accord focused initially on renovating the shrine at Garm Ab, in the north of the District, believed to heal the body and wash away sin,[103] turning only to security and reconciliation months later, when credibility and confidence allowed. The intent to move from conflict management into genuine resolution should also be signalled clearly, and events that may make these shifts more likely should be tracked (see point 6 discussed under 'How will negotiations be tracked and handed over?'). Populations who do not feel secure, or have reason to doubt the credibility of their interlocutors may hedge their bets and pursue multiple strategies, for entirely rational reasons. In such circumstances, confidence-building measures must be specific and verifiable without requiring a public change of allegiance as this draws reprisals before a political shift is likely. At a particular point in a transition, this capacity to corroborate credibility may not be available, which risks manipulation.

Analyse negotiating partners, assuming multi-polar identity and structure unless shown otherwise

It would be wrong to apply any universal distinction between 'local' and 'foreign' opponents. Interviewees confirm that Sangin's Alikozai were involved in attacks on NATO forces and active in the narcotics trade even while pursuing negotiations with the Afghan Government.[104] There may be few visible distinguishing identifiers visible to combat personnel. Nevertheless, in the context of political progress there is an 'extremely important difference between insurgents who originate from villages within the same district where they fight (local guerrillas) and insurgents who fight outside their district-of-origin'[105] because locals 'represent key members of society the international presence is trying to stabilize'.[106] Considering the Sangin Accord, the 'Taliban' side, actually included at least five overlapping elements, few of which were in the District regularly, and some of whom negotiated with each other. These were: local Alikozai; at least two local groups, rivals of the Alikozai, who fought them and the Afghan Government; 'foreign' Taliban appointees based in Sangin; exiled leaders in Lashkar Gah and other urban centres, including in Pakistan; and finally Taliban Provincial and Quetta Shura

[103] Interviews with Sangin Alikozai and Ishaqzai, Subjects 1, 4, and 7, 2012. With thanks and acknowledgement to Professors Antonio Giustozzi and Theo Farrell, who provided all interviews with Taliban members and Sangin residents from field research conducted in 2012 and 2013.

[104] Multiple confirmations in interview transcripts shared by Professors Antonio Giustozzi and Theo Farrell, from field research conducted in 2012 and 2013.

[105] Kilcullen, 'Measuring progress in Afghanistan', p. 28.

[106] Kilcullen, 'Measuring progress in Afghanistan', p. 28. Kilcullen addresses his advice primarily to military commanders, but I have replaced his term 'unit' with 'international presence' to reflect the civilian–military team present in Sangin.

members. This 'hedging of one's bets, in identity, location, profession... is a powerful warning to anyone operating with policies or data collection and categorisation mechanisms that do not allow this plurality'.[107] This adds another level of complexity for practitioners, and increases dependence on local expertise. So, allocation of responsibility for politics according to District administrative boundaries risks diluting capacity to resolve multi-faceted social grievances.

Decide acceptable compromises that support post-transition leaders

American Secretary of State George Shultz wrote, 'the success of negotiations is attributable not to a particular procedure chosen but to the readiness of the parties to exploit opportunities, confront hard choices, and make fair and mutual concessions'.[108] There is an important semantic element here. It is essential to determine whether you have the capacity and backing to take actions *that the other side(s) perceives to be concessions*—it is not essential that you do. This matters, because 'if parties that perceive themselves to be of equal power and the negotiators share a cooperative motivational orientation, the more effectively they are likely to function', compared to competitive approaches.[109] 'By giving a sense of equality to the weaker' they will be 'less impelled to seek compensating advantages in other, more disruptive ways'.[110] These types of strategies require careful explanation and handling, as there is a risk that audiences recognize negotiated outcomes differently. The domestic narrative is especially important, and complex.[111]

Control and oversight of negotiation—especially during transition from an international presence to a supported government—remains a critical area for study and training, as doctrine is clear:

> where the host nation government is functioning it is essential that intervening headquarters work effectively with the agencies of the host nation in order to develop and implement politically acceptable and culturally appropriate settlement. The host nation should be encouraged to take 'ownership' of such

107 Mark Beautement, 'Review: Fragments of the Afghan Frontier', *e-International Relations*, 16 May 2012, <http://www.e-ir.info/2012/05/16/review-fragments-of-the-afghan-frontier/>.

108 US Secretary of State George Shultz quoted in Zartman, 'Ripeness: the hurting stalemate and beyond', p. 226.

109 I. William Zartman and Jeffrey Z. Rubin, eds, *Power and Negotiation* (Ann Arbor: University of Michigan Press, 2002), p. 18.

110 Zartman and Rubin, *Power and Negotiation*, p. 289.

111 For example Mark Beautement, 'We're winning sir, we just don't believe it yet: public perception and modern military operations', in *Comparative Perspectives on Civil-Military relations in conflict zones*, edited by M. Williams and K. Clouston (RUSI Occasional Paper, 2006), <http://www.rusi.org/downloads/assets/Cusps_Report.pdf>.

settlements as part of the process of winning the consent of the people. The planning of transitions should reflect this.[112]

This implies a counter-argument, that where the host government is not working, settlements may be best avoided, unless there is a temporary conflict management imperative—or unless the settlement improves governance, perhaps through the wholesale co-option of respected and capable opponents.

Consider theory, use it, but do not be bound unnecessarily

Ripeness and other negotiation theories suggest triggers for analysts to monitor. The MHS is 'optimally associated with an impending, past, or recently avoided catastrophe' because this sharpens the perceptual awareness of the pain that is associated with defeat.[113] The failed uprising in 2007 could satisfy this definition for Sangin's Alikozai, as could the Taliban's failure to address local concerns after the spring 2010 floods. Positive progress after the change in Afghan Government District Governor, and two changes in Taliban Shadow Governor, 'suggests that a change in leadership is often needed to pull away from failed policies'.[114] The uprising, the flooding, high-impact military targeting, or the announcement of the NATO surge, prompted 'a return to rationality when a sudden striking event—a "shock"—jolts the mind and stimulates rethinking'.[115] These factors could also support Druckman and Green's reformulation of ripeness to include a 'stalemate... on the level of legitimacy... in addition to the more dynamically evolving stalemate on the level of power'.[116]

As originally conceived, the requirement in Zartman's theory for both sides to perceive a military stalemate creates problems for explaining how a military force that considers itself dominant can support a genuine negotiated political reconciliation. Later evolutions of ripeness theory, such as Dean Pruitt's readiness theory,[117] can offer scenarios in which the stalemate felt by each party could be constructed from a wide range of differing military and non-military stabilization calculations, for example on security, public service delivery, the credibility of leaders and elites, economics, or political power. The very act of dialogue, or offer of it, could establish a political equilibrium if the opposition's power advantage depended on isolating a community through intimidation.

112 British Army, *Field Manual Vol. 1. Part 10 Countering Insurgency*, para. 7–5.

113 Zartman, 'Ripeness: the hurting stalemate and beyond', p. 228.

114 Lieberfeld (1999); Mitchell (2000); Stedman (1991) quoted in Pruitt, *Whither Ripeness Theory?*, p. 4.

115 Bercovitch, Diehl, and Goertz, (1997); Mitchell (2000) quoted in Pruitt, *Whither Ripeness Theory?*, p. 4.

116 Druckman and Green (1995), quoted in Zartman, 'Ripeness: the hurting stalemate and beyond', p. 236.

117 Pruitt, *Whither Ripeness Theory?*, p. 7.

How will negotiations be tracked and handed over?

Practitioners should consider dynamic transition as normal, rather than a special event at the end of intervention: priorities will change. These events can also change the conditions for a future agreement.

Consistency, informed by institutional memory, is essential. What you (and your organization) promised and what is delivered are linked directly to the credibility required simply to reach credible representatives for negotiation. As US Marine Corps General Larry Nicholson said so appositely, 'you can surge troops and equipment, but you can't surge trust. That has to be earned.'[118] US doctrine sets high expectations for the Political Officer here, requiring them to 'influence and inform the perceptions, allegiances, attitudes, actions, and behaviours of all principal participants in the Area of Operation, and in the regional, international and domestic audiences as well'.[119] Strong political strategy rests on a shared vision that meets local and international objectives, and contains credible elements that can be sustained after transition for 'it is through an approach which seeks to unify essentially voluntary efforts that political primacy is achieved'.[120]

Mediation may take time to moderate conflict significantly—typically 8–12 months—and may increase conflict in the short term.[121] However, once a decision has been taken for a negotiation to support transition, the stability of the agreement requires changes in the military approach. When, and how, civilian and then local officials leading negotiation influence this is a critical area for training and study.

> In the summer of 2011, a leak revealed that CIA analysts had assessed the state of the war, district by district, and reached the conclusion that it was stalemated. But their view was countered by General David Petraeus, the outgoing US commander in Afghanistan, as well as General John Allen, who was taking over from him. They each added a note to the CIA report to say they disagreed with the intelligence agency's findings.[122]

[118] Rajiv Chandrasekaran, 'In Afghanistan's Garmser district, praise for a U.S. official's tireless work', *Washington Post*, 14 August 2011, <http://www.washingtonpost.com/world/national-security/in-afghanistans-garmser-district-praise-for-a-us-officials-tireless-work/2011/07/29/gIQA2CcODJ_story.html>. US doctrine refers to this role as the Political Advisor, but the UK used Political Officer (POLO), perhaps to avoid confusion with the UK's Policy Advisors (POLADs) deployed into headquarters staffs to work for military commanders, largely on defence policy issues. The General commended Carter Malkasian, the Provincial Reconstruction Team's District Political Officer for Garmser in Helmand.

[119] British Army, *Field Manual Vol 1. Part 10 Countering Insurgency*, para. 4–4.

[120] British Army, *Field Manual Vol 1. Part 10 Countering Insurgency*, para. 3–5.

[121] Philip A. Schrodt, Ömür Yilmaz, and Deborah J. Gerner, *Evaluating 'Ripeness' and 'Hurting Stalemate' in Mediated International Conflicts: An Event Data Study of the Middle East, Balkans, and West Africa* (Center for International Political Analysis: University of Kansas, 2003), pp. 10–12.

[122] David Ignatius quoted in Jonathan Steele, 'A tale of two retreats: Afghan transition in historical perspective', *Central Asian Survey* 32, no. 3 (2013): p. 311.

Disagreements can be problematic, even before prioritizing the views of the host nation. It is particularly important that policy describes when communication with other parties is permitted, and that a distinction is considered between informal dialogue and exploratory discussion, and formal bargaining and negotiation over specific conditions.

Plan for turbulent transitions, ensuring negotiations promote social cohesion

As the concentration of military force is diluted by withdrawal, some may use violence to re-open the struggle for social and political pre-eminence. Ecologist Eric Berlow applied his complexity modelling theories and software to the NATO campaign strategy for Afghanistan. Demonstrating novel network analysis, he showed that most critical actions to influence popular support for the government are non-violent and fall into two broad categories, 'active engagement with ethnic rivalries and religious beliefs, and fair, transparent economic development and provisioning of services.... Others are non-actionable (like the harshness of the terrain), and a small minority are military.'[123] These actions are rooted in regular, effective communication that repairs communities and engages populations detached from central government. This is essential since 'the collapse of social cohesion is the Taliban's most powerful enabler. And their operations and methods are deliberately designed to exacerbate it'.[124] Practitioners should consider the distinction between a formal negotiating process and communication that fosters this social strength, improving the reach of any agreement. If outreach evolves into a negotiation, theorists have some lessons for the structure and scope of an agreement.

Derouen, Lea, and Wallensteen have analysed the duration of civil war peace agreements and conclude that, '[l]ess costly concessions by government of military integration and autonomy increase the duration of peace agreements'.[125] Caroline Hartzell has considered the stability of agreements in intrastate wars, and shows that while 'destroying opposing groups' organizations has little effect on the duration of the peace, an agreement among rivals to share power can help prolong the peace'.[126] Nevertheless, eliminating sanctuaries that give active support remains central, when seeking a solution

[123] Eric Berlow, 'Simplifying complexity' [online video], *TED*, July 2010, <http://www.ted.com/talks/eric_berlow_how_complexity_leads_to_simplicity.html>.

[124] Lieutenant Colonel Christopher Kolenda, 'Winning Afghanistan at the community level: A rejoinder to Volney F. Warner and "C"', *Joint Force Quarterly* 56 (2010): p. 27.

[125] Karl Derouen, Jenna Lea, and Peter Wallensteen, 'The duration of civil war peace agreements', *Conflict Management and Peace Science* 26, no. 4 (2009): p. 367.

[126] Caroline Hartzell, 'Explaining the stability of negotiated settlements to intrastate wars', *Journal of Conflict Resolution* 43, no. 1 (1999): p. 3; Caroline Hartzell, 'Settling civil wars: Armed

within defined boundaries.[127] Transitions in military approach therefore underpin negotiating progress, say from 'kill or capture', to coercion, to the provision of security guarantees for opponents susceptible to co-option, or to semi-autonomy, power-sharing, or integration. These mirror the evolution in mindset ripeness theory anticipates, from zero-sum coercion to mutually enticing opportunity, and require military organizations—and those that comment on their achievements—to consider a shared outcome as a success.

Prioritize effective implementation, and make promises you can keep

While ripeness theory concentrates on the conditions present at the opening of negotiations, getting the politics around negotiated agreements right includes at least four stages: (1) pre-negotiation and credibility building to prepare for negotiation; (2) striking an agreement, usually formally; (3) communicating the pledges, and implementing the provisions of the deal; (4) managing the consequences, and evolving it when required.

Retaining a record of promises made by individuals, and organizations, is an excellent way of tracking credibility risks. Different cultures accord varying respect to positions of authority, or the conduct of the individual—regardless of their office. This appears to apply after agreements have been made, especially over military provisions. Hoddie and Hartzell showed that 'peace proved durable in seven of the eight cases in which post-civil war states with agreements requiring military measures fully implemented this aspect'.[128] Establishing sunset clauses, or expiry dates to specific proposals or whole agreements can also apply pressure. 'The Dayton peace talks ended well because [US negotiator Richard] Holbrooke gave the Bosnian Muslims an ultimatum: If you don't sign the agreement in one hour, we close the talks down for good.'[129] They also offer re-negotiation opportunities that head off violent responses to changing power relationships. 'Some of the most stable civil war settlements were preceded by a rapid succession of agreements. For example, there were seven agreements in El Salvador and 14 in Guatemala within a very short period.'[130]

opponents' fates and the duration of the peace', *Conflict Management and Peace Science* 26, no. 4 (2009): p. 347.

[127] Connable, *How Insurgencencies End*, pp. 34–5.

[128] Matthew Hoddie and Caroline Hartzell, 'Civil War Settlements and the Implementation of Military Power-Sharing Arrangements', *Journal of Peace Research* 40, no. 3 (2003): p. 313.

[129] Stephen Sestanovich, 'What would Richard Holbrooke do?', *Politico Magazine*, 9 December 2013, <http://www.politico.com/magazine/story/2013/12/what-would-richard-holbrooke-do-100879_Page2.html>.

[130] Derouen et al., 'The duration of civil war peace agreements', p. 371.

Final thoughts

Effective implementation requires sustained unity of purpose and consistency of method. Political analysis focused on negotiated conflict resolution should also consider a social trajectory, extending beyond military intervention. The past gives context to grievance, explaining who may lose and gain—and how they may resist—if military intervention crystalizes power relations at a particular point. Field research shows, for example, that Upper Sangin Valley elders recognized that Ishaqzai residents held land titles to the contested village of Jushalay, but Alikozai Mujahedeen used that canal area to repel Soviet tanks, and simply did not withdraw. It is perhaps unsurprising that 30 years later people who felt disenfranchised fought those who had the capacity to right a perceived wrong, but appeared to support its permanence. It is a peculiar threat to large organizations, that people can consider all actions as deliberate, based on perfect institutional memory. 'You've been coming here for 200 years,' said Sangin elders in 2010—how can you not remember who everyone is?'[131]

Post-transition stability relies on functioning relationships between local political and military officials. As the foreign presence steps back, will the political representative be able to lead reconciliation by harnessing a range of military and civil resources? The co-opting of communities wholesale may require a proven security guarantee, independent from international forces. The alignment of interests is undoubtedly helped by clear, local aspirations for territorial control and a degree of semi-autonomy. Though this chapter has made much of tribal labels, I would counsel against any single-identity categorization. Yet, in this case the ancient historical ties to definable territory dominated by one group (that need not be tribally-determined in future) offers a strong overlap between Western and local conceptualizations of power and interest, focused on physical geography. There are 'many paths up the mountain',[132] and so it is not wise to assert universal theories specifying how or when negotiations should be used in transitions. However, the Sangin Accord highlights five points to consider in future.

1. Generating and sustaining the option for agreement (and then seeing benefits) requires significant time—often longer than military and development strategies.
2. Communication aligns understanding and interests essential for formal bargaining; this exploratory work need not depend on military advantage.

[131] Heard repeatedly by the author during participant observation between 2009 and 2010.

[132] Nathan Springer, 'Many paths up the mountain: Population-centric COIN in Afghanistan', *Small Wars Journal* (2010), <http://smallwarsjournal.com/blog/journal/docs-temp/443-springer.pdf>.

Figure 15.2. Sangin District Governor Faisal Haq conducts a *shura* (council meeting) in 2009. UK Provincial Reconstruction Team Stabilisation Advisor Phil Weatherill looks on. Photo: Eros Hoagland

Figure 15.3. The Sangin Valley from the air, looking northwards, date unknown. The Kajaki Road (Route 611) is clearly visible to the right, with the population living mostly in the thin fertile strip between the highway and the Helmand River. The western tip of the larger, prominent range of hills marks the northern most point of the District, and the site of the important shrine at Garm Ab. Photo: Crown copyright 2010

Figure 15.4. The Upper Sangin Valley looking southwards from the Kajaki Dam, date unknown. The impact of irrigation on the landscape is shown perfectly by the contrasting colours of the terrain either side of the Kajaki Road. Land and water access were heavily contested at times. Photo: Crown copyright 2010

3. Local conflict drivers, relationships, and implementation are critical to wider strategy, especially if local solutions do not cascade from top-level engagement.
4. Negotiation should be about conflict resolution; but unequal or temporary agreements to manage conflict remain policy options.
5. Partisan approaches to conflict and relationship-building may inhibit wider stability, where a patchwork of polarizing agreements cannot be aggregated.

These are intensely detailed and complex issues, and understanding them socially, politically, and linguistically requires an enormous amount of effort. It is therefore beholden upon policy-makers to consider very carefully before undertaking a negotiation especially at the local level. Even if an opportunity exists to strike a deal, not taking it remains a legitimate choice. If reconciliation through negotiation is sought, however, political work focused on long-term stability should support arbitration and stabilization by creating agreements than can be aggregated together. Developing relationships with narrow sections of a society may breed segregation and inflammatory advantage between communities that are supposed to reconcile with themselves, threatening stability before and after international political, development, and military actors transition control and depart.[133]

[133] Mark Beautement, 'Peace in whose time? Ripeness and the Sangin Accord, Helmand Province, Afghanistan, 2006–2011', forthcoming PhD thesis (King's College London, 2014).

Figure 15.5. British and American forces plan combined operations, 2010. Lieutenant Colonel Paul James (Royal Marines) explains the lie of the land in Sangin to incoming United States Marine Corps personnel, in August 2010. Together, they designed the combined operations that preceded the Sangin Accord. Photo: Mark Beautement

Figure 15.6. The Sangin District Council deliberates on the business of the day, Winter 2009. Sitting left to right: Mayor, NDS, elder, Police, District Governor, UK battlegroup commander Lieutenant Colonel Nick Kitson (3 RIFLES). Off camera: Stabilisation Advisor Phil Weatherill, Political Officer Mark Beautement, interpreters. Photo: Mark Beautement

THE TIMES
Afghanistan

News | Opinion | Business | Money | Sport | Life | Arts | Puzzles | Papers

Afghan tribal elders promise to stop attacks on troops in Sangin

Article | Graphic

Jerome Starkey Kabul
Last updated January 4 2011 12:01AM

American and Afghan officials claim to have brokered a landmark peace deal in Sangin, the town in central Helmand which has been the location of almost a third of Britain's Afghan fatalities.

Members from the Taliban after voluntarily handing over their weapons and joining the government in Sangin district of Helmand

Figure 15.7. *The Times* newspaper announces the Sangin Accord, 4 January 2011. Jerome Starkey's article in *The Times* covering Helmand Provincial Governor Gulab Mangal's public announcement of the Sangin Accord, 4 January 2011. Image from a screen capture: <http://www.thetimes.co.uk/tto/news/world/asia/afghanistan/article2861680.ece>.

References

'Afghan peace jirga backs Karzai Taliban talks proposal', *BBC News*, 4 June 2010, <http://www.bbc.co.uk/news/10234823>.

'Afghanistan: Sangin insurgents agree to stand up to Taliban', *The Telegraph*, 4 January 2011, <http://www.telegraph.co.uk/news/worldnews/asia/afghanistan/8238031/Afghanistan-Sangin-insurgents-agree-to-stand-up-to-Taliban.html>.

Arnson, Cynthia, 'The political economy of war', in *Rethinking the Economics of War: The Intersection of Need, Creed, and Greed*, edited by Cynthia Arnson and I. William Zartman (Johns Hopkins University Press: Baltimore, 2005), pp. 1–22.

Autesserre, Séverine, *The Trouble with the Congo: Local Violence and the Failure of International Peacebuilding* (New York: Cambridge University Press, 2010).

Barfield, Thomas, *Afghanistan: A Cultural and Political History* (Oxford: Princeton University Press, 2010).

Beautement, Mark, 'Peace in Whose Time? Ripeness and the Sangin Accord, Helmand Province, Afghanistan, 2006–2011', forthcoming Ph.D thesis (King's College London, 2014).

Beautement, Mark, 'Review: Fragments of the Afghan frontier', *e-International Relations*, 16 May 2012, <http://www.e-ir.info/2012/05/16/review-fragments-of-the-afghan-frontier/>.

Beautement, Mark, 'We're winning sir, we just don't believe it yet: public perception and modern military operations', in *Comparative Perspectives on Civil-Military relations in conflict zones*, edited by M. Williams and K. Clouston (RUSI Occasional Paper, 2006), <http://www.rusi.org/downloads/assets/Cusps_Report.pdf>.

Berlow, Eric, 'Simplifying Complexity' [online video], *TED*, July 2010, <http://www.ted.com/talks/eric_berlow_how_complexity_leads_to_simplicity.html>.

Bishop, Patrick, *3 PARA* (London: HarperPress 2007).

'Bomb explosion "kills Afghan MP"', *BBC News*, 19 March 2009, <http://news.bbc.co.uk/1/hi/world/americas/7952333.stm>.

Braithwaite, Rodric, *Afghantsy: The Russians in Afghanistan 1979–1989* (London: Profile Books, 2011).

'Britain stirs clan lords to fight the Taliban', *The Australian*, 14 August 2010, <http://www.theaustralian.com.au/news/world/britain-stirs-clan-lords-to-fight-taliban/storye6frg6so-1225905055147>.

British Army, *Field Manual Vol. 1. Part 10 Countering Insurgency* (London: The Stationery Office, October 2009).

Campbell, John, *Successful Negotiation: Trieste* (Princeton: Princeton University Press, 1976).

Chandrasekaran, Rajiv, 'In Afghanistan's Garmser district, praise for a U.S. official's tireless work', *Washington Post*, 14 August 2011, <http://www.washingtonpost.com/world/national-security/in-afghanistans-garmser-district-praise-for-a-us-officials-tireless-work/2011/07/29/gIQA2CcODJ_story.html>.

Chandrasekaran, Rajiv, *Little America, The War within the War for Afghanistan* (London: Bloomsbury, 2012).

Chesterman, Simon, 'Transitional administration, state-building and the United Nations', in *Making States Work: State failure and the crisis of government*, edited by Simon Chesterman, Michael Ignatieff, and Ramesh Thakur (New York: United Nations University Press, 2005), pp. 339–58.

Clarke, Michael, ed., *The Afghan Papers: Committing Britain to War in Helmand 2005–06*, Whitehall Paper 77 (London: RUSI, 2011).

Coghlan, Tom, 'The Taliban in Helmand: an oral history', in *Decoding the New Taliban*, edited by Antonio Giustozzi (London: Hurst, 2009), pp. 119–53.

Connable, Ben and Martin Libicki, *How Insurgencies End* (RAND National Defense Research Institute, 2010), <http://www.rand.org/content/dam/rand/pubs/monographs/2010/RAND_MG965.pdf>.

Derouen, Karl, Jenna Lea, and Peter Wallensteen, 'The duration of civil war peace agreements', *Conflict Management and Peace Science* 26, no. 4 (2009): pp. 367–87.

DeYoung, Karen, 'U.S attempts to restart peace talks with the Taliban', *The Washington Post*, 3 February 2013, <http://articles.washingtonpost.com/2013-02-03/world/36728713_1_taliban-negotiators-taliban-office-taliban-leaders>.

Druckman, Daniel and Justin Green, 'Playing two games: Internal negotiations in the Philippines', in *Elusive Peace: Negotiating an End to Civil Wars*, edited by I. W. Zartman (Washington, DC: The Brookings Institution, 1995), pp. 299–331.

Fall, Bernard, 'The theory and practice of insurgency and counterinsurgency', *Naval War College Review* 17, no. 8 (1965): pp. 21–38.

Giddens, Anthony, *The Constitution of Society: Outline of the theory of Structuration* (Cambridge: Polity Press, 1986).

Hartzell, Caroline, 'Explaining the stability of negotiated settlements to intrastate wars', *Journal of Conflict Resolution* 43, no. 1 (1999): pp. 3–22.

Hartzell, Caroline, 'Settling civil wars: Armed opponents' fates and the duration of the peace', *Conflict Management and Peace Science* 26, no. 4 (2009): pp. 347–65.

Hoddie, Matthew and Caroline Hartzell, 'Civil war settlements and the implementation of military power-sharing arrangements', *Journal of Peace Research* 40, no. 3 (2003): pp. 303–20.

Jihadology.net, 'New statement from Qārī' Yūsef Aḥmadī, the spokesman of the Islamic Emirate of Afghanistan: Regarding the Rumors of Ceasefire in Sangin District', 5 January 2011, <http://jihadology.net/2011/01/05/new-statement-from-qari-yusef-a%E1%B8%A5madi-the-spokesman-of-the-islamic-emirate-of-afghanistan-regarding-the-rumors-of-ceasefire-in-sangin-district/>.

Johnson, Robert, '*Mizh der beitabora khalqi-i*': A comparative study of Afghan-Pashtun perspectives on negotiating with the British and the Soviets, 1839–1989', *Journal of Imperial and Commonwealth History* 39, no. 4 (November 2011): pp. 551–70.

Johnson, Thomas H. and Matthew C. DuPee, 'Analysing the new Taliban Code of Conduct (Layeha): an assessment of changing perspectives and strategies of the Afghan Taliban', *Central Asian Survey* 31, no. 1 (2012): pp. 77–91.

Jones, Seth and Arturo Munoz, 'Afghanistan's Local War: Building Local Defense Forces' (Santa Monica: RAND Corporation, 2010), <http://www.rand.org/pubs/monographs/MG1002.html>.

Kilcullen, David, 'Measuring Progress in Afghanistan', 2009, <http://literature-index.wikispaces.com/file/view/Kilcullen-COIN+Metrics.pdf>.

Kolenda, Lieutenant Colonel Christopher, 'Winning Afghanistan at the community level: A rejoinder to Volney F. Warner and "C"', *Joint Force Quarterly* 56 (2010): pp. 25–31.

MacAskill, Euan, 'US claims to have driven Taliban out of Sangin', *The Guardian*, 8 March 2011, <http://www.guardian.co.uk/world/2011/mar/08/us-afghanistan-sangin-taliban-claim>.

Marsden, Magnus and Benjamin D. Hopkins, *Fragments of the Afghan Frontier* (London: Hurst, 2012).

Martin, Mike, *A Brief History of Helmand* (Warminster: British Army, 2011).

Nissenbaum, Dion and Hashim Shukoor, 'U.S. Marines report peace deal with tribe in Afghan hot spot', *McClatchy Newspapers Washington Bureau*, 3 January 2011, <http://www.mcclatchydc.com/2011/01/03/v-print/106135/us-marines-report-peace-deal-with.html>.

Pannell, Ian, 'UK troops leave Helmand's Sangin', *BBC News*, 20 September 2010, <http://www.bbc.co.uk/news/uk-11367931>.

Pruitt, Dean, *Whither Ripeness Theory? Working Paper No. 25* (George Mason University: Institute for Conflict Management and Resolution, 2005).

Saunders, Harold H., 'We need a larger theory of negotiation: The importance of pre-negotiation phases', *Negotiation Journal* 1, no. 3 (1985): pp. 249–62.

Schrodt, Philip A., Ömür Yilmaz, and Deborah J. Gerner, *Evaluating 'Ripeness' and 'Hurting Stalemate' in Mediated International Conflicts: An Event Data Study of the Middle East, Balkans, and West Africa* (Center for International Political Analysis: University of Kansas, 2003).

Semple, Michael, *Reconciliation in Afghanistan* (Washington, DC: United States Institute of Peace, 2009).

Sestanovich, Stephen, 'What would Richard Holbrooke do?', *Politico Magazine*, 9 December 2013, <http://www.politico.com/magazine/story/2013/12/what-would-richard-holbrooke-do-100879_Page2.html>.

Simpson, Emile, *War from the Ground Up: Twenty-First-Century Combat as Politics* (London: Hurst, 2012).

Springer, Maj. Nathan, 'Many paths up the mountain: Population-centric COIN in Afghanistan', *Small Wars Journal* (2010), <http://smallwarsjournal.com/blog/journal/docs-temp/443-springer.pdf>.

Stanikzai, Zainullah, 'Ceasefire agreed in Sangin', *Pajhwok Afghan News*, 2 January 2011, <http://www.pajhwok.com/en/2011/01/02/ceasefire-agreed-sangin>.

Steele, Jonathan, 'A tale of two retreats: Afghan transition in historical perspective', *Central Asian Survey* 32, no. 3 (2013): pp. 306–17.

Tariq, Mohammed O., 'Tribal Security System (*Arbakai*) in Southeast Afghanistan', Crisis States Occasional Paper No. 7 (London: Crisis States Research Centre, 2008).

'Time not ripe for peace talks: Pentagon', *Pajhwok Afghan News*, 6 October 2010, <http://www.pajhwok.com/en/2010/10/06/time-not-ripe-peace-talks-pentagon-0>.

United Kingdom Parliament, 'Corrected Transcript of Oral Evidence to the United Kingdom House of Commons Foreign Affairs Committee HC 514-i: The United Kingdom's Foreign Policy towards Afghanistan and Pakistan', 13 October 2010, <http://www.publications.parliament.uk/pa/cm201011/cmselect/cmfaff/514/514.pdf>.

Urban, Mark, 'Newsnight: ingredients making Sangin so lethal', *BBC News*, 8 March 2010, <http://news.bbc.co.uk/1/hi/programmes/newsnight/8555922.stm>.

USAID Afghanistan, 'Hilmand Food Zone Project', 2013, <http://afghanistan.usaid.gov/en/USAID/Activity/255/Hilmand_Food_Zone_Project_HFZP>.

US Army, *Field Manual 3–24: Counterinsurgency* (Washington, DC: Department of the Army, 2006).

Watts, Stephen, Caroline Baxter, Molly Dunigan, and Christopher Rizzi, *The Uses and Limitations of Small-scale Military Interventions* (Santa Monica: RAND Corporation, 2012).

Weatherill, Phil, 'Note from the Field: Targeting the centre of gravity—adapting stabilisation in Sangin', *RUSI Journal* 156, no. 4 (2011): pp. 90–8.

Williams, Mike, 'How the British presence in Sangin restored trust in government', *The Guardian*, 20 September 2010, <http://www.guardian.co.uk/commentisfree/2010/sep/20/british-forces-in-sangin>.

Zartman, I. William, ed., *Elusive Peace: Negotiating an End to Civil Wars* (Washington, DC: The Brookings Institution, 1995).

Zartman, I. William, *Ripe for resolution: Conflict resolution in* Africa, 2nd edn (New York: Oxford University Press, 1989).

Zartman, I. William, 'Ripeness: the hurting stalemate and beyond', in *Conflict Resolution after the Cold War*, edited by D. Druckman and P. Stern (Washington, DC: National Academy Press, 2000), pp. 225–50.

Zartman, I. William, 'The Structuralist Dilemma in Negotiation', *Research Group in International Security*, January 1997, <http://id.cdint.org/content/documents/The_Structuralist_Dilemma_in_Negotiation.pdf>.

Zartman, I. William, 'The timing of peace initiatives: Hurting stalemates and ripe moments', *The Global Review of Ethnopolitics* 1, no. 1 (2001): pp. 8–18.

Zartman, I. William and Maureen Berman, *The Practical Negotiator* (New Haven: Yale University Press, 1982).

Zartman, I. William and Jeffrey Z. Rubin, eds, *Power and Negotiation* (Ann Arbor: University of Michigan Press, 2002).

16

Local and tactical political accommodation

Evidence from Afghanistan

Antonio Giustozzi

Introduction

Throughout the on-going Afghan conflict, there have been regular press reports about government officials, police, and army collaboration or collusion with the insurgents. From 2012, as Western disengagement from the Afghan conflict was finally underway, tactical accommodation started being paid greater attention because of its growing implications for both the withdrawal of foreign troops and for the final outcome of the conflict. Different schools of thought emerged. One argued that widespread tactical accommodation was potentially positive, because it could be conducive to an eventual peace deal, or to piecemeal reconciliation of insurgents with the government.[1] Another school of thought argued instead that tactical accommodation was a serious risk factor for Western personnel, based on the experience of Afghan armed units actively collaborating with the enemy against International Security Assistance Force (ISAF) units.[2] Finally, there were those arguing that tactical deal-making could even undermine the reliability of the security forces and lead to government collapse after the completion of ISAF's withdrawal.[3]

This chapter is an attempt to assess available evidence about local and tactical accommodation in Afghanistan and on that basis evaluate its potential impact.

[1] Personal communication with Western diplomats, Kabul, 2011.

[2] See the American officers interviewed in David Axe, 'Turncoats: How the Taliban Undermines and Infiltrates the Afghan Local Police', *Wired*, 23 May 2013, <http://www.wired.com/dangerroom/2013/05/turncoats/all/>.

[3] See, among others: International Crisis Group, 'Afghanistan: The Long, Hard Road to the 2014 Transition', *Asia Report*, no. 236, Kabul/Bruxelles, 8 October 2012.

The future, of course, cannot be predicted with any degree of accuracy, but a range of most likely scenarios can be developed. Accommodation does not only involve officers of the security forces, but also civilian officials of the Afghan government. Moreover, it is not just a matter of insurgents having a policy of co-opting government officials into deals, but also of government agencies (chiefly the National Directorate of Security, NDS) and Western intelligence organizations trying to do the same with individual insurgent commanders or insurgent groups/factions. As a result, it is not just accommodation *per se* which matters, but its actual shape and content.

In general, it is in the logic of accommodation that it does not get widely publicized by its protagonists, at least as long as a conflict is occurring. Writing about accommodation while a conflict is on-going implies having to rely on partial evidence, some of which is likely to be flawed or biased. One has therefore to be careful about drawing conclusions on the basis of such evidence, unless it is possible to find confirmation of it. This chapter is based on information obtained directly or indirectly from all sides in the conflict. As will be noted, in its general lines the information provided by the different parties to the conflict matches, even if it is often impossible to confirm details or individual cases.

How widespread is accommodation?

By 2012 agreements between armed opposition groups and government forces were reported by ISAF's intelligence as being a 'common occurrence'. Prisoners interrogated by ISAF extensively discussed army, militia, NDS, and police collaboration with them, revealing outright coordination; weapons transfers; intelligence sharing; release of Taliban prisoners; and occasional incorporation of Afghan units into Taliban operations. The most common examples are informal ceasefires.[4]

A military intelligence source reported in mid-2012 that at least 50 local deals involving the armed opposition and government armed forces had been identified.[5] Accommodation seemed to affect all branches of the Afghan state, but not in the same measure.

Police

Taliban commanders in Helmand alleged the existence of ceasefires in several districts of Helmand in 2011, involving district governors and police.[6] Even in

[4] 'State of the Taliban: Detainee Perspectives', Bagram: TF-3-10 (ISAF secret), 6 January 2012.
[5] Personal communication with government official of a Western European country, July 2012.
[6] Interviews with Taliban commander in Helmand, Autumn 2011.

many districts of north-eastern Afghanistan, the Taliban claim to have a number of Afghan National Police (ANP) officers and patrolmen cooperating with them.[7] The question remains whether this information is accurate or not. Independent witnesses confirmed that at least in some cases collaboration appears to have taken place. A bus driver in Helmand, for example, reported carrying Taliban in his bus and observing police at roadblocks ignoring these passengers, while asking others for identification. A trader in a town in Helmand reported observing Taliban roaming around the Bazaar unarmed, shopping, and being ignored by the police.[8]

Sources in ISAF confirmed cases of collaboration and accommodation. Often eyewitnesses have reported instances of police collaboration with the Taliban, or at least passive tolerance of their activities.[9] There were also reports of police helping the Taliban carry out attacks against US units.[10]

Even if the number of individuals involved in the worst incidents (murder of foreign troops) was small, it appears that sometimes investigations highlighted widespread complicity. After the killing of five British soldiers in Nad-i Ali in November 2009, a 'wholesale clear' of the district's police force was carried out, leaving in place only 30 of the 150 policemen.[11] In Nawa in 2010 the police split between supporters and opponents of the district police chiefs accused of having links to the Taliban. Four of the 100 policemen in the district, known to oppose the police chief, were murdered in unclear circumstances in a matter of days. Eventually the police chief was forced to leave by the district council and the governor.[12]

In some cases the police seemed to be cooperating with the Taliban on a commercial basis. Wardak police, for example, lost 160 weapons to the Taliban in alleged clashes during 2005–06, and the suspicion was that they sold them for cash.[13] Another instance was reported in Helmand in 2013.[14]

In several cases such collaboration appears to have reached the stage of ceasefires. Pro-active police officers sometimes allege that they are isolated in their struggle with the insurgents and are singled out for attacks while

[7] Interviews with Taliban cadres and commander in Kunduz, Baghlan, and Takhar, Autumn 2012.

[8] Interviews carried out in Helmand, Autumn 2011.

[9] 'Police let Taleban take us away: freed Afghan', *Agence France Press*, 10 December 2007.

[10] Eric Schmitt, 'Afghan Officials Aided an Attack on U.S. Soldiers', *New York Times*, 3 November 2008, <http://www.nytimes.com/2008/11/04/world/asia/04military.html?pagewanted=all&_r=0>.

[11] Toby Harnden, *Dead Men Risen: The Welsh Guards and the Defining Story of Britain's War in Afghanistan* (London: Quercus, 2011), p. 486.

[12] Bing West, *The Wrong War: Grit, Strategy, and the Way Out of Afghanistan* (New York: Random House, 2011), p. 186.

[13] Interview with former government official, Kabul, March 2009.

[14] See the Panorama series programme 'Mission Accomplished? Secrets of Helmand', BBC 2, 2013.

surrounding district police stations are quiet.[15] According to United Nations (UN) sources, many Chiefs of Police in the districts of the south and south-east had contacts with the Taliban and developed agreements with them.[16] In August 2008 there were reports of the Marjah police having opened negotiations with the Taliban.[17] Diplomatic sources highlighted that even in the north, deal-making between the police and the Taliban might be a problem, as for example in the case of Almar's border police.[18] Evidence of collaboration between Laghman's police and the Taliban was reported in 2010.[19] In Helmand the British often suspected the police of passing on information on British troops to the Taliban.[20] The Danes also suspected the police of collusion with the Taliban.[21]

At the Ministry of Interior (MoI), high-ranking officers admit that in some areas there might be informal ceasefires with the armed opposition.[22] Another high-ranking officer stated that the MoI knew about these deals, but also that hard evidence was difficult to come by.[23] According to the Chief of Staff of the MoI, officers were sometimes removed for cooperating with the enemy.[24] In 2006 a police officer in Kandahar alleged that the Chief of Police of five districts of Kandahar city had contacts with the Taliban. One of them was in fact the cousin of a Taliban commander, but was protected by a high-ranking MoI official on the basis of their shared Alokozai background.[25] A source within the MoI even believed that an important provincial Chief of Police had links to the Taliban, but was protected by one of the southern strongmen.[26]

Accommodation was sometimes interpreted by observers as the result of local interests prevailing over the desire of those in the political leadership to fight one another. In an area of Kunar opposed to Bajaur in 2010, the police and the Taliban were mainly from the same tribes. As a fight would inevitably result in casualties on both sides, and potential revenge attacks, the police

[15] Aryn Baker, 'Policing Afghanistan', *Time*, 21 October 2008, <http://content.time.com/time/world/article/0,8599,1852296,00.html>.

[16] Interview with UN official, Kabul, October 2010.

[17] Sam Kiley, *Desperate Glory: At War in Helmand with Britain's 16 Air Assault Brigade* (London: Bloomsbury, 2009), p. 228.

[18] Interview with foreign embassy official, November 2010.

[19] Douglas Saltmarshe and Abhilash Medhi, 'Local Governance in Afghanistan: A View from the Ground', Kabul, Afghanistan Research and Evaluation Unit Synthesis Paper, 2011, <http://www.areu.org.af/Uploads/EditionPdfs/1114E%20Local%20Governance%20in%20Afghanistan%20SP%202011.pdf>.

[20] Stuart Tootal, *Danger Close* (London: John Murray, 2009), p. 106; Patrick Bishop, *3 Para* (London: Harper Perennial, 2007), p. 187; Sean Rayment, *Into the Killing Zone* (London: Constable, 2008) pp. 76, 92; British officer cited in James Fergusson, *A Million Bullets* (London: Bantam Press, 2008), p. 68; Jake Scott, *Blood Clot: In Combat with the Patrols Platoon, 3 Para, Afghanistan 2006* (Solihull: Helion & Company, 2008), p. 175; Harnden, *Dead Men Risen*, p. 102.

[21] Bishop, *3 Para*, p. 238.

[22] Interview with high ranking Ministry of Interior official, Kabul, November 2010.

[23] Interview with high ranking Ministry of Interior official, November 2010.

[24] Interview with senior Ministry of Interior source, Kabul, October 2007.

[25] Interview with police officer, Kandahar, January 2006.

[26] Interview with high ranking Ministry of Interior official, November 2011.

might have tried to avoid fighting as much as possible.[27] In other cases further considerations were at play. In Arghandab, Kandahar in 2008–09 the police reportedly made a deal with the Taliban because of the weak ISAF presence.[28]

Army

The Taliban claim that 2,000 members of the Afghan National Army (ANA) forces belong to their underground organization. Beyond that, there would also be substantial numbers of ANA officers who have signed ceasefires or collaboration agreements.[29] Sources in the ANA military intelligence estimate that as much as 25 per cent of the army might be involved in some sort of accommodation, collaboration, or contact with the armed opposition of the intelligence services of rival countries.[30] While this seems to be an exaggeration, some cases of alleged collaboration have made it to the media. The most discussed case of accommodation between the Taliban and the ANA was in Uruzgan in 2012, on the basis that ANA units were not taking casualties while police and ISAF were.[31] These allegations led to an Afghan Ministry of Defence (MOD) investigation, even if the MOD denied the claims.[32] In other cases ISAF units grew suspicious of the units they were partnering or mentoring because they seemed to never get hit.[33] In one interview in the *Sunday Times*, an Afghan Lieutenant admitted to having made a deal with the Taliban in Ghazni in 2012: 'The plan is simple,' said Wali. 'When the Taliban attack the convoys we stay in our bases. If the Taliban capture something valuable then they share it with us later.'[34]

Another interviewee in Baghlan justified his own accommodation with the Taliban with allegations that ISAF itself has deals with the Taliban or the Pakistanis:

> When I understand this situation, I also thought with myself why I lost my two brothers and why I am fighting with [the] Taliban? I have [a] checkpoint in Dandi

[27] West, *The Wrong War*, p. 124.
[28] Interview with Canadian Task Force Kandahar officer, April 2010.
[29] Taliban source in Peshawar, contacted April 2013.
[30] Interview with Afghan General, Kabul, April 2013.
[31] Rory Callinan and Ali Safi, 'Fears over Afghan army, Taliban collusion', *Sydney Morning Herald*, 16 July 2012, <http://www.smh.com.au/federal-politics/political-news/fears-over-afghan-army-taliban-collusion-20120715-224dm.html>.
[32] 'Defense Ministry to Investigate Claims of ANA, Taliban 'Truce in Uruzgan', *TOLOnews.com*, 16 July 2012, <http://tolonews.com/en/afghanistan/6892-defense-ministry-to-investigate-claims-of-ana-taliban-truce-in-uruzgan->.
[33] Dianna Cahn, 'Troops fear corruption outweighs progress of Afghan forces', *Stars and Stripes*, 9 December 2009, <http://www.stripes.com/news/troops-fear-corruption-outweighs-progress-of-afghan-forces-1.97195>.
[34] Miles Amoore and Christina Lamb, 'Afghan troops and Taliban in pact to loot Nato convoys', *Sunday Times*, 20 May 2012, <http://www.thesundaytimes.co.uk/sto/news/world_news/Afghanistan/article1042275.ece>.

> Ghori District in Mangal village of Baghlan province and I also deal with [the] Taliban not to fight with them and they will not fight with us, it is because if the foreigner[s] are not fighting with [the] Taliban, how [do] we fight them because the foreigner has everything such as air force, modern weapon[s] and other logistics.[35]

Local police and militias

A variety of militias operate in Afghanistan, ranging from some officially incorporated into the police (Afghan Local Police, ALP) to semi-official groups recognized by provincial governors (called *Arbakis* in some areas), to entirely unofficial groups which belong to strongmen linked to the Kabul government. Mapping these groups is already problematic, even more so tracking any links to the armed opposition. Some ALP units belonged to the armed opposition in the past and in some cases have been suspected of maintaining such links.[36]

In north-eastern Afghanistan, virtually all the Taliban provincial and district cadres interviewed in 2012 claimed to have some men inside the ranks of the ALP and of the *Arbakis*.[37] ISAF sources have been reporting the suspected disloyalty of ALP units, such as one group in the heavily disputed district of Zari (Kandahar). American army sources believe, on the basis of intercepted radio communications, that some ALP units maintain relations with the Taliban because they are uncertain about the final outcome of the conflict and want to hedge their bets.[38]

Most semi-official and unofficial militias are affiliated with one of the old anti-Taliban organizations, which contributed to the defeat of the Taliban regime in 2001.[39] Despite this pedigree, accommodation with the insurgents is far from unknown even among their ranks. Off the record, members of Jamiat-i Islami often complain about the alleged collaboration of several local strongmen linked to Junbesh-i Milli and the Taliban. The Jamiati's also accuse government representatives of occasionally facilitating or colluding with the insurgents against Jamiat.[40] While these accusations *per se* mean little, given

[35] Interview with ANA Officer in Baghlan Province, March 2013.

[36] Quil Lawrence, 'In Afghanistan, Some Former Taliban Become The Police', *NPR*, 13 January 2012, <http://www.npr.org/2012/01/13/145049649/in-afghanistan-some-former-taliban-become-the-police>; Rod Nordland, 'Some Police Recruits Impose "Islamic Tax" on Afghans', *The New York Times*, 12 June 2011, <http://www.nytimes.com/2011/06/13/world/asia/13police.html?pagewanted=all&_r=0>; Afghanistan Independent Human Rights Commission (AIHRC), 'From Arbaki to Local Police', Kabul, 2012.

[37] Interviews carried out during Autumn and Winter 2012–13 in Kunduz, Baghlan, and Takhar.

[38] Axe, 'Turncoats: How the Taliban Undermines and Infiltrates the Afghan Local Police'.

[39] The two main such groups were Jamiat-i Islami of Professor Rabbani and Junbesh-i Milli of General Dostum.

[40] 'Afghan governor claims some officials involved in killing of jihadi figures', Text of report by privately-owned Afghan *Ariana TV* on 2 June 2012. A wing of Hizb-i Islami was legalized in 2005 and obtained several appointments to government positions. In the 1990s, Hizb-i Islami was the main enemy of Jamiat-i Islami in the civil war, until the Taliban emerged in 1994.

the rivalry between Jamiat and Junbesh, both General Dostum and the Taliban confirm that in 2010 a meeting between the General and the leading Uzbek Taliban in Faryab took place; the Taliban say that Dostum gave them weapons to destabilize the province, Dostum said that they invited him to lead them against the central government. Dostum has been openly telling Western diplomats that he would consider a deal with the Taliban if marginalized from the central government; some of Dostum's associates have been venting similar threats for years, and Dostum himself has expressed the possibility of a separate deal with the Taliban if Kabul continue excluding him from negotiations with them. Dostum is also known to have entertained contacts with the Taliban in Jowzjan.[41] Sources close to Dostum indicated that some Taliban commanders had close relations with him: Haji Rashid in Dasht-i Laili, despite having joined the Taliban, was still loyal to Dostum and was funded by him as of 2012; Mullah Malang Akhund was another in Jowzjan.[42] Other examples included Fataullah Khan's links with some insurgents in Qaysar of Faryab; the connection between the district governor of Almar Mohammad Omar and the Taliban; and the facilitation of Taliban movements by Faqir and Kamal Khan in Jowzjan and Sar-i Pul.[43]

However, even among the ranks of Jamiat, accommodation or collaboration with the Taliban has taken place. Many accuse Mir Alam, a strongman in Kunduz province, of having cooperated with the Taliban in the assassination of some of these *arbaki* (tribal militia); Mir Alam did not hide the fact to his entourage that he also maintained relations with the Taliban. In Baghlan, collaboration between some ALP units and the Taliban was reported: there were armed clashes between the ALP and the ANP, most seriously in September 2011 when the US Special Operations Forces (SOF) had to intervene, and the tension of the situation might have contributed to encouraging some ALP units to maintain a relationship with the Taliban against their common Jamiati enemies.[44]

In southern Afghanistan rumours have long been circulating concerning the collaboration of former Helmand Governor Sher Mohammed Akhundzada with the Taliban after his removal from the governorship at the end of 2005, at the insistence of the British.[45] Taliban sources indicate a complex picture of Sher Mohammed's accommodation with powerful factions within

[41] Interview with adviser to General Dostum, September 2013; Meeting with official of international organisation, April 2012.

[42] Adviser to General Dostum, interviewed Spring 2012.

[43] Interview with security officers of development agency, July 2012; ISAF source, contacted September 2011.

[44] Meeting with international organization official, October 2011; interview with former commander of Sayyid Mansur, Kabul, April 2012; interview with militia commander from Takhar, Mazar, April 2012; interview with Afghan intellectual from Takhar, October 2010.

[45] Personal communication with British Ministry of Defence, Foreign and Commonwealth Office, and Department for International Development personnel, 2006–11.

the Taliban, in particular Abdul Qayyum Zakir's, which led eventually to the creation of a new Taliban network led by one former associate of Sher Mohammed, Mullah Ibrahim. At the same time other Taliban factions (linked to Akhtar Mansur) continued to view Sher Mohammed and his family as arch-enemies.[46] Taliban sources also indicate that part of this accommodation was Taliban facilitation for the electoral campaign of Sher Mohammed's brother in the 2010 parliamentary elections, at a time when the official policy of the Taliban was sabotaging the elections violently.[47]

National Directorate of Security (NDS)

Obtaining verifiable information about the NDS and potential accommodation with the armed opposition is particularly difficult. A former Taliban commander in Musa Qala, now hostile to the movement, says in this regard:

> [The Taliban] have agents in the government to inform them about the plans and programs of the officials. There were 200 to 250 agents of [the] Taliban in the intelligence service of [the] government when I was leader of a group of Taliban. Their number must have been increased by now. Same is the case of [the] national army and police.[48]

Military intelligence sources in ISAF believe that a number of NDS officers have reached personal deals with the armed opposition, but the author is unaware of any deals involving whole NDS stations.[49]

Government officials

The Taliban claim that at least four provincial governors as of early 2013 had made formal deals with the Taliban to collaborate with them and pass on information. Several district governors would have made similar deals. It appears that such governors were rewarded with special treatment by the Taliban: the governors of Sangin and Musa Qala allegedly managed in 2010 to negotiate the downscaling of the anti-election campaign of the Taliban.[50] Observers on the ground in Helmand also believe that some deals of this kind may be in place, having observed the behaviour of the Taliban in government-controlled district centres and bazaars.[51] Some government officials have been

[46] Interviews with Taliban commanders in Helmand, Spring 2012.
[47] Interviews with Taliban cadres and commander in Helmand, Spring 2013.
[48] Interview with former Taliban commander in Musa Qala, Spring 2012.
[49] ISAF military intelligence source, September 2011.
[50] Taliban sources in Peshawar, April 2013; interviews with Taliban commanders, Helmand, Spring 2012; interviews with Taliban commanders, Helmand, 2013.
[51] Interviews with elders, drivers, and traders in Helmand, Autumn 2011.

accused of collaborating with Hizb-i Islami as well, as in the case of the Kapisa Governor (2007–10), Abu Bakr.[52]

Apart from formal deal-making, ad hoc deals are reported to exist between government officials and individual insurgent commanders of factions, without official sponsorship from the Taliban leadership. Reports of this kind were already popping up in 2004, when the Taliban were just in the early stages of mounting their insurgency effort.[53]

In northern Afghanistan examples of this behaviour have included government officials and strongmen tolerating the expansion of the insurgency and even encouraging it with the purpose of sending signals to their rivals or to the central government.[54] Examples of this include Governor Atta's links with Taliban commander Atta Mohammed (homonymous of Governor Atta) over smuggling operations but also as a tool to intimidate some elements of the Pashtun population hostile to both the Taliban and Atta.[55]

Lower level officials in the Afghan administrative structure are also reported to be reaching accommodation with the insurgents. The administrative sector where such deals have apparently been most common is in education.[56] Taliban sources claimed that the negotiations over local agreements included direct talks between local Taliban representatives and high-level representatives of the Ministry of Education (MoE) on several occasions starting in early 2010.[57] An MoE source confirmed the negotiations and indicated that the Taliban were divided over how to deal with the issue of an agreement with the MoE. Some Taliban opposed re-opening schools, while others were in favour; the two groups reportedly 'fought and killed and wounded each other' (see below for some confirmation of this by Taliban sources). Many Taliban would be in favour of an agreement which guaranteed the Taliban's changes to the curriculum, in the textbooks, and in the teaching staff. The 'Afghan Taliban' also wanted: more Islamic subjects; 'Afghan' teachers [meaning no exchange teachers from abroad; though they would probably be scarce in rural areas, this point also implies a threat against Westernized Afghan teachers]; and

[52] Maria Abi-Habib, 'U.S. Blames Senior Afghan in Deaths', *Wall Street Journal*, 1 April 2012, <http://online.wsj.com/article/SB10001424052702303404704577311522824172282.html>.

[53] For the case of governor Muhammad Ali Jalali in Paktika see: P. Constable, 'Border Offensive Has Paktika Residents on Edge', *The Washington Post*, 15 March 2004.

[54] Meeting with security officer of an international organization, Mazar-i Sharif, April 2012; Meeting with security officer of international organization, Mazar-i Sharif, July 2012.

[55] Interview with security officials of an aid organization, Mazar-i Sharif, July 2012.

[56] The following comments on accommodation involving the Afghan Ministry of Education are based on Antonio Giustozzi and Claudio Franco, 'The on-going battle for the schools' (Berlin: Afghanistan Analyst Network, 2013), <http://www.afghanistan-analysts.org/wp-content/uploads/2013/06/20130610_AAN_Taleban_and_Schools_FINAL.pdf>.

[57] Interviews with Taliban cadres in Wardak, December 2012; interview with senior Taliban cadre, Peshawar, December 2012.

gender separation for teachers and students [that is the prerequisite of the *Layeha*].

For the MoE, the most controversial of the Taliban's demands was the request for curriculum changes. Within the 'Afghan Taliban', some had problems with the re-opening of girls' schools, while others were more amenable to the idea, but only under certain conditions.[58]

Although no formal agreement was reached with the Taliban, some of the 'Afghan Taliban' networks reportedly promised the MoE not to attack schools, despite opposition from within the Taliban ranks. MoE sources concur with sources within the Peshawar Shura structure, indicating that these networks included at least part of the Peshawar Shura, while (as stated above) Taliban sources indicate that some components of the Quetta Shura (at least Naim's) also wish to refrain from attacking schools.[59] Overall, according to the MoE, the situation concerning schools improved greatly after 2009: the number of closed schools declined from 4,000 before communication started between the MoE and the Taliban in early 2010, to 1,247 in September 2012 and 471 in March 2013.[60] The Taliban themselves claimed to have allowed the re-opening of 100 schools in the first 11 months of 2012, after having closed them under the accusation of spreading pro-government propaganda and violating Taliban rules.

The re-opening of the schools was not a gracious concession of the Taliban, as there were many strings attached. The Peshawar Education Commission kept a record of how many teachers were fired between January and November 2012 at what they claim was the request of the Taliban (2,385), and how many were hired on the same basis (1,265).[61] The rules imposed by the Taliban in the accommodations to re-open schools are the following:

1. It is the right of human beings to get education, but:
2. in those areas which are under the control of the Islamic Emirate of Afghanistan, every Afghan can open schools but they must contact the Taliban's academic administration [that is the Taliban's provincial or district education commissioners].
3. In those areas which have schools or where schools are opening, the books, teachers and lessons must be under Taliban observation. The lessons should be delivered as dictated by the Taliban.

[58] Interview with Ministry of Education advisor, October 2012.

[59] The allegations against ISI paying the Taliban or insurgents to attack schools are circulated widely and were known in detail even to students (interview with Sayed Abad student, October 2012).

[60] Interview with Ministry of Education advisor, October 2012; 'Still 471 Schools Remain Closed', *Ariana News*, 19 March 2013.

[61] Interviews with senior Taliban cadre, Peshawar, September and December 2012.

4. The Taliban does not allow those subjects which are against *jihad*, women's freedom [as defined by the Taliban], and Muslims.
5. Male teachers don't have the right to teach to female students and female teachers don't have right to teach to male students.
6. In education the focus must be on Islamic subjects such as *Quran-e Sharif, Fiqh, Aqaid, Hadith,* and Arabic subjects. This must be from the first class to the end of education.
7. The teachers must be Afghans.
8. The clothes of teachers and students must be Islamic style.
9. The administrator of every school must give a monthly report to the academic responsible for that area and tell the teachers not to motivate students against Islam and *jihad*.
10. The teacher who works against Islam and *jihad* must be punished and fired from the job.
11. Those schools which are against the Taliban and *jihad* will be closed.
12. Girls who are going to school and studying with boys must be warned two times; if they do not stop going to such classes, they must be killed.
13. Teachers, who make programmes and courses for girls and help them to fight against their right, must be warned; if not then that teacher must be killed too.[62]

There have been claims that the Education Commission is involved in paying salaries as well. According to Taliban sources in Wardak, the MoE is required to pay the salaries of teachers who are hired on the Taliban's recommendations, through the local Taliban education commissions, which then proceed to pay the teachers. This, however, has not been independently confirmed. Additional conditions mentioned by the Taliban in Wardak include an increase in government funding for religious schools (*madrasas*) (the Taliban want at least ten functioning *madrasas* in each province); the abstention of the MoE from stopping students from joining the Taliban; and the abolition of English classes for girls.[63] Schools opened with Taliban authorization are reported to have Taliban informers (typically three, according to the Taliban), who report to the local education commissioner on what is occurring in the school. If a school does not comply with the rules imposed by the Taliban, the

[62] Interview with Taliban District Governor, October 2012. These 'rules' were not contained in the 2011 edition of the *Layeha*, but appear in the new edition that was approved in 2012 but has not been widely circulated at the time of writing. The *Layeha* is in fact a compilation of rules issued by the Taliban from time to time, so these specific rules might have been issued separately from the *Layeha* to be integrated into the next edition of the *Layeha*.

[63] Interviews with two Taliban cadres in Wardak, December 2012.

commission in Peshawar may order the school to be closed and, failing that, attacks on education staff. The district and provincial education commissions, in principle, do not have the authority to order closures or attacks.[64]

Accommodation with the armed opposition affects other government organizations, even if to a lesser degree. The Taliban claim that several government health officials have made deals with them, giving access to hospitals and clinics to injured Taliban.[65] At least one case could be identified of a government judge who also doubled up as a Taliban judge.[66]

Policies and practices

The Taliban

Taliban sources confirm that it was always common Taliban practice to obtain ammunition and even weapons from the ANA and the ANP in exchange for a treatment of favour, as well as purchasing such equipment for cash, particularly where Taliban supply lines are weak or non-existent, as in the north.[67] Vice versa, ceasefires have not always been authorized. Cases of collusion were occurring even when the Taliban leadership was discouraging collaboration with strongmen and government forces. The Taliban involved in such deals might not report them to the leadership, or described them as part of their efforts to recruit supporters. In some cases such deals appear to have included tip offs in exchange for economic benefits.[68]

This changed in 2011 as the Taliban issued a decree to regulate the 'reconciliation' of government officials with the Taliban. As a consequence, official agreements between the Taliban and government officials began to be signed.[69] Still, unauthorized deal-making continued to be severely punished, particularly when it conflicted with strong policy lines dictated by the leadership. For instance, in early 2013 the Military Commissioner of Wardak province, Fahim, was sacked and arrested over his alleged deal with the Minister of Education Faruq Wardak, who offered him cash in exchange for supporting the electoral process.[70] In particular, deals which involved the exchange of cash behind the backs of the Taliban leadership were susceptible to severe punishment: Taliban sources indicated the sacking of the shadow governor of Herat in 2012, following allegations that he received money from the Italian

64 Interviews with two district Taliban military commissioners, December 2012.
65 Interviews with Taliban cadres in north-eastern Afghanistan, Autumn 2012–Winter 2012/13.
66 Taliban source in Peshawar, contacted April 2013.
67 Interviews with Taliban commander in the north-east, Autumn 2012.
68 Meeting with ISAF officers, September 2011.
69 'State of the Taliban: Detainee Perspectives'.
70 Interviews with Taliban cadres in Wardak, Spring 2013.

intelligence service to avoid targeting Italian units.[71] Taliban sources also allege that government officials who make formal deals with the Taliban and start working regularly for them are paid regular salaries, on top of the official one.[72]

The Taliban's intimidation and targeted killing campaign seems to have been initially designed to simply disrupt the government and eventually lead to its collapse. The 2011 decree, however, suggests a change, with intimidation and targeted killings becoming much more integrated in an effort to reach accommodation with government officials. The leadership, in fact, changed the rules concerning the prosecution of government collaborators recently, to avoid the targeting of Taliban friends.[73]

The government

The Afghan government does not have an official policy of reaching accommodation with insurgents (apart from reconciling them). Some Ministries have, however, tried to reach accommodation with the Taliban and other insurgent groups, with varying degrees of success.

The MoE acknowledges that such accommodation is taking place, even if it maintains that agreements with the Taliban on re-opening schools are brokered by local community elders, sometimes through the school protection *shuras* organized by the MoE.[74] However, several sources in the MoE and within the Taliban also confirm that direct discussions between the MoE and the Taliban took place, perhaps following contacts between the Taliban and elders.[75] MoE efforts to reach out to the Taliban leadership in Quetta and Peshawar started in 2010. MoE representatives were dispatched to Pakistan to negotiate a reduction of violence against schools.[76] They talked with Taliban leaders, but did not reach a formal agreement. The MoE denies having issued any guidelines concerning negotiations with the Taliban, which is likely to be true, given the absence of a comprehensive deal with them.[77]

MoE officials have gone on record as saying that, although they have reached local understandings with the Taliban, no comprehensive deal has been achieved:

[71] Taliban source in Quetta, contacted August 2012.

[72] Interviews with Taliban commander in Helmand, Autumn 2011.

[73] Taliban source in Peshawar, contacted September 2012.

[74] See Antonio Giustozzi and Claudio Franco, 'The battle for the schools' (Berlin: Afghanistan Analyst Network, 2012) <http://www.afghanistan-analysts.org/wp-content/uploads/downloads/2012/10/2011TalebanEducation.pdf, 10ff>.

[75] Meeting with Ministry of Education official, Kabul, April 2013.

[76] Meeting with Ministry of Education official, Kabul, April 2013.

[77] Meeting with Ministry of Education official, Kabul, April 2013.

> Mohammad Sediq Patman, a deputy education minister said the government has to be flexible in order to keep schools open. In areas where the Taliban had more control, sometimes the government lets them influence what subjects are taught and even allows them to check student attendance, Patman said. 'There was no deal between the government and the Taliban, but only in order to keep the schools open and running the Education Ministry had shown flexibility to this issue,' he said.[78]

Taliban sources indicate that the Ministry of Public Health (as well as NGOs and aid organizations) has made deals with the Taliban over access and freedom to operate.[79]

Apart from official policies, one can imagine how many government officials might have felt that they could make their lives easier by agreeing to local arrangements. Awareness that negotiations were going on at the highest level is likely to have encouraged and legitimized individual deal-making too. In addition, many village elders favoured and encouraged deal-making as a way to create islands of peace in the countryside and may have put pressure on government officials to follow this path.[80]

The NDS and some high rank police officers also had their own policy of reaching accommodation with the insurgents, but with the aim of splitting and weakening the insurgency, not to make life easier for their own organizations. This policy in fact resembles much more the Taliban's official policy, than the deals reached by civilian government organizations. Information about this policy is scant because, for obvious reasons, it is not being debated in the public domain. Taliban factions, however, often accuse each other of having reached accommodation agreements with the government or with foreigners; in recent years Akhtar Mansur's alliance within the Quetta Shura has regularly been accused by hard-line Taliban of slowing down its combat operations or even suspending them following talks or even cash payments.[81] External observers familiar with the Taliban in the south reported in 2012 that for several months fighters from Mansur's and from Baradar's network disappeared from the contested areas.[82]

Implications for the wider economy of the conflict

In sum, on both sides of the conflict there has been a planned policy to reach accommodation with portions of the enemy forces in order to weaken and

[78] Nick P. Walsh, 'Taliban Tightens Grip on Afghan Schools', *CNN*, 22 May 2012, <http://edition.cnn.com/2012/05/22/world/asia/afghanistan-taliban-schools/index.html>.
[79] Interview with high level Taliban cadre in Quetta, September 2012.
[80] Interviews with village elders in various Afghan provinces, April 2013.
[81] Interviews with Taliban cadres in Peshawar and Quetta, Summer 2012.
[82] Observation by Afghan researcher, Helmand and Kandahar, Summer 2012.

split them, as well as vulnerability to the enemy achieving the same. Arguably the side which has the greatest cohesiveness and strongest chain of command and control is bound to benefit most from this type of local deal-making. Few observers doubt the fact that the government is not very cohesive. Indeed the multiplication of local deals has not brought much benefit to the Afghan Peace and Reconciliation Programme (APRP) efforts yet.

Taliban cohesiveness is still a matter of debate. In 2012 and early 2013 in particular, the Taliban underwent a series of rather crippling crises, in part due to the disappearance of Mullah Omar as an active leader, who had been able to keep the movement united.[83] Several attempts to reunify the movement and resolve internal conflict have taken place, but as of June 2013 the final result was still in doubt.

The widespread practice of accommodation means that the first side in the conflict to face a serious internal crisis will be in serious trouble, because there will be an easy way out for its rank-and-file, who might want to opt out. Western disengagement makes it likely that the government side will be the first to suffer an internal crisis, but should the government survive, the Taliban might well undergo its own crisis. A similar pattern occurred in 1988–90. In the 1980s accommodation was also widely practised by both the pro-Soviet government and the Mujahedeen opposition; then too there were official policies of using accommodation to infiltrate and weaken the enemy, as well as personal deal-making growing out of concern for one's own future. The competition to turn accommodation deals to each side's favour continued throughout the war and arguably each side benefited more from it in different phases of the war. The government side benefited most after it managed to survive the Mujahedeen's onslaught in 1988–89, until the collapse of the Soviet Union completely undermined its credibility as a deal-making partner. In 1988–89 and from the summer of 1991 onwards, accommodation played instead into the hands of the Mujahedeen. Government officials who had started authorized contacts with opposition members in order to convince them to switch sides or at least to reach ceasefires then used those same contacts to negotiate their own collaboration agreement with the insurgents. While accommodation agreements by government officials already existed in the early stages of the war, the reconciliation policy launched by the government in 1987 contributed to making accommodation deals more common.[84]

In sum, strategically driven tactical accommodation with the enemy is another way of waging war, more than a way to seek peace. Unauthorized

[83] See Antonio Giustozzi, 'Turmoil within the Taliban: A Crisis of Growth?', *Central Asia Policy Brief*, no. 7 (Elliott School of International Affairs, George Washington University), January 2013.

[84] See Antonio Giustozzi, *War, Politics and Society in Afghanistan, 1978–1992* (London: Hurst, 2000).

local deals are often centred on how to benefit from the war, not ending it (whether through a peace deal or total victory). In addition, unauthorized local deals aiming to profiteer from the war certainly do not favour state-building in Afghanistan, even in the long-term. In some cases there might be a genuine thirst for peace driving local accommodation; however, there is little evidence that local deal-making may favour the emergence of wider peace agreements, as political leaderships are driven by their own interests and aims.

References

Abi-Habib, Maria, 'U.S. Blames Senior Afghan in Deaths', *Wall Street Journal*, 1 April 2012, <http://online.wsj.com/article/SB10001424052702303404704577311522824172282.html>.

'Afghan governor claims some officials involved in killing of jihadi figures', Text of report by privately-owned Afghan *Ariana TV* on 2 June 2012.

Afghanistan Independent Human Rights Commission (AIHRC), 'From Arbaki to Local Police', Kabul, 2012.

Amoore, Miles and Christina Lamb, 'Afghan troops and Taliban in pact to loot Nato convoys', *Sunday Times*, 20 May 2012, <http://www.thesundaytimes.co.uk/sto/news/world_news/Afghanistan/article1042275.ece>.

Axe, David, 'Turncoats: How the Taliban Undermines and Infiltrates the Afghan Local Police', *Wired*, 23 May 2013, <http://www.wired.com/dangerroom/2013/05/turncoats/all/>.

Baker, Aryn, 'Policing Afghanistan', *Time*, 21 October 2008, <http://content.time.com/time/world/article/0,8599,1852296,00.html>.

Bishop, Patrick, *3 Para* (London: Harper Perennial, 2007).

Cahn, Dianna, 'Troops fear corruption outweighs progress of Afghan forces', *Stars and Stripes*, 9 December 2009, <http://www.stripes.com/news/troops-fear-corruption-outweighs-progress-of-afghan-forces-1.97195>.

Callinan, Rory and Ali Safi, 'Fears over Afghan army, Taliban collusion', *Sydney Morning Herald*, 16 July 2012, <http://www.smh.com.au/federal-politics/political-news/fears-over-afghan-army-taliban-collusion-20120715-224dm.html>.

Constable, P., 'Border Offensive Has Paktika Residents on Edge', *The Washington Post*, 15 March 2004.

'Defense Ministry to Investigate Claims of ANA, Taliban "Truce" in Uruzgan', *TOLOnews.com*, 16 July 2012, <http://tolonews.com/en/afghanistan/6892-defense-ministry-to-investigate-claims-of-ana-taliban-truce-in-uruzgan->.

Fergusson, James, *A Million Bullets* (London: Bantam Press, 2008).

Giustozzi, Antonio, 'Turmoil within the Taliban: A Crisis of Growth?', *Central Asia Policy Brief*, no. 7 (Elliott School of International Affairs, George Washington University), January 2013.

Giustozzi, Antonio, *War, Politics and Society in Afghanistan, 1978–1992* (London: Hurst, 2000).

Giustozzi, Antonio and Claudio Franco, 'The battle for the schools' (Berlin: Afghanistan Analyst Network, 2012), <http://www.afghanistan-analysts.org/wp-content/uploads/downloads/2012/10/2011TalebanEducation.pdf>.

Giustozzi Antonio and Claudio Franco, 'The on-going battle for the schools' (Berlin: Afghanistan Analyst Network, 2013), <http://www.afghanistan-analysts.org/wp-content/uploads/2013/06/20130610_AAN_Taleban_and_Schools_FINAL.pdf>.

Harnden, Toby, *Dead Men Risen: The Welsh Guards and the Defining Story of Britain's War in Afghanistan* (London: Quercus, 2011).

International Crisis Group, 'Afghanistan: The Long, Hard Road to the 2014 Transition', *Asia Report*, no. 236, Kabul/Bruxelles, 8 October 2012.

Kiley, Sam, *Desperate Glory: At War in Helmand with Britain's 16 Air Assault Brigade* (London: Bloomsbury, 2009).

Lawrence, Quil, 'In Afghanistan, Some Former Taliban Become The Police', *NPR*, 13 January 2012, <http://www.npr.org/2012/01/13/145049649/in-afghanistan-some-former-taliban-become-the-police>.

Nordland, Rod, 'Some Police Recruits Impose "Islamic Tax" on Afghans', *The New York Times*, 12 June 2011, <http://www.nytimes.com/2011/06/13/world/asia/13police.html?pagewanted=all&_r=0>.

'Police let Taleban take us away: freed Afghan', *Agence France Press*, 10 December 2007.

Rayment, Sean, *Into the Killing Zone* (London: Constable, 2008).

Saltmarshe, Douglas and Abhilash Medhi, 'Local Governance in Afghanistan: A View from the Ground', Kabul, Afghanistan Research and Evaluation Unit Synthesis Paper, 2011, <http://www.areu.org.af/Uploads/EditionPdfs/1114E%20Local%20Governance%20in%20Afghanistan%20SP%202011.pdf>.

Schmitt, Eric, 'Afghan Officials Aided an Attack on U.S. Soldiers', *New York Times*, 3 November 2008, <http://www.nytimes.com/2008/11/04/world/asia/04military.html?pagewanted=all&_r=0>.

Scott, Jake, *Blood Clot: In Combat with the Patrols Platoon, 3 Para, Afghanistan 2006* (Solihull: Helion & Company, 2008).

'State of the Taliban: Detainee Perspectives', Bagram: TF-3-10 (ISAF secret), 6 January 2012.

'Still 471 Schools Remain Closed', *Ariana News*, 19 March 2013.

Tootal, Stuart, *Danger Close* (London: John Murray, 2009).

Walsh, Nick P., 'Taliban Tightens Grip on Afghan Schools', *CNN*, 22 May 2012, <http://edition.cnn.com/2012/05/22/world/asia/afghanistan-taliban-schools/index.html>.

West, Bing, *The Wrong War: Grit, Strategy, and the Way Out of Afghanistan* (New York: Random House, 2011).

17

The changing role of contractors in security transition in Southern Afghanistan

James Dunsby

The role of contractors in modern warfare has, in the last ten years, received a vast amount of attention from academics, policy-makers, and the media.[1] There have been a host of biographies and similar personal narratives focusing on the modern 'corporate warrior'. Each work has an agenda: for the academic, the intention is to find regulation; for the media, it is finding controversy; and for the popular author who may have 'been there and done that', the objective is to convey a sense of adventure. The differences of opinion highlight the varied roles that contractors play in modern warfare, from guarding VIPs to engaging, controversially, in offensive operations, but their crucial role within security transition has been overlooked. This chapter outlines the roles that contractors play during and after security transition in southern Afghanistan and supports the contractors' perception that their tasking will initially remain unchanged, but their future will be determined by the limitations of the paymaster and the uncertainty of the security situation. However, if they remain in Afghanistan after the International Security Assistance Force (ISAF) has departed, they will exist in a state that is already comfortable with both the concept and practicalities of private force. There is therefore an opportunity for contractors who are industry experts to fill a capability gap once coalition forces depart and compliment the objectives of transition rather than work against them.

Studies on the growth of Private Security/Military Companies (PSC/PMC) in the last ten years are numerous and the historic links they have from

[1] The author lost his life in tragic circumstances in 2013 when this chapter was in draft form. The final edits have been made by the editors, but the spirit of the original work has been preserved.

mercenary to corporate warrior are increasingly well documented.[2] The role they have played in asset and convoy protection, logistics, medical support, training and mentoring, and intelligence gathering and dissemination during periods of armed conflict is widely understood, but what of their role during transition and in the 'nebulous' world of post-conflict environments, in particular the case of southern Afghanistan? To answer these questions three main areas will be examined: first, who are the contractors in Afghanistan and what is their relationship with the military? This section focuses on how both the military and the contractors view transition and the disconnect that exists between them because of language and the 'end date vs end state' scenario. Secondly, how does the role of the contractor fit in with the UK's broader strategy on transition and what opportunities might be available for contractors post-transition to help develop Afghanistan's security forces? Thirdly, what are the main concerns for contractors operating independently from both a private and a military perspective? This chapter has deliberately focused on southern Afghanistan due to the author's familiarity with the experience of UK forces, and their requirement to use routes through this area during the phased withdrawal. The use of private force has also become a norm in southern Afghanistan which, it will be argued, could potentially allow for a smoother transition towards privatized security in the short-term, but reinforces the argument made frequently that Afghanistan will once again become dominated by private militias once Western forces depart.

During transition, in the United Kingdom armed forces joint doctrine, there are five key questions to consider: Why is transition taking place? What functions are fulfilled by critical enablers of the security transition? Who are the potential partners and key stakeholders in the transition? When should the security transition take place? How will transition options be developed, negotiated and implemented? Contractors are both key partners and stakeholders and have served alongside UK forces in Afghanistan since operations began and have played a vital role in logistical support since modern armies were first raised. Not to include or consider them in any form of planning when confronting the daunting task of re-deployment would undermine the intervention strategy after years of valuable, hard-earned experience and waste industry knowledge.

[2] Deborah Avant, *The Market for Force: The Consequences of Privatizing Security* (Cambridge: Cambridge University Press, 2005); Christopher Kinsey, *Corporate Soldiers and International Security: The Rise of Private Military Companies* (Oxford: Routledge, 2006); Sarah Percy, *Mercenaries: The History of a Norm in International Relations* (Oxford: Oxford University Press, 2007); Thomas Jager and Gerhard Kummel, eds, *Private Military and Security Companies: Chances, Problems, Pitfalls and Prospects* (Weisbaden: VS Verlag, 2007). For more recent discussions of the ethical dilemma of private security see: James Pattison, *The Morality of Private War: The Challenge of Private Security and Private Military Companies* (Oxford: Oxford University Press, 2014).

Definitions of contractors and private security

There are three main types of private force in the international system: mercenaries, Private Military Companies (PMCs), and Private Security Companies (PSCs).[3] Mercenaries are well understood but the difference between them and the more recent PMCs and PSCs is less so. PMCs have been described as tightly organized corporate structures that provide military services including offensive operations and often possess a wider strategic objective in return for payment. PMCs have enjoyed only a brief moment of glory on the world stage but their use has fallen out of favour with many host and donor nations. They developed in the Middle East and Africa, often led by retired Western military personnel to solve either the security dilemmas of host nations or those of third parties by proxy. Examples include retired SAS founder David Stirling's Watchguard in the 1960s, Executive Outcomes and Sandline in the 1990s. The success of these groups and their legacy is still hotly debated and their dubious reputation is born from the personal ambitions of many of the company's leadership and the arrangements that were made for payment, which, on some occasions, was linked to the mineral wealth of the country.

PSCs developed from the business model of PMCs in that they are similarly organized but stop short of offensive operations as part of their services. Sarah Percy distinguishes between PSCs and PMCs on the basis that the former claim to use force only in self-defence, if at all, often deploying personnel unarmed.[4] This has been the case along the ground lines of communication in Pakistan where Western and sub-contracted Pakistani contractors have provided unarmed security for ISAF convoys up until the point that armed security takes over at the Afghan border. Examples of PSCs operating in Afghanistan are UK-based firms such as Olive Group, Aegis, Group4 Security, and Control Risks, and US firms such as White Eagle, Blue Hackle, and Dyncorp. There also exist a host of Afghan Companies and some Western-owned companies with Afghan business support based in Afghanistan. These are known as Risk Management Companies (RMCs)[5] and differ from PSCs in that they have a much smaller cohort of Westerners providing a mentoring service to Afghan PSCs or the Afghan military. For the purpose of this chapter, the term contractors will refer to all those companies providing some form of support to

[3] Sarah Percy, 'Morality and regulation', in *From Mercenaries to Market: The Rise and Regulation of Private Military Companies*, edited by Simon Chesterman and Chia Lehnardt (Oxford: Oxford University Press, 2005), p. 12.

[4] Sarah Percy, 'Private security companies and civil wars', *Civil Wars* 11, no. 1 (2009): pp. 57–8.

[5] During President Karzai's crackdown on PSCs in late 2010, all existing Western PSCs were forced to reduce in strength and re-badge as Risk Management Companies (RMCs). The strength of these companies was then to be replaced by a national security force known as the Afghan Public Protection Force (APPF). However, this force should not be confused with the APPF in Wardak Province which was a different scheme and similar to the Afghan Local Police (ALP).

the ISAF mission, and the term PSCs will be used to encompass companies that provide physical security in Afghanistan and also provide security support services such as logistics.

Transition

Despite the apparent clarity of the definition of 'transition', the practical difficulties of implementing security transition seem to lack definable boundaries. It is, in short, as one of the editors of this volume suggest, an 'exit plan for the disengagement and ultimate withdrawal of external parties from a state or territory'.[6] However, although the aim of withdrawing and leaving in place a strong government with a capable security apparatus is clear, transition remains nebulous due to the actors that are involved, the geo-political setting that they must act in, and the friction that is an inevitable part of all military conflicts. A great deal has been written on the concept of transition in order to broaden our understanding so that we may better appreciate the new asymmetric battle space. Due consideration has been given to the Afghan National Security Forces (ANSF),[7] local and national power brokers, and the wider instruments of the Afghan government, but a detailed understanding of what role ISAF's greatest practical ally, the contractor, might play is strangely absent. It is a hard fact, that, as Western militaries continue to cut defence budgets, the remit of contractors will continue to grow and widen and may potentially, in the future, take on roles more akin to their mercenary forefathers. This widening remit has led to an expansion of literature on their future role within the state, regulation, and their place within the varied State of Forces Agreements (SOFA) or Bilateral Security Agreement (BSA), governing foreign militaries in conflict zones. The 'Western way of war' has yet not devolved back to a state of using security contractors in the conventional military sense on a wide scale. In the initial phases of an operation it is still the state's standing military forces that engages the enemy, seizes and then holds ground, but contractors now follow closely on their heels and fulfil a range of roles in support of prolonged operations. During security transition, withdrawal, and after intervention, the role of the security contractor is not as well understood possibly because a culture of 'pay and forget' has become the prevalent attitude, and when we look towards southern Afghanistan there are no templates that can be imposed.

[6] Personal communication with R. Johnson.

[7] The ANSF includes all forces either under the control of the Ministry of the Interior (MoI) or the Ministry of Defence (MoD).

'End states' vs 'end dates' and the military–contractor disconnect

To the contractor, transition from a business perspective is clear cut. It is about reinvestment, renewal, or redeployment but there exists a clear disconnect between the military and the contractor community that frustrates their relationship. This is a simple issue of language. Rarely within the business world are problems viewed by their social, historic, ethnic religious, and tribal roots.[8] For the Western military, operating amongst the people, more comprehensive definitions are required. This question of language can then lead to a question of moral motivation, perhaps one of the greatest sources of mistrust between contractors and the military. Studies of private security contractors and those that provide support functions will often place these organizations within the wider historical narrative and their development from PMCs and mercenaries. It is barely understood within the military how these organizations have adapted to suit the new security nexus and the specific needs of donor states. As a result, the motivations for these organizations and the individuals within them are still understood as driven solely by the mercenary's desire for profit. It is true that a business must make a favourable increment but to suggest that an individual's performance will be somewhat inferior to that of a soldier loyal to the state is misleading. In a recent study of US contractor support in Iraq, by far the most often cited reasons for working in the security sector were to 'face and meet new challenges' (74.9 per cent) and to 'help others' (64.6 per cent). About one-third of respondents hoped that their work would make a difference (38.0 per cent) and saw their contractor service as a way to serve their country (31.3 per cent) possibly in their own way. Only one-quarter (25.2 per cent) of respondents indicated that they were driven by the desire to make money.[9] This study must of course be caveated. Rarely will an individual who is conditioned to being paid a regular salary by the military be willing to work in the private sector and to risk his or her life without substantial compensation. Their statements do not take into account the remarkable phenomenon of the surge in voluntarism that occurred in response to 9/11, whereby private security firms were inundated with applications from anguished citizens, and anyone with security training could acquire a position within a PSC and then subsequently deploy overseas. However, the situation is very different in Afghanistan. Contractors are no longer paid the same amounts they were during the heady days of the 'Baghdad dash for cash' and the role has become increasingly professionalized.

[8] Malcolm Hugh Patterson, *Privatising Peace: A Corporate Adjunct to United Nations Peacekeeping and Humanitarian Operations* (Basingstoke: Palgrave Macmillan, 2009), p. 141.

[9] Volker Franke and Marc von Boemcken, 'Guns for hire: motivations and attitudes of private security contractors', *Armed Forces & Society* 37, no. 4 (2011): p. 735.

Many seeking the contractors' 'lifestyle', particularly from the UK, are often retired middle to senior ranking military commissioned and non-commissioned officers and vacancies are highly sought after. Their private motivations aside, failure to complete a task within a deadline and to a budget will often result in the loss of their position with little to no warning, whereas, in a state's regular armed forces, sacking is not a common outcome.

Acknowledging the issue of 'end state vs end dates' is crucial to our understanding of the military/contractor disconnect that exists when it comes to transition.[10] The contractor is quite simply paid to fulfil a contract and most contracts in the business world have an end date. Within a security context, contracts are expected to be implemented within a time-frame and will then either be renewed as necessary or re-commissioned through a bidding process within a clear timetable. End states are of paramount importance to the military, whereas to a contractor working in an environment such as Afghanistan, the end date is a greater priority simply because as a business there exist a number of key questions based on a timescale: how long will they need to fulfil subcontractual requirements; how much time do they have to work on moving stock and as a result, what will they keep and write-off or gift aid; how will they redeploy, and where? Whereas the redeployment of members of the UK military will often be back to the UK or Germany, usually with a period of extended leave, the contractor will need to seek new business opportunities that could see them deploying to other insecure conflict zones, none of which will be clear at that time. However, contractors and the military can work together towards an end state as well. If we look closely at three of the key principles of transition as laid out by the *Transition Planning Handbook*[11] we can see areas where contractors may indeed assist the end state scenario.

Developing the ANSF

The private security sector in southern Afghanistan focuses on the PSCs and Host Nation Trucking services (HNT) that have been in operation between Kandahar and Camp Bastion and also along the southern route to Herat. In the absence of foreign state militaries, this is an area that can only really be maintained and developed either by foreign private enterprise or the Afghan government and its national security forces.

[10] Timothy Clack and Robert Johnson, *Land Tactical Transitions: Key Judgements*, Joint LIFC/CCW Report 2011, p. 2.

[11] ABCA, *Transition Planning Handbook*, 371 (ABCA Publication, 2012).

According to Peter Wilson there are two distinct elements to any discussion on the private sector in Security Sector Reform. The first element is to view the private sector as a target for reform particularly with regard to regulation. The second is to understand what contribution the private sector can make as instruments of reform, particularly in providing training and mentoring services. It is therefore important to distinguish between internal and external security actors.[12] In southern Afghanistan, the international drawdown will create a gap in the development of the ANSF therefore allowing external actors to play a major role and perhaps even to mentor not only the ANSF but internal security contractors as well.

Contractors have in the past been used to great effect to train local forces during armed conflict and during transition. However, their reputation has suffered due to the role of PMCs in Africa and particularly the allegations against Military Professionals Resources Inc. (MPRI) in training and then fighting alongside Croatian troops in Kosovo.[13] This example has highlighted the problems associated with 'mission creep', in this case where a private company is utilized to provide training and mentoring services, but are later accused of actually leading and fighting alongside the state military. This is certainly not a new phenomenon, nor is it necessarily something to fear so long as the company is supporting the apparatus of a recognized and legitimate government. However, unless there is a clear mandate, PSCs should probably not become involved in deliberate offensive operations in support of the ANSF. Nevertheless, if security deteriorates, they may not always have a choice.

Critics, such as Marc von Boemcken, note that PSCs cannot be expected to become involved in *peace*-keeping activities as the very nature of their business and the maximization of profits depends on sustaining an overall sense of insecurity, which, in turn, will guarantee a continual demand for their protective and deterrent services.[14] There have indeed been instances in the past of Afghan contractors on the road between Herat and Camp Bastion setting fire to their own vehicles and selling on the cargo, generally fuel. Although this can be classed as simple banditry rather than being a case of 'mission creep' or military action by PSCs, it does help to create a greater sense of insecurity than is actually the case.

Contractors must therefore possess a very clear mandate: will their support to the government of Afghanistan be of a training and advisory nature or could provision be made for a direct role in military operations? In some cases

[12] Peter Wilson, 'Private security actors, donors and SSR', in *Private Actors and Security Governance*, edited by Alan Bryden and Marina Caparini (New Brunswick: Transaction Publishers, 2006), p. 248.
[13] Avant, *The Market for Force*, pp. 101–4.
[14] Marc von Boemcken, 'Liaisons Dangereuses: The Cooperation between Private Security Companies and Humanitarian Aid Agencies', in *Private Military and Security Companies*, ed. Jager and Kummel, p. 268.

an absence of Western military uniforms may be welcome, especially given the traditional hostility to Western armies and the habitual presence of local militias within Afghanistan. Afghan culture does not hold the same reservations about private force as Iraq. Iraq had a tradition of a strong standing army that was linked to the protection of the state. Many Iraqis believed that armed private contractors were members of the CIA or linked with other Western intelligence agencies ensuring both distrust and also legitimizing them as targets.[15] Afghanistan is far more comfortable with the idea of contracted security given its history of militias and lack of a standing army. Nevertheless, Western contractors have not enjoyed the same levels of freedom in Afghanistan, having to register directly with the government rather than with a Coalition authority. There are few incidents of contractors killing innocent civilians or their actions going unchecked in Afghanistan.

The advantages that arise by using PSCs over the military are well documented but within the Afghan context a clear plus is their consistency, as contractors are often stationed in the country for extended periods and are not subject to six-month rotation cycles like regular Western troops.[16] This arguably gives contractors a greater degree of situational awareness than their military counterparts. In fact contractors often echo the same feelings of frustration as ANSF commanders when they are forced to work on an enduring footing with ISAF forces that only spend a limited time in a country. Tim Spicer argues that contractors actually raise the standards of behaviour amongst local forces who, if allowed to go unchecked, would extract compensation from the civilian population due to long-standing ethnic and tribal rivalries. Contractors, it is argued, are less involved and therefore more objective and 'professional'.[17] Nonetheless, according to the US State Department, military training of local forces is most effective when it is conducted by uniformed personnel who also tend to act as better role models.[18] This is where the issue of uniformed and non-uniformed personnel becomes blurred as some US contractors will wear a similar uniform to that of the US military. For Afghans, it is difficult to differentiate between Western forces and the nuances in their approaches.

Afghanistan's government could potentially relinquish its monopoly on violence altogether by reverting to a traditional norm where security is in the hands of militias, and therefore effectively privatized. This could happen

[15] Pratap Chatterjee, *Iraq Inc, A Profitable Occupation* (New York: Seven Stories Press, 2004), p. 132.

[16] Patterson, *Privatising Peace*, p. 71.

[17] Tim Spicer, *An Unorthodox Soldier: Peace and War and the Sandline Affair* (Edinburgh: Mainstream Publishing, 2003), p. 24.

[18] Elke Krahmann, 'Transitional states in search of support', in *From Mercenaries to Market*, ed. Chesterman and Lehnardt, p. 107.

naturally or deliberately, as in the case of Bulgaria in 1991 where the state responded to the employment needs of unemployed military and security guards by privatizing its security.[19] However, sharing this monopoly of violence with non-state entities can weaken government legitimacy, as was proven with the dissatisfaction of the Northern Alliance and Pashtun warlords after the overthrow of the Taliban regime.[20] Many believe it would make more sense bolstering the Afghan Uniformed Police (AUP) or the Afghan National Army (ANA) than investing in the private security sector. Nevertheless, there is strong evidence from both Afghanistan and Iraq that contractors could be used to continue to train and mentor the ANSF for the foreseeable future so long as funding does not run out and contractors are centrally administered.

Gradualism in the transfer responsibility

One of the most important areas that will require contractors to hand over land security responsibilities to the ANSF is through the provision and management of logistics, convoy security, and static site protection. Logistical support to the ANSF is a logical area that PSCs could take over during transition and after withdrawal.[21] The importance of PSCs in logistics is valued. ISAF recognize: 'Transition requires significant logistic effort in both planning and execution; the inclusion of logistic planners from the outset will help to maintain momentum.' They also acknowledge: 'Critical to the logistic effort throughout the process will be the continuation of HN logistic capacity building. This involves developing logistic capacity through the provision of assistance and support and interaction with contractors/other agencies in enabling the necessary personnel skills and infrastructure requirements.'[22]

The logistical capabilities of the Afghan security forces are weak. Historically, logistics is often the last element to be developed during any security reform programme. A nation such as Afghanistan that had no standing professional army and that regularly defaulted to the use of militias, be they ad-hoc or established by the government, will base its supply chain and its support services around the availability of local resources.[23] This has the potential to be poorly managed and could end up isolating the Afghan security forces from the civilian population if its procurement methods are not

[19] Alan Bryden, 'Approaching the privatisation of security from a security governance perspective', in *Private Actors and Security Governance*, ed. Bryden and Caparini, p. 9.

[20] Albrecht Schnabel, 'Insurgencies, Security Governance and the International Community', in *Private Actors and Security Governance*, ed. Bryden and Caparini, p. 80.

[21] Interview with Andy Bearpark, 3 March 2013.

[22] ABCA, *Transition Planning Handbook*, pp. 2–5.

[23] See Rob Johnson, *The Afghan Way of War* (London: Hurst, 2011).

carried out effectively. Although an efficient logistical support network is a primary concept of Western military thinking, within the ANSF it is only secondary to the actual business of military operations. Understanding logistics demands numeracy and literacy levels not generally found amongst the senior non-commissioned ranks one would expect to find on the front line of logistical planning. Within the ANSF, a fully indigenous logistical capability would be forced to rely on local trucking companies for movement, and would be dependent on privatized warehousing. This is achieved in Pakistan, although not perfectly, through agencies such as the National Logistics Cell (NCL) where registered trucking companies can be contracted for national and military purposes. This system relies on an established command and control structure with a clear military foundation. The ANSF would need to subcontract route and static site security or take on this role themselves; a notion that, even among Western militaries, is becoming outdated. Many Western companies could fulfil this role, providing that security could be delivered by either an effective Afghan-led privatized guard force or their own security units.

Fulfilling the logistical requirements for an entire military along with its force protection could mean that PSCs have to take on offensive roles. Another obvious responsibility for contractors would be the provision of medical and aviation support, and the latter is already an established business in Afghanistan.[24] However, to bring these assets together would require a high level of coordination between contractors and the ANSF, and no such provision exists at the time of writing.

The problem of contractor coordination could potentially be solved by establishing a contractor coordination cell based around a central body that synchronized not only the local logistic elements of the Afghan security forces but also the Western contractors who remain in the country. The Iraq example is an obvious one. In May 2004 Aegis was awarded a $293 million contract to act as a central hub to coordinate contractor activity under what became known as the 'Matrix Contract'. The idea was to create a Reconstruction Operations Centre (ROC) that would be fully computerized and linked directly to the US military satellite system in order to track convoys and security teams. This also acted as a central intelligence fusion centre and ensured that Aegis analysts could create regular intelligence summaries based on the reports

[24] The distinction must be made between Aviation Support and Air Support. In this context aviation support consists of fixed wing and rotary airlift capabilities employed within a logistical role such as moving troops and equipment, and performing other non-warlike roles. Air Support is the direct assistance that would be given by fixed wing or rotary to military operations and could encompass both logistical support and offensive operations. In the last 20 years, PSCs have provided air support quite effectively. Executive Outcomes provided Angolan forces with very effective offensive air support which, it could be argued, ended up breaking the resistance of UNITA in the 1990s.

that filtered through from the contractors.[25] However, membership was not mandatory and in some cases companies did not sign up as it was feared the sharing of intelligence would weaken their competitive edge. The impression of the performance of this centre was varied especially with regard to the quality of the shared intelligence.[26] Be that as it may, the model is effective and suggests that if private companies were not to play a significant part in the practical aspects of security, their management expertise could be utilized to coordinate a nationalized state security apparatus.

The rise of the Afghan Public Protection Force (APPF) represents Afghanistan's attempt at nationalizing their private security and, although greeted with some suspicion, it has the opportunity to provide a sound foundation for the privatization of Afghan security in the future.[27] Many contractors, although frustrated with its slow progress, believe this is indeed a step in the right direction and have done a great deal to support it.[28] A similar venture was trialled in Iraq with the awarding of a contract to the British firm Erinys to recruit, train, and mentor the Iraqi Oil Protection Force, which, at its height numbered an estimated 16,000 personnel. However the force all but collapsed through corruption once it was handed over to Iraqi control.[29] The APPF has had similar issues with corruption given that such an organization is a central hub for the administration of contracts awarded to protect assets which are themselves incredibly valuable. If Western security firms are going to be contracted to either mentor or administer the APPF this will itself require a further level of transition if it is to become a nationalized force. As Erinys experienced, if this takes place too quickly without an effective transition plan then the force becomes disaffected through mal-administration. The consequent loss of effective leadership can fuel further corruption and inefficiency.

Some effort has been made towards coordinating the duties of the APPF, who allowed major contractors, both Western and Afghan, to place bids for their responsibilities. This included the management of the individual contracts. Despite the standard of the Western applicants, many of whom had run these types of centres before, the contract went to an Afghan company.

[25] Christopher Kinsey, *Private Contractors and the Reconstruction of Iraq: Transforming Military Logistics* (Oxford: Routledge, 2009), pp. 83–5.

[26] Jan Stober, 'Contracting in the fog of war... private security providers in Iraq: A principle–agent analysis', in *Private Military and Security Companies*, ed. Jager and Kummel, p. 128.

[27] It was announced in late 2010 that a new force known as the Afghan Public Protection Force (APPF) would take on the role of all Western- and Afghan-owned PSCs by providing both convoy and static site security from March 2012. The basic idea was that all current PSCs would re-register and rebrand, and would continue to own various contracts but would utilize APPF personnel as the actual physical guard force.

[28] The APPF Working Group has been assisted in many areas by contractors who manage route and static site security, most notably Supreme.

[29] Erinys, *The Erinys Iraq Oil Protection Force: Infrastructure Security in a Post-Conflict Environment*, 2005, <www.erinys.net/download/i/mark_dl/u/... /erinys-opf.pdf>.

Although this is a step in the right direction as it complements the 'Afghan first' strategy, the mood in Kabul amongst Western contractors was that Afghan officials were scrabbling for any last minute opportunities to make a cash windfall.[30] The creation of an effective command element for the APPF could be an excellent opportunity for ISAF to carry out transition and withdrawal from Afghanistan, whilst being secure in the knowledge that host nation trucking and other contractor tasks will be employed effectively, and intelligence will continue to be gathered along the lines of communication. Brigadier Richard Iron (retired), who was a British soldier before becoming a security contractor in Iraq after Western transition, commented that:

> For any such idea to work post-Afghan transition, it needs to gain the support of GIROA [the Government of the Islamic Republic of Afghanistan]. The support that the US provided to Matrix would need to be provided by the Afghan authorities, including intelligence feeds and triggering security force reaction to incidents. Only GIROA can make international companies working in Afghanistan sign up to, and pay for, this kind of organisation. Money can come from elsewhere of course (such as international donors) but it needs to be fed through the Afghan authorities if the system is to work.[31]

Christopher Kinsey believes, however, that intelligence sharing and war fighting should remain in the hands of state military forces and should not be outsourced completely.[32] Nevertheless, a limited intelligence mentoring role could work, and Afghanistan requires an efficient logistics service free of the corruption that plagues its existing apparatus.

Private companies and responsible government

Inevitably, as contracts come to an end, reinvestment, redeployment, or renewal becomes the focus of the private sector. Contractors may wish to reinvest part or all of their business in that of the host nation. This could be done by providing engineering and construction services, basing security operations in Afghanistan (as opposed to the UK, US, or UAE) and continuing to subcontract trucking services. Renewal of contracts could occur in three ways: under different standards and caveats with the host government; with a new single third country donor; or with an international force. The contractors Kellog Brand & Root (KBR) have suggested that the support services that it

[30] Interview with Security Contractor, January 2010.

[31] Interview with Brigadier Richard Iron (retired), 13 March 2013.

[32] Kinsey, *Private Contractors and the Reconstruction of Iraq*, p. 149. Kinsey's opinions are concerned very much with outsourcing intelligence within the state structure.

provides to UK forces in Camp Bastion would simply transfer to the US force that remains, and they would literally 'wave off' the UK forces as they redeployed (similar to what occurred in Basra).[33] Contractor redeployment is an inevitable eventual outcome but might not necessarily occur at the same time as UK or other ISAF troops are withdrawing. Concern was raised by one leading UK service provider that the redeployment plan did not actually include contractors, as one might have hoped, as part of a 'whole force' concept. However, companies will generally redeploy their personnel as and when required. Supreme Global Services commented that:

> Those companies that have invested in infrastructure in the country and who have strong ties to the country will want to continue to serve Afghanistan. However, companies cannot be driven by political ideals but by their own shareholders. They will want to know that the capital risk that they incur will mean acceptable profit. Therefore, the financing of industry's future role will be key. Industry will seek a steady and reliable paymaster. The Afghan government has already highlighted that it will need upwards of $7bn per annum from overseas donors if it is to secure its fledgling democracy. Most of this funding will be needed to procure the same services provided at no cost today by NATO.[34]

PSCs may also be used to greater effect alongside non-governmental organizations (NGOs). As NGOs are generally concerned with preserving their status as independent and impartial actors, rarely do they cooperate with national military forces. They prefer to defer security matters to a PSC whom they regard as apolitical.[35] There is no reason why PSCs, including logistic providers, will not continue to utilize the NGO market as the reason to remain in southern Afghanistan. Given that these organizations are usually centrally administered in Kabul with outlying stations throughout the country, their inclusion in a ROC-type fusion centre and continued engagement would be hugely beneficial for those Western forces restrained by where they can operate in a post-conflict Afghanistan.

However one views it, transition needs to be seen as less conclusive since it will involve a degree of reinvestment, redeployment, or renewal. Any contractors who remain in Afghanistan will be representing, indirectly, the UK and should be viewed as a valuable 'force multiplier'. The opportunity therefore exists for them to work closely with the Afghan government providing security, private industry, and governmental experts who can continue to support and develop the Afghan state.

[33] Interview with Kellog Brand & Root, 7 March 2013.

[34] Supreme Global Services, 'Defence Management', <http://www.defencemanagement.com/article.asp?id=552&content_name=Logistics&article=18895>.

[35] Boemcken, 'Liaisons Dangereuses', p. 267.

Concerns

Afghanistan is not an easy country to operate in or withdraw from. It is restricted by a southern line of communication through a temperamental Pakistan, a restricted and expensive northern route, an overloaded air corridor, and a host of other associated issues, all causing immense friction to the supply chain and the process of withdrawal. The lines of communication through Pakistan have been closed periodically, as in 2010, and sometimes for months. Internal political struggles, peace marches, US incursions and drone strikes, cross-border artillery duels, border crossing raids on both sides, flooding, criminal activity, rising transport duties, corruption, and stifling bureaucracy add to the friction. This means that the contracting community have been nervous about their options for redeployment. Much of the customs paperwork is dealt with by contractors themselves in Kabul and relies on varying degrees of liaison between the central government, the Afghan Customs Police, the Ministry of Finance, and ISAF HQ. As ISAF draws down, contractors may not have the necessary weight behind them in meeting exit deadlines when dealing with customs paperwork and Afghan officials. Redeployment also needs to correspond with the drawdown of security assets or make allowance for the renewal of private security contracts to provide convoy security either directly through the host nation or through existing contracts. If NATO cannot secure Pakistan's unflinching support along the lines of communication, the re-deployment options open to contractors will be limited and will inevitably result in a great deal of equipment being left behind. Many contractors may indeed wish to do this anyway as it would not be cost effective to bring home material that has had its lifespan degraded by the Afghan climate and which would not meet industry regulations in the UK or abroad.

The lack of a clear end date to contractors is a major concern as it is with those who manage those contracts. Although a rough time-frame was given, the approximate withdrawal date fell long before some prime UK contracts were due to end. The problem for the future is: should contracts be renewed in the light of a shorter deployment time; and will prime contractors be willing to do this or should new contractors be considered to take on the role of transition?[36] Those who manage UK contracts from Camp Bastion have already noted that many large construction companies that have been in Afghanistan for some years are starting to withdraw their personnel as contracts are not being renewed or new work is not being put up for tender. This is particularly worrying as any work that will need to be done as part of the

[36] Interview with DSCOM.

hand-over process will probably fall to local Afghan contractors who will not be vetted, increasing the stress on force protection.[37]

'Mission creep' is a very real concern when outsourcing security: the issue that PSCs will turn more towards PMCs especially as they take on more Afghan personnel is not an unlikely scenario. An issue that can both divide and actively isolate the people of Afghanistan from their government would be through the use of less well-regulated or constrained Private Security Details (PSDs). During and post transition there is a risk that PSCs, by highlighting and inflating the sense of insecurity, may increase. PSCs may be tempted to shift the focus to providing close protection for VIPs and therefore move attention from collective security to individualized and reactive services such as personal protection.[38] This concentration on the individual could undermine notions of local community security. The transfer of PSCs to Afghan personnel could in turn, given Afghanistan's history of militias, lead to warlordism and protection rackets based on extortion and bribery. To some extent this already occurs, although many of these groups are signed up to state-sponsored projects such as the Afghan registered RMCs, APPF, or Afghan Local Police (ALP). There will simply be little incentive once the reach of the ISAF security umbrella decreases and eventually dissolves, for private Afghan units to hold true to their original contractual obligation.

Conclusion

Within Task Force Helmand, four principles for transition were identified: to fight, build, talk, and commit.[39] Within the first principle of 'fight', training, mentoring, the provision of quick reaction forces, and the transition of intelligence and support systems have been identified as having priority. Contractors have a clearly definable role as supporting organizations. PSC involvement in development projects and investment are part of the 'build' principle, and contractors have long been involved in the 'talk' principle through close liaison. So long as it remains financially viable and security needs remain, there is no reason why contractors cannot 'commit' to a long-term engagement in Afghanistan. Nevertheless, a number of further questions could be added to any planning estimate when considering the role of contractors in security transition: what is their primary role and how could this fulfil key ISAF interests? What are their strengths and weaknesses? What are their interests in transition? Are they perceived as a legitimate partner in the

[37] Interview with MoD Contracts body, Camp Bastion, November 2012.

[38] Elke Krahmann, *States, Citizens and the Privatisation of Security* (New York: Cambridge University Press, 2009), p. 280.

[39] Clack and Johnson, *Land Tactical Transitions*, p. 9.

eyes of the wider host nation population? Do they have, or could they develop, appropriate accountability mechanisms that are effective to GIRoA? Would they, or could they, conduct the function in a sustainable manner?[40]

The role of contractors it is perceived, will, during the early stages of any transition, remain largely unchanged for their operational deployment period. They will continue to mentor and develop both the private security sector and state forces, and they will continue to provide support services to the interventionist forces that remain in the country. However, in Afghanistan, these roles could be developed much further especially with regard to the support contractors may give the ANSF or the Afghan private security sector. The issue becomes one of priority. Will the Afghan government and the international community concentrate their efforts on developing a national standing military and police force or will it be easier for the already existing Afghan PSCs to take on a more active role in state security? Historically, private force has prospered on the peripheries of urban centres in Afghanistan, basing themselves in the relative protection of the countryside, free from state interference and controlling transport routes. Despite the advantages of using PSCs to train and mentor state forces, and to provide active logistics support, the concerns of handing over all private security and its support services to indigenous hands are considerable. If funding is not forthcoming from local governments or the international community, it seems inevitable that it will be provided through other nefarious means. It is likely that, in such circumstances, links to the insurgency will be able to develop unchecked.

Contractors and Western military forces face challenges characterized by differences in business priorities and the requirements of an 'end state' or an 'end date'. However many of the issues they face are of a similar nature. Both face the problems associated with redeployment, and the legacy of reinvestment and renewal, but as long as these issues are highlighted in good time, long before the final truck departs Camp Bastion, then both the military and the contractor community might be able to understand the roles each might play in a successful security transition in the future.

References

ABCA, *Transition Planning Handbook*, 371 (ABCA Publication, 2012).

Avant, Deborah, *The Market for Force: The Consequences of Privatizing Security* (Cambridge: Cambridge University Press, 2005).

Boemcken, Marc von, 'Liaisons Dangereuses: The Cooperation between Private Security Companies and Humanitarian Aid Agencies', in *Private Military and Security Companies: Chances, Problems, Pitfalls and Prospects*, edited by Thomas Jager and Gerhard Kummel (Weisbaden: VS Verlag, 2007), pp. 259–72.

[40] Joint Doctrine Note 6/10, 'Security Transitions', November 2010.

Bryden, Alan, 'Approaching the privatisation of security from a security governance perspective', in *Private Actors and Security Governance*, edited by Alan Bryden and Marina Caparini (New Brunswick: Transaction Publishers, 2006), pp. 3–19.

Chatterjee, Pratap, *Iraq Inc, A Profitable Occupation* (New York: Seven Stories Press, 2004).

Clack, Timothy and Robert Johnson, *Land Tactical Transitions: Key Judgements*, Joint LIFC/CCW Report 2011.

Erinys, *The Erinys Iraq Oil Protection Force: Infrastructure Security in a Post-Conflict Environment*, 2005, <www.erinys.net/download/i/mark_dl/u/ . . . /erinys-opf.pdf>.

Franke, Volker and Marc von Boemcken, 'Guns for hire: motivations and attitudes of private security contractors', *Armed Forces & Society* 37, no. 4 (2011): pp. 725–42.

Jager, Thomas and Gerhard Kummel, eds, *Private Military and Security Companies: Chances, Problems, Pitfalls and Prospects* (Weisbaden: VS Verlag, 2007).

Johnson, Rob, *The Afghan Way of War* (London: Hurst, 2011).

Kinsey, Christopher, *Corporate Soldiers and International Security: The Rise of Private Military Companies* (Oxford: Routledge, 2006).

Kinsey, Christopher, *Private Contractors and the Reconstruction of Iraq: Transforming Military Logistics* (Oxford: Routledge, 2009).

Krahmann, Elke, *States, Citizens and the Privatisation of Security* (New York: Cambridge University Press, 2009).

Patterson, Malcolm Hugh, *Privatising Peace: A Corporate Adjunct to United Nations Peacekeeping and Humanitarian Operations* (Basingstoke: Palgrave Macmillan, 2009).

Pattison, James, *The Morality of Private War: The Challenge of Private Security and Private Military Companies* (Oxford: Oxford University Press, 2014).

Percy, Sarah, *Mercenaries: The History of a Norm in International Relations* (Oxford: Oxford University Press, 2007).

Percy, Sarah, 'Morality and regulation', in *From Mercenaries to Market: The Rise and Regulation of Private Military Companies*, edited by Simon Chesterman and Chia Lehnardt (Oxford: Oxford University Press, 2005), pp. 11–28.

Percy, Sarah, 'Private security companies and civil wars', *Civil Wars* 11, no. 1 (2009): pp. 57–74.

Schnabel, Albrecht, 'Insurgencies, Security Governance and the International Community', in *Private Actors and Security Governance*, edited by Alan Bryden and Marina Caparini (New Brunswick: Transaction Publishers, 2006), pp. 65–85.

Spicer, Tim, *An Unorthodox Soldier: Peace and War and the Sandline Affair* (Edinburgh: Mainstream Publishing, 2003).

Stober, Jan, 'Contracting in the fog of war... private security providers in Iraq: a principle–agent analysis', in *Private Military and Security Companies: Chances, Problems, Pitfalls and Prospects*, edited by Thomas Jager and Gerhard Kummel (Weisbaden: VS Verlag, 2007), pp. 121–34.

Wilson, Peter, 'Private security actors, donors and SSR', in *Private Actors and Security Governance*, edited by Alan Bryden and Marina Caparini (New Brunswick: Transaction Publishers, 2006), pp. 247–60.

18

'Gripping and Touching' the Afghan National Security Forces

Tactical and operational experiences during Operation Herrick 16

Oliver Lewis and Andrew Britton

Introduction

In October 2011 the International Security Assistance Force (ISAF) campaign in Afghanistan shifted from direct counter-insurgency in partnership with the Afghans to 'security force assistance' (SFA): supporting the Afghan government and security forces to conduct their own counter-insurgency operations. Defined by ISAF, security force assistance is 'the unified action to generate, employ, and sustain Afghan security forces to support the government and people of Afghanistan'.[1] From the perspective of military planners, the very outcome of the campaign hinged on the effectiveness of assistance provided to the ANSF (Afghan National Security Forces) and the degree to which armed groups and the countryside could be brought under governmental control. From April to October 2012, Operation Herrick 16 saw 12 Mechanized Brigade interpret and implement SFA with an unparalleled focus on Afghan priorities, while enabling Afghan-led operations. The commanders and staff officers responsible for ensuring that Task Force Helmand would be capable of delivering SFA, through advising and assistance teams, had to balance the demands of higher NATO headquarters, domestic UK military and political imperatives, US domestic considerations, force

[1] Headquarters International Security Assistance Force, *ISAF Commander's Security Force Assistance Concept* (2011). Hereafter cited as: HQ ISAF, *Concept*.

protection against 'insider attacks', and—crucially—the Afghan's appetite for counter-insurgency operations and its imperatives in Helmand Province.

'All ethnography', claimed Geertz, 'is part philosophy and a good deal of the rest is confession.'[2] As participants and observers of Operation Herrick 16 we are aware of the process of building meaning and understanding of time in the field; what Williams described thus: '[u]nderstanding emerges out of interaction between me as a researcher and the situation within which I find myself—out of the questions that emerge from my response to the situation'.[3] At MOB (Main Operating Base) Lashkar Gah, a fortified military camp in the capital city of Helmand Province, we had distinct roles to play in the headquarters of Task Force Helmand that afforded us more freedom than most to ask questions. We were not researchers, but the nature of our roles—as the staff officer responsible for planning the immediate operational future (Britton) and as the Brigade Commander's 'constructive contrarian' (Lewis)—necessitated that we interrogate and justify our opinions and assumptions, and those of subordinate units, the commanders, and the multiple levels of higher headquarters within Afghanistan and in the UK. This chapter is our 'confessional tale' as participants: in an international, inter-connected massive military bureaucracy; in an operational campaign in Helmand; as lobbyists and apologists for a Task Force Helmand-centric view of the ISAF campaign; and as individuals engaged in an attempt at reflexivity on our time in the field. There is a degree of mimesis in our tale; as authors we are engaging in a reflexive exercise about a period of time when the institutions of the campaign in Afghanistan were undergoing their own reflective phase about ISAF's operational design and purpose. Implicit in both was a recognition of the past failures of the intervention.

Most commentators would conclude that the coalition and ISAF have struggled with the campaign since 2001. Decades of conflict have atomized Afghan society; central government is weak and perceived as illegitimate; corruption is endemic; security forces are unreliable and in many cases badly trained, corrupt, poor, and illiterate. The conflict is against a well-established insurgency with deep roots, reliable sources of funds, and sanctuary in Pakistan. Unequivocal success in this context has eluded ISAF, despite the enormous expenditure of 'blood and treasure'. The change in the operational design of the Afghanistan campaign in 2011 to a clearly articulated concept of security force assistance is ISAF's confessional moment—a *mea culpa* rendition made flesh in operational doctrine. SFA is the manifestation of military catharsis, with the key documents authorized by General Allen in the final months of

[2] Clifford Geertz, *The Interpretation of Cultures* (New York: Basic Books, 1973), p. 25.

[3] Anne Williams, 'Reading feminism in fieldnotes', in *Feminist Praxis: Research, Theory, and Epistemology in Feminist Sociology*, edited by Liz Stanley (New York: Routledge, 1990), p. 2.

2011 serving a threefold purpose: as an acceptable expression of catharsis; a (self-)recognition of military limitations in the Afghanistan mission; and an attempt at reconciling the military's need for tactical and operational successes with broader strategies.

Issued in 2011 from the four-star[4] ISAF headquarters, two short letters signified the change in campaign design to SFA, and we will quote extensively from them in the course of this chapter. The first document served as an introduction to SFA and set out some key themes and behaviours required of the approach.[5] The second document was divided into a number of bullet-points arranged under three headings: mission, mindset, and approach.[6] The content of these letters have subsequently been included in *The ISAF Security Force Assistance Guide.*[7] The contextual argument for the shift to SFA was that 'the combination of reducing coalition forces, increasing Afghan capability, and transition requires an evolution in the relationship between the international community and the government of Afghanistan'.[8] The 'surge' in troops of the previous year had, it was argued, provided the space for the Afghan security forces to develop to a level at which they should gradually and increasingly take over from ISAF, hopefully in concord with the political transition of areas to fully autonomous Afghan government control. As the document argued that 'a secure environment is required to set the conditions for long-term economic development, effective rule of law, and the other functions of legitimate government' the shift towards SFA was therefore 'the logical progression in the execution of ISAF's campaign to enable the Afghans to take the lead for their own security'.[9] Even more explicitly, this logical progression from ISAF leading the counter-insurgency fight, to the Afghans leading it, is 'the only successful way of delivering a permanent security solution and ensuring the transition is made irreversible by the Afghan security forces'.[10] Operation Herrick 16 was understood as likely to be the 'high-watermark' of the UK contribution to the ISAF campaign and consequently the last operational deployment in which the UK would have sufficient troops, resources, political will, and points of leverage with our Afghan interlocutors necessary to shape the lasting security context in Helmand. More than many others, Herrick 16 was the final point to set the conditions for the successful conclusion and drawdown of the UK campaign.

[4] Commanded by a four-star general. [5] HQ ISAF, *Concept.*

[6] Headquarters International Security Assistance Force, *ISAF Commander's Security Force Assistance Principles* (2011). Hereafter cited as: HQ ISAF, *Principles.*

[7] Headquarters International Security Assistance Force, *ISAF Security Force Assistance Guide*, 2013, <https://ronna.apan.org/CAAT/Shared%20Documents/20130505_NIU_SFA_Guide.pdf>.

[8] HQ ISAF, *Concept.* [9] HQ ISAF, *Concept.* [10] HQ ISAF, *Concept.*

Concepts and commands

As commander of ISAF, General John Allen said in January 2012 that 'SFA is the single most important concept that ISAF will implement in more than ten years of the campaign—it reflects a fundamental milestone in the campaign and change in relationship with the ANSF'.[11] SFA changed the campaign plan, initially more as a speech act than immediately altering military behaviour, but the consequences of cascading the concept and its accompanying principles down the chain of command did result in a very significant shift in approach for the British-led operation in central Helmand. Whereas a command directive[12] could have immediate affect on military units, the issuing of a concept that sought a changed 'mindset' necessitated a period of socialization[13] of the idea, interpretation by the constituent commands, and the dissemination of documents to tens of thousands of individuals geographically isolated and connected by slow computing networks.

Words not only say something, but 'do something'.[14] The documents that narrate the process of enacting security force assistance did so as a *change* in the ISAF mission that contain a series of explicitly performative utterances: General Allen, as commander of ISAF, was appropriate for the invocation of the particular procedure invoked. The procedure itself encountered a number of complications, some general and some specific to the military and expeditionary context. The utterance existed within a hierarchical organization, and had as its point of origin the head of that organization; the directive that SFA was a change to be promulgated was legitimate and must be executed by all participants *correctly*, and *completely*. Infelicity was possible but only by some failure by those tasked with its execution; security force assistance could be executed badly or implemented only in part and it falls to the military chain of command to attempt to enforce a change in concept. That SFA must be understood correctly was raised in the documents:

> It is also essential to develop a common framework of understanding which translates the theoretical concept of Security Force Assistance into a language

[11] HQ ISAF, *Principles*.

[12] Such an order was experienced during Operation Herrick 16 to cease temporarily some advising activities while direction to take on the 'insider threat' was considered.

[13] In military doctrine-writing organizations, 'socialization' generally refers to a period of time in which an early draft of a document is widely distributed in order to draw in as many critical comments as possible. The aspiration is that if an uncomfortable or disliked idea is circulated long enough, opposition will gradually decrease.

[14] John L. Austin, *How to Do Things with Words* (Cambridge, MA: Harvard University Press, 1962), p. 25.

readily understood and accepted by the military and civilian agencies supporting the Afghan security forces.[15]

However, the security force assistance documents of late 2011 and early 2012 were irregular forms of military knowledge that are not easily interpreted by the institution: it is ambiguous as to where the 'order' is in the concept that compels military leaders further down the chains of command to comprehend individually how to 'operationalize' security force assistance in the absence of further explicit direction from higher commands. For much of the summer of 2012, whilst we had been involved in meetings and informal discussions, the issuing of the detailed SFA orders from the regional headquarters was delayed by some months, leaving the British to carry on with their own 'operationalized' version. Such orders were the currency of headquarters and the usual means for enacting changes in the way the campaign was to be run. Typically, less transient forms of military knowledge were organized and disseminated through field manuals that employ an instantly recognizable structure that provided 'clear direction'—courses of action to undertake under certain conditions or in certain contexts.[16] Such a manual describing SFA[17] was produced in October 2012 for the Herrick 17 audience. Nevertheless, military doctrine contains utterances that are explicitly performative and constative: the issued security force assistance documents did not arrange knowledge with the same degree of simplicity or clarity and it is difficult to judge whether the utterances require action. For the headquarters of Herrick 16 (and the beginning of Herrick 17 in September and October 2012) this lack of clarity created significant breaks in coherence and some dissonance in operational-level planning.

This was made more manifest following the receipt of a draft 'unified implementation plan' (UIP) from the three-star command—ISAF Joint Command (IJC)—who had interpreted General Allen's concept into a more conventional military planning format that was intended to bring coherence across the force. It is from the UIP that we draw the title of our article: 'gripping and touching' were the terms used to describe the relative proximity that ISAF advisors and soldiers were to have with their interlocutors in the Afghan security forces. 'Gripping' was used for close support, when the advisors would be living with their Afghan partners or at the very least visiting with them daily. 'Touching' was intended to describe a lighter footprint, where the advising unit would only visit with their Afghan counterpart

[15] HQ ISAF, *Concept*.

[16] Josef T. Ansorge, 'Spirit of War: A Field Manual', *International Political Sociology* 4, no. 4 (2010): p. 374.

[17] Land Stabilisation and COIN Centre, 'UK Security Force Assistance in Afghanistan', October 2012.

infrequently. In Task Force Helmand and for the UK, touching had variously been described as 'patrolling to advise' and, initially and somewhat optimistically, 'commuting to work'. In the headquarters and for most of the British contingent, the language was perceived as farcical and laden with unintended innuendo. In one example, during a video conference with a senior British officer in the UK, the general spoke harshly about 'all this touching and feeling the ANSF'.

However, taking the form of a 'draft' implementation plan, the ambiguity for our headquarters persisted. Still, there had not been orders, and so—in the absence of contrary direction—the task force in Helmand continued with its extant plans and the approach to advising that it understood as most suitable for its area of operations (AO). Whether passivity in the face of ambiguity is infelicity is debatable. In our minds, as participants in and observers of this phase of the campaign, the headquarters and commanders pursued the correct course of action in refraining from making changes to the British advising pattern too rashly. Advising is an acutely delicate process, where individual relationships are paramount to the local success of the operation and for the safety of military and diplomatic personnel operating in the province. Some of the enduring criticisms of the British advising profile were about its paucity—it is challenging to form strong bonds in a six-month tour—and there was a conversation in the headquarters regarding the dangers of 'lifting off' the effort of advising. In terms of force protection, it was believed that less contact with the Afghan security forces could expose the task force to greater mortal danger as daily interaction increased mutual trust. But that is an incomplete frame: some of the most forceful and well-received arguments were mostly legitimate and sometimes paternalistic concerns and guilt about abandoning those Afghan soldiers and policeman that were our friends and allies. Nonetheless, while reading the SFA documents at the headquarters, it was felt that Task Force Helmand was already following many of the principles outlined by General Allen. For example, the SFA document states that,

> [there] is no single approach. ISAF will provide assistance to all ANSF [Afghan National Security Force] entities. Do not solely focus on the ANA [Afghan National Army] because it is comfortable to do so. The ANP [Afghan National Police] are not the ANA, nor are they the NDS [National Directorate of Security].[18]

Task Force Helmand believed that it was pursuing an approach most suited to the operational environment of central Helmand, which necessitated advising at a lower level for longer. That other ISAF units across Afghanistan were advising at a higher level at the same time was not perceived as a problem,

[18] HQ ISAF, *Principles*.

but more a reflection of their lower troop densities. However, this does highlight some of the inconsistencies in the subsequent application of security force assistance: while 'there is no single approach' to advising, there is, however, a parallel requirement for 'a common approach' and 'unified action' across all of ISAF. Simultaneously, we were required to conduct operations as both particular to the task force and Helmand, and general to ISAF and Afghanistan.

Receiving a draft plan from the three-star headquarters (IJC) was indicative of the highly complex chains of command present in the ISAF campaign. As a result of time and competing national and international imperatives, agendas, and interests, the command structure to which the Helmand task force headquarters was subject had grown complex. Furthermore, with an explicit desire for transition from ISAF to the Afghan security forces, there was clearly to be a significant shift of power and realignment of the expectations at every level of command: this was never going to be a simple process. Confusingly, the Helmand task force headquarters was subject to three distinct 'chains of command': UK national, with a chain via Kabul; another UK command direct to the Permanent Joint Headquarters (PJHQ) in Northwood; and NATO operational command, via Headquarters Regional Command (South West) (RC (SW)). The headquarters was trying to support the Afghan chain of command. We worked very closely with the headquarters of 3/215 Brigade of the Afghan National Army (ANA), the regional chief of the Afghan National Police (ANP) and the chiefs of the three districts in our area of operations; specifically, the local commander of the Afghan Civil Order Police (ANCOP), the regional and district chiefs of the National Directorate for Security (NDS), and on occasion, local commanders of the Afghan Border Police (ABP). The headquarters also had to coordinate with the Provincial Reconstruction Team (PRT) co-located with Task Force Helmand in Lashkar Gah, who themselves reported to the British Embassy in Kabul (and back to home departments in Whitehall); the Ministry of Defence's Operations Directorate in Whitehall via the task force's political advisor (POLAD); and the supporting logistic commander based in Camp Bastion. And there were more in addition. Each of these chains worked well enough in isolation, and had done for some time, with a regular flow of directives, back-briefs, updates, and a network of embedded liaison officers. Occasionally difficulties could be experienced when the multiple masters required competing or differing responses to any given issue. Then, the result could be what one could describe as a 'wicked' problem—one where no obvious solution could be found due to competing and mutually exclusive outcomes. An example of this could be the highly political issues of the UK policy towards detainees and the Afghan Local Police (ALP) programme. But generally, pragmatism won the day and the system just 'worked'.

Cultural change

At the time of our deployment, Task Force Helmand's headquarters was subject to a set of dynamics driving action and reaction that are worth exploring. First, the task force's operational design was to pursue relentlessly and defeat the insurgent, wherever they were to be found, in order to create space and time for the Afghan security forces to stand on their own. Where possible this would be done on the periphery, in order to take the violence away from the population centres, and give the local inhabitants the impression that Helmand was increasingly peaceful, and that it was due to the Afghan security forces being in charge (as they were, in the population centres). Secondly, there was the clear need to drawdown UK forces in accordance with the UK 'Transition Plan' which was constructed and owned by PJHQ. Thirdly, it was important for the UK to appear to be acting in accordance with a steady, coherent national course, plan, or strategy. Fourthly, it was important not to be seen to be dancing to an American tune; the impression of UK sovereignty and autonomy over its actions and deployed troops, and that associated credibility, was politically significant. Nevertheless, there was a clear imperative to follow orders through the NATO operational chain of command, under Major General Gurganus, the US commander of Regional Command (South West). Simultaneously there was an obvious requirement to follow orders from the UK's national chain of command. Finally, there was a necessity to have credibility with our own troops, many of whom were risking their lives every day. The latter would occasionally be emphasized by a national political requirement to have our troops operate under the best possible force protection profile, to minimize their exposure to unnecessary risk. The shift to SFA contradicted some of these dynamics, complemented some, and reinforced others—without necessarily adding a great deal of further clarity. For example, security force assistance requires that ISAF push the Afghan security forces forward and supports them in exposing themselves to the risk associated with independent military operations. Simultaneously, as stated in the SFA document, 'this does not mean the cessation of all combat operations by coalition forces, who will still be required to fight alongside their Afghan counterparts until the threat is diminished'.[19] Consequently, flexibility of mind in planning our own and supporting Afghan operations was a constant and challenging imperative for the headquarters.

In a broader sense, the conversation in the task force headquarters in Helmand was reflective, self-critical, and acutely aware of past failures in, and possible risks to, the British effort. The complexity of the campaign was

[19] HQ ISAF, *Concept.*

obvious and there would often be intellectual discussions, accompanied with a great many complaints, about how the British military culture, institutional characteristics, and policy constraints meant that the campaign could not always be executed in the most effective manner. At this late stage in the campaign, many officers in the headquarters believed that it was too late for problems to be addressed by technical resources and equipment, and instead it was our cultures that were the greatest danger to a successful mission, closely followed by a sense that the campaign was 'hostage to fortune' of a long list of factors completely outside our control. The headquarters was fully cognizant of the popular criticisms that were present in many scholarly articles and public commentaries about the mission in Helmand, and, to mention but a few: the six-month tour duration; the relatively small number of Dari and Pashtu speakers in the force; being wedded to company, battlegroup, and brigade structures; the requirement to be 'soldier-diplomats' and deliver development aid; and the requirement for knowledge of complex Afghan national, provincial, and district politics and society.

An inherent contradiction can exist in military hierarchies. Ostensibly, military forces are immensely flexible: they can be tasked and will take corresponding action in very short time-frames. But once engaged in 'steady state' activity, institutional conservatism can predominate (perhaps in common with most organizations). In this climate, orders from higher headquarters that require substantive change are often not received with overwhelming positivity. Over time these behaviours can be reinforced by practice and become the norm, leading to institutional inertia. This inertia can be exacerbated by having large headquarters with a high number of staff officers, as found at regional command in Afghanistan. Typically, with several hundred staff, the large regional headquarters would produce correspondingly large operational orders, if only because each branch chief and staff officer therein felt compelled to produce quantities of detailed staff work. One of the authors recalls leading the writing of a combined operation order for the regional headquarters in Kandahar in 2008. The resulting order was several hundred pages of masterful and detailed work, but it was never going to be enacted in full by a hard-pressed British brigade headquarters in central Helmand, with its own set of dynamics and realities.

One of the reasons that implementing the shift towards security force assistance was problematic was that the fundamental nature of the change was not grasped immediately, and it was seen as mere re-branding. SFA was to be carried out simultaneously to and as part of a bitter, protracted counter-insurgency fight on the ground. Its scope was vast, as the security forces must act jointly, and with other government institutions. Indeed, SFA had to encompass not just the Afghan security forces but the entire security enterprise:

> [SFA supports] Afghan security ministries to build institutional capacity; to Afghan training bases to provide education and professional development; [and] to the deployed force, by providing advisory and assistance teams.[20]

However because it was underway in the midst of a conflict, it required that operational imperatives be balanced with the development of the Afghan security forces and associated government ministries. In the words of the SFA document, 'Security Force Assistance is conducted in the Afghan security ministries all the way down to the squad on patrol'.[21] Consequently in the headquarters and within the task force, there was inertia to be overcome (as every sinew was being strained to locate and defeat the insurgents). Furthermore, after 15 previous iterations, the headquarters was a highly efficient machine for warfighting. Yet we had to stop doing it, or at least shift our focus and approach. The operational design for Herrick 16 incorporated this shift intelligently, but it would still take time for the mindset of all the practitioners to change. Time for cultural change, however, is not a comfortable or easily accommodated concept in military operations and so policing this shift to SFA was, as ISAF directed us: 'the responsibility of each and every individual supporting the ISAF mission, both military and civilian'.[22]

Cognizant of many of the problems we have discussed, the SFA instructions identified the danger for campaign success of an unusually large number of parallel and possibly competing chains of command. There are often and repeated statements about the importance of 'coherence', a 'single plan', a 'common approach'. SFA requires:

> unified action to ensure that support is applied appropriately across all the Afghan security forces... and developing all elements of the Afghan security forces in parallel.[23]

Moreover, and within even greater force of language, unified action and a common approach are achieved through:

> **One Command and one mission**.... Do not build alternative chains of command or ad hoc organizations. Use simple and unambiguous command and control systems that mirror the Afghan's chain of command and then support them at every level.[24]

Observing the vast interrelated and byzantine network of commands operating during the campaign in Afghanistan, the behaviour desired from the deductions within the SFA documents were, arguably, impossible for the military to enact. Consequently, the SFA documents were serving multiple purposes: some were commands and behaviours that the constituent components of ISAF

[20] HQ ISAF, *Concept*. [21] HQ ISAF, *Principles*. [22] HQ ISAF, *Concept*.
[23] HQ ISAF, *Principles*. [24] HQ ISAF, *Principles*.

should or could implement; others served as admissions of guilt, as points of failure for the military, or were caused by factors and actors outside of the military's control.

Military knowledge and catharsis

As Campbell observes, the concluding phase of war or military campaigns is accompanied by books and commentaries that attempt to 'make sense' of the events: the texts often deploy theatrical keywords of 'tragedy', 'inferno', 'death', and 'drama'.[25] A summary observation of recent book titles about the decade-long campaign in Afghanistan supports Campbell's observation—amongst others we have *The Inside Story of the Chaotic Struggle for Afghanistan* (2012) and *Dead Men Risen* (2011). More than the publisher's struggle for a snappy title, the titles are revealing in the drama they purport to describe, the author's privileged access or unknown stories that they will reveal, and how they are *the* definitive account: 'if you only read one, read this one'. The shift to SFA and its written words are a process of internal military emplotment: they arrange the 'facts' to become components of a particular narrative, a tragic narrative from which the valiant are engaged in a difficult struggle to recover, learning from past failures, and fighting not only an unconventional enemy but also tragic characteristics of our own institutions and culture. Aristotle observed that we take pleasure even in unpleasant things, and the distinction between the pleasure of poetry and the pleasure of tragedy is that the latter creates pleasure through the representation of disagreeable emotions, especially pity and fear, and allowing a process of *catharsis*—the release of the negative emotions.[26] Lacan argued that gazing upon an issue or object is sustained most readily when the object of attention produces not only anxiety but also pleasure.[27] Tragedy is pleasurable in its purgation, allowing the participants (typically the audience) to feel relief from the bitter imitation.[28] In an effective tragedy, the audience feels pity for good people undergoing underserved suffering, and fear because we see tragedy happening to someone like ourselves. A successful plot, Aristotle advocated, 'should be so constructed that even without seeing the play, anyone who merely hears the events unfold will shudder and feel pity as a result of what is happening'.[29] The SFA documents write an incomplete narrative of the campaign and draw deductions

[25] Patricia Molloy, 'Theatrical release: catharsis and spectacle in Welcome to Sarajevo', *Alternatives* 25, no. 1 (2000): p. 75.

[26] Aristotle, *Poetics* (New York: Norton, 1982), p. 50.

[27] Jacques Lacan, *The Four Fundamental Concepts of Psychoanalysis* (New York: Norton, 1981), pp. 181–3.

[28] Molloy, 'Theatrical release', p. 83.

[29] Molloy, 'Theatrical release', p. 84.

from the military story that have been painful to acknowledge, particularly those deductions that are plain for all to see and yet institutionally, socially, politically, or materially impossible to implement.

The military is a highly structured organization that nonetheless allows a degree of resistance precisely because it is a modern, professionalized system of domination that is far more bureaucratic than would perhaps be assumed by most outsiders. Power relations within the military do leave space for practices of freedom, and, arguably, the forms of power and the requirements of military participants 'are possible only insofar as the subjects are free'.[30] As in other domains of domination, the power relations of the modern military operating in Afghanistan are dependent on acts of resistance within itself. Some of the sanctioned acts of resistance in military organizations are perceived as institutional learning. The manner in which the UK Ministry of Defence (MOD) manages knowledge is not only through the construction and dissemination of doctrine, but also in the identification and internalization of 'lessons'. Such is the prolificacy of lessons in the MOD and single-services, that framed on the wall of one organization with responsibility for some institutional learning, was the humorous indictment that, 'the MOD's ongoing lessons learnt programme has identified we haven't learned the lessons we identified last time'. In the language of policy, the MOD understands lessons as analysis drawn from previous experience that imparts new knowledge, which can be used to inform recommendations or actions. Organizations within the MOD and the single-services with a responsibility for lessons, and the lessons processes themselves, provide the military with an invaluable and *legitimate* process for reflection and self-criticism. Far from being suppressed, drawing 'lessons' from experience on operations is institutionalized and encouraged behaviour—with the accompanying policy and doctrine describing how the process should be conducted. The deductions drawn from lessons are intended, once scrutinized (or 'staffed'), to change how the military behave. For example, the cross-government 'Stabilisation Unit' has a dedicated lessons team that is charged with supporting stabilization efforts 'through the effective collection, analysis and dissemination of lessons.... Lessons are based on the experience of people working in the field'.[31] Much of the new direction within the SFA documents are deductions drawn from such lessons, and one bullet-point under 'approach' explicitly addresses that ISAF must be a 'learning organisation':

> Share best practices; explain to others what has worked.... Ensure continuity, chart progress and pass relevant information to your replacement, so that they

[30] Michel Foucault, *Foucault Live: Interviews, 1961–1984* (New York: Semiotext(e), 1996), p. 441.

[31] UK Stabilisation Unit, accessed 15 May 20013, <http://www.stabilisationunit.gov.uk/about-us/more-about-the-unit.html>.

can tailor their own pre-deployment training to accurately reflect the events on the ground.[32]

Given the mortal requirements of the profession, it should come as no surprise that the military has a function and processes for institutional learning: there is an industry of 'making sense' of military campaigns. The defence bureaucracy has formalized programmes of 'historical-based decision making' and 'evidence-based decision making' that are intended to support policy-makers in making the most informed decisions possible by giving them access to a wide variety of analyses, deductions, and evidence-sets. Defence perceives itself as a learning organization and so believes in the Enlightenment notion that humankind has the ability to reason about its fate and to impact upon the future.

However, knowledge in the military is intentionally simplified. It is removed from its geographic, temporal, and intellectual context and rendered universal[33] in order to be easily applicable across multiple operating environments. The desire is for a standard set of military behaviours and courses of action that are transferable across time and space, with every possible campaign and form of war accounted for by sets of military knowledge. According to Scott, these simplifications within state institutions

> represent techniques for grasping a large and complex reality; in order for officials to be able to comprehend aspects of the ensemble, that complex reality must be reduced to schematic categories. The only way to accomplish this is to reduce an infinite array of detail to a set of categories that will facilitate summary descriptions, comparisons, and aggregation'.[34]

The security force assistance concept is a simple set of changes in behaviour drawn out of deductions formed by collating the dominant descriptions of the military's experiences, mostly the perceived failures, of over 10 years of campaigning in Afghanistan. With monumental differences in physical and human terrain, a strategic and policy context that has been absent or in constant flux, alongside cultural divergences within and between military contingents, the ability to give written form to failure is a significant achievement of resistance and reflection.

To perceive the enactment of the process of security force assistance as only a clear desire for change in the course(s) of action risks misinterpreting what it is these documents are 'doing', or only seeing them as attempting to achieve something explicit—a change in mission—rather than serving some additional purpose to the institution. The utterance and documents of

[32] HQ ISAF, *Principles*. [33] Ansorge, 'Spirit of War: A Field Manual', p. 369.
[34] James Scott, 'Cities, people and language', in *The Anthropology of the State*, edited by Aradhana Sharma and Akhil Gupta (Oxford: Blackwell, 2006), p. 259.

security force assistance are a moment of reflection and catharsis through which the military organization is attempting to 'make sense' of the strategic narrative for the campaign in Afghanistan compared with the 'reality on the ground'. The peculiar construct of the documents arranges knowledge as a narrative, with declarations, exposition, and deductions that are intended to inform decision-making within the military organization. The security force assistance concepts are not doctrine, but a collection of painful lessons.

Gazing at the ANSF and gazing at ourselves

After 2003, Western military campaigning shifted away from a focus only on physical surroundings (nature and typography) to terms that focus on social and human relations—the 'human terrain'. In Task Force Helmand there was a small cadre of 'cultural advisors' (CULADs) who were present both at the headquarters and assigned to work alongside the battlegroup commanders. During the period of our deployment, the CULADs became known as 'cultural specialists (human terrain)' (CS(HT)), or colloquially as 'See Shit'. Consequently, the military gaze sought cultural awareness and valued cultural sensitivity (at least in theory). The 'approach' section of the SFA documents expended many words emphasizing and reiterating the absolute requirement of constructing operations and understanding how our actions impacted on the Afghans and their ability to conduct independent operations:

> **This is Afghanistan.** Don't template assistance based on your own background or prejudice. Approach every problem from an Afghan perspective.... Observe and understand the cultural norms, their systems and processes before offering advice. Sustainable solutions will be ones that Afghans can embrace as their own.[35]

For Operation Herrick 16, 'Afghan-led' was one of the most vital considerations running throughout the deployment and many of our activities were intended to embed this in our thinking and to be checked against this mindset. For example, on all of the task force's briefing material—usually a Microsoft PowerPoint slide—was the tagline of the deployment, 'WITH the ANSF, FOR the people, AGAINST the insurgent'. The task force commander saw a great deal of his task as ensuring and enabling Afghan ownership of the security plan and he did so by regular (sometimes daily) meetings with his Afghan interlocutors in Helmand—the importance of 'key leader engagement' was definitely understood and prioritized by the commander and the task force. Consequently, for Task Force Helmand some of the lessons identified in

[35] HQ ISAF, *Principles*.

the SFA documents had already been embedded in the brigade's behaviour. For example, one directive stated:

> **Don't allow cultural differences to divide us.** Operating according to Afghan priorities and timelines may involve periods of relative inactivity: be comfortable with this. Relationships are incredibly valuable. Chatting and drinking chai isn't a distraction or an unproductive use of your time; view it as the time where you arrive at a mutual understanding of where you're going and how you are collectively going to get there.[36]

How this intention for Afghan-ownership was made manifest in Helmand was through supporting the leaders of the Helmand security forces in formulating an approach to operations that, according to the SFA principles later set out, is based entirely on Afghan needs and not influenced by British or ISAF demands:

> **SFA is based on Afghan needs.** Afghan needs and requirements are just that. Their solutions must be durable, consistent and sustainable.... Developing professionalism and leadership will have far greater and a more lasting effect than developing tactics.[37]

This approach to operations led to the production of a map of Helmand with geographic spaces marked out and afforded a colour based on the priority assigned to them by the Afghan leadership of Helmand. The task force understood this as the *realistic* intent of our Afghan interlocutors and therefore it assisted the commander and staff in the 'when', 'how', 'where', and 'with whom' to plan combined operations. It was a creed that all our activities were to be based on how best to support the Afghan security forces. The task force's efforts were assessed at a regular meeting between senior figures in Helmand and their Afghan counterparts, namely the Central Helmand Security Shura.[38] This meeting was deliberately Afghan-led and increasingly only facilitated by the task force with support from the Helmand Provincial Reconstruction Team. This process is a good example of the headquarters practising another of the SFA mindset requirements:

> **Better that the Afghans do something adequately than we do it perfectly.** Ask and then listen to how the Afghans will conduct operations, and then assist them accordingly; increase their capability along the way. Your effect is measured by how well the ANSF develop, not the number of times you successfully complete a task, acquire resources, or the number of suggestions you make.[39]

[36] HQ ISAF, *Principles*. [37] HQ ISAF, *Principles*.

[38] By the military in Afghanistan, the word *shura* was used to describe any general meeting, council, or consultation between themselves and any Afghan counterparts.

[39] HQ ISAF, *Principles*. This is a line borrowed from T. E. Lawrence's advice on conducting guerilla operations.

However, because of the complicated command chains already mentioned, and the subsequent enforcement of greater scrutiny from the regional command, the existence of this *shura* caused tensions between the British-led task force and the American-led regional command as to which ISAF headquarters was the appropriate interlocutor for the senior Afghan security figures in Helmand. This tension highlights an enduring problem of our advising efforts in Afghanistan generally, and Helmand in particular: the advising space is heavily crowded with many officers and commanders who wish to advise or otherwise communicate with an Afghan official of a comparative authority. In another example of catharsis, this is a problem well known to ISAF and articulated in the SFA documents:

> **One Afghan, one advisor.** Define the sphere of influence for every Afghan unit, official and leader. Avoid multiple and overlapping advisory chains. Determine who owns the relationship and then allow that individual to develop it.... Do not confuse quantity with quality.[40]

This is a further example of how the institutional culture of the military complicates or perhaps renders impossible the pursuit of the ideal as recognized and outlined in pieces of military knowledge. Outwardly, the cultural knowledge desired is that of the Afghan security forces, politicians, and wider Afghan society. However, an inevitable corollary of an emerging cultural lexicon is that it becomes to a degree reflexive: the military become interested in their own culture, sensitive to structural and cultural failures that inhibit ability to conduct the mission. Taking this observation further, the military seeks out an understanding of how its culture creates difficulties in interacting with Afghan culture, and therefore makes purely military tasks much more complicated. In the extreme, cultural differences that are beyond the military's ability to control or change could result in mission failure. Consequently, it is entirely feasible that one narrative within the SFA is that the military are not entirely to blame for the perceived failure of some components of its mission precisely because it only has limited cultural control.

By expanding the domain of military intelligence into cultural awareness, the demand for information is insatiable and almost infinitely broadened. It is not just the enemy that Task Force Helmand was required to 'collect' intelligence on, but with the onset of increasing attacks by insurgents disguised in Afghan security force uniforms (known as the 'insider threat'), the focus was drawn to our partners in the Afghan security forces. With political sensitivity in mind, there is a distinction drawn between forces 'red' (enemy), 'green' (friendly), and 'blue' (ourselves) and the gaze on the Afghan security forces was described and understood more in cultural terms of understanding and

[40] HQ ISAF, *Principles*.

influence rather than in the traditional martial language of collecting information on and targeting the enemy. This cognitive distinction was hugely challenging for a military force already operating with a different culture and with multinational allies. The complexity is increased to mental exhaustion when the military have to understand their Afghan allies as friendly forces who may be infiltrated by enemy forces, potentially without any outwardly visible 'indicators' of that threat: there is nothing to *see* of the threat until it has been carried out, increasing the feeling of anxiety and an absence of understanding. This concern is echoed in the SFA documents and is drawn out of the military obsession—especially in Afghanistan—with situational awareness. A key part of the SFA approach is therefore to:

> **Maintain the Sensory Network.** As force levels reduce, our traditional situational awareness will decline.... Locals have an advantage, culturally and linguistically, over ISAF and can access information that you will never leverage.[41]

The idea of the panopticon is useful for understanding the British experience in Helmand, 'everyone is watched, according to his position within the system, by all or by certain of the others. Here we have an apparatus of total and mobile distrust'.[42] There is no ultimate scrutineer in the Helmand campaign who can reveal an accurate and trustworthy picture: however, as the single point at which multiple communications converge, the task force commander could, with extraordinary capacity, come closer than most. The amount of information produced in a given day was more than any one person could usefully interpret, and so Krips encapsulates this aspect of the headquarters (and countless others involved in the Afghanistan campaign) in theoretical language, where orders, instructions, intelligence, and cultural assessments, and so on, come:

> from everyone and everywhere and yet from no one and nowhere, a heteroglossia of voices that depends for its appearance of univocality upon a retrospective interpretative gesture by each and every audience member as s/he struggles to make sense of the inchoate stream of signs that assail her/his ears from all sides.[43]

Taking Krips' argument further, the articles of military knowledge of Helmand and Afghanistan become indeterminate because there is no absolute point of truth; the indeterminacy creates a space and requirement for practices of freedom as the military interpret—'make sense'—of the huge amount of information traffic about the campaign. The cathartic set of SFA documents are an act of resistance attempting to form a coherent narrative of the

[41] HQ ISAF, *Principles*. [42] Foucault, *Foucault Live*, p. 235.
[43] Henry Krips, 'The politics of the gaze: Foucault, Lacan and Žižek', *Culture Unbound* 2 (2010): p. 97.

military's past in Afghanistan with the hope of providing the simplistic sets of behaviours required to continue to make sense of the remaining period of the campaign. Moreover, the documents are intended to help the military to 'let go', to move on, and 'step away', leaving and trusting the Afghan security forces to carry on the fight. This in itself is a considerable challenge to military culture, as, morally, the fight can still be seen as ISAF's responsibility (particularly after all the expenditure of blood and treasure), and it can require considerable conscious effort to trust our Afghan partners. This cultural difficulty goes some way to illuminating why the insider threat was such a brutally simple and yet effective insurgent tactic.

However, we believe it would be invidious not to record the very tangible progress made by our Afghan colleagues throughout Herrick 16, often leading to a sense of surprise and professional admiration amongst the staff and soldiers of the task force. The Afghans' appetite to take on the leadership of the campaign was evident. Such was the capability of, in particular, the ANA in central Helmand that they were well ahead of the capacity levels envisaged by the SFA doctrine, which required us to have the following mindset:

> **Their failure is not your failure**. Have the confidence and patience to allow your counterpart to lead and to learn through self-discovery and to determine their own shortcomings. The Afghans will get the occasional bloody nose and you must ensure that they learn from the experience. However, ISAF must not stand by and watch them being knocked down.[44]

These occasions were very rare, and when a 'bloody nose' was received, the Afghan response was usually far swifter than ISAF could have enacted. With an embedded culture of military pride, it was always going to be unlikely that ISAF assistance would be called for. The doctrine foresaw a period of gradually reducing support:

> **It is ok to say 'no'**. Just because you can, don't always provide enablers that the ANSF will not have access to, post transition. The routine provision of these assets will only stall the Afghans' ability to develop their own enablers.[45]

In fact the Afghan security forces were well advanced in their capabilities, and their requests for support were carefully assessed and rationed. One of the most enduring positives of the campaign will be the capacity that has been built in the Afghan security apparatus. In this sense SFA predicts correctly the Afghan appetite and facility for prosecuting a successful campaign and ensuring the viability of the current Afghan state.

[44] HQ ISAF, *Principles*. [45] HQ ISAF, *Principles*.

Conclusion

This chapter speaks to the heart of transition in Afghanistan. The authors experienced a time in the campaign where a tipping point was reached, following what can be seen as the high-watermark of British military feats of arms in the counter-insurgency campaign. Over a short space of time, the mindset and approach of thousands of soldiers had to change fundamentally, while 'in contact' with their enemy: from expending maximum energy on defeating the insurgent, to expending the same energy on supporting the Afghan government and its security forces to defeat the insurgents, and on their terms.

Simultaneously, we felt that the shift in the campaign, intellectually, to a stated mission that placed the Afghans in the lead was the military's cathartic moment. It was an admission of past failures, not all within the control of the actors on the ground, with a genuine desire to drive cultural changes within our own organization that would bring our operational planning to a point of being attuned to the realistic priorities of our Afghan allies, who, rightly, should decide on the future of their country. In attempting to shift ISAF from pure warfighting to the institutional development of the Afghan security forces, the British Army had thought about the problems of supporting armed groups who had yet to fully develop the checks and balances against predation or their excesses, let alone the nightmarish difficulties of creating and sustaining supply and logistics chains across hostile territory amidst endemic corruption. Faced with this, there are many dedicated people, Afghan and ISAF, who have struggled in extremely difficult circumstances, morally and mortally, to reform the Afghan security apparatus into effective policing and military units that will protect the Afghan people. The criticisms that this change came too late in the decade-long campaign may have some accuracy, but to use that criticism as mere fatalistic cynicism is—in our eyes—unacceptable.

References

Ansorge, Josef T., 'Spirit of War: A Field Manual', *International Political Sociology* 4, no. 4 (2010): pp. 362–79.

Aristotle, *Poetics* (New York: Norton, 1982).

Austin, John L., *How to Do Things with Words* (Cambridge, MA: Harvard University Press, 1962).

Foucault, Michel, *Foucault Live: Interviews, 1961–1984* (New York: Semiotext(e), 1996).

Geertz, Clifford, *The Interpretation of Cultures* (New York: Basic Books, 1973).

Headquarters International Security Assistance Force, *ISAF Commander's Security Force Assistance Concept* (2011).

Headquarters International Security Assistance Force, *ISAF Commander's Security Force Assistance Principles* (2011).

Headquarters International Security Assistance Force, *ISAF Security Force Assistance Guide*, 2013, <https://ronna.apan.org/CAAT/Shared%20Documents/20130505_NIU_SFA_Guide.pdf>.

Krips, Henry, 'The politics of the gaze: Foucault, Lacan and Žižek', *Culture Unbound* 2 (2010): pp. 91–102.

Lacan, Jacques, *The Four Fundamental Concepts of Psychoanalysis* (New York: Norton, 1981).

Land Stabilisation and COIN Centre: 'UK Security Force Assistance in Afghanistan', October 2012.

Molloy, Patricia, 'Theatrical release: catharsis and spectacle in Welcome to Sarajevo', *Alternatives* 25, no. 1 (2000): pp. 75–90.

Scott, James, 'Cities, people and language', in *The Anthropology of the State*, edited by Aradhana Sharma and Akhil Gupta (Oxford: Blackwell, 2006), pp. 53–83.

UK Stabilisation Unit, accessed 15 May 2013, <http://www.stabilisationunit.gov.uk/about-us/more-about-the-unit.html>.

Williams, Anne, 'Reading feminism in fieldnotes', in *Feminist Praxis: Research, Theory, and Epistemology in Feminist Sociology*, edited by Liz Stanley (New York: Routledge, 1990), pp. 253–61.

19

'Insider'/'outsider' policing

Observations on the role of UK Police (MDP) in Afghanistan and the application of 'lessons learnt'

Georgina Sinclair

Introduction

> One of the most important lessons to me regarding Tactical Transitions is that it must impact on how UK Police plans and does international policing assistance in the future, which includes working with the military. The aspiration of the UK in the future and how it supports fragile countries needs to be established with mechanisms that support the current strategies rather than learning and relearning the lessons every time we (the UK) become involved in such work.
>
> Head Afghan Police Unit, Ministry of Defence Police, 2012[1]

The global policing community has been increasingly invited to contribute to international policing missions since the 1990s. Policing post-conflict and fragile states forms a core component of US and European security sector reform strategies and the export of policing systems and styles has subsequently been undertaken by members of both the developed and the developing world. The UK's involvement in international policing (from both the state and corporate sectors) has increased during the post-Cold War era with the rise of transnational security threats and the global 'war on terror',

[1] I would like to extend my gratitude to the Ministry of Defence Police for their support in the preparation of this chapter and in particular to Alistair Eivers for all his assistance in providing the necessary material and organizing my visit to Wethersfield in November 2012. I would also like to thank Clive Emsley who read several drafts of this chapter and made helpful comments and suggestions.

attracting greater scholarly attention across the disciplines.[2] International policing though is not a new phenomenon and can be traced to the development of British colonial policing in the nineteenth century and the early secondment of British police to the empire and commonwealth (and further afield) to provide a range of policing services, advisory and diplomatic roles. The use of international police has been described as 'police strangers' engaging with local communities and their own police, although this retains early inferences to the colonial and post-colonial context.[3] A more useful term might be 'outsider' policing (of insiders) which could be applied to international policing assistance as a description of how international police (or military and services police—as outsiders) have engaged with 'insiders' (citizens and local police).

In this chapter the focus is on one facet of the 'UK Police PLC'—the Ministry of Defence Police (widely known as the MDP) that has carved out a particular niche in international policing assistance since the mid-1990s. In more recent years, the MDP has provided nearly half of all the UK police who have served on official overseas secondments, and since 2007 has supported UK policing efforts in Afghanistan in both Helmand and Kabul. Here I draw on MDP's Afghanistan experiences under Operation Herrick and reflect on the role of stakeholders and providers at the UK end and in Afghanistan. In this case an opportunity presented to improve the provision of international policing services at the centre, to identify those 'lessons needing to be learnt' in theatre within an integrated military-police approach to police monitoring, mentoring, and advising. This may provide an opportunity to harness lessons learnt

[2] See for example: David Bayley and Robert Perito, *The Police in War: Fighting insurgency, terrorism, and violent crime* (Boulder, CA: Lynne Rienner Publishers, 2010); Ben Bowling and James Sheptycki, *Global Policing* (London: Sage, 2012); Graham Ellison and Nathan Pino, *Globalization, Police Reform and Development: Doing it the Western Way? Transnational Crime, Crime Control and Security* (Basingstoke: Palgrave Macmillan, 2012); Georgina Sinclair, 'Exporting the UK Police "Brand": The RUC-PSNI and the International Agenda', *Policing: A Journal of Policy and Practice* 6, no. 1 (2012): pp. 55–66.

[3] Colonial policing has been linked to the concept of 'policing strangers' to describe the policing of a community by police who had been brought in from the 'outside' to police that community. In essence this concept has referred to coercive mechanisms of control stemming from scholarly interpretations of policing in nineteenth century Ireland, and its transfer to the Empire and Commonwealth. The term is still in use in relation to the colonial and post-colonial eras and relates to the contemporary period in relation to the policing of mobile populations, ethnic minorities both in the national and international contexts. More recently, 'policing by strangers' has been loosely applied to problems inherent within community policing (See M. Brogden, 'Community policing as cherry pie', in *Policing across the World: Issues for the twenty-first century*, edited by R. Mawby (London: UCL Press, 1999), pp. 167–86). However as a theoretical concept it remains deeply problematic and there has been little engagement with the shifting of 'coercion' and 'consent' paradigms over time and the blurring of policing boundaries. This extends to community policing which remains an amorphous concept although nonetheless an essential mechanism by which policing can be theorized. Policing in stable democratic societies is predominantly concerned with the implementation and practice of this globally accepted philosophy of community policing and this has been extended to the international arena.

to any future overseas policing missions within post-conflict and fragile states and may benefit the development of international policing and rule of law doctrine more broadly.

The role of the UK Police and international policing

International police assistance has become something of a growth industry, with requests for UK policing from the UN, the EU, the Organisation for Security and Cooperation in Europe (OSCE), and other multinational organizations, as well as the governments of individual countries—often those with long-standing historic links to the Commonwealth.[4] The rationales underpinning the UK's delivery of international policing are generally articulated through foreign policy and international agreements relating to defence, diplomacy, and the strengthening of fragile states. The UK's continued involvement in 'formal' international policing missions is highlighted by the government's pledge to distribute 0.7 per cent of national income as aid from 2013. The *National Security Strategy*, published in October 2010 to correlate with the *Strategic Defence and Security Review*, noted the wider security risks which included terrorism, instability and conflict overseas, and transnational crime.[5]

One key historic legacy of UK police *and* policing, which has a continuing impact upon the provision of UK officers for international missions, has been the lack of a 'national police service' and by extension a central coordination point for stakeholders. Supplying UK policing is heavily reliant on a cross-departmental approach within Whitehall which poses particular challenges. A traditionally interactive and sometimes adversarial approach to policy development in the UK is reflected within the different agendas relating to UK policing, and this is compounded by there being no international policing or rule of law strategy equivalent to the Ministry of Defence's (MOD) Defence Engagement Strategy. All Home Office and MOD police can technically provide official international police assistance which is governed by different legal provisions: section 26 of the Police Act 1996 (England and Wales), the equivalent section 12A of the Police (Scotland) Act 1967, and section 8 of the Police (Northern Ireland) Act 2000 in Northern Ireland. The 2008 Policing

[4] In UK policing terminology, a distinction should be made between international policing and policing internationally: the former relating to international policing assistance offered within a multi-lateral context (e.g. United Nations led missions) whilst the latter refers to bilateral arrangements between UK police (e.g. College of Policing (International Academy) or individual constabularies) and an overseas police force to deliver training, or the types of international activities undertaken by Interpol.

[5] Cabinet Office, *A Strong Britain in an Age of Uncertainty*, Cm 7953 (London: HMSO, 2010); Cabinet Office, *Securing Britain in an Age of Uncertainty: The Strategic Defence and Security Review*, Cm 7948 (London: HMSO, 2010), p. 22.

Green Paper supported the creation of an International Policing Assistance Board (IPAB), chaired by the Association of Chief Police Officers (ACPO) International portfolio holder (Chief Constable Colin Port until January 2013) 'to help coordinate and focus activity where it is most in the national and international interests of the UK'.[6] Established in 2009, this senior cross-departmental and police advisory body has a primary objective of facilitating and enhancing UK police assistance overseas from government departments, individual police services, and agencies and to provide a key coordination point for the referral process between government departments and the police service. However, IPAB's terms of reference does not include counter-terrorism or operational policing in an international environment. In recognizing this fragmentation coupled with a lack of direct funding, ACPO International Affairs was established in June 2010 to become the central coordination for all international policing. It has continued to face real challenges.

Since the late 1990s there has been an increased demand for the use of UK police (serving and retired officers) within missions that stem directly from UK foreign policy: this involves both the Foreign and Commonwealth Office's (FCO) conflict-related policing assistance (e.g. Kosovo, Iraq, and Afghanistan) and the Department for International Development's (DfID) increased 'investment' in broader security and access to justice programmes, as well as a myriad of bilateral missions. Currently the FCO through the Stabilisation Unit (SU) and on behalf of Her Majesty's Government (HMG) supports the secondment of UK police officers to: the EU Police Mission in Afghanistan (EUPOL Afghanistan); the EU Monitoring Mission in Georgia (EUMM Georgia); the EU Integrated Rule of Law Mission for Iraq (EUJUST LEX Iraq); the EU Rule of Law Mission in Kosovo (EULEX Kosovo); and the NATO Training Mission—Afghanistan (NTMA) and so on. The activities of the FCO, DfID, and the MOD have been supported by the cross-departmental Stabilisation Unit since 2004 and its SU Policing Team (SUPT) set up in April 2011. Currently the pool of UK officers eligible for an overseas deployment stands at several hundred with 47 successful applicants currently accepted for 2012–13. UK officers are drawn from across all constabularies (England and Wales and Scotland) and include the MDP.[7] Within this pool of officers eligible for an overseas deployment, the MDP has played an ever-increasing role since the mid-1990s within post-conflict, fragile, and transitional states.

[6] Interview with Chief Constable Colin Port (ACPO International Affairs Portfolio Holder), 5 December 2012.

[7] Extracted from research material collected by Georgina Sinclair and Clive Emsley during the course of an ESRC-funded project, *Exploring UK Policing Practices as a blueprint for democratic police reform: the overseas deployment of UK Police Officers, 1989–2009* (2010–2012).

The MDP and international policing

The MDP was established in 1971 from an amalgamation of the Admiralty, War Office, and Air Ministry Constabularies. In 1996 it became a defence agency within the MDP and in 2004 expanded to include the MOD Guard Service and was renamed the MOD Police and Guarding Agency (MDPGA). MDP has status under the Ministry of Defence Police Act (1987) which defines the jurisdiction of the force and confers constabulary power on its officers of whom a large number carry firearms, unlike Home Office police. MDP officers are recruited, trained, and attested in the same way as Home Office and other police, and their duties must conform to national policing standards. As well as their role in providing armed guarding at key defence sites, counter-terrorism activities, protection of defence personnel and property, and uniformed general policing, the MDP provides services such as criminal and fraud investigation to the MOD, and specialist capabilities such as waterborne security for HM Dockyards and HM Naval Bases. It also has one of the largest dog sections in the UK (23 sections), and is the only UK police service able to work fully in a chemical, biological, radioactive, or nuclear environment. At a local level, joint investigations or operations with other law enforcement agencies or other public bodies are commonplace (e.g. cross-use of resources such as crime scene investigators, transport, intelligence, etc. and 'routine' interaction with other UK police forces).[8]

Although the MDP has been one of the largest *civil* police forces in the UK it has received scant academic attention, and despite issues of nationalizing the UK police, there has been no thought given to the role of 'special police forces' (which includes the MDP), which already have a national operational jurisdiction.[9] MDP has retained a reputation of providing 'guarding duties' at MOD sites, but there is a distinct lack of awareness of its many other duties and responsibilities that necessitate public interface and by extension community policing. This is particularly true of the force's considerable public order management expertise with MDP officers having been seconded to all major public order incidents in the past 30 years. Traditionally, therefore, MDP has and can provide support to all of the UK's police forces and has its own Operation Support Units.

Whilst the MDP could be described as a specialist police force and thus may be perceived as 'niche' in comparison with other UK police forces, MDP officers consider that they are an integral part of UK Police PLC.[10] Their

[8] Ministry of Defence Police and Guarding Agency (MOGDA), *Annual Report 2011–2012* (Braintree: Wethersfield), pp. 8–12.

[9] See: Les Johnston, 'An unseen force: the Ministry of Defence Police in the UK', *Policing and Society* 3, no. 1 (1992): pp. 23–40.

[10] Author interview with ACC Robert Chidley, Wethersfield, 9 November 2012.

niche policing skills extend to the international arena which MDP today promotes as a 'specialization' noting that the force 'deploys the largest number of officers of any UK police force on secondments to organizations such as the United Nations (UN), European Union and other organisations involved in international peacekeeping missions'.[11] Since 2000 the MDP have deployed a total of 595 officers across 13 different countries to provide international policing assistance. Their involvement in overseas missions was partly triggered from the UNMIK mission to Kosovo (2000–07) when MDP cohorts (with RUC–PSNI officers) were deployed. Following UNMIK, MDP officers were then seconded under the EU's EULEX mission. Their initial involvement in UNMIK was linked to the need for UK officers with armed capability who could rapidly deploy to an overseas theatre.[12] Few international missions to which UK police have been seconded have required police under full executive authority policing (East Timor is one other example), although all international missions require officers to carry weapons for self-protection. In the main, MDP have provided monitoring, mentoring, and advising which broadly speaking translates into 'training other police'. In addition, senior MDP with expertise in police intelligence, cybercrime, fraud, and criminal investigations have been seconded as police advisors to missions in Iraq, Kosovo, Bosnia, Georgia, Afghanistan, and the Sudan, and as community police officers to the Pitcairn Islands. Their role in Afghanistan under Operation Herrick has been a departure from the MDP's prior policing experiences in the international arena and where they have been able to operate in conditions of high security threat alongside the military, providing a bridging function to help prepare the ground for handing over to an incoming civilian deployment.

MDP involvement in international policing missions since 2000 has been described as having become an 'institutional reflex',[13] supported by the creation of a centralized deployment hub (International Police Secondments Office (IPSO)) which until 2008 managed the recruitment, deployment, pre-deployment training, and debriefings and so on of all police personnel seconded overseas. From 2008 IPSO has managed the deployment of MDP officers under Operation Herrick whilst all other missions are handled through the Stabilisation Unit (including all EU and UN missions). IPSO has been staffed by four MDP officers and three police personnel, and, for a period of time, extended its own pre-deployment training material and equipment to all Home Office police deployed overseas. This has now ceased as the Stabilisation Unit has become the central coordination point for international policing assistance

[11] MODGA, *Annual Report 2011–2012*, p. 7.
[12] Sinclair, 'Exporting the UK Police "Brand"', p. 59.
[13] Author interview with Inspector Alistair Eivers, Wethersfield, 8 November 2012.

delivery. However, the MDP mission in Afghanistan has been wholly managed by the MDP's Afghanistan Police Unit and the MOD's Support to Operations (S20) team. The terms and conditions, duty of care, and allowances differ from those of SU deployed officers (Home Office police).

International policing in Afghanistan

Afghanistan has provided the framework for a complex range of international debates within which international policing, and by extension the deployment of MDP, forms one segment. The international community has committed huge resources to a range of stabilization and reconstruction programmes in Afghanistan in the past decade. In 2013 the Afghans will assume the lead for security and by the end of 2014 will have full responsibility across Afghanistan. Yet a recent International Crisis Group report posited that there was a real possibility that rule of law may not be maintained during the 2014 election period noting, it 'will at best result in deep divisions and conflicts within the ruling elite that Afghan insurgency will exploit. At worst, it could trigger extensive unrest, fragmentation of the security services and perhaps even a much wider civil war'.[14] Indeed the threats to human security at this time of transition have continued to fluctuate throughout certain parts of the country. This has necessitated counter-insurgency and security management approaches rather than moving from the quasi-militaristic to a community policing style that might in the longer term build legitimacy with the local community. The need for counter-insurgency solutions has also been at the heart of the Afghan government's strategy and 'to many observers, EUPOL's stated objective of introducing a democratic, civilian model of policing seemed too sophisticated and ambitious within the context of an escalating war situation'.[15]

Security Sector Reform (SSR) programmes in Afghanistan were marshalled by the 2001 Bonn Agreement, leading to intensive capacity and capability building programmes which were spread over different stages. In the first instance SSR focused on the (re)establishment of the rule of law and in providing physical and human security throughout the country in order to enhance the Afghan government's legitimacy. Then the focus shifted to localizing security approaches by enabling local Afghan military and police to gradually take over all security functions from the international players.

[14] International Crisis Group, 'Afghanistan: the Long, Hard Road to the 2014 Transition', *Asia Report* 236 (2012): p. 4.

[15] L. Peral, 'The EU Police Mission in Afghanistan (EUPOL Afghanistan)', in *European Security & Defence Policy, the First 10 Years*, edited by Giovanni Grevi, Damien Holly, and Daniel Keohane (New York: Institute for Security Studies, 2009), p. 332.

In 2006, the international community launched 'Afghanistan Compact' which provided a framework for cooperation between the Afghan government and the international community of donor states, signalling greater partnership and emphasizing Afghan ownership of the process. Importantly 'Compact' highlighted areas, including police reform, that had previously been side-lined and, as a result, mooted that by 2010 both the Afghan National Police (ANP) and the Afghan Border Police (ABP) should be fully functional with a combined force of 62,000 male and female officers. It also emphasized that policy-making (in policing terms) should be the remit of the Afghan government, although it offered no clear strategies on how these objectives should be met.[16] Compact strategies advanced through the development of two Afghan National Police strategies: the first in 2009 and the second in 2011, although it has taken a considerable time for the Afghans to develop a general consensus in relation to the development of future policing doctrine. The 'new' Afghan National Police Strategy (2011) provided:

> strategic guidance for the continued development of the operational capability of the Ministry in order to meet current and future challenges relating to the stabilization and security of our Nation. The National Police Strategy specifies objectives for continued development of the police, law enforcement activities, and associated systems. It draws upon applicable Afghan law and national-level documents including the Afghan Constitution, Police Law, National Security Policy (NSP), Afghan National Development Strategy (ANDS), and National Threat Assessment (NTA) to determine the missions, roles, and responsibilities of the Ministry.[17]

Meeting the objectives laid out in the National Police Strategy relies in part on the coordination efforts of international stakeholders in providing assistance. The input and strategies of these stakeholders are overseen by the International Police Coordination Board (IPCB), chaired by the MOI with eight board members: EUPOL, United Nations (UNAMA), ISAF, NATO, US Embassy, CSTC-A, EUSR, and the European Commission. The IPCB mandate 'directs, prioritizes and coordinates the international effort for institutional and police reform in the wider context of rule of law in Afghanistan' providing a platform to identify challenges and problem solve.[18]

Behind the reform of the ANP and development of a new police strategy, international policing assistance has been provided by a range of international stakeholders although the United States has provided the majority of training and support. The EU became more actively involved in November 2005 when

[16] Felix Heiduk, 'Policing Mars or Venus? Comparing European and US approaches to police assistance', *European Security* 20, no. 3 (2011): p. 372.

[17] Islamic Republic of Afghanistan, Ministry of Interior Affairs, Deputy Minister for Strategy and Policy, Department of Strategy, *National Police Plan for Solar Years 1390–1391* (Kabul, 2011), p. 6.

[18] International Police Coordination Board of Afghanistan, accessed 5 January 2013, <http://www.ipcbafghanistan.com>.

the EU Council signed the EU Afghanistan Joint Declaration committing to a new EU-Afghan partnership; EUPOL was established under Council Joint Action 2007/369/CFSP on 15 June 2007 with a mandate extended (from 2010) to 31 May 2013 and the UN Security Council Resolution 1746 agreed to the EU launching of a police mission. The EU took over key partner status for police reform from Germany, launching a policing mission that aimed to draw together all non-US approaches; but in its early stages this led to the international policing structures becoming hugely complicated and, as a consequence, they were subsumed by Combined Security Transition Command-Afghanistan (CSTC-A).[19] EUPOL's principal stated objective has been to

> contribute to the establishment under Afghan ownership of sustainable and effective civilian policing arrangements, which will ensure appropriate interaction with the wider criminal justice system, in keeping with the policy advice and institution-building work of the Union, Member States and other international actors... support[ing] the reform process towards a trusted and efficient police service, which works in accordance with international standards within the framework of the rule of law and respect for human rights.[20]

The EUPOL mission monitors, mentors, advises, and trains at the level of the Afghan Ministry of Interior, Afghan Ministry of Justice, Afghan Attorney General's Office, and regions and provinces with seconded personnel from 22 EU member states with additional support provided from Canada, Croatia, New Zealand, and Norway.[21]

From the onset EUPOL was criticized for its reactive rather than proactive approach and more seriously, for failing to create a global vision of police reform; it is also possible that the lack of coherence and strategic direction impacted upon the operational level. The patchy approach to providing police assistance in Afghanistan led Heiduk to comment: 'There is no "Europe" in Afghanistan, European Police as a common framework for a "European" approach to police reform in Afghanistan has been replaced by a wide array of different, often contradictory police reform policies carried out by individual member states... dwarfed by that of the US'.[22] Whilst US Focused District Development (FDD) training programmes have emphasized counter-insurgency and counter-terrorist training, they have not moved sufficiently beyond security-oriented, militaristic styles of policing to include community-policing efforts to build future community trust and legitimacy. A greater emphasis on community styles of policing has been found within European policing projects, although the

[19] See: International Crisis Group, Policing in Afghanistan: Still Searching for a Strategy, *Crisis Group Asia Briefing* 85, 18 December 2008.
[20] European Council Decision 2010/279/CFSP, Article 2, 18 May 2010.
[21] See: EUPOL Afghanistan, accessed 21 September 2013, <http://www.euppol-afg.eu>.
[22] Heiduk, 'Policing Mars or Venus', p. 367.

EUPOL approach has been heavily fragmented with individual countries emphasizing their own policing priorities. Some European donors, including EUPOL, the UK, and Germany favour a greater emphasis on developing a community-based model of policing, whilst Italy and France highlight the value of gendarmerie-style forces in counter-insurgency and stabilization environments.[23]

This is further complicated by a US vision that views policing through the lens of paramilitary or security-oriented support to the Afghan National Army (ANA) and ISAF counter-insurgency operations through NATO sponsored programmes which do not necessarily sit comfortably with EUPOL's overall remit, despite the fact that the US, unlike a number of European countries, does not have gendarmerie units. Many of these issues have arisen in the last few years and whilst EUPOL may provide work of 'generally good quality [in] meeting real needs in terms of civilian policing . . . it is quite clear [from all our witnesses] that the job will take at least 5 to 10 years longer . . . '.[24] Yet there are some signs of cohesion amongst the international stakeholders with, for example, the establishment of a staff training college in Kabul by EUPOL, in collaboration with the NATO Training Mission (Afghanistan) (NTM-A), German Police Project Team (Afghanistan) (GPPT), and the Afghan National Police Training General Command. This initially came under the leadership of Lieutenant General Patang and delivered training and education for police officers of all ranks recognized at command levels—Gold, Silver, and Bronze or Strategic, Operational, and Tactical.[25] It has currently been described as successful in providing 'real' training opportunities for the ANP and will become a regional hub for the delivery of state of the art programmes.[26]

The UK has deployed both serving and retired police officers to Afghanistan across the range of international missions: EUPOL and NTMA missions in Kabul and the Provincial Reconstruction Team (PRT) in Helmand (the Afghanistan Police Unit has deployed since 2008) with up to approximately 50 officers per year. Numerically this is vastly inferior to many of the other donor states, although the UK has contributed heads of mission including the head of the Kabul Police Staff College, senior police advisors to the MOI, and Chief of Police Trainers to NTMA. The integrated training approach provided by the MDP, services police, and the military under Operation Herrick has laid a possible blueprint for police–military cooperation within hostile environments for future international policing assistance.

[23] Sinclair and Emsley, *Exploring UK Policing Practices*, 2010–2012.

[24] House of Lords, European Union Committee, 'The EU's Afghan Police Mission', *8th Report of Session 2010–2011* (London: The Stationery Office Ltd, 2011), p. 8.

[25] See: EUPOL Afghanistan, accessed 21 September 2013, <http://www.euppol-afg.eu>.

[26] Author Interview with Chief Supt. Brian Johnston, 19 September 2012.

Development of MDP–military integrated approach to MMA under Operation HERRICK

Traditionally the MDP policing environment has provided opportunities to develop a close working relationship with the military (though clearly not within hostile or post-conflict environments). Outside the domestic context there is general recognition across UK police (including MPD) that police–military cooperation is an essential ingredient of international missions in achieving police primacy which the military recognize as the 'ultimate goal' when undertaking stabilization programmes. They acknowledge that this is typically achieved at a later stage as the operating environment may well preclude the implementation of civil styles of policing, and, since the UK has no equivalent of a gendarmerie or paramilitary model of policing, military commanders are often brought in to provide policing and interior security matters. Whilst a 'clear difference' is assumed between the combat and policing roles, post-conflict and hostile environments require that the UK military adapt to both.[27] UK police (and in particular the MDP) can potentially provide part of that bridge between semi-military policing styles and civil–community styles of policing if the resources are made available and sufficient officers deployed. Indeed in recent joint exercises undertaken between the military and police, a possible operational framework was developed for use within international missions, although a formal doctrine is not yet in place.[28]

It is widely accepted that police reform often comes under the remit of broader security sector reform (SSR). The two are increasingly promoted in post-conflict, transitional, and fragile states as a means of providing a stable environment within which wider social, economic and political development can take place. Yet the international community has been slow to recognize the importance of police (as international actors) within post-conflict situations.[29] In addition the UK police have no formal international policing policy nor have they developed an international policing doctrine aligned with other stakeholders.[30] This has arisen partly from the police operating *ad hoc* to transfer their experiences from domestic policing to the implementation of international reform programmes. As such military-policing roles

[27] Ministry of Defence (MOD), 'Security and Stabilisation: the Military Contribution', *Joint Doctrine Publication* (JDP) *3–40*, 2009, ch. 4, p. 10.

[28] Author interview with Chief Supt. Rob Hoblin, Wethersfield, 8 November 2012 and ACC Rod Hansen, Portishead, 22 August 2012.

[29] With reference to this point see for example: Tonita Murray, 'Police-building in Afghanistan: A case study of civil security reform', *International Peacekeeping* 14, no. 1 (2007): pp. 108–26; Beth Greener, *The New International Policing (Global Issues)* (Basingstoke: Palgrave Macmillan, 2009).

[30] Andy Pritchard and Georgina Sinclair, 'International Police Assistance: Globalising UK Policing Practices', *Policing UK 2013*: *Priorities and Pressures: a year of transformation* (London: Witan Publishing, 2012), p. 101.

within international environments may become blurred, with the military often taking the lead. The military have, however, engaged with the development of a doctrine that accepts that both UK military and civilian agencies should work collaboratively and as part of a multinational and inter-agency approach within stabilization programmes more broadly.[31] There is tacit agreement that all parties working within the security sector must build close working relationships if reform programmes are to be successful. Afghanistan at a time of transition has provided an opportunity for the practical application of these concepts.

Integrating police–military approaches to international policing assistance in Afghanistan under Operation Herrick was partly the 'brainchild' of Colonel Iain Smailes, a Royal Dragoons Guard officer with extensive international experience since the 1990s, which included working alongside the UK police in different theatres including Sierra Leone and Kenya. Smailes had also had the experience of working alongside the MDP in Kosovo and following earlier tours in Afghanistan approached the MDP in 2006 with the idea that they could 'operate within the military bubble' under Operation Herrick. Smailes later noted that: 'The work being undertaken by the MDP in Afghanistan is at the very forefront of the Government's thinking; the National Security Strategy was clear in its ambition to "develop our national capabilities . . . ensur[ing] that all these capabilities—military and civilian, security and development—are fully integrated to deliver effect in risky or hostile environments"'.[32] Initially the MDP 'borrowed and paid' for Smailes' assistance (as staff) for a period of 18 months through terms of reference agreed by the MOD.

In the first instance, the MDP (with Smailes) carried out a scoping exercise to determine whether the MDP *could* be deployed to Helmand under Operation Herrick. This rested on the extent to which the MDP could ensure that 'risk' to their officers was mitigated: MDP's duty of care (DoC) procedures differ from Home Office police and could potentially allow the deployment of officers to forward operating bases (FOBs). The first scoping exercise brought Smailes, Inspector Colin Aitken, and Chief Inspector Tony Sherridan (then head of the International Policing Secondments Office (IPSO)) to Afghanistan. Their official assessment was that MDP could create a policing unit that would operate out of FOBs at Lashkar Gah, Babaji, Nahre Saraj, and Nad-e Ali. The MDP units would provide integrated mentoring and training, alongside the military and services police, to the ANP 'to help change the policing

[31] MOD, *Joint Doctrine Publication 3–40*, 2009, p. vi.
[32] Author interview with Col. Iain Smailes, Beaconsfield, 2 October 2012.

culture and management with support for Afghan laws and customs and to help transfer policing responsibility in Helmand to the ANP'.[33] This first scoping exercise led to a joint request from the 2nd Permanent Under-Secretary of State and the Vice Chief of Defence Staff to propose an MDP (Afghan Police) unit to provide monitoring, mentoring, and advising (MMA) to senior ANP officers, and to help oversee MMA to patrolmen and non-commissioned officers—previously the domain of the military and services police (Royal Military Police (RMP) and Royal Airforce Police (RAP). Once approval had been given, two further scoping missions were undertaken by senior MDP officers with Smailes to ensure that the venture was feasible and in full alignment with the then National Security Strategy. In the intervening period between the two scoping exercises undertaken in 2007, the MDP's Chief Constable Stephen Love formally agreed to the deployment of MDP officers, the formation of the Afghan Police Unit (APU) and to 'own that risk'.[34] In November 2007, agreement was given by David Miliband (then Foreign Secretary) and Des Browne (then Defence Secretary) that the MDP could deploy to PRT Helmand.

Of an original 84 officers who put forward their candidature for the APU, an initial six (plus two reserve) were deployed in January 2008 headed by Assistant Chief Constable Robert Chidley.[35] The initial pre-deployment training undertaken in January 2008 was initiated by Smailes over a one and a half day period and concentrated on 'working with the military in hostile environments' and hence was described as having been 'heavy on military ethos'.[36] This implied that the MDP would be 'protected' by the military (though the MDP were armed for self-protection) and would integrate their approaches to MMA within military objectives. The reality of course was that the numbers of MDP deployed to Helmand (between 20–40 officers) was, and has remained, in the minority compared to the numbers of the military. However, 'bringing blue thinking into a green environment' became a key investment area for the MDP, crystallized by the development of an 'International Gold Strategy Policy' in 2010 which included the full support of the MDP's contribution to the 'Afghanistan effort' and ensured 'the maintenance of the capability to respond and deploy MDP resources to overseas deployments more effectively and quickly than other UK police forces'.[37]

[33] Smailes, 2 October 2012.
[34] Author interview with Chief Constable Stephen Love, Wethersfield, 9 November 2012.
[35] Eivers, 8 November 2012; Chidley, 9 November 2012; Smailes, 2 October 2012.
[36] Eivers, 8 November 2012. [37] See Appendix i.

'Lessons identified' and 'lessons learnt'?

From the outset, the MDP identified the key issues that needed to be addressed which included a greater awareness of the challenges the MDP faced in managing the transition period. This contributed to significant changes in the recruitment and selection procedures; tailor-made pre-deployment training for MDP officers; the development of an integrated police–military approach to MMA through the use of the 'Concept of District Level Operations'; the introduction of 'hot' debriefings; and the development of the MDP's international policing gold strategy. The MDP's approach, encouraged by Smailes, was to identify the challenges as they arose and to feed the 'lessons learnt' into subsequent deployments.

The MDP continued to sharpen their recruitment and selection procedures from 2008. It implemented more thorough checks of individual MDP officers for information relating to personal and professional skills base; security vetting, health checks and tests specific to a deployment to a forward operating base. The latter stemmed from the need to ensure that an officer was professionally and personally competent, and capable of operating within a hostile environment; those who are not can then be weeded out. Criticism has been levied in the past about poor recruitment and selection procedures, and some officers have had to return home.[38] MDP standardized the use of a 'Statement of Civilian Personnel Policy' in support of operations and the MOD's duty of care processes as an insurance guarantee with 'welfare forms' provided to the officer's spouse/partner giving details of how the family could contact the MOD if needed. Additional health checks and fitness assessments have become an integral part of selection and recruitment. By 2009, MDP IPSO staff had developed a specific 'course acclimatization exercise' to run alongside the pre-deployment training course. It included completing 1.5 miles in full body armour in 22 minutes; and completing 1.5 miles cross-country with full kit and carrying a stretcher (four officers) for 90 metres. Failure to complete the acclimatization course has resulted in officers being barred from deployment.[39]

One principal criticism of pre-deployment training levied by UK police officers has been the paucity of training material that is both police mission and police context specific. Particular areas that officers perceived as requiring more thorough analysis included not only police–military cooperation (UK specific) within democratic police reform (in its broadest sense) but also an understanding of other international players: in particular the US military and

[38] Sinclair and Emsley, *Exploring UK Policing Practices*, 2010–2012.
[39] Author interview with Inspector David Mcilwraith, Wethersfield, 8 November 2012 and access to relevant IPSO material.

US Marines and their approach to delivering police training.[40] During the first 2008 pre-deployment training programme, Smailes recognized that there needed to be a focus on the UK military experiences in Afghanistan to ensure that MDP–military cooperation could be built and sustained within a hostile environment: 'We needed to eliminate tensions between the military and police in the UK prior to mission. . . . It was not just a question of applying what had been delivered in the past which was basically lack of pre-deployment briefs, just a here is your uniform, a few injections and you have passed your pistol test now off you go!'[41] This triggered a review of the 'International Policing Programme pre-deployment training course', which has been substantially revised since 2008. Training took place over a 4-day period and was supported by an extensive 'Support 2 Operations' pack prepared for each officer. MDP/APU considered that this approach to the preparation of training was both 'organic' and 'holistic'. The courses were individually tailored to the mission and the context of that mission (within the wider remit of Operation Herrick); in addition all feedback received from officers who have undertaken the training was embedded on an ongoing basis to improve course content.[42]

On their immediate return from mission and prior to returning 'home', all officers completed an 'Operation Herrick Feedback Questionnaire'. This has been designed semi-quantitatively to cover all aspects of pre-deployment training, operational involvement in theatre, experiences with local police and military, stakeholders, military and international police/military, and more specifically the aims of the mission. The responses provided to this questionnaire were then used to model the individual 'hot debrief' carried out by a police member of IPSO within 48 hours of the individual officer's return to the UK. These face-to-face debriefs typically encompassed all elements of the pre-deployment training; kit and financial issues; deployment (e.g. information and briefings, flight information and flights, arrival in theatre, expectations and realities); lessons learnt; operational issues; professional and personal development; end of tour; and possible re-application.[43] The findings from these 'hot' debriefings were fed directly into subsequent training programmes and (if necessary) the application and selection processes. In addition they have been used to refine the processes undertaken at ground level to deliver the 'Concept of District Level Operations' within Helmand Province under Operation Herrick.

[40] Sinclair and Emsley, *Exploring UK Policing Practices*, 2010–2012.
[41] Smailes, 2 October 2012.
[42] Mcilwraith, 8 November 2012 and access to relevant IPSO material.
[43] Author interview with Inspector Bob Locke, Wethersfield, 8 November 2012; Mcilwraith, 8 November 2012; Eivers, 8 November 2012; Chidley, 9 November 2012.

'Concept of District Level Operations'

The Afghan National Policing plan states that:

> [T]he training and education of the police is critical to enhancing the capacities and capabilities of the Afghan National Police. The focus of this training and education should be on core police operations based on community policing, the Afghan National Police code of conduct, the detection and prevention of crime, ensuring security and public safety, adherence to core values, and protecting public property.[44]

Despite this clear cut message there have been numerous initiatives over the past decade to train, restructure, and mentor the different branches of Afghanistan's police to ensure that local police are able to fully take over their role in the future.

Whilst the responsibility for police mentoring and training has rested predominantly with the military in Afghanistan, the UK military argues that the aspiration is for community policing styles with 'clear separation between the roles of the police and the military... [for] community policing models assume consent which is unlikely to be achievable in the midst of violent conflict'.[45] Therefore in the post-conflict and early stabilization stages 'care should be taken to ensure that [the ANP] are not over-faced before they are demonstrably capable'. Training and mentoring in this early stage could include static guarding and border security tasks, patrolling secured areas, facilitating local contacts to gain intelligence and so on.[46] Within this, the MDP–military 'concept of district level operations' integrated approach to MMA may be perceived as just another initiative. However, in relation to UK policing overseas this has been a unique example of providing integrated MMA across the police–military divide within a hostile environment.

As demonstrated within Figure 19.1, police-related MMA is delivered simultaneously across the full local police spectrum (patrolmen, non-commissioned officers, and senior officers at district/provincial level). It has been recognized that bringing 'outsiders' (international military, services police, and police) to 'insiders' (local police) to deliver MMA is complex in the extreme and rests on transparent and constant dialogue involving all parties and the shared use of intelligence in the form of military, police, intelligence briefings, and so on.[47] This concept has been designed to ensure that first, MMA is *not* delivered in silos but across the police–military divide and that this delivery involves *all* ANP officers of all ranks. Secondly it is clear that all parties providing MMA

44 *National Policing Plan for Solar Years 1390–1391*, 2011, p. 14.
45 MOD, *Joint Doctrine Publication 3–40*, 2009, pp. 6–14.
46 MOD, *Joint Doctrine Publication 3–40*, 2009, pp. 5–9.
47 Smailes, 2 October 2012.

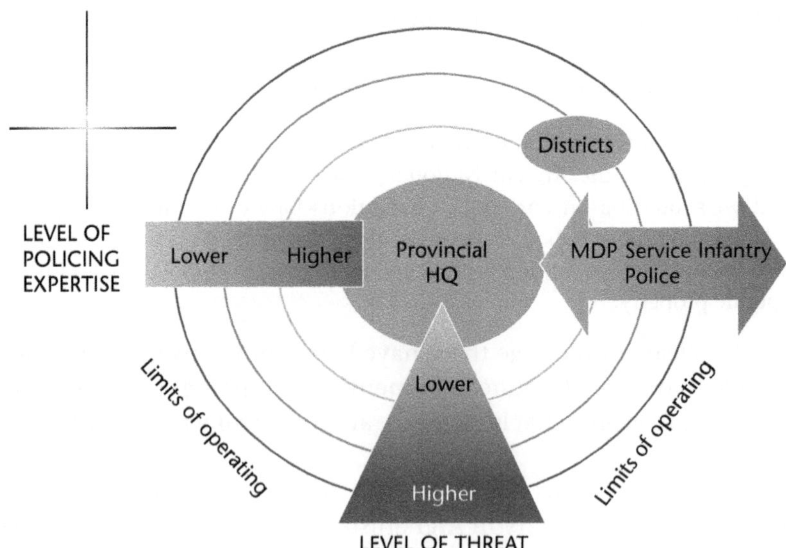

Figure 19.1. MDP—Operation Herrick—concept of district level operations (Crown copyright)

(UK military, services police, and MDP) have to work to their *own* level of risk and operational limits, which are variable, to ensure that progress is steady and continual rather than 'stop and start' as can be the case if levels of risk are deemed too high for the police to remain operational.

Thus the military are perceived as operating within the highest level of risk geographically as demonstrated by the outer layers, whilst MDP (in relation to their different level of risk) operate solely at the core. In practical terms this means that the MDP operate in far smaller locations whilst the military (and Services Police) can operate in a wider vicinity. Moreover, bringing the MDP (in physical terms) from the inner to the outer layers necessitates (once again) clear channels of communication ensuring that risk factors are mitigated. This has taken the form of regular briefings across all the MMA providers at local and district level.[48] Thirdly, the actual delivery of MMA and specific elements of training (see Table 19.1 for examples) runs from the outer layers where the level of policing expertise required is considered to be at its lowest, to the inner core where the level of policing expertise is perceived to be at its most complex. In theory this means that the 'outer ring' provides military-led 'green training'; the middle ring provides predominantly services police-led training, and the inner ring is MDP led. In practical terms, however, the extent of 'problem solving' required within both 'green' and 'blue' training requires a fairly meshed approach to MMA. Ensuring that a balance is achieved between

[48] Smailes, 2 October 2012.

Table 19.1. Examples of MMA provided within the concept of district level operations (Crown copyright)

OUTER RING Military led	MIDDLE RING Services Police led	INNER RING MDP led
Ground Holding (human saftey + security skills)	Basic evidence gathering/ secure evidence in crime scene	MMA middle-ranking to senior ANP at district/provincial level
Patrolling—Human safety/security skills	Forensics	Problem solving in line with ANP requests/dictated by events at district/provincial level
Securing/cordoning an area (e.g. checkpoints;road blocks; house)	Personal and saftey training 'sustainment training'	Working towards ANP plan (e.g. National Policing Plan)
Checkpoints (person search; vehicles search) Containment checkpoint (health and hygiene; latrines; personal hygiene; food distribution) Sentry checkpoints (sleep)	Women Police e.g. searches at checkpoints	Working towards all forward planning provided by Afghan Government (National Level)
Logistics (weapons; equipment; fuel)		
Survival skills (firearms—direct; advance to contact)		

the delivery of 'harder' green policing skills (outer perimeter) and the 'softer' blue police mentoring delivered at the core has necessitated 'the fullest and frankest' of police–military cooperation which the MDP have pushed to achieve despite the changing and often escalating levels of threat experienced in Helmand.[49]

Concluding observations

In any country, either democratized, developing, in transition, or post-conflict, training and mentoring institutions play a key role in fostering police management, professionalization, and modernization. Whenever the police undergo structural reform or when policing processes and procedures are altered, the questions are always: was it effective and why, will it endure, and can it be applied elsewhere? In consideration of MDP experiences since 2008 under Operation Herrick the following observations can be made.

This was the first experience of UK 'civilian' police (MDP) working alongside the military in Afghanistan within a hostile environment where the

[49] Eivers, 8 November 2012; Chidley and Love, 9 November 2012.

conditions/risk limitations had been set to enable an integrated approach to help build the rule of law. In terms of supporting the operational effort in Afghanistan through the deployment of serving MDP officers, the 'end of year key priority performance report' noted that MDP had 'achieved 100% of HMG/MOD approved requirements for Afghanistan National Police capacity building'. By extension, MDPGA had continued to support all international policing missions as requested by the Foreign and Commonwealth Office in support of wider defence and UK foreign policy initiatives.[50] Yet the provision of officers has been limited in relation to the military and with current drawdown underway, the MDP as of January 2013 had only 16 officers deployed under Operation Herrick until September 2013 with a final withdrawal completed by January 2014. This experience, therefore, has been undertaken at a micro level, which raises questions as to its real impact on the ground.

The importance, however, of creating a future police–military mechanism for the implementation of integrated approaches to the delivery of MMA cannot be underestimated. In terms of gaining front-line policing experiences and consolidating police–military cooperation (however limited), senior MDP have gauged that the Afghanistan experience has allowed them to bring their corporate knowledge of international policing missions to a specific hostile environment. By extension, in identifying those challenges posed by Operation Herrick (including recruitment, pre-deployment training, and in-theatre delivery of policing services) lessons have been learnt which have been applied to MMA/training more broadly and, more specifically, to working closely alongside the military.[51] This has been perceived as a real opportunity to mesh green/military and blue/policing skills and jointly to problem solve within a hostile environment. As a concept it is believed that this approach could be deployed in other theatres not only to ensure police–military cooperation (in UK terms) but to enable the range of 'outsiders' to deliver integrated MMA to 'insiders'.[52]

However, when gauging the 'success' or 'failure' of this approach from an international perspective, and particularly from the viewpoint of the ANP, this becomes far more problematic. The opinion of MPD officers who have deployed under Herrick is that any element of success remains fragile; delivery, implementation, and the legacy of the range of policing skills (from green to blue) has often been reliant on the local senior Afghan police and their personal interest in bringing about change, which in turn is dependent upon the local political and social context. Some MDP officers have been

[50] MODGA, *Annual Report 2011–2012*, p. 16. [51] Chidley and Love, 9 November 2012.

[52] These concluding comments are drawn from author interviews undertaken with MDP officers returning from Helmand 2011–13.

highly critical of the failure of international stakeholders to adequately reflect 'the Afghan Way' within training and mentoring doctrine until too late. The plethora of international players and their individualistic approaches to MMA coupled with a lack of Afghan ownership has stalled progress. This has been complicated by the sheer mass of police 'outsiders' as compared to 'insiders' riddled by rivalries and tensions from the myriad of international organizations present in Afghanistan. In addition, senior ANP in Helmand are also often construed as outsiders when deployed from other provinces.

More broadly international policing assistance as delivered by the UK faces real challenges in terms of the future provision of serving UK police and this includes any future deployment of MDP officers. With the current plethora of changes to the structure of UK policing (e.g. the advent of Police and Crime Commissioners, the unification of policing in Scotland, the College of Policing, and the demise of the National Policing Improvement Agency), international policing may well be placed on the back burner. Currently the Home Office is undertaking a considerable cost-cutting exercise for all of its services (including the police), which may impact upon international policing assistance if the decrease in numbers of officers in the UK prevents sparing an officer for an overseas mission. (This may certainly be the case for the MDP which is undergoing a reduction in a similar vein to Home Office forces.) Unless and until the Cabinet choses to focus on international policing and commit additional funding and the creation of an official international policing and rule of law strategy, any decision will come as the result of interaction between departments and valiant attempts by ACPO International Affairs (with very few resources) to maintain the flow of serving UK officers overseas. Additionally international policing *or* policing internationally is becoming increasingly complex with the involvement of international institutions (e.g. the Organization for Security & Cooperation in Europe (OSCE) and the United Nations), the corporate sector, and a global approach to operational cooperation spearheaded in the UK by the Serious Organised Crime Agency (and its future replacement). This has the potential to make the problems identified and lessons learnt in one hostile environment or post-conflict theatre much more difficult to apply elsewhere, and the lack of any clear and official UK international policing policy can only serve to compound the difficulties.

References

Bayley, David and Robert Perito, *The Police in War: Fighting insurgency, terrorism, and violent crime* (Boulder, CO: Lynne Rienner Publishers, 2010).

Bowling, Ben and James Sheptycki, *Global Policing* (London: Sage, 2012).

Brogden, M., 'Community policing as cherry pie', in *Policing across the World: Issues for the twenty-first century*, edited by R. Mawby (London: UCL Press, 1999): pp. 167–86.

Cabinet Office, *A Strong Britain in an Age of Uncertainty: The National Security Strategy*, Cm 7953 (London: HMSO, 2010).

Cabinet Office, *Securing Britain in an Age of Uncertainty: The Strategic Defence and Security Review*, Cm 7948 (London: HMSO, 2010).

Ellison, Graham and Nathan Pino, *Globalization, Police Reform and Development: Doing it the Western Way? Transnational Crime, Crime Control and Security* (Basingstoke: Palgrave Macmillan, 2012).

Greener, Beth, *The New International Policing (Global Issues)* (Basingstoke: Palgrave Macmillan, 2009).

Heiduk, Felix, 'Policing Mars or Venus? Comparing European and US approaches to police assistance', *European Security* 20, no. 3 (2011): pp. 363–83.

House of Lords, European Union Committee, *The EU's Afghan Police Mission*, 8th Report of Session 2010–2011 (London: The Stationery Office Ltd, 2011).

International Crisis Group, 'Afghanistan: the Long, Hard Road to the 2014 Transition', *Asia Report* 236, 2012.

International Crisis Group, 'Policing in Afghanistan: Still Searching for a Strategy', *Crisis Group Asia Briefing* 85, 18 December 2008.

International Police Coordination Board of Afghanistan, accessed 5 January 2013, <http://www.ipcbafghanistan.com>.

Islamic Republic of Afghanistan, Ministry of Interior Affairs, Deputy Minister for Strategy and Policy, Department of Strategy, *National Police Plan for Solar Years 1390–1391* (Kabul, 2011).

Johnston, Les, 'An unseen force: the Ministry of Defence Police in the UK', *Policing and Society* 3, no. 1 (1992): pp. 23–40.

Ministry of Defence Police, *Talk Through; the Magazine of the Ministry of Defence Police*, Issue 136 (Braintree, Ministry of Defence Police Wethersfield, 2008).

Ministry of Defence Police, *Talk Through; the Magazine of the Ministry of Defence Police*, 40th Anniversary Issue, Issue 149 (Braintree: Ministry of Defence Police Wethersfield, 2011).

Ministry of Defence Police and Guarding Agency, *Annual Report 2011–2012* (London: HMSO, 2012).

Ministry of Defence, *Partnering Indigenous Forces: A Discussion paper by DCDC* (Ministry of Defence, undated).

Ministry of Defence, 'Security and Stabilisation: the Military Contribution', *Joint Doctrine Publication* (JDP) *3–40*, 2009.

Ministry of Defence and Stabilisation Unit, 'Security Transitions', *Joint Doctrine Note 6/10*, 2010.

Murray, Tonita, 'Police-Building in Afghanistan: A Case Study of Civil Security Reform', *International Peacekeeping* 14, no. 1 (2007): pp. 108–26.

Peral, L., 'The EU Police Mission in Afghanistan (EUPOL Afghanistan)', in *European Security & Defence Policy, the First 10 Years*, edited by Giovanni Grevi, Damien Holly, and Daniel Keohane (New York: Institute for Security Studies, 2009).

Perito, Robert, 'Afghanistan's police: the weak link in security sector reform', *Special Report 227* (Washington, DC: United States Institute of Peace, 2009).

Perito, Robert, 'Police in peace and stability operations: Evolving US policy and practice', *International Peacekeeping* 15, no. 1 (2008): pp. 51–66.

Pritchard, Andy and Georgina Sinclair, 'International Police Assistance: Globalising UK Policing Practices', in *Policing UK 2013: Priorities and Pressures: a year of transformation* (London: Witan Publishing, 2013), pp. 100–2.

Sinclair, Georgina, 'Exporting the UK Police "Brand": The RUC-PSNI and the International Agenda', *Policing: A Journal of Policy and Practice* 6, no. 1 (2012): pp. 55–66.

Sinclair, Georgina, 'Globalising British Policing', in *The History of Policing*, edited by Clive Emsley (Aldershot: Ashgate, 2011), vol. IV.

Web sources

<http://www.mod.uk/DefenceInternet/AboutDefence/WhatWeDo/SecurityandIntelligence/MDPGA/MinistryOfDefencePolice.htm>.

<http://www.mod.uk/DefenceInternet/AboutDefence/CorporatePublications/SecurityandIntelligencePublications/MODPoliceCommitteeMtgMins/>.

<http://www.ipcbafghanistan.com/>.

<http://www.eupol-afg.eu/>.

Appendix i AA

AP

Force Orders

28 July 2010

FO 110/10—International Policing Gold Strategy

GREEN—We fully support

1. Making a full contribution to the Afghanistan effort as part of the over-riding priority of Secretary of State.
2. The maintenance of the capability to respond and deploy MDP resources to overseas deployments more effectively and quickly than other UK police forces.
3. The inclusion of competency and experience gained on overseas duties, as part of the evidence base for promotion (and other selection competitions).
4. The need to plan the re-integration of staff returning from overseas, particularly seeking to exploit, maintain, and develop their enhanced skills for the benefit of the Agency.

AMBER—We will strike a reasonable balance between

5. Ensuring the maintenance of the effectiveness of our UK tasks, whilst supporting Defence/UK objectives overseas.

RED—We will not support

6. Deployments, unless ACC(OS) has confirmed that there is a police task to be done, MDP officers are capable of doing it, required safety standards are met and that full external funding is confirmed.
7. Deployments to forward posts in Afghanistan, unless they meet and can maintain the Chief Constable's 'Support to Operations' (S2O) standards.
8. Deployments, where a Chief Officer has identified that an unacceptable business risk would be created.
9. Further deployments of Chief Inspectors and above to roles other than Afghanistan, unless there is a very strong business case that over-rides the Amber criteria.

20

The other side of COIN

New challenges for British police and military in the twenty-first century

Lindsay Clutterbuck

Introduction

Transition in Afghanistan formed a core focus of British and US forces between 2011 and 2014. Essentially, this involved the handing over of responsibility for security to the Afghan government, army, and police. During the transition the number of British bases reduced from 137 in 2011, to just 11 in 2013.[1] As the British military involvement in Afghanistan draws to a close it is important to reflect on experiences and their impacts not least because the British Army is currently undertaking its most comprehensive restructuring in living memory.

This chapter looks at the symbiotic relationship that has existed in British military counter-insurgency history with the other side of COIN (counter-insurgency), namely the contribution made to it by police and policing. It briefly sets out why police and policing are a key element and how they became so, particularly when it comes to the role of Police HUMINT (Human Intelligence) activity. This historical approach is bolstered by personal observations made on research visits to Helmand. Both of these contribute to some concluding thoughts and suggestions that focus on the UK approach to policing in Helmand and why there needs to be a radical rethink if the British Army and the UK police are to meet elsewhere the new challenges of counter-insurgency, stability operations, and security sector reform in the twenty-first century.

[1] Richard Norton-Taylor, 'UK's fleet of Merlin helicopters to return home from Afghanistan', *The Guardian*, 4 June 2013, <http://www.guardian.co.uk/uk/2013/jun/04/uk-merlin-helicopters-return-afghanistan>.

Police and policing have been an integral part of the British response to preventing and countering civil conflict, insurgency, and terrorism since the establishment of organized police forces in the early years of the nineteenth century, first in what is now Ireland and then on the British mainland.[2] Individuals at all levels were responsible for this development, from politicians such as Sir Robert Peel to the police officers themselves and by the beginning of the twentieth century, the concept of policing in the form of organized, uniformed police forces was well established in Ireland, Britain, the Empire, and the Commonwealth. The way that these forces were organized and operated differed but each was based on one of three models of policing.

British and Irish models of police and policing

At first sight, the responsibilities assigned by the legislation that created both the rural Constabulary-type police forces in Ireland and Metropolitan-type forces in Britain appear very similar. They encompassed the prevention and detection of crime and the prevention of disorder, plus the suppression of disturbances or disorder when it occurred. Both also had a functional remit to carry out what would later become known as 'internal security' duties. However, there were marked differences in the priorities assigned to these duties by the two types of police forces and, consequently, there were substantial differences in how they were equipped and trained to carry them out.

In brief, the organization in Ireland of the Irish Constabulary (and after it was awarded the accolade of 'Royal', the Royal Irish Constabulary (RIC)), derived primarily from its task of restoring civil order in rural areas where it had broken down and to deterring and preventing its recurrence. It was therefore characterized by its military ethos, with police officers living together in barracks, routinely being armed with rifles and subjected to military style discipline. In this way, disorder was suppressed and internal security maintained. The British model of policing, initially beginning with the Metropolitan Police in London in 1829, was derived from it but took a different trajectory in its development. It was characterized from the start by its civilian ethos and its commitment to policing by consent, and when this was no longer possible, to the restoration of public peace and order without first resort to the use of military weapons, that is, the rifle and the bayonet. Its main emphasis was on the prevention of crime and the preservation of the peace.

Also emerging in the nineteenth century, with roots in both the Irish and the British models, was a third model of police and policing, namely the

[2] Lindsay Clutterbuck, 'Countering Irish terrorism in Britain: Its origin as a police function', *Terrorism and Political Violence* 8, no. 1 (Spring 2006): pp. 95–118.

colonial model. The main characteristics of colonial model police forces were their civil-like police style, with officers trained and equipped for police work, dealing with public disorder, and carrying out internal security duties but these forces had 'a dual role as defenders of a colony and as upholders of the law'.[3] Consequently they also formed an integral part of the defence forces of the territory and were trained and equipped for this more military-like role. This approach to policing shows a greater affinity with the Royal Irish Constabulary, militarized/gendarmerie model than it does to the British and Dublin civil police-like model, leading a Deputy Under-Secretary of State for the Colonies to state 'that the really effective influence upon the development of colonial police forces during the nineteenth century was not that of the police of Great Britain, but that of the Royal Irish Constabulary.'[4]

The colonial model of police and policing

The Irish Constabulary initially, and later the RIC, acted as a source of recruitment for the police of the colonies and other parts of the Empire, particularly to serve in the role of officers. This key role was recognized formally by the Colonial Office in 1907 when all officers of commissioned rank in the Crown Colonies were required to attend training at the RIC Depot in Phoenix Park, Dublin. During 1936, the Colonial Police Service was set up as part of a wider reorganization of British government to bring cohesion and raise standards across the police forces of over 40 diverse 'Colonies, Protectorates and Trust Territories administered under the Colonial Office'.[5] By 1939, each of them had an established police force based on the colonial police model (with local variations) but whose core responsibilities included the prevention and detection of crime, the suppression of internal disturbances, and the defence of the Colony against external aggression.[6]

Despite the impact of the Second World War on many Colonial and Dominion police forces, in particular the Japanese invasion and occupation of Malaya and Singapore in South East Asia, British Colonial-style police and policing was usually re-established once hostilities had ceased. As the move towards

[3] Georgina Sinclair and C. A. Williams, 'Home and away: The Cross-Fertilization between 'Colonial' and 'British' policing, 1921–1985', *Journal of Imperial and Commonwealth History* 35, no. 2 (2007): pp. 221–38.

[4] Sir Charles Jeffries, *The Colonial Police* (London: Max Parrish, 1952), p. 30. The Irish Constabulary were given the 'Royal' accolade after successfully dealing in 1867 with an insurrection in Ireland where Irish-American veterans of the US Civil War were prominent in its organization and leadership.

[5] Jeffries, *The Colonial Police*, frontispiece.

[6] Georgina Sinclair, *At the End of the Line: Colonial policing and the imperial endgame, 1945–1980* (Manchester: Manchester University Press, 2006), pp. 3–5.

statehood and independence from Britain gathered momentum in a number of countries from 1945 onwards, a number of these police forces played central roles during major civil conflicts, campaigns of terrorism, and insurgencies.

In the post-war period, lasting to the turn of this century, Britain engaged in countering ten significant low-intensity conflicts that are generally accepted as 'insurgencies', plus a greater number of lesser engagements on a smaller scale and categorized as 'police actions', for example as a consequence of the Chinese communist government inspired violence in Hong Kong and the New Territories during 1967.[7] Since the invasions of Afghanistan in 2001 and Iraq in 2003, two more campaigns can be added to this list (see Table 20.1).[8]

There are many factors relevant to the pursuit of a COIN campaign and Table 20.1 sets out in a matrix twelve post-Second World War counter-insurgency campaigns, plus six factors relevant to how the campaigns were pursued and, in particular, the critical elements within them that relate to police and policing. These include whether the concept of police primacy over the military was applied (by military support being authorized as 'Military Aid to the Civil Power'—MACP); whether the local police were under British control or direction (usually as a consequence of a pre-existing colonial-style police force); and whether the local police possessed an intelligence gathering capability (usually provided by the local police Special Branch). Upon examination, in at least eight of them the local civil police and the British military operated together in a coordinated and integrated way and did so as a central plank of an overall COIN strategy.

When looked at holistically, the factors shown in Table 20.1 highlight a fundamental shift from the pattern established during the post-Second World War insurgencies and conflicts to what is a 'new normality' over the last 20 years. This new paradigm is most pronounced in Iraq and Afghanistan. In essence, for at least 50 years, the UK could rely on the presence of a recognizable police force and policing approach that could be built upon and restructured to counter any current outbreak of conflict. Not only is this no longer the case, it is clear that without it, controlling or even influencing a partner nation police force to operate in the most effective way to the benefit of all is extremely challenging.

This problem was highlighted in the campaigns in Bosnia/Kosovo, Iraq, and Afghanistan as the UK found itself participating not only as part of a wider coalition but also where its military presence in the country was through the circumstances of invasion and occupation and not through consensual

[7] Sinclair, *At the End of the Line*, pp. 179–82.

[8] The *Army Staff College Official Handbook on Counter Revolutionary Warfare* also includes Eritrea (1949) and Togoland (1957) as 'counter insurgency actions'. Cited in Frank Ledwidge, *Losing Small Wars: British military failure in Iraq and Afghanistan* (New Haven and London: Yale University Press, 2011), p. 153.

Table 20.1. Presence of high level factors relevant to police and policing during the main conflicts and insurgencies since World War II (Crown copyright)

Police relevant strategic factors	British control of local police & policing	Principle of Police primacy applied	Effective local Police HUMINT capability present or developed	Local Police & British military operations routinely integrated	British military employed in country as MACP	British military presence post-invasion/ intervention
Insurgency & Date						
Java & Sumatra 1945–1947	Colony of Netherlands					✓
Palestine 1945–1948	✓	✓	✓	✓	✓	
Malaya 1948–1957	✓	✓	✓	✓	✓	
Kenya 1952–1956	✓	✓	✓	✓	✓	
Cyprus 1955–1959	✓	✓	✓		✓	
Muscat & Oman 1958–1959	✓		✓	✓	✓	
Brunei & Borneo 1962–1966	✓		✓	✓		
Aden & South Arabia 1964–1967	✓	✓Aden	✓	✓	✓	
Northern Ireland 1971–2007	✓	✓	✓	✓	✓	
Bosnia & Kosovo 1992–2000				UN-led		✓
Iraq 2003–2009				Coalition-led		✓
Afghanistan 2001–2014				NATO & US-led		✓

MACP. The critical consequence is that 'upon occupation the military force loses the strategic initiative.... The initiative moves to the occupied who can choose to cooperate with the occupiers or not... and if they have popular support, those that choose not to cooperate... can mount their own destructive tactical offensives [to] drain and exhaust the stronger military occupier'.[9] The difficulties for the military can be compounded where the legitimacy of the existing local police force is already denied or rejected by the local population.

Another of the missing factors from recent and current British counter-insurgency campaigns has been the absence of an effective local police HUMINT capability that can contribute to the overall intelligence picture or the development of one. Retired General Rupert Smith is clear in his belief that intelligence leading to targeted action is the way for the military to operate during 'wars among the people'; 'For the rule of law to be supported and enhanced such that the people support it, the military measures must be focused on the lawbreakers. This demands good information and intelligence, precision in the attack or arrest, and a successful prosecution.'[10] The next section will look at how the police have played an integral role in contributing to this end during counter-insurgency campaigns of the past.

Police HUMINT as a facet of counter-insurgency

There are many aspects of police and policing that are key components in any wider campaign designed to counter an insurgency. For example, military forces may try to 'dominate' the areas in which they operate and to achieve this, troops are sent out to patrol. At its most fundamental, day-to-day police work is built upon interacting with the local communities they serve and to carry out this function, uniformed police officers also engage in their own type of patrol activity.

In times of internal conflict and insurgency, the beneficial contribution of patrolling as a tactic and the critical contribution the police can make by using it has been recognized. David Kilcullen, encapsulates it with the words: 'The first rule of deployment in counterinsurgency is to be there.... So your first order of business is to establish presence.'[11] Sepp puts this into a wider context: 'Constant patrolling by government forces establishes an official

[9] General Sir Rupert Smith, *The Utility of Force: The art of war in the modern world* (London: Penguin Books, 2006), p. 274.

[10] Smith, *The Utility of Force*, p. 380.

[11] David Kilcullen, 'Twenty-eight Articles: Fundamentals of Company Level Counterinsurgency', *Military Review* (May/June 2006): pp. 103–8. Reprinted with updated comments from the author in *Counterinsurgency* (Oxford: Oxford University Press, 2010), pp. 29–50.

presence that enhances security and builds confidence in the government. Patrolling is a basic tenet of policing, and in the last 100 years all successful counterinsurgencies have employed this fundamental security practice.'[12] Activity such as patrolling in order to gain intelligence also tends to be more effective if it in turn is driven and informed by intelligence. Intelligence may be the single most important commodity for not only mounting counter-insurgency operations but also in defeating the overall insurgency.

A comparative analysis of 30 recent resolved insurgencies is unequivocal in concluding that when it comes to assessing the effectiveness of the counter measures used to try and resolve them, '[t]here is strong evidence in support of the criticality of intelligence'.[13] From this it can be argued that the gathering and development of both information and intelligence to drive operations against the insurgents is an area of COIN activity in which the police have a unique and prominent role to play.

The highest tier of intelligence gathering is conducted at the national level by organizations dedicated to the task, utilizing sophisticated technology and highly trained human resources to carry it out. However, in addition to this, countering terrorism and civil conflict requires the acquisition and processing of very localized, community-based information and intelligence. It is here that the police can make a significant contribution to counter-insurgency and counter-terrorism operations. They can do so on three levels. At the first level, there is the collection of overt information that is freely available to those who are able to move among the community, observe, ask pertinent questions and understand the significance of what they see and hear.[14] The second level is the collection of information provided discreetly and in confidence by members of the local community on local events, personalities, and incidents. The final level is secret intelligence, predominantly human intelligence (HUMINT), gathered clandestinely from within the community. All of these products must be fused with the higher tier intelligence product if a holistic picture is to be obtained and used to drive security force activities.

Uniform police officers can gather information when carrying out their core duties and their presence in the local community also provides an opportunity for individuals to pass on information to them. Arrangements can also be made for them to be contacted by specialized police officers operating covertly. Police HUMINT officers operating clandestinely can recruit and run

[12] Kalev Sepp, 'Best Practices in Counter Insurgency', *Military Review* (May/June 2005): p. 11, <http://www.au.af.mil/au/awc/awcgate/milreview/sepp.pdf>.

[13] Christopher Paul, Colin P. Clarke, and Beth Grill, *Victory Has a Thousand Fathers: Qualitative comparative analysis of 30 recent resolved insurgencies* (Santa Monica: RAND Corporation, 2010).

[14] Lindsay Clutterbuck, 'An overview of violent Jihad in the UK: Radicalisation and the state response', in *Understanding Violent Radicalisation: Terrorist and Jihadist Movements in Europe*, edited by Magnus Ranstorp (London: Routledge, 2010), p. 161.

sources in their local area and act as a conduit to feed this local level intelligence product up to the higher regional and national levels.

The police should ideally be organized, trained, and equipped to contribute across all three of these levels as '[i]ntelligence operations that detect insurgents and lead to their arrest and prosecution are the single most important practice to protect the population.'[15] When all this is done in conjunction with the capabilities and experience the military can bring to intelligence collection during insurgency, then significant progress is possible.

As well as the police playing a crucial role in countering civil conflict and insurgency, police and policing is also very effective against terrorist groups. An analysis conducted by RAND of 648 terrorist groups active since 1968 was able to state that: '[a]gainst terrorist groups that cannot or will not make a transition to nonviolence, policing is likely to be the most effective strategy (40%)'.[16] This is in contrast to the stark figure that military force has been the primary reason for the demise of terrorist groups in only 7 per cent of the cases examined.[17]

The reasons for this are succinctly set out in the report:

> Police and intelligence services have better training and information to penetrate and disrupt terrorist organisations than do such institutions as the military. They are the primary arm of the government focused on internal security matters. Local police and intelligence agencies usually have a permanent presence in cities, towns and villages; a better understanding of the threat environment in these areas; and better human intelligence.[18]

In addition, Thomas Mockaitis makes the telling point that '[a] government threatened by insurgency usually faces significant criminality as well. Given the nexus that often develops between these two threats, a strategy to fight one must also tackle the other.'[19] Crime and criminality are in the domain of the police, not the military.

The concept of police intelligence gathering to prevent community violence, civil disorder, and terrorism is not a new one and it was utilized in both Britain and Ireland from the middle of the nineteenth century onwards. It quickly became an integral part of police activities whether the force was organized according to the Irish, British, or colonial police models. As a function, it became institutionalized within a specific police structure known as 'Special Branch'. During the twentieth century Special Branch

[15] Sepp, 'Best Practices in Counter Insurgency', p. 9.

[16] Seth Jones and Martin Libicki, *How Terrorist Groups End: Lessons for countering al Qa'ida* (Santa Monica: RAND Corporation, 2008), pp. 18–19.

[17] Jones and Libicki, *How Terrorist Groups End*, pp. 18–19.

[18] Jones and Libicki, *How Terrorist Groups End*, pp. xiii–xvii.

[19] Thomas Mockaitis, *Resolving Insurgencies* (US Army War College Strategic Studies Institute, 2011), pp. 68–9.

came to be an integral part of all UK police forces and in many others across the British Empire and colonies.

The period after the First World War saw a number of events and developments that were to have a profound effect on the efforts made to counter the wave of colonial insurgencies that gathered strength after 1945. The first of these was the Irish War of Independence from 1919 until the British withdrawal in 1921. Both sides fought with the knowledge that intelligence could be decisive and the Irish Republican Army (IRA) under Michael Collins were relentless in stopping the RIC and the detectives of the Dublin Metropolitan Police (DMP) 'G' Division (also known as 'Crime Special') from collecting it. A deliberate strategy of 'ruthless war' was devised to counter the threat posed to local IRA volunteers by policemen who had an intimate knowledge of the area where they were stationed and its inhabitants.[20] At the same time, efforts were made to convince them that at the least they should not act against the IRA but where possible should covertly assist. Policemen who could pass on useful information to the IRA were encouraged to do so.

When Ireland gained its independence in 1921, the RIC was disbanded and replaced by a new force, the Civic Guard (*Garda Síochána*). Over 700 ex-RIC and DMP officers, British Army ex-soldiers (including some from the RIC 'Auxilliaries', who had a fearsome reputation for violence and were known as the 'Black and Tans') and new young recruits looking for adventure had signed up by April 1922 to form a new unit to police the British Mandate in Palestine. They were known as the Palestine Gendarmerie (British Section) and their role was to assist the small Palestine Police Force by augmenting the Palestine Gendarmerie (Palestine Section), whose activities consisted mainly of patrolling and protecting the northern border.[21] A reorganization in 1926 led to the disbandment of the British Section, with the transfer of some of its best men to the police force, while the Palestine Gendarmerie became the 'Trans-Jordan Frontier Force', a more overtly paramilitary force organized on Indian Army lines. Both the Palestine Police Force and the Trans-Jordan Frontier Force were disbanded in 1948 when Israel became independent.[22]

The importance of Palestine for British police and military officers as a 'training ground' in the policing and countering of civil conflict within societies riven with national, ethnic, religious, and tribal fault lines should be recognized. After their disbandment in 1948, many were recruited to take their knowledge, experience, and expertise with them to other countries

[20] T. Ryle Dwyer, *The Squad and the Intelligence Operations of Michael Collins* (Dublin: Mercier Press, 2010), pp. 20–1.

[21] Edward Horne, *A Job Well Done: A History of the Palestine Police Force* (Sussex: Book Guild, 1982), pp. 76–97.

[22] James Lunt, *Imperial Sunset: Frontier soldiering in the 20th century* (London: Macdonald, 1981), pp. 67–70.

where they were to prove invaluable in the succession of insurgencies that began to break out. In terms of the police, approximately 1,400 men from the Palestine police transferred directly to other Colonial forces, with 709 going to Malaya, 113 to Kenya, 80 to Cyprus, and 40 to Aden.[23] As can be seen, half of them went to Malaya, a British colony that had been in the grip of a communist inspired insurgency since 1945 and usually referred to as the 'Malayan Emergency'.

The insurgency in Malaya was the first instance where a number of existing elements concerned with policing, military operations, and the role of government first came together and began to develop. Foremost among them was the firm principle of the primacy of civil government (and hence the police), while military forces were required always to act in support of the civil power (see also Table 20.1).[24] To reinforce this arrangement,

> [t]he Malayan government made clear that the Special Branch was to be regarded as its main agency and that it reported to the civilian police. As such, it was responsible for providing the government not only with political and security intelligence, but also, more importantly, with operational or combat intelligence on which the security forces could mount counterinsurgency operations.[25]

Crucially, this also meant there was no separate intelligence role for the military, although by the end of 1954 a government review noted that '[s]ome 30 military intelligence officers have been integrated with the Special Branch. Their role is to assist in the collation and presentation of tactical intelligence for emergency operations.'[26]

It would be misleading to assess the effectiveness of the security forces in the early stages of the Emergency in 1948 compared to its later stages. Initially, there was a great amount of work to be done in transforming the counterinsurgency response into one that stood a good chance of succeeding and first and foremost was the recognition at the highest levels that a huge transformation was needed. It was clear to the British government that '[t]he first priority is the re-organisation and build-up of the police force. During this time, the ring must be held by the Army....'[27] Sir Richard Catling, a Senior Assistant Commissioner in the Malayan Police, commented on the situation he found on his arrival at the beginning of the insurgency:

[23] Sinclair and Williams, 'Home and away', pp. 221–38.

[24] Leon Comber, *Malaya's Secret Police 1945–60* (Melbourne: Monash University Press, 2008), p. 11.

[25] Comber, *Malaya's Secret Police 1945–60*, p. 11.

[26] Comber, *Malaya's Secret Police 1945–60*, pp. 88–9.

[27] Memorandum to the Cabinet from Secretary of State for the Colonies 'Situation in Malaya', 20 November 1951, Annex 1, p.1, para. 2, CAB 129-48-0-0026, The National Archives (TNA).

> as always happens in these situations—it happened in Palestine, it happened in Malaya, it happened in Kenya, it happened in Cyprus—there was a lot of reorganizing, training and retraining to be done, new equipment to be acquired, new brains to be acquired, new systems to be worked out and applied and of course, the basic method of correlating the activities of administration, army and police so there was a maximum push against the adversary.[28]

Even before British military involvement in Malaya ended with the country gaining its independence in 1957, there followed a series of counter-insurgency and counter-insurgency-like campaigns in number of countries (see Table 20.1). In terms of the role of the police and policing, they tended to fall into the more-or-less familiar pattern established in Malaya. Space precludes closer examination but in August 1969, after a long build-up of violence and terrorism in Northern Ireland that was eventually almost to overwhelm the Royal Ulster Constabulary (RUC), the British Army were deployed to help contain it. Sam Bradley, Deputy Chief Constable of the RUC at this time, is quoted as saying that 'it was not a question of the military coming to the aid of the civil power; the military took over and for eight years thereafter the police did what the army asked them to do.'[29] Indeed, it was not until 1974 that the decision was finally made not to replace the RUC as a force but 'to build up its role and reduce but not withdraw army involvement.'[30]

From this low point, over the following 20 years, police primacy was re-established as the RUC were built up into both an effective police force and in conjunction with the British military, one whose expertise in counter-terrorism became second to none. By the time of the invasion of Iraq in March 2003, the concept of the army working in close cooperation with the police to defeat terrorism in Northern Ireland was perhaps even then beginning to fade from institutional memory. It now seems clear that there had been no military planning or resources devoted to the issue of police and policing in Iraq in the aftermath of the invasion and the downfall of the regime of Saddam Hussein, and no consideration given to the potential role of the British Army in supporting and operating with it.

This led to a wholly new set of circumstances as there was no local police force in the area of British operations, not even an embattled and underperforming one, to neatly slot into the tried and tested British COIN template. Steps were taken to try and correct this but it appears that UK attempts to create a police force in Basra relied heavily for its personnel on local militias

[28] John Nagl, *Learning to Eat Soup with a Knife: Counterinsurgency lessons from Malaya and Vietnam* (Chicago: University of Chicago Press, 2005), p. 80.

[29] Chris Ryder, *The RUC—1922–2000: A force under fire* (London: Arrow Books, 2000), p. 114.

[30] Ryder, *The RUC—1922–2000: A force under fire*, p. 131.

whose loyalties lay with their own leadership. As time passed, they became increasingly hostile to the British presence.

The most notorious of these militia dominated police units was the Serious Crimes Unit (SCU) in Basra. According to a British 'senior military officer', they would 'dress in police uniform, use police cars, police pistols and will murder just for political or criminal gain. The SCU are a significant part of death squad activity in Basra.'[31] Identifying and learning the lessons of Basra to ensure the situation is not repeated will be painful but essential. To emphasize the importance of this task, as the British Army turned its attention to its new task in Helmand province, Afghanistan, the issue of the lack of an organized police force operating to any meaningful concept of policing rapidly became apparent once more.

Police and policing in a contemporary insurgency: Afghanistan

Building capacity and capability in the police

The first part of this chapter delineated briefly the integral role that police and policing have played in countering insurgencies and terrorism over at least the last 150 years, and the evolution of the relationships and interactions that are required between the police and military forces to achieve it. Throughout this period, police HUMINT has constantly proved its worth in dismantling terrorist and insurgent groups and in its contribution to the wider aim of defeating the insurgency.

The second part of this chapter is based on a series of interviews and conversations with British and US military and Afghan police officers, plus personal observations made during regular visits to Helmand province since 2010 and, from 2012, to a number of other provinces in Afghanistan. It is therefore very much a personal perspective focused on the relevance of police HUMINT to the counter-insurgency effort.

The lesson identified by Sir Richard Catling in Malaya, that countering an insurgency inevitably seems to require comprehensive organizational re-development before all the necessary resources can be accurately focused on the task at hand, is as relevant today in Afghanistan as it was in the time-period and across the insurgencies to which he refers. In terms of police and policing, the challenge is to determine how the UK can build the capability and capacity in the Afghan police forces in Helmand province to enable them to perform effectively during on-going insurgency and terrorism while at the

[31] 'Rogue police officers seized in Basra', *Daily Telegraph*, 23 December 2006, cited in Ledwidge, *Losing Small Wars*, pp. 33–4.

same time preparing them to better serve their communities by performing the functions and tasks expected of them as a police force.

The second phase of British military involvement in Afghanistan began in April 2006 when 16 Air Assault Brigade were deployed to Helmand Province and for the first time, the British military became engaged in a counter-insurgency campaign. Time and space preclude a full examination of events and circumstances since then but, by 2010, the criticality of police and policing to a successful counter-insurgency campaign had been generally recognized, although arguably it was 'too little and too late'. The question for the British and US military primarily became one of how quickly they could build counter-insurgency capability and capacity in the partner nation police force (the Afghan National Police—ANP). The more difficult but equally crucial issue of how to prepare them to better serve their communities by competently and reliably performing the functions and tasks expected of them as a police force received less attention. The approach eventually adopted in Helmand was to utilize both British military units operating in theatre and civil police seconded from the UK, operating as part of the UK Stability Unit, to deliver to the ANP both training and on-the-job mentoring.

Building on past experience of counter-insurgency, the approach in Helmand should have been for the British military to focus on partnering and advising the police in the conduct of joint operations and how to coordinate their own operations with the military, plus training and mentoring them with the appropriate military knowledge and skills they needed to defend themselves and their communities. The British civil police contribution should have been to advise and mentor senior ANP officers on operational police matters and to train and mentor rank and file ANP officers in order to inculcate and develop their police knowledge, expertise, and skills.

However, it became normal practice in Helmand for British and US military officers to be appointed their own battalion 'Police Mentoring and Advisory Group' (PMAG) or its equivalent. It was established for the duration of their tour and its role was to mentor and advise local senior police officers from the ANP.[32] Very few members of these teams had any police experience or police training. The senior Afghan police officers (usually mentored by the officer heading the team) were often of a higher rank than their military mentor and may already have had many years of police experience. Even more problematically, they too may have had little or no previous police experience. In either case, it is hard to envision how an army officer acting as a mentor could contribute to their development as senior police officers.

[32] The British and US military titles tend to change regularly over time. The word 'Police' is usually followed by 'liaison', 'mentoring', 'advisory', or 'training', used either singly or in varying combinations.

A significant disadvantage to a military-only approach is that the task of mentoring an ANP officer first and foremost requires a relationship to be built with them. The experiences of police mentors in Iraq and elsewhere in Afghanistan has shown that a natural way for empathy and understanding to be established is by drawing on and sharing the relevant experiences the mentors have gained in their own career as police officers. Many of these are almost universal and hence common ground can be found in policing in countries as apparently diverse as the UK and Afghanistan. Once a working relationship has been established, then relevant police-related stories can continue to be used to pass on and reinforce points of learning as required.

To compound the problems encountered with one-to-one mentoring, there are only a limited number of senior ANP officers to be mentored and British officers were in competition with their equivalent in the US military to achieve 'face time' with them. US military mentors of the ANP were often appointed in the same haphazard circumstances as their British counterparts, although the greater US use of military reservists increases the opportunity for the US military to find and utilize officers with a police background. A further advantage is that they can also directly use the services of US police officers who are in Helmand as part of the Law Enforcement Professional Programme (LEPP) and who are attached as required to military units as part of the USMC Province Police Advisory Team (PPAT) or a 'Rule of Law' unit in a US Army Security Forces Advise and Assist Team (SFAAT).

At the same time as the British and US military police training effort is being delivered, to fulfil their mission British civil police mentors also need access to the ANP senior officers.[33] UK police have been operating in Helmand since 2008 and from 2011 they have worked within the UK Stability Unit. Consequently, they are independent of the British military. Despite this relatively long commitment, there is still no real UK policy in place to govern their role. When on the ground, they are entirely dependent on the British military to escort them safely and securely to their mentees and when their escort leaves a location, they must leave with them. As military concerns always take precedence with the PMAG (including making sure their own requirement to mentor the ANP is fulfilled), the civil police mentoring of Afghan senior officers tends to be fitted in if there is any time left when this is completed.

The circumstances thus described only touch upon the difficult and complex task of delivering relevant and effective capability and capacity building measures to partner nation police. Individual military and police officers, from the UK and the US do their best to carry out what is asked of them in difficult and dangerous circumstances, and there is no doubt that progress has been

[33] They are drawn from volunteers across a number of Police Forces in the UK. The largest number come from the Ministry of Defence Police (MDP).

made in the provision of basic training to the rank and file of the ANP. There is also day-to-day cooperation and coordination at an operational level with the ANP through the medium of the Operations Command Centre Province (OCCP). However, in light of the almost universal acknowledgement that intelligence, and particularly police HUMINT, can be a critical factor in countering insurgencies and terrorism, it is instructive to examine how this central tenet of counter-insurgency is implemented in Helmand, in both the operational and training spheres.

Building police HUMINT capability and capacity

There is a widespread military recognition of both the need for intelligence and that police-derived HUMINT should be an integral part of police operations, as well as contributing to the wider counter-insurgency intelligence picture: 'War amongst the people is conducted best as an intelligence and information operation.... We need the information so as to achieve the deterrent of the law [and] evidential information in sufficient depth for a successful prosecution.'[34] However, there is ambivalence when it comes to following this through to its logical conclusion, namely the need to prepare the partner nation police to carry out this function over the long-term.

With regard to police and policing, the US Army and Marine Field Manual on insurgency is unequivocal. It both recognizes the principle that '[t]he primary frontline COIN force is often the police—not the military. The primary COIN objective is to enable local institutions. Therefore, supporting the police is essential.'[35] It goes on to highlight their applicability to counter-insurgency: '[f]ew military units can match a good police unit in developing an accurate human intelligence picture of their A[rea of] O[perations]. Because of their frequent contact with the populace, police often are the best force for countering small insurgent bands supported by the local populace.'[36] This view of the insurgency as being very local and hence its vulnerability to police activity has recently been reinforced.

A report based on nearly 80 interviews with Afghans from numerous Provinces, all of whom identified themselves as active Taliban insurgents, gives an insight into their activities and seems to confirm its 'localized' nature.[37] The study found that insurgents deliberately travelled some distance away from their own communities to engage in attacks and relied on these sources for

[34] Smith, *The Utility of Force*, p. 390.

[35] *The US Army—Marine Corps Counterinsurgency Field Manual*, Field Manual (FM) No. 3–24 and Warfighting Publication No. 3–33.5 (Chicago: University of Chicago Press, 2007), para. 6–90, p. 229.

[36] FM3-24, para. 6–91, p. 229.

[37] Andrew Garfield and Alicia Boyd, 'Understanding Afghan insurgents: motivations, goals, and the reconciliation and reintegration process', accessed 2 May 2013, *Foreign Policy Research Institute E-Notes*, <http://www.fpri.org/docs/Garfield_understanding_Afghan_insurgents.pdf>.

money and supplies. On returning home after the 'fighting season', they felt secure from denunciation in their own communities and therefore made little effort to conceal their presence or where their sympathies lay.

These insights give an indication of the potential impact 'bottom up' police HUMINT operations could have when carried out by properly trained and organized local police departments. If the insurgents operate away from the communities where they are known, then they have to operate in areas where others will see them as strangers. Community and perhaps tribal loyalties will be weaker and hence HUMINT on their activities may be easier to obtain. In addition, long-term absences of individuals from their own community may make them visible as insurgents to police 'eyes and ears' activity during routine patrolling.

In Helmand, neither the British military nor the UK civil police were involved in training or structured on-the-job mentoring activity to ensure that police HUMINT can be generated by the ANP and utilized in counter-insurgency operations. However, this was not the case with the US military. In 2008 in Iraq, the United States Marine Corps (USMC) implemented an experimental mission known as the Legacy Program. It was designed to test the concept of building HUMINT capacity in a partner nation police organization and initially, it was introduced by Multi National Force—West (MNF-W) in Anbar province, Iraq. The programme was later extended by Multi National Force—Iraq (MNF-I) to four more provinces in the north of Iraq and on its completion in 2010, the concept was considered successful enough by the USMC to be taken with them on their deployment to Afghanistan.

Originally operating under the auspices of Regional Command—South West (RC-SW) in Helmand province, the programme was soon taken up by the International Security Assistance Force—Afghanistan (ISAF), expanding first into Kandahar province and then across a number of other provinces in the east of the country and into Kabul itself. While the programme is controlled and managed by the US military, the training and mentoring of the partner nation police officers was designed and carried out by former civil police officers from the UK, many of whom were able to draw on relevant experience obtained over many years from working in Northern Ireland, Iraq, and Kosovo. The Legacy Program operated as an integral part of the wider Rule of Law effort and was of proven merit in the short-term against the insurgency day-to-day and, in the longer term, in assisting the Afghans to build the organizational systems and structures necessary to continue with this type of work after the drawdown and exit of US and ISAF forces.

No-one is better able to gather HUMINT in Afghanistan than the Afghans themselves and the HUMINT they already generate will become an increasingly vital resource in the post-transition future. Experience in Iraq has shown that during transition, as the military footprint is reduced, local HUMINT becomes almost the only way for military commanders to find out what is going on locally at ground level 'outside the wire'. However, building police HUMINT capability and capacity takes effort, resources, and, most importantly, time. Consequently, efforts to create and sustain such a capability need to have started well before the transition phase. Indeed, if they are not in place by then, it is going to be too late to try and create them.

Conclusion

In the context of the UK, the origins and development of police and policing since the early nineteenth century are intricately linked to the need to deal with the outbreaks of insurgency, terrorism, and civil conflict that have occurred throughout the histories of Britain, Ireland, and in the wider British Empire. As a consequence, during the second half of the twentieth century, the British military were able to operate in foreign countries that were also British colonies in the knowledge that there would be (eventually) an effective police force that understood their own role and that of the military and hence could operate competently in a coordinated counter-insurgency campaign. There has now been a shift from this paradigm, most markedly from 2003 onwards in Iraq and from 2006 in Afghanistan. Not only were there no familiar police forces in place that could be revamped for the task in hand, where police forces were in place, they were corrupt, ineffective, and, at their worst, actively hostile towards any efforts to reform or even influence them.

This is where a new challenge for the twenty-first century lies. When required, how can the UK build the capability and capacity in partner nation police forces to enable them to perform effectively during on-going civil conflict, insurgency, and terrorism while at the same time preparing them to better serve their communities by performing the functions and tasks expected of them as a police force? To begin this process, there should be a fundamental rethink of how police-like the British military need to become in these circumstances and conversely, how military-like the UK civil police need to be if they are to participate in any meaningful way.

The necessity for the military to alter its approach when engaged in conducting 'operations amongst the people' has been set out by Rupert Smith:

> To reach the desired outcome the currency of [military] deterrence must be changed from that necessary to achieve order under law, the aimed bullet, to that necessary to achieve justice within the law, evidential information leading to a prosecution and sentence.[38]

[38] Smith, *The Utility of Force*, p. 380.

If this is to be the case, a review should be undertaken to examine whether the UK is better served by soldiers who can also act effectively in the realm of police and policing or whether it is preferable to train, equip, and employ civil police to deliver policing in a militarized environment. In the latter case, it may be more effective if the civil police were embedded or aligned with the Army PMAG, working alongside and mentoring them in police and policing, rather than competing with them for the attention of each ANP mentee.

The employment in Afghanistan of 'Gendarmerie-type' units from France, Italy, Turkey, Romania, and the Netherlands will have generated a wealth of experience that should be tapped to see what could usefully be learned and applied to the UK perspective. Others have already explored this concept. A proposal outlining the need for a US civilian 'Stability Force' was first put forward just prior to the invasion of Iraq but the idea was taken no further.[39] A later study prepared on behalf of the US Army in 2009 examined the US need for a 'Stability Police Force', how one could be created, and the mission it would fulfil.[40]

The creation of a standing, deployable British military/police capability is not an option in the current political and economic climate but there could be another way to deliver what is required. The new 'Army Reserve' could have a role to play, once it emerges from the current reorganization. Perhaps a Reserve battalion, specializing in 'Rule of Law' and Security Sector Reform and utilizing as its personnel Army reserves with relevant backgrounds, could be established to train, operate, and be deployed as a single unit as part of the new 'Adaptable Force' structure. The Military Stabilisation Support Group (MSSG) set up in 2008 could form the basis for this and the UK police forces could have a role to at least train and support them in this role.[41]

The ability of the UK in the future to build capability and capacity for police HUMINT operations, and to do so in conjunction with partner nation police forces, must not be neglected if the new challenges of police and policing in militarized or conflict environments are to be addressed.

References

Clutterbuck, Lindsay, 'Countering Irish terrorism in Britain: Its origin as a police function', *Terrorism and Political Violence* 8, no.1 (Spring 2006): pp. 95–118.

[39] Michael Gordon and General Bernard Trainor, *Cobra II: The inside story of the invasion and occupation of Iraq* (New York: Vintage Books, 2007), Appendix, pp. 661–5.

[40] Terrence Kelly, Seth Jones, James Barnett, Keith Crane, Robert Davis, and Carl Jensen, *A Stability Police Force for the United States: Justifications and options for creating U.S. capabilities* (Santa Monica: RAND Corporation, 2009).

[41] Ledwidge, *Losing Small Wars*, pp. 232–3.

Clutterbuck, Lindsay, 'An overview of violent Jihad in the UK: Radicalisation and the state response', in *Understanding Violent Radicalisation: Terrorist and Jihadist Movements in Europe*, edited by Magnus Ranstorp (London: Routledge, 2010), pp. 144–67.

Comber, Leon, *Malaya's Secret Police 1945–60* (Melbourne: Monash University Press, 2008).

Dwyer, T. Ryle, *The Squad and the Intelligence Operations of Michael Collins* (Dublin: Mercier Press, 2010).

Garfield, Andrew and Alicia Boyd, 'Understanding Afghan insurgents: Motivations, goals, and the reconciliation and reintegration process', *Foreign Policy Research Institute E-Notes*, accessed 2 May 2013, http://www.fpri.org/docs/Garfield_understanding_Afghan_insurgents.pdf.

Gordon, Michael and General Bernard Trainor, *Cobra II: The inside story of the invasion and occupation of Iraq* (New York: Vintage Books, 2007).

Horne, Edward, *A Job Well Done: A History of the Palestine Police Force* (Sussex: Book Guild, 1982).

Jeffries, Sir Charles, *The Colonial Police* (London: Max Parrish, 1952).

Jones, Seth and Martin Libicki, *How Terrorist Groups End: Lessons for countering al Qa'ida* (Santa Monica: RAND Corporation, 2008).

Kelly, Terrence, Seth Jones, James Barnett, Keith Crane, Robert Davis, and Carl Jensen, *A Stability Police Force for the United States: Justifications and options for creating U.S. capabilities* (Santa Monica: RAND Corporation, 2009).

Kilcullen, David, *Counterinsurgency* (Oxford: Oxford University Press, 2010).

Ledwidge, Frank, *Losing Small Wars: British military failure in Iraq and Afghanistan* (New Haven and London: Yale University Press, 2011).

Lunt, James, *Imperial Sunset: Frontier soldiering in the 20th century* (London: Macdonald, 1981).

Mockaitis, Thomas, *Resolving Insurgencies* (US Army War College Strategic Studies Institute, 2011).

Nagl, John, *Learning to Eat Soup with a Knife: Counterinsurgency lessons from Malaya and Vietnam* (Chicago: University of Chicago Press, 2005).

Norton-Taylor, Richard, 'UK's fleet of Merlin helicopters to return home from Afghanistan', *The Guardian*, 4 June 2013, <http://www.guardian.co.uk/uk/2013/jun/04/uk-merlin-helicopters-return-afghanistan>.

Paul, Christopher, Colin Clarke, and Beth Grill, *Victory Has a Thousand Fathers: Qualitative comparative analysis of 30 recent resolved insurgencies* (Santa Monica: RAND Corporation, 2010).

Ryder, Chris, *The RUC—1922–2000: A force under fire* (UK: Arrow Books, 2000).

Sepp, Kalev, 'Best practices in counter insurgency', *Military Review*, May–June 2005, <http://www.au.af.mil/au/awc/awcgate/milreview/sepp.pdf>.

Sinclair, Georgina, *At the End of the Line: Colonial policing and the imperial endgame, 1945–1980* (Manchester: Manchester University Press, 2006).

Sinclair, Georgina and C. A. Williams, 'Home and Away: The Cross-Fertilization between 'Colonial' and 'British' Policing, 1921–1985', *Journal of Imperial and Commonwealth History* 35, no. 2 (2007): pp. 221–38.

Smith, General Sir Rupert, *The Utility of Force: The art of war in the modern world* (London: Penguin Books, 2006).

US Army-Marine Corps Counterinsurgency Field Manual, Field Manual No. 3–24 and Warfighting Publication No. 3–33.5 (Chicago: University of Chicago Press, 2007).

Glossary

ABP	Afghan Border Police
ALP	Afghan Local Police
ANA	Afghan National Army
ANCOP	Afghan Civil Order Police
ANP	Afghan National Police
ANSF	Afghan National Security Forces
APRP	Afghan Peace and Reconciliation Programme
AUP	Afghan Uniformed Police
BBC	British Broadcasting Corporation
CIA	Central Intelligence Agency
COIN	Counter-Insurgency
CP	Check Point
CT	Counter Terrorism
DDR	Disarmament, Demobilisation and Reintegration
DFID	Department for International Development
DOD	Department of Defense
DOS	Department of State
EOC	Emergency Operations Council
EU	European Union
FATA	Federally Administered Tribal Areas
FCO	Foreign and Commonwealth Office
FOB	Forward Operating Base
GIRoA	Government of the Islamic Republic of Afghanistan
HMEP	Helmand Monitoring and Evaluation Programme
HMG	Her Majesty's Government (United Kingdom)
HPRT	Helmand Provincial Reconstruction Team
ICRC	International Committee of the Red Cross/Crescent
ICT	International Combined Team

IED	Improvised Explosive Device
IIG	Iraq Information Group
INA	Indian National Army
INGO	International Non-Governmental Organisation
IPAB	International Policing Assistance Board
ISAF	International Security Assistance Force
ISI	Inter-Services Intelligence (Pakistan)
KAR	King's African Rifles
MDP	Ministry of Defence Police
MOD	Ministry of Defence
MoE	Ministry of Education
MoI	Ministry of Interior
NATO	North Atlantic Treaty Organisation
NCA	National Crime Agency
NDS	National Directorate of Security
NGO	Non-Governmental Organisation
NWFP	North-West Frontier Provinces
OECD	Organisation for Economic Cooperation and Development
OMLT	Operational Mentoring and Liaison Teams
OSCE	Office for Security and Cooperation in Europe
PB	Patrol Base
PJHQ	Permanent Joint Head Quarters
PSYOPS	Psychological Operations
RAF	Royal Air Force
RC	Regional Command
RM	Royal Marines
RN	Royal Navy
SB	Special Branch
SF	Special Forces
SFA	Security Force Assistance
SIS	Secret Intelligence Service
SOCA	Serious Organised Crime Agency
SOF	Special Operations Force
SSR	Security Sector Reform
TFH	Task Force Helmand
TTP	Tehrik-i-Taliban Pakistan

UN	United Nations
USAID	United States Agency for International Development
USMC	United States Marine Corps
WMD	Weapon of Mass Destruction

Index